CHILTON BOOK COMPANY

REPAIR MANUAL

BMW
1970-88

All U.S. and Canadian models of 1600 • 2000 • 2002 • 2002tii •
2500 • 2800 • 2800CS • Bavaria • 3000CS • 3.0CS • 3.0S •
3.0CSi • 318i • 320i • 325e • 325es • 325iS • 325i • 325iX • M3 •
528e • 528i • 530i • 525i • 533i • 524td • 535i • 535is • M5 •
630CSi • 633i • 633CSi • 635CSi • M6 • L6 • 733i • 735i • L7

Sr. Vice President	Ronald A. Hoxter
Publisher and Editor-In-Chief	Kerry A. Freeman, S.A.E.
Managing Editors	Peter M. Conti, Jr. □ W. Calvin Settle, Jr., S.A.E.
Assistant Managing Editor	Nick D'Andrea
Senior Editors	Richard J. Rivele, S.A.E. □ Ron Webb
Director of Manufacturing	Mike D'Imperio
Manager of Manufacturing	John F. Butler
Editor	Peter M. Conti, Jr.

CHILTON BOOK COMPANY

ONE OF THE DIVERSIFIED PUBLISHING COMPANIES,
A PART OF CAPITAL CITIES/ABC, INC.

CONTENTS

GENERAL INFORMATION and MAINTENANCE

ENGINE PERFORMANCE and TUNE-UP

ENGINE and ENGINE OVERHAUL

EMISSION CONTROLS

FUEL SYSTEM

CHASSIS ELECTRICAL

DRIVE TRAIN

SUSPENSION and STEERING

BRAKES

BODY

MECHANIC'S DATA

SAFETY NOTICE

Proper service and repair procedures are vital to the safe, reliable operation of all motor vehicles, as well as the personal safety of those performing repairs. This book outlines procedures for servicing and repairing vehicles using safe, effective methods. The procedures contain many NOTES, CAUTIONS and WARNINGS which should be followed along with standard safety procedures to eliminate the possibility of personal injury or improper service which could damage the vehicle or compromise its safety.

It is important to note that repair procedures and techniques, tools and parts for servicing motor vehicles, as well as the skill and experience of the individual performing the work vary widely. It is not possible to anticipate all of the conceivable ways or conditions under which vehicles may be serviced, or to provide cautions as to all of the possible hazards that may result. Standard and accepted safety precautions and equipment should be used during cutting, grinding, chiseling, prying, or any other process that can cause material removal or projectiles.

Some procedures require the use of tools specially designed for a specific purpose. Before substituting another tool or procedure, you must be completely satisfied that neither your personal safety, nor the performance of the vehicle will be endangered.

Although the information in this guide is based on industry sources and is as complete as possible at the time of publication, the possibility exists that the manufacturer made later changes which could not be included here. While striving for total accuracy, Chilton Book Company cannot assume responsibility for any errors, changes, or omissions that may occur in the compilation of this data.

PART NUMBERS

Part numbers listed in this reference are not recommendations by Chilton for any product by brand name. They are references that can be used with interchange manuals and aftermarket supplier catalogs to locate each brand supplier's discrete part number.

SPECIAL TOOLS

Special tools are recommended by the vehicle manufacturer to perform their specific job. Use has been kept to a minimum, but where absolutely necessary, they are referred to in the text by the part number of the tool manufacturer. These tools can be purchased, under the appropriate part number, from BMW of North America, Inc. or an equivalent tool can be purchased locally from a tool supplier or parts outlet. Before substituting any tool for the one recommended, read the SAFETY NOTICE at the top of this page.

ACKNOWLEDGMENTS

Chilton Book Company expresses its appreciation to BMW of North America, Inc.; Bayerische Motoren Werke AG Munich, AB Volvo Göteborg; and the Ford Motor Company for the technical information and illustrations contained within this manual.

Chilton's Repair Manual: BMW 1970–88
ISBN 0-8019-7941-2 pbk.
Library of Congress Catalog Card No. 88-43185

General Information and Maintenance

HOW TO USE THIS BOOK

Chilton's Repair and Tune-Up Guide for the BMW is intended to teach you more about the inner working of your automobile and save you money on its upkeep. Chapters 1 and 2 will probably be the most frequently used in the book. The first chapter contains all the information that may be required at a moment's notice. Aside from giving the location of various serial numbers and the proper towing instructions, it also contains all the information on basic day-to-day maintenance that you will need to ensure good performance and long component life. Chapter 2 contains the necessary tune-up procedures to assist you not only in keeping the engine running properly and at peak performance levels, but also in restoring some of the more delicate components to operatingg condition in the event of a failure. Chapters 3 through 10 cover repairs (rather than maintenance) for various portions of your car, with each chapter covering either one separate system or 2 related systems. The appendix then lists general information which may be useful in rebuilding the engine or performing some other operation on any car.

When using the Table of Contents, refer to the bold listings for the subject of the chapter and the smaller listings (or the index) for information on a particular component.

In general, there are 3 things a proficient mechanic has which must be allowed for when a non-professional does work on his/her car. These are:

1. A sound knowledge of the construction of the parts he is working with; their order of assembly, etc.

2. A knowledge of potentially hazardous situation; particularly how to prevent them.

3. Manual dexterity.

This book provides step-by-step instructions and illustrations whenever possible. Use them carefully and wisely—don't just jump headlong into disassembly. When there is doubt about being able to readily reassemble something, make a careful drawing of the component before taking it apart. Assembly always look simple when everything is still assembled.

"CAUTIONS," "WARNINGS" and "NOTES" will be provided where appropriate to help prevent you from injuring yourself or damaging your car. Consequently, you should always read through the entire procedure before beginning the work so as to familiarize yourself with any special problems which may occur during the given procedure. Since no number of warnings could cover every possible situation, you should work slowly and try to envision what is going to happen in each operation ahead of time.

When it comes to tightening things, there is generally a slim area between too loose to properly seal or resist vibration and so tight as to risk damage or warping. When dealing with major engine parts, or with any aluminum component, it pays to buy a torque wrench and go by the recommended figures.

When reference is made in this book to the "right side" or the "left side" of the car, it should be understood that the positions are always to be viewed from the front seat. This means that the left side of the car is the driver's side and the right side is the passenger's side. This will hold true through out the book, regardless of how you might be looking at the car at the time.

We have attempted to eliminate the use of special tools whenever possible, substituting more readily available hand tools. However, in some cases, the special tools are necessary. These tools can usually be purchased from your local BMW dealer or from an automotive parts store.

Always be conscious of the need for safety in your work. Never get under a car unless it is

firmly supported by jackstands or ramps. Never smoke near, or allow flame to get near the battery or the fuel system. Keep your clothing, hands and hair clear of the fan and pulleys when working near the engine if it is running. Most importantly, try to be patient, even in the midst of an argument with a stubborn bolt; reaching for the largest hammer in the garage is usually a cause for later regret and more extensive repair. As you gain confidence and experience, working on your car will become a source of pride and satisfaction.

TOOLS AND EQUIPMENT

It would be impossible to catalog each and every tool that you may need to perform all the operations included in this book. It would also not be wise for the amateur to rush out and buy an expensive set of tools on the theory that he may need one of them at some time. The best approach is to proceed slowly, gathering together a good quality set of those tools that are used most frequently. Don't be mislead by the low cost of bargain tools. It is far better to spend a little more for quality, name brand tool. Forged wrenches, 6- or 12-point sockets and fine-tooth ratchets are by far preferable to their less expensive counterparts. As any good mechanic can tell you, there are few worse experiences than trying to work on a car or truck with bad tools. Your monetary savings will be far outweighed by frustration and mangled knuckles.

Begin accumulating those tools that are used most frequently; those associated with routine maintenance and tune-up. In addition to the normal assortment of screwdrivers and pliers, you should have the following tools for routine maintenance jobs:

1. Metric wrenches, sockets and combination open end/box end wrenches
2. Jackstands for support
3. Oil filter wrench
4. Oil filler spout or funnel
5. Grease gun for chassis lubrication
6. Hydrometer for checking the battery
7. A low flat pan for draining oil
8. Lots of rags for wiping up the inevitable mess

In addition to these items there are several others which are not absolutely necessary, but handy to have around. These include a transmission funnel and filler tube, a drop light on a long cord, an adjustable wrench and a pair of slip joint pliers.

A more advanced set of tools, suitable for tune-up work, can be drawn up easily. While the tools are slightly more sophisticated, they need not be outrageously expensive. The key to these purchases is to make them with an eye towards adaptability and wide range. A basic list of tune-up tools could include:

1. Tachometer/dwell meter
2. Spark plug gauge and gapping tool
3. Feeler gauges for valve and point adjustment
4. Timing light

A tachometer/dwell meter will ensure accurate tune-up work on cars without electronic ignition. The choice of a timing light should be made carefully. A light which works on the DC current supplied by the car battery is the best choice; it should have a xenon tube for brightness. Since some later models have an electronic ignition system, the timing light should have an inductive pickup which clamps around the No. 1 spark plug cable (the timing light illustrated has one of these pickups).

In addition to these basic tools, there are several other tools and gauges which, though not particularly necessary for basic tune-up work, you may find to be quite useful. These include:

1. A compression gauge. The screw-in type is slower to use but eliminates the possibility of a faulty reading due to escaping pressure
2. A manifold vacuum gauge
3. A test light
4. A combination volt/ohmmeter
5. An induction meter, used to determine whether or not there is current flowing through a wire. An extremely helpful tool for electrical troubleshooting.

Finally, you will find a torque wrench necessary for all but the most basic of work. The beam-type models are perfectly adequate. The click-type (breakaway) torque wrenches are more accurate, but are also much more expensive and must be periodically recalibrated.

SPECIAL TOOLS

Normally, the use of special factory tools is avoided for repair procedures, since these are not readily available for the do-it-yourself mechanic. When it is possible to perform the job with more commonly available tools, it will be pointed out, but occasionally, a special tool was designed to perform a specific function and should be used. Before substituting another tool, you should be convinced that neither you safety nor the performance of the vehicle will be compromised.

Some special tools are available commercially from major tool manufacturers. Others can be purchased from your dealer.

The special tools required for work on your BMW are confined primarily to rebuilding the cylinder head. A compression frame permits all the valves to be opened fully at once for easy camshaft removal. There are also guide pins

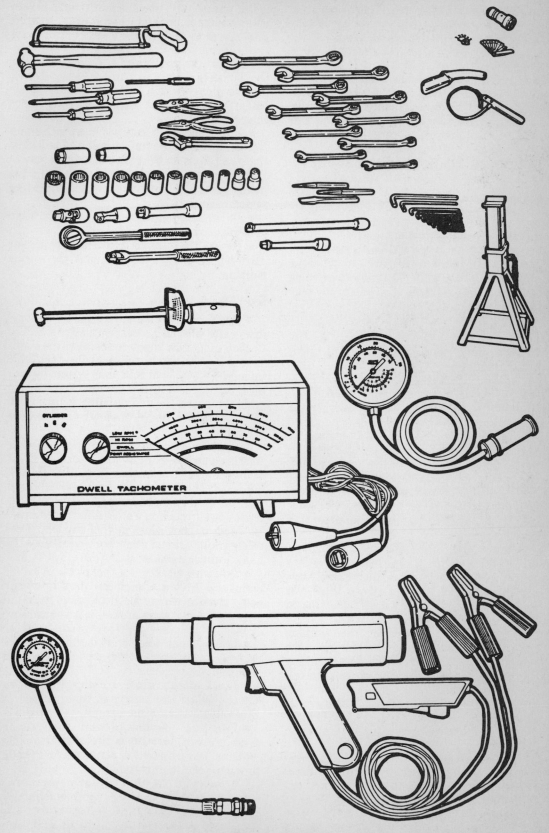

You need only a basic assortment of hand tools for most maintenance and repair jobs

used for removal of the rocker shaft assembly, and various punches used in removing and installing valve guides. These tools will be described and pictured in the procedures to which they apply.

No special tools are required for routine maintenance or minor work except the valve adjusting rod, which is included in the BMW tool kit supplied with the car.

SERVICING YOUR VEHICLE SAFELY

It is virtually impossible to anticipate all of the hazards involved with automotive maintenance and service, but care and common sense will prevent most accidents.

The rules of safety for mechanics range from "don't smoke around gasoline," to "use the proper tool for the job." The trick to avoiding injuries is to develop safe work habits and take every possible precaution.

DOS

- Do keep a fire extinguisher and first aid kit within easy reach.
- Do wear safety glasses or goggles when cutting, drilling, grinding or prying, even if you have 20-20 vision. If you wear glasses for the sake of vision, they should be made of hardened glass that can serve also as safety glasses, or wear safety goggles over your regular glass.
- Do shield your eyes whenever you work around the battery. Batteries contain sulphuric acid. In case of contact with the eyes or skin, flush the area with water or a mixture of water and baking soda and get medical attention immediately.
- Do use safety stands for any undercar service. Jacks are for raising vehicles, safety stands are for making sure the vehicle stays raised until you want to come down. Whenever the car is raised, block the wheels remaining on the ground and set the parking brake.
- Do use adequate ventilation when working with any chemicals or hazardous material. Like carbon monoxide, the asbestos dust resulting from brake lining wear can be poisonous in sufficient quantities.
- Do disconnect the negative battery cable when working on the electrical system. The secondary ignition system can contain up to 40,000 volts.
- Do follow manufacturer's directions whenever working with potentially hazardous materials. Both brake fluid and antifreeze are poisonous if take internally.
- Do properly maintain your tools. Loose hammer heads, mushroomed punches and chisels, frayed or poorly grounded electrical cords, excessively worn screwdrivers, spread wrenches (open end), cracked sockets, slipping ratchets, or faulty droplight sockets can cause accidents.
- Do use the proper size and type of tool for the job being done.
- Do when possible, pull on a wrench handle rather than push on it, and adjust your stance to prevent a fall.
- Do be sure that adjustable wrenches are tightly closed on the nut or bolt and pulled so that the face is on the side of the fixed jaw.
- Do select a wrench or socket that fits the nut or bolt. The wrench or socket should sit straight, not cocked.
- Do strike squarely with a hammer; avoid glancing blows.
- Do set the parking brake and block the drive wheels if the work requires the engine running.

Don'ts

- Don't run an engine in a garage or anywhere else without proper ventilation—EVER! Carbon monoxide is poisonous; it takes a long time to leave the human body and you can build up a deadly supply of it in your system by simply breathing in a little every day. You may not realize you are slowly poisoning yourself. Always use power vents, windows, fans or open the garage door.
- Don't work around moving parts while wearing a necktie or other loose clothing. Short sleeves are much safer than long, loose sleeves; hard-toed shoes with neoprene soles protect your toes and give a better grip on slippery surfaces. Jewelry such as watches, fancy belt buckles, beads or body adornment of any kind is not safe working around a car. Long hair should be hidden under a hat or cap.
- Don't use pockets for tool boxes. A fall or bump can drive a screwdriver deep into your body. Even a wiping cloth hanging from the back pocket can wrap around a spinning shaft or fan.
- Don't smoke when working around gasoline, cleaning solvent or other flammable material.
- Don't smoke when working around the battery. When the battery is being charge, it gives off explosive hydrogen gas.
- Don't use gasoline to wash your hands; there are excellent soaps available. Gasoline contains lead, and lead can enter the body through a cut, accumulating in the body until you are very ill. Gasoline also removes all the natural oils from the skin so that bone dry hands will suck up oil and grease.
- Don't service the air conditioning system unless you are equipped with the necessary

tools and training. The refrigerant, R-12, is extremely cold when compressed, and when released into the air will instantly freeze any surface it contacts, including your eyes. Although the refrigerant is normally non-toxic, R-12 becomes a deadly poisonous gas in the presence of an open flame. One good whiff of the vapors from buring refrigerant can be fatal.

HISTORY

BMW (Bavarian Motor Works) began its life in 1916 as a builder of aircraft engines (called the "Bavarian Aircraft Works"), although the name was changed to the present one only a year later. The company logo which still appears several places on each car represents a propeller spinning against a blue sky. Thus, the high performance associated with BMW engines has its origin in the necessity to minimize weight in an aircraft. BMW's first car was a vehicle produced by the Dixi automobile works which BMW purchased in 1928.

In 1933, BMW produced its first in-house design, the BMW 303. This model series began two BMW traditions which are well known — the 6-cylinder engine and twin kidney grills. By the end of the 30s, BMW was making the 328, which featured an engine using a light allow head, with V-type overhead values and hemi-head combustion chambers.

BMW's history as a major manufacturer of performance cars was eclipsed by the destruction of the Munich plant in World War II. The 50s were dominated by the extremes — the too-large 501, and the Isetta with a BMW motorcycle engine propelling it. Neither brought much profit to the company.

In 1959 Dr. Herbert Quant invested heavily in the company to save it from a sale of assets. In 1961, the 1500 was introduced, in the tradition of the later models. This "new wave" of 4-cylinder sports sedans has become recognized for its high output, low displacement and fuel efficient engine and light and compact chassis-body, which offers excellent road holding and braking. With the introduction of the 530i in 1975, BMW began to be associated with luxury-performance cars as well as sports sedans.

SERIAL IDENTIFICATION NUMBER

Vehicle

On 1970-74 models, this number is stamped on a plate attached to the upper steering column and on a Certification Label located on the edge of the driver's door. On most 1975 and later models, the number is located at the left end of the dashboard, visible through the wind-

On most late models, the serial number can be found on the left side of the instrument panel, visible through the windshield

Typical serial number and ID plate location—1600, 2000, 2002, 320i, 528e, 528i and 530i

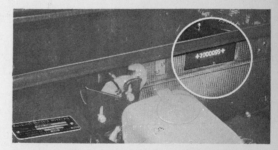

Typical serial number (circle) and ID plate location—2500, 2800, Bavaria, 3000, 3.0 and 733i

Typical serial number and ID plate location—630CSi and 633CSi

shield. The vehicle serial number and the vehicle identification plate are also found in various other locations in the engine compartment.

1600, 2000, 2002, 2002tii, ALL 3, 5 AND 7 SERIES

On these models, the vehicle serial number can be found stamped into the right front fender apron, while the vehicle identification plate can be found attached to the right front wheel arch, near the shock tower.

2500, 2800, BAVARIA, 3.0CS, 3.0C AND 3.0Si

On these models, the vehicle serial number can be found stamped into the top, right side of the firewall in the engine compartment. The vehicle identification plate can be found attached to the right front wheel arch, near the shock tower.

630CSi, 633csi, 635csi AND M6

On these models, the vehicle serial number can be found stamped into the top, right side of the firewall, facing the passenger compartment. The vehicle identification plate can be found attached to the right front wheel arch, near the shock tower.

Engine

This serial number is stamped ont he left, rear side of the engine itself, usually above the starter motor.

Engine serial number location—typical of all models

Engine Identification

Year	Model	Engine Displacement cu. in. (cc/liter)	Engine Series Identification	No. of Cylinders	Engine Type
1970	1600	96 (1573)	—	4	OHC
	2000,2002Ti	121 (1990)	—	4	OHC
	2500	152 (2493)	—	6	OHC
	2800,CS	170 (2788)	—	6	OHC
	Bavaria	170 (2788)	—	6	OHC
1971	1600	96 (1573)	—	4	OHC
	2000,2002,Ti	121 (1990)	—	4	OHC
	2500	152 (2493)	—	6	OHC
	2800,3000,CS	170 (2788)	—	6	OHC
	Bavaria	170 (2788)	—	6	OHC
1972	2000,2002	121 (1990)	—	4	OHC
	2002 Tii	121 (1990)	—	4	OHC
	2800,3000,CS	170 (2788)	—	6	OHC
	Bavaria	170 (2788)	—	6	OHC
1973	2000,2002	121 (1990)	—	4	OHC
	2002Tii	121 (1990)	—	4	OHC
	Bavaria	170 (2788)	—	6	OHC
	3.0,CS,S,Si	182 (2985)	—	6	OHC
1974	2002	121 (1990)	—	4	OHC
	2002Tii	121 (1990)	—	4	OHC
	Bavaria	170 (2788)	—	6	OHC
	3.0, CS, S, Si	182 (2985)	—	6	OHC

Engine Identification (cont.)

Year	Model	Engine Displacement cu. in. (cc/liter)	Engine Series Identification	No. of Cylinders	Engine Type
1975	2002	121 (1990)	—	4	OHC
	3.0,CS,S	182 (2985)	—	6	OHC
	530i	182 (2985)	—	6	OHC
			—		OHC
1976	2002	121 (1990)	—	4	OHC
	3.0,CS,S	182 (2985)	—	6	OHC
	530i	182 (2985)	—	6	OHC
	630CS	182 (2985)	—	6	OHC
1977	320i	121 (1990)	—	4	OHC
	530i	182 (2985)	—	6	OHC
	630CSi	182 (2985)	—	6	OHC
1978	320i	121 (1990)	—	4	OHC
	530i	182 (2985)	—	6	OHC
	630CSi	182 (2985)	—	6	OHC
	633CSi	196 (3210)	—	6	OHC
	733i	196 (3210)	—	6	OHC
1979	320i	121 (1990)	—	4	OHC
	528i	170 (2788)	—	6	OHC
	633CSi	196 (3210)	—	6	OHC
	733i	196 (3210)	—	6	OHC
1980	320i	107 (1766)	—	4	OHC
	528i	170 (2788)	—	6	OHC
	633CSi	196 (3210)	—	6	OHC
	733i	196 (3210)	—	6	OHC
1981	320i	107 (1766)	—	4	OHC
	528i	170 (2788)	—	6	OHC
	633CSi	196 (3210)	—	6	OHC
	733i	196 (3210)	—	6	OHC
1982	320i	108 (1766/1.8)	—	4	OHC
	325e	165 (2693/2.7)	M20B27	6	OHC
	528e	165 (2693/2.7)	M20B27	6	OHC
	533i	196 (3210/3.2)	M30B32	6	OHC
	633CSi	196 (3210/3.2)	M30B32	6	OHC
	733i	196 (3210/3.2)	M30B32	6	OHC
1983	320i	108 (1766/1.8)	—	4	OHC
	325e	165 (2693/2.7)	M20B27	6	OHC
	528e	165 (2693/2.7)	M20B27	6	OHC
	533i	196 (3210/3.2)	M30B32	6	OHC
	633CSi	196 (3210/3.2)	M30B32	6	OHC
	733i	196 (3210/3.2)	M30B32	6	OHC

Engine Identification (cont.)

Year	Model	Engine Displacement cu. in. (cc/liter)	Engine Series Identification	No. of Cylinders	Engine Type
1984	318i	108 (1766/1.8)	M10B18	4	OHC
	325e	165 (2693/2.7)	M20B27	6	OHC
	528e	165 (2693/2.7)	M20B27	6	OHC
	533i	196 (3210/3.2)	M30B32	6	OHC
	633CSi	196 (3210/3.2)	M30B32	6	OHC
	733i	196 (3210/3.2)	M30B32	6	OHC
1985	318i	108 (1766/1.8)	M10B18	4	OHC
	325e	165 (2693/2.7)	M20B27	6	OHC
	528e	165 (2693/2.7)	M20B27	6	OHC
	524td	149 (2443/2.4)	M21D24	6	OHC
	533i	196 (3210/3.2)	M30B32	6	OHC
	633CSi	196 (3210/3.2)	M30B32	6	OHC
	733i	196 (3210/3.2)	M30B32	6	OHC
1986	325e	165 (2693/2.7)	M20B27	6	OHC
	528e	165 (2693/2.7)	M20B27	6	OHC
	524td	149 (2443/2.4)	M21D24	6	OHC
	535i	209 (3428/3.4)	M30B34	6	OHC
	635CSi	209 (3428/3.4)	M30B34	6	OHC
	735i	209 (3428/3.4)	M30B34	6	OHC
1987	325	165 (2693/2.7)	M20B27	6	OHC
	325i	152 (2494/2.5)	M20B25	6	OHC
	528e	165 (2693/2.7)	M20B27	6	OHC
	325iS	152 (2494/2.5)	M20B25	6	OHC
	535i	209 (3428/3.4)	M30B34	6	OHC
	635CSi	209 (3428/3.4)	M30B35MZ	6	OHC
	735i	209 (3428/3.4)	M30B35MZ	6	OHC
	M5	210.6 (3453/3.5)	S38Z	6	DOHC
	M6	210.6 (3453/3.5)	S38Z	6	DOHC
1988	325	165 (2693/2.7)	M20B27	6	OHC
	528e	165 (2693/2.7)	M20B27	6	OHC
	325i	152 (2494/2.5)	M20B25	6	OHC
	325iS	152 (2494/2.5)	M20B25	6	OHC
	325iX	152 (2494/2.5)	M20B25	6	OHC
	535i	209 (3428/3.4)	M30B34	6	OHC
	635CSi	209 (3428/3.4)	M30B35MZ	6	OHC
	L6	209 (3428/3.4)	M30B35MZ	6	OHC
	735i	209 (3428/3.4)	M30B35MZ	6	OHC
	M3	140.4 (2302/2.3)	S14	4	DOHC
	M5	210.6 (3453/3.5)	S38Z	6	DOHC
	M6	210.6 (3453/3.5)	S38Z	6	DOHC

ROUTINE MAINTENANCE

Air Cleaner

All the dust present in the air is kept out of the ening by means of the air cleaner filter element. Proper maintenance is vital, as a clogged element not only restricts the airflow and thus the power, but can also cause premature engine wear.

Removing the filter element—carbureted engines

The filter element should be cleaned or replaced every 15,000 miles (24,000 km), or more often if the car is driven in dusty areas. The condition of the element should be checked periodically; if it appears to be overly dirty or clogged, shake it; if this does not help, the element must be replaced.

NOTE: *The paper element should not be cleaned or soaked with gasoline, cleaning solvent or oil.*

CLEANING OR REPLACING THE FILTER ELEMENT

Carbureted Engines

The air filter on these engines sits on top of the carburetor, usually towards the center of the engine compartment. To remove the filter element, simply unsnap the housing cover and lift out the element.

Clean the element by lightly shaking it against the palm of your hand (blowing with compressed air is also acceptable). If the filter element remains clogged after cleaning, replace it.

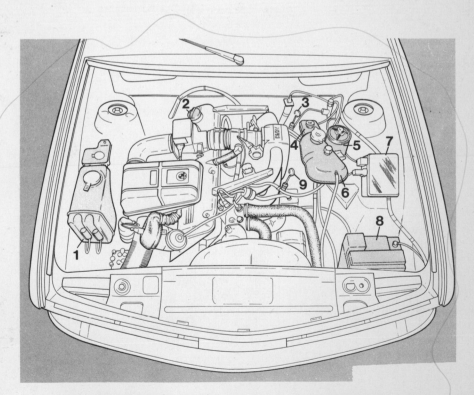

1. Fluid tank for windshield washer
2. Engine oil filler
3. Dipstick for automatic transmission
4. Fludi tank for brake and clutch hydralic
5. Fluid tank for power steering
6. Coolant tank
7. Fuse box
8. Battery
9. Dipstick for engine oil

Underhood view—1983 and later 5 series vehicles

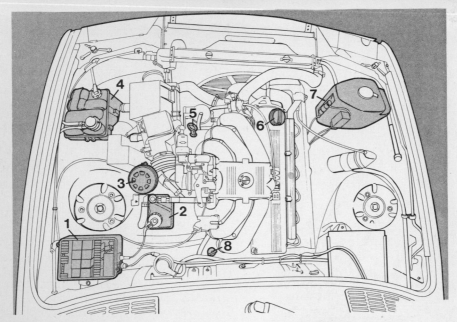

1. Fuse box
2. Fluid tank for brake and clutch hydraulic systems
3. Fluid tank for power steering
4. Coolant tank
5. Dipstick for engine oil
6. Engine oil filler
7. Fluid tank for windshield washer
8. Dipstick for automatic transmission

Underhood view—1983 and later 3 series vehicles

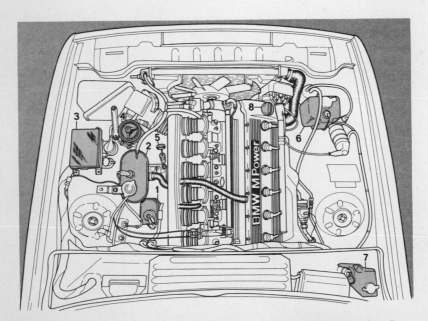

1. Fluid tank for brake and clutch hydraulic systems
2. Coolant tank
3. Fuse box
4. Fluid-tank for power steering
5. Dipstick for engine oil
6. Fluid tank for windshield washer
7. Fluid tank for intensive cleanser
8. Engine oil filler

Underhood view—M6

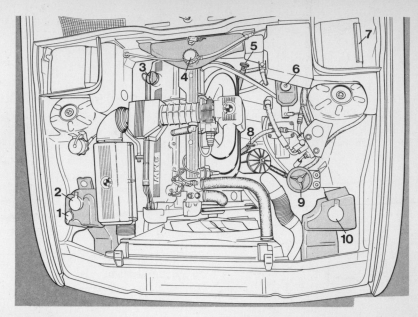

1. Fluid tank for intensive cleanser
2. Fluid tank for windshield washer
3. Engine oil filler
4. Coolant tank
5. Dipstick for automatic transmission
6. Fluid tank for brake and clutch hydraulic systems
7. Fuse box
8. Dipstick for engine oil
9. Fluid tank for brake booster servo and power steering
10. Fluid tank for fog and headlight washer

Underhood view—1983 and later 7 series vehicles

Removing the air filter element—2002tii

Remove the two bolts fastening this valve and its companion to the bracket near the injection pump—320i

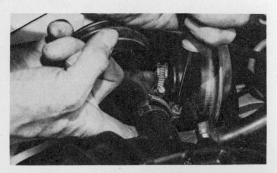

On the 320i, first loosen the clamp attaching the hose from the vacuum limiting valve to the air intake duct

Remove the square-type filter element—633CSi shown, others similar

Fuel Injected Engines

2002tii

This model utilizes a long cylindrical air cleaner housing with 2 separate filters in each end; it is located in the left side of the engine compartment. To remove, unsnap each end from the main body of the housing and lift out the filter elements. Clean in the same manner as described for carbureted engines.

320i

This model utilizes a square air filter element and housing, located in the left, front side of the engine compartment.

To remove, loosen the clamp connecting the vacuum limiting valve to the air intake duct. Next, remove the 2 bolts fastening this valve and its companion valve, the cold start valve, to the bracket near the injection pump. Unsnap the over-center catches and, while holding the 2 valves out of the way, pull the filter element up and out of the air cleaner housing. Clean in the same manner as described for carbureted engines.

6-CYLINDER MODELS

The air filter element on all 6-cylinder models is removed in basically the same manner. Unsnap the 2 over-center catches and split the 2 halves of the housing apart. Lift the element upward slightly to separate it from the lower half of the housing and then slide it out of the opening between the 2 halves.

NOTE: *When replacing the square type element used on most later models, always make sure that the arrow indicating airflow direction points toward the engine (or into the manifold) when positioning the filter. Also make sure that the rubber border on the element is properly positioned around the lower case half before closing the catches.*

Clean in the same manner as described for carbureted engines.

Fuel Filter
Gasoline Engines

FUEL SYSTEM SERVICE PRECAUTION

Gasoline is extremely volatile and can easily be ignited. Work on fuel system parts only when the engine is cold. Keep all other sources of ignition away. Carefully observe all precautions given in the procedures as to clamping fuel lines, collecting fuel in a metal container, and disposing of it in a safe manner. Always relieve fuel system pressure before unclamping lines, as fuel injection systems maintain very high pressure, even when the engine is off. This pressure is enough to cause the fuel to

spray from the line that is being opened. If the fuel is allowed to spray from the line it could be ignited by a spark. Pressurized fuel spray could also squirt into your eyes and cause severe injury.

RELIEVING FUEL SYSTEM PRESSURE

To relieve the pressure in fuel injected systems, first find the fuel pump relay plug, located on the cowl. Unplug the relay, leaving it in a safe position where the connections cannot ground. If necessary, tape the plug in place or tape over the connector prongs with electrical tape. Then, start the engine and operate it until it stalls. Crank the engine for 10 seconds after it stalls to remove any residual pressure.

REMOVAL AND INSTALLATION

Carbureted Models

1600, 2000, 2002, 2002tii, 2500, 2800, BAVARIA, 3000CS, 3.0CS and 3.0S

On all carbureted models, the fine mesh filter screen in the fuel pump is removed at 8,000 mile (13,000 km) intervals for cleaning. On 1600 models, this is accomplished by removing the 8mm cover plate bolt. On all other models, this is accomplished by removing the filter sieve retaining bolt (13mm). Discard the old sealing ring and wash out the filter sieve in clean gasoline or kerosene. On 1600 models, clean the cov-

Removing the fuel pump cover plate—1600

Removing the fuel pump filter sieve retaining bolt—all carbureted models but the 1600

er plate also. On all others, replace the filter sieve using a new sealing ring, and tighten the retaining bolt. At this time, check that the 6 cheese headed screws on the fuel pump are evenly tightened with a screwdriver.

Fuel Injected models

FILTER CLEANING

On all fuel injected models, a total of 3 fuel filters must be cleaned or replaced at 40,000 mile (64,000 km) intervals, the fourth, or main filter should be serviced at least every 8,000 (13,000 km) miles. They consist of a fine mesh filter in the fuel tank pick-up screen, a fine mesh filter in the electric fuel pump, an in line main fuel filter in the front of the engine compartment and another fine mesh filter in the mechanical fuel injection pump.

To clean the fuel tank pick-up screen, the following procedure is used:

1. Remove the right hand floor panel that covers the fuel tank in the trunk.

Fuel tank pick-up screen—fuel injected models

Removing the mesh filter in the injection pump

Main fuel filter—fuel injected models

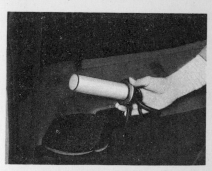

Removing the mesh strainer in the fuel tank—320i

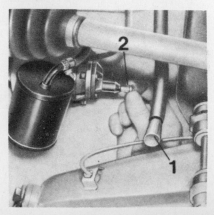

Removing the mesh filter in the electric fuel pump— (1) plugged fuel line, (2) filter

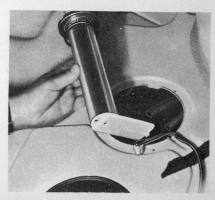

Removing the mesh strainer in the fuel tank—530i

2. Loosen t the hose clamps and disconnect the fuel lines from the pick-up unit.

3. Using 2 screwdrivers, turn the pickup unit counterclockwise in its bayonet mount until it releases. Lift out the pick-up unit.

4. Clean the fine mesh pick-up screen.

5. Reverse the above procedure to install, taking care to install a new sealing ring on the pick-up unit.

To clean the fine mesh filter in the electric fuel pump, the following procedure is used:

1. Locate the fuel pump underneath the car near the differential housing.

2. Loosen t the hose clamp on the fuel feed pipe. Disconnect and plug the end of the feed pipe with a suitable object.

3. Pull out the thimble-sized, bag-type fine mesh filter from the pump and clean it in clean gasoline or kerosene.

4. Reverse the above procedure to install.

To replace the in line main fuel filter, the following procedure is used:

1. Loosen both hose clamps and the filter retaining clamp. Mark the fuel line for reassembly.

NOTE: *Battery removal may facilitate better access to the fuel filter.*

2. Disconnect and plug both fuel lines, remove and discard the old filter.

3. Install a new filter, taking care to note the prescribed direction of flow shown on the filter label.

To clean the fine mesh filter in the fuel injection pump, the following procedure is used:

1. Remove the 17mm hollow screw in the fuel inlet pipe.

2. Clean the thimble-sized fine mesh filter located in the hollow screw using clean gasoline or kerosene.

3. Reverse the above procedure to install.

MESH STRAINER IN FUEL TANK

On the 320i, remove the rear seat to gain access to this unit. On the 3, 5 and 7 series models, remove the left luggage compartment floor panel. On the 3.0Si and 6 series models, remove the right side luggage compartment floor panel. On all models, first disconnect the electrical connector. Then, on 320i and 3.0Si models, remove bolts or nuts, detach hoses, and pull the pump/sensor unit out of the tank,. On the remaining models, unplug hoses, and turn the unit counter clockwise using screwdrivers as levers.

The strainer should then be cleaned in fresh gasoline. Be careful about the fire hazard related to using gasoline as a solvent. Install the unit in reverse order, using a new gasket and making sure to plug in hoses securely and check for

Removing the full flow fuel filter—530i

Removing the full flow filter—3.0Si

leaks before replacing the luggage compartment cover or sear.

FULL FLOW FILTER

These filters are located as follows:

• 318i, 320i, 325e, 325es, 325i, 325is, 325ix, M3—near the electric fuel pump on the left side of the rear axle

• 528e—above the rear suspension next to the fuel pump

• 528i, 530i, 630CSi, 633CSi, 635CSi, M6—above the rear suspension, left rear

• 3.0Si—left, front wheel arch, under the fusebox

• 535i, 535is, M5, 733i—above and slightly to the left of the rear axle

To replace this unit, loosen the hose clamps, remove the unit, and then replace it with a new one, making sure the arrow indicating direction of flow is facing the same direction as with the old unit (away from the tank). See the "Maintenance Intervals" chart for frequency of service.

FUEL PUMP STRAINER (3.0SI ONLY)

Loosen the intake clamp hose (1) on the fuel pump, which is located above the right rear halfshaft. Remove the fine mesh, basket type filter located inside the hose connection, and clean it in fresh fuel. This should be performed when the full flow filter is replaced.

Fuel Filter—Diesel Engine

REMOVAL AND INSTALLATION

1984-86 524Td

1. Loosen the bleeder screw located on top of the filter mounting fitting with a regular screw-

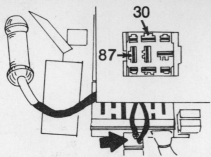

Jumper terminals 30 and 87 to run the fuel transfer pump and prime the fuel system

driver. Place a container under the filter and loosen the drain cock to drain a small amount of fuel (this will keep fuel from spilling when the filter is removed).

2. Disconnect the plug on the water level sensor. Unscrew the filter with a standard oil filter strap wrench.

3. Remove the water level sensor from the old filter and move it over to the new one.

4. Thoroughly coat the seal on top of the new filter with clean fuel. Start the filter onto the threads, turn it until the gasket touches, and then turn it just one half turn more by hand.

5. Disconnect the plug for the fuel transfer pump. Open the bleeder screw. Jumper terminals 30 and 87. When fuel that is bubble-free runs out of the bleed screw, tighten it. Remove the jumper and reconnect the plug.

6. Start the engine and operate it to check for leaks. Tighten the filter just a bit further, if necessary.

DRAINING WATER FROM THE SYSTEM

Due to the chemical make up of diesel fuel it is prone to hold water. The fuel filter in the diesel fuel system is designed to separate this water from the fuel before it reaches the injection system.

Periodically this water must be removed from the filter canister or the filter will become full of water, causing water to enter the injection system. The water can be drained as follows:

Hold a half pint container under the bleeder screw and open the drain cock. See Step 5 of the procedure above for fuel filter replacement, and activate the fuel transfer pump as described there. Then, press the drain adapter in to open it. Drain until pure fuel runs out.

PCV Valve and Evaporative Canister
SERVICE

The BMW employs crankcase ventilation and evaporative canister systems which do not re-

quire fresh air for their operation. This eliminates the need for periodic replacement of the PCV valves and canister filters generally associated with other types of systems.

Battery

SPECIFIC GRAVITY (EXCEPT MAINTENANCE FREE BATTERIES)

At least once a year, check the specific gravity of the battery. It should be between 1.20 and 1.26 at room temperature.

The specific gravity can be checked with the use of an hydrometer, an inexpensive instrument available from many sources, including auto parts stores. The hydrometer has a squeeze bulb at one end and a nozzle at the other. Battery electrolyte is sucked into the hydrometer until the float is lifted from its eat. The specific gravity is then read by noting the position of the float. Generally, if after charging, the specific gravity between any 2 cells varies more than 50 points (0.050), the battery is bad and should be replaced.

It is not possible to check the specific gravity in this manner on sealed ("maintenance free") batteries. Instead, the indicator built into the top of the case must be relied on to display any signs of battery deterioration. If the indicator is dark, the battery can be assumed to be OK. If

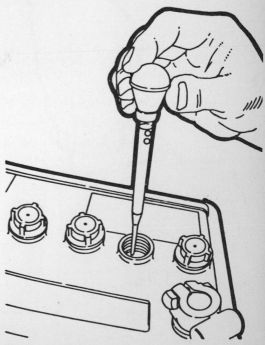

Specific gravity can be checked with an hydrometer

the indicator is light, the specific gravity is low, and the battery should be charged or replaced.

CABLES AND CLAMPS

Once a year, the battery terminals and the cable clamps should be cleaned. Loose the clamps and remove the cable, negative cable first. On batteries with posts on top, the use of a puller

Clean the inside of the clamps with a wire brush, or the special tool

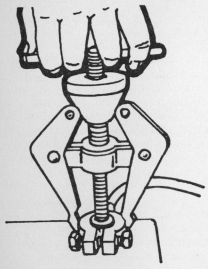

Pullers make clamp removal easier

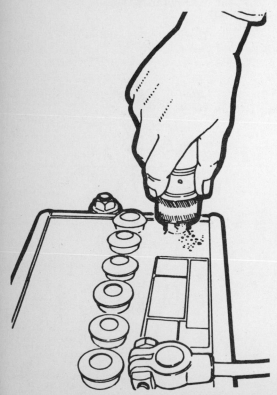

Clean the posts with a wire brush, or a terminal cleaner made for the purpose (shown)

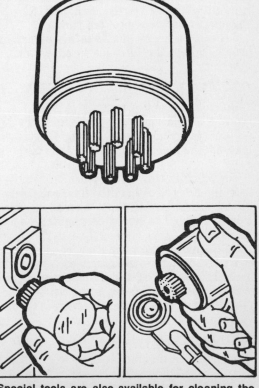

Special tools are also available for cleaning the posts and clamps on side terminal batteries

specially made for that purpose is recommended. These are inexpensive, and available in auto parts stores. Side terminal battery cables are secured with a bolt.

Clean the cable clamps and the battery terminal with a wire brush, until all corrosion, grease, etc. is removed and the metal is shiny. It is especially important to clean the inside of the clamp thoroughly, since a small deposit of foreign material or oxidation will prevent a sound electrical connection and inhibit either starting or charging. Special tools are available for cleaning these parts, one type for conventional batteries and another type for side terminal batteries.

Before installing the cables, loosen the battery holddown clamp or strap, remove the battery and check the battery try. Clear it of any debris, and check it for soundness. Rust should be wire brushed away, and the metal given a coat of anti-rust paint. Replace the battery and tighten the holddown clamp or strap securely, but be careful not to over tighten, which will crack the battery case.

After the clamps and terminals are clean, reinstall the cables, negative cable last, do not hammer on the clamps to install. Tighten the clamps securely, but do not distort them. Give the clamps and terminals a thin external coat of grease after installation, to retard corrosion.

Check the cable at the same time that the terminals are cleaned. If the cable insulation is cracked or broken, or if the ends are frayed, the cable should be replaced with a new cable of the same length and gauge.

NOTE: *Keep flame or sparks away from the battery; it gives off explosive hydrogen gas. Battery electrolyte contains sulphuric acid. If you should splash any on your skin or in your eyes, flush the affected area with plenty of clear water; if it lands in your eyes, get medical help immediately.*

REPLACEMENT

When it becomes necessary to replace the battery, select a battery with a rating equal to or greater than the battery originally installed. Deterioration, embrittlement and just plain aging of the battery cables, starter motor, and associated wires makes the battery's job harder in successive years. The slow increase in electrical resistance over time makes it prudent to install a new battery with a greater capacity than the old.

BATTERY LEVEL

Check the battery fluid level (except in Maintenance Free batteries) at least once a month, more often in hot weather or during extended periods of travel. The electrolyte level should be up to the bottom of the split ring in each cell. All batteries are equipped with an "eye" in the cap of one cell. If the "eye" glows or has an amber color to it, this means that the level is low and only distilled water should be added. Do not ad anything else to the battery. If the "eye" has a dark appearance the battery electrolyte level is high enough. It is also wise to check each cell individually.

If water is added during freezing weather, the car should be driven several miles to allow the electrolyte and water to mix. Otherwise the battery could freeze.

If the battery becomes corroded, a solution of baking soda and water will neutralize the corrosion. This should be washed off after making sure that the caps are securely in place. Rinse the solution off with cold water.

Some batteries were equipped with a felt terminal washer. This should be saturated with engine oil approximately every 6,000 miles (9,600 km). This will also help to retard corrosion.

If a "fast" charger is used while the battery is in the car, disconnect the battery before connecting the charger.

CAUTION: *Keep flame or sparks away from the battery; it gives off explosive hydrogen gas.*

TESTING THE MAINTENANCE FREE BATTERY

All later model cars are equipped with maintenance free batteries, which do not require normal attention as far as fluid level checks are concerned. However, the terminals require periodic cleaning, which should be performed at least once a year.

Charging Rate Amps	Time
75	40 min
50	1 hr
25	2 hr
10	5 hr

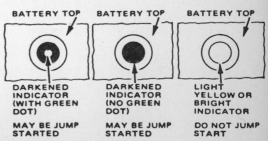

DARKENED INDICATOR (WITH GREEN DOT)
MAY BE JUMP STARTED

DARKENED INDICATOR (NO GREEN DOT)
MAY BE JUMP STARTED

LIGHT YELLOW OR BRIGHT INDICATOR
DO NOT JUMP START

Maintenance–free batteries contain their own built–in hydrometer

Battery	Test Load
Y85–4	130 amps
R85–5	170 amps
R87–5	210 amps
R89–5	230 amps

The sealed top battery cannot be checked for charge in the normal manner, since there is no provision for access to the electrolyte. To check the condition of the battery:

1. If the indicator eye on top of the battery is dark, the battery has enough fluid. If the eye is light, the electrolyte fluid is too low and the battery must be replaced.

2. If a green dot appears in the middle of the eye, the battery is sufficiently charged. Proceed to Step 4. If no green dot is visible, charge the battery as in Step 3.

3. Charge the battery at this rate.

CAUTION: *Do not charge the battery for more than 50 amp/hours. If the green dot appears, or if electrolyte squirts out of the vent hole, stop the charge and proceed to Step 4.*

It may be necessary to tip the battery from side to side to get thee green dot to appear after charging.

4. Connect a battery load tester and a voltmeter across the battery terminals (the battery cables should be disconnected from the battery). Apply a 300 amp load to the battery for 15 seconds to remvoe the surface charge. Remove the load.

5. Wait 15 seconds to allow the battery to recover. Apply the appropriate test load, as specified in the following chart:

Apply the load for 15 seconds while reading the voltage. Disconnect the load.

6. Check the results against the following chart. If the battery voltage is at or above the specified voltage for the temperature listed, the battery is good. If the voltage falls below what's listed, the battery should be replaced.

Air Intake Preheat Flap

Every 8,000 miles (13,000 km) on 1970-74 models check the function of the air intake flap as follows:

1. With the engine cold, remove the fresh air intake line at the air cleaner. The outside temperature should be cool, preferably 70°F (21°C) or below.

2. Start the engine and immediately observe the flap. It should close tightly. Shut the engine off and verify that the valve opens all the way.

Belts

INSPECTION

Belts should be inspected for both tension and condition at intervals of 12,500 miles

(20,000 km) and shortly after replacement. Belt tension is checked by applying pressure (about 10-15 lbs..) with your thumb midway between 2 pulleys. The belt should deflect (stretch) about ½-¾" for each 10" of distance between pulley centers. The belt should spring tight, not sag-

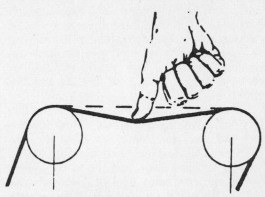

Belt deflection can be tested with your thumb

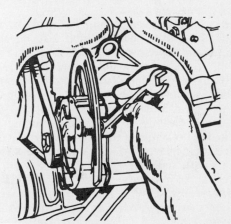

To adjust belt tension or to replace belts, first loosen the component's mounting and adjusting bolts slightly

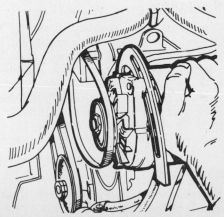

Push the component toward the engine and slip off the belt

HOW TO SPOT WORN V-BELTS

V-Belts are vital to efficient engine operation—they drive the fan, water pump and other accessories. They require little maintenance (occasional tightening) but they will not last forever. Slipping or failure of the V-belt will lead to overheating. If your V-belt looks like any of these, it should be replaced.

This belt has deep cracks, which cause it to flex. Too much flexing leads to heat build-up and premature failure. These cracks can be caused by using the belt on a pulley that is too small. Notched belts are available for small diameter pulleys.

Cracking or weathering

Oil and grease on a belt can cause the belt's rubber compounds to soften and separate from the reinforcing cords that hold the belt together. The belt will first slip, then finally fail altogether.

Softening (grease and oil)

Glazing is caused by a belt that is slipping. A slipping belt can cause a run-down battery, erratic power steering, overheating or poor accessory performance. The more the belt slips, the more glazing will be built up on the surface of the belt. The more the belt is glazed, the more it will slip. If the glazing is light, tighten the belt.

Glazing

The cover of this belt is worn off and is peeling away. The reinforcing cords will begin to wear and the belt will shortly break. When the belt cover wears in spots or has a rough jagged appearance, check the pulley grooves for roughness.

Worn cover

This belt is on the verge of breaking and leaving you stranded. The layers of the belt are separating and the reinforcing cords are exposed. It's just a matter of time before it breaks completely.

Separation

ging or having play, but not so tight that it requires tremendous effort to get a slight deflection. Excessive belt tension may wear the bearings of the accessory being driven, or may stretch and crack the belt, while insufficient tension will cause slippage and glazing.

Inspect the belt for separation between the outer surface and the Vee, and for radial cracks, which usually begin at the inner surface. The driving surfaces should be rough, slightly cross-hatched because they are fabric covered. If the surface is perfectly smooth, the belt has slipped, and this has caused overheating. A glazed belt cannot offer a sufficient amount of friction to carry the load without excessive tension. Belts which show cracks or glazing should be replaced.

REPLACEMENT

First, a few rules:

1. Replace belts with the proper part. A belt of the wrong length will have to be pried on if too short, a procedure that will seriously damage the belt even before it turns around once, or which may prevent sufficient tightening to compensate for wear long before the belt has really worn out. If you must use a belt that is just a little too short, you might be able to avoid stretching it during installation by completely dismounting the driven accessory, working the belt around the pulleys, and then remounting the accessory.

2. Replace the multiple belts in sets only, as work belts stretch and mixing stretched belts with new ones will prevent even division of the load.

3. Do not attempt to change belt tension or rotate an accessory for belt replacement without loosening both the adjustment bolt (the bolt which runs in a slitted bracket) and the pivot bolt. Do not pry belts on to avoid rotating the drive accessory.

4. Do not pry the driven accessory with a heavy metal bar if you can get sufficient belt tension by hand. This applies especially to aluminum castings or air/fluid pumps, where distortion of the housing can be a critical problem. If you must pry, pry on a substantial steel bracket only or, failing that, on the part of the casting the adjusting bolt screws into. Some accessory mounting brackets are designed with a slit or square hole into which you can insert a socket drive for tensioning purposes.

To replace a belt, first locate the pivot bolt. This holds the unit to the engine block or to a short bracket which has only a hole—no slot. If the pivot bolt does not use a nut welded onto the back of the accessory or a bracket you will have to apply wrenches at both ends—to both the bolt and nut to loosen this bolt. Loosen t the

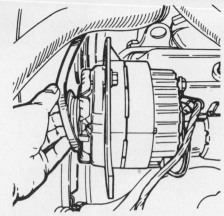
Slip the new belt over the pulley

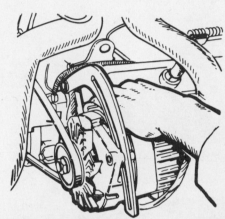
Pull outward on the component and tighten the mounting bolts

bold slightly—don't release all tension, as you will want the accessory to stay securely mounted to get an accurate tension adjustment later.

Then, loosen the adjusting bolt. This passes through a long slot in a bracket and usually runs right into threads cut into the main body of the accessory. Now, all belt tension will be gone.

Next, move the accessory all the way toward the engine, and pull off the belt. Position the new blet around all the pulleys. Make sure it tracks in all the pulley grooves and, if there are multiple pulleys or pulleys and belts involved, make sure the belt runs in pulleys which are directly in line with one another.

Be ready to tighten the adjusting bolt, pull or pry the accessory away from the engine until the tension is correct (see above). and then tighten the adjusting bolt, finally, tighten the pivot bolt.

NOTE: *When installing a new belt (one run less than 10 minutes) put a little extra tension on it to allow for stretch and seating in the pulley Vees during break-in. About 30-40 per-*

HOW TO SPOT BAD HOSES

Both the upper and lower radiator hoses are called upon to perform difficult jobs in an inhospitable environment. They are subject to nearly 18 psi at under hood temperatures often over 280°F., and must circulate nearly 7500 gallons of coolant an hour—3 good reasons to have good hoses.

Swollen hose

A good test for any hose is to feel it for soft or spongy spots. Frequently these will appear as swollen areas of the hose. The most likely cause is oil soaking. This hose could burst at any time, when hot or under pressure.

Cracked hose

Cracked hoses can usually be seen but feel the hoses to be sure they have not hardened; a prime cause of cracking. This hose has cracked down to the reinforcing cords and could split at any of the cracks.

Frayed hose end (due to weak clamp)

Weakened clamps frequently are the cause of hose and cooling system failure. The connection between the pipe and hose has deteriorated enough to allow coolant to escape when the engine is hot.

Debris in cooling system

Debris, rust and scale in the cooling system can cause the inside of a hose to weaken. This can usually be felt on the outside of the hose as soft or thinner areas.

cent extra tension will do. Instead of deflecting as much as ¾", the belt should deflect a little less than ½" for each 10" of distance between the pulley centers. Recheck tension of new belts several days after installation in case of stretch.

Hoses

Worn hoses will feel brittle, the lower hose may be permanently narrowed at one point from suction, or may appear frayed or cracked. New hoses will be springy and pliable yet firm, the rubber surface will be solid and smooth, and there will be no evidence of string reinforcements showing through.

REPLACEMENT

1. Put a bucket of about 2 gallons capacity under the radiator drain (some models are so equipped) or the radiator end of the lower hose (if there's no drain plug). Remove the drain plus or loosen the hose clamp and pull the bottom of the hose off the radiator connection. Remove the radiator soap.

CAUTION: *When draining the coolant, keep in mind that cats and dogs are attracted by the ethylene glycol antifreeze, and are quite likely to drink any that is left in an uncovered container or in puddles on the ground. This will prove fatal in sufficient quantity. Always drain the coolant into a sealable container. Coolant should be reused unless it is contaminated or several years old.*

2. If a heater hose is being replaced, turn the rotary heater control to "Warm" and allow any water contained in the heater core and hoses to drain.

3. Loosen t the clamps at both ends of the hoses. Work the hose ends off the radiator or heater core and engine block connections.

4. Install the new hose in reverse order. If the hose has certain bends molded into it, make sure to position the hose so that it does not become crimped at these points. Also, install new hose clamps onto the hose from both ends before sliding hose ends onto connections. Make sure hoses slide all the way onto the connectors. Make sure you then slide the clamps over the lips on the connectors but not all the way at the ends of the hoses.

5. Tighten the clamps securely, and then refill the cooling system as described below.

Cooling System

COOLANT CHECK AND CHANGE

On systems without a coolant recovery tank, the engine coolant level should be maintained 1-2" below the bottom of the radiator filler neck when the engine is at air temperature and 1" below the bottom of the filler neck when the engine is hot.

On systems with a coolant recovery tank, maintain the coolant level at the level marks on the recovery bottle.

For best protection against freezing and overheating, maintain an approximate 50% water and 50% ethylene glycol antifreeze mixture in the cooling system. Do not mix different brands of antifreeze to avoid possible chemical damage to the cooling system.

Avoid using water that is known to have a high alkaline content or is very hard, except in emergency situations. Drain and flush the cooling system as soon as possible after using such water.

CAUTION: *Cover the radiator cap with a thick cloth before removing it from a radiator in a vehicle that is hot. Turn the cap counterclockwise slowly until pressure can be heard escaping. Allow all pressure to escape from the radiator before completely removing the radiator cap. It is best to allow the engine to cool if possible, before removing the radiator cap.*

NOTE: *Never add cold water to an overheated engine while the engine is not running.*

After filling the radiator, run the engine until it reaches normal operating temperature, to make sure that the thermostat has opened and all the air is bled from the system.

DRAINING, FLUSHING AND REFILLING

CAUTION: *When draining the coolant, keep in mind that cats and dogs are attracted by the ethylene glycol antifreeze, and are quite likely to drink any that is left in an uncovered container or in puddles on the ground. This will prove fatal in sufficient quantity. Always drain the coolant into a sealable container. Coolant should be reused unless it is contaminated or several years old.*

To drain the cooling system, allow the engine to cool down **BEFORE ATTEMPTING TO REMOVE THE RADIATOR CAP**. Then turn the cap until it hisses. Wait until all pressure is off the cap before removing it completely.

CAUTION: *To avoid burns and scalding, always handle a warm radiator cap with a heavy rag.*

1. At the dash, set the heater TEMP control lever to the fully HOT position.

2. With the radiator cap removed, drain the radiator by loosening the petcock at the bottom of the radiator. Locate any drain plugs in the block and remove them. Flush the radiator with water until the fluid runs clear.

3. Close the petcock and replace the plug(s), then refill the system with a 50/50 mix of ethylene glycol antifreeze. Fill the system to ¾-1¼"

from the bottom of the filler neck. Reinstall the radiator cap.

NOTE: *If equipped with a fluid reservoir tank, fill it up to the MAX level.*

4. Operate the engine at 2,000 rpm for a few minutes and check the system for signs of leaks.

RADIATOR CAP INSPECTION

Allow the engine to cool sufficiently before attempting to remove the radiator cap. Use a rag

On models without a coolant recovery tank, the coolant level should be even with the bottom of the filler neck

If the engine is hot, cover the radiator cap with a rag

Some radiator caps have pressure release levers

to cover the cap, then remove by pressing down and turning counterclockwise to the first stop. If any hissing is noted (indicating the release of pressure), wait until the hissing stops completely, then press down again and turn counterclockwise until the cap can be removed.

CAUTION: *DO NOT attempt to remove the radiator cap while the engine is hot. Severe personal injury from steam burns can result.*

Check the condition of the radiator cap gasket and seal inside of the cap. The radiator cap is designed to seal the cooling system under normal operating conditions which allows the build up of a certain amount of pressure (this pressure rating is stamped or printed on the cap). The pressure in the system raises the boiling point of the coolant to help prevent overheating. If the radiator cap does not seal, the boiling point of the coolant is lowered and overheating will occur. If the cap must be replaced, purchase the new cap according to the pressure rating which is specified for your vehicle.

Prior to installing the radiator cap, inspect and clean the filler neck. If you are reusing the old cap, clean it thoroughly with clear water. After turning the cap on, make sure the arrows align with the overflow hose.

Air Conditioner
GENERAL SERVICING PROCEDURES

The most important aspect of air conditioning service is the maintenance of pure and adequate charge of refrigerant in the system. A refrigeration system cannot function properly if a significant percentage of the charge is lost. Leaks are common because the severe vibration encountered in an automobile can easily cause a sufficient cracking or loosening of the air conditioning fittings. As a result, the extreme operating pressures of the system force refrigerant out.

The problem can be understood by considering what happens to the system as it is operated with a continuous leak. Because the expansion valve regulates the flow of refrigerant to the evaporator, the level of refrigerant there is fairly constant. The receiver/drier stores any excess of refrigerant, and so a loss will first appear there as a reduction in the level of liquid. As this level nears the bottom of the vessel, some refrigerant vapor bubbles will begin to appear in the stream of liquid supplied to the expansion valve. This vapor decreases the capacity of the expansion valve very little as the valve opens to compensate for its presence. As the quantity of liquid in the condenser decreases, the operating pressure will drop there and throughout the high side of the system. As the R-12 continues to be expelled, the pressure

available to force the liquid through the expansion valve will continue to decrease, and, eventually, the valve's orifice will prove to be too much of a restriction for adequate flow even with the needle fully withdrawn.

At this point, low side pressure will start to drop, and severe reduction in cooling capacity, marked by freeze-up of the evaporator coil, will result. Eventually, the operating pressure of the evaporator will be lower than the pressure of the atmosphere surrounding it, and air will be drawn into the system wherever there are leaks in the low side.

Because all atmospheric air contains at least some moisture, water will enter the system and mix with the R-12 and the oil. Trace amounts of moisture will cause sludging of the oil, and corrosion of the system. Saturation and clogging of the filter/drier, and freezing of the expansion valve orifice will eventually result. As air fills the system to a greater and greater extend, it will interfere more and more with the normal flows of refrigerant and heat.

A list of general precautions that should be observed while doing this follows:

1. Keep all tools as clean and dry as possible.
2. Thoroughly purge the service gauges and hoses of air and moisture before connecting them to the system. Keep them capped when not in use.
3. Thoroughly clean any refrigerant fitting before disconnecting it, in order to minimize the entrance of dirt into the system.
4. Plan any operation that requires opening the system beforehand in order to minimize the length of time it will be exposed to open air. Cap or seal the open ends to minimize the entrance of foreign material.
5. When adding oil, pour it through an extremely clean and dry tube or funnel. Keep the oil capped whenever possible. Do not use oil that has not been kept tightly sealed.
6. Use only refrigerant 12. Purchase refrigerant intended for use in only automotive air conditioning system. Avoid the use of refrigerant 12 that may be packaged for another use, such as cleaning, or powering a horn, as it is impure.
7. Completely evacuate any system that has been opened to replace a component, other than when isolating the compressor, or that has leaked sufficiently to draw in moisture and air. This requires evacuating air and moisture with a good vacuum pump for at least one hour.

If a system has been open for a considerable length of time it may be advisable to evacuate the system for up to 12 hours (overnight).

8. Use a wrench on both halves of a fitting that is to be disconnected, so as to avoid placing torque on any of the refrigerant lines.

ADDITIONAL PREVENTIVE MAINTENANCE CHECKS

Antifreeze

In order to prevent heater core freeze-up during A/C operation, it is necessary to maintain permanent type antifreeze protection of $+15°F$ ($-9°C$) or lower. A reading of $-15°F$ ($-26°C$) is ideal since this protection also supplies sufficient corrosion inhibitors for the protection of the engine cooling system.

WARNING: *Do not use antifreeze longer than specified by the manufacturer.*

Radiator Cap

For efficient operation of an air conditioned car's cooling system, the radiator cap should have a holding pressure which meets manufacturer's specifications. A cap which fails to hold these pressure should be replaced.

Condenser

Any obstruction of or damage to the condenser configuration will restrict the air flow which is essential to its efficient operation. It is therefore, a good rule to keep this unit clean and in proper physical shape.

NOTE: *Bug screens are regarded as obstructions.*

Condensation Drain Tube

This single molded drain tube expels the condensation, which accumulates on the bottom of the evaporator housing, into the engine compartment.

If this tube is obstructed, the air conditioning performance can be restricted and condensation buildup can spill over onto the vehicle's floor.

SAFETY WARNINGS

The air conditioner is filled with refrigerant R-12, which produces very high pressure even when the system is not operating. Not only can a component broken by mishandling crack or break explosively, but the escaping refrigerant will immediately drop to 27°F ($-33°C$), causing severe frostbite to any part of the body exposed nearby. The problem is worsened by the fact that refrigerant systems employ thin sections of light alloys to transfer heat efficiently – thus, components are readily damaged by inexperienced mechanics.

Thus, we recommend that you make not attempt whatever to repair any component on the air conditioning system. If a refrigerant component must be moved to gain access to another part, we recommend you leave at least the part of the job involving the refrigerant component to someone with the specialized training, tools,

and experience to handle the job safely. However, if you are going to work on the system yourself, you must be very careful and use common sense before making any repairs.

CHECKING THE SYSTEM

Once a year, before hot weather sets in, it is advisable to check the refrigerant charge in the air conditioner system. This may be accomplished by looking at the sight glass located in the engine compartment on the right fender well. First, wipe the sight glass clean with a cloth wrapped around the eraser end of a pencil. Connect a tachometer to the engine with the positive line connected to the distributor side of the ignition coil and the negative line connected to a good ground, such as the steering box. Have a friend operate the air conditioner controls while you look at the sight glass. Have your friend set the dash panel control to **MAX** cooling. Start the engine and idle at 1,500 rpm. While looking at the sight glass, signal your friend to turn the blower switch to the **HIGH** position. If a few bubbles appear immediately after the blower is turned on and then disappear, the system is sufficiently charged with refrigerant. If, on the other hand, a large amount of bubbles has operated for a few seconds, then the system is in need of additional refrigerant. If no bubbles appear at all, then there is either sufficient refrigerant in the system, or it is bone

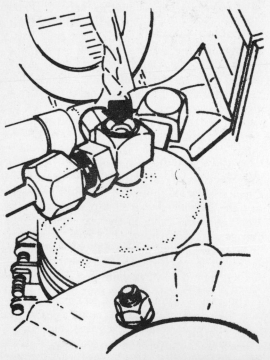

Air conditioner sight glass location—528i shown, others similar

dry. The way to clear this question up is to have your friend turn the unit **OFF** and **ON** (engine running at 1,500 rpm) about every 10 seconds or so while you look at the sight glass. This will cycle the magnetic clutch. If the system is properly charged, bubbles will appear in the sight glass a few seconds after the unit is turned off and disappear when it is turned on although they may linger awhile in extremely hot weather. If no bubbles appear when the unit is in the **OFF** position, then the system should be serviced by an authorized dealer and checked for leaks. Do not operate the unit if you suspect that the refrigerant has leaked out.

USING THE BAR GAUGE MANIFOLD

WARNING: *Refrigerant work is usually performed by highly trained technicians. Improper use of the gauges can result in a leakage of refrigerant liquid, damage to the compressor, or even explosion of a system part. The do-it-yourselfer must be very careful to insure that he proceeds with extreme care and understands what he is doing before proceeding. The best insurance for safety is a complete understanding of the system and proper techniques for servicing it. A careful study of a complete text such as CHILTON'S GUIDE TO AIR CONDITIONING SERVICE AND REPAIR, book part No. 7580, is the best insurance against either dangerous or system-damaging problems.*

To use the bar gauge manifold, follow the procedures outlined below.

1. It is first necessary to clear the manifold itself of air and moisture, especially if the fittings have been left open. You should follow this procedure, unless you know that the hoses and gauge manifold have recently been bled with refrigerant and capped off tightly. Otherwise, you may actually force air and moisture into the system when you are testing or charging it. Begin with both the service valves on the refrigerant gauge set *closed*.

  a. First, tap a can of refrigerant. To do this, first unscrew the tap's cutting tool all the way. Turn the rotatable locking lever so it leaves one side of the collar assembly open. Then, slide the tap onto the top of the can so the collar tabs fit over the rim that runs around the top of the can. Turn the locking lever so that it secures the collar. Then, turn the cutting tool all the way down to tap the can.

  b. Remove any plugs that may be present and then screw the *center* hose to the screw fitting on top of the tap. Now, slightly loosen the plugs in the ends of the other 2 lines.

  c. Sit the can of refrigerant down right side up on a flat surface. *Make sure the can does not*

get pulled up off the surface as you work, or you could be splattered by liquid refrigerant. Then, open the tap by unscrewing the tapping tool handle all the way. Crack both of the bar gauge manifold valves just a little--just until you hear a slight hiss at the plug at the end of the hose on either side. Allow the refrigerant to enter the system until you are sure it has reached the ends of the hoses (30 seconds). Tighten the plugs at the bottom of the hoses and then *immediately* turn off both manifold valves.

2. Using a wrench if the cap has flats, uncap the low and high pressure, Schrader valve type fittings for the system. The low pressure fitting is located on the suction port of the compressor. In a typical mounting of the unit with the ports facing the front of the car, this is the lower port. You'll find that there is a line connecting with this port that comes from the evaporator (located behind the cowl). The high pressure fitting is located on the muffler, which, in turn is located on the line coming out of the commmpressor and heading toward the condenser. There is a low pressure gauge on the left side of the manifold, which shows pressures up to about 100 psi *and* vacuum. Connect the line on this side to the low pressure side of the system. The gauge on the right or high pressure side of the manifold reads only pressure and, typically, the scale goes up to 500 psi. or higher. If you are shopping for gauges, you can use a conventional set which has only 2 gauges. There are some gauge sets available that have 3 gauges on them, these are for specific types of compressors that are not used on these vehicles.

On many newer systems, the threads on high and low pressure Schrader valves are of different sizes to prevent improper hookup.

If you have an older set of gauges, you can get an adapter or a different hose that will convert your gauges to the new thread sizes. Consult a heating, air conditioning and refrigeration supply source.

WARNING: *When making connections, start the threads carefully and, once you are sure they are not crossthreaded, turn the fitting as fast as you can in order to avoid getting sprayed by refrigerant. Sometimes the Schrader valve will open early--before the fitting is tight, and this will cause a little refrigerant to be sprayed out.*

3. Use of the gauges once they are bled and installed typically includes reading high and low side pressures with both valves closed, charging the system with the low side valve cracked partly open, and discharging it with both valves partly open. Refer to the section just below on "Charging the System" for specifics.

4. To disconnect the gauges, turn the fittings as quickly as possible so as to close the Schrader valves as quickly as possible. Note that liquid refrigerant and oil may be sprayed out for a short time as this is done, especially on the low pressure side. Turn the fittings by reaching down from above, as liquid will be sprayed out underneath the gauge connection. Less refrigerant will be sprayed out on the high side if the connection is broken a few minutes after the system is turned off. Cap the open ends of the gauges immediately. If, for any reason, the ends are left open for a minute or 2, repeat the bleeding procedure above. Tightly cap the system openings right away.

DISCHARGING THE SYSTEM

NOTE: *Fluorocarbon refrigerants like ihat used in car air conditioners damage the upper atmosphere, destroying its ability to screen off dangerous solar radiation. For this reason, air conditioning service shops will soon be required to use special charging/evacuating stations to condense and recover refrigerants rather than releasing them to the atmosphere. While these environmental regulations may not apply to the do-it-yourselfer, you may wish to have your system discharged by a professional equipped to recover the refrigerant if you are concerned about the environment.*

1. Connect the gauges to the high and low sides of the system, as described above. Do not connect a refrigerant can to the center hose.

2. Insert the center hose into a glass bottle with an opening that is slightly larger in diameter than the hose. *Do not attempt to cap or seal the opening in the top of the bottle in any way.* This bottle will collect oil discharged from the system so that it can be measured and replaced when the system is recharged. Make sure you keep the bottle upright to avoid spilling any of this oil out.

3. Make sure the compressor is turned off and remains off throughout the procedure. Crack the low side manifold valve until refrigerant gas is expelled at a steady, moderate rate. Don't open the valve all the way, or too much refrigerant oil will be expelled from the system.

4. As refrigerant pressure drops and the gas begins to be expelled only very slowly, open the low side manifold valve more and more to compensate and keep the refrigerant moving out of the system.

5. Once *all* the pressure is discharged, slowly open the high side service valve, repeating Steps 3 and 4 until the system is clear. Close it after any pressure has escaped.

6. Disconnect the gauges and recap the openings. Retain the bottle of oil. If you have the sys-

tem evacuated and recharged by a professional, give him the bottle of oil. He will measure the amount it contains and replace it with a like amount.

CHARGING THE SYSTEM

WARNING: *Charging the system can prove to be very dangerous. You must satisfy yourself that you are fully aware of all risks before starting. Although most systems use a high pressure cutoff switch for the compressor, overcharging the system, attempting to charge it when it contains air, or charging it when there is inadequate cooling of the condenser could cause dangerous pressures to develop if this switch should fail. Overcharging could also damage the compressor.*

The safest way to charge the system is with a set of gauges installed and reading both low and high side pressures so that you can monitor pressures throughout the procedure. It is best to refer to a text on refrigeration and air conditioning first, so that you understand what will happen. Using the simple hose sold for do-it-yourself charging of the system can be safe, provided 3 precautions are taken:

a. Make sure the system has been completely evacuated by a professional with a good vacuum pump. Eliminating air in the system is a vital step toward maintaining safe pressures during the charging process and ensuring reliable and effective operation later.

b. Charge the system with precisely the amount of refrigerant it is specified to use *and no more*. Consult the label on the compressor. Purchase the right number of cans. You can precisely estimate what percentage of a can has been charged into the system by noting the frost line on the can.

c. Run the engine at a moderate speed during charging (not too fast), valve the refrigerant into the system at a controlled rate, and keep a fan blowing across the condenser at all times.

Charge the system by following these steps:

1. Make sure the system has been completely evacuated with a good vacuum pump. This should be done with gauges connected and the pump must be able to create a vacuum of 28-29 in. Hg near sea level. Lower this specification one in. Hg for each 1,000 feet above sea level at your location.

2. Connect the gauges as described above, including tapping in a new can of refrigerant. If you are using a gaugeless hose that is part of a charging kit, follow the directions on the package; in any case, make sure to hook up the hose to the low pressure side of the system--to the accumulator or POA valve.

3. Situate a fan in front of the condenser and use it to blow air through the condenser and radiator throughout the charging process.

4. Unless the system has a sight glass, get the exact refrigerant capacity off the compressor label. Make sure you have only the proper number of cans available to help avoid unnecessary overcharge.

5. It will speed the process to place the cans, top up, in warm water. Use a thermometer and make sure the water is *not over 120°F*. You will need to warm the water as the process goes on. Monitor the temperature to make sure it does not go too high, as warm water will almost immediately create excessive pressure inside the can—pressure that will not be reflected in gauge readings. Make sure the cans *always* stay top up. This requires a lot of attention because as the cans run low on refrigerant, they begin to float and may turn upside down. Charging the system with the can upside down may cause liquid refrigerant to enter the system, damaging the compressor. If the bar gauge manifold or charging line suddenly frosts up, check the position of the can immediately and rectify it, if necessary!

6. Start the process with the engine off. Open the charging valve (if you are using a kit) or the low side bar gauge manifold valve slightly until the pressures equalize. Then, close the charging valve or bar gauge manifold back off. Place an electric fan in front of the condenser. Then, start the engine and run it at idle speed or just very slightly above. Turn the blower to the lowest speed. Then, turn the air conditioner on in the normal operating mode. If the system has no refrigerant in it, the low pressure cutout switch on the compressor will keep it from starting until some pressure is created in the system.

7. If you're working with a charging kit, follow the manufacturer's instructions as to how far to open the charging valve. If you're working with a bar gauge manifold, and the system has a lot of refrigerant in it (you're just topping it off) follow the rest of this step. Otherwise, skip to 8. Note the operating pressure (the average if the compressor is cycling). Then, open the manifold valve until system low side pressure rises 10 psi. Throughout the charging procedure, maintain this pressure by opening or closing the valve to compensate for changes in the temperature of the refrigerant can. Also, keep your eye on the high side pressure and make sure it remains at a moderate level (usually less than 200 psi).

8. Gradually open the valve on the suction (left) side of the bar gauge manifold, as you watch the low side gauge. Allow the pressure to build until the compressor comes on and runs

continuously. Keep permitting it to rise until it reaches 50 psi. Then, carefully control the position of the valve to maintain this pressure. You will have to change the position of the valve to compensate for cooling of the refrigerant can and surrounding water and to help empty the can.

9. When the first can runs out of refrigerant, close off the manifold valve or charging line valve. Tap in a new can, immerse it in liquid, keeping it right side up, and then open the charging line valve if you're working without gauges. If you are working with gauges, open the valve on the tap and then open the low side manifold valve as described in Step 8 to maintain the pressure as before.

10. Continue with the process until the last can is hooked up. Measure in a fraction of a can, if necessary, by watching the frost line on the can and stopping appropriately. Watch for the time when bubbles just disappear from the sight glass. If you're just topping off the system, stop charging just after this occurs. Otherwise, this is a sign that you should expect the system to be completely charged and find that you have just about measured the right amount of refrigerant in. Be ready to stop charging! If you're just topping off the system, turn off the charging valve or low side manifold valve and then run the system with the fan on high and the engine accelerated to about 1,500 rpm to check the charge. If bubbles appear, charge the system slightly more until just after all the bubbles disappear.

11. When charging is complete, turn off the manifold or charging line valves and any valve on the can. Disconnect the low side line *at the suction line and not at the gauges*, grabbing the connection from above, watching for liquid refrigerant to spray out, and unscrewing the connection as fast as you can. Turn off the engine and allow the pressure on the high side to drop until it stabilizes. Then, disconnect the high side gauge connection (if necessary) as quickly as possible. Cap both system openings and all gauge openings as soon as possible.

Windshield Wipers

Intense heat from the sun, snow, and ice, road oils and the chemicals used in windshield washer solvent combine to deteriorate the rubber wiper refills. The refills should be replaced about twice a year or whenever the blades begin to streak or chatter.

WIPER REFILL REPLACEMENT

Normally, if the wipers are not cleaning the windshield properly, only the refill has to be replaced. The blade and arm usually require replacement only in the event of damage. It is not necessary (except on new Tridon® refills) to remove the arm or the blade to replace the refill (rubber part), though you may have to position the arm higher on the glass. You can do this turning the ignition switch on and operating the wipers. When they are positioned where they are accessible, turn the ignition switch off.

There are several types of refills and your vehicle could have any kind, since aftermarket blades and arms may not use exactly the same type refill as the original equipment.

Most Anco® styles use a release button that is pushed down to allow the refill to slide out of the yoke jaws. The new refill slides in and locks in place.

Some Trico® refills are removed by locating where the metal backing strip or the refill is wider. Insert a small screwdriver blade between the frame and metal backing strip. Press down to release the refill from the retaining tab.

Other Trico® blades are unlocked at one end by squeezing 2 metal tabs, and the refill is slid out of the frame jaws. When the new refill is installed, the tabs will click into place, locking the refill.

The polycarbonate type is held in place by a locking lever that is pushed downward out of the groove in the arm to free the refill. When the new refill is installed, it will lock in place automatically.

The Tridon® refill has a plastic backing strip with a notch about 1" (25mm) from the end. Hold the blade (frame) on a hard surface so that the frame is tightly bowed. Grip the tip of the backing strip and pull up while twisting counterclockwise. The backing strip will snap out of the retaining tab. Do this for the remaining tabs until the refill is free of the arm. The length of these refills is molded into the end and they should be replaced with identical types.

No matter which type of refill you use, be sure that all of the frame claws engage the refill. Before operating the wipers, be sure that no part of the metal frame is contacting the windshield.

Tires and Wheels

Tires should be checked weekly for proper air pressure. A chart, located either in the glove compartment or on the driver's or passenger's door, gives the recommended inflation pressures. Maximum fuel economy and tire life will result if the pressure is maintained at the highest figure given on the chart. Pressures should be checked before driving since pressure can increase as much as 6 pounds per square inch (psi) due to heat buildup. It is a good idea to have your own accurate pressure gauge, be-

cause not all gauges on service station air pumps can be trusted. When checking pressures, do not neglect the spare tire. Note that some spare tires require pressures considerable higher than those used in the other tires.

While you are about the task of checking air pressure, inspect the tire treads for cuts, bruises and other damage. Check the air valves to be sure that they are tight. Replace any missing valve caps.

Check the tires for uneven wear that might indicate the need for front end alignment or tire rotation. Tires should be replaced when a tread wear indicator appears as a solid band across the tread.

When buying new tires, give some thought to the following points, especially if you are considering a switch to larger tires or a different profile series:

1. All 4 tires must be of the same construction type. This rule cannot be violated. Radial, bias, and bias-belted tires must not be mixed.

2. The wheels should be correct width for the tire. Tire dealers have charts of tire and rim compatibility. A mismatch will cause sloppy handling and rapid tire wear. The tread width should match the rim width (inside bead to inside bead) within an inch. For radial tires, the rim width should be 80% or less of the tire (not tread) width.

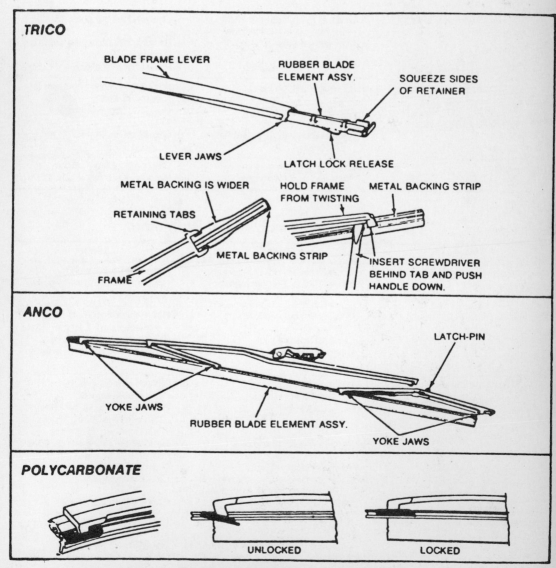

The three types of wiper blade retention

3. The height (mounted diameter) of the new tires can change speedometer accuracy, engine speed at a given road speed, fuel mileage, acceleration, and ground clearance. Tire manufacturers furnish full measurement specifications.

4. The spare tire should be usable, at least for short distance and low speed operation, with the new tires.

5. There shouldn't be any body interference when loaded, on bumps, or in turns.

Tread depth can be checked with an inexpensive gauge

Troubleshooting Basic Tire Problems

Problem	Cause	Solution
The car's front end vibrates at high speeds and the steering wheel shakes	• Wheels out of balance • Front end needs aligning	• Have wheels balanced • Have front end alignment checked
The car pulls to one side while cruising	• Unequal tire pressure (car will usually pull to the low side) • Mismatched tires • Front end needs aligning	• Check/adjust tire pressure • Be sure tires are of the same type and size • Have front end alignment checked
Abnormal, excessive or uneven tire wear See "How to Read Tire Wear"	• Infrequent tire rotation • Improper tire pressure • Sudden stops/starts or high speed on curves	• Rotate tires more frequently to equalize wear • Check/adjust pressure • Correct driving habits
Tire squeals	• Improper tire pressure • Front end needs aligning	• Check/adjust tire pressure • Have front end alignment checked

Troubleshooting Basic Wheel Problems

Problem	Cause	Solution
The car's front end vibrates at high speed	• The wheels are out of balance • Wheels are out of alignment	• Have wheels balanced • Have wheel alignment checked/adjusted
Car pulls to either side	• Wheels are out of alignment • Unequal tire pressure • Different size tires or wheels	• Have wheel alignment checked/adjusted • Check/adjust tire pressure • Change tires or wheels to same size
The car's wheel(s) wobbles	• Loose wheel lug nuts • Wheels out of balance • Damaged wheel • Wheels are out of alignment • Worn or damaged ball joint • Excessive play in the steering linkage (usually due to worn parts) • Defective shock absorber	• Tighten wheel lug nuts • Have tires balanced • Raise car and spin the wheel. If the wheel is bent, it should be replaced • Have wheel alignment checked/adjusted • Check ball joints • Check steering linkage • Check shock absorbers
Tires wear unevenly or prematurely	• Incorrect wheel size • Wheels are out of balance • Wheels are out of alignment	• Check if wheel and tire size are compatible • Have wheels balanced • Have wheel alignment checked/adjusted

TIRE ROTATION

Tire rotation is recommended every 6,000 miles (9,600 km) or so, to obtain maximum tire wear. The pattern you use depends on whether or not your car yhas a usable spare. Radial tires should not be cross-switched (from one side of the car to the other); they last longer if their direction of rotation is not changed. Snow tires sometimes have directional arrows molded into the side of the carcass; the arrow shows the direction of rotation. They will wear very rapidly if the rotation is reversed. Studded tires will lose their studs if their rotational direction is reversed.

A penny works as well as anything for checking tire tread depth; when you can see the top of Lincoln's head, it's time for a new tire

Tire Size Comparison Chart

"Letter" sizes			Inch Sizes	Metric-inch Sizes		
"60 Series"	"70 Series"	"78 Series"	1965–77	"60 Series"	"70 Series"	"80 Series"
		Y78-12	5.50-12, 5.60-12 6.00-12	165/60-12	165/70-12	155-12
		W78-13	5.20-13	165/60-13	145/70-13	135-13
		Y78-13	5.60-13	175/60-13	155/70-13	145-13
			6.15-13	185/60-13	165/70-13	155-13, P155/80-13
A60-13	A70-13	A78-13	6.40-13	195/60-13	175/70-13	165-13
B60-13	B70-13	B78-13	6.70-13	205/60-13	185/70-13	175-13
			6.90-13			
C60-13	C70-13	C78-13	7.00-13	215/60-13	195/70-13	185-13
D60-13	D70-13	D78-13	7.25-13			
E60-13	E70-13	E78-13	7.75-13			195-13
			5.20-14	165/60-14	145/70-14	135-14
			5.60-14	175/60-14	155/70-14	145-14
			5.90-14			
A60-14	A70-14	A78-14	6.15-14	185/60-14	165/70-14	155-14
	B70-14	B78-14	6.45-14	195/60-14	175/70-14	165-14
	C70-14	C78-14	6.95-14	205/60-14	185/70-14	175-14
D60-14	D70-14	D78-14				
E60-14	E70-14	E78-14	7.35-14	215/60-14	195/70-14	185-14
F60-14	F70-14	F78-14, F83-14	7.75-14	225/60-14	200/70-14	195-14
G60-14	G70-14	G77-14, G78-14	8.25-14	235/60-14	205/70-14	205-14
H60-14	H70-14	H78-14	8.55-14	245/60-14	215/70-14	215-14
J60-14	J70-14	J78-14	8.85-14	255/60-14	225/70-14	225-14
L60-14	L70-14		9.15-14	265/60-14	235/70-14	
	A70-15	A78-15	5.60-15	185/60-15	165/70-15	155-15
B60-15	B70-15	B78-15	6.35-15	195/60-15	175/70-15	165-15
C60-15	C70-15	C78-15	6.85-15	205/60-15	185/70-15	175-15
	D70-15	D78-15				
E60-15	E70-15	E78-15	7.35-15	215/60-15	195/70-15	185-15
F60-15	F70-15	F78-15	7.75-15	225/60-15	205/70-15	195-15
G60-15	G70-15	G78-15	8.15-15/8.25-15	235/60-15	215/70-15	205-15
H60-15	H70-15	H78-15	8.45-15/8.55-15	245/60-15	225/70-15	215-15
J60-15	J70-15	J78-15	8.85-15/8.90-15	255/60-15	235/70-15	225-15
	K70-15		9.00-15	265/60-15	245/70-15	230-15
L60-15	L70-15	L78-15, L84-15	9.15-15			235-15
	M70-15	M78-15				255-15
		N78-15				

Note: Every size tire is not listed and many size comparisons are approximate, based on load ratings. Wider tires than those supplied new with the vehicle, should always be checked for clearance.

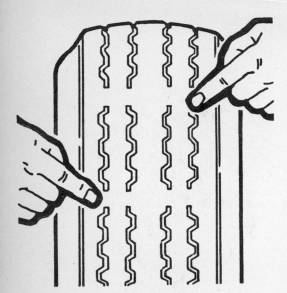

Tread wear indicators will appear when the tire is worn out

NOTE: *Mark the wheel position or direction of rotation on radial tires or studded snow tires before removing them.*

STORAGE

Store the tires at the proper inflation pressure if they are mounted on wheels. Keep them in a cool dry place, laid on their sides. If the tires are stored in the garage or basement, do not let them stand on a concrete floor; set them on strips of wood.

FLUIDS AND LUBRICANTS

Fuel and Engine Oil Recommendations

OIL

Gasoline Engines

The SAE (Society of Automotive Engineers) grade number indicates the viscosity of the engine oil and thus its ability to lubricate at a given temperature. The lower the SAE grade number, the lighter the oil; the lower the viscosity, the easier it is to crank the engine in cold weather.

Oil viscosities should be chosen from those oils recommended for the lowest anticipated temperature during the oil change interval.

Multi-viscosity oils (10W-30, 20W-50, etc.) offer the important advantage of being adaptable to temperature extremes. They allow easy starting at low temperatures, yet they give good protection at high speeds and engine temperatures. This is a decided advantage in changeable climates or in long distance touring.

The API (American Petroleum Institute) designation indicates the classification of engine oil used under certain given operating conditions. Only oils designated for use "Service SF" should be used. Oils of the SF type perform a variety of functions inside the engine in addition to their basic function as a lubricant. Through a balanced system of metallic detergents and polymeric dispersants, the oil prevents the formation of high and low tempera-

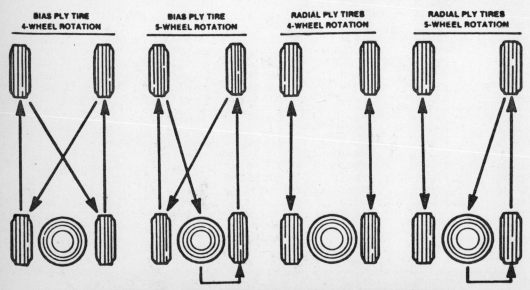

Tire rotation diagrams; note that radials should not be cross–switched

Capacities

Year	Model	Engine Crankcase		Transmission (pts.)			Drive Axle (pts.)	Fuel Tank (gal.)	Cooling System (qts.)
		With Filter	Without Filter	4-Spd	5-Spd	Auto.			
1970	1600	4.5	4.25	2.1	—	3.6	1.7 ①	12.1	7.4
	2000	4.5	4.25	2.1	—	3.6	1.7 ①	12.1	7.4
	2002,Tii	4.5	4.25	2.1	—	3.6	1.7 ①	12.1	7.4
	2800,CS	6.1	5.3	2.5	—	3.2	2.6	19.8 ②	12.7
	2500	6.1	5.3	2.5	—	3.2	2.6	19.8	12.7
1971	1600	4.5	4.25	2.1	—	3.6	1.7 ①	12.1	7.4
	2000,2002,Tii	4.5	4.25	2.1	—	3.6	1.7 ①	12.1	7.4
	2500	6.1	5.3	2.5	—	3.2	2.6	19.8	12.7
	2800,CS	6.1	5.3	2.5	—	3.2	2.6	19.8 ②	12.7
	Bavaria	6.1	5.3	2.5	—	3.2	2.6	19.8	12.7
1972	2000,2002,Tii	4.5	4.25	2.1	—	3.6	1.7 ①	12.1	7.4
	Bavaria	6.1	5.3	2.5	—	3.2	2.6	19.8	12.7
	3000CS	6.1	5.3	2.5	—	3.2	2.6	15.4	12.7
1973	2000,2002,Tii	4.5	4.25	2.1	—	3.6	1.9	13.5	7.4
	3.0CS,S,Si	5.3	5.0	2.5	—	3.8	3.4	16.5	12.7
	Bavaria	6.1	5.3	2.5	—	3.2	2.6	19.8	12.7
1974	2002	4.5	4.25	2.1	—	3.6	1.9	13.5	7.4
	Bavaria	6.1	5.3	2.5	—	3.2	2.6	19.8	12.7
	3.0CS,S,Si	5.3	5.0	2.5	—	3.8	3.4	16.5	12.7
1975	2002	4.5	4.25	2.8	—	3.6	1.9	13.5	7.4
	3.0CS,S,Si	5.3	5.0	2.5	—	3.8	3.4	16.5	12.7
	530i	6.0	5.25	2.3	—	4.2	3.4	16.4	12.7
1976	2002	4.5	4.25	2.8	—	3.6	1.9	13.5	7.4
	3.0CS,S,Si	5.3	5.0	2.5	—	3.8	3.4	16.5	12.7
	530i	6.0	5.25	2.3	—	4.2	3.4	16.4	12.7
1977	320i	4.5	4.25	2.2	—	4.2	2.0	15.9	7.4
	530i	6.0	5.25	2.3	—	4.2	3.4	16.4	12.7
	630CSi	6.0	5.25	2.3	—	4.2	3.2	16.4	12.7
1978	320i	4.5	4.25	2.2	—	4.2	2.0	15.9	7.4
	530i	6.0	5.25	2.3	—	4.2	3.4	16.4	12.7
	633CSi	6.0	5.3	2.3	—	4.2	3.2	16.4	12.7
	733i	6.0	5.3	2.3	—	4.0	3.8	22.5	12.7
1979	320i	4.5	4.25	2.2	—	4.2	2.0	15.9	7.4
	528i	6.0	5.25	2.3	—	4.2	3.4	16.4	12.7
	633CSi	6.0	5.3	2.3	—	4.2	3.2	16.4	12.7
	733i	6.0	5.3	2.3	—	4.0	3.8	22.5	12.7
1980	320i	4.5 ③	4.25 ④	2.2	—	4.2	1.9	15.3	7.4
	528i	6.0	5.25	2.3	—	4.2	3.4	16.4	12.7
	633CSi	6.0	5.3	2.3	—	4.2	3.2	16.4	12.7

Capacities (cont.)

Year	Model	Engine Crankcase — With Filter	Engine Crankcase — Without Filter	Transmission (pts.) — 4-Spd	Transmission (pts.) — 5-Spd	Transmission (pts.) — Auto.	Drive Axle (pts.)	Fuel Tank (gal.)	Cooling System (qts.)
1980	733i	6.0	5.3	2.3	—	4.0	3.8	22.5	12.7
1981	320i	4.5 ③	4.25 ④	2.2	—	4.2	1.9	15.3	7.4
	528i	6.0	5.25	2.3	—	4.2	3.4	16.4	12.7
	633CSi	6.0	5.3	2.3	—	4.2	3.2	16.4	12.7
	733i	6.0	5.3	2.3	—	4.0	3.8	22.5	12.7
1982	320i	4.5 ③	4.25 ④	2.2	—	4.2	1.9	15.3	7.4
	528e	4.5	4.2	3.4	—	4.2	3.8	16.6	12.7
	633CSi	6.0	5.25	2.4	—	4.2	3.2	16.5	12.7
	733i	6.0	5.25	2.4	—	4.0	3.8	22.5	12.7
1983	320i	4.5 ③	4.25 ④	2.2	—	4.2	1.9	15.3	7.4
	528e	4.5	4.2	—	3.4	4.2	3.8	16.6	12.7
	533i	6.0	5.3	—	2.65	6.3	3.6	16.6	12.7
	633CSi	6.0	5.25	2.4	—	4.2	3.2	16.5	12.7
	733i	6.0	5.25	—	2.4	4.0	3.8	22.5	12.7
1984	318i	4.5	4.2	—	2.4	6.3	1.9	14.5	7.4
	528e	4.5	4.2	—	3.4	4.2	3.8	16.6	12.7
	533i	6.0	5.3	—	2.65	6.3	3.6	16.6	12.7
	633CSi	6.0	5.25	2.4	—	4.2	3.2	16.5	12.7
	733i	6.0	5.25	—	2.4	4.0	3.8	22.5	12.7
1985	318i	4.5	4.2	—	2.4	6.3	1.9	14.5	7.4
	325e	4.5	4.2	—	2.4	6.3	3.4	14.5	7.4
	325es	4.5	4.2	—	2.4	6.3	3.4	14.5	7.4
	528e	4.5	4.2	—	3.4	4.2	3.8	16.6	12.7
	524td	6.1	5.3	—	3.4	6.4	4.0	16.6	12.7
	535i	6.1	5.3	—	3.4	6.4	4.0	16.6	12.7
	635CSi	6.1	5.3	—	3.4	6.4	4.0	16.6	12.7
	735i	6.1	5.3	—	3.4	6.4	4.0	22.5	12.7
1986	325e	4.5	4.2	—	2.4	6.3	3.4	14.5	7.4
	325es	4.5	4.2	—	2.4	6.3	3.4	14.5	7.4
	524td	6.1	5.3	—	3.4	6.4	4.0	16.6	12.7
	528e	4.5	4.2	—	3.4	4.2	3.8	16.6	12.7
	535i	6.1	5.3	—	3.4	6.4	4.0	16.6	12.7
	635CSi	6.1	5.3	—	3.4	6.4	4.0	16.6	12.7
	735i	6.1	5.3	—	3.4	6.4	4.0	22.5	12.7
1987	325	4.5	4.2	—	2.6	6.4	3.6	15.3	12.7
	528e	4.5	4.2	—	3.4	6.4	3.8	16.6	11.6
	535i	6.1	5.3	—	3.4	6.4	4.0	16.6	12.7
	635CSi	6.1	5.3	—	3.4	6.4	4.0	16.6	12.7
	735i	6.1	5.3	—	3.4	6.4	3.6	21.4	12.7

Capacities (cont.)

Year	Model	Engine Crankcase		Transmission (pts.)			Drive Axle (pts.)	Fuel Tank (gal.)	Cooling System (qts.)
		With Filter	Without Filter	4-Spd	5-Spd	Auto.			
1987	M5	6.1	5.3	—	2.6	6.4	4.0	16.6	12.7
	M6	6.1	5.3	—	2.6	6.4	4.0	16.6	12.7
1988	325	4.5	4.2	—	2.6	6.4	3.6	16.4	11.6
	325i	5.0	4.75	—	2.6	6.4 ⑤	3.6 ⑥	16.4	11.0
	325iS	5.0	4.75	—	2.6	6.4 ⑤	3.6 ⑥	16.4	11.0
	325iX	5.0	4.75	—	2.6	6.4 ⑤	3.6 ⑥	16.4	11.0
	528e	4.5	4.2	—	3.4	6.4	3.8	16.6	11.6
	535i	6.1	5.3	—	2.6	6.4	4.0	16.6	11.6
	535iS	6.1	5.3	—	2.6	6.4	4.0	16.6	12.7
	635CSi	6.1	5.3	—	3.4	6.4	4.0	16.6	12.7
	L6	6.1	5.3	—	3.4	6.4	4.0	16.6	12.7
	735i	6.1	5.3	—	2.6	6.4	4.0	21.4	12.7
	M3	5.0	4.75	—	2.6	6.4	3.6	16.4	NA
	M5	6.1	5.3	—	2.6	6.4	4.0	16.6	12.7
	M6	6.1	5.3	—	2.6	6.4	4.0	16.6	12.7
	750iL	7.9	6.8	—	2.6	6.4	4.0	21.4	12.7

NA—Not available
① 1600-2 Short neck differential up to chassis no. 15678-45
2002 Long neck differential up to chassis no. 1664750—capacity of 2.1 pts.
② 2800CS—15.4 gals
③ With chrome plated guide tube for dipstick—4.25
④ With chrome plated guide tube for dipstick—4.0
⑤ 325iX Transfer case—1.1
⑥ 325iX Front drive axle—1.5

ture deposits and also keeps sludge and particles of dirt in suspension. Acids, particularly sulfuric acid, as well as other byproducts of combustion, are neutralized. Both the SAE grade number and the API designation can be found on top of the oil can.

For recommended oil viscosities, refer to the chart.

CAUTION: *Non-detergent or straight mineral oils should not be used in your car.*

Diesel Engines

Engine oil, meeting API specification **SF/CD** is recommended. You can use either SAE 30W or SAE 10W-40 weight oils.

Fuel

Gasoline Engines

For the years 1970-74, premium grade fuel is recommended. The actual octane required varies with the year and modle.

For the years 1975-79, octane requirements are standardized at 87 AKI (which means "Anti-Knock Index"), which is an average of "Motor" and "Research" octane ratings. All BMWs made in the 1975-79 model years, except the 528i, use regular, leaded fuel, as afterburning of the exhaust occurs in an ordinary manifold or thermal reactor.

The 528i, and all 1980 and later models have been designed to run on unleaded fuel. The use of a leaded fuel in a car requiring unleaded fuel will plug the catalytic converter and render it inoperative. It will also increase exhaust backpressure to the point where engine output will be severely reduced. In all cases, the minimum octane rating of the unleaded fuel being used must be at least 91 RON (87 CLC). Al unleaded fuels sold in the U.S. are required to meet this minimum rating.

The use of a fuel too low in octane (a measurement of anti-knock quality) will result in spark knock. Since many factors such as altitude, terrain, air temperature and humidity affect operating efficiency, knocking may result

even though the recommended fuel is being used. If persistant knocking occurs, it may be necessary to switch to a high grade of fuel. Continuous or heavy knocking may result in engine damage.

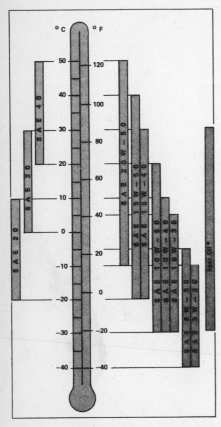

* Special oils individually approved by BMW (low-friction lubricants)

Oil viscosity chart

NOTE: *Your engine's fuel requirement can change with time, mainly due to carbon buildup, which will in turn change the compression ratio. If your engine pings, knocks, or runs on, switch to a higher grade of fuel. Sometimes just changing brands will cure the problem. If it becomes necessary to retard the timing from the specifications don't change it more than a few degrees. Retarded timing will reduce power output and fuel mileage, in addition to increasing the engine temperature.*

DIESEL ENGINES

No.2 automotive diesel fuel with a cetane rating of 40 is sufficient for most localities. In colder areas, No.1 can be used during periods of extreme cold.

Engine
OIL LEVEL CHECK

Every time you stop for fuel, check the engine oil as follows:

1. Make sure the car is parked on level ground.

2. When checking the oil level it is best for the engine to be at normal operating temperature, although checking the oil immediately after stopping will lead to a false reading. Wait a few minutes after turning off the engine to allow the oil to drain back into the crankcase.

3. Open the hood and locate the dipstick on the left side of the engine compartment. Pull the dipstick from its tube, wipe it clean and then reinsert it.

4. Pull the dipstick out again and, holding it horizontally, read the oil level. The oil should be between the 2 marks on the dipstick. If the oils

Recommended Lubricants

Item	Lubricant
Engine Oil	API "SE" or "SF"
Manual Transmission	SAE 80W or SAE 80W/90 (non-hypoid)
Automatic Transmission	DEXRON® or DEXRON® 11 ATF
Rear Axle–Standard	SAE 90W GL-5
Power Steering Reservoir	DEXRON® ATF
Brake Fluid	DOT 4
Antifreeze	Ethylene Glycol
Front Wheel Bearings	Wheel Bearing Grease
Clutch Linkage	Engine Oil
Hood and Door Hinges	Engine Oil
Chassis Lubrication	NLGI #1 or NLGI #2
Lock Cylinders	WD-40 or Powdered Graphite

is below the upper mark, add oil of the proper viscosity through the capped opening in the top of the cylinder head cover.

5. Replace the dipstick and check the oil level again after adding any oil. Be careful not to over fill the crankcase. Approximately one quart of oil will raise the level from the lower mark to the upper mark. Excess oil will generally be consumed at an accelerated rate.

OIL AND FILTER CHANGE

The oil should be changed every 4 months or 6,000 miles (9,600 km) in all models. Make sure that you change the oil based on whichever interval comes first.

The oil drain plug is located on the bottom, right hand side of the oil pan (bottom of the engine, underneath the car). The oil filter is located on the left side of all engines.

The mileage figures given are the BMW recommended intervals assuming normal driving and conditions. If your car is used under dusty, polluted or off-road conditions, change the oil and filter more often than specified. The same goes for cars driven in stop-and-go traffic or only for short distances at a time. Always drain the engine oil after the engine has been running long enough to bring it up to normal operating temperature. Hot oil will flow easier and more contaminants will be removed along with the oil than if it were drained cold. To change the oil and filter:

CAUTION: *Prolonged and repeated skin contact with used engine oil, with no effort to remove the oil, may be harmful. Always follows these simple precautions when handling used motor oil:*

1. Avoid prolonged skin contact with used motor oil.

2. Remove oil from skin by washing thoroughly with soap and water or waterless hand cleaner. Do not use gasoline, thinners or other solvents.

3. Avoid prolonged skin contact with oil-soaked clothing.

1. Run the engine until it reaches normal operating temperature.

2. Jack up the from t of the car and support it on safety stands.

3. Slide a drain pan of at least 6 quarts capacity under the oil pan.

4. Loosent he drain plug with a 19mm wrench. Turn the plug out by hand. By keeping an inward pressure on the plug as you unscrew it, oil won't escape past the threads and you can remove it without being burned by hot oil.

5. Allow the oil to drain completely and then install the drain plug. Don't over tighten the plug, or you'll by buying a new pan or a trick replacement plug for stripped threads.

6. Using a strap wrench, remove the oil filter. Keep in mind that it's holding about 1 quart of dirty, hot oil.

7. Empty the old filter into the drain pan and dispose of the filter.

8. Using a clean rag, wipe off the filter adapter on the engine block. Be sure that the rag doesn't leave any lint which could clog an oil passage.

9. Coat the rubber gasket ont he filter with fresh oil. Spin it onto the engine by hand; when the gasket touches the adapter surface, give it another ½-¾ turn. No more, or you'll squash the gasket and it will leak.

10. Refill the engine with the correct amount of fresh oil. See the "Capacities" chart.

11. Check the oil level on the dipstick. It is normal for the level to be a bit above the full

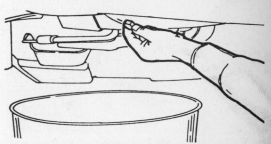

By keeping an inward pressure on the plug as you unscrew it, oil won't escape past the threads

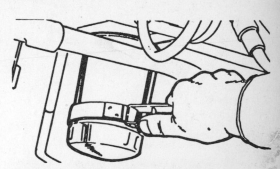

Remove the oil filter with a strap wrench

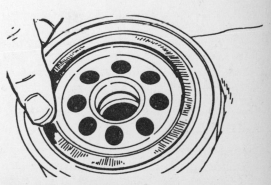

Coat the new oil filter gasket with clean oil

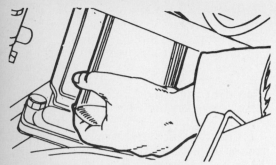

Install the new oil filter by hand

The oil filler cap is located on the cam cover on all engines

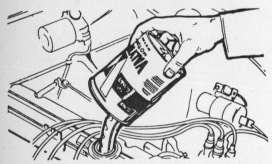

Add oil through the capped opening in the cylinder head cover

mark. Start the engine and allow it to idle for a few minutes.

CAUTION: *Do not run the engine above idle speed until it has built up oil pressure, indicated when the oil light goes out.*

12. Shut off the engine, allow the oil to drain for a minute, and check the oil level. Check around the filter and drain plug for any leaks, and correct as necessary.

Diesel Engine oil change

1. Place the drip pan beneath the oil filter.
2. Remove the drain plug from the filter housing.

3. Remove the 2 housing cover attaching nuts and remove the cover and filter cartridge.
4. Clean the cover in a safe solvent and dry it thoroughly.
5. Install a new gasket on the cover.
6. Install the cover and new filter cartridge. Tighten the cover nut and drain plug to 15 ft.lbs.

NOTE: *Certain operating conditions may warrant more frequent oil changes. If the vehicle is used for short trips, where the engine does not have a chance to fully warm up before it is shut off, water condensation and low temperature deposits may make it necessary to change to oil sooner. If the vehicle is used mostly in stop-and-go traffic, corrosive acids and high temperature deposits may necessitate shorter oil changing intervals. The shorter intervals also apply to industrial or rural areas where high concentrations of dust and other airborne particulate matter contaminate the oil. Finally, if the car is used for towing trailers, a severe load is placed on the engine causing the oil to thin out sooner, making necessary the shorter oil changing intervals.*

Manual Transmission
LEVEL CHECK

The oil in the manual transmission should be checked at least every 6,000-7,500 miles (9,600-12,000 km).

1. With the car parked on a level surface, remove the filler plug from the side of the transmission housing.
2. If the lubricant begins to trickle out of the hole, there is enough and you need not go any further. Otherwise, carefully insert your finger (watch out for sharp threads) and check to see if the oil is up to the edge of the hole.
3. If not, add oil through t he hole until the level is at the edge of the hole. Most gear lubricants come in a plastic squeeze bottle with a nozzle; making additions simple. You can also use a common kitchen baster. Use only standard non hypoid-type gear oil—SAE 80W or SAE 80W/90.
4. Replace the filler plug, run the engine and check for leaks.

DRAIN AND REFILL

1. The oil must be hot before it is drained. Drive the car until the engine reaches normal operating temperature.
2. Remove the filler plug to provide a vent.
3. Place a large container underneath the transmission and then remove the 17mm drain plug.
4. Allow the oil to drain completely. Clean

the magnetic drain plug of any excessive metal particles and replace it; tighten it until it is just snug.

5. Fill the transmission with the proper lubricant as detailed earlier in this chapter. Refer to the "Capacities" chart for the correct amount of lubricant.

6. When the oil level is up to the edge of the filler hole, replace the filler plug. Drive the car for a few minutes, stop, and check for any leaks.

Automatic Transmission
FLUID LEVEL CHECK

Check the automatic transmission fluid level at least every 12,500 miles (20,000 km). The dipstick can be found int he rear of the engine compartment. The fluid level should be checked only when transmission is hot (normal operating temperature). The transmission is considered hot after about 20 miles (30 km) of highway driving.

1. Park the car on a level surface with the engine idling. Shift the transmission into Neutral and set the parking brake.

2. Remove the dipstick, wipe it clean and then reinsert it firmly. Be sure that it has been pushed all the way in. Remove the dipstick again and check the fluid level while holding it horizontally. With the engine running, the fluid level should be between the 2 marks on the dipstick.

3. If the fluid level is below the second mark, add DEXRON®II automatic transmission fluid through the dipstick tube. This is easily done with the aid of a funnel. Check the level often as you are filling the transmission. Be extremely careful not to over fill it. Overfilling will cause slippage, seal damage and overheating. Approximately one pint of ATF will raise the fluid level from one mark to the other.

NOTE: *Always use DEXRON®II ATF. The use of ATF Type F or any other fluid will cause severe damage to the transmission. The fluid on the dipstick should always be a bright red color, If it is discolored (brown or black) or smells burnt, serious transmission troubles, probably due to overheating, should be suspected. The transmission should be inspected by a qualified technician to locate the cause of the burnt fluid.*

DRAIN AND REFILL

The procedures for automatic transmission fluid drain and refill, filter change and band adjustment are all detailed in Chapter 7.

Transfer Case
FLUID RECOMMENDATION
1988-89 325ix

This is the only 4-wheel drive available from BMW. The transfer case contains 1.1 pts. of DEXRON®II ATF. This is the factory reccomended fluid to use is the transfer case.

DRAIN AND REFILL

The transfer case has a drain plug that is removed to drain the fluid. To fill the transfer case, open the filler plug located on the top edge of the case and add the fluid. The fluid should flow from the filler hole, this is how you know it is full.

Drive Axle
LEVEL CHECK
Rear Axle

The oil in the differential on models through 1974 should be checked at least every 8,000 miles (13,000 km); 12,500 miles (20,000 km) for 1975 and later models.

1. With the car on a level surface, remove the filler plug from the side of the differential.

2. If the oil begins to trickle out of the hole, there is enough. Otherwise, carefully insert your finger (watch out for sharp threads) into

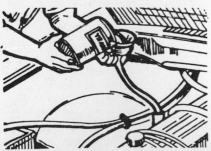

Add automatic transmission fluid through the dipstick tube

Rear axle fluid filler plug (side) and drain plug (bottom) locations

the hole and check that the oils is up to the bottom edge of the filler hole.

3. If not, add oil through t he hole until the level is at the edge of the hole. Most gear oils come in a plastic squeeze bottle with a nozzle; making additions is simple. You can also use a common kitchen baster. Use only standard GL-5 hypoid-type gear oil, SAE 90W.

DRAIN AND REFILL

There is not recommended change interval for the rear axle but it is always a good idea to change the fluid if you have purchased the car used or if it has been drive in water high enough to reach the axle.

1. Park the car on a level surface and set the parking brake.

2. Remove the filler plug (10mm Allen wrench).

3. Place a large container underneath he rear axle. Remove the drain plug (10mm Allen wrench) at the bottom of the differential and allow all lubricant to drain into the pan.

4. When all lubricant has drained out, clean and replace the drain plug.

5. Refill with the proper grade and quantity of lubricant as detailed earlier in this chapter. Replace the filler plug, run the car and then check for any leaks.

Cooling System

It's a good idea to check the coolant level every time that you stop for fuel. If the engine is hot, let it cool for a few minutes and then check the level following the procedure given earlier in this chapter.

Check the freezine protection rating at least once a year, preferably just before the winter sets in. This can be done with an antifreeze tester (most service stations will have one on hand and will probably check it for you, if not, they are available at an auto part store). Maintain a protection rating of at least $-20°F$ ($-29°C$) to prevent engine damage as a result of freezing and to assure the proper engine operating temperature.

DRAIN AND REFILL

The cooling system should be drained, thoroughly flushed and then refilled at least every 30,000 miles (48,000 km). This should be done with the engine cold.

1. Remove the radiator cap.
CAUTION: *Make sure the system is well below operating temperature before removing the cap!*

2. Turn the heater control to **WARM.**

3. Loosen t the radiator end clamp on the lower radiator hose, and pull the hose off the radiator connector.

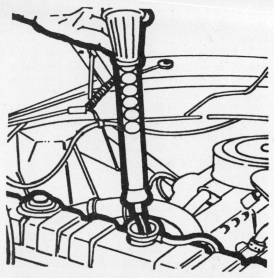

Coolant protection can be checked with a simple, float—type tester

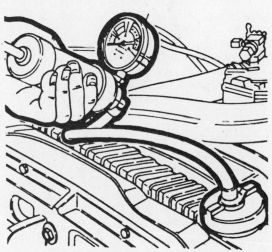

The system should be pressure tested at least once a year

4. Remove the 19mm plug from the right rear of the engine block.

5. To refill the system, first replace the drain plug and reconnect the radiator hose and clamp it.

6. On 6-cylinder engines, loosen the bleeder screw ont eh thermostat housing. On all engines, make sure the heater control is still in the **WARM position.**

7. Fill the system with at least a 35% mix if antifreeze and water and then replace the filler cap, turning it to the second stop. Start the engine and run it at 2,500 rpm until normal operating temperature is reached, and then stop it. Watch for water to come out at the bleed point

and close the bleeder screw as soon as this happens.

8. Start the engine after a wait of at least 1 minute and then run it at 4,000 rpm for 30 seconds. Release the throttle and make sure heat comes from the heater at idle speed. Then, shut off the engine again.

9. If necessary, allow the engine to cool until the temperature gauge needle is in the center of the white zone; then, refill the radiator of 4-cylinder engines to a point within ¾″ of the cap, or refill the overflow tank of 6-cylinder engines to a point within 1⅞″ of the filler cap.

Clutch and Brake Master Cylinder

LEVEL CHECK

On all but the 1600 models, the fluid reservoir services both he brake and clutch master cylinder. On the 1600, no fluid is involved in clutch operation. The fluid level should be checked at every oil change.

Master cylinder reservoir location—1600, 2002

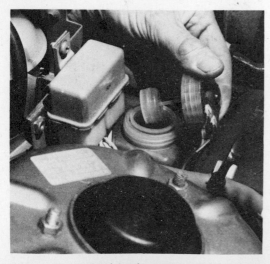

Combination brake/clutch master cylinder location (528i)

Wipe the reservoir cap and surrounding area clean. Make sure the level is up to the full marker (the reservoir is translucent). If necessary, add DOT 4 specification fluid that is brand new (do not attempt to reuse fluid). Be careful not to drop any dirt into the fluid, and avoid spilling fluid on the paint work, or wipe it up immediately if it spills. Make sure the vent hole used in earlier type reservoirs is clean by blowing through it.

Steering Fluid

LEVEL CHECK

On 1970-74 models, at 8,000 mile (13,000 km) intervals, check the level of oil in the steering box. Pry up the plastic plug on the steering gear top cover and check to see that the oil level reaches the lower edge of the filler aperture. Top up as necessary with SAE 90 hypoid gear oil.

On 4-cylinder models build in 1975 and later years, the vehicle is equipped with a rack and pinion unit which requires only greasing. ON 1975 and later 6-cylinder vehicles (with the exception of the 528e), check the power steering fluid as follows at every oil change:

1. With the engine off, remvoe the wing nut

Remove the wing nut on top of the power steering fluid reservoir (late model cars with six cylinder engines)

Location of the felt wick in the end of the distributor shaft

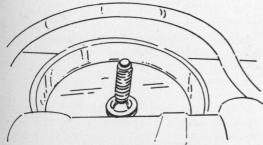

Pull the cap off and watch the fluid level

28 81 02 431 00

The level of the power steering fluid is checked with a dipstick on the 528e

located at the top of the reservoir. The oil level should be just above the mark on the reservoir. If necessary, refill with a DEXRON®II type automatic transmission fluid.

2. Start the engine and watch the fluid level. If it drops to below the level of the line, add fluid until the level just reaches the line. The, shut the engine off and observe that the fluid level rises to slightly above the line.

3. Reinstall the reservoir cover, making sure the seal seats properly. Check for any leaks in the steering box.

The 528e has a translucent plastic reservoir similar to a brake master cylinder reservoir. To check the fluid level in this reservoir, simply

unscrew the cap and check that the level is between the 2 marks on the dipstick. If not, add fluid in the manner already described for previous models.

Chassis Greasing

The steering rods, suspension joints and ball joints of BMW suspension are maintenance free. The only chassis items that require attention are the distributor on systems with conventional contacts, the throttle linkage, and, on early models, the halfshafts.

Throttle Linkage

Apply a few drops of engine oil to the joints and bearings of throttle linkage and, on injected models with the distributor type pump (4-cylinder engine only), oil the joints and bearing points of the injection pump and throttle butterflies.

Distributor

At periodic intervals, fill the oil cup on the side of the distributor with light engine oil; grease the cam lobes and fiber heel on the contacts with distributor grease; and lubricate the advance mechanism by applying 2-3 drops of light oil to the felt wick in the end of the distributor shaft.

NOTE: *Take care not to allow or grease to contaminate the breaker points. Contamination may result in misfiring or accelerated contact point erosion.*

OUTSIDE VEHICLE MAINTENANCE

Lock Cylinders

Apply graphite lubricant sparingly thought the key slot. Insert the key and operate the lock several times to be sure that the lubricant is worked into the lock cylinder.

Door Hinges and Hinge Checks

Spray a silicone lubricant on the hinge pivot points to eliminate any binding conditions. Open and close the door several times to be sure that the lubricant is evenly and thoroughly distributed.

Body Drain Holes

Be sure that the drain holes in the doors and rocker panels are cleared of obstruction. A small screwdriver can be used to clear them of any debris.

Front Wheel Bearings

ADJUSTMENT

The front wheels each rotate on a set of opposed, tapered roller bearings as shown in the accompanying illustration. The grease retainer at the inside of the hub prevents lubricant from leaking into the brake drum.

1. Raise and support the front end on jackstands.
2. Remove the grease cap and remove excess grease from the end of the spindle.
3. Remove the cotter pin and nut lock shown in the illustration.
4. Rotate the wheel, hub and drum assembly while tightening the adjusting nut to 17-25 ft. lbs. in order to seat the bearings.
5. Back off the adjusting nut ½, then retighten the adjusting nut to 10-15 in. lbs.
6. Locate the nut lock on the adjusting nut so that the castellations on the lock are lined up with the cotter pin hole in the spindle.
7. Install the new cotter pin, bending the ends of the cotter pin around the castellated flange of the nut lock.
8. Check the wheel for proper rotation, then install the grease cap. If the wheel still does not rotate properly, inspect and clean or replace the wheel bearings and cups.

REMOVAL, REPACKING, AND INSTALLATION

NOTE: *Sodium-based grease is not compatible with lithium-based grease. Read the package labels and be careful not to mix the two types. If there is any doubt as to the type of grease used, completely clean the old grease from the bearing and hub before replacing.*

Before handling the bearings, there are a few things that you should remember to do and not to do.

Remember to DO the following:
● Remove all outside dirt from the housing before exposing the bearing.
● Treat a used bearing as gently as you would a new one.
● Work with clean tools in clean surroundings.
● Use clean, dry canvas gloves, or at least clean, dry hands.
● Clean solvents and flushing fluids are a must.
● Use clean paper when laying out the bearings to dry.
● Protect disassembled bearings from rust and dirt. Cover them up.
● Use clean rags to wipe bearings.
● Keep the bearings in oil-proof paper when they are to be stored or are not in use.
● Clean the inside of the housing before replacing the bearing.

Do NOT do the following:
● Don't work in dirty surroundings.
● Don't use dirty, chipped or damaged tools.
● Try not to work on wooden work benches or use wooden mallets.
● Don't handle bearings with dirty or moist hands.
● Do not use gasoline for cleaning; use a safe solvent.
● Do not spin-dry bearings with compressed air. They will be damaged.
● Do not spin dirty bearings.
● Avoid using cotton waste or dirty cloths to wipe bearings.
● Try not to scratch or nick bearing surfaces.
● Do not allow the bearing to come in contact with dirt or rust at any time.

1. Raise and support the front end on jackstands.
2. Remove the wheel cover. Remove the wheel.
3. Remove the caliper from the disc and wire it to the underbody to prevent damage to the brake hose. See Chapter 9.
4. Remove the grease cap from the hub. Then, remove the cotter pin, nut lock, adjusting nut and flat washer from the spindle. Remove the outer bearing assembly from the hub.
5. Pull the hub and disc assembly off the wheel spindle.
6. Remove and discard the old grease retainer. Remove the inner bearing cone and roller assembly from the hub.
7. Clean all grease from the inner and outer bearing cups with solvent. Inspect the cups for pits, scratches, or excessive wear. If the cups are damaged, remove them with a drift.
8. Clean the inner and outer cone and roller assemblies with solvent and shake them dry. If the cone and roller assemblies show excessive wear or damage, replace them with the bearing cups as a unit.
9. Clean the spindle and the inside of the hub with solvent to thoroughly remove all old grease.

10. Covering the spindle with a clean cloth, brush all loose dirt and dust from the brake assembly. Remove the cloth carefully so as to not get dirt on the spindle.

11. If the inner and/or outer bearing cups were removed, install the replacement cups on the hub. Be sure that the cups seat properly in the hub.

12. It is imperative that all old grease be removed from the bearings and surrounding surfaces before repacking. The new lithium-based grease is not compatible with the sodium base grease used in the past.

13. Install the hub and disc on the wheel spindle. To prevent damage to the grease retainer and spindle threads, keep the hub centered on the spindle.

14. Install the outer bearing cone and roller assembly and the flat washer on the spindle. Install the adjusting nut.

15. Adjust the wheel bearings by torquing the adjusting nut to 17-25 ft. lbs. with the wheel rotating to seat the bearing. Then back off the adjusting nut ½ turn. Retighten the adjusting nut to 10-15 in. lbs. Install the locknut so that the castellations are aligned with the cotter pin hole. Install the cotter pin. Bend the ends of the cotter pin around the castellations of the locknut to prevent interference with the radio static collector in the grease cap. Install the grease cap.

11. Install the wheels.

12. Install the wheel cover.

JUMP STARTING

The chemical reaction in a battery produces explosive hydrogen gas. This is the safe way to jump start a dear battery, reducing the chances of an accidental spark that could cause an explosion.

Jump Starting Precautions

1. Be sure both batteries are of the same voltage.

2. BE sure both batteries are of the same polarity (have the same grounded terminal).

3. Be sure the vehicles are not touching.

4. Be sure the vent cap holes are not obstructed.

5. Do not smoke or allow sparks around the battery.

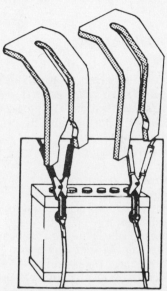

Side terminal batteries occasionally pose a problem when connecting jumper cables. There frequently isn't enough room to clamp the cables without touching sheet metal. Side terminal adaptors are available to alleviate this problem and should be removed after use.

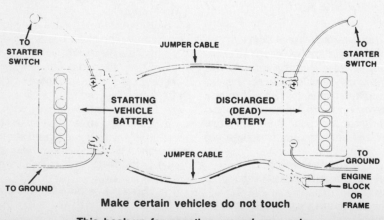

Make certain vehicles do not touch

This hook-up for negative ground cars only

6. In cold weather, check for frozen electrolyte in the battery.

7. Do not allow electrolyte on your skin or clothing.

Jump Starting Procedure

1. Determine voltages of the 2 batteries; they must be the same.

2. Bring the starting vehicle close (they must not touch) so that the batteries can be reached easily.

3. Turn off all accessories and both engines. Put both cars in **NEUTRAL** or **PARK** and set the handbrake.

4. Cover the cell caps with a rag. Do not cover terminals.

5. If the terminals on the run down battery are heavily corroded, clean them.

6. Identify the positive and negative posts on both batteries and connect the cables in the order shown.

7. Start the engine of the starting vehicle and run it at fast idle. Try to start the car with the dead battery. Crank it for no more than 10 seconds at a time and let it cool off for 20 seconds in between tries.

8. If it doesn't;t start in 3 tries, there is something else wrong.

9. Disconnect the cables in the reverse order.

10. Replace the cell cover and dispose of the rags.

PUSHING AND TOWING

Pushing is not recommended for your BMW. The bumpers were not designed for this purpose. Possible mismatching of number heights, especially around turns and over undulating road surfaces, may result in rearend body damage to your car.

BMWs may be towed, however, by attaching a 2 rope or chain to the towing loop attached to the chassis/frame near the front crossmember. Never attach a tow chain or rope to the bumper.

If you BMW fails to start, it may be started with jumper cables, or, if equipped with manual transmission, by tow-starting. When tow-starting a car, the towing vehicle should start out smoothly and be driven at an even speed to keep slack out of the tow line. Switch the ignition to the **ON** position (not the START position) and depress the clutch pedal. On older models, pull out the choke if the engine is cold. Place the transmission in Third gear and, as the towing car picks up speed, gradually release the clutch. Once the engine fires, depress the clutch pedal and feather the gas, so as to not collide with the friend who is towing you.

If the car is in a reasonable state of tune but the battery is dead, the car may be started with the use of jumper cables.

CAUTION: *All models are equipped with 12 volt negative ground electrical systems. Make sure that the car (or battery) that is supplying the jump has the same system. Always connect the positive cable of the assist battery to the positive pole of the car battery, and connect the negative cable of the assist battery to a good ground in your car's engine compartment. The idea here is to keep sparks away from you car's battery, as the battery does emit explosive hydrogen and oxygen gases.*

If all else fails, the car will have to be towed to a garage. If the car is equipped with automatic transmission, a few special precautions must be taken to prevent the transmission from being damaged. The car must be towed with the selector lever in the **NEUTRAL** position. The car my be towed a maximum distance of 30 miles (50 km) at a maximum towing speed of 25-30 mph. If the car must be towed a greater distance or at a greater speed then stated above, either the driveshaft must be disconnected or an additional 2.1 pts.. of DEXRON®II must be added to the transmission (to be drained immediately after towing). Cars with automatic transmission may not be started by towing.

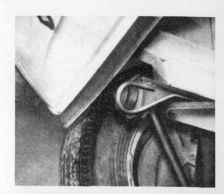

Front towing sling

Rear towing sling

Jackstand correctly positioned under front support area

JACKING

Always use the jack supplied with the car according to the safety warnings, remembering especially to block the wheel opposite the jack with the chock provided.

If the car is to be lifted or supported by axle stands below the outer body seam, place them immediately adjacent to the reinforcement points used for the jack which is supplied with the car.

If the car is to be supported via the front axle beam or final drive, use a suitable fixture such as a thick, durable block of wood to spread weight and avoid damaging these assemblies.

TRAILER TOWING

If you are installing a trailer hitch and wiring on your car, there are a few thing that you ought to know.

Trailer Weight

Trailer weight is the first, and most important, factor in determining whether or not your vehicle is suitable for towing the trailer you have in mind. The horsepower-to-weight ratio should be calculated. The basic standard is a ratio of 35:1. That is, 35 pounds of GVW for every horsepower.

To calculate this ratio, multiply you engine's rated horsepower by 35, then subtract the weight of the vehicle, including passengers and luggage. The resulting figure is the ideal maximum trailer weight that you can tow. One point to consider: a numerically higher axle ratio can offset what appears to be a low trailer weight. If the weight of the trailer that you have in mind is somewhat higher than the weight you just calculated, you might consider changing your rear axle ratio to compensate.

Hitch Weight

There are three kinds of hitches: bumper mounted, frame mounted, and load equalizing.

Bumper mounted hitches are those which attach solely to the vehicle's bumper. Many states prohibit towing with this type of hitch, when it attaches to the vehicle's stock bumper, since it subjects the bumper to stresses for which it was not designed. Aftermarket rear step bumpers, designed for trailer towing, are acceptable for use with bumper mounted hitches.

Frame mounted hitches can be of the type which bolts to two or more points on the frame, plus the bumper, or just to several points on the frame. Frame mounted hitches can also be of the tongue type, for Class I towing, or, of the receiver type, for classes II and III.

Load equalizing hitches are usually used for large trailers. Most equalizing hitches are welded in place and use equalizing bars and chains to level the vehicle after the trailer is hooked up.

The bolt-on hitches are the most common, since they are relatively easy to install.

Check the gross weight rating of your trailer. Tongue weight is usually figured as 10% of gross trailer weight. Therefore, a trailer with a maximum gross weight of 2,000 lb. will have a maximum tongue weight of 200 lb. Class I tarilers fall into this category. Class II trailers are those with a gross weight rating of 2,000-3,500 lb., while Class III trailers fall into the 3,500-6,000 lb. category. Class IV trailers are those over 6,000 lb. and are for use with fifth wheel trucks, only.

When you've determined the hitch that you'll need, follow the manufacturer's installation instructions, exactly, especially when it comes to fastener torques. The hitch will subjected to a lot of stress and good hitches come with hardened bolts. Never substitute an inferior bolt for a hardened bolt.

Wiring

Wiring the car for towing is fairly easy. There are a number of good wiring kits available and these should be used, rather than trying to design your own. All trailers will need brake lights and turn signals as well as tail lights and side marker lights. Most states require extra marker lights for overwide trailers. Also, most states have recently required back-up lights for trailers, and most trailer manufacturers have been building trailers with back-up lights for several years.

Additionally, some Class I, most Class II and just about all Class III trailers will have electric brakes.

Add to this number an accessories wire, to

operate trailer internal equipment or to charge the trailer's battery, and you can have as many as seven wires in the harness.

Determine the equipment on your trailer and buy the wiring kit necessary. The kit will contain all the wires needed, plus a plug adapter set which included the female plug, mounted on the bumper or hitch, and the male plug, wired into, or plugged into the trailer harness.

When installing the kit, follow the manufacturer's instructions. The color coding of the wires is standard throughout the industry.

One point to note: some domestic vehicles, and most imported vehicles, have separate turn signals. On most domestic vehicles, the brake lights and rear turn signals operate with the same bulb. For those vehicles with separate turn signals, you can purchase an isolation unit so that the brake lights won't blink whenever the turn signals are operated, or, you can go to your local electronics supply house and buy four diodes to wire in series with the brake and turn signal bulbs. Diodes will isolate the brake and turn signals. The choice is yours. The isolation units are simple and quick to install, but far more expensive than the diodes. The diodes, however, require more work to install properly, since they require the cutting of each bulb's wire and soldering in place of the diode.

One, final point, the best kits are those with a spring loaded cover on the vehicle mounted socket. This cover prevent dirt and moisture from corroding the terminals. Never let the vehicle socket hang loosely; always mount it securely to the bumper or hitch.

Cooling
ENGINE

One of the most common, if not THE most common, problems associated with trailer towing is engine overheating.

With factory installed trailer towing packages, a heavy duty cooling system is usually included. Heavy duty cooling systems are available as optional equipment on most vehicles, with or without a trailer package. If you have one of these extra-capacity systems, you shouldn't have any overheating problems.

If you have a standard cooling system, without an expansion tank, you'll definitely need to get an aftermarket expansion tank kit, preferably one with at least a 2 quart capacity. These kits are easily installed on the radiator's overflow hose, and come with a pressure cap designed for expansion tanks.

Another helpful accessory is a Flex Fan. These fan are large diameter units are designed to provide more airflow at low speeds, with blades that have deeply cupped surfaces. The blades then flex, or flatten out, at high speed, when less cooling air is needed. These fans are far lighter in weight than stock fans, requiring less horsepower to drive them. Also, they are far quieter than stock fans.

If you do decide to replace your stock fan with a flex fan, note that if your car has a fan clutch, a spacer between the flex fan and water pump hub will be needed.

Aftermarket engine oil coolers are helpful for prolonging engine oil life and reducing overall engine temperatures. Both of these factors increase engine life.

While not absolutely necessary in towing Class I and some Class II trailers, they are recommeded for heavier Class II and all Class III towing.

Engine oil cooler systems consist of an adapter, screwed on in place of the oil filter, a remote filter mounting and a multi-tube, finned heat exchanger, which is mounted in front of the radiator or air conditioning condenser.

TRANSMISSION

An automatic transmission is usually recommended for trailer towing. Modern automatics have proven reliable and, of course, easy to operate, in trailer towing.

The increased load of a trailer, however, causes an increase in the temperature of the automatic transmission fluid. Heat is the worst enemy of an automatic transmission. As the temperature of the fluid increases, the life of the fluid decreases.

It is essential, therefore, that you install an automatic transmission cooler.

The cooler, which consists of a multi-tube, finned heat exchanger, is usually installed in front of the radiator or air conditioning compressor, and hooked inline with the transmission cooler tank inlet line. Follow the cooler manufacturer's installation instructions.

Select a cooler of at least adequate capacity, based upon the combined gross weights of the car and trailer.

Cooler manufacturers recommend that you use an aftermarket cooler in addition to, and not instead of, the present cooling tank in your car's radiator. If you do want to use it in place of the radiator cooling tank, get a cooler at least two sizes larger than normally necessary.

One note: the transmission cooler can, sometimes, cause slow or harsh shifting in the transmission during cold weather, until the fluid has a chance to come up to normal operating temperature. Some coolers can be purchased with or retrofitted with a temperature bypass valve which will allow fluid flow through the cooler only when the fluid has reached operating temperature, or above.

Engine Performance and Tune-Up

2

TUNE-UP PROCEDURES

In order to extract the full measure of performance and economy from your engine it is essential; that it is properly tuned at regular intervals. A regular tune-up will keep your car's engine running smoothly and will prevent the annoying breakdowns and poor performance associated with an untuned engine.

NOTE: *All models built before 1980 used a conventional breaker point ignition system except for the 633CSi and the 733i. All models built after 1980 utilize a pointless electronic ignition system.*

A complete tune-up should be performed at least every 15,000 miles (12,000 miles for early models) or 12 months, whichever comes first. This interval should be halved if the car is operated under severe conditions such as trailer towing, prolonged idling, start-and-stop driving, or if starting or running problems are noticed. It is assumed that the routine maintenance described in Chapter 1 has been kept up, as this will have a decided effect on the results of a tune-up. All of the applicable steps of a tune-up should be followed in order, as the result is a cumulative one.

If the specifications on the underhood tune-up sticker in the engine compartment of your car disagree with the "Tune-Up Specifications" chart in this chapter, the figures on the sticker must be used. The sticker often reflects changes made during the production run.

Spark Plugs

A typical spark plug consists of a metal shell surrounding a ceramic insulator. A metal electrode extends downward through the center of the insulator and protrudes a short distance. Located at the end of the plug and attached to the side of the outer metal shell is the side electrode. This side electrode bends in at 90° merely provides a gap across which the current can arc. The coil produces 20,000-25,000 V (electronic ignition systems produce considerable more voltage than the standard type, approximately

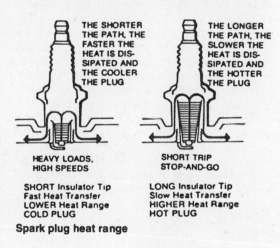

THE SHORTER THE PATH, THE FASTER THE HEAT IS DISSIPATED AND THE COOLER THE PLUG

THE LONGER THE PATH, THE SLOWER THE HEAT IS DISSIPATED AND THE HOTTER THE PLUG

HEAVY LOADS, HIGH SPEEDS

SHORT Insulator Tip
Fast Heat Transfer
LOWER Heat Range
COLD PLUG

SHORT TRIP STOP-AND-GO

LONG Insulator Tip
Slow Heat Transfer
HIGHER Heat Range
HOT PLUG

Spark plug heat range

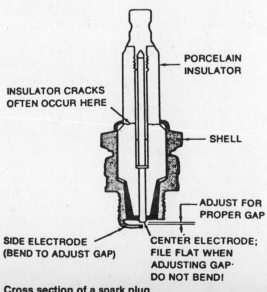

PORCELAIN INSULATOR

INSULATOR CRACKS OFTEN OCCUR HERE

SHELL

ADJUST FOR PROPER GAP

SIDE ELECTRODE (BEND TO ADJUST GAP)

CENTER ELECTRODE; FILE FLAT WHEN ADJUSTING GAP. DO NOT BEND!

Cross section of a spark plug

Gasoline Engine Tune-Up Specifications

Year	Model	Engine Displacement cu. in. (cc)	Spark Plugs Type	Spark Plugs Gap (in.)	Distributor Dwell Angle (deg)	Distributor Point Gap (in.)	Ignition Timing (deg.) ▲■● MT	Ignition Timing (deg.) ▲■● AT	Compression Pressure (psi)*	Fuel Pump (psi)	Idle Speed (rpm) MT	Idle Speed (rpm) AT	Valve Clearance In.	Valve Clearance Ex.
1970	1600	96 (1573)	①	.024	61–66	.016	25B @ 1400		142	3.0–3.6	1000	1000	.0059–.0079	.0059–.0079
	2000,2002,Tii	121 (1990)	W175T30	.024	59–66	.016	25B @ 1400		142	3.0–3.6	900	900	.006–.008	.006–.008
	2500	152 (2493)	W175T2	.024	35–41	.016	22B @ 1700		142	2.8–3.5	900	900	.010–.012	.010–.012
	2800,CS	170 (2788)	WG160T30	.024	35–41	.015	22B @ 1700		149	2.8–3.5	900	900	.010–.012	.010–.012
	Bavaria	170 (2788)	WG160T30	.024	35–41	.015	22B @ 1700		149	2.8–3.5	900	900	.010–.012	.010–.012
1971	1600	96 (1573)	①	.024	61–66	.016	25B @ 1400		142	3.0–3.6	1000	1000	.0059–.0079	.0059–.0079
	2000,2002	121 (1990)	W175T30	.024	59–66	.016	25B @ 1400		142	3.0–3.6	900	900	.006–.008	.006–.008
	2500	152 (2493)	W175T2	.024	35–41	.016	22B @ 1700		149	2.8–3.5	900	900	.010–.012	.010–.012
	Bavaria	170 (2788)	WG160T30	.024	35–41	.015	22B @ 1700		149	2.8–3.5	900	900	.010–.012	.010–.012
1972	2000,2002Tii	121 (1990)	W175T30	.024	59–66	.016	25B @ 1400		142	3.0–3.6 ②	900	900	.006–.008	.006–.008
	Bavaria	170 (2788)	WG160T30	.024	35–41	.015	22B @ 1700		149	2.8–3.5	900	900	.010–.012	.010–.012
	3000CS	170 (2788)	WG160T30	.024	35–41	.015	22B @ 1700		149	2.8–3.5	900	900	.010–.012	.010–.012
1973	2000,2002Tii	121 (1990)	W175T30	.024	59–66	.016	25B @ 1400		142	3.0–3.6 ②	900	900	.006–.008	.006–.008
	3.0CS,S,Si	182 (2985)	W145T30	.024	35–41	.015	22B @ 1700		149	2.8–3.5	900	900	.010–.012	.010–.012

Gasoline Engine Tune-Up Specifications (cont.)

Year	Model	Engine Displacement cu. in. (cc)	Spark Plugs Type	Gap (in.)	Distributor Dwell Angle (deg)	Point Gap (in.)	Ignition Timing ▲ (deg.)■● MT	AT	Compression Pressure (psi)*	Fuel Pump (psi)	Idle Speed (rpm) MT	AT	Valve Clearance In.	Ex.
1973	Bavaria	170 (2788)	WG160T30	.024	35–41	.015	22B @ 1700		149	2.8–3.5	900	900	.010–.012	.010–.012
1974	2000,2002,Tii	121 (1990)	W175T30	.024	59–66	.016	25B @ 1400		142	3.0–3.6 ②	900	900	.006–.008	.006–.008
	Bavaria	170 (2788)	WG160T30	.024	35–41	.015	22B @ 1700		149	2.8–3.5	900	900	.010–.012	.010–.012
	3.0CS,S,Si	182 (2985)	W145T30	.024	35–41	.015	22B @ 1700		149	2.8–3.5	900	900	.010–.012	.010–.012
1975	2002,Tii	121 (1990)	W175T30	.024	59–66	.016	25B @ 1400		142	3.0–.36 ②	900	900	.006–.008	.006–.008
	3.0CS,S,Si	182 (2985)	W145T30	.024	35–41	.015	22B @ 1700		149	29–31	900	900	.010–.012	.010–.012
	530i	182 (2985)	W145T30	.024	35–41	.014	22B @ 1700 (2700)		149	35	950	950	.010–.012	.010–.012
1976	2002,Tii	121 (1990)	W175T30	.024	59–66	.016	25B @ 1400		142	3.0–3.6 ②	900	900	.006–.008	.006–.008
	3.0CS,S,Si	182 (2985)	W145T30	.024	35–41	.015	22B @ 1700		149	29–31	900	900	.010–.012	.010–.012
	630CS 530i	182 (2985)	W145T30	.024	35–41	.014	22B @ 1700 (2700)		149	35	950	950	.010–.012	.010–.012
1977	320i	121 (1990)	W145T30	.024	59–65	.014	25B @ 2200 (2400)		128	67–74	950	950	.006–.008	.006–.008
	530i	182 (2985)	W145T30	.024	35–41	.014	22B @ 1700 (2700)		149	35	950	950	.010–.012	.010–.012
	630CSi	182 (2985)	W145T30	.024	35–41	.014	22B @ 1700 (2700)		114	35	950	950	.010–.012	.010–.012
1978	320i	121 (1990)	W145T30	.024	59–65	.014	25B @ 2200 (2400)		128	67–74	950	950	.006–.008	.006–.008

Year	Model										
	530i	182 (2985)	W145T30	.024	35–41 .014	22B @ 1700 (2700)	149	35	950	950	.010–.012	.010–.012
	633CSi	196 (3210)	W145T30	.025	Electronic ③	22B @ 2400 (2750)	114	37	950	950	.010–.012	.010–.012
	733i	196 (3210)	W145T30	.025	Electronic ③	22B @ 2400 (2750)	114	37	950	950	.010–.012	.010–.012
1979	320i	121 (1990)	W125T30	.027	59–65 .014	25B @ 2200 (2400)	128	67–74	950	950	.006–.008	.006–.008
	528i	170 (2788)	W125T30	.024	Electronic ③	22B @ 2100	142	35	900	900	.010–.012	.010–.012
	633CSi	196 (3210)	W145T30	.025	Electronic ③	22B @ 2400 (2750)	114	37	950	950	.010–.012	.010–.012
	733i	196 (3210)	W145T30	.025	Electronic ③	22B @ 2400 (2750)	114	37	950	950	.010–.012	.010–.012
1980	320i	107 (1766)	WR9DS	.024	Electronic ③	25B @ 2200	128	67–74	850	900	.006–.008	.006–.008
	528i	170 (2788)	WR9DS	.024	Electronic ③	22B @ 2100	142	35	900	900	.010–.012	.010–.012
	633CSi	196 (3210)	WR9DS	.024	Electronic ③	22B @ 1650	114	35	900	900	.010–.012	.010–.012
	733i	196 (3210)	WR9DS	.024	Electronic ③	22B @ 1650	114	35	900	900	.010–.012	.010–.012
1981	320i	107 (1766)	WR9DS	.024	Electronic ③	25B @ 2200	128	67–74	850	900	.006–.008	.006–.008
	528i	170 (2788)	WR9DS	.024	Electronic ③	22B @ 2100	142	35	900	900	.010–.012	.010–.012
	633CSi	196 (3210)	WR9DS	.024	Electronic ③	22B @ 1650	114	35	900	900	.010–.012	.010–.012
	733i	196 (3210)	WR9DS	.024	Electronic ③	22B @ 1650	114	35	900	900	.010–.012	.010–.012
1982	320i	108 (1766)	WR9DS	0.024	Electronic ③	25B @ 2200	128	64–74	850	900	0.007	0.007
	325e	165 (2693)	WR9LS	0.024	Electronic ③	④	142	33–38	④	④	0.010	0.010
	528e	165 (2693)	WR9LS	0.024	Electronic ③	④	142	33–38	④	④	0.010	0.010

Gasoline Engine Tune-Up Specifications (cont.)

Year	Model	Engine Displacement cu. in. (cc)	Spark Plugs Type	Spark Plugs Gap (in.)	Distributor Dwell Angle (deg)	Distributor Point Gap (in.)	Ignition Timing ▲ (deg.)■● MT	Ignition Timing ▲ (deg.)■● AT	Compression Pressure (psi)*	Fuel Pump (psi)	Idle Speed (rpm) MT	Idle Speed (rpm) AT	Valve Clearance In.	Valve Clearance Ex.
1982	533i	196 (3210)	WR9LS	0.024	Electronic ③		④	④	114	35	④	④	0.011	0.011
	633CSi	196 (3210)	WR9LS	0.024	Electronic ③		④	④	114	35	④	④	0.011	0.011
	733i	196 (3210)	WR9LS	0.024	Electronic ③		④	④	114	35	④	④	0.011	0.011
1983	320i	10B (1766)	WR9DS	0.024	Electronic ③		25B @ 2200	25B @ 2200	128	64–74	850	900	0.007	0.007
	325e	165 (2693)	WR9LS	0.024	Electronic ③		④	④	149	33–38	④	④	0.010	0.010
	528e	165 (2693)	WR9LS	0.024	Electronic ③		④	④	149	33–38	④	④	0.010	0.010
	533i	196 (3210)	WR9LS	0.024	Electronic ③		④	④	149	35	④	④	0.012	0.012
	633CSi	196 (3210)	WR9LS	0.024	Electronic ③		④	④	149	35	④	④	0.012	0.012
	733i	196 (3210)	WR9LS	0.024	Electronic ③		④	④	149	35	④	④	0.012	0.012
1984	318i	108 (1766)	WR9DS	0.024	Electronic ③		④	④	149	43	750	750	0.008	0.008
	325e	165 (2693)	WR9LS	0.024	Electronic ③		④	④	149	33–38	700	700	0.010	0.010
	528e	165 (2693)	WR9LS	0.024	Electronic ③		④	④	149	33–38	700	700	0.010	0.010
	533i	196 (3210)	WR9LS	0.024	Electronic ③		④	④	149	35	700	700	0.012	0.012
	633CSi	196 (3210)	WR9LS	0.024	Electronic ③		④	④	149	35	700	700	0.012	0.012
	733i	196 (3210)	WR9LS	0.024	Electronic ③		④	④	149	35	700	700	0.012	0.012
1985	318i	108 (1766)	WR9DS	0.033	Electronic ③		④	④	149	43	750	750	0.008	0.008
	325e	165 (2693)	WR9LS	0.029	Electronic ③		④	④	149	33–38	700	700	0.010	0.010
	528e	165 (2693)	WR9LS	0.029	Electronic ③		④	④	149	33–38	700	700	0.010	0.010
	533i	196 (3210)	WR9LS	0.024	Electronic ③		④	④	149	35	700	700	0.012	0.012
	633CSi	196 (3210)	WR9LS	0.024	Electronic ③		④	④	149	35	700	700	0.012	0.012
	535i	209 (3428)	WR9LS	0.029	Electronic ③		④	④	149	43	800	800	0.012	0.012
	635CSi	209 (3428)	WR9LS	0.029	Electronic ③		④	④	149	43	800	800	0.012	0.012
	733i	196 (3210)	WR9LS	0.024	Electronic ③		④	④	149	35	700	700	0.012	0.012

Year	Model	Displacement cu in (cc)	Spark Plugs Type	Gap (in)	Ignition Timing						Idle Speed		Valve Clearance	
1986	735i	209 (3428)	WR9LS	0.029	Electronic ③	④	④	149	43		800	800	0.012	0.012
	325e	165 (2693)	WR9LS	0.029	Electronic ③	④	④	149	33–38		700	700	0.010	0.010
	528e	165 (2693)	WR9LS	0.029	Electronic ③	④	④	149	33–38		700	700	0.010	0.010
	535i	209 (3428)	WR9LS	0.029	Electronic ③	④	④	149	43		800	800	0.012	0.012
	635CSi	209 (3428)	WR9LS	0.029	Electronic ③	④	④	149	43		800	800	0.012	0.012
	535i	209 (3428)	WR9LS	0.029	Electronic ③	④	④	149	43		800	800	0.012	0.012
1987	325	165 (2693)	WR9LS	0.029	Electronic ③	④	④	149	33–38		700	700	0.010	0.010
	528e	165 (2693)	WR9LS	0.029	Electronic ③	④	④	149	33–38		700	700	0.010	0.010
	325i	152 (2494)	W8LCR	0.029	Electronic ③	④	④	149	43		720	720	0.010	0.010
	325iS	152 (2494)	W8LCR	0.029	Electronic ③	④	④	149	43		720	720	0.010	0.010
	535i	209 (3428)	WR9LS	0.029	Electronic ③	④	④	149	43		800	800	0.012	0.012
	635CSi	209 (3428)	WR9LS	0.029	Electronic ③	④	④	149	43		800	800	0.012	0.012
	735i	209 (3428)	WR9LS	0.029	Electronic ③	④	④	149	43		800	800	0.012	0.012
	M5	210.6 (3453)	X5DC	0.029	Electronic ③	④	④	149	43		800	—	0.013	0.013
	M6	210.6 (3453)	X5DC	0.029	Electronic ③	④	④	149	43		800	—	0.013	0.013
1988	325	165 (2693)	WR9LS	0.027	Electronic ③	④	④	149	36		720	720	0.010	0.010
	528e	165 (2693)	WR9LS	0.027	Electronic ③	④	④	149	36		720	720	0.010	0.010
	325i	152 (2494)	WR9LS	0.027	Electronic ③	④	④	149	43		760	760	0.010	0.010
	325iS	152 (2494)	WR9LS	0.027	Electronic ③	④	④	149	43		760	760	0.010	0.010
	325iX	152 (2494)	WR9LS	0.027	Electronic ③	④	④	149	43		760	760	0.010	0.010
	535i	209 (3428)	WR9LS	0.027	Electronic ③	④	④	149	43		800	800	0.012	0.012
	635CSi	209 (3428)	WR9LS	0.027	Electronic ③	④	④	149	43		800	800	0.012	0.012
	L6	209 (3428)	WR9LS	0.027	Electronic ③	④	④	149	43		800	800	0.012	0.012
	M3	140.4 (2302)	WR9LS	0.027	Electronic ③	④	④	149	43		880	—	0.012	0.012
	M5	210.6 (3453)	WR9LS	0.027	Electronic ③	④	④	149	43		850	—	0.013	0.013
	M6	210.6 (3453)	WR9LS	0.027	Electronic ③	④	④	149	43		850	—	0.013	0.013

Gasoline Engine Tune-Up Specifications (cont.)

| Year | Model | Engine Displacement cu. in. (cc) | Spark Plugs | | Distributor | | Ignition Timing ▲ (deg.)■● | | Compression Pressure (psi)* | Fuel Pump (psi) | Idle Speed (rpm) | | Valve Clearance | |
			Type	Gap (in.)	Dwell Angle (deg)	Point Gap (in.)	MT	AT			MT	AT	In.	Ex.
1988	735iL	209 (3428)	W8LCR	0.027	Electronic ③	Electronic ③	④	④	149	43	④	④	0.012	0.012
	750i	304 (4988)	F8LCR	0.027	Electronic ③	Electronic ③	④	④	176	43	700	700	NA	NA

NOTE: The underhood specifications sticker often reflects tune-up specification changes made in production. Sticker figures must be used if they disagree with those in this chart.

NA Not available

B Before Top Dead Center

*When analyzing compression figures, look for uniformity between cylinders

▲ See text for procedures

● Figures in parenthesis are for California

■ All figures are Before Top Dead Center

① Bosch W200T30 or WG190T30

② 2002Tii—21–29 psi.

③ Although not adjustable the air gap should be checked periodically. The gap should be .012–.028, if not within specification the unit should be replaced.

④ Motronic injection system—controlled by computer, please refer to the underhood sticker for specifications

Diesel Engine Tune-Up Specifications

Year	Engine Displacement cu. in. (cc)	Valve Clearance		Intake Valve Opens (deg.)	Injection Pump Setting (deg.)	Injection Nozzle Pressure (psi)		Idle Speed (rpm)	Cranking Compression Pressure (psi)
		Intake (in.)	Exhaust (in.)			New	Used		
1985	149 (2443)	0.012	0.012	NA	3.5B	2133–2470	1920	750	284
1986	149 (2443)	0.012	0.012	NA	3.5B	2133–2247	1920	750	284

B Before Top Dead Center
NA Not available

50,000 volts), which travels to the distributor where it is distributed through the spark plug wires to the plugs. The current passes along the center electrode and, in so doing, ignites the air/fuel mixture in the combustion chamber. All plugs used in recent models have a resistor built into the center electrode to reduce interference to any nearby radio and television receivers. The resistor also cuts down on erosion of plug electrodes caused by excessively long sparking. Resistor spark plug wiring is original equipment on all such models.

Spark plug life and efficiency depend upon the condition of the engine and the temperatures to which the plug is exposed. Combustion chamber temperatures are affected by many factors such as compression ratio of the engine, fuel/air mixtures, exhaust emission equipment, and the type of driving you do. Spark plugs are designed and classified by number according to the heat range at which they will operate most efficiently. The amount of heat that the plug absorbs is determined by the length of the lower insulator. The longer the insulator (it extends farther into the engine), the hotter the plug will operate; the shorter it is, the cooler it will operate. A plug that has a short path for heat transfer and remains too cool will quickly accumulate deposits of oil and carbon since it is not hot enough to burn them off. This leads to plug fouling and consequently to misfiring. A plug that has a long path for heat transfer will have no deposits but, due to the excessive heat, the electrodes will burn away quickly and, in some instances, pre-ignition may result. Pre-ignition takes place when plug tips get so hot that they glow sufficiently to ignite the fuel/air mixture before the spark does. This early ignition will usually cause a pinging (sounding much like castanets) during low speeds and heavy loads. In severe cases, the heat may become enough to start the fuel/air mixture burning throughout the combustion chamber rather than just to the front of the plus as in normal operation. At this time, the piston is rising in the cylinder making its compression stroke. The burning mass is compressed and an explosion results producing tremendous pressure. Something has to give, and it does—pistons are often damaged. Obviously, this detonation (explosion) is a destructive condition that can be avoided by installing a spark plug designed and specified for your particular engine.

A set of spark plugs usually requires replacement after 10,000-12,500 miles depending on the type of driving, BMW reccomends that spark plugs be checked and changed if necessary at 12,500 mile intervals. The electrode on a new spark plug has a sharp edge but, with use, this edge becomes rounded by erosion causing the plug gap to increase. In normal operation, plug gap increases about 0.025mm in every 1,000-2,000 miles (1,600-3,200 km). As the gap increases, the plug's voltage requirement also increases. It requires a greater voltage to jump the wider gap and about 2 to 3 times as much voltage to fire a plug at high speeds and acceleration than at idle.

Worn plugs become obvious during acceleration. Voltage requirement is greater during acceleration and a plug with an enlarged gap may require more voltage than the coil is able to produce. As a result, the engine misses and sputters until acceleration is reduced. Reducing acceleration reduces the plug's voltage requirement and the engine runs smoother. Slow, city driving is hard on plugs. The long periods of idle experience in traffic creates an overly rich gas mixture. The engine isn't running fast enough to completely burn the gas and, consequently, the plugs are fouled with gas deposits and engine idle becomes rough. In many cases, driving under the right conditions can effectively clean these fouled plugs.

NOTE: *There are several reasons why a spark plug will foul and you can usually learn which is at fault by just looking at the plug. A few of the most common reasons for*

Troubleshooting Engine Performance

Problem	Cause	Solution
Hard starting (engine cranks normally)	• Binding linkage, choke valve or choke piston	• Repair as necessary
	• Restricted choke vacuum diaphragm	• Clean passages
	• Improper fuel level	• Adjust float level
	• Dirty, worn or faulty needle valve and seat	• Repair as necessary
	• Float sticking	• Repair as necessary
	• Faulty fuel pump	• Replace fuel pump
	• Incorrect choke cover adjustment	• Adjust choke cover
	• Inadequate choke unloader adjustment	• Adjust choke unloader
	• Faulty ignition coil	• Test and replace as necessary
	• Improper spark plug gap	• Adjust gap
	• Incorrect ignition timing	• Adjust timing
	• Incorrect valve timing	• Check valve timing; repair as necessary
Rough idle or stalling	• Incorrect curb or fast idle speed	• Adjust curb or fast idle speed
	• Incorrect ignition timing	• Adjust timing to specification
	• Improper feedback system operation	• Refer to Chapter 4
	• Improper fast idle cam adjustment	• Adjust fast idle cam
	• Faulty EGR valve operation	• Test EGR system and replace as necessary
	• Faulty PCV valve air flow	• Test PCV valve and replace as necessary
	• Choke binding	• Locate and eliminate binding condition
	• Faulty TAC vacuum motor or valve	• Repair as necessary
	• Air leak into manifold vacuum	• Inspect manifold vacuum connections and repair as necessary
	• Improper fuel level	• Adjust fuel level
	• Faulty distributor rotor or cap	• Replace rotor or cap
	• Improperly seated valves	• Test cylinder compression, repair as necessary
	• Incorrect ignition wiring	• Inspect wiring and correct as necessary
	• Faulty ignition coil	• Test coil and replace as necessary
	• Restricted air vent or idle passages	• Clean passages
	• Restricted air cleaner	• Clean or replace air cleaner filler element
	• Faulty choke vacuum diaphragm	• Repair as necessary
Faulty low-speed operation	• Restricted idle transfer slots	• Clean transfer slots
	• Restricted idle air vents and passages	• Clean air vents and passages
	• Restricted air cleaner	• Clean or replace air cleaner filter element
	• Improper fuel level	• Adjust fuel level
	• Faulty spark plugs	• Clean or replace spark plugs
	• Dirty, corroded, or loose ignition secondary circuit wire connections	• Clean or tighten secondary circuit wire connections
	• Improper feedback system operation	• Refer to Chapter 4
	• Faulty ignition coil high voltage wire	• Replace ignition coil high voltage wire
	• Faulty distributor cap	• Replace cap
Faulty acceleration	• Improper accelerator pump stroke	• Adjust accelerator pump stroke
	• Incorrect ignition timing	• Adjust timing
	• Inoperative pump discharge check ball or needle	• Clean or replace as necessary
	• Worn or damaged pump diaphragm or piston	• Replace diaphragm or piston

Troubleshooting Engine Performance (cont.)

Problem	Cause	Solution
Faulty acceleration (cont.)	• Leaking carburetor main body cover gasket	• Replace gasket
	• Engine cold and choke set too lean	• Adjust choke cover
	• Improper metering rod adjustment (BBD Model carburetor)	• Adjust metering rod
	• Faulty spark plug(s)	• Clean or replace spark plug(s)
	• Improperly seated valves	• Test cylinder compression, repair as necessary
	• Faulty ignition coil	• Test coil and replace as necessary
	• Improper feedback system operation	• Refer to Chapter 4
Faulty high speed operation	• Incorrect ignition timing	• Adjust timing
	• Faulty distributor centrifugal advance mechanism	• Check centrifugal advance mechanism and repair as necessary
	• Faulty distributor vacuum advance mechanism	• Check vacuum advance mechanism and repair as necessary
	• Low fuel pump volume	• Replace fuel pump
	• Wrong spark plug air gap or wrong plug	• Adjust air gap or install correct plug
	• Faulty choke operation	• Adjust choke cover
	• Partially restricted exhaust manifold, exhaust pipe, catalytic converter, muffler, or tailpipe	• Eliminate restriction
	• Restricted vacuum passages	• Clean passages
	• Improper size or restricted main jet	• Clean or replace as necessary
	• Restricted air cleaner	• Clean or replace filter element as necessary
	• Faulty distributor rotor or cap	• Replace rotor or cap
	• Faulty ignition coil	• Test coil and replace as necessary
	• Improperly seated valve(s)	• Test cylinder compression, repair as necessary
	• Faulty valve spring(s)	• Inspect and test valve spring tension, replace as necessary
	• Incorrect valve timing	• Check valve timing and repair as necessary
	• Intake manifold restricted	• Remove restriction or replace manifold
	• Worn distributor shaft	• Replace shaft
	• Improper feedback system operation	• Refer to Chapter 4
Misfire at all speeds	• Faulty spark plug(s)	• Clean or replace spark plug(s)
	• Faulty spark plug wire(s)	• Replace as necessary
	• Faulty distributor cap or rotor	• Replace cap or rotor
	• Faulty ignition coil	• Test coil and replace as necessary
	• Primary ignition circuit shorted or open intermittently	• Troubleshoot primary circuit and repair as necessary
	• Improperly seated valve(s)	• Test cylinder compression, repair as necessary
	• Faulty hydraulic tappet(s)	• Clean or replace tappet(s)
	• Improper feedback system operation	• Refer to Chapter 4
	• Faulty valve spring(s)	• Inspect and test valve spring tension, repair as necessary
	• Worn camshaft lobes	• Replace camshaft
	• Air leak into manifold	• Check manifold vacuum and repair as necessary
	• Improper carburetor adjustment	• Adjust carburetor
	• Fuel pump volume or pressure low	• Replace fuel pump
	• Blown cylinder head gasket	• Replace gasket
	• Intake or exhaust manifold passage(s) restricted	• Pass chain through passage(s) and repair as necessary
	• Incorrect trigger wheel installed in distributor	• Install correct trigger wheel

Troubleshooting Engine Performance (cont.)

Problem	Cause	Solution
Power not up to normal	• Incorrect ignition timing • Faulty distributor rotor • Trigger wheel loose on shaft • Incorrect spark plug gap • Faulty fuel pump • Incorrect valve timing • Faulty ignition coil • Faulty ignition wires • Improperly seated valves • Blown cylinder head gasket • Leaking piston rings • Worn distributor shaft • Improper feedback system operation	• Adjust timing • Replace rotor • Reposition or replace trigger wheel • Adjust gap • Replace fuel pump • Check valve timing and repair as necessary • Test coil and replace as necessary • Test wires and replace as necessary • Test cylinder compression and repair as necessary • Replace gasket • Test compression and repair as necessary • Replace shaft • Refer to Chapter 4
Intake backfire	• Improper ignition timing • Faulty accelerator pump discharge • Defective EGR CTO valve • Defective TAC vacuum motor or valve • Lean air/fuel mixture	• Adjust timing • Repair as necessary • Replace EGR CTO valve • Repair as necessary • Check float level or manifold vacuum for air leak. Remove sediment from bowl
Exhaust backfire	• Air leak into manifold vacuum • Faulty air injection diverter valve • Exhaust leak	• Check manifold vacuum and repair as necessary • Test diverter valve and replace as necessary • Locate and eliminate leak
Ping or spark knock	• Incorrect ignition timing • Distributor centrifugal or vacuum advance malfunction • Excessive combustion chamber deposits • Air leak into manifold vacuum • Excessively high compression • Fuel octane rating excessively low • Sharp edges in combustion chamber • EGR valve not functioning properly	• Adjust timing • Inspect advance mechanism and repair as necessary • Remove with combustion chamber cleaner • Check manifold vacuum and repair as necessary • Test compression and repair as necessary • Try alternate fuel source • Grind smooth • Test EGR system and replace as necessary
Surging (at cruising to top speeds)	• Low carburetor fuel level • Low fuel pump pressure or volume • Metering rod(s) not adjusted properly (BBD Model Carburetor) • Improper PCV valve air flow • Air leak into manifold vacuum • Incorrect spark advance • Restricted main jet(s) • Undersize main jet(s) • Restricted air vents • Restricted fuel filter • Restricted air cleaner • EGR valve not functioning properly • Improper feedback system operation	• Adjust fuel level • Replace fuel pump • Adjust metering rod • Test PCV valve and replace as necessary • Check manifold vacuum and repair as necessary • Test and replace as necessary • Clean main jet(s) • Replace main jet(s) • Clean air vents • Replace fuel filter • Clean or replace air cleaner filter element • Test EGR system and replace as necessary • Refer to Chapter 4

plug fouling, and a description of the fouled plug's appearance, can be found in the color insert in this book.

Accelerate your car to the speed where the engine begins to miss and then slow down to the point where the engine smooths out. Run at this speed for a few minutes and then accelerate again to the point of engine miss. With each repetition this engine miss should occur at increasingly high speeds and then disappear altogether. Do not attempt to shortcut this procedure by hard acceleration. This approach will compound problems by fusing deposits into a hard permanent glaze. Dirty, fouled plugs may be cleaned by sandblasting. Many shops have a spark plug sandblaster. After sandblasting, the electrode should be filed to a sharp, square shape and then gapped to specifications. Gapping a plug too close will produce a rough idle while gapping it too wide will increase its voltage requirement and cause missing at high speeds and during acceleration.

The type of driving you do may require a change in spark plug heat range. If the majority of your driving id done in the city and rarely at high speeds, plug fouling may necessitate changing to a plug with a heat range one number higher than that specified by the car manufacturer.

One the other hand, if your car were used almost exclusively for long distance high speed driving, the specified plus might be too hot resulting in rapid electrode wear and dangerous preignition. In this case, it might be wise to change to a colder plug. If the car is used for abnormal driving (as in the examples above), or the engine has been modified for higher performance, then a change to a plug of a different heat range may be necessary. With a modified car it is always wise to go to a colder plug as a protection against pre-ignition. It will require more frequent plug cleaning, but destructive detonation during acceleration will be avoided.

REMOVAL

When you're removing spark plugs, you should work on one at a time. Don't start by removing the plug wires all at once because unless you number them, they're going to get mixed up. On some models though, it will be more convenient for you to remove all the wires before you start to work on the plugs. If this is necessary, take a minute before you begin and number the wires with tape before you take them off. The time you spend here will pay off later on.

1. Twist the spark plug boot and remove the boot from the plug. You may also use a plug wire removal tool designed especially for this purpose. Do not pull on the wire itself. When

Twist and pull on the rubber boot to remove the spark plug wires; never pull on the wire itself

Plugs that are in good condition can be filed and reused

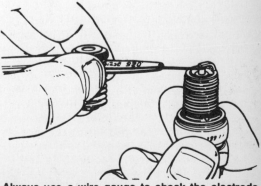

Always use a wire gauge to check the electrode gap

Adjust the electrode gap by bending the side electrode

the wire has been removed, take a wire brush and clean the area around the plug. Make sure that all the grime is removed so that none will enter the cylinder after the plug has been removed.

2. Remove the plug using the proper size socket, extensions, and universals as necessary. For all engines, use a $^{13}/_{16}''$ spark plug socket.

NOTE: *All BMW cylinder heads are made of aluminum. Be very careful when removing the plugs so as not to strip the threads.*

3. If removing the plus is difficult, drip some penetrating oil on the plug threads, allow it to work, then remove the plug. Also, be sure that the socket is straight on the plug, especially on those hard to reach plugs.

INSPECTION

Check the plugs for deposits and wear. If they are not going to be replaced, clean the plugs thoroughly. Remember that any kind of deposit will decrease the efficiency of the plug. Plugs can be cleaned on a spark plug cleaning machine, which can sometimes be found in service stations, of you can do an acceptable job of cleaning with a stiff brush.

NOTE: *Refer to the color insert "Fuel Economy and Tune-Up Tips" for examples of problem spark plugs.*

If the plugs are cleaned, the electrodes must be filed flat. Use an ignition point file, not an emery board or the like, which will leave deposits. The electrodes must be filed perfectly flat with sharp edges; rounded edges reduce the spark plug voltage by as much as 50%.

Check spark plug gap before installation. The ground electrode (the L-shaped one connected to the body of the plug) must be parallel to the center electrode and the specified size wire gauge (see "Tune-Up Specification") should pass through the gap with a slight drag. Always check the gap on new plugs, too; they are not always set correctly at the factory. Do not use a flat feeler gauge when measuring the gap, because the reading will be inaccurate. Wire gapping tools usually have a bending tool attached. Use that to adjust the side electrode until the proper distance is obtained. Absolutely never bend the center electrode. Also, be careful not

to bend the side electrode too far or too often; it may weaken and break off within the engine, requiring removal of the cylinder head to retrieve it.

INSTALLATION

1. Lubricate the threads of the spark plugs with a drop of oil. Install the plugs and tighten them hand-tight. Take care not to cross-thread them.

2. Tighten the spark plugs with the socket. Do not apply the same amount of force you would use for a bolt, just snug them in. If a torque wrench is available, tighten to 17-21 ft. lbs.

3. Install the wires on their respective plugs. Make sure the wire are firmly connected. You will be able to feel them click into place.

RETHREADING

Should you encounter uneven or unduly stiff resistance when removing or installing the spark plugs in the head, the threads may be stripped or cross-threaded. This will necessitate either rethreading of the existing threads or the installation of a Heli-Coil®. Consult the "Engine Rebuilding" section in Chapter 3 for details on these procedures.

Checking and Replacing Spark Plug Wires

Every 15,000 miles, inspect the spark plug wires for burns, cuts, or breaks in the insulation. Check the boots and the nipples on the distributor cap. Replace any damaged wiring.

Every 45,000 miles or so, the resistance of the wires should be checked with an ohmmeter. Wires with excessive resistance will cause misfiring, and may make the engine difficult to start in damp weather. Generally, the useful life of the cables is 45,000-60,000 miles.

To check resistance, remove the distributor cap, leaving the wires in place. Connect one lead of an ohmmeter to an electrode within the cap; connect the other lead to the corresponding spark plug terminal (remove it from the spark plug for this test). Replace any wire which shows a resistance over 30,000Ω.

Generally speaking, resistance should not be over 25,000Ω, and 30,000Ω must be considered the outer limit of acceptability.

It should be remembered that resistance is also a function of length; the longer the wire, the greater the resistance. Thus, if the wires on your car are longer than the factory originals, resistance will be higher, quite possibly outside these limits.

When installing new wires, replace them one at a time to avoid mixups. Start by replacing the

longest one first. Install the boot firmly over the spark plug. Route the wire over the same path as the original. Insert the nipple firmly onto the tower on the distributor cap, then install the cap cover and latches to secure the wires.

FIRING ORDERS

To avoid confusion, replace spark plug wires one at a time.

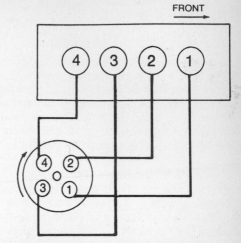

4 cylinder firing order: 1–3–4–2—2002tii

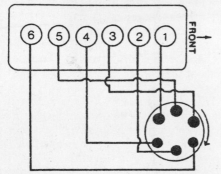

6 cylinder firing order: 1–5–3–6–2–4—2500, 2800, 3000, 3.0 and Bavaria

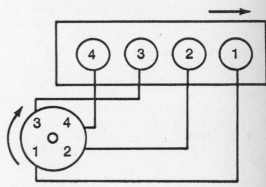

4 cylinder firing order: 1–3–4–2—1600, 2000, 2002 and 1977–79 320i

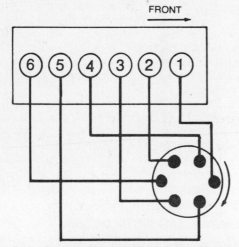

6 cylinder firing order: 1–5–3–6–2–4—528i, 530i, 630CSi and 1978–81 633CSi and 733i

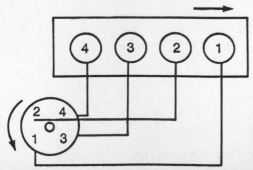

4 cylinder firing order: 1–3–4–2—1980–82 320i

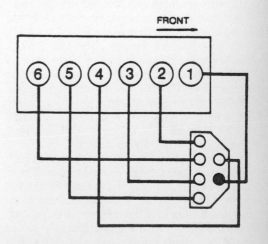

325, 325e, 325i, 528e, 533i, 535i, M5, and 1982 and later 633CSi, 635CSi, M6, and 733i, 735i
Firing order: 1–5–3–6–2–4

POINT-TYPE IGNITION

Breaker Points and Condenser

The points function as a circuit breaker for the primary circuit of the ignition system. The ignition coil must boost the 12 volts of electrical pressure supplied by the battery to as much as 25,000 volts in order to fire the plugs. To do this, the coil depends on the points and the condenser to make a clean break in the primary circuit.

The coil has both primary and secondary circuits. When the ignition is turned on, the battery supplies voltage through the coil and onto the points. The points are connected to ground, completing the primary circuit. As the current passes through the coil, a magnetic field is created in the iron center core of the coil. When the cam in the distributor turns, the points open, breaking the primary circuit.

The magnetic field in the primary circuit of the coil then collapses and cuts through the secondary circuit windings around the iron core. Because of the physical principle called "electromagnetic induction," the battery voltage is increased to a level sufficient to fire the spark plugs.

When the points open, the electrical charge in the primary circuit tries to jump the gap created between the 2 open contacts of the points. If this electrical charge were not transferred elesewhere, the metal contacts of the points would start to change rapidly.

The function of the condenser is to absorb excessive voltage from the points when they open and thus prevent the points from becoming pitted or burned.

If you have ever wondered why it is necessary to tune-up your engine occasionally, consider the fact that the ignition system must complete the above cycle each time a spark plug fires. On a 4-cylinder, 4-cycle engine, 2 of the 4 plugs must fire once for every engine revolution. If the idle speed of your engine is 800 revolutions per minute (800 rpm), the breaker points open and close 2 times each revolution. For every minute your engine idles, your points open and close 1,600 times (2 × 800 = 1,600). And that is just at idle. What about at 60 mph?

There are 2 ways to check breaker point gap: with a feel gauge or with a swell meter. Either way you set the points, you are adjusting the amount of time (in degrees of distributor rotation) that the points will remain open. If you adjust the points with a feeler gauge, you are setting the maximum amount the points will open when the rubbing block on the points is on a high point of the distributor cam. When you adjust the points with a dwell meter, you are measuring the number of degrees (of distributor cam rotation) that the points will remain closed before they start to open as a high point of the distributor cam approaches the rubbing block of the points.

If you still do not understand how the points function, take a friend, go outside, and remove the distributor cap from your engine. Have your friend operate the starter (make sure the transmission is not in gear) as you look at the exposed parts of the distributor.

There are two rules that should always be followed when adjusting or replacing points. The points and condenser are a matched set; never replace one without replacing the other. If you change the point gap or swell of the engine, you also change the ignition timing. Therefore, if you adjust the points, you must also adjust the timing.

NOTE: *Certain 1978-79 and virtually all 1980 and later BMWs are equipped with electronic, breakerless ignition systems. See the following section for maintenance procedures.*

1. Disconnect the high tension wire from the top of the distributor and the coil.

2. Remove the distributor cap by prying off the spring clips on the sides of the cap.

3. Remove the rotor from the distributor shaft by pulling it straight up. Examine the condition of the rotor. If it is cracked or the metal tip is excessively worn or burned, it should be replaced. Clean the top with fine emery paper.

4. Pry open the contacts of the points with a screwdriver and check the condition of the contacts. If they are excessively worn, burned or pitted, they should be replaced.

5. If the points are in good condition, adjust them and replace the rotor and the distributor cap. If the points need to be replaced, follow the replacement procedure given below.

REMOVAL AND INSTALLATION

On 1970-74 cars, BMW recommends that the breaker points be inspected and adjusted every

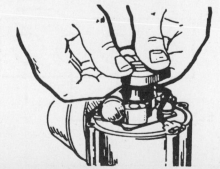

Pull the rotor straight up to remove it

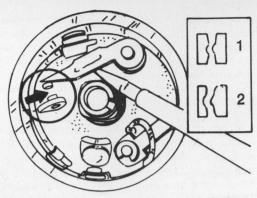

Examining condition of breaker points. Mild pitting (1) is acceptable. Excessive transfer (2) is unacceptable.

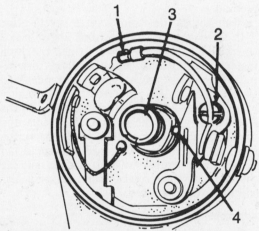

Breaker point attachment and lubrication points: (1) primary connection, (2) hold-down screw, (3) advance mechanism lubrication wick, (4) breaker arm rubbing block

Install the point set on the breaker plate and then attach the wires

6 months or 8,000 miles. If, upon inspection, the points prove to be faulty, they must be replaced with the condenser as a unit. On later models, replace the points every 12,500 miles, if the car is so equipped.

CAUTION: *Make sure that the ignition is off!*

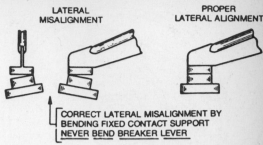

CORRECT LATERAL MISALIGNMENT BY BENDING FIXED CONTACT SUPPORT NEVER BEND BREAKER LEVER

Check the points for proper alignment after installation

The usual procedure is to replace the condenser each time the point set is replaced. Although this is not always necessary, it is easy to do at this time and the cost is negligible. Every time you adjust or replace the breaker points, the ignition timing must be checked and, if necessary, adjusted. No special equipment other than a feeler gauge is required for point replacement or adjustment, but a dwell meter is strongly advised. A magnetic screwdriver is handy to prevent the small points and condenser screws from falling down into the distributor.

1. Remove the coil high tension wire from the top of the distributor cap. Remove the distributor cap and place it our of the way. Remove the rotor from the distributor shaft by pulling up.

2. Disconnect the electrical lead to the condenser, loosen the condenser bracket retaining screw and slide out the condenser.

3. Disconnect the point set electrical lead.

4. Remove the points assembly attaching screws and then remove the points. A magnetic screwdriver or one with a holding mechanism will come in handy here, so that you don't drop a screw into the distributor and have to remove the entire distributor to retrieve it.

After points are removed, wipe off the cam and apply new cam lubricant. If you don't the points will wear out in a few thousand miles.

5. Slip the new set of points onto the locating dowel and install the screws that hold the assembly onto the plate. Don't tighten them all the way yet, since you'll only have to loosen them to set the point gap.

6. Install the new condenser and attache the condenser lead to the points.

7. Set the point gap and dwell (see the following sections).

ADJUSTMENT

1. If the contact points of the assembly are not parallel, bend the stationary contact so that they make contact across the entire surface of the contacts. Bend only the stationary bracket

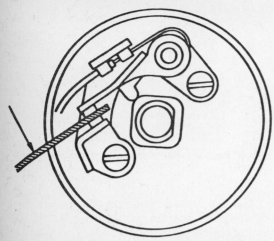

The arrow indicates the feeler gauge used to check the point gap

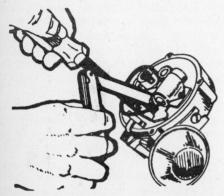

Use a screwdriver to lever the points closer together or farther apart

part of the point assembly; not the movable contact.

2. Turn the engine until the rubbing block of the points is on one of the high points of the distributor cam. You can do this by either turning the ignition switch to the start position and releasing it quickly ("bumping" the engine) or by using a wrench on the bolt which holds the crankshaft pulley to the crankshaft.

3. Place the correct size feeler gauge between the contacts (see the "Tune-Up" chart). Make sure that it is parallel with the contact surfaces.

4. With your free hand, insert a screwdriver into the eccentric adjusting slot, then twist the screwdriver to either increase and decrease the gap to the proper setting.

5. Tighten the adjustment lockscrew and recheck the contact gap to make sure that it didn't change when the lockscrew was tightened.

6. Replace the rotor and distributor cap, and the high tension wire which connects the top of the distributor and the coil. Make sure that the rotor is firmly seated all the way onto the distributor shaft and that the of the rotor is aligned with the notch in the shaft. Align the tab in the base of the distributor cap with the notch in the distributor body. Make sure that the end of the high tension wire is firmly placed in the top of the distributor and the coil.

DWELL ANGLE

The dwell angle or cam angle is the number of degrees that the distributor cam rotates while the points are closed. There is an inverse relationship between dwell angle and point gap. Increasing the point gap will decrease the swell angle and vice versa. Checking the swell angle with a meter is a far more accurate method of measuring point opening than the feeler gauge method.

After setting the point gap to specification with a feeler gauge as described above, check the swell angle with a meter. Attach the dwell meter according to the manufacturer's instruction sheet. The negative lead is grounded and the positive lead is connected to the primary wire terminal which runs from the coil to the distributor. Start the engine, let it idle and reach operating temperature, and observe the dwell on the meter. The reading should fall within the allowable range. If it does not, the gap will have to be reset or the breaker points will have to be replaced.

Adjustment

Dwell can be checked with the engine running or cranking. Decrease dwell by increasing the point gap; increase by decreasing the gap. Dwell angle is simply the number of degrees of

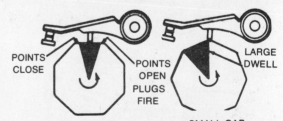

POINTS CLOSE — POINTS OPEN PLUGS FIRE — LARGE DWELL

NORMAL DWELL-NORMAL GAP   SMALL GAP EXCESSIVE DWELL

SMALL DWELL

WIDE GAP INSUFFICIENT DWELL

Dwell angle

distributor shaft rotation during which the points stay closed. Theoretically, if the point gap is correct, the dwell should also be correct or nearly so. Adjustment with a dwell meter produces more exact, consistent results since it is a dynamic adjustment. If dwell varies more than 3° from idle speed to 1,750 engine rpm, the distributor is worn and will probably require adjustment.

1. Adjust the points with a feeler gauge as previously described.

2. Connect the dwell meter to the ignition circuit as per the manufacturer's instructions. One lead of the meter is connected to a ground and the other lead is connected to the distributor post on the coil. An adapter is usually provided for this purpose.

3. If the dwell meter has a set line on it. adjust the meter to zero the indicator.

4. Start the engine.

NOTE: *Be careful when working on any vehicle while the engine is running. Make sure that the transmission is in Neutral and that the parking brake is applied. Keep hands, clothing, tools and the wires of the test instruments clear of the rotating fan blades.*

5. Observe the reading on the dwell meter. If the reading is within the specified range, turn off the engine and remove the dwell meter.

NOTE: *If the meter does not have a scale for 4-cylinder engines, multiply the 8-cylinder reading by 2.*

6. If the reading is above the specified range, the breaker point gap is too small. If the reading is below the specified range, the gap is too large. In either case, the engine must be stopped and the gap adjusted in the manner previously covered.

After making the adjustment, start the engine and check the reading on the dwell meter. When the correct reading is obtained, disconnect the dwell meter.

7. Check the adjustment of the ignition timing.

ELECTRONIC IGNITION

CAUTION: *The engine should be turned off or the battery cable disconnected when ignition system components are replaced or engine test equipment is connected to the ignition system, because of a dangerous current that can be present in the primary and secondary circuits. Personal injury could occur.*

All 528i, 633CSi, 733i and 1980 and later 320i models are equipped with a Bosch transistorized ignition system. The 528e and all 1982 and later models are all equipped with a Digital Motor Electronics (DME) engine control sys-

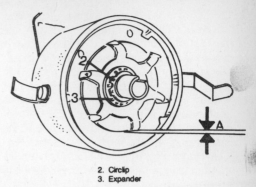

2. Circlip
3. Expander

Measuring the air gap (A) on the electronic ignition system

tem. DME is basically an onboard computer – a microprocessor that controls many more engine related functions than would a conventional system.

Although no adjustment is possible, the air gap on the 1980-1984 models with the electronic distributors can and should be checked periodically.

NOTE: *On all 1984-88 models there is no adjustment possible.*

This is the gap between the rotor wheel (NOT the one directly underneath the distributor cap) and the stator. It should be measured when a tooth of each is lined up and should be in the range of 0.30-0.70mm. If found not to be within specifications, the distributor or certain components thereof will require replacement.

Tune-up maintenance to either system is usually limited to checking the condition of the ignition wires, distributor cap and rotor. Except for ignition timing (where applicable) normal adjustments and maintenance to either of these systems is unnecessary.

Ignition Timing

Ignition timing is the measurement, in degrees of crankshaft rotation, of the point at which the spark plugs fire in each of the cylinders. It is measure in degrees before or after Top Dead Center (TDC) of the compression stroke.

Because it takes a fraction of a second for the spark plug to ignite the mixture in the cylinder, the spark plug must fire a little before the piston reaches TDC. Otherwise, the mixture will not be completely ignited as the piston passes TDC and the full power of the explosion will not be used by the engine.

The timing measurement is given in degrees of crankshaft rotation before the piston reaches

TDC (BTDC). If the setting for the ignition timing is 5° BTDC, the spark plus must fire 5° before each piston reaches TDC. This only holds true, however, when the engine is at idle speed.

As the engine speed increases, the pistons go faster. The spark plugs have to ignite the fuel even sooner if it is to be complete ignited when the piston reaches TDC. To do this, the distributor has 2 means to advance the timing of the spark as the engine sped increases: a set of centrifugal weights within the distributor, and a vacuum diaphragm, mounted on the side of the distributor.

If the ignition is set too far advanced (BTDC), the ignition and expansion of the fuel in the cylinder will occur too soon and tend to force the piston down while it is still traveling up. This causes engine ping. If the ignition spark is set too far retarded, after TDC (ATDC), the piston will have already passed TDC and started on its way down when the fuel is ignited. This will cause the piston to be forced down for only a portion of its travel. This will result in poor engine performance and lack of power.

If the distributor has been removed for any reason, and the timing has been disturbed, the engine may be timed statically to obtain an initial setting. This will ensure that the dynamic timing adjustment will be an easier operation. Simply crank the engine until the No. 1 cylinder is at the top dead center (TDC) position and that piston is on its compression stroke. At this point both intake and exhaust valves for that cylinder will be closed (clearance at rocker arm), the engraved notch in the distributor rotor will align with the notch in the distributor housing (cap removed), the No. 1 piston will be at the top of it stroke, the notch in the camshaft flange will align with the notch in the cylinder head (valve cover removed), and the **OT** or first notch in the crankshaft pulley will align with the raised ridge in the center of the timing case cover. If necessary, loose the distributor clamp bolt and rotate the distributor housing so that the 2 marks coincide. This will at least guarantee that the engine will start so that a dynamic timing adjustment may be performed.

Another method of static timing is the 12 volt test light method. Connect a test light between the distributor primary connection and ground. With the point gap correctly set and the timing marks aligned, rotate the distributor housing counterclockwise slightly until the breaker points just start to open. With the ignition switch turned on, the test light will light the moment the points open. Tighten the distributor holddown clamp slightly in this position and proceed to the dynamic timing adjustment.

Timing marks consist of a notch on the rim of the timing hole in the flywheel housing and a steel ball pressed into the flywheel itself. The

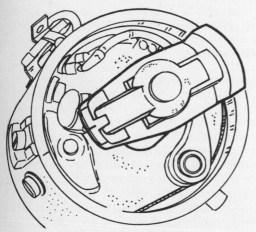

Notch on rotor aligning with notch on distributor housing with No. 1 cylinder at top dead center (TDC)

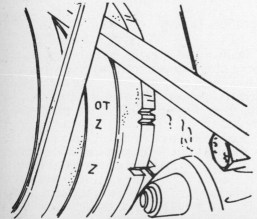

"OT" mark on first notch aligning with raised ridge on timing cover with No. 1 at top dead center (TDC)

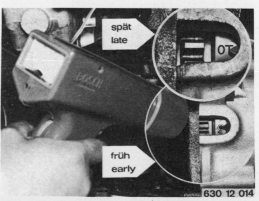

630 12 014

Aiming the timing light at the window in the flywheel housing

notch corresponds to the position of the piston in the number 1 cylinder. A stroboscopic (dynamic) timing light is used, which is hooked into the circuit of the No. 1 cylinder spark plug. Every time the spark plug fires, the timing light flashes. By aiming the timing light at the timing marks, the exact position of the piston within the cylinder can be read, since the stroboscopic flash makes the mark on the pulley appear to be standing still. Proper timing is indicated when the notch is aligned with the steel ball on the flywheel.

There are 3 basic types of timing light available. The first is a simple neon bulb with 2 wire connections (one for the spark plug and one for the plug wire, connecting the light in series). This type of light is quite dim, and must be held closely to the marks to be seen, but it is inexpensive. The second type of light operates from the car battery. Two alligator clips connect to the battery terminals, while a third wire connects to the spark plug with an adapter. This type of light is more expensive, but the xenon bulb provides a nice bright flash which can even be seen in sunlight. The third type replaces the battery source with 110 volt house current. Some timing lights have other functions built into them, such as dwell meters, tachometers, or remote starting switches. These are convenient, in that they reduce the tangle of wires under the hood, but may duplicate the functions of tools you already have.

If your BMW has electronic ignition, you should use a timing light with an inductive pickup. This pickup simply clamps onto the No. 1 plug wire, eliminating the adapter. It is not susceptible to crossfiring or false triggering, which may occur with a conventional light, due to the greater voltages produced by electronic ignition.

NOTE: *Ignition timing on late model vehicles, is constantly being adjusted by the Motronics (DME) engine control system. No manual timing adjustment is necessary or possible.*

In order to set the ignition timing dynamically, the engine must be at operating temperature and running at a specified rpm (see the "Tune-Up Specifications" chart). A stroboscopic timing light and tachometer are needed for this operation. First, disconnect and plug the vacuum line(s) at the distributor. After attaching a timing light and tachometer according to the manufacturer's instructions, raise the idle speed to that listed in the "Tune-Up Specifications" chart under "Ignition Timing". Most timing lights are battery powered. The read and black leads are connected to the positive and negative battery terminals, respectively. Then, the trigger lead is either connected in series between No. 1 spark plug and No. 1 plug wire, or if an indication type trigger is used (this is usually a black, plastic claw) it is simply clamped around No. 1 plug wire without disconnecting it from the plug.

With the idle speed adjusted to the proper rpm (see "Idle Speed and Mixture Adjustment" later in this chapter) for purposes of ignition timing, direct the stroboscopic timing light beam straight down through the opening in the flywheel housing flange adjacent to the starter, and align the steel ball pressed into the flywheel with the timing mark on the flywheel housing. Loosen the distributor holddown bolt and rotated the distributor as necessary. After the adjustment has been made tighten the holddown bolt and recheck the timing at the specified rpm to make sure that the setting was not disturbed during tightening. After the ignition timing is properly set.

Computer Controlled Ignition Timing Chart

Car/Model	Unit Number	RPM	Timing BTDC
325e	0261200021	650–750	4-12
325e	0261100007	650–750	6-12
528e	0261200007	650–750	4-12
528e	0261200021	650–750	6-12
	0261200027		
533i	0261200008	650–750	6-14
535i	0261200059	750–850	10–16
M5	0261200079	800–900	−3-3 ①
633CSi	0261200008	650–750	10-16
635CSi	0261200059	750–850	10-16
M6	0261200079	800–900	−3-3 ①
733i	0261200008	600–700	6-14
735i	0261200059	700–800	10-6

① That is −3° after top dead center to 3° before top dead center

IGNITION TIMING CHECK

Vehicles with Electronic Ignition

Although the timing on vehicles equipped with the Motoronic control unit can not be adjusted, the timing can still be checked.

On cars with the Motronic control unit, the timing can be adjusted in a fairly straight forward manner. However, the only cure for improper timing is to replace the control unit. Also, timing must be within a certain range, as the computer changes the timing slightly to allow for various changes in operating condition. In other words, the timing does not have to be right on the mark, but anywhere in the specified range.

The engine should bve at normal operating temperature and the operation should be perfromed at normal room temperatures. The engine rpm should be within the specified range under the control of the computer.

Look up the control unit number on the unit itself. On 3, 5 and 6 series vehicles, the unit is in the glove box; on the 7 series, it is in the right side speaker cutout.

Find the control unit number on the underside of the unit and then reference that number to the on the Computer Controlled Ignition Timing Chart. Then connect a tachometer and a timing light to the engine (connect the timing to the No. 1 cylinder). Start the engine and check the rpm. If it is not correct see the appropriate checks under Idle Speed and Mixture Adjustment. Operate the timing light to see if the timing is within the range specified on the chart. If it is significantly outside of the range the control unit must be replaced.

VALVE LASH

ADJUSTMENT

All Gasoline Engines Except
1987-88 M3, M5, M6

All BMW gasoline engines except for the 1987-88 M series, dual overhead camshaft designs are equipped with an overhead camshaft operating the intake and exhaust valves through rocker arm linkage.

Valve lash on these engines should be adjusted at 8,000 mile or 12,500 mile intervals, depending on the year of the car. See the Owner's Manual. It is important to adjust the lash to make up for wear in the valve train, which will cause noisy valve operation and reduced power, or, in some cases, excessive tightness in the valve train, which can cause the valves to burn and may even reduce compression. The BMW features a unique adjuster design that makes it

easy to hold the required dimension while tightening the locknut; thus, valve adjustment is unusually easy.

1. Make sure the engine is as cold as possible. It need not actually sit overnight, but must be cool to the touch (under 95°F [35°C]). Several hours should be allowed for cooling if the engine started out at operating temperature.

2. Remove the valve cover. This will require, in some cases, removal of the air cleaner or main air intake hose, and disconnecting the PCV line or other vacuum lines. Note that the valve cover is secured to the cylinder head by cap nuts, while bolts attach it to the timing cover on the front of the engine. make sure you remove all the fasteners. Then, lift the cover straight off.

3. The engine must be rotated to a position

Removing the cam cover-to-timing cover bolts

4 Cylinder Engines

To Adjust Cylinder:	Put This Cylinder at Overlap Position
1	4
3	2
4	1
2	3

6 Cylinder Engines

To Adjust Cylinder:	Put This Cylinder at Overlap Position
1	6
5	2
3	4
6	1
2	5
4	3

that will ensure that there will be no closing effect from the camshaft when the valves are adjusted. This requests a different position for the adjustment of each cylinder. The charts below list the cylinder to be adjusted in the first (left hand) column, and the cylinder whose valves must be watched while postioning the engine in the right hand column. Cylinders are numbered from front to rear, 1 through 4 or 1 through 6. The engine may be rotated by rolling the car in third gear (if it is equipped with a manual transmission) or by installing a socket wrench on the bolt which attaches the front pulley and rotating the ring with the wrench. The valve of the cylinder to be adjusted (left hand column) will be in the fully closed position, so that you can wiggle the rockers up and down slightly die to clearance in the valve train, when the engine is in the proper position. The valve in the cylinder to be watched while rotating the engine

Tightening the cam cover capnuts. Don't forget the bolts, located at the front of the cover and going into the engine timing cover

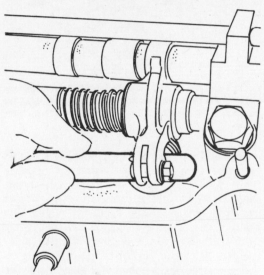

Checking valve clearance with a *flat* feeler gauge

Adjusting valves with bent rod. Secure the adjustment with the locknut (1)

(right hand column) must be in the overlap position. At this position, both valves will be slightly open. For example, to position the engine for adjustment of the valves on No. 1 cylinder, watch cylinder No. 4 on 4-cylinder engines, and cylinder No. 6 on 6-cylinder engines. As you rotate the engine in the direction of normal rotation, you'll note a point at which the valve on the right side of the engine (the exhaust valve) begins closing (moving upward). If you crank very slowly, you'll note that, just before the exhaust valve has closed, the intake begins opening. You want to stop rotating the engine when the valves are both open about the same amount. Now, you are ready to adjust cylinder NO. 1, as described in the next 2 steps.

4. Check the clearances on one of the valves with a feeler gauge that falls within the limits given in the "Tune-Up Specifications" chart. For example, if the dimension is 0.25-0.30mm, use a 0.28mm gauge. The gauge should pass through between the valve and the outer end of the rocker with a slight resistance (don't check between the camshaft and rocker, at the center of the engine). If there is any doubt about the clearance, check with the gauges equivalent to the minimum and maximum specifications. If the specification is, for example, 0.25-0.30mm, and the 0.25mm gauge passes through, but the 0.30mm gauge will not, the valve meets specification and will not need adjustment. If the clearance is not right, insert the bent wire tool supplied with the car (these may also be purchased at an automotive supply store or you can make one yourself with a piece of coat hanger) into the small hole in the adjusting cam, which is located in the outer end of the rocker arm. Then, use a 10 mm wrench to loosen the adjust-

ing locknut, also located on the end of the rocker. Rotate the adjusting can with the wire as you slide the gauge between the can and valve. When the gauge will go in between the valve and adjusting cam and can be slid back and forth with just a slight resistance, hold the position of the cam with the adjusting wire and then tighten the locknut.

5. Recheck the clearance to make sure it has not changed—if the minimum and maximum dimension gauges behave as described in the step above, the adjustment is correct.

6. Repeat the adjustment for the other valve on cylinder No. 1, located directly across from the one you've already adjusted.

7. Then, rotate the engine to the next cylinder listed in the left hand column of the appropriate chart above, watching the valve of the cylinder listed in the right hand column. When the engine is positioned for this cylinder, adjust the valves for it as described in Steps 4, 5 and 6. Then, proceed with the next cylinder in the left hand column in the same way, until all 4- or 6-cylinders have had their valves adjusted.

8. Replace the valve cover using a new gasket. Tighten the cover cap nuts or bolts a very little at a time and alternately in order to bring the cam cover down onto the gasket evenly in all areas. Be careful not to overtighten the cover cap nuts/bolts.

9. Reconnect all disconnected hoses and, if necessary, replace the air cleaner.

M3, M5 and M6

NOTE: *To perform this procedure, a special tool is needed to depress the valves against spring pressure to gain access to the valve adjusting discs. Use BMW Tool 11 3 170 or equivalent. Also needed are: compressed air to lift valve adjusting discs that must be replaced out of the valve tappet; an assortment of adjusting discs of various thicknesses and a precise outside michrometer.*

1. Make sure the engine is overnight cold. Remove the rocker cover.

2. Turn the engine until the No. 1 cylinder intake valve cams are both straight up. The intake cam is labeled **A** on the head.

3. Then, slide a flat feeler gauge in between each of the cams and the adjacent valve tappet. Check to see if the clearance is within the specified range. If it is, proceed with checking the remaining clearances as described starting in Step 8. If not, switch gauges and measure the actual clearance. When actual clearance is achieved, proceed with Steps 4-7.

4. Turn the tappets so the grooves machined into their edges are aligned as shown. Looking at the valves from the center of the engine, the right hand tappet's groove should be at about 5

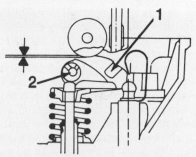

A back-up wrench should be used at (1) when adjusting valves. The locknut that holds the adjusting eccentric is at (2). "V" shows the valve clearance

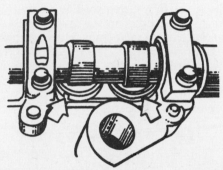

On M5 and M6 DOHC engines, rotate the valve tappets so the grooves machined in the tops are facing as shown before attempting to measure valve clearance

o'clock and the left hand tappet's groove should be at about 7 o'clock. Use the end of the special tool required for the camshaft involved—in this case the **A** or intake camshaft (the exhaust camshaft end is labeled **E** on the engine and tool). Slide the proper end of the tool, going from the center of the engine outward, under the cam, with the heel of the tool pivoting on the inner side of the camshaft valley. Force the handle downward until the handle rests on the protrusion on the center of the cylinder head.

5. Use compressed air to pop the disc out of the tappet. Read the thickness dimension on the disc.

6. Determine the thickness required as follows:

a. If the valve clearance is too tight, try the next thinner disc.

b. If the valve clearance is too loose, try the next thicker disc.

7. Slip the thinner or thicker disc into the tappet *with the letter facing downward*. Rock the valve spring depressing tool out and remove it. Then, recheck the clearance. Change the disc again, if necessary, until the clearance falls within the specified range.

8. Turn the engine in firing order sequence (1-5-3-6-2-4 for the 6-cylinder engines or, for

the M3 1-3-4-2), turning the crankshaft forward ⅓ of a turn each time to get the intake cams to the upward position for each cylinder. Measure the clearance as in Step 3 and, if it is outside the specified range, follow Steps 4-7 to adjust either or both valves. Repeat this for all the intakes, and then turn the engine until No. 1 cylinder exhaust valves are upward.

9. Follow the same sequence for all the exhaust valves, going through the firing order, checking clearance as described in Step 3 and adjusting the valves as in Steps 4-7. Note that it is necessary, however, to use the opposite end of the special tool—the end marked **E** to depress the exhaust valves.

10. When all the clearances are in the specified range, replace the cam cover, start the engine, and check for leaks.

Diesel Engine

1. Remove the rocker cover.

2. Rotate the engine (using a socket on the crankshaft pulley nut) until the No. 1 cylinder is at TDC on the firing stroke. Line up the timing marks and also ensure that both No. 1 cylinder valves are loose; if they are not, turn the engine 360°.

3. Use the 12mm backup wrench on the nut shown in the illustration. Then, loosen the locknut. Slide a flat feeler gauge of the proper size (0.30mm) into the gap shown in the illustration. If it is necessary to change the clearance, rotate the eccentric, making sure the clearance is always taken up by turning the eccentric toward the operator or away from the centerline of the engine. Tighten the nut, and recheck the clearance, readjusting it if necessary. Repeat this step for the other valve on No. 1 cylinder.

4. Repeat the step above for each cylinder. Turn the engine ⅓ turn forward and adjust each cylinder in the firing order of 1-5-3-6-2-4.

5. Replace the valve rocker cover.

Idle Speed and Mixture Adjustment

With the advent of emission control legislation on the Federal level as well as emission equipment state inspection legislation, it has become increasingly important that carburetor adjustment do not violate the letter of the law. The only way to make sure that the idle mixture setting remains at a legal level is to have it checked with an exhaust analyzer of known accuracy. This is an extremely expensive electronic device which your BMW dealer or a reputable independent garage is required to have on hand to make these adjustments. Therefore, it is recommended that the mixture adjustment be referred to them.

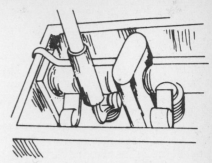

Tighten the adjusting nut with special tools 11 1 1809 and 00 2 050 or equivalent (524td)

NOTE: *The idle speed and mixture can be adjusted ONLY with the aid of a CO meter. If this tool is not available, do not attempt any of the following procedures. The idle mixture can be adjusted ONLY with the aid of a CO meter on most models; on the 318i, it can be adjusted ONLY with a BMW digital mixture adjustment unit 12 6 400. Idle speed is not adjustable on any model with the Motronic control unit except the M5 and M6. If idle speed is incorrect, either the idle valve or the idle control unit must be replaced.*

SOLEX 38 PDSI, 40PDSI, and 40 PDSIT

1. Run the engine until it reaches operating temperature. Disconnect the air pump outlet hose (leading from the air pump to the exhaust manifold) at the air pump.

2. Adjust the idle speed to 1000 rpm with the idle speed screw.

3. Wit a CO meter attached to the exhaust pipe of the car, turn the idle mixture adjustment screw to obtain a reading of 0.7% CO ± 1% CO. This should compute to a 75.5% combustion efficiency reading.

4. Reset idle to 1000 rpm, as necessary, and reconnect the air pump outlet hose.

SOLEX 32/32 DIDTA

1. Run the engine until it reaches operating temperature.

2. Adjust the idle speed by turning the idle air by-pass control screw until the reading is 850-950 rpm.

3. With a CO meter attached to the exhaust pipe of the car, turn idle mixture control screw to obtain a reading of 0.8-1.2% Co.

4. Return the idle speed to that rpm listed on the engine compartment sticker.

ZENITH 35/40 INAT TWIN CARBURETORS

NOTE: *Making this adjustment requires a carburetor synchronizing meter with caps which replace the effect of the air cleaner on*

each carburetor, and a CO meter with taps designed to connect with the BMW exhaust manifolds.

1. Run the engine until it reaches operating temperature. Remove the plugs from the exhaust manifolds and insert the test probes.

2. Remove the air cleaner (note that engine rpm will drop about 100 rpm).

3. Disconnect the throttle linkage rod at the ball stud (2) near the rear carburetor.

4. Install the 2 caps over the carburetor tops, and connect them to the synchronizer. Now, adjust the 2 idle screws (3 and 4) (the larger screws near the base of each carburetor) to get an idle rpm of 900-1000 and a reading of 0 on the synchronizing meter. If the meter shows

Solex 32/32 DIDTA carburetor details: dashpot (1), and vacuum hose (2)

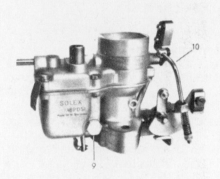

1. Cold start butterfly
2. Float chamber breather
3. Fuel inlet
4. Idling adjustment screw
5. Vacuum regulator connection

6. Idling jet
7. Idling mixture control screw
8. Accelerator pump
9. Main jet closure plug
10. Cold start connecting link

Solex 38 PDSI, 40 PDSI adjustment locations

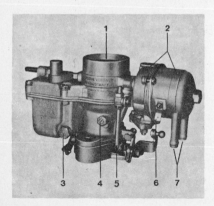

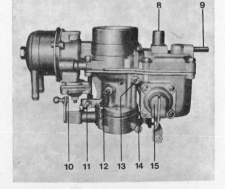

1. Cold start butterfly
2. Automatic choke
3. Main jet cover screw
4. Venturi retaining screw
5. Choke connecting linkage
6. Terminal for electric heating of automatic choke

7. Collant unions for heating of automatic choke
8. Float chamber breather
9. Fuel feed
10. Vacuum diaphragm housing
11. Idling speed adjusting screw

12. Vacuum regulator connection
13. Idling jet
14. Idling mixture adjusting screw
15. Accelerator pump

Solex 40 PDSIT adjustment locations

greater vacuum on one side than the other, adjust the screws in opposite directions in equal amounts, adjusting the screw of the carburetor with the higher vacuum in the clockwise direction.

5. Adjust the idle mixture screws 5 and 6 (the smaller screws near the idle screws) in or out to bring the CO content in the exhaust under each carburetor to 1.95-2.05%.

6. If this changes the idle speed, reset the idle screws as described above. Then, read the

CO meter and, if necessary, readjust the mixture screws as necessary. Continue in this manner until both idle speed (including balance) and mixture are within specification.

7. Finally, stop the engine, reinstall the air cleaner, disconnect exhaust probes and reinstall the plugs, and reconnect the throttle linkage. When reconnecting the throttle linkage, adjust the length of the connecting rod with the knurled nut so that the rod can be connected without changing idle speed.

1. Cold start butterfly
2. Breather tube
3. Fuel inlet
4. Fuel return valve
5. Vacuum bore for distributor and return valve
6. Accelerator pump
7. Electromagnetic idling shutoff valve
8. Idle air by-pass control screw
9. Idling mixture control screw
10. Throttle valve adjusting screw (do not adjust)
11. Connection for electric choke heater
12. Automatic choke
13. Connection for coolant heating of the automatic choke
14. Vacuum diaphragm housing
15. Electromagnetic starter valve

Solex 32/32 DIDTA adjustment locations

Adjusting idle speed and mixture on twin carburetor models. Stop screws (7) are *not* to be disturbed (see text for identification of remaining adjustment screws and linkage parts).

KUGELFISCHER MECHANICAL FUEL INJECTION
2002tii

1. Run the engine until it reaches operating temperature. Remove the cap from the top of the throttle butterfly port.

2. Adjust the idle speed by turning the idling speed screw to obtain an 850-950 rpm reading.

3. With a CO meter attached to the exhaust pipe of the car, turn the throttle stop (throttle butterfly air adjustment screw) to obtain a reading of 2.0-3.0% CO. Turning the screw in clockwise will lean the mixture and turning counterclockwise will richen the mixture.

4. Grabbing hold of the throttle linkage, take the engine through its rpm range a few times and see if to returns to idle properly. If necessary, readjust each screw (Steps 2 and 3) until the CO reading and idle speed remain constant.

5. Return the idle speed to the rpm listed on the engine compartment sticker.

Adjusting CO level with special tool. Hole plug shown—320i

320i

1. Run the engine until it reaches normal operating temperature.

2. Adjust the engine idle speed with the screw located near the throttle valve linkage.

3. Detach the exhaust check valve and plug the hose.

4. To adjust the CO, remove the plug from the fuel distributor and with a special wrench, adjust the CO level to a maximum of 2.0% for the 49 state vehicles or 3.5% for the California cars.

5. Reconnect the exhaust check valve hose and check the idle speed.

530i

1. Run the engine until it reaches normal operating temperature.

2. Disconnect the hose from the collector to the charcoal filter. Do not plug the line.

NOTE: *The hose is located between the first and second air induction tubes.*

Kugelfischer fuel injection adjustment locations: (1) idling speed screw, (2) air adjustment screw

Location of the idle speed screw (320i)

Removal of hoses before adjustment of CO level—530i

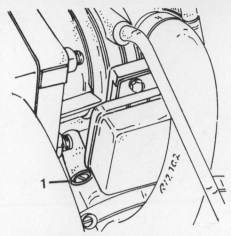

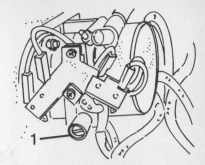

Idle speed adjustment screw—530i

Idle speed adjustment screw—528i

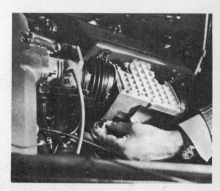

Location of CO adjusting screw—528i

CO level adjusting screw location—530i

3. Disconnect the air pump hose at the air pump and plug the line.

4. Adjust the idle speed by turning the screw on the side of the throttle housing.

5. The CO level should be between 1.5-3.0% at idle speed.

6. If necesary, adjust the CO to specifications with the idle air screw located ont eh air volume control, bu turning the screw to the left or right.

7. Reconnect the hoses.

528i

1. Adjust the idle speed to the proper specifications. The idle screw is on the side of the throttle body housing. Turning it clockwise will decrease the idle and counterclockwise will increase it.

2. Remove the CO test plug at the rear of the exhaust manifold and connect a CO meter. Start the engine and run it until operating tem-

Remove plus (3) and use special tool 13-1-060 or equivalent to adjust the CO level with the screw in the bottom of the air intake sensor—530i, 630CSi, 633CSi, and 733i

perature is reached. Measure the CO reading. CO must be 0.2-0.8% (by volume).

3. Disconnect the connector for the oxygen sensor from the wiring harness. The connector is on the right side of the firewall in the engine compartment. The CO valve should not change.

4. If CO is not to specification, adjust the mixture by turning the adjusting screw, located low on the airflow meter. Adjust for 0.5% CO.

5. Reconnect the oxygen sensor and check CO again. If CO does not meet specification, have the car checked by someone professionally trained to troubleshoot the injection system.

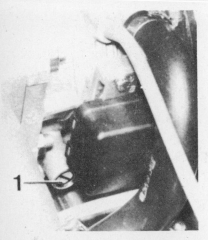

Idle speed screw location—630i, 633i and 733i

630 13 065

Disconnect the carbon filter hose (top arrow) and the air hose (bottom arrow)—630CSi, 633CSi and 733i

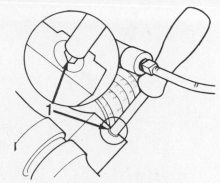

Drilling the anti-tamper plug on the 318i

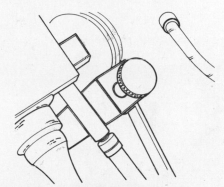

Special tool adjusting the CO on 318i

6. Disconnect the test probe and reinstall the test plug into the exhaust manifold.

7. Recheck the idle speed.

318i

NOTE:Several special tools are required to drill out the anti-tamper plug for the adjustment screw and to turn the adjustment screw. Get a new anti-tamper plug before beginning work.

1. The engine must be run until is is at operating temperature. Ignition timing and valve clearances must be correct. Connect the BMW digital mixture measurement unit 12 6 400 or equivalent according to the instrument instructions. Disconnect the hose going to the active carbon filter on the throttle housing and do not plug the open connections.

2. Operate the engine at least 3000 rpm for at least 30 seconds to ensure that the oxygen sensor is at operating temperature.

3. Disconnect the oxygen sensor wire, and fasten it where it cannot touch a ground. The nominal value to be looked for will now appear in the test unit's display. Make note of it and then reconnect the oxygen sensor into the test unit. The actual value will appear in the display. If the actual value is within plug or minus 0.3 volt of the nominal value, CO is within tolerance. If not, proceed as follows.

4. Drill a hole through the tamper plug with a special tool 13 1 092 or equivalent. Then screw special tool 13 1 094 or equivalent into the plug, and use the slide hammer on the tool to draw the plug out.

5. Use a special tool 13 1 060 to turn the adjusting screw to bring the actual valve to within 0.3 volt of the nominal value plug or minus. Turn off the engine, disconnect the test unit and reconnect the oxygen sensor wire to the oxygen sensor. Replace the anti-tamper plug with a new one.

325, 325e, 325i and 325iS

1. Disconnect the hose, leading from the throttle housing, that goes to the carbon canister. Do not plug the openings. Remove the bolts on either side of the exhaust manifold plug.

2. Remove the plug in the exhaust manifold, install the test nipple BMW part No. 13 0 100 or equivalent and connect the CO tester 13 0 070 or equivalent into the open nipple.

3. With the engine valve clearances correctly adjusted, ignition timing correct and the engine at operating temperature, measure the CO percentage at idle speed. CO nominal value is 0.2-1.2%.

4. If the CO level is within the specified range, disconnect the test unit, replace the plug in the exhaust manifold, and conclude the test. If not, adjust the CO as described below.

5. Turn off the engine and then unplug the oxygen sensor plug. Drill a hole in the anti-tamper plug in the throttle body with special tool No. 13 1 092 or equivalent. Then screw the special extractor tool No. 13 1 094 or equivalent into the hole drilled into the plug and draw the plug out with the impact mass. Finally, use an adjustment tool 13 1 060 or 13 1 100 or equivalent to turn the adjustment, with the engine running, until the CO meets nominal values.

6. When the adjustment is complete, install a new anti-tamper plug, and reconnect the oxygen sensor plug and the carbon canister hose. Also, remove the nipple in the exhaust manifold and replace the plug. Reinstall the exhaust manifold bolts.

528e

1. Pull the canister purge hose off the solenoid shown in the illustration, leaving the connections unplugged.

2. Connect the CO meter 13 0 070 or equivalent to the manifold via the nipple 13 0 100.

3. Follow Steps 3-6 of the procedure for the 325 above. All are identical including the CO nominal value. Remember to reconnect the canister purge hose to the solenoid.

633CSi AND 733i

1982

1. Run the engine to normal operating temperature.

2. Disconnect the throttle housing-to-activated carbon filter hose. Disconnect and plug the air hose at the air pump.

3. Adjust the idle speed to specifications with the idle adjusting screw, located in the side of the throttle housing.

4. Adjust the CO to 1.5-3.0% at idle. Remove the cap from the air flow sensor and with the aid of a special tool, or short screwdriver, turn the bypass air screw located in the air flow sensor, until the CO level is as specified.

5. Reconnect the 2 hoses.

533i, 535i, 633CSi, 635CSi, 733i AND 735i

1983-89

1. Make sure the idle speed is correct. The engine must be hot. Disconnect the evaporative

emissions canister purge hose at the bottom of the solenoid mounted on the firewall. Leave the openings unplugged.

2. Unscrew the bolts on the exhaust manifold and install a nipple (part No. 13 0 100 or equivalent) and connect the CO test unit 13 0 070 or equivalent. CO should be 0.2-1.2%. If CO is not within limits, adjust it as described below.

3. Turn off the engine and unplug the oxygen sensor plug. Then, remove the air flow sensor by removing the air cleaner and removing the 3 mounting bolts to separate the airflow sensor from it.

4. Use special tool 13 1 092 or equivalent to remove the anti-tamper plug. Use this tool to drill a hole in the plug and then use 13 1 094 or equivalent to pull it. The second tool should be screwed into the hole already drilled; use the slide hammer to pull the plug out.

5. Once the plug is removed, install the air flow sensor back onto the air cleaner and reinstall the air cleaner. With the engine idling hot and the oxygen sensor plug still disconnected, measure the CO and adjust it with Tool 13 1 060 or 13 1 100 or equivalent. The CO level must meet the nominal value of 0.2-1.2%.

6. Once the level is adjusted, stop the engine and reconnect the oxygen sensor plug. Then, remove the air flow sensor, put it on a bench, and install a new anti-tamper plug. Reinstall the airflow sensor and air cleaner. Reconnect the canister purge hose to the solenoid.

M5 AND M6

1. Make sure the engine is at operating temperature, and that the air cleaner is in reasonably clean condition. All basic engine tuning factors (spark plug condition and gap, valve adjustment, ignition timing, etc.) must be correct.

2. Adjust the idle speed by turning the screw shown in the illustration.

3. To adjust CO, first remove the cap located at the center of the top surface of the airflow

On the M5 and M6 engines, adjust idle speed by turning this screw (1)

sensor. Use a special tool 13 1 100 to turn the airflow control screw in the airflow sensor, accessible after the anti-tamper cap is removed. CO must be 0.4-1.2%.

4. Install a new cap when CO meets specification.

M3

NOTE: *This test must be performed at essentially sea level altitude. In an area well above sea level, it will be necessary to use a BMW Service tester or equivalent device from another source and run the test with the system's altitude correction box connected.*

1. Make sure the engine is at operating temperature, and that the air cleaner is in reasonably clean condition. All basic engine tuning factors (spark plug condition and gap, valve adjustment, ignition timing, etc.) must be correct. Turn off all accessories.

2. A special electrical fitting (BMW special tool 13 4 010 or equivalent) is required to disable the Motronic control system's throttle valve switch. Pull off the electrical connector leading to the throttle valve switch. Then, plug the special tool into the open end of the connector.

3. Adjust the idle speed to specification by turning the screw located just above the **M** on the valve cover. Make sure to restore the throttle valve switch when the idle speed is correct.

4. Make sure the engine is in good basic tune, including proper spark plug gap and valve clearances. The engine must be at operating temperature.

● On cars with no test openings in the exhaust manifold:

  a. With a CO meter in the tailpipe, disconnect the oxygen sensor so it no longer influences the mixture produced by the injection system. CO level should be zero. If there is a CO reading, it is necessary to get a special adjusting screw cap remover BMW special tool 13 1 011 or equivalent and an adjusting tool 13 1 100 or equivalent.

  b. The adjusting screw cap is located on the top surface of the airflow sensor; the adjusting screw is accessible in the aperture underneath. Remove the cap with the cap remover and then turn the adjusting screw slowly to correct the CO value to 0. Reinstall the cap and reconnect the oxygen sensor.

● On cars with a test opening in the exhaust manifold:

  a. Remove the plug in the exhaust manifold and put the probe of the CO meter into the opening. Disconnect the oxygen sensor so it no longer influences the mixture produced by the injection system. CO level should be 0.8-1.2%. If the CO reading is outside the

nominal value range, it is necessary to get a special adjusting screw cap remover BMW special tool 13 1 011 or equivalent and an adjusting tool 13 1 100 or equivalent.

  b. The adjusting screw cap is located on the top surface of the airflow sensor; the adjusting screw is accessible in the aperture underneath. Remove the cap with the cap remover and then turn the adjusting screw slowly to correct the CO value to 0.8-1.2%. Reinstall the cap and reconnect the oxygen sensor.

Idle Speed
Diesel Engines
ADJUSTMENT

1. Valve clearance must be correct. Run the engine until it reaches operating temperature. Make sure all electrical accessories are shut off. Check to make sure the throttle lever is resting on the idle adjusting screw. Shut the engine off.

2. Check the play between the throttle lever and the knurled screw. It should be 0.30-0.50mm. Hold the hexagonal nut associated

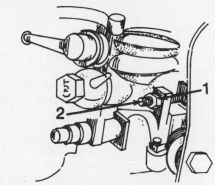

Loosen the locknut (1) and turn the adjusting screw (2) to adjust the idle on the diesel engine

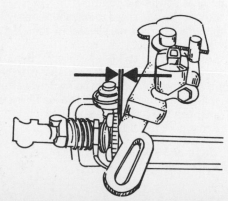

Check the play "S" between the knurled screw and the throttle lever (524 td)

with the screw with the knurled head, and then turn that screw until the play is correct.

3. Loosen the locknut (1) and turn the adjusting screw (2) to give the correct idle speed. Tighten the locknut.

4. Repeat the clearance check of Step 2. If not to specification, readjust the clearance as in Step 3. On cars with automatic transmission, check the distance from the linkage to the rear injection pump flange and adjust if necessary (see the section below covering transmission linkage adjustments).

Engine and Engine Overhaul

UNDERSTANDING THE ENGINE ELECTRICAL SYSTEM

The engine electrical systems can be broken down into 3 separate and distinct systems:
1. The starting system
2. The charging system
3. The ignition system.

Battery and Starting System

The battery is the first link in the chain of mechanisms which work together to provide cranking of the automobile engine. In most modern cars, the battery is a lead-acid electrochemical device consisting of 6 2-volt (2V) subsections connected in series so the unit is capable of producing approximately 12V of electrical pressure. Each subsection, or cell, consist of a series of positive and negative plates held a short distance apart in a solution of sulfuric acid and water. The 2 types of plates are of dissimilar metals. This causes a chemical reaction to be set up, and it is this reaction which produces current flow from the battery when its positive and negative terminals are connected to an electrical appliance such as a lamp or motor. The continued transfer of electrons would eventually convert the sulfuric acid in the electrolyte to water, and make the 2 plates identical in chemical composition. As electrical energy is removed from the battery, its voltage output tends to drop. Thus, measuring battery voltage and battery electrolyte composition are 2 ways of checking the ability of the unit to supply power. During the starting of the engine, electrical energy is removed from the battery. However, if the charging circuit is in good condition and the operating conditions are normal, the power removed from the battery will be replaced by the generator (or alternator) which will urrent. Generally, the major power supply cable that leaves the battery goes directly to the starter, while other electrical system needs are supplied by a smaller cable. During the starter operation, power flows from the battery to the starter and is grforce electrons back through the battery, reversing the normal flow, and restoring the battery to its original chemical state.

The battery and starting motor are linked by very heavy electrical cables designed to minimize resistance to the flow of counded through the car's frame and the battery's negative ground strap.

The starting motor is a specially designed, direct current electric motor capable of producing a very great amount of power for its size. One thing that allows the motor to produce a great deal of power is its tremendous rotating speed. It drives the engine through a tiny pinion gear (attached to the starter's armature), which drives the very large flywheel ring gear at a greatly reduced speed. Another factor allowing it to produce so much power is that only intermittent operation is required of it. Thus, little allowance for air circulation is required, and the windings can be built into a very small space.

The starter solenoid is a magnetic device which employs the small current supplied by the starting switch circuit if the igniton switch. This magnetic action moves a pluger which mechanically engages the starter and electrically closes the heavy switch which connects it to the battery. The starting switch circuit consists of the starting switch contained withing the ignition switch, a transmission neutral safety switch or clutch pedal switch, and the wiring necessary to connect these with the starter solenoid or relay.

A pinion, which is a small gear, is mounted to a one-way drive clutch. This clutch is plined to the starter armature shaft. When the igniton switch is moved to the **START** position, the solenoid plunger slides the pinion toward the flywheel ring gear via a collar and spring. If the

teeth on the pinion and flywheel match properly, the pinion will engage the flywheel immediately. If the gear teeth butt one another, the spring will be compressed and will force the gears to mesh as soon as the starter turns far enough to allow them to do so. As the solenoid plunger reaches the end of its travel, it closes the contacts that connect the battery and starter and then the engine is cranked.

As soon as the engine starts, the flywheel ring gear begins turning fast enough to drive the pinion at an extremely high rate of speed. At this point, the one-way clutch begins allowing the pinion to spin faster than the starter shaft so that the starter will not operate at excessive speed. When the ignition switch is released from the starter position,t he solenoid is de-energized, and a spring contained within the solenoid assembly pulls the gear out of mesh and interrupts the current flow to the starter.

Some starters employ a separate relay, mounted away from the starter, to switch the motor and solenoid current on and off. The relay thus replaces the solenoid electrical switch, but does not eliminate the need for a solenoid mounted ont he starter used to mechanically engage the starter drive gears. The relay is used to reduce the amount of current the starting switch must carry.

The Charging System

The automobile charging system provides electrical power for operation of the vehicle's ignition and starting systems and all the electrical accessories. The battery serves as an electrical surge or storage tank, sorting (in chemical form) the energy originally produced by the engine-driven generator. The system also provides a means of regulator generator output to protect the battery f rom being overcharged and to avoid excessive voltage to the accessories.

The storage battery is a chemical device incorporating parallel lead plates in a tank containing a sulfuric acid-water solution. Adjacent plates are slightly dissimilar, and the chemical reaction of the 2 dissimilar plates produces electrical energy when the battery is connected to a load such as the starter motor. The chemical reaction is reversible, so that when the generator is producing a voltage (electrical pressure) greater than that produced gby the battery, electricity is forced into the battery, and the battery is returned to its fully charged state.

The vehicle's generator is driven mechanically, through V belts, by the engine crankshaft. It consists of 2 coils of fine wire, one stationary (the "stator") , and one movable ("the rotor"). The rotor may also be known as the "armature," and consist of fine wire wrapped around an iron core which is mounted on a shaft. The

electricity which flows through the 2 coils of wire(provided initially by the battery in some cases) creates an intense magnetic field around both rotor and stator, and the interaction between t the 2 fields creates voltage, allowing the generator to power the accessories and charge the battery.

There are 2 types of generators; the earlier is the direct current (DC) type. The current produced by the DC generator is generated in the armature and carried off the spinning armature by stationary brushes contacting the commutator. The commutator is a series of smooth metal contact plates on the end of the armature. The commutator plates, which are separated from one another by a verys hort gap, are connected to the armature circuits so that current will flow in one direction only in the wires carrying the generator output. The generator startor consists of 2 stationary coils of wire which draw some of the output current of the generator to form a powerful magnetic field and create the interaction of fields which generates the voltage. The generator field is wired in series with the regulator.

New automobiles use alternating current generators of "alternators" bcause they are more efficient, can be rotated at higher speeds, and have fewer brush problems. In an alternator, the field rotates while all the current produced passes only through the stator windings. The brushes bear against continuous slip rings rather than a commutator. This causes the current produced to periodically reverse the direction of its flow. Diodes (electrical one-way switches) block the flow of current from traveling in the wrong direction. A series of diodes is wired together to permit the alternating floor of the stator to ve converted to a pulsating, but uni-directional flow at the alternator output. The alternator's field is wired in series with the voltage regulator.

The regulator consists of several circuits. Easy circuit had a core, or magnetic coil of wire, which operates a switch. Each switch is connected to ground through one or more resistors. The coil of wire responds directly to system voltage. When t the voltage reaches the required level, the magnetic field creasted by the winding of wire closes the switch and inserts a resistance into the generator field circuit, thus reducing the output. the contacts of the switch cycle open and close many times each second to precisely control voltage.

While alternators are self-limiting as far as maximum current is concerned, DC generators emply a current regulating circuit which responds directly to the total amount of current flowing through the generator circuit rather than than to the output voltage. The current

regulator is similar to the voltage regulator except that all system current must flow through the energizing coil on its way to the various accessories.

SAFETY PRECAUTIONS

Observing these precautions will ensure safe handling of the electrical system components, and will avoid damage to the vehicle's electrical system:

1. Be absolutely sure of the polarity of a booster battery before making connections. Connect the cables positive to positive, and negative to negative. Connect positive cables first and then make the last connection to a ground ont he body of the booster vehicle so that arcing cannot ignite hydrogen gas that may have accumulated near the battery. Even momentary connection of a booster battery with the polarity reversed will damage alternator diodes.

2. Disconnect both vehicle battery cables before attempting to charge a battery.

3. Never ground the alternator or generator output or battery terminal. Be cautious when using metal tools around a battery to avoid creating a short circuit between the terminals.

4. Never ground the field circuit between t the alternator and regulator.

5. Never run an alternator or generator without load unless the field circuit is disconnected.

6. Never attempt to polarize an alternator.

7. Keep the regulator cover in place when taking voltage and current limiter readings.

8. Use insulated tools when adjusting the regulator.

9. Whenever DC generator-to-regulator wires have been disconnected, the generator must be repolarized. To do this with an externally grounded, light duty generator, momentarily place a jumper wire between the battery terminal and the generator terminal of the regulator. With an internally grounded heavy duty unit, disconnect the wire to the regulator field terminal and touch the regulator battery terminal with it.

Troubleshooting the Electronic Ignition System

1. Pull the high tension wire out of the center of the distributor cap and hold it within about ⅜″ of a good ground. If there is a spark, proceed to Step 2; otherwise, follow the lettered steps below:

   a. Pull the black/red wire off the starter terminal #16 and connect a voltmeter between the connector ont the wire and a good ground. Operate the starter and read the voltage on the meter. Then read the voltage across the battery terminals, also with the starter operating. If the voltage read at the end of the black/red wire is significantly below battery voltage, repair the wire or connectors as necessary.

   b. Detach transmitter wires at the plugs near the control unit and measure the voltage coming from the transmitter (in the dis-

1. Ignition coil
2. Resistors
3. Starter
4. Control unit
5. Distributor
7. Multiple plug to control unit terminal 1
8. Ignition switch
9. Battery

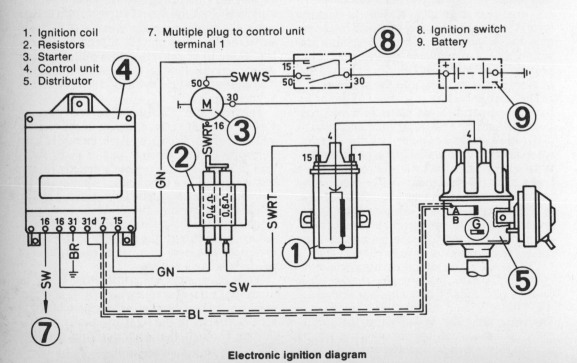

Electronic ignition diagram

tributor). The voltmeter should be set ont the most sensitive scale: the red connector going to connection 7, and the black to 31d. At cranking speed, voltage should be at least 0.05 volts. If not, check the gap between rotor and stator with engine turned so as to align teeth; it should be 0.35-0.68mm. Replace defective parts as necessary. Replace the transmitter wiring, if defective, or replace the pulse transmitter, if necessary.

2. inspect spark plugs, distributor cap and rotor, and ignition wires, and replace defective parts as necessary.

3. Measure the voltage between t the coil primary terminal leading to the control unit (1) and ground. If there is less than 2 volts, go on with the next step. Otherwise:

    a. Check for voltage at the plug going into control unit terminal 15. If there is not voltage, repair the igniton switch.

    b. Check for voltage at the plug going into control unit terminal 16. If ther is no voltage, repair the wire leading from ignition coil terminal 1 to terminal 16.

    c. Check to see that the control unit is properly grounded (terminal 31). If not, repair the ground connection.

If none of these checks reveal the problem, or if making the required repairs still results in more than 2 volts as read in Step 3, repalce the control unit.

4. Measure the voltage between igniton coil terminal 15 and ground. It should be more than 3 volts. Otherwise, replace a defective resistor of igniton coil.

5. If the above teste are passed, the engine should start. Adjust igniton timing as described in the previous chapter. Then, connect a dwell meter between coil terminal 1 and ground. Check the dwell angle at 1500 rpm and at 6000 rpm. The figures should be 32-53° at 1500 and 43-56° at 6000. If dwell is incorrect, substitute a new or known good pulse transmitter. If dwell is still incorrect, replace the control unit.

Digital Motor Electronic (DME) Engine Control System

The DME, or Motronic, engine control system is used on the 1982 528e, 633CSi and 733i and all later models. It is a complicated, precision system. Troubleshooting is best left to a trained service technician who is familiar with this system.

Ignition Coil
PRIMARY RESISTANCE CHECK

To check the coil primary resistance, connect an ohmmeter across the coil primary terminals and read the resistance on the low scale. Note whether an external ballast resistor is used. The procedure for breaker point igniton systems and electronic ignition systems is the same except that the resistance for breaker point ignitions should be 1.7-2.1 ohms and the resistance of the electronic igniton should be between 0.4-0.7 ohms.

SECONDARY RESISTANCE CHECK

To check the coil secondary resistance, connect an ohmmeter across the distributor side of the coil and the coil tower. Read the resistance on the high scale, resistance should be between 4,000-10,000 ohms on breaker point ignition systems. The procedure for breaker point ignition systems and electronic igniton systems is the same except that the resistance of the electronic igniton should be between 7,700-9,300 ohms.

REMOVAL AND INSTALLATION

To remove the ignition coil, first disconnect the ignition lead and the coil wire. Lossen the screw retaining the ignition coil in its bracket. Slide the coil from the bracket and remove it. Slide the replacement coil into position and tighten the bracket screw. Connect the ignition lead and the coil wire.

Distributor
REMOVAL AND INSTALLATION
4-Cylinder Engines Except M3

1. Prior to removal, using paint, chalk or a sharp instrument, scribe alignment marks showing the relative position of the distributor body to its mount on the rear of the cylinder head.

2. Following the firing order illustration (Chapter 2), mark each spark plug wire with a

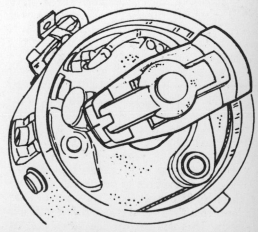

Notches on distributor body and rotor aligning with the No. 1 piston TDC

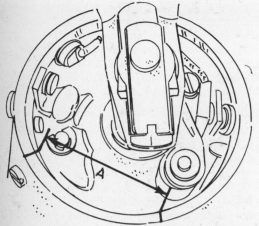

Position of the rotor prior to distributor installation. (A) 1.4 in.

dab of pint or chalk noting its respective cylinder. It will be easier and faster to install the distributor and get the firing order right if you leave the plug wires in the cap.

3. Pull up and disconnect the secondary wire (high tension cable leading front the coil to the center of the distributor cap), and remove the spark plug loom retaining nut(s) from the cylinder head cover. Disconnect the vacuum line(s) from the vacuum capsule.

4. Disconnect the primary wire (low tension wire running from one of the coil terminals to the side of the distributor) at the distributor.

5. Unsnap the distributor cap retaining clasps and lift off the cap and wire assembly.

6. Now, with the aid of a remote starter switch or a friend, "bump" the starter a few times until the No. 1 piston is at Top Deat Center (TDC) of its compression stroke, At this time, the notch scribed on the metal tip of the distributor rotor must be aligned with a corresponding notch scribed on the distributor case. Before removing the distributor, make sure that these 2 marks coincide as per the illustration.

7. Loosen the clamp bolt at the base of the distributor (where it slides into its mount) and lift the distributor up and out. You will notice that the rotor turns clockwise as the distributor is removed. This is because the distributor is gear driven and must be compensated for during installation.

8. Reverse the above procedure to install the distributor. Remember to rotate the rotor approximately 35mm counterclockwise (see illustration) from the notch scribed in the distributor body. This will ensure that when the distributor is fully seated in its mount, the marks will coincide. Adjust the igniton timing as de-

scribed in Chapter 2. Tighten the clamp bolt to 8 ft. lbs.

6-Cylinder Engines 1970-81

1. Pull the vacuum hoses for advance and retard off the distributor, as required.

2. With chalk or paint, mark the relationship between the distributor body and the cylinder head. Then, rotate the engine untilt he line on the tip of the rotator id directly in line with the notch in the distributor housing (this puts the engine at TDC for No. 1 cylinder). Make sure that the TDC timing marks on the flywheel or balancer pulley are in line.

3. Loose the clamp bolt at the bottom of the distributor.

4. Unscrew the mounting bracket screw for the electrical connector on the distributor body, pull the mounting bracket off, and unplug the connector.

5. Pull the distributor out of the cylinder head.

6. To install, first position the rotor about 25-38mm counterclockwise from the notch in the distributor housing. Then, position the distributor body so the alignment marks you made in Step 1 are aligned. Insert the distributor into

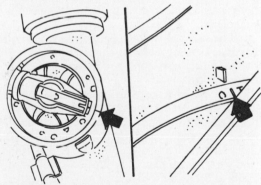

Alignment of the rotor with the electronic distributor housing and alignment of the balancer pulley TDC mark with the timing housing lug, before distributor removal

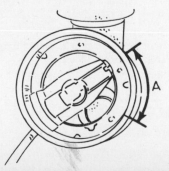

Distance (A) rotor moves from the housing mark during the removal of the electronic distributor

the head. If necessary, shift the top of the rotor just slightly one way or the other to get the distributor and camshaft gears to mesh properly; otherwise, the distributor cannot be inserted into the head.

7. When the distributor is fully seated, reconnect the electrical connector and all vacuum lines and install the cap. Adjust the igniton timing as described in Chapter 2.

6-Cylinder Engines 1982-88
And M3 4-Cylinder Engine

1982 6-cylinder engines are quipped with the Motronic (DME) engine control system. The distributor on these models is contained within the engine itself. Other than distributor cap and rotor removal and installation, no general service is possible.

INSTALLING THE DISTRIBUTOR IF TIMING HAS BEEN DISTURBED

Sometimes, the engine is accidentally turned over while the distributor is removed, in this case, it will be necessary to find TDC position for NO. 1 cylinder before installing the distributor. First, go the the "Valve Lash Adjustment" procedure in Chapter 2, remove the cam cover,and set the position of the engine as described there for adjustment of the valve for No. 1 cylinder. Check the exact position of the crankshaft via the timing marks on the flywheel or front pulley, and obtain exact alignment as indicated by them. Then, proceed to uninstall the distributor as described above.

Alternator

ALTERNATOR PRECAUTIONS

Several precautions must be observed with alternator equipped vehicles to avoid damaging the unit. They are as follows:

• If the battery is removed for any reason, make sure that it is reconnected with the correct polarity. Reversing the battery connections may result in damage to the one-way rectifiers.

• When utilizing a booster battery as a starting aid, always connect it as follows: positive to positive, and negative (booster battery) to a good ground on the engine the car being started. Note that on the 1982 733i, the No. 5 fuse must be pulled out of the fuse panel before using a booster battery, or the onboard computer may be damaged.

• Never use a fast charger as a booster to start cars with alternating-current (AC) circuits.

• When servicing the battery with a fast charger, always disconnect the battery cables.

• Never attempt to polarize an alternator.

• Avoid long soldering times when replacing

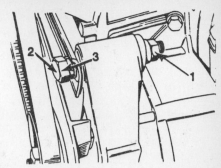

Loosen the locknut (1) at the rear of the alternator, and then turn the bolt (3) and tighten to 4.0–4.3 ft. lb. Hold the bolt in position while tightening the nut—318i

diodes or transistors. Prolonged heat is damaging to alternators.

• Do not use test lamps of more than 12 volts for checking diode continuity.

• Do not short across or ground any of the terminals on the alternator.

• The polarity of the battery, alternator, and regulator must be matched and considered before making any electrical connections within the system.

• Never operate the alternator on an open circuit. Make sure that all connections within the circuit are clean and tight.

• Turn off the ignition switch and then disconnect the battery terminals when performing any service on the electrical system or charging the battery.

• Disconnect the battery ground cable if arc welding is to be done on any part of the car.

CHARGING SYSTEM TROUBLESHOOTING

There are many possible ways in which the charging system can malfunction. Often the source of a problem is difficult to diagnose, requiring special equipment and a good deal of experience. This is usually not the case, however, where the charging system fails completely and causes the dash board warning light to come on or the battery to become dead. To troubleshoot a complete system failure only two pieces of equipment are needed: a test light, to determine that current is reaching a certain point; and a current indicator (ammeter), to determine the direction of the current flow and its measurement in amps.

This test works under three assumptions:

1. The battery is known to be good and fully charged.

2. The alternator belt is in good condition and adjusted to the proper tension.

3. All connections in the system are clean and tight.

NOTE: *In order for the current indicator to*

give a valid reading, the car must be equipped with battery cables which are of the same gauge size and quality as original equipment battery cables.

1. Turn off all electrical components on the car. Make sure the doors of the car are closed. If the car is equipped with a clock, disconnect the clock by removing the lead wire from the rear of the clock. Disconnect the positive battery cable from the battery and connect the ground wire on a test light to the disconnected positive battery cable. Touch the probe end of the test light to the positive battery post. The test light should not light. If the test light does light, there is a short or open circuit on the car.

2. Disconnect the voltage regulator wiring harness connector at the voltage regulator. Turn on the ignition key. Connect the wire on a test light to a good ground (engine bolt). Touch the probe end of a test light to the ignition wire connector into the voltage regulator wiring connector. This wire corresponds to the **I** terminal on the regulator. If the test light goes on, the charging system warning light circuit is complete. If the test light does not come on and the warning light on the instrument panel is on, either the resistor wire, which is parallel with the warning light, or the wiring to the voltage regulator, is defective. If the test light does not come on and the warning light is not on, either the bulb is defective or the power supply wire form the battery through the ignition switch to the bulb has an open circuit. Connect the wiring harness to the regulator.

3. Examine the fuse link wire in the wiring harness from the starter relay to the alternator. If the insulation on the wire is cracked or split, the fuse link may be melted. Connect a test light to the fuse link by attaching the ground wire on the test light to an engine bolt and touching the probe end of the light to the bottom of the fuse link wire where it splices into the alternator output wire. If the bulb in the test light does not light, the fuse link is melted.

4. Start the engine and place a current indicator on the positive battery cable. Turn off all electrical accessories and make sure the doors are closed. If the charging system is working properly, the gauge will show a draw of less than 5 amps. If the system is not working properly, the gauge will show a draw of more than 5 amps. A charge moves the needle toward the battery, a draw moves the needle away from the battery. Turn the engine off.

5. Disconnect the wiring harness from the voltage regulator at the regulator at the regulator connector. Connect a male spade terminal (solderless connector) to each end of a jumper wire. Insert one end of the wire into the wiring harness connector which corresponds to the **A**

terminal on the regulator. Insert the other end of the wire into the wiring harness connector which corresponds to the **F** terminal on the regulator. Position the connector with the jumper wire installed so that it cannot contact any metal surface under the hood. Position a current indicator gauge on the positive battery cable. Have an assistant start the engine. Observe the reading on the current indicator. Have your assistant slowly raise the speed of the engine to about 2,000 rpm or until the current indicator needle stops moving, whichever comes first. Do not run the engine for more than a short period of time in this condition. If the wiring harness connector or jumper wire becomes excessively hot during this test, turn off the engine and check for a grounded wire in the regulator wiring harness. If the current indicator shows a charge of about three amps less than the output of the alternator, the alternator is working properly. If the previous tests showed a draw, the voltage regulator is defective. If the gauge does not show the proper charging rate, the alternator is defective.

REMOVAL AND INSTALLATION

All 1970-81 Models

1. Disconnect the battery cables at the battery. On some models, it may be necessary to remove the battery for clearance. If so, remove it.

2. Remove the stabilizer bar, if necessary on 2002tii models.

3. Mark any individual electrical leads that could be installed to the wrong terminal on reinstallation. Then, pull off any multiple connectors, To disconnect individual leads, remove rubber covers, remove attaching nuts, and pull leads off.

4. Remove the bolt which runs in the slotted

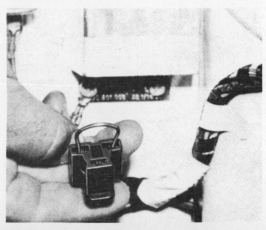

Disconnecting multiple plug from regulator

Alternator electrical connections—2002 series

adjusting bar and loosen the mounting bolt. Slide the unit toward the engine, remove the bolt and then remove the main mounting bolt and remove the alternator from the engine.

5. In installation, first locate the alternator in its normal position and install the main mounting bolt loosely. Then, install the fan belt onto the alternator pulley; position the sliding bracket appropriately and install the mounting bolt for that bracket. Finally, tension the fan belt as described in Chapter 1.

6. Remake all electrical connections. Install the stabilizer bar or battery if necessary; reconnect the battery.

All 1982-88 Models

1. Disconnect the battery ground cable.

2. Disconnect the wires from the rear of the alternator, marking them for later installation. Note that there is a ground wire on some models. On the 735i, remove the cap and then disconnect the positive terminal at the junction box on the fender well. On the 325, M3, 633CSi, 635CSi, 733i and 735i, it may be easier to remove the alternator mounting bolts, turn it, and then remove the wires.
On the M5 and M6:

    a. Unscrew the nut and loosen the hose clamp. Pull of the plug. Then, lift out the air cleaner and airflow sensor.

    b. Make sure the engine is cool. Place a pan underneath and then disconnect the lower radiator hose.

    • On the 1988-89 325, and the M3 and 528e, remove the airflow sensor.

    • On the 735i, make sure the engine is cool. Place a pan underneath and then disconnect the lower radiator hose.

3. Loosen the adjusting and pivot bolts, and remove the belt on those models with a standard mounting system. If the alternator has the tensioning bolt described in Step 4, loosen the lockbolt, turn the tensioning bolt so as to eliminate belt tension and then remove the belt. Remove the bolts and remove the alternator. On the 633CSi, 635CSi, 733i and 735i, it may be necessary to loosen the fan cowl to get at the mounting bolts. On the 535i, it may be necessary to disconnect a power steering line that runs near the alternator.

4. Installation is the reverse of removal. Adjust the belt tension to approximately ⅜", measured between the balancer and the alternator pulley. On all 1984-88 models, a unique tensioning system is used. See the illustration for the 318i; the other models are similar. The tensioning bolt on the front of the alternator must be turned so as to tension the belt, using a torque wrench, until the torque is approximately 5 ft. lbs. Then, hold the adjustment with one wrench while tightening the locknut at the rear of the unit. Make sure that, if the unit has a ground wire on the alternator, it has been reconnected. On the M5 and M6 and 735i, make sure to reconnect the radiator hose, refill and bleed the cooling system. On the M5, M6, and 528e securely reinstall the air cleaner and airflow sensor. On the 528e, if the power steering line had to be disconnected, reconnect it securely, refill, and bleed the system.

Regulator

REMOVAL AND INSTALLATION

1. Disconnect the negative battery cable.

2. Disconnect the multiple connector from the bottom of the regulator.

3. Remove the phillips head hold down screws and ground wires.

4. Lift off the regulator. If you are replacing it with another unit, make sure that the color coding is the same: yellow tape — nonsuppressed (radio), white or green tape — suppressed (radio).

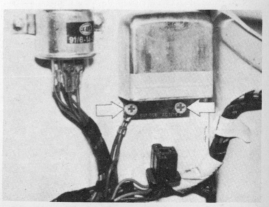

Voltage regulator installation

5. To install, position the regulator and ground wires, install the retaining screws, connect the multiple connector and lastly, the negative battery cable.

Models with Integral Regulator

On these models, the regulator and carbon brushes are an integral assembly, and the regulator cannot be adjusted. Simply remove the 2 mounting screws, one located at either end of

Remove the two screws and remove the carbon brush holder—models with integral regulator

the unit, remove it, and replace it in reverse otder. During installation, make sure brushes are located flat on the slip rings and then install mounting screws.

VOLTAGE ADJUSTMENT

NOTE: *The voltage regulators used on most BMW's are non-adjustable; the procedure below describes the means of adjusting the regulators used on 4-cylinder models build up until 1975. Tools required include a voltmeter, an ohmmeter, a tachometer, and test equipment which will permit you to isolate the battery and alternator front the rest of the vehicle's electrical system (called a "battery post adapter"), and a load rheostat to permit loading the system a set amount.*

Install the battery post adapter on the positive post of the battery. Connect the voltmeter across the battery. Hook up the tachometer. With all electrical accessories turned off the battery post adaptor switch closed, start the engine. Open the post adapter switch as soon as the engine is started. Adjust engine speed to 2500 rpm, and load the system with a ¼ ohm resistance. With the voltage reading stabilized, any figure between 13.5 and 14.8 volts is acceptable. If the reading is unacceptable, remove the regulator cover and adjust the armature spring tension until the voltmeter reads 14.0 volts.

Troubleshooting Basic Charging System Problems

Problem	Cause	Solution
Noisy alternator	• Loose mountings • Loose drive pulley • Worn bearings • Brush noise • Internal circuits shorted (High pitched whine)	• Tighten mounting bolts • Tighten pulley • Replace alternator • Replace alternator • Replace alternator
Squeal when starting engine or accelerating	• Glazed or loose belt	• Replace or adjust belt
Indicator light remains on or ammeter indicates discharge (engine running)	• Broken fan belt • Broken or disconnected wires • Internal alternator problems • Defective voltage regulator	• Install belt • Repair or connect wiring • Replace alternator • Replace voltage regulator
Car light bulbs continually burn out—battery needs water continually	• Alternator/regulator overcharging	• Replace voltage regulator/alternator
Car lights flare on acceleration	• Battery low • Internal alternator/regulator problems	• Charge or replace battery • Replace alternator/regulator
Low voltage output (alternator light flickers continually or ammeter needle wanders)	• Loose or worn belt • Dirty or corroded connections • Internal alternator/regulator problems	• Replace or adjust belt • Clean or replace connections • Replace alternator or regulator

Starter

REMOVAL AND INSTALLATION

All 1970-82 Models

1. Disconnect the battery ground cable. Then, disconnect the starter main power cable at the solenoid by removing the nut and washer, and pulling the connection off the terminal.

2. On injected 4-cylinder models, remove the intake cowl from the mixture control unit. On 6-cylinder injected models, remove No. 6 intake tube.

3. Pull off the 2 solenoid connectors, noting the colors attached to each terminal. On 4-cylinder models, disconnect the mounting bracket at the block by removing the 2 bolts. Remove the front Allen screw on the 528e.

4. Remove the starter mounting bolts from the transmisison and remove the unit.

All 1983-88 Models

1. Disconnect the battery ground cable.

2. On fuel injection 6-cylinder models with 6 identical intake tubes, it may be necessary to remove No. 6 intake tube for clearance. On injected 4-cylinder models, remove the intake cowl from the mixture control unit. On the 318i, remove the wire holding bracket.

On the 325 up to 1987:

a. Disconnect the positive terminal at the junction box on the fender well. Then, remove the air cleaner with the flow sensor.

b. Unscrew the air collector bracket that's in the way.

c. Unscrew the nut that fastens a wiring bracket near the starter.

CAUTION: *When draining the coolant, keep in mind that cats and dogs are attracted by the ethylene glycol antifreeze, and are quite*

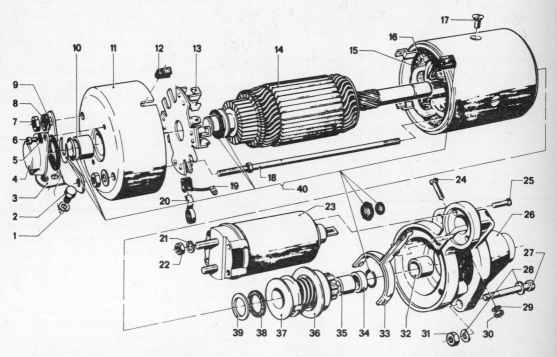

1. Spring ring	12. Rubber bushing	21. Lockwasher	31. Hex nut
2. Screw	13. Brush support	22. Nut	32. Bearing shell
3. Support angle	plate	23. Magnetic coupler	33. Switch lever
4. Cover cap	14. Armature	switch	34. Stop face ring
5. Lockwasher	15. Insulating strip	24. Cylinder screw	35. Bearing shell
6. Cylinder head	16. Excitation winding	25. Countersunk screw	36. Gears
screw	17. Countersunk screw	26. Drive bearing with	37. Guide ring
7. Hex nut	18. Cylinder head	bearing shell	38. Sleeve
8. Lockwasher	screw	27. Screw	39. Washer shim
9. Washer	19. Carbon brush set	28. Lockwasher	40. Parts set
10. Bearing shell	20. Compression	29. Lockwasher	
11. Collector bearing	spring	30. Hex nut	

Exploded view of typical Bosch starter

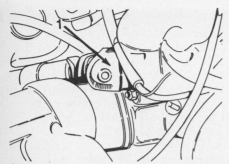

In 318i starter removal, remove the nut and detach the bracket (1)

likely to drink any that is left in an uncovered container or in puddles on the ground. This will prove fatal in sufficient quantity. Always drain the coolant into a sealable container. Coolant should be reused unless it is contaminated or several years old.

d. Make sure the engine is cool and then drain the coolant into a clean container. Disconnect the heater hose that runs near the starter. Remove the coolant pipe if doing so is necessary for clearance.

On the 1988 325 and the M3: Remove the air cleaner and airflow sensor. Then, remove the mounting bolts for the bracket for the air collector and remove it.

On the 528e:

a. Remove the air cleaner and airflow sensor.

b. Disconnect the electrical leads. Remove the 3 bolts and remove the mounting bracket.

On the 533i and 535i: Make sure the engine is cool. Drain some coolant from the cooling system and then remove the expansion tank.

CAUTION: *When draining the coolant, keep in mind that cats and dogs are attracted by the ethylene glycol antifreeze, and are quite likely to drink any that is left in an uncovered container or in puddles on the ground. This will prove fatal in sufficient quantity. Always drain the coolant into a sealable container. Coolant should be reused unless it is contaminated or several years old.*

On the 633CSi and 635CSi:

a. Make sure the engine is cool and drain some coolant out. Disconnect the heater hose that is near the starter.

CAUTION: *When draining the coolant, keep in mind that cats and dogs are attracted by the ethylene glycol antifreeze, and are quite likely to drink any that is left in an uncovered container or in puddles on the ground. This will prove fatal in sufficient quantity. Always drain the coolant into a sealable container. Coolant should be reused unless it is contaminated or several years old.*

b. Operate the brake pedal hard 20 times. Disconnect the power steering line that would otherwise prevent access to the starter.

c. Cut off the straps and remove the solenoid switch insulating cover, located right near the solenoid.

On the M5 and M6:

a. Remove the exhaust manifold as described later in this section.

b. Cut off the straps and remove the solenoid switch insulating cover, located right near the solenoid.

3. Remove the starter solenoid wire leads, marking them for later installation unless they have already been removed. On 4-cylinder models, disconnect the mounting bracket at the block. On the 1988-89 325 and the M3, drain coolant out of the engine and then disconnect the heater hose located near the starter; also unscrew and remove the coolant pipe if necessary for clearance.

CAUTION: *When draining the coolant, keep in mind that cats and dogs are attracted by the ethylene glycol antifreeze, and are quite likely to drink any that is left in an uncovered container or in puddles on the ground. This will prove fatal in sufficient quantity. Always drain the coolant into a sealable container. Coolant should be reused unless it is contaminated or several years old.*

NOTE: *Remove the accelerator cable holder on automatic transmission equipped vehicles.*

4. Unbolt and remove the starter. On the 325 up to 1987, the lower nut can be removed more easily from underneath. On late model 533 and 535i, 733i and 735i, M5 and M6, it may be necessary to use a box wrench with an angled handle to unscrew the main starter mounting bolts. On the 528e, 633CSi and 635CSi, the final mounting bolt must be removed from underneath. On the 1988 325 and the M3, the starter must be pulled out from above.

5. Installation is the reverse of removal. Make sure to reconnect all hoses and refill and bleed the cooling system or power steering system. Where the solenoid switch cover has been unstrapped, reinstall it with new straps to locate it properly for electrical safety.

STARTER OVERHAUL

Brush Replacement

1. On 4-cylinder starters, remove the support bracket. Remove the 2 screws and remove the dust cap.

2. Remove the lockwasher, shims, and gasket or seal.

3. Unscrew the pole housing through bolts and remove the cap.

4. Lift out positive side brushes and then remove the brush plate, noting how the housing bolts pass through the locating slits in the plate.

5. Unsolder brushes from the exterior coil and brush plate and resolder new brush connections in place.

6. Assemble in reverse order. On 630, 633, and 733 models, check endplay at the front of the armature. It should be 0.10-0.15mm. If the play is excessive, correct it by inserting additional shims under the dust cap.

Starter Drive Replacement

The starter must be disassembled to replace the starter drive. A circlip retains the drive gear

Disassemble the starter in numbered order (typical of six cylinder starters)

Troubleshooting Basic Starting System Problems

Problem	Cause	Solution
Starter motor rotates engine slowly	• Battery charge low or battery defective	• Charge or replace battery
	• Defective circuit between battery and starter motor	• Clean and tighten, or replace cables
	• Low load current	• Bench-test starter motor. Inspect for worn brushes and weak brush springs.
	• High load current	• Bench-test starter motor. Check engine for friction, drag or coolant in cylinders. Check ring gear-to-pinion gear clearance.
Starter motor will not rotate engine	• Battery charge low or battery defective	• Charge or replace battery
	• Faulty solenoid	• Check solenoid ground. Repair or replace as necessary.
	• Damage drive pinion gear or ring gear	• Replace damaged gear(s)
	• Starter motor engagement weak	• Bench-test starter motor
	• Starter motor rotates slowly with high load current	• Inspect drive yoke pull-down and point gap, check for worn end bushings, check ring gear clearance
	• Engine seized	• Repair engine
Starter motor drive will not engage (solenoid known to be good)	• Defective contact point assembly	• Repair or replace contact point assembly
	• Inadequate contact point assembly ground	• Repair connection at ground screw
	• Defective hold-in coil	• Replace field winding assembly
Starter motor drive will not disengage	• Starter motor loose on flywheel housing	• Tighten mounting bolts
	• Worn drive end busing	• Replace bushing
	• Damaged ring gear teeth	• Replace ring gear or driveplate
	• Drive yoke return spring broken or missing	• Replace spring
Starter motor drive disengages prematurely	• Weak drive assembly thrust spring	• Replace drive mechanism
	• Hold-in coil defective	• Replace field winding assembly
Low load current	• Worn brushes	• Replace brushes
	• Weak brush springs	• Replace springs

Continue six cylinder starter disassembly in numbered order. See illustration above. No. 9 is the brush holder

on the the armature shaft and must be removed before the drive gear can be replaced.

1. Remove the field coil wires from the solenoid and remove the solenoid mounting bolts.

2. Disengage the solenoid plunger from the starter drive and remove the solenoid from the starter motor.

3. Remove the small dust cap from the end of the motor.

4. Remove the C-clip, shims and gasket from the end of the starter motor shaft.

5. Remove the two long pole housing screws from the housing. Lift off the pole housing cap, the brushes and the brush plate.

6. Remove the intermediate bearing screws and remove the pole housing.

7. Remove the rubber seal and washer from the engaging lever housing.

8. Remove the engaging lever screw and pull the armature out of the drive bearing.

9. Push back the thrust washer or thrust bearing race on the drive pinion end of the motor shaft in order to remove the C-clip retainer.

10. Remove the starter drive pinion and bracket.

11. Install the starter pinion and bracket. Secure them on the shaft with the thrust washer and C-clip. Lubricate the coarse threads, engaging ring and bearing with high temperature silicone grease.

12. Install the armature and shaft into the drive bearing, making sure that the tabs of the engaging lever are installed over the engaging ring. Lubricate the engaging lever with silicone grease.

13. Install the washer and rubber seal into the engaging lever housing, making sure the tabs on the seal and washer point toward the armature.

14. Position the pole housing so that the groove faces toward the rubber pad and install the pole housing into the drive bearing. Secure the screws with Loctite® No. 270.

15. Check the commutator bearing for looseness and then guide the field coil wires into the rubber seal.

16. Install the pole housing screws through the pole housing cap and locating slots in the brush plate. Install the brushes and pole housing cap on the starter.

17. Check armature axial play to 0.10-0.15mm (0.10-0.20mm on 1983-89 models) and correct any excessive play with additional shims.

18. Install end gasket, shims and C-clip on the end of the motor shaft. Install the dust cover on the end of the starter motor (over the shaft, end gasket and shims).

19. Install the solenoid on the starter and attach the field coil wires to the solenoid.

SOLENOID REPLACEMENT

1. With the starter out of the car, disconnect the field coil connection (at the bottom of the solenoid).

2. Unscrew the solenoid mounting screws from the front of the front housing. Then, pull the solenoid unit upward to disengage the solenoid plunger from the shift lever, and pull the unit off the starter.

3. Install in the reverse order of removal.

Battery

REMOVAL AND INSTALLATION

1. Turn the engine off. Disconnect both battery cables (negative first).

2. Loosen the angled clamp screw, located in front of the battery. Then, shift the retaining bracket away from the battery and remove the unit.

3. To install, reverse the removal procedure, making sure the retaining bracket has the bat-

Positioning solenoid eyelet into engaging arm

Location of battery clamp screw—typical

tery tightly clamped in place before tightening the clamp screw.

NOTE: *Make sure you connect terminals plus-to-plus and minus-to-minus, or damage to the alternator will result.*

4. Apply petroleum jelly to the connections.

ENGINE MECHANICAL
Design

The 2 liter engines are 4-cylinder, in-line designs, while all larger engines are 6-cylinder in-line designs. The block is made of a special gray iron, while the heads are of aluminum alloy to save weight. The crankshafts are of forged steel and are nitrite hardened. 4-cylinder engines use 8 counterweights, while 6-cylinders use 12, for optimum balance. 4-cylinder engines use 5 main bearings while the 6-cylinders employ 7; all main bearings are of replaceable, 3 layer design.

The cylinder heads employ valves located in an inverted Vee pattern, allowing the use of hemispherical combustion chambers for optimum, swirl assisted combustion with minimum heat transfer to the cylinder head. This kind of combustion chamber also allows for use of the largest possible valves. The valves are actuated by a single, nitrite hardened overhead camshaft. Since they are not located directly below the shaft, they are actuated via light alloy rockers. This makes valve adjustment procedure very simple-the only special tool required is a simple piece of wire. Valve adjustments are made via a unique cam,located in the end of the rocker arm and in effect, pinched between sections of it. Since the adjusting cams are separate from the adjusting lockbolts and nuts, and since the lockbolts are prevented from turning via a flat at one end, it is easy to tighten down on the adjustment mechanism without changing the clearance. This minimizes the time required in performing the adjustment. Other engine features that prolong life are the use of

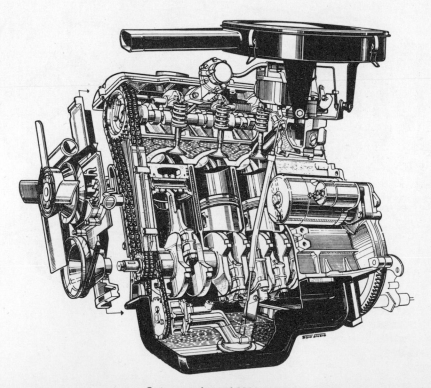

Cutaway view of 2002 engine

chromium plated rings and valve stems, and forged connecting rods.

The ourstanding feature of BMW engines is maximum output per cubic inch. This is possible through painstaking design of camshafts, valves, and the crossflow form taken by the intake and exhaust systems; the ramtype manifolds used on later models; the use of fuel injection on later models, which permits elimination of the restricting effect of the carburetor venturi; and on all engines, the toughness and precise balance required to permit high run up to 6,400 rpm, and are rated for a constant 6,000 rpm (except for the 528e). The result is high performance without the fuel economy penalty usually associated with it.

Engine Overhaul Tips

Most engine overhaul procedures are fairly standard. In addition to specific parts replacement procedures and complete specifications for your individual engine, this chapter also is a guide to accept rebuilding procedures. Examples of standard rebuilding practice are shown and should be used along with specific details concerning your particular engine.

Competent and accurate machine shop services will ensure maximum performance, reliability and engine life.

In most instances it is more profitable for the do-it-yourself mechanic to remove, clean and inspect the component, buy the necessary parts and deliver these to a shop for actual machine work.

On the other hand, much of the rebuilding work (crankshaft, block, bearings, piston rods, and other components) is well within the scope of the do-it-yourself mechanic.

TOOLS

The tools required for an engine overhaul or parts replacement will depend on the depth of your involvement. With a few exceptions, they will be the tools found in a mechanic's tool kit (see Chapter 1). More in-depth work will require any or all of the following:

- A dial indicator (reading in thousandths) mounted on a universal base
- Micrometers and telescope gauges
- Jaw and screw-type pullers
- Scraper
- Valve spring compressor
- Ring groove cleaner
- Piston ring expander and compressor
- Ridge reamer

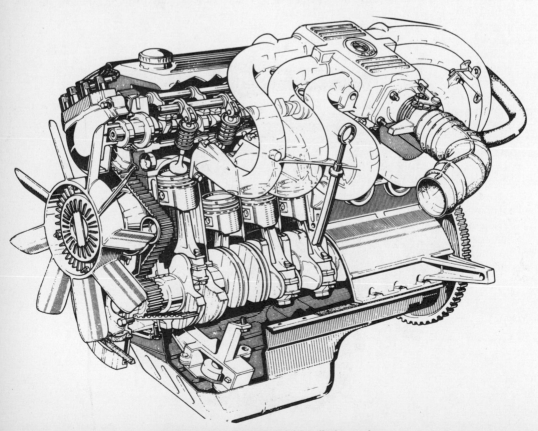

Cutaway view of later model 6 cylinder engine

- Cylinder hone or glaze breaker
- Plastigage®
- Engine stand

The use of most of these tools is illustrated in this chapter. Many can be rented for a one-time use from a local parts jobber or tool supply house specializing in automotive work.

Occasionally, the use of special tools is called for. See the information on Special Tools and Safety Notice in the front of this book before substituting another tool.

INSPECTION TECHNIQUES

Procedures and specifications are given in this chapter for inspecting, cleaning and assessing the wear limits of most major components. Other procedures such as Magnaflux® and Zyglo® can be used to locate material flaws and stress cracks. Magnaflux® is a magnetic process applicable only to ferrous materials. The Zyglo® process coats the material with a fluorescent dye penetrant and can be used on any material Check for suspected surface cracks can be more readily made using spot check dye. The dye is sprayed onto the suspected area, wiped off and the area sprayed with a developer. Cracks will show up brightly.

OVERHAUL TIPS

Aluminum has become extremely popular for use in engines, due to its low weight. Observe the following precautions when handling aluminum parts:

- Never hot tank aluminum parts (the caustic hot tank solution will eat the aluminum.
- Remove all aluminum parts (identification tag, etc.) from engine parts prior to the tanking.
- Always coat threads lightly with engine oil or anti-seize compounds before installation, to prevent seizure.
- Never over-torque bolts or spark plugs especially in aluminum threads.

Stripped threads in any component can be repaired using any of several commercial repair kits (Heli-Coil®, Microdot®, Keenserts®, etc.).

When assembling the engine, any parts that will be frictional contact must be prelubed to provide lubrication at initial start-up. Any product specifically formulated for this purpose can be used, but engine oil is not recommended as a prelube.

When semi-permanent (locked, but removable) installation of bolts or nuts is desired, threads should be cleaned and coated with Loctite® or other similar, commercial non-hardening sealant.

REPAIRING DAMAGED THREADS

Several methods of repairing damaged threads are available. Heli-Coil® (shown here),

Keenserts® and Microdot® are among the most widely used. All involve basically the same principle—drilling out stripped threads, tapping the hole and installing a prewound insert—making

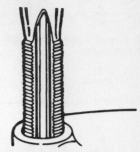

With the tap supplied, tap the hole to receive the thread insert. Keep the tap well oiled and back it out frequently to avoid clogging the threads

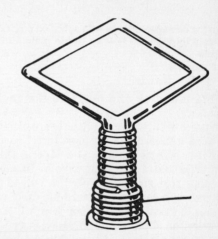

Screw the threaded insert onto the installation tool until the tang engages the slot. Screw the insert into the tapped hole until it is ¼–½ turn below the top surface. After installation break off the tang with a hammer and punch

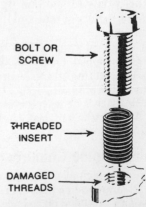

BOLT OR SCREW →

THREADED INSERT →

DAMAGED THREADS →

Damaged bolt holes can be repaired with thread repair inserts

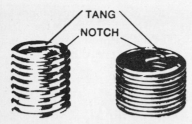

Standard thread repair insert (left) and spark plug thread insert (right)

Drill out the damaged threads with specified drill. Drill completely through the hole or to the bottom of a blind hole

welding, plugging and oversize fasteners unnecessary.

Two types of thread repair inserts are usually supplied: a standard type for most Inch Coarse, Inch Fine, Metric Course and Metric Fine thread sizes and a spark lug type to fit most spark plug port sizes. Consult the individual manufacturer's catalog to determine exact applications. Typical thread repair kits will contain a selection of prewound threaded inserts, a tap (corresponding to the outside diameter threads of the insert) and an installation tool. Spark plug inserts usually differ because they require a tap equipped with pilot threads and a combined reamer/tap section. Most manufacturers also supply blister-packed thread repair inserts separately in addition to a master kit containing a variety of taps and inserts plus installation tools.

Before effecting a repair to a threaded hole, remove any snapped, broken or damaged bolts or studs. Penetrating oil can be used to free frozen threads; the offending item can be removed with locking pliers or with a screw or stud extractor. After the hole is clear, the thread can be repaired, as follows:

Checking Engine Compression

A noticeable lack of engine power, excessive oil consumption and/or poor fuel mileage measured over an extended period are all indicators of internal engine war. Worn piston rings, scored or worn cylinder bores, blown head gas-

kets, sticking or burnt valves and worn valve seats are all possible culprits here. A check of each cylinder's compression will help you locate the problems.

As mentioned in the Tools and Equipment section of Chapter 1, a screw-in type compression gauge is more accurate that the type you simply hold against the spark plug hole, although it takes slightly longer to use. It's worth it to obtain a more accurate reading. Follow the procedures below for gasoline and diesel engined trucks.

GASOLINE ENGINES

1. Warm up the engine to normal operating temperature.
2. Remove all spark plugs.
3. Disconnect the high tension lead from the ignition coil.
4. On fully open the throttle either by operating the carburetor throttle linkage by hand or by having an assistant floor the accelerator pedal.
5. Screw the compression gauge into the no.1 spark plug hole until the fitting is snug.

NOTE: *Be careful not to crossthread the plug hole. On aluminum cylinder heads use extra care, as the threads in these heads are easily ruined.*

6. Ask an assistant to depress the accelerator pedal fully on both carbureted and fuel injected trucks. Then, while you read the compression gauge, ask the assistant to crank the engine two or three times in short bursts using the ignition switch.
7. Read the compression gauge at the end of each series of cranks, and record the highest of these readings. Repeat this procedure for each of the engine's cylinders. Compare the highest reading of each cylinder to the compression pressure specification in the Tune-Up Specifications chart in Chapter 2. The specs in this chart are maximum values.

A cylinder's compression pressure is usually acceptable if it is not less than 80% of maximum. The difference between each cylinder should be no more than 12-14 pounds.

8. If a cylinder is unusually low, pour a tablespoon of clean engine oil into the cylinder through the spark plug hole and repeat the compression test. If the compression comes up after adding the oil, it appears that the cylinder's piston rings or bore are damaged or worn. If the pressure remains low, the valves may not be seating properly (a valve job is needed), or the head gasket may be blown near that cylinder. If compression in any two adjacent cylinders is low, and if the addition of oil doesn't help the compression, there is leakage past the head

Standard Torque Specifications and Fastener Markings

In the absence of specific torques, the following chart can be used as a guide to the maximum safe torque of a particular size/grade of fastener.

- There is no torque difference for fine or coarse threads.
- Torque values are based on clean, dry threads. Reduce the value by 10% if threads are oiled prior to assembly.
- The torque required for aluminum components or fasteners is considerably less.

U.S. Bolts

SAE Grade Number	1 or 2			5			6 or 7		
Number of lines always 2 less than the grade number.									
Bolt Size (Inches)—(Thread)	**Maximum Torque**			**Maximum Torque**			**Maximum Torque**		
	Ft./Lbs.	Kgm	Nm	Ft./Lbs.	Kgm	Nm	Ft./Lbs.	Kgm	Nm
¼ — 20	5	0.7	6.8	8	1.1	10.8	10	1.4	13.5
— 28	6	0.8	8.1	10	1.4	13.6			
5/16 — 18	11	1.5	14.9	17	2.3	23.0	19	2.6	25.8
— 24	13	1.8	17.6	19	2.6	25.7			
⅜ — 16	18	2.5	24.4	31	4.3	42.0	34	4.7	46.0
— 24	20	2.75	27.1	35	4.8	47.5			
7/16 — 14	28	3.8	37.0	49	6.8	66.4	55	7.6	74.5
— 20	30	4.2	40.7	55	7.6	74.5			
½ — 13	39	5.4	52.8	75	10.4	101.7	85	11.75	115.2
— 20	41	5.7	55.6	85	11.7	115.2			
9/16 — 12	51	7.0	69.2	110	15.2	149.1	120	16.6	162.7
— 18	55	7.6	74.5	120	16.6	162.7			
⅝ — 11	83	11.5	112.5	150	20.7	203.3	167	23.0	226.5
— 18	95	13.1	128.8	170	23.5	230.5			
¾ — 10	105	14.5	142.3	270	37.3	366.0	280	38.7	379.6
— 16	115	15.9	155.9	295	40.8	400.0			
⅞ — 9	160	22.1	216.9	395	54.6	535.5	440	60.9	596.5
— 14	175	24.2	237.2	435	60.1	589.7			
1 — 8	236	32.5	318.6	590	81.6	799.9	660	91.3	894.8
— 14	250	34.6	338.9	660	91.3	849.8			

Metric Bolts

Relative Strength Marking	4.6, 4.8			8.8		
Bolt Markings						
Bolt Size Thread Size x Pitch (mm)	**Maximum Torque**			**Maximum Torque**		
	Ft./Lbs.	Kgm	Nm	Ft./Lbs.	Kgm	Nm
6 x 1.0	2–3	.2–.4	3–4	3–6	4–.8	5–8
8 x 1.25	6–8	.8–1	8–12	9–14	1.2–1.9	13–19
10 x 1.25	12–17	1.5–2.3	16–23	20–29	2.7–4.0	27–39
12 x 1.25	21–32	2.9–4.4	29–43	35–53	4.8–7.3	47–72
14 x 1.5	35–52	4.8–7.1	48–70	57–85	7.8–11.7	77–110
16 x 1.5	51–77	7.0–10.6	67–100	90–120	12.4–16.5	130–160
18 x 1.5	74–110	10.2–15.1	100–150	130–170	17.9–23.4	180–230
20 x 1.5	110–140	15.1–19.3	150–190	190–240	26.2–46.9	160–320
22 x 1.5	150–190	22.0–26.2	200–260	250–320	34.5–44.1	340–430
24 x 1.5	190–240	26.2–46.9	260–320	310–410	42.7–56.5	420–550

Test and Procedure	Results and Indications	Proceed to
Attach a vacuum gauge to the intake manifold beyond the throttle plate. Start the engine, and observe the action of the needle over the range of engine speeds.	See below.	**See below**

 INDICATION: normal engine in good condition

Normal engine
Gauge reading: steady, from 17–22 in./Hg.

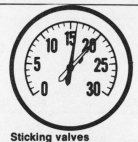 INDICATION: sticking valves or ignition miss

Sticking valves
Gauge reading: intermittent fluctuation at idle

 INDICATION: late ignition or valve timing, low compression, stuck throttle valve, leaking carburetor or manifold gasket

Incorrect valve timing
Gauge reading: low (10–15 in./Hg) but steady

 INDICATION: improper carburetor adjustment or minor intake leak.

Carburetor requires adjustment
Gauge reading: drifting needle

 INDICATION: ignition miss, blown cylinder head gasket, leaking valve or weak valve spring

Blown head gasket
Gauge reading: needle fluctuates as engine speed increases

 INDICATION: burnt valve or faulty valve clearance. Needle will fall when defective valve operates

Burnt or leaking valves
Gauge reading: steady needle, but drops regularly

 INDICATION: choked muffler, excessive back pressure in system

Clogged exhaust system
Gauge reading: gradual drop in reading at idle

 INDICATION: worn valve guides

Worn valve guides
Gauge reading: needle vibrates excessively at idle, but steadies as engine speed increases

White pointer = steady gauge hand

Black pointer = fluctuating gauge hand

gasket. Oil and coolant water in the combustion chamber can result from this problem. There may be evidence of water droplets on the engine dipstick when a head gasket has blown.

DIESEL ENGINES

Checking cylinder compression on diesel engines is basically the same procedure as on gasoline engines except for the following:

1. A special compression gauge adaptor suitable for diesel engines (because these engines have much greater compression pressures) must be used.

2. Remove the injector tubes and remove the injectors from each cylinder.

NOTE: *Don't forget to remove the washer underneath each injector; otherwise, it may get lost when the engine is cranked.*

3. When fitting the compression gauge adaptor to the cylinder head, make sure the bleeder of the gauge (if equipped) is closed.

4. When reinstalling the injector assemblies, install new washers underneath each injector.

Engine Removal and Installation

Most engine repair work may be performed with the engine installed in the car. The only operations that should require removal of the engine are crankshaft removal, or any exten-

The screw-in type compression gauge is more accurate

Diesel engines require a special compression gauge adaptor

sive cylinder block overhaul. Remember than on all 1600, 2000 and 2002 series models, the engine and tranmission should be removed as a unit.

Before setting out to tear out your engine, and tying up both yourself and your BMW, there are a few preliminary steps that should be taken. Jot down those engine and chassis numbers (see Chapter 1) and make a trip to your parts dealer to order all those gaskets, hoses, belts, filters, etc. (i.e., exhaust manifold-to-head pipe flange gasket) that are in need of replacement. This will help avoid last minute or weekend parts dashes that can tie up a car even longer. Also, have enough oil, antifreeze, transmission fluid, etc. (see "Capacities" chart) on hand for the job. If the car is still running, have the engine, engine compartment, and underbody steam cleaned. The less dirt, the better. Have all of the necessary tools together. These should include a sturdy hydraulic jack and a pair of jackstands of sufficient capacity, a chain/pulley engine hoist of sufficient test strength, a wooden block and small jack to support the oil pan or transmission, a can of penetrating fluid to help loosen rusty nuts and bolts, a few jars and plastic containers to store and identify used engine hardware, and a punch or bottle of brush paint to matchmark adjacent parts, to aid in reassembly. Once you have all of your parts, tools, and fluids together, proceed with the task.

Engine
REMOVAL AND INSTALLATION
1600, 2000 and 2002

1. Open the hood and trace the outline of the hood hinge mounts on the hood.

2. Cover the fenders with gender aprons. With the help of an assistant, remove the hood hinge bolts and lift off the hood. Place the hood away from the work area or it may become damaged.

3. Open the drain cocks at the bottom of the radiator and at the rear right hand side of the engine block. Drain the cooling system (remove the radiator cap to speed the process).

CAUTION: *When draining the coolant, keep in mind that cats and dogs are attracted by the ethylene glycol antifreeze, and are quite likely to drink any that is left in an uncovered container or in puddles on the ground. This will prove fatal in sufficient quantity. Always drain the coolant into a sealable container. Coolant should be reused unless it is contaminated or several years old.*

4. Place a drip pan (5 qt. capacity) under the oil pan and remove the engine oil drain plug. Drain the crankcase.

General Engine Specifications

Year	Model	Engine Displacement cu. in. (cc)	Fuel System Type	Net Horsepower @ rpm	Net Torque @ rpm (ft. lbs.)	Bore x Stroke (in.)	Compression Ratio	Oil Pressure @ rpm
1970	1600	96 (1573)	Solex 38 PDSI	105 @ 5500	91 @ 3000	3.307 x 2.795	8.6:1	57 @ 4000
	2000,2002	121 (1990)	Solex 38 PDSI	113 @ 5800	116 @ 3000	3.504 x 3.130	8.5:1	57 @ 4000
	2500	152.1 (2493)	Zenith 35 INAT	170 @ 6000	176 @ 3700	3.386 x 2.820	9.0:1	71 @ 6400
	2800,CS Bavaria	170.1 (2788)	Zenith 35 INAT	192 @ 6000	174 @ 3700	3.386 x 3.150	9.0:1	71 @ 6400
1971	1600	96 (1573)	Solex 38 PDSI	105 @ 5500	91 @ 3000	3.307 x 2.795	8.6:1	57 @ 4000
	2000,2002	121 (1990)	Solex 38 PDSI	113 @ 5800	116 @ 3000	3.504 x 3.130	8.5:1	57 @ 4000
	2500	152.1 (2493)	Zenith 35 INAT	170 @ 6000	176 @ 3700	3.386 x 2.820	9.0:1	71 @ 6400
	2800,CS Bavaria	170.1 (2788)	Zenith 35 INAT	192 @ 6000	174 @ 3700	3.386 x 3.150	9.0:1	71 @ 6400
1972	2000,2002	121 (1990)	Solex 38 PDSI	113 @ 5800	116 @ 3000	3.504 x 3.130	8.5:1	57 @ 4000
	2002Tii	121 (1990)	Kugel Fisher Inj.	125 @ 5500	127 @ 4000	3.504 x 3.130	9.0:1	57 @ 4000
	2800,3000CS Bavaria	170.1 (2788)	Zenith 35 INAT	192 @ 6000	174 @ 3700	3.386 x 3.150	9.0:1	71 @ 6400
1973	2000,2002	121 (1990)	Solex 32 DIPTA	98 @ 5500	100 @ 3500	3.504 x 3.130	8.3:1	57 @ 4000
	2002Tii	121 (1990)	Kugel Fisher Inj.	125 @ 5500	127 @ 4000	3.130 x 3.130	9.0:1	57 @ 4000
	3.0	182 (2985)	Zenith 35 INAT	180 @ 6000	188 @ 3700	3.504 x 3.149	9.0:1	71 @ 6000
1974	2000,2002	121 (1990)	Solex 32 DIPTA	98 @ 5500	100 @ 3500	3.504 x 3.130	8.3:1	57 @ 4000
	2002Tii	121 (1990)	Kugel Fisher Inj.	125 @ 5500	127 @ 4000	3.504 x 3.130	9.0:1	57 @ 4000
	3.0	182 (2985)	Zenith 35 INAT	180 @ 6000	188 @ 3700	3.504 x 3.149	9.0:1	71 @ 6000
1975	2002,Tii	121 (1990)	Solex 32 DIPTA	98 @ 5500	100 @ 3500	3.504 x 3.130	8.3:1	57 @ 4000
	3.0	182 (2985)	EFI ①	200 @ 5500	200 @ 4000	3.504 x 3.149	9.0:1	71 @ 6000
	530i, 630CSi	182 (2985)	EFI ③	176 @ 5500	188 @ 4500	3.504 x 3.150	8.1:1	71 @ 6000
1976	2002,Tii	121 (1990)	Solex 32 DIPTA	98 @ 5500	100 @ 3500	3.504 x 3.130	8.3:1	57 @ 4000
	3.0	182 (2985)	EFI ①	200 @ 5500	200 @ 4000	3.504 x 3.149	9.0:1	71 @ 6000
	530i, 630CSi	182 (2985)	EFI ③	176 @ 5500	188 @ 4500	3.504 x 3.150	8.1:1	71 @ 6000
1977	320i	121 (1990)	EFI ②	110 @ 5800	112 @ 3750	3.504 x 3.150	8.2:1	57 @ 4000
	530i, 630CSi	182 (2985)	EFI ③	176 @ 5500	188 @ 4500	3.504 x 3.150	8.1:1	71 @ 6000
1978	320i	121 (1990)	EFI ②	110 @ 5800	112 @ 3750	3.504 x 3.150	8.2:1	57 @ 4000
	530i, 630CSi	182 (2985)	EFI ③	176 @ 5500	188 @ 4500	3.504 x 3.150	8.1:1	71 @ 6000
	633CSi, 733i	196 (3210)	EFI ③	176 @ 5500	192 @ 4000	3.504 x 3.386	8.0:1	71 @ 6000

General Engine Specifications (cont.)

Year	Model	Engine Displacement cu. in. (cc)	Fuel System Type	Net Horsepower @ rpm	Net Torque @ rpm (ft. lbs.)	Bore x Stroke (in.)	Compression Ratio	Oil Pressure @ rpm
1979	320i	121 (1990)	EFI ②	110 @ 5800	172 @ 3750	3.504 x 3.150	8.2:1	57 @ 4000
	528i	170.1 (2788)	EFI ③	169 @ 5500	166 @ 4500	3.386 x 3.150	8.2:1	71 @ 6000
	633CSi, 733i	196 (3210)	EFI ③	176 @ 5500	192 @ 4000	3.504 x 3.386	8.0:1	71 @ 6000
1980	320i	107 (1766)	EFI ②	101 @ 5800	100 @ 4500	3.504 x 2.793	8.8:1	57 @ 4000
	528i	170.1 (2788)	EFI ③	169 @ 5500	166 @ 4500	3.386 x 3.150	8.2:1	71 @ 6000
	633CSi, 733i	196 (3210)	EFI ③	174 @ 5200	184 @ 4200	3.504 x 3.386	8.0:1	71 @ 6000
1981	320i	107 (1766)	EFI ②	101 @ 5800	100 @ 4500	3.504 x 2.793	8.8:1	57 @ 4000
	528i	170.1 (2788)	EFI ③	169 @ 5500	166 @ 4500	3.386 x 3.150	8.2:1	71 @ 6000
	633CSi, 733i	196 (3210)	EFI ③	174 @ 5200	184 @ 4200	3.504 x 3.386	8.0:1	71 @ 6000
1982	320i	108 (1766)	EFI ④	101 @ 5800	100 @ 4500	3.504 x 2.793	8.8:1	57 @ 4000
	325e	165 (2693)	EFI ④	121 @ 4250	170 @ 3250	3.307 x 3.189	9.0:1	71 @ 5000
	528e	165 (2693)	EFI ④	121 @ 4250	170 @ 3250	3.307 x 3.189	9.0:1	71 @ 5000
	533i	196 (3210)	EFI ④	181 @ 6000	195 @ 4000	3.504 x 3.386	8.8:1	64 @ 4000
	633CSi	196 (3210)	EFI ④	181 @ 6000	195 @ 4000	3.504 x 3.386	8.8:1	64 @ 4000
	733i	196 (3210)	EFI ④	181 @ 6000	195 @ 4000	3.504 x 3.386	8.8:1	64 @ 4000
1983	320i	108 (1766)	EFI ④	101 @ 5800	100 @ 4500	3.504 x 2.793	8.8:1	57 @ 4000
	325e	165 (2693)	EFI ④	121 @ 4250	170 @ 3250	3.307 x 3.189	9.0:1	71 @ 5000
	528e	165 (2693)	EFI ④	121 @ 4250	170 @ 3250	3.307 x 3.189	9.0:1	71 @ 5000
	533i	196 (3210)	EFI ④	181 @ 6000	195 @ 4000	3.504 x 3.386	8.8:1	64 @ 6000
	633CSi	196 (3210)	EFI ④	181 @ 6000	195 @ 4000	3.504 x 3.386	8.8:1	64 @ 6000
	733i	196 (3210)	EFI ④	181 @ 6000	195 @ 4000	3.504 x 3.386	8.8:1	64 @ 6000
1984	318i	108 (1766)	EFI ④	101 @ 5800	103 @ 4500	3.504 x 2.793	9.0:1	64 @ 4000
	325e	165 (2693)	EFI ④	121 @ 4250	170 @ 3250	3.307 x 3.189	9.0:1	71 @ 5000
	528e	165 (2693)	EFI ④	121 @ 4250	170 @ 3250	3.307 x 3.189	9.0:1	71 @ 5000
	533i	196 (3210)	EFI ④	181 @ 6000	195 @ 4000	3.504 x 3.386	8.8:1	64 @ 6000
	633CSi	196 (3210)	EFI ④	181 @ 6000	195 @ 4000	3.504 x 3.386	8.8:1	64 @ 6000
	733i	196 (3210)	EFI ④	181 @ 6000	195 @ 4000	3.504 x 3.386	8.8:1	64 @ 6000
1985	318i	108 (1766)	EFI ④	101 @ 5800	103 @ 4500	3.504 x 2.793	9.0:1	64 @ 4000
	325e	165 (2693)	EFI ④	121 @ 4250	170 @ 3250	3.307 x 3.189	9.0:1	71 @ 5000
	528e	165 (2693)	EFI ④	121 @ 4250	170 @ 3250	3.307 x 3.189	9.0:1	71 @ 5000
	524td	149 (2443)	DFI	114 @ 4800	155 @ 2400	3.15 x 3.19	22:1	71 @ 6000
	533i	196 (3210)	EFI ④	181 @ 6000	195 @ 4000	3.504 x 3.386	8.8:1	64 @ 6000
	633CSi	196 (3210)	EFI ④	181 @ 6000	195 @ 4000	3.504 x 3.386	8.8:1	64 @ 6000
	733i	196 (3210)	EFI ④	181 @ 6000	195 @ 4000	3.504 x 3.386	8.8:1	64 @ 6000
	535i	209 (3428)	EFI ④	182 @ 5400	213 @ 4000	3.62 x 3.38	8.0:1	71 @ 6000
	635CSi	209 (3428)	EFI ④	182 @ 5400	213 @ 4000	3.62 x 3.38	8.0:1	71 @ 6000
	735i	209 (3428)	EFI ④	182 @ 5400	213 @ 4000	3.62 x 3.38	8.0:1	71 @ 6000
1986	325e	165 (2693)	EFI ④	121 @ 4250	170 @ 3250	3.307 x 3.189	9.0:1	71 @ 5000
	528e	165 (2693)	EFI ④	121 @ 4250	170 @ 3250	3.307 x 3.189	9.0:1	71 @ 5000
	524td	149 (2443)	DFI	114 @ 4800	155 @ 2400	3.15 x 3.19	22:1	71 @ 6000

General Engine Specifications (cont.)

Year	Model	Engine Displacement cu. in. (cc)	Fuel System Type	Net Horsepower @ rpm	Net Torque @ rpm (ft. lbs.)	Bore x Stroke (in.)	Compression Ratio	Oil Pressure @ rpm
1986	535i	209 (3428)	EFI④	182 @ 5400	213 @ 4000	3.62 x 3.38	8.0:1	71 @ 6000
	635CSi	209 (3428)	EFI④	182 @ 5400	213 @ 4000	3.62 x 3.38	8.0:1	71 @ 6000
	735i	209 (3428)	EFI④	182 @ 5400	213 @ 4000	3.62 x 3.38	8.0:1	71 @ 6000
1987	325	165 (2693)	EFI④	121 @ 4250	170 @ 3250	3.307 x 3.189	9.0:1	71 @ 5000
	528e	165 (2693)	EFI④	121 @ 4250	170 @ 3250	3.307 x 3.189	9.0:1	71 @ 5000
	325iS	152 (2494)	EFI④	167 @ 5800	164 @ 4300	3.307 x 2.953	8.8:1	71 @ 5000
	325iS	152 (2494)	EFI④	167 @ 5800	164 @ 4300	3.307 x 2.953	8.8:1	71 @ 5000
	535i	209 (3428)	EFI④	182 @ 5400	213 @ 4000	3.62 x 3.38	8.0:1	71 @ 6000
	635CSi	209 (3428)	EFI④	208 @ 5700	225 @ 4000	3.62 x 3.38	9.0:1	64 @ 6200
	735i	209 (3428)	EFI④	208 @ 5700	225 @ 4000	3.62 x 3.38	9.0:1	64 @ 6200
	M5	210.6 (3453)	EFI④	256 @ 6500	239 @ 4500	3.67 x 3.30	9.8:1	71 @ 6900
	M6	210.6 (3453)	EFI④	256 @ 6500	239 @ 4500	3.67 x 3.30	9.8:1	71 @ 6900
1988	325	165 (2693)	EFI④	121 @ 4250	170 @ 3250	3.307 x 3.189	9.0:1	71 @ 5000
	528e	165 (2693)	EFI④	121 @ 4250	170 @ 3250	3.307 x 3.189	9.0:1	71 @ 5000
	325i	152 (2494)	EFI④	167 @ 5800	164 @ 4300	3.307 x 2.953	8.8:1	71 @ 6000
	325iS	152 (2494)	EFI④	167 @ 5800	164 @ 4300	3.307 x 2.953	8.8:1	71 @ 6000
	325iX	152 (2494)	EFI④	167 @ 5800	164 @ 4300	3.307 x 2.953	8.8:1	71 @ 6000
	535i	209 (3428)	EFI④	182 @ 5400	213 @ 4000	3.62 x 3.38	8.0:1	71 @ 6100
	635CSi	209 (3428)	EFI④	208 @ 5700	225 @ 4000	3.62 x 3.38	9.0:1	64 @ 6200
	L6	209 (3428)	EFI④	208 @ 5700	225 @ 4000	3.62 x 3.38	9.0:1	64 @ 6200
	735i	209 (3428)	EFI④	208 @ 5700	225 @ 4000	3.62 x 3.38	9.0:1	64 @ 6200
	M3	104.4 (2302)	EFI④	194 @ 6750	166 @ 4750	3.67 x 3.30	10.5:1	71 @ 7250
	M5	210.6 (3453)	EFI④	256 @ 6500	239 @ 4500	3.67 x 3.30	9.8:1	71 @ 6800
	M6	210.6 (3453)	EFI④	256 @ 6500	239 @ 4500	3.67 x 3.30	9.8:1	71 @ 6800

EFI Electronic Fuel Injection
DFI Diesel Fuel Injection
① EFI—Bosch Electronic Injection
② EFI—Bosch K-Jetronic Fuel Injection
③ EFI—Bosch L-Jetronic Fuel Injection
④ EFI—Bosch Motronic Injection

Valve Specifications

Year	Engine Displacement cu. in. (cc)	Seat Angle (deg.)	Face Angle (deg.)	Spring Test Pressure (lbs.)	Spring Installed Height (in.)	Stem-to-Guide Clearance (in.) Intake	Stem-to-Guide Clearance (in.) Exhaust	Stem Diameter (in.) Intake	Stem Diameter (in.) Exhaust
1970–72	96 (1573)	45	45.5	64 @ 1.48	1.171 ①	0.0010–0.0020	0.0015–0.0030	0.3149	0.3149
	121 (1990)	45	45.5	64 @ 1.48	1.171 ①	0.0010–0.0020	0.0015–0.0030	0.3149	0.3149
	152.1 (2493)	45	45.5	64 @ 1.48	1.171 ①	0.0010–0.0020	0.0015–0.0030	0.3149	0.3149
	170.1 (2788)	45	45.5	64 @ 1.48	1.171 ①	0.0010–0.0020	0.0015–0.0030	0.3149	0.3149

Valve Specifications (cont.)

Year	Engine Displacement cu. in. (cc)	Seat Angle (deg.)	Face Angle (deg.)	Spring Test Pressure (lbs.)	Spring Installed Height (in.)	Stem-to-Guide Clearance (in.)		Stem Diameter (in.)	
						Intake	Exhaust	Intake	Exhaust
1973–76	121 (1990)	45	45.5	64 @ 1.48	1.171 ①	0.0010–0.0020	0.0015–0.0030	0.3149	0.3149
	170.1 (2788)	45	45.5	64 @ 1.48	1.171 ①	0.0010–0.0020	0.0015–0.0030	0.3149	0.3149
	182 (2985)	45	45.5	64 @ 1.48	1.171 ①	0.0010–0.0020	0.0015–0.0030	0.3149	0.3149
1977–81	121 (1990)	45	45.5	64 @ 1.48	1.171 ①	0.0010–0.0020	0.0015–0.0030	0.3149	0.3149
	107 (1766)	45	45.5	64 @ 1.48	1.171 ①	0.0010–0.0020	0.0015–0.0030	0.3149	0.3149
	182 (2985)	45	45.5	64 @ 1.48	1.171 ①	0.0010–0.0020	0.0015–0.0030	0.3149	0.3149
	170.1 (2788)	45	45.5	64 @ 1.48	1.171 ①	0.0010–0.0020	0.0015–0.0030	0.3149	0.3149
	196 (3210)	45	45.5	64 @ 1.48	1.171 ①	0.0010–0.0020	0.0015–0.0030	0.3149	0.3149
1982	108 (1766)	45	45.5	64 @ 1.48	1.71 ①	0.0010–0.0020 ②	0.0010–0.0020 ②	0.3149	0.3149
	165 (2693)	45	45	NA	NA	0.006	0.006	0.275	0.275
	196 (3210)	45	45.5	64 @ 1.48	1.71 ①	0.0010–0.0020 ②	0.0010–0.0020 ②	0.3149	0.3149
1983	108 (1766)	45	45.5	64 @ 1.48	1.71 ①	0.0010–0.0020 ②	0.0010–0.0020 ②	0.3149	0.3149
	165 (2693)	45	45	NA	NA	0.031 ③	0.031 ③	0.3149	0.3149
	196 (3210)	45	45.5	64 @ 1.48	1.71 ①	0.031 ③	0.031 ③	0.3149	0.3149
1984	108 (1766)	45	45.5	64 @ 1.48	1.71 ①	0.031 ③	0.031 ③	0.3149	0.3149
	165 (2693)	45	45	NA	NA	0.031 ③	0.031 ③	0.275	0.275
	196 (3210)	45	45.5	64 @ 1.48	1.71 ①	0.031 ③	0.031 ③	0.3149	0.3149
1985	108 (1766)	45	45.5	64 @ 1.48	1.71 ①	0.031 ③	0.031 ③	0.3149	0.3149
	149 (2443)	45	NA	NA	NA	0.031 ③	0.031 ③	0.275	0.275
	165 (2693)	45	45	NA	NA	0.031 ③	0.031 ③	0.275	0.275
	209 (3248)	45	45.5	64 @ 1.48	1.71 ①	0.031 ③	0.031 ③	0.3149	0.3149
1986	149 (2443)	45	NA	NA	NA	0.031 ③	0.031 ③	0.275	0.275
	165 (2693)	45	45	NA	NA	0.031 ③	0.031 ③	0.275	0.275
	209 (3248)	45	45.5	64 @ 1.48	1.71 ①	0.031 ③	0.031 ③	0.3149	0.3149
1987	152 (2494)	45	45.5	64 @ 1.48	1.71 ①	0.031 ③	0.031 ③	0.3149	0.3149
	165 (2693)	45	45	NA	NA	0.031 ③	0.031 ③	0.275	0.275
	209 (3428)	45	45.5	64 @ 1.48	1.71 ①	0.031 ③	0.031 ③	0.3149	0.3149
	210.6 (3453)	45	NA	NA	NA	0.025 ③	0.031 ③	0.276	0.276
1988	140.4 (2302)	45	NA	NA	NA	0.025 ③	0.031 ③	0.276	0.276
	152 (2494)	45	NA	NA	NA	0.031 ③	0.031 ③	0.275	0.275

Valve Specifications (cont.)

Year	Engine Displacement cu. in. (cc)	Seat Angle (deg.)	Face Angle (deg.)	Spring Test Pressure (lbs.)	Spring Installed Height (in.)	Stem-to-Guide Clearance (in.)		Stem Diameter (in.)	
						Intake	Exhaust	Intake	Exhaust
1988	165 (2693)	45	NA	NA	NA	0.031 ③	0.031 ③	0.275	0.275
	209 (3248)	45	NA	NA	NA	0.031 ③	0.031 ③	0.315	0.315
	210.6 (3453)	45	NA	NA	NA	0.025 ③	0.031 ③	0.276	0.276
	304 (4988)	45	NA	NA	NA	0.020 ③	0.020 ③	0.275	0.275

① A dimension of 1.8110 applies to some springs, depending upon manufacturer. Figure given is free height
② Wear limit: .006 in.
③ Tilt clearance

Crankshaft and Connecting Rod Specifications
All measurements are given in inches.

Year	Engine Displacement cu. in. (cc)	Crankshaft				Connecting Rod		
		Main Brg. Journal Dia.	Main Brg. Oil Clearance	Shaft End-play	Thrust on No.	Journal Diameter	Oil Clearance	Side Clearance
1970–72	96 (1573)	2.3622 ③	0.0012–0.0027	0.003–0.007	④	1.8898	0.0009–0.0027	0.0016
	121 (1990)	2.3622 ③	0.0012–0.0027	0.003–0.007	④	1.8898	0.0009–0.0027	0.0016
	152.1 (2493)	2.3622 ③	0.0012–0.0027	0.003–0.007	④	1.8898	0.0013–0.0027	0.0016
	170.1 (2788)	2.3622 ③	0.0012–0.0027	0.003–0.007	④	1.8898	0.0013–0.0027	0.0016
1973–76	121 (1990)	2.3622 ③	0.0012–0.0027	0.003–0.007	④	1.8898	0.0009–0.0031	0.0016
	170.1 (2788)	2.3622 ③	0.0012–0.0027	0.003–0.007	④	1.8898	0.0013–0.0027	0.0016
	182 (2985)	2.3622 ③	0.0012–0.0077	0.003–0.007	④	1.8898	0.0013–0.0027	0.0016
1977–81	121 (1990)	2.3622 ③	0.0012–0.0027	0.003–0.007	④	1.8898	0.0009–0.0027	0.0016
	107 (1766)	2.3622 ③	0.0012–0.0027	0.003–0.007	④	1.8898	0.0009–0.0031	0.0016
	182 (2985)	2.3622 ③	0.0012–0.0027	0.003–0.007	④	1.8898	0.0013–0.0027	0.0016
	170.1 (2788)	2.3622 ③	0.0012–0.0027	0.003–0.007	④	1.8898	0.0009–0.0027	0.0016
	196 (3210)	2.3622 ③	0.0012–0.0027	0.003–0.007	④	1.8898	0.0009–0.0031	0.0016
1982	108 (1766)	2.3622	0.0012–0.0027	0.003–0.007	3	1.8898	①	0.0016
	165 (2693)	2.3622	0.0012–0.0027	0.003–0.007	4	1.8898	①	0.0016
	196 (3210)	2.3622	0.0012–0.0027	0.003–0.007	4	1.8898	①	0.0016
1983	108 (1766)	2.3622	0.0012–0.0027	0.003–0.007	3	1.8898	0.0012–0.0028	0.0016
	165 (2693)	2.3622	0.0012–0.0027	0.003–0.007	4	1.7717	0.0012–0.0028	0.0016

Crankshaft and Connecting Rod Specifications (cont.)

All measurements are given in inches.

Year	Engine Displacement cu. in. (cc)	Crankshaft				Connecting Rod		
		Main Brg. Journal Dia.	Main Brg. Oil Clearance	Shaft End-play	Thrust on No.	Journal Diameter	Oil Clearance	Side Clearance
1983	196 (3210)	2.3622	0.0012–0.0027	0.003–0.007	4	1.8898	0.0012–0.0028	0.0016
1984	108 (1766)	2.1654	0.0012–0.0027	0.003–0.007	3	1.8898	0.0012–0.0028	0.0016
	165 (2693)	2.3622	0.0012–0.0027	0.003–0.007	4	1.7717	0.0012–0.0028	0.0016
	196 (3210)	2.3622	0.0012–0.0027	0.003–0.007	4	1.8898	0.0012–0.0028	0.0016
1985	108 (1766)	2.1654	0.0012–0.0027	0.003–0.007	3	1.8898	0.0012–0.0028	0.0016
	149 (2443)	②	0.0008–0.0018	0.0031–0.0064	4	1.7707–1.7713	0.0008–0.0022	—
	165 (2693)	2.3622	0.0012–0.0027	0.003–0.007	4	1.7717	0.0012–0.0028	0.0016
	209 (3428)	2.3622	0.0012–0.0027	0.003–0.007	4	1.8898	0.0012–0.0028	0.0016
1986	149 (2443)	②	0.0008–0.0018	0.0031–0.0064	4	1.7707–1.7713	0.0008–0.0022	0.0016
	165 (2693)	2.3622	0.0012–0.0027	0.003–0.007	4	1.7717	0.0012–0.0028	0.0016
	209 (3428)	2.3622	0.0012–0.0027	0.003–0.007	4	1.8898	0.0012–0.0028	0.0016
1987	152 (2494)	2.3622	0.0012–0.0027	0.030–0.007	4	1.7717	0.0012–0.0028	0.0016
	165 (2693)	2.3622	0.0012–0.0027	0.003–0.007	4	1.7717	0.0012–0.0028	0.0016
	209 (3428)	2.3622	0.0012–0.0027	0.003–0.007	4	1.8898	0.0012–0.0028	0.0016
	210.6 (3453)	2.3622	0.0012–0.0027	0.003–0.007	4	1.88877–1.88940	0.0012–0.0028	0.0016
1988	140.4 (2302)	2.1653	0.0012–0.0028	0.0033–0.0068	3	1.88877–1.88940	0.0012–0.0028	0.0016
	152 (2494)	2.3622	0.0012–0.0027	0.0033–0.0068	4	1.7717	0.0012–0.0028	0.0016
	165 (2693)	2.3622	0.0012–0.0027	0.0033–0.0068	4	1.7717	0.0012–0.0028	0.0016
	209 (3428)	2.3622	0.0012–0.0027	0.0033–0.0068	4	1.8898	0.0012–0.0028	0.0016
	210.6 (3453)	2.3622	0.0012–0.0027	0.0033–0.0068	4	1.88877–1.88940	0.0012–0.0028	0.0016
	304 (4988)	2.9521–2.9523	0.0010–0.0030	0.0033–0.0068	—	1.7707–1.7713	0.0006–0.0023	0.0016

NOTE: BMW does not specify side clearance. The figure given expresses maximum permissible deviation from parallel of connecting rod bearing bores, with the shells 150mm or 5.905 in. apart

① 528i, 530i, 533i, 630CSi—0.0009–0.0027
   320i, 733i—0.0009–0.0031
   528e—0.0013–0.0027
② Yellow—2.3616–2.3618
   Green—2.3613–2.3615

White—2.3611–2.3613
③ 1970–76 four cylinder models: 2.1654
④ Four cylinder models: 3
   Six cylinder models: 4

Piston and Ring Specifications (cont.)

All measurements are given in inches.

Year	Engine Displacement cu. in. (cc)	Piston Clearance	Ring Gap			Ring Side Clearance		
			Top Compression	Bottom Compression	Oil Control	Top Compression	Bottom Compression	Oil Control
1970	96 (1573)	0.0018	0.008– 0.020	0.008– 0.016	0.010– 0.016	0.002– 0.003	0.001– 0.002	0.001– 0.002
	121 (1990)	0.0018	0.012– 0.018	0.008– 0.016	0.010– 0.020	0.002– 0.004	0.002– 0.003	0.001– 0.002
	152.1 (2493)	0.0016	0.012– 0.018	0.012– 0.018	0.010– 0.016	0.0006– 0.0011	0.0005– 0.0009	0.0004– 0.001
	170.1 (2788)	0.0016	0.012– 0.018	0.012– 0.018	0.010– 0.016	0.0006– 0.0011	0.0005– 0.0009	0.0004– 0.001
1971	96 (1573)	0.0018	0.008– 0.020	0.008– 0.016	0.010– 0.016	0.002– 0.003	0.001– 0.002	0.001– 0.002
	121 (1990)	0.0018	0.012– 0.018	0.008– 0.016	0.010– 0.020	0.002– 0.004	0.002– 0.003	0.001– 0.002
	152.1 (2493)	0.0016	0.012– 0.018	0.012– 0.018	0.010– 0.016	0.0006– 0.0011	0.0005– 0.0009	0.0004– 0.001
	170.1 (2788)	0.0016	0.012– 0.018	0.012– 0.018	0.010– 0.016	0.0006– 0.0011	0.0005– 0.0009	0.0004– 0.001
1972	121 (1990)	0.0018	0.012– 0.018	0.008– 0.016	0.010– 0.020	0.002– 0.004	0.002– 0.003	0.001– 0.002
	170.1 (2788)	0.0016	0.012– 0.018	0.012– 0.018	0.010– 0.016	0.0006– 0.0011	0.002– 0.003	0.001– 0.002
1973	121 (1990)	0.0018	0.012– 0.018	0.008– 0.016	0.010– 0.020	0.002– 0.004	0.002– 0.003	0.001– 0.002
	170.1 (2788)	0.0016	0.012– 0.018	0.012– 0.018	0.010– 0.016	0.0006– 0.0011	0.0005– 0.0009	0.0004– 0.001
	182 (2985)	0.0016	0.012– 0.018	0.008– 0.018	0.010– 0.016	0.0024– 0.0036	0.0012– 0.0024	0.001– 0.002
1974	121 (1990)	0.0018	0.012– 0.018	0.008– 0.016	0.010– 0.020	0.002– 0.004	0.002– 0.003	0.001– 0.002
	170.1 (2788)	0.0016	0.012– 0.018	0.012– 0.018	0.010– 0.016	0.0006– 0.0011	0.0005– 0.0009	0.0004– 0.001
	182 (2985)	0.0016	0.012– 0.018	0.008– 0.018	0.010– 0.016	0.0024– 0.0036	0.0012– 0.0024	0.001– 0.002
1975	121 (1990)	0.0018	0.0012– 0.018	0.008– 0.016	0.010– 0.020	0.002– 0.004	0.002– 0.003	0.001– 0.002
	182 (2985)	0.0016	0.012– 0.018	0.008– 0.018	0.010– 0.016	0.0024– 0.0036	0.0012– 0.0024	0.001– 0.002
1976	121 (1990)	0.0018	0.0012– 0.018	0.008– 0.016	0.010– 0.020	0.002– 0.004	0.002– 0.003	0.001– 0.002
	182 (2985)	0.0016	0.012– 0.018	0.008– 0.018	0.010– 0.016	0.0024– 0.0036	0.0012– 0.0024	0.001– 0.002
1977	121 (1990)	0.0018	0.0012– 0.018	0.008– 0.016	0.010– 0.020	0.002– 0.004	0.002– 0.003	0.001– 0.002
	182 (2985)	0.0016	0.012– 0.018	0.008– 0.018	0.010– 0.016	0.0024– 0.0036	0.0012– 0.0024	0.001– 0.002
1978	121 (1990)	0.0018	0.0012– 0.018	0,008– 0.016	0.010– 0.020	0.002– 0.004	0.002– 0.003	0.001– 0.002
	182 (2985)	0.0016	0.012– 0.018	0.008– 0.018	0.010– 0.016	0.0024– 0.0036	0.0012– 0.0024	0.001– 0.002

Piston and Ring Specifications (cont.)

All measurements are given in inches.

Year	Engine Displacement cu. in. (cc)	Piston Clearance	Ring Gap			Ring Side Clearance		
			Top Compression	Bottom Compression	Oil Control	Top Compression	Bottom Compression	Oil Control
1978	196 (3210)	0.0018	0.012–0.020	0.008–0.016	0.010–0.016	0.0024–0.0036	0.0012–0.0024	0.0008–0.0028
1979	121 (1990)	0.0018	0.012–0.018	0.008–0.016	0.010–0.020	0.002–0.004	0.002–0.003	0.001–0.002
	170.1 (2788)	0.0016	0.012–0.018	0.012–0.018	0.010–0.016	0.0006–0.0011	0.0005–0.0009	0.0004–0.001
	196 (3210)	0.0018	0.012–0.020	0.008–0.016	0.010–0.016	0.0024–0.0036	0.0012–0.0024	0.0008–0.0020
1980	107 (1766)	0.0018	0.012–0.018	0.008–0.016	0.010–0.020	0.002–0.008	0.002–0.003	0.001–0.002
	170.1 (2788)	0.0016	0.012–0.018	0.012–0.018	0.010–0.016	0.0006–0.0011	0.0005–0.0009	0.0004–0.001
	196 (3210)	0.0018	0.012–0.020	0.008–0.016	0.010–0.016	0.0024–0.0036	0.0012–0.0024	0.0008–0.0020
1981	107 (1766)	0.0018	0.012–0.018	0.008–0.016	0.010–0.020	0.002–0.004	0.002–0.003	0.001–0.002
	170.1 (2788)	0.0016	0.012–0.018	0.012–0.018	0.010–0.016	0.0006–0.0011	0.0005–0.0009	0.0004–0.001
	196 (3210)	0.0018	0.012–0.020	0.008–0.016	0.010–0.016	0.0024–0.0036	0.0012–0.0024	0.0008–0.0020
1982	108 (1766)	0.0018	0.0120–0.0180	0.0080–0.0160	0.0100–0.0200	0.002–0.004	0.002–0.003	0.001–0.002
	165 (2693)	0.0004–0.0016	0.0120–0.0200	0.0120–0.0200	0.0100–0.0200	0.0016–0.0028	0.0012–0.0024	0.0008–0.0017
	196 (3210)	0.0018	0.0120–0.0200	0.0080–0.0160	0.0024–0.0036	②	①	—
1983	108 (1766)	0.0018	0.0120–0.0180	0.0080–0.0160	0.0100–0.0200	0.002–0.004	0.002–0.003	0.001–0.002
	165 (2693)	0.0004–0.0016	0.0120–0.0200	0.0120–0.0200	0.0100–0.0200	0.0016–0.0028	0.0012–0.0024	0.0008–0.0017
	196 (3210)	0.0008–0.0020	0.0120–0.0280	0.0080–0.0160	0.0100–0.0200	0.0020–0.0032	0.0016–0.0028	0.0008–0.0028
1984	108 (1766)	0.0008–0.0020	0.0120–0.0280	0.0080–0.0160	0.0100–0.0200	0.0024–0.0035	0.0012–0.0028	0.0008–0.0024
	165 (2693)	0.0004–0.0016	0.0120–0.0200	0.0120–0.0200	0.0100–0.0200	0.0016–0.0028	0.0012–0.0024	0.0008–0.0017
	196 (3210)	0.0008–0.0020	0.0120–0.0280	0.0080–0.0160	0.0100–0.0200	0.0020–0.0032	0.0016–0.0028	0.0008–0.0028
1985	108 (1766)	0.0008–0.0020	0.0120–0.0280	0.0080–0.0160	0.0100–0.0200	0.0024–0.0035	0.0012–0.0028	0.0008–0.0024
	149 (2443)	0.0010–0.0013	0.0008–0.0016	0.0080–0.0160	0.0100–0.0200	0.0024–0.0025	0.0020–0.0031	0.0012–0.0024
	165 (2693)	0.0004–0.0016	0.0120–0.0200	0.0120–0.0200	0.0100–0.0200	0.0016–0.0028	0.0012–0.0024	0.0008–0.0017
	209 (3428)	0.0008–0.0020	0.0120–0.0020	0.0080–0.0160	0.0100–0.0200	0.020–0.032	0.0016–0.0028	0.0008–0.0020
1986	149 (2443)	0.0008–0.0020	0.0120–0.0200	0.0080–0.0160	0.0100–0.0200	0.020–0.032	0.0016–0.0028	0.0008–0.0020

Piston and Ring Specifications (cont.)

All measurements are given in inches.

Year	Engine Displacement cu. in. (cc)	Piston Clearance	Ring Gap			Ring Side Clearance		
			Top Compression	Bottom Compression	Oil Control	Top Compression	Bottom Compression	Oil Control
1986	165 (2693)	0.0004–0.0016	0.0120–0.0200	0.0120–0.0200	0.0100–0.0200	0.0016–0.0028	0.0012–0.0024	0.0008–0.0017
	209 (3428)	0.0008–0.0020	0.0120–0.0020	0.0080–0.0160	0.0100–0.0200	0.020–0.032	0.0016–0.0028	0.0008–0.0020
1987	152 (2494)	0.0004–0.0016	0.0120–0.0200	0.0120–0.0200	0.0100–0.0200	0.0016–0.0028	0.0012–0.0024	0.0008–0.0017
	165 (2693)	0.0004–0.0016	0.0120–0.0200	0.0120–0.0200	0.0100–0.0200	0.0016–0.0028	0.0012–0.0024	0.0008–0.0017
	209 (3428)	0.0008–0.0020	0.0120–0.0200	0.0080–0.0160	0.0100–0.0200	0.020–0.032	0.0016–0.0028	0.0008–0.0020
	210.6 (3453)	0.0012–0.0024	0.0120–0.0220	0.0120–0.0220	0.0100–0.0200	0.0024–0.0035	0.0024–0.0035	0.0008–0.0020
1988	140 (2302)	0.0012–0.0024	0.0120–0.0220	0.0120–0.0220	0.0100–0.0200	0.0024–0.0035	0.0024–0.0035	0.0008–0.0020
	152 (2494)	0.0004–0.0016	0.0120–0.0200	0.0120–0.0200	0.0100–0.0200	0.0016–0.0028	0.0012–0.0024	0.0008–0.0017
	165 (2693)	0.0004–0.0016	0.0120–0.0200	0.0120–0.0200	0.0100–0.0200	0.0016–0.0028	0.0012–0.0024	0.0008–0.0017
	209 (3428) ③	0.0008–0.0020	0.0120–0.0200	0.0080–0.0160	0.0100–0.0200	0.020–0.032	0.0016–0.0028	0.0008–0.0020
	209 (3428) ④	0.0008–0.0020	0.008–0.018	0.016–0.026	0.016–0.024	0.0016–0.0028	0.0012–0.0024	0.0008–0.0022
	210.6 (3453)	0.0012–0.0024	0.0120–0.0220	0.0120–0.0220	0.0100–0.0200	0.0024–0.0035	0.0024–0.0035	0.0008–0.0020
	304 (4988)	0.0004–0.0013	0.0080–0.0160	0.008–0.016	0.0100–0.0200	0.0016–0.0025	0.0012–0.0028	0.0008–0.0022

① Mahle: .0008–.0020
KS: .0012–.0024
② Mahle: .0020–.0032

KS: .0016–.0028
③ B34 used in 535i
④ B35 used in 6 and 7 series cars

Troubleshooting the Serpentine Drive Belt

Problem	Cause	Solution
Tension sheeting fabric failure (woven fabric on outside circumference of belt has cracked or separated from body of belt)	• Grooved or backside idler pulley diameters are less than minimum recommended • Tension sheeting contacting (rubbing) stationary object • Excessive heat causing woven fabric to age • Tension sheeting splice has fractured	• Replace pulley(s) not conforming to specification • Correct rubbing condition • Replace belt • Replace belt
Noise (objectional squeal, squeak, or rumble is heard or felt while drive belt is in operation)	• Belt slippage • Bearing noise • Belt misalignment • Belt-to-pulley mismatch • Driven component inducing vibration • System resonant frequency inducing vibration	• Adjust belt • Locate and repair • Align belt/pulley(s) • Install correct belt • Locate defective driven component and repair • Vary belt tension within specifications. Replace belt.

Troubleshooting the Serpentine Drive Belt (cont.)

Problem	Cause	Solution
Rib chunking (one or more ribs has separated from belt body)	• Foreign objects imbedded in pulley grooves • Installation damage • Drive loads in excess of design specifications • Insufficient internal belt adhesion	• Remove foreign objects from pulley grooves • Replace belt • Adjust belt tension • Replace belt
Rib or belt wear (belt ribs contact bottom of pulley grooves)	• Pulley(s) misaligned • Mismatch of belt and pulley groove widths • Abrasive environment • Rusted pulley(s) • Sharp or jagged pulley groove tips • Rubber deteriorated	• Align pulley(s) • Replace belt • Replace belt • Clean rust from pulley(s) • Replace pulley • Replace belt
Longitudinal belt cracking (cracks between two ribs)	• Belt has mistracked from pulley groove • Pulley groove tip has worn away rubber-to-tensile member	• Replace belt • Replace belt
Belt slips	• Belt slipping because of insufficient tension • Belt or pulley subjected to substance (belt dressing, oil, ethylene glycol) that has reduced friction • Driven component bearing failure • Belt glazed and hardened from heat and excessive slippage	• Adjust tension • Replace belt and clean pulleys • Replace faulty component bearing • Replace belt
"Groove jumping" (belt does not maintain correct position on pulley, or turns over and/or runs off pulleys)	• Insufficient belt tension • Pulley(s) not within design tolerance • Foreign object(s) in grooves • Excessive belt speed • Pulley misalignment • Belt-to-pulley profile mismatched • Belt cordline is distorted	• Adjust belt tension • Replace pulley(s) • Remove foreign objects from grooves • Avoid excessive engine acceleration • Align pulley(s) • Install correct belt • Replace belt
Belt broken (Note: identify and correct problem before replacement belt is installed)	• Excessive tension • Tensile members damaged during belt installation • Belt turnover • Severe pulley misalignment • Bracket, pulley, or bearing failure	• Replace belt and adjust tension to specification • Replace belt • Replace belt • Align pulley(s) • Replace defective component and belt
Cord edge failure (tensile member exposed at edges of belt or separated from belt body)	• Excessive tension • Drive pulley misalignment • Belt contacting stationary object • Pulley irregularities • Improper pulley construction • Insufficient adhesion between tensile member and rubber matrix	• Adjust belt tension • Align pulley • Correct as necessary • Replace pulley • Replace pulley • Replace belt and adjust tension to specifications
Sporadic rib cracking (multiple cracks in belt ribs at random intervals)	• Ribbed pulley(s) diameter less than minimum specification • Backside bend flat pulley(s) diameter less than minimum • Excessive heat condition causing rubber to harden • Excessive belt thickness • Belt overcured • Excessive tension	• Replace pulley(s) • Replace pulley(s) • Correct heat condition as necessary • Replace belt • Replace belt • Adjust belt tension

Troubleshooting Engine Mechanical Problems

Problem	Cause	Solution
External oil leaks	• Fuel pump gasket broken or improperly seated	• Replace gasket
	• Cylinder head cover RTV sealant broken or improperly seated	• Replace sealant; inspect cylinder head cover sealant flange and cylinder head sealant surface for distortion and cracks
	• Oil filler cap leaking or missing	• Replace cap
	• Oil filter gasket broken or improperly seated	• Replace oil filter
	• Oil pan side gasket broken, improperly seated or opening in RTV sealant	• Replace gasket or repair opening in sealant; inspect oil pan gasket flange for distortion
	• Oil pan front oil seal broken or improperly seated	• Replace seal; inspect timing case cover and oil pan seal flange for distortion
	• Oil pan rear oil seal broken or improperly seated	• Replace seal; inspect oil pan rear oil seal flange; inspect rear main bearing cap for cracks, plugged oil return channels, or distortion in seal groove
	• Timing case cover oil seal broken or improperly seated	• Replace seal
	• Excess oil pressure because of restricted PCV valve	• Replace PCV valve
	• Oil pan drain plug loose or has stripped threads	• Repair as necessary and tighten
	• Rear oil gallery plug loose	• Use appropriate sealant on gallery plug and tighten
	• Rear camshaft plug loose or improperly seated	• Seat camshaft plug or replace and seal, as necessary
	• Distributor base gasket damaged	• Replace gasket
Excessive oil consumption	• Oil level too high	• Drain oil to specified level
	• Oil with wrong viscosity being used	• Replace with specified oil
	• PCV valve stuck closed	• Replace PCV valve
	• Valve stem oil deflectors (or seals) are damaged, missing, or incorrect type	• Replace valve stem oil deflectors
	• Valve stems or valve guides worn	• Measure stem-to-guide clearance and repair as necessary
	• Poorly fitted or missing valve cover baffles	• Replace valve cover
	• Piston rings broken or missing	• Replace broken or missing rings
	• Scuffed piston	• Replace piston
	• Incorrect piston ring gap	• Measure ring gap, repair as necessary
	• Piston rings sticking or excessively loose in grooves	• Measure ring side clearance, repair as necessary
	• Compression rings installed upside down	• Repair as necessary
	• Cylinder walls worn, scored, or glazed	• Repair as necessary
	• Piston ring gaps not properly staggered	• Repair as necessary
	• Excessive main or connecting rod bearing clearance	• Measure bearing clearance, repair as necessary
No oil pressure	• Low oil level	• Add oil to correct level
	• Oil pressure gauge, warning lamp or sending unit inaccurate	• Replace oil pressure gauge or warning lamp
	• Oil pump malfunction	• Replace oil pump
	• Oil pressure relief valve sticking	• Remove and inspect oil pressure relief valve assembly
	• Oil passages on pressure side of pump obstructed	• Inspect oil passages for obstruction

Troubleshooting Engine Mechanical Problems (cont.)

Problem	Cause	Solution
No oil pressure (cont.)	• Oil pickup screen or tube obstructed • Loose oil inlet tube	• Inspect oil pickup for obstruction • Tighten or seal inlet tube
Low oil pressure	• Low oil level • Inaccurate gauge, warning lamp or sending unit • Oil excessively thin because of dilution, poor quality, or improper grade • Excessive oil temperature • Oil pressure relief spring weak or sticking • Oil inlet tube and screen assembly has restriction or air leak • Excessive oil pump clearance • Excessive main, rod, or camshaft bearing clearance	• Add oil to correct level • Replace oil pressure gauge or warning lamp • Drain and refill crankcase with recommended oil • Correct cause of overheating engine • Remove and inspect oil pressure relief valve assembly • Remove and inspect oil inlet tube and screen assembly. (Fill inlet tube with lacquer thinner to locate leaks.) • Measure clearances • Measure bearing clearances, repair as necessary
High oil pressure	• Improper oil viscosity • Oil pressure gauge or sending unit inaccurate • Oil pressure relief valve sticking closed	• Drain and refill crankcase with correct viscosity oil • Replace oil pressure gauge • Remove and inspect oil pressure relief valve assembly
Main bearing noise	• Insufficient oil supply • Main bearing clearance excessive • Bearing insert missing • Crankshaft end play excessive • Improperly tightened main bearing cap bolts • Loose flywheel or drive plate • Loose or damaged vibration damper	• Inspect for low oil level and low oil pressure • Measure main bearing clearance, repair as necessary • Replace missing insert • Measure end play, repair as necessary • Tighten bolts with specified torque • Tighten flywheel or drive plate attaching bolts • Repair as necessary
Connecting rod bearing noise	• Insufficient oil supply • Carbon build-up on piston • Bearing clearance excessive or bearing missing • Crankshaft connecting rod journal out-of-round • Misaligned connecting rod or cap • Connecting rod bolts tightened improperly	• Inspect for low oil level and low oil pressure • Remove carbon from piston crown • Measure clearance, repair as necessary • Measure journal dimensions, repair or replace as necessary • Repair as necessary • Tighten bolts with specified torque
Piston noise	• Piston-to-cylinder wall clearance excessive (scuffed piston) • Cylinder walls excessively tapered or out-of-round • Piston ring broken • Loose or seized piston pin • Connecting rods misaligned • Piston ring side clearance excessively loose or tight • Carbon build-up on piston is excessive	• Measure clearance and examine piston • Measure cylinder wall dimensions, rebore cylinder • Replace all rings on piston • Measure piston-to-pin clearance, repair as necessary • Measure rod alignment, straighten or replace • Measure ring side clearance, repair as necessary • Remove carbon from piston

Troubleshooting Engine Mechanical Problems (cont.)

Problem	Cause	Solution
Valve actuating component noise	• Insufficient oil supply	• Check for: (a) Low oil level (b) Low oil pressure (c) Plugged push rods (d) Wrong hydraulic tappets (e) Restricted oil gallery (f) Excessive tappet to bore clearance
	• Push rods worn or bent	• Replace worn or bent push rods
	• Rocker arms or pivots worn	• Replace worn rocker arms or pivots
	• Foreign objects or chips in hydraulic tappets	• Clean tappets
	• Excessive tappet leak-down	• Replace valve tappet
	• Tappet face worn	• Replace tappet; inspect corresponding cam lobe for wear
	• Broken or cocked valve springs	• Properly seat cocked springs; replace broken springs
	• Stem-to-guide clearance excessive	• Measure stem-to-guide clearance, repair as required
	• Valve bent	• Replace valve
	• Loose rocker arms	• Tighten bolts with specified torque
	• Valve seat runout excessive	• Regrind valve seat/valves
	• Missing valve lock	• Install valve lock
	• Push rod rubbing or contacting cylinder head	• Remove cylinder head and remove obstruction in head
	• Excessive engine oil (four-cylinder engine)	• Correct oil level

Troubleshooting the Cooling System

Problem	Cause	Solution
High temperature gauge indication—overheating	• Coolant level low	• Replenish coolant
	• Fan belt loose	• Adjust fan belt tension
	• Radiator hose(s) collapsed	• Replace hose(s)
	• Radiator airflow blocked	• Remove restriction (bug screen, fog lamps, etc.)
	• Faulty radiator cap	• Replace radiator cap
	• Ignition timing incorrect	• Adjust ignition timing
	• Idle speed low	• Adjust idle speed
	• Air trapped in cooling system	• Purge air
	• Heavy traffic driving	• Operate at fast idle in neutral intermittently to cool engine
	• Incorrect cooling system component(s) installed	• Install proper component(s)
	• Faulty thermostat	• Replace thermostat
	• Water pump shaft broken or impeller loose	• Replace water pump
	• Radiator tubes clogged	• Flush radiator
	• Cooling system clogged	• Flush system
	• Casting flash in cooling passages	• Repair or replace as necessary. Flash may be visible by removing cooling system components or removing core plugs.
	• Brakes dragging	• Repair brakes
	• Excessive engine friction	• Repair engine
	• Antifreeze concentration over 68%	• Lower antifreeze concentration percentage
	• Missing air seals	• Replace air seals
	• Faulty gauge or sending unit	• Repair or replace faulty component

Troubleshooting the Cooling System (cont.)

Problem	Cause	Solution
High temperature gauge indicaiton— overheating (cont.)	• Loss of coolant flow caused by leakage or foaming • Viscous fan drive failed	• Repair or replace leaking component, replace coolant • Replace unit
Low temperature indication— undercooling	• Thermostat stuck open • Faulty gauge or sending unit	• Replace thermostat • Repair or replace faulty component
Coolant loss—boilover	• Overfilled cooling system • Quick shutdown after hard (hot) run • Air in system resulting in occasional "burping" of coolant • Insufficient antifreeze allowing coolant boiling point to be too low • Antifreeze deteriorated because of age or contamination • Leaks due to loose hose clamps, loose nuts, bolts, drain plugs, faulty hoses, or defective radiator • Faulty head gasket • Cracked head, manifold, or block • Faulty radiator cap	• Reduce coolant level to proper specification • Allow engine to run at fast idle prior to shutdown • Purge system • Add antifreeze to raise boiling point • Replace coolant • Pressure test system to locate source of leak(s) then repair as necessary • Replace head gasket • Replace as necessary • Replace cap
Coolant entry into crankcase or cylinder(s)	• Faulty head gasket • Crack in head, manifold or block	• Replace head gasket • Replace as necessary
Coolant recovery system inoperative	• Coolant level low • Leak in system • Pressure cap not tight or seal missing, or leaking • Pressure cap defective • Overflow tube clogged or leaking • Recovery bottle vent restricted	• Replenish coolant to FULL mark • Pressure test to isolate leak and repair as necessary • Repair as necessary • Replace cap • Repair as necessary • Remove restriction
Noise	• Fan contacting shroud • Loose water pump impeller • Glazed fan belt • Loose fan belt • Rough surface on drive pulley • Water pump bearing worn • Belt alignment	• Reposition shroud and inspect engine mounts • Replace pump • Apply silicone or replace belt • Adjust fan belt tension • Replace pulley • Remove belt to isolate. Replace pump. • Check pulley alignment. Repair as necessary.
No coolant flow through heater core	• Restricted return inlet in water pump • Heater hose collapsed or restricted • Restricted heater core • Restricted outlet in thermostat housing • Intake manifold bypass hole in cylinder head restricted • Faulty heater control valve • Intake manifold coolant passage restricted	• Remove restriction • Remove restriction or replace hose • Remove restriction or replace core • Remove flash or restriction • Remove restriction • Replace valve • Remove restriction or replace intake manifold

NOTE: *Immediately after shutdown, the engine enters a condition known as heat soak. This is caused by the cooling system being inoperative while engine temperature is still high. If coolant temperature rises above boiling point, expansion and pressure may push some coolant out of the radiator overflow tube. If this does not occur frequently it is considered normal.*

CAUTION: *The EPA warns that prolonged contact with used engine oil may cause a number of skin disorders, including cancer! You should make every effort to minimize your exposure to used engine oil. Protective gloves should be worn when changing the oil. Wash your hands and any other exposed skin areas as soon as possible after exposure to used engine oil. Soap and water, or waterless hand cleaner should be used.*

5. Place a drip pan (2 qt. capacity) under the transmission. Remove the drain plug (manual and automatic transmission) and drain the transmission.

6. Disconnect the cables and remove the battery.

7. Remove the mounting bolts, vacuum control hose(s), breather hoses and tubes, and intake air hose from the air cleaner, marking them for reassembly. Remove and disassemble the air cleaner.

8. On carbureted version, remove the preheating air regulation housing and hose assembly from the front panel.

9. Disconnect the radiator hoses at the thermostat and water pump. On 2002A models, disconnect and plug the transmission cooler lines

1. Clamp spring
2. Return spring
3. Wire retainer

Disconnecting downshift linkage—2002A

1. Return spring
2. Clamp spring
3. Control rod

Disconnecting throttle linkage—carbureted models

Connecting engine hoist

Disconnecting throttle linkage—2002tii models

Removing right hand engine mount

at the radiator. Remove the radiator retaining bolts and carefully lift out the radiator.

10. Disconnect the multiple plug from the alternator, and remove the B† cable from the alternator and starter. Mark them for reassembly. Tag and disconnect the coolant temperature sensor.

Removing left hand engine mount

Removing transmission support crossmember

Adjusting clearance of engine mount

11. Disconnect the throttle linkage. On the 2002A, disconnect the cable from the automatic choke and the thermo-start valve. Also on the 2002A, detach the plug from the starter lock and pull the cable loom out of the retainer at the transmission. Detach the coolant hoses from the automatic choke housing. On manual choke models, disconnect the choke cable from its lever and the cable sleeve from the cable clamp and pull out the cable. On all 2002 and 2002A models equipped with the Solex 32/32 DIPTA carburetor, disconnect the wire for the electric choke, and the leads for the EGR system. On the 2002A, disconnect the downshift linkage by detaching the clamp spring, return spring, lifting out the wire retainer, disconnecting the linkage ball, and pulling the torsion shaft towards the front.

12. Disconnect and plug the fuel line at the tank side of the fuel pump. On 2002tii models, disconnect the fuel hose at the injection pump. On tii models, remove the main fuel filter from its mount on the front panel. Also on 2002tii models, disconnect the fuel reflow hose.

13. On models equipped with the emission control air pump, disconnect the vacuum line

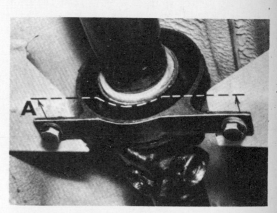

Preloading center support bearing housing

Head pipe support bracket

from the check (non-return) valve at the intake manifold.

14. Disconnect the heater hoses at the return flow connection and cylinder head.

15. Disconnect and label the wire connector from the oil pressure switch, the distributor primary connection, and the ground strap at the engine transmission flange. On 2002tii models, disconnect the cable from the thermotime switch. Also on 2002tii models, disconnect and label the vacuum hose from the air container and the cable from the start valve. Release the cable from the cable clamps on the cam cover.

16. Disconnect the coil high tension lead front he center of the distributor cap. On 2002tii models, pull out the induction transmitter from the coil. On all models, remove the distributor cap and rotor.

17. On manual transmission models, remove the shifter by sliding the shifter boot up along with t he foam rubber ring and inner sealing boot. Lift the leaf spring out of the selector head. On models with a pivot-ball on the shift lever end, pull up the rubber boot and gasket to remove the snap-ring and shift lever.

18. Using a hydraulic floor jack of sufficient capacity for the vehicles weight, raise the front of the car, and position jackstands beneath the reinforced box members adjacent to the 2 front jacking points (front of each rocker panel).

   CAUTION: *Before climbing under the car, make sure that the jackstands are secure. Test their stability by attempting to rock the car back and forth, forward and sideways.*

19. Disconnect the head pipe from the exhaust manifold. Disconnect the head pipe support and the front muffler mounting screws.

20. Disconnect the driveshaft from the transmission flange by releasing the self-locking nuts and bolts from the rotoflex coupling. Tie up the driven shaft so that it does not fall out of the transmission. Disconnect the backup light wires from their terminals, and the speedometer cable from the transmission.

21. On the 2002 series models, remove the hydraulic line bracket from the clutch housing, but do not disconnect the line from the slave cylinder. Disconnect the return spring from the throwout lever. Pull back the dust cover and remove the snap-ring from the slave cylinder. Then pull the slave cylinder forward and remove the pushrod.

22. On 1600 models, detach the pullrod on the intermediate shaft. Detach the bearing support from the engine support. Then remove the intermediate shaft.

23. On 2002A models, remove the selector lever. Also lift out the circlip and detach the selector rod from the selector lever. Disconnect the back-up light neutral start switch lead.

24. Support the weight of the transmission with a floor jack and a block or wood. Attach lifting eyes to strong mounting points at the front and rear of the engine. Hook up an engine houst to the eyelets and take the slack out of the host chain.

25. Remove the left and right-hand engine mount bolts. Remove the bolts retaining the driveshaft center support bearing to the body. Remove the c-bolts for the transmission support crossmember. The engine/transmission unit should now be free. Check to make sure that all wires, hoses, etc. are disconnected. Remove the windshield washer reservoir.

26. Carefully, tilt the transmission down and the front of the engine up. Lift the engine out with the front raised. Lower the car, and push it back out from under the engine. Lower the engine onto a stand, workbench, or other suitable sturdy work surface.

27. Reverse the above procedure to install using the following installation notes:

   a. When bolting the engine of the 1600, 2002, and 2002A in place, make sure that the right engine mount support stop is adjusted so that a 3mm clearance exists as per the illustration.

   b. When installing the center driveshaft support bearing mount, preload the bearing mount by adjusting it forward 2mm in its eccentric bolt holes. Make sure that the driveshaft bolts are torqued to 21.8 ft. lbs.

   c. When connecting the pullrod to the intermediate shaft, make sure that the bearing support is aligned at a 90° angle to the engine before tightening the mounting screws.

   d. When hooking up the exhaust system, make sure that the following sequence is used: first connect the head pipe to the manifold, then loosen the head pipe support

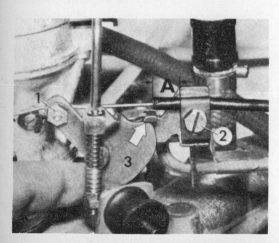

Proper installation of manual choke linkage

mount on the transmission (2) so that it rests tension-free against the pipe, then tighten the support mount on the transmission (2) and (1) and finally tighten the support bracket on the head pipe (3).

e. Adjust the clutch free-play while the car is up in the air following the procedure given in Chapter 7.

f. When m installing the shift lever, make sure that the gearshift pin is installed in its lever with the bolt positioned in the centering recess of the pin. Also make sure that the breather holes in the shifter dust boot face down.

g. When filling the radiator, make sure that the heater control is set to the **HOT** position.

h. When filling the automatic transmisison on the 2002A, follow the instructions for filling under "Changing the Transmission Oil" in Chapter 1.

i. When hooking up the choke on 1970-71 1600-2 and 2002 models, make sure that the choke handle on the dash is at its bottom notch. Then press the fast idle lever (3) against the stop, and tighten the clamp screw (1). The sleeve must project exactly 15mm (distance "A") for the choke flap to close fully.

2500, 2800, Bavaria, 3000 and 3.0 Carbureted Models

1. Scribe the hood hinge locations and remove the hood. Disconnect and remove the battery.

2. Remove the air cleaner and hoses.

3. Drain the cooling system, disconnect the hoses and remove the radiator.

CAUTION: *When draining the coolant, keep in mind that cats and dogs are attracted by the ethylene glycol antifreeze, and are quite likely to drink any that is left in an uncovered container or in puddles on the ground. This will prove fatal in sufficient quantity. Always drain the coolant into a sealable container. Coolant should be reused unless it is contaminated or several years old.*

Removal and installation of six cylinder engines—typical

Removal and installation of four cylinder engines—typical

4. Remove the windshield washer reservoir and the fan.

5. Disconnect the electrical wiring from the engine components, tagging them for later installation.

6. Disconnect the accelerator linkage and unbolt the exhaust pipe from the exhaust manifold.

7. Remove the front lower apron and loosen both engine mounting retaining nuts.

8. Remove the front lower apron and loosen both engine mount retaining nuts.

9. On vehicles with power steering, remove the pump from the mounting brackets and more the pump out of the way. Do not remove the lines.

10. Raise and support the vehicle.

11. Remove the transmission. Refer to "Transmission Removal and Installation." See Chapter 7.

12. On manual transmission cars, remove the slave cylinder form the clutch housing, leaving the pressure hose attached.

13. Lower the car and attach a lifting sling to the engine.

14. Be sure that all wires, hoses and linkages are disconnected and remove the engine.

15. Install the engine assembly into the vehicle, be careful to position it correctly in the engine mount locations.

16. Loosely install the engine mount retaining nuts. Raise and safely support the vehicle and install the transmission, being careful to align it with the engine.

17. Install the engine to transmission bolts and tighten the engine mount nuts. Remove the lifting device from the engine and lower the vehicle.

18. On manual transmission vehicles, install the clutch slave cylinder to the transmission housing. Install the power steering pump to the

brackets and reconnect the exhaust pipe to the exhaust manifold.

19. Install the accelerator linkage and all electrical wiring and hoses to the engine.

20. Install the windshield reservoir and the cooling fan. Install the air cleaner and hoses. Install the battery, hoses and belts. Raise and safely support the vehicle then install the front lower apron. Lower the vehicle.

21. With the aid of a helper, install the hood, aligning the scribe marks made during disassembly.

3.0 Fuel Inject Models

Follow the engine removal and isntallatin procedures for carburetor equipped models. The following procedures pertain specifically to fuel injection models.

1. Separate the electrical connection for the fuel injection wire loom by removing the 3 retaining screws.

2. Remove the wire leads from the relays, sensors, and switches. Mark the wire connections for installaiton.

3. Remove the transmission, if equipped with an automatic transmission. If equipped with a manual transmission, the engine can be removed with the transmission attached.

1984-85 318i

1. Remove the transmission as detailed later.
2. Scribe hood hinge locations on the hood, and then remove it.
3. Detach the 2 mounting bolts and remove the power steering pump with hoses attached. Suspend the pump securely so that hoses will not be damaged.
4. Looking at the top of the air conditioning compressor, loosen the 2 outer bolts (bolts screwing into the compressor) and remove the 2 bolts fastening the mounting bracket to the engine. Then, support the unit and remove the hinge nut and bolt form the bottom of the unit. Finally, pull the unit away from the engine and support it to avoid putting strain on refrigerant hoses.

NOTE: *Do not disconnect any air conditioning hoses!*

5. Remove the radiator cap and drain coolant. Detach radiator hoses. Then, on air conditioned cars, disconnect the wires at the temperature switches. Unscrew and remove the cover located at the left side of the radiator (driver's side). Unscrew and disconnect transmission oil cooler lines at the radiator (automatic only), and plug openings. Finally, remove the mounting bolt located at the top, lift the radiator upward until it clears the rubber mounts on the bottom, and remove it.

CAUTION: *When draining the coolant, keep*

in mind that cats and dogs are attracted by the ethylene glycol antifreeze, and are quite likely to drink any that is left in an uncovered container or in puddles on the ground. This will prove fatal in sufficient quantity. Always drain the coolant into a sealable container. Coolant should be reused unless it is contaminated or several years old.

6. Disconnect both battery leads and the battery-to-alternator wire. Disconnect the engine ground strap.

7. Open clips that hold the wiring harness

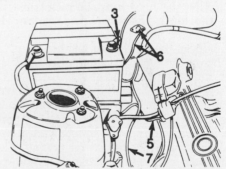

Remove bolts (1 and 2), then remove the bolt at the base of the A/C compressor—1984–87 318i

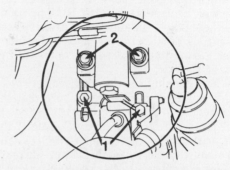

Disconnect wire (3) and ground (5), pull off plugs on temperature sensor (6), and on oxygen sensor (7)—318i

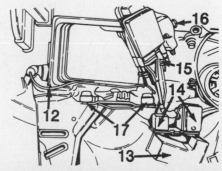

Disconnect wire (12), lift off cap (13) and remove relay (14), disconnect plug (15), open hose strap (16). Loosen nuts (17) and remove the air cleaner—318i

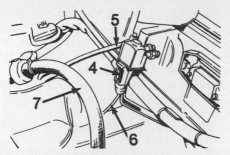

On the 318i, pull off the plug (4) and vacuum hoses (5 and 6). Detach vacuum hose (7). When installing, make sure (5) goes to the distributor, and (6) to the intake manifold.

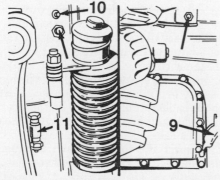

Disconnect the ground strap (9), and engine shock absorber (11) on the 318i. During installation, note that the pin (10) must fit into a bore in the axle carrier.

running along the fender just behind the battery. Disconnect plugs from the temperature sensor and oxygen sensor.

8. Remove the glovebox liner. Unplug plugs at the idle control and L-Jetronic units. Unplug the connector that also comes out of this harness. Then, pull the harness through into the engine compartment.

9. Disconnect all 3 coil wires and wire to the electronic ignition unit. Take the wires out of the clips mounted nearby.

10. At the air cleaner, disconnect the wire mounted on the side of the air cleaner housing, and disconnect the plug. Lift off the L-shaped cap of the relay mounted nearby, and then remove the relay. Loosen the strap and disconnect the inlet hose. Loosen the 2 mounting nuts and remove the air cleaner.

11. Go to the relay box mounted in between the cowl and suspension strut on the driver's side. Remove the top of the box and lift out and disconnect the plug on the outboard side. Remove the rubber guard from the TCI control unit nearby and pull off the plug connected to that. Open both associated wire straps.

12. Going to the rear of the intake manifold,

unscrew the clamp and pull off the large vacuum hose. Label and then disconnect the small vacuum hoses running to the distributor and intake manifold.

13. Disconnect the throttle cable. Remove the hose clamp and hose nearby.

14. Detach fuel hoses at the injection system, and with them the associated hose holder. Collect fuel in a metal pan.

15. Attach a suitable hoist to hooks at front and rear of the engine and support the engine securely.

16. Detach both engine mounts and the vibration damper. Lift out the engine, taking care not to permit the engine to shift and hit anything on the way out.

17. Install the engine in reverse order, keeping these points in mind:

　　a. The locating mandrel on the front of the engine must be guided into the front suspension carrier.

　　b. Adjust the throttle cable for smooth operation.

　　c. Adjust the fan, air conditioning compressor, and power steering pump drive belts.

1977-79 320i

1. Raise and support the vehicle. Remove the transmission (See "Transmission Removal and Installation" in Chapter 7). Disconnect the exhaust pipe from the exhaust manifold.

2. Remove the hood, after scribing the hinge locations.

3. Drain the cooling system, disconnect the hoses and remove the radiator. Remove the intake air panel.

CAUTION: *When draining the coolant, keep in mind that cats and dogs are attracted by the ethylene glycol antifreeze, and are quite likely to drink any that is left in an uncovered container or in puddles on the ground. This*

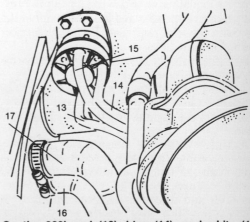

On the 320i, red (13), blue (14), and white (15) hoses, and the heater hoses (16 and 17)

will prove fatal in sufficient quantity. Always drain the coolant into a sealable container. Coolant should be reused unless it is contaminated or several years old.

4. Tag and disconnect the lines to the injector valves.

5. Disconnect all electrical wires from the engine, marking them for installation.

6. Disconnect all fuel and vacuum lines and mark them for installation.

7. Disconnect the accelerator cable. Disconnect the battery cables and remove the battery.

8. Attach a lifting sling to the engine. Remove the retaining nuts from the left and right engine mounts and the upper engine damper, located on the left side of the engine.

9. Carefully raise and remove the engine.

10. Install the engine into the engine compartment, aligning the motor mounts in their appropriate position. Install the motor mount retaining nuts and install the upper engine damper.

11. Connect all of the electrical wiring. Connect the fuel lines and vacuum hoses. Install the radiator and connect all hoses.

12. Install the air intake panel. Connect the exhaust pipe to the exhaust manifold. Raise and safely support the vehicle and install the transmission, carefully aligning it with the engine. With the aid of a helper, install the hood aligning the scribe marks made before removing the engine.

1980-82 320i

1. Remove the transmission as detailed in Chapter 7.

2. Scribe lines around the hood hinges and then remove the hood.

3. Disconnect the upper and lower radiator hoses and then remove the radiator.

4. Unscrew and remove the air filter housing.

5. On models equipped with air conditioning, detach the compressor and position it out of the way with the wires attached. Do not disconnect the refrigerant lines.

6. Disconnect the battery cables (negative cable first) and remove the battery.

7. Disconnect all fuel lines at the fuel distributor. Pull the hose off the charcoal canister. Disconnect the ground wire form the front axle carrier.

8. Unscrew the retaining nut and lift the accelerator cable from the holders toward the side. Push the nipple out toward the rear and then disconnect the cable.

9. Tag and disconnect all remaining wires and hoses which may interfere with engine removal.

10. Lift out the relay socket and then pull out

the 2 relays to the side of the housing. Disconnect the plug underneath and then lift out the wire harness from its holder on the wheel arch.

11. Open the glove box and disconnect the plug on the left-hand side. Pull the harness out through the hole in the firewall (into the engine compartment) Pull the harness out of its holders.

12. Attach an engine hoist to the front and rear of the engine.

13. Unbolt the left engine mount and the upper engine damper.

14. Unbolt the right engine mount and lift out the engine.

15. Install the engine into the engine compartment and install the motor mount nuts.

16. Slide the electrical harness in through the firewall and connect it to the control unit.

17. Connect all the wires and hoses to the engine components, making sure to properly route the wiring.

18. Install the accelerator cable and its retaining nut. When installing the accelerator cable, push the cable through the eye on the lever, attach it and then press the nipple into the eye. Attach the cable to the holder.

19. Connect the fuel lines and the vacuum lines. Install the radiator and connect the hoses.

20. On models equipped with air conditioning install the compressor and connect the wiring to it.

21. Install the air filter housing. With the aid of an assistant, install the hood, aligning the scribe marks made on the hood.

1982-87 325, 325e, 325i, 325is and 1988 325ix

1. Disconnect the battery ground cable. Remove the transmission as described in Chapter 7.

2. Without disconnecting hoses, loosen and

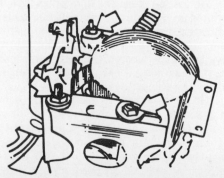

Remove the 3 arrowed bolts and remove the compressor—M3

remove the 3 power steering pump bolts and re-move the pump and belts and support the pump out of the way.

3. Remove the drain plug and remove the coolant from the radiator. Then, remove the radiator (see the appropriate procedure).

CAUTION: *When draining the coolant, keep in mind that cats and dogs are attracted by the ethylene glycol antifreeze, and are quite likely to drink any that is left in an uncovered container or in puddles on the ground. This will prove fatal in sufficient quantity. Always drain the coolant into a sealable container. Coolant should be reused unless it is contaminated or several years old.*

4. Without disconnecting hoses, remove the 3 mounting bolts and remove the air conditioner compressor and drive belt and support the compressor out of the way.

5. Remove the through-bolts to disconnect the engine hood supports and then open the hood and support it securely.

CAUTION: *The hood must be propped in a secure manner! If it falls during work serious injury could result.*

6. Remove the trim panel inside the glovebox.

On 325e models:

a. Disconnect the plugs going to the engine control computer; 2 are located in the wiring, and one directly on the unit.

b. Unscrew the idle control unit near the main control computer and pull off its plugs. On automatic transmission-equipped cars, disconnect the plug leading to the vehicle wiring harness.

On 325i and iS models:

a. Pull the main, multiprong plug off the control unit. Also unplug one plug in a wire coming into the unit, located below the unit and to the left.

b. If the car has an automatic transmission, disconnect the plug for the main wiring harness.

7. Lift out and disconnect the plug for the oxygen sensor and 2 additional wires nearby. Pull off the temperature sensor plug. Disconnect the 3 other connections for this harness, which are nearby. Then, loosen the straps and pull this harness into the engine compartment.

8. Remove the coolant expansion tank. Pull off the ignition coil high tension and low tension wires. Disconnect the wiring harness.

9. **On 325e models:**

a. Disconnect the accelerator cable and cruise control cable. Pull off the vacuum hoses going to the throttle body. Loosen the clamp and pull off the large air intake hose.

b. Disconnect the plugs near the air cleaner. Lift out the relay. Pull off the cover and

disconnect the wiring harness plug at the fusebox. Disconnect the wiring harness.

c. Unscrew the mounting nuts and remove the air cleaner and airflow sensor as a unit.

On 325i and iS models:

a. Near the air cleaner, next to the strut mount in the wheel well, there is an L-shaped relay box. Unplug it and remove it.

b. Loosen the clamp on the air intake hose.

c. Disconnect the multiprong connector from the airflow sensor (integral with the air cleaner). Then, open all the fasteners associated with this wiring harness so that it will not interfere with engine removal.

d. Disconnect the mounting nuts and remove the air cleaner/airflow sensor unit.

e. Disconnect the large, multiprong plug at the rear of the engine, near the firewall. Then, open all the fasteners associated with this wiring harness as well. Also, disconnect the 2 vacuum hoses nearby.

f. Disconnect the accelerator cable. If the car has cruise control, disconnect the cruise control cable as well. Also disconnect the large vacuum line supplying the cruise control servo on these cars.

10. On 1982-85 325e cars, disconnect the multiprong plug at the fusebox and open all the fasteners associated with this wiring harness. On 1986-87 models lift out and unscrew the large, multi-prong plug at the firewall and then open up the fasteners associated with its harness.

11. Unscrew the fuel lines, pull off the hose and disconnect the fuel filter.

12. Disconnect both heater hoses. Disconnect the engine ground strap. Unbolt the engine mounts.

13. Lift out the engine with a suitable hoist, using hooks at front and rear.

14. To install, reverse the procedures used for removal and lower the engine into the engine compartment. When the engine is positioned, the guide pin must fit in the bore of the axle carrier. Torque the mounting bolts on the front axle carrier (small bolt) to 18-20 ft. lbs.; the larger bolt to 31-35 ft. lbs. The mount-to-bracket bolts are torqued to 31-35 ft. lbs. Engine-to-bracket mounts are torqued to (small bolt) 16-17 ft. lbs., (large bolt) 31-35 ft. lbs.

15. Connect the fuel lines, use new hose clamps to connect the fuel lines to the fuel filter. Connect all of the multiprong plugs and all vacuum hoses.

16. Connect the accelerator cable and cruise control cable to the throttle body and adjust the accelerator cable and cruise control cable.

17. Install the coolant recovery tank, use a new hose clamp on the coolant expansion tank.

18. Install the air cleaner and reconnect all

electrical plugs. Connect and install the L-shaped relay box on the wheel well.

19. Reconnect the wiring to the main control unit and install the idle control unit.

20. Install the air conditioning compressor and power steering pump, properly route the accessory drive belt. Adjust the belt tension.

21. Install the radiator and connect the hoses.

22. Install the transmission as described in Chapter 7.

23. Install the hood support and lower the hood.

24. Make sure all fluid levels are correct before starting the engine. Bleed air from the cooling system.

1988 325, 325e, 325i, 325is and 325ix

1. Disconnect the battery ground cable. Remove the transmission as described in Chapter 7.

2. Without disconnecting hoses, loosen and remove the 3 power steering pump bolts and remove the pump and belts and support the pump out of the way.

3. Remove the drain plug and remove the coolant from the radiator. Then, remove the radiator (see the appropriate procedure). Unbolt and remove the fan from the engine. Store it in an upright position.

CAUTION: *When draining the coolant, keep in mind that cats and dogs are attracted by the ethylene glycol antifreeze, and are quite likely to drink any that is left in an uncovered container or in puddles on the ground. This will prove fatal in sufficient quantity. Always drain the coolant into a sealable container. Coolant should be reused unless it is contaminated or several years old.*

4. Without disconnecting hoses, remove the 4 mounting bolts (they run through the compressor body) and remove the air conditioner compressor and drive belt and support the compressor out of the way.

5. Remove the through-bolts to disconnect the engine hood supports and then open the hood and support it securely.

CAUTION: *The hood must be propped in a secure manner! If it falls during work serious injury could result.*

6. Disconnect the accelerator cable. If the car has cruise control, disconnect the cruise control cable. If the car has an automatic transmission, disconnect the throttle cable leading to the transmission.

7. Pull the large, multiprong plug off the airflow sensor (an integral part of the air cleaner). Loosen the clamp and disconnect the air intake hose at the airflow sensor. Remove the 2 mounting nuts and remove the air cleaner/airflow sensor unit.

8. Disconnect the coolant expansion tank hose. Disconnect the large, multiprong connector near ther air intake hose.

9. The diagnosis plug is a large, screw-on connector located near the thermostat and associated hoses. Unscrew and disconnect this connector.

10. Disconnect the 2 large coolant hoses connecting to the thermostat.

11. Make sure the engine is cold. Place a metal container under the connection to collect fuel; then, disconnect the fuel line at the connection right near the thermostat housing by unscrewing it. Unfasten the fuel line clip about a foot away from this connection.

12. Disconnect the 2 electrical plugs near the diagnosis plug connector. Disconnect the bracket for the dipstick guide tube.

13. Remove the 2 bolts which attach 2 water pipes going to the engine to mounting brackets.

14. Disconnect the 2 heater hoses at the heater core (near the firewall). Remove the coolant hose running to the top of the block.

15. Place a metal container under the connection to collect fuel; then, disconnect the remaining fuel hose supplying the engine injectors. Disconnect the 3 electrical connectors nearby.

16. Remove the bolt from the mounting brace connecting with the cylinder head.

17. Mark and then disconnect the 2 electrical leads from the starter. Unbolt the starter and lift it out from above.

18. Place a metal container under the connection to collect fuel; then, disconnect the fuel pipe that runs right near the starter.

19. Label electrical connectors on the alternator. Then, pull off the rubber caps for the 2 connectors which are attached with nuts and remove the nuts and any washers. Disconnect the plug-on connector.

20. Disconnect the electrical leads for the coil. Loosen the clips attaching the leads under the distributor and pull the harness away to the left. Disconnect the oil pressure sending unit.

21. Place a drain pan underneath the 2 connections and then disconnect the oil cooler pipes at the crankcase by unscrewing the flare nut fittings.

22. Take the cover off the relay box. Then, lift out the relays and their mounting sockets. Place the relays and associated wiring on top of the engine so they will come out with it.

23. Loosen its mounting clamp and then remove the carbon canister. There is a plate nearby to which a number of electrical leads are connected. Remove the mounting screws and move the plate aside so that it will clear the dipstick guide tube when the engine is removed.

24. Remove the 2 bolts that fasten the wiring harness to the firewall. Then, disconnect the engine ground strap.

25. Remove both engine mount through-bolts. Lift out the engine with a suitable hoist, using hooks at front and rear.

26. To install, reverse the procedures used for removal and lower the engine into the engine compartment. When the engine is positioned, the guide pin must fit in the bore of the axle carrier. Torque the mounting bolts on the front axle carrier (small bolt) to 18-20 ft. lbs.; the larger bolt to 31-35 ft. lbs. The mount-to-bracket bolts are torqued to 31-35 ft. lbs. Engine-to-bracket mounts are torqued to (small bolt) 16-17 ft. lbs., (large bolt) 31-35 ft. lbs.

27. Connect the fuel lines, use new hose clamps to connect the fuel lines to the fuel filter. Connect all of the multiprong plugs and all vacuum hoses.

28. Connect the accelerator cable and cruise control cable to the throttle body and adjust the accelerator cable and cruise control cable.

29. Install the coolant recovery tank, use a new hose clamp on the coolant expansion tank.

30. Install the air cleaner and reconnect all electrical plugs. Connect and install the relays in the relay box.

31. Reconnect the wiring to the main control unit and install the idle control unit.

32. Install the air conditioning compressor and power steering pump, properly route the accessory drive belt. Adjust the belt tension.

33. Install the radiator and connect the hoses.

34. Install the transmission as described in Chapter 7.

35. Install the hood support and lower the hood.

36. Make sure all fluid levels are correct before starting the engine. Bleed air from the cooling system.

M3

1. Disconnect the battery ground cable. Remove the transmission as described in Chapter 7.

2. Remove the splash guard from underneath the engine. Put a drain pan underneath and then drain coolant from both the radiator and block.

CAUTION: *When draining the coolant, keep in mind that cats and dogs are attracted by the ethylene glycol antifreeze, and are quite likely to drink any that is left in an uncovered container or in puddles on the ground. This will prove fatal in sufficient quantity. Always drain the coolant into a sealable container. Coolant should be reused unless it is contaminated or several years old.*

3. Loosen the hose clamps at either end of the air intake hose leading to the air intake sensor. Pull off the hose. Then, pull both electrical connectors off the air cleaner/airflow sensor unit. Remove both mounting nuts and remove the unit.

4. Disconnect the accelerator and cruise control cables. Unscrew the nuts mounting the cable housing mounting bracket and set the housings and bracket aside.

5. Loosen the clamp and disconnect the brake booster vacuum hose.

6. Loosen the clamp and disconnect the other end of the booster vacuum hose at the manifold. Remove the nut from the intake manifold brace.

7. Loosen the hose clamp and disconnect the air intake hose at the manifold. Then, remove all 6 nuts attaching the manifold assembly to the outer ends of the intake throttle necks and remove the assembly.

8. Put a drain pan underneath and then loosen the hose clamps and disconnect the coolant expansion tank hoses. Disconnect the engine ground strap.

9. Disconnect the ignition coil high tension lead. Then, label and disconnect the 2 plugs on the front of the block, nearby. Remove the nut fastening another lead farther forward of the 2 plugs and move the lead aside so it will not interfere with engine removal.

10. Label and then disconnect the 2 plugs from the rear of the alternator. Label the 2 additional leads and then remove the nuts and disconnect those leads. It's best to reinstall nuts once the leads are removed to keep them from being mixed up.

11. Remove the cover for the electrical connectors from the starter. Label the leads and then remove the attaching nuts and disconnect them. Reinstall the nuts.

12. There is a wire running to a connector on the oil pan to warn of low oil level. Pull off the connector, unscrew the carrier for the lead, and then pull the lead out from above. Pull off the 2 connectors near where the lead for the low oil warning system ran and unclip the wires from the carrier.

13. Find the vacuum hose leading to the fuel pressure regulator. Pull it off. Label and then disconnect the 2 plugs nearby. Unscrew the mounting screw for another electrical lead connecting with the top of the block and remove the lead and its carrier.

14. There is a vacuum hose connecting with one of the throttle necks. Disconnect it and pull it out of the intake manifold bracket. Pull off the electrical connector nearby. Pull out the rubber retainer, and then pull the idle speed control out and put it aside. The engine wiring

harness is located nearby. Take it out of its carriers.

15. All the fuel injectors are plugged into a common plate. Carefully and evenly pull the plate off the injectors, pull it out past the pressure regulator, and lay it aside.

16. Loosen the clamp and then disconnect the PCV hose. Label and then disconnect the 2 fuel lines connecting with the injector circuit (it's important to label them so that they can be installed correctly!). Put a drain pan underneath and then disconnect the heater hose from the cylinder head.

17. Loosen the clamp near the throttle necks and then pull the engine wiring harness out and put it aside. Put a drain pan underneath and then disconnect the heater hose that connects to the block.

18. Loosen the mounting clamp for the carbon canister, slide it out of the clamp, and place it aside with the hoses still connected.

19. Note the routing of the 2 oil cooler lines where they connect at the base of the oil filter. Label them if necessary. Put a drain pan underneath and then unscrew the flared connectors for the 2 lines.

20. Unbolt and remove the fan. Store it in an upright position. See the appropriate procedure later in this section and remove the radiator.

21. Support the power steering pump. Remove the adjusting bolt and disconnect and remove the belt. Then, remove the 2 sets of nuts and bolts on which the unit hinges. Pull the unit aside and hang it so there will not be strain on the hoses.

22. Remove the adjusting bolt for the air conditioning compressor and disconnect and remove the belt. Then, remove the nut at one end of the hinge bolt and pull the bolt out, suspending the compressor to reduce the load on the bolt and to keep it from falling. Move the compressor aside and hang it so there will not be strain on the hoses.

23. Remove the through-bolts to disconnect the engine hood supports and then open the hood and support it securely.

CAUTION: *The hood must be propped in a secure manner! If it falls during work serious injury could result.*

24. Suspend the engine with a lifting crane via the hooks at the front and rear of the cylinder head. Then, remove the nuts for the engine mounting bolts. The mounts are on the axle carrier and the nut is at the top on the left and on the bottom on the right. Then, carefully lift the engine out of the compartment, avoiding contact between it and the components remaining in the car.

25. Keep these points in mind during installation:

a. Torque the engine mounting bolts to 32.5 ft. lbs.

b. Adjust the belt tension for the air conditioning compressor and power steering pump drive belts to give ½-¾" deflection.

c. Torque the oil cooler line flare nuts to 25 ft. lbs.

d. When reconnecting the intake manifold to the throttle necks, inspect and, if necessary, replace the O-rings. Torque the mounting nuts to 78 in. lbs.

26. To install, reverse the procedures used for removal and lower the engine into the engine compartment. When the engine is positioned, the guide pin must fit in the bore of the axle carrier. Torque the mounting bolts on the front axle carrier (small bolt) to 18-20 ft. lbs.; the larger bolt to 31-35 ft. lbs. The mount-to-bracket bolts are torqued to 31-35 ft. lbs.

27. Install the intake manifold assembly and connect the fuel lines, use new hose clamps to connect the fuel lines to the fuel filter. Connect all of the multiprong plugs and all vacuum hoses.

28. Connect the accelerator cable and cruise control cable to the throttle body and adjust the accelerator cable and cruise control cable.

29. Install the coolant recovery tank, use a new hose clamp on the coolant expansion tank.

30. Install the air cleaner and reconnect all electrical plugs. Connect and install the relays in the relay box.

31. Reconnect the wiring to the main control unit and install the idle control unit.

32. Install the air conditioning compressor and power steering pump, properly route the accessory drive belt. Adjust the belt tension.

33. Install the radiator and connect the hoses.

34. Install the transmission as described in Chapter 7.

35. Install the hood support and lower the hood.

36. Make sure all fluid levels are correct before starting the engine. Bleed air from the cooling system.

524td

1. Remove the transmission as detailed in Chapter 7.

2. Remove the adjusting and hinge bolts for the power steering pump support the pump out of the way securely without placing any strain on the hoses.

3. Remove the adjusting and hinge bolts for the air conditioning compressor; support the compressor out of the way without placing any strain on the hoses (do not attempt to disconnect them!)

4. Remove the drain plug from a block, and drain the coolant. Then, remove the radiator as

described later in this section. Remove the circlip and disconnect the power lead, nearby.

CAUTION: *When draining the coolant, keep in mind that cats and dogs are attracted by the ethylene glycol antifreeze, and are quite likely to drink any that is left in an uncovered container or in puddles on the ground. This will prove fatal in sufficient quantity. Always drain the coolant into a sealable container. Coolant should be reused unless it is contaminated or several years old.*

5. Remove the ground wires from the hood. Disconnect the gas pressure hood props and

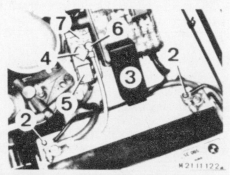

Disconnect the primary electrical wire (2), lift off the cover (3) and remove the plugs (4, 5), disconnect the wire (6) and remove the preheat control

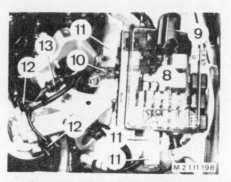

Remove the cover and cap (8, 9), disconnect the plug (10) and remove the relays (11), and disconnect the pugs (12, 13)

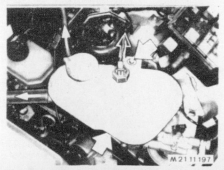

Remove the coolant recovery bottle

then securely prop up the engine hood so it is wide open.

6. Disconnect the negative and positive battery leads.

7. Disconnect the primary electrical connection (2). Lift off the cover (3) and pull off plugs (4) and (5). Disconnect the wire (6). Remove the preheating time control (7).

8. Remove the coolant overflow tank by disconnecting wiring and the coolant hose, removing the 2 mounting nuts, and then pulling it off the mounting studs.

9. Remove the cover (8) and cap (9). Disconnect the plug (10). Then, pull off all 3 relays (11).

10. Disconnect plugs at (12) and (13). Remove the wiring harness fasteners at the body.

11. Disconnect the accelerator and cruise control cables.

12. Disconnect the fuel hoses running between the injection pump and the filter system (supply and return).

13. Disconnect the 5 vacuum hoses connecting to the rear of the engine block.

14. Disconnect the plug near the rear of the cylinder head and disconnect the ground wire nearby.

15. Disconnect the water hoses for the heater.

16. Disconnect the hoses going into the air cleaner. The large air intake hose is twisted to release it prior to removing it. Unscrew the wingnuts, release the clamps, and remove the air cleaner.

17. Place a bucket underneath the oil cooler and then disconnect both oil lines. Disconnect the manifold pressure line going to the turbo wastegate.

18. Disconnect the multi-prong plug on the control unit in the glovebox. Disconnect the engine wiring harness and pull it into the engine compartment.

19. Disconnect the wiring running near one of the engine mounts. Disconnect the engine ground strap.

20. Attach a lifting sling to the engine lifting hoods. Apply tension enough to support the engine. Pull the center-bolts out of both engine mounts and remove the engine.

21. To install, guide the engine into the engine compartment, carefully. The engine mounting system has a guidepin that must be fitted into a corresponding bore in the front axle to locate the engine properly for installing of the mount through-bolts.

22. Connect the electrical leads to the control unit and the ground strap to the body.

23. Connect the oil cooler lines and connect the pressure line to the turbocharger. Install the air cleaner and connect all hoses to the air cleaner assembly.

24. Reconnect the water hoses to the heater. Connect the vacuum lines to the rear of the engine block. Connect the fuel lines between the injection pump and the filler system.

25. Connect the accelerator and cruise control cables. Connect all the plugs and wiring at the relay box and the timed heater unit.

26. Install the radiator and all hoses. Reattach the air conditioning compressor and the power steering pump.

27. Install the transmission as described in Chapter 7. Install the hood support struts.

28. Top off all of the fluids. Connect the battery cables. Run the engine and check for proper timing and idle.

530i and 528i

1. Raise and support the vehicle. Remove the transmission. (See transmission removal in Chapter 7. Disconnect the exhaust pipe at the exhaust manifold.

2. Remove the power steering pump and place it out of the way along the inner fender panel. Leave the hoses attached.

3. Lower the vehicle, scribe the hood hinge location and remove the hood.

4. Remove the air cleaner with the duct work attached. Disconnect and remove the air volume control.

5. Disconnect and remove the battery.

6. Disconnect all electrical wires and connectors. Mark the wires and connector for installation.

7. Disconnect all vacuum hoses, marking them for installation.

8. Drain the cooling system, disconnect the hoses and remove the radiator.

CAUTION: *When draining the coolant, keep in mind that cats and dogs are attracted by the ethylene glycol antifreeze, and are quite likely to drink any that is left in an uncovered container or in puddles on the ground. This will prove fatal in sufficient quantity. Always drain the coolant into a sealable container. Coolant should be reused unless it is contaminated or several years old.*

9. Disconnect the accelerator linkage.

10. Install a lifting sling on the engine.

11. Remove the left and right engine mount retaining nuts and washers.

12. Carefully lift the engine from the engine compartment.

13. To install, reverse the procedures used for removal and lower the engine into the engine compartment. When the engine is positioned, the guide pin must fit in the bore of the axle carrier. Torque the mounting bolts on the front axle carrier (small bolt) to 18-20 ft. lbs.; the larger bolt to 31-35 ft. lbs. The mount-to-bracket bolts are torqued to 31-35 ft. lbs. Engine-to-bracket mounts are torqued to (small bolt) 16-17 ft. lbs., (large bolt) 31-35 ft. lbs.

14. Connect the fuel lines, use new hose clamps to connect the fuel lines to the fuel filter. Connect all of the multiprong plugs and all vacuum hoses.

15. Install the air conditioning compressor and power steering pump, properly route the accessory drive belt. Adjust the belt tension.

16. Install the radiator and connect the hoses.

17. Install the transmission as described in Chapter 7.

18. Install the hood support and lower the hood.

19. Make sure all fluid levels are correct before starting the engine. Bleed air from the cooling system.

528e

1. Remove the transmisison as detailed in Chapter 7. Disconnect the exhaust pipe from the exhaust manifold.

2. Remove the splash guard.

3. With the hoses stall attached, remove the power steering pump and position it out of the way.

4. Unscrew the drain plug on the engine block, remove the upper and lower radiator hoses and drain the cooling system. After draining, remove the radiator.

CAUTION: *When draining the coolant, keep in mind that cats and dogs are attracted by the ethylene glycol antifreeze, and are quite likely to drink any that is left in an uncovered container or in puddles on the ground. This will prove fatal in sufficient quantity. Always drain the coolant into a sealable container. Coolant should be reused unless it is contaminated or several years old.*

5. With the refrigerant hoses still connected,

On the 530i, hoses are coded as follows: 2-blue, 3-black, 4-white, 5-white, 6-black. Also disconnect hose 8 at the blowoff valve and hose 9 at the fuel pressure governor

remove the air conditioning compressor and position it out of the way.

6. Disconnect the gas pressure springs, scribe around the hinges and then remove the hood.

7. Disconnect the battery cables (negative first) and remove the battery.

8. Disconnect the accelerator and cruise control cables. Disconnect all hoses from the throttle housing (make sure you tag them all). Disconnect the air duct.

9. Remove the air filter housing along with the air flow sensor.

10. Tag and disconnect all remaining liens, hoses and wires which may interfere with engine removal.

11. Tag and disconnect all plugs and wires attached to the control unit in the glove box. Unscrew the straps ont the firewall and pull the wire harness through to the engine compartment.

12. Disconnect the engine ground strap and then loosen both engine mounts.

13. Attach an engine lifting hoist to the front and rear of the engine, remove the engine mount bolts and then lift out the engine.

14. To install, reverse the procedures used for removal and lower the engine into the engine compartment. When the engine is positioned, the guide pin must fit in the bore of the axle carrier. Torque the mounting bolts on the front axle carrier (small bolt) to 18-20 ft. lbs.; the larger bolt to 31-35 ft. lbs. The mount-to-bracket bolts are torqued to 31-35 ft. lbs.

15. Connect all of the electrical wiring and all vacuum hoses.

16. Connect the accelerator cable and cruise control cable to the throttle body and adjust the accelerator cable and cruise control cable.

17. Install the air cleaner and reconnect all electrical plugs.

18. Reconnect the wiring to the main control unit.

19. Install the air conditioning compressor and power steering pump, properly route the accessory drive belt. Adjust the belt tension.

20. Install the radiator and connect the hoses.

21. Install the transmission as described in Chapter 7.

22. Install the hood support and lower the hood.

23. Make sure all fluid levels are correct before starting the engine. Bleed the air from the cooling system.

630CSi

1. Raise and support the vehicle and remove the transmisison. (See "Transmission Removal and Installation" in Chapter 7.) Disconnect the exhaust pipe at the manifold.

2. Remove the power steering pump and place it out of the way. Leave the hoses attached.

3. If equipped with air conditioning, remove the compressor and place it aside. Do not remove the hoses.

4. Scribe the hood hinge locations and remove the hood.

5. Drain the cooling system, disconnect the hoses and remove the radiator.

CAUTION: *When draining the coolant, keep in mind that cats and dogs are attracted by the ethylene glycol antifreeze, and are quite likely to drink any that is left in an uncovered container or in puddles on the ground. This will prove fatal in sufficient quantity. Always drain the coolant into a sealable container. Coolant should be reused unless it is contaminated or several years old.*

6. Remove the air cleaner housing at the wheel hosue.

7. Remove the electrical wires and connectors from the engine components. Tag the wires and connectors.

NOTE: *The fuel injection control box is located either in the glove box or behind the right side kick panel. Remove the plug and thread the wire and connector through the hole in the firewall and into the engine compartment.*

8. Tag and disconnect all plugs and wires attached to the control unit in the glove box. Unscrew the straps ont the firewall and pull the wire harness through to the engine compartment.

9. Disconnect the engine ground strap and then loosen both engine mounts.

10. Attach an engine lifting hoist to the front and rear of the engine, remove the engine mount bolts and then lift out the engine.

On the 630CSi and 633CSi, hoses are coded as follows: 3-red from EGR valve and red capped electric valve; 4-blue from EGR valve/pressure converter; 5-red from throttle housing and red capped electric valve; 6-white from collector/distributor electric switching valve

11. To install, reverse the procedures used for removal and lower the engine into the engine compartment. When the engine is positioned, the guide pin must fit in the bore of the axle carrier. Torque the mounting bolts on the front axle carrier (small bolt) to 18-20 ft. lbs.; the larger bolt to 31-35 ft. lbs. The mount-to-bracket bolts are torqued to 31-35 ft. lbs.

12. Connect all of the electrical wiring and all vacuum hoses.

13. Connect the accelerator cable and cruise control cable to the throttle body and adjust the accelerator cable and cruise control cable.

14. Install the air cleaner and reconnect all electrical plugs.

15. Reconnect the wiring to the main control unit.

16. Install the air conditioning compressor and power steering pump, properly route the accessory drive belt. Adjust the belt tension.

17. Install the radiator and connect the hoses.

18. Install the transmission as described in Chapter 7.

19. Install the hood support and lower the hood.

20. Make sure all fluid levels are correct before starting the engine. Bleed the air from the cooling system.

533i, 535i, 633CSi and 635CSi

1. Disconnect both battery connections (negative first). There is a lead coming from the engine to the positive battery terminal. Disconnect it at the battery. On the 600 Series cars, disconnect the ground strap.

2. Unscrew the ground strap for the hood. Support the hood securely and then disconnect the gas props. Then, raise the hood until it is vertical and securely fasten it in place.

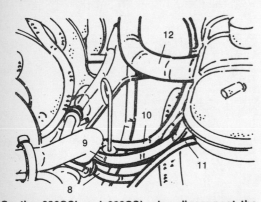

On the 630CSi and 633CSi, also disconnect the hoses shown, which are routed/coded as follows: 8-white from booster blowoff valve to white capped valve; 9-black from booster blowoff valve to blue capped valve; 10-blue from booster blowoff valve to blue capped valve; 11-red from pressure converter to EGR valve. Also detach overflow tank hose (12)

3. Remove the transmission as described later in this section. With the engine cool, place a clean container underneath the coolant drain plug in the side of the block. Remove the plug and drain all coolant from the block. Remove the fan and radiator.

CAUTION: *When draining the coolant, keep in mind that cats and dogs are attracted by the ethylene glycol antifreeze, and are quite likely to drink any that is left in an uncovered container or in puddles on the ground. This will prove fatal in sufficient quantity. Always drain the coolant into a sealable container. Coolant should be reused unless it is contaminated or several years old.*

4. Support the power steering pump. Remove the 3 mounting bolts and then hang the pump out of the way in a position that will not put stress on the hoses.

5. Support the air conditioning compressor. Remove the 3 mounting bolts and then hang the compressor out of the way in a position that will not put stress on the hoses.

On the 533i and 633i:

a. Pull off the plug at the airflow sensor and remove associated wiring. Remove the hoses and pipes connected to the air cleaner and airflow sensor. If it looks like it will be confusing to reconnect all hoses to the proper connections, label them. Then, remove the nuts and remove the airflow sensor and air cleaner as an assembly.

b. Pull off the plugs on the idle control and Digital Motor Electronics control in the glove box. Pull the wires through into the engine compartment. Disconnect the ground wire associated with the DME. Disconnect the oxygen sensor. Disconnect the DME wiring harness on the firewall.

c. Disconnect both (+) and (-) low tension and the high tension wire from the coil. Disconnect the wires from the solenoid nearby. Pull the wiring harness out of the holders. On the 633i, also disconnect the harness at the fuse box.

On the 535i and 635i:

a. Pull the wire leading to the oxygen sensor out of the clips under the floor. Disconnect the sensor at the exhaust pipe.

b. Pull off the plug at the airflow sensor and remove associated wiring. Remove the hoses and pipes connected to the air cleaner and airflow sensor. If it looks like it will be confusing to reconnect all hoses to the proper connections, label them. Then, remove the nuts and remove the airflow sensor and air cleaner as an assembly.

c. Pull the large, multiprong plug off the Digital Motor Electronics box in the glove compartment. Disconnect the smaller plug

that's connected to the same harness and plugged in nearby. Then, run the entire harness back into the engine compartment.

d. Disconnect the engine ground wire located at the rear of the block. Unclip the harness for the DME from the firewall.

e. Disconnect both (+) and (−) low tension and the high tension wire from the coil. Disconnect the wires from the solenoid nearby. Pull the wiring harness out of the holders.

6. Pull off the fuse box cover and the cap nearby. Remove the 3 relays (they have metal covers) on one side of the fusebox. Then, disconnect the wiring harness that leads into the fusebox. On the 635i, unclamp the harness where it is clamped to the fender well and remove the diagnosis socket (located right near the fusebox).

7. Disconnect the accelerator and cruise control cables.

8. Unclamp and remove the coolant hose that leads to the expansion tank. Disconnect the fuel return line nearby, collecting any fuel in a metal container for safe disposal. Unclip the wiring harness clips on the 2 wires that run through this area of the engine compartment.

9. Disconnect the fuel supply line, collecting any fuel in a metal container for safe disposal. Disconnect the 2 heater hoses at connections nearby.

10. Pull the main vacuum supply hose off at the intake manifold.

11. Disconnect the remaining main coolant hose and plug it.

12. Install a lifting sling to the 2 hooks on top of the engine. Unbolt the left side engine mount. Remove the main engine ground strap. Unbolt the right side engine mount. Carefully pull the engine out of the compartment.

13. To install, reverse the procedures used for removal and lower the engine into the engine compartment. When the engine is positioned, the guide pin must fit in the bore of the axle carrier. Torque the mounting bolts on the front axle carrier (small bolt) to 18-20 ft. lbs.; the larger bolt to 31-35 ft. lbs. The mount-to-bracket bolts are torqued to 31-35 ft. lbs.

14. Install the intake manifold assembly and connect the fuel lines, use new hose clamps to connect the fuel lines to the fuel filter. Connect all of the multiprong plugs and all vacuum hoses.

15. Connect the accelerator cable and cruise control cable to the throttle body and adjust the accelerator cable and cruise control cable.

16. Install the coolant recovery tank, use a new hose clamp on the coolant expansion tank.

17. Install the air cleaner and reconnect all electrical plugs. Connect and install the relays in the relay box.

18. Reconnect the wiring to the main control unit and install the idle control unit.

19. Install the air conditioning compressor and power steering pump, properly route the accessory drive belt. Adjust the belt tension.

20. Install the radiator and connect the hoses.

21. Install the transmission as described in Chapter 7.

22. Install the hood support and lower the hood.

23. Make sure all fluid levels are correct before starting the engine. Bleed air from the cooling system.

M5 and M6

1. Disconnect the battery negative cable. Then, disconnect the positive cable. Scribe matchmarks and then remove the hood.

2. Remove the fan. Remove the drain plugs in the block and radiator. Disconnect the hoses and remove the radiator.

CAUTION: *When draining the coolant, keep in mind that cats and dogs are attracted by the ethylene glycol antifreeze, and are quite likely to drink any that is left in an uncovered container or in puddles on the ground. This will prove fatal in sufficient quantity. Always drain the coolant into a sealable container. Coolant should be reused unless it is contaminated or several years old.*

3. Support the power steering pump. Remove the 3 mounting bolts and then hang the pump out of the way in a position that will not put stress on the hoses.

4. Support the air conditioning compressor. Remove the 3 mounting bolts and then hang the compressor out of the way in a position that will not put stress on the hoses.

5. Remove the transmission as described later in this section.

6. Remove the attaching bolt and, with an appropriate puller, remove the vibration damper from the front of the engine.

7. Remove the 2 bolts at either end and remove the cross brace that runs under the engine. Remove the heat shield nearby.

8. Disconnect the electrical connector going to the airflow sensor. Pull the electrical leads out of the wiring holders. Loosen the hose clamp for the air intake hose. Remove the mounting nut for the air cleaner. Then, remove the air cleaner and airflow sensor as an assembly.

9. Disconnect the large vacuum hose at the bottom of the intake manifold.

10. Disconnect the PCV hoses where they connect to the top of the manifold. Disconnect the throttle cable that runs across the top of the manitold, and the hose running near the front.

Remove the bolts fastening the manifold to the outer ends of the intake tubes and remove it.

11. Working inside the glove compartment, disconnect the plug that connects to the Digital Motor Electronics control. Then, guide the leads through and into the engine compartment. Disconnect the high tension lead and the 2 low tension leads at the coil. Then, unfasten the wiring harness holders for the harness running to the coil where the harness runs along the fender well.

12. Disconnect the fuel hose connection at the rear of the fuel manifold on top of the engine, and collect fuel in a metal container for safe disposal. Disconnect the vacuum hose that runs along the firewall nearby.

13. Disconnect the plugs for the reference mark and speed sensors. Disconnect the hoses on the coolant expansion tank.

14. Working on the fuse box, pull off the large electrical connector. Pull off the diagnosis socket. Disconnect the remaining leads.

15. Disconnect the heater hoses near the firewall. Using a backup wrench, disconnect the 2 lines at the oil cooler. Disconnect the low pressure fuel line at the pressure regulator.

16. Disconnect the starter leads. Cut the straps and remove the solenoid heat shield.

17. Attach a lifting sling to the engine and support the assembly with a crane. Disconnect the ground lead. Then, disconnect the left side engine mount, removing the nut from underneath and then unscrewing the bolt out the top. Do the same for the right mount (the nut is underneath). Carefully lift the engine out of the compartment, tilting the front of the engine upward for clearance.

18. Suspend the engine with a lifting crane via the hooks at the front and rear of the cylinder head. Then, remove the nuts for the engine mounting bolts. The mounts are on the axle carrier and the nut is at the top on the left and on the bottom on the right. Then, carefully lift the engine out of the compartment, avoiding contact between it and the components remaining in the car.

19. Keep these points in mind during installation:

    a. Torque the engine mounting bolts to 32.5 ft. lbs.

    b. Adjust the belt tension for the air conditioning compressor and power steering pump drive belts to give ½-¾″ deflection.

    c. Torque the oil cooler line flare nuts to 25 ft. lbs.

    d. When reconnecting the intake manifold to the throttle necks, inspect and, if necessary, replace the O-rings. Torque the mounting nuts to 785 in. lbs.

20. To install, reverse the procedures used for removal and lower the engine into the engine compartment. When the engine is positioned, the guide pin must fit in the bore of the axle carrier. Torque the mounting bolts on the front axle carrier (small bolt) to 18-20 ft. lbs.; the larger bolt to 31-35 ft. lbs. The mount-to-bracket bolts are torqued to 31-35 ft. lbs.

21. Install the intake manifold assembly and connect the fuel lines, use new hose clamps to connect the fuel lines to the fuel filter. Connect all of the multiprong plugs and all vacuum hoses.

22. Connect the accelerator cable and cruise control cable to the throttle body and adjust the accelerator cable and cruise control cable.

23. Install the coolant recovery tank, use a new hose clamp on the coolant expansion tank.

24. Install the air cleaner and reconnect all electrical plugs. Connect and install the relays in the relay box.

25. Reconnect the wiring to the main control unit and install the idle control unit.

26. Install the air conditioning compressor and power steering pump, properly route the accessory drive belt. Adjust the belt tension.

27. Install the radiator and connect the hoses.

28. Install the transmission as described in Chapter 7.

29. Install the hood support and lower the hood.

30. Make sure all fluid levels are correct before starting the engine. Bleed air from the cooling system.

1982 733i

1. Raise and support the vehicle and remove the transmission. (See "Transmission Removal and Installation" in Chapter 7.) Disconnect the exhaust pipe at the exhaust manifold or thermal reactor.

2. Remove the clutch housing from the engine.

3. Remove the power steering pump and place it out of the way. Do not disconnect the hoses.

4. If equipped with air conditioning, remove the compressor and place it out of the way. Do not disconnect the hoses.

5. Remove th damper bracket from the crankcase and lower the vehicle.

6. Scribe the hood hinge locations and remove the hood.

7. Drain the cooling system, disconnect the hoses and remove the radiator.

CAUTION: *When draining the coolant, keep in mind that cats and dogs are attracted by the ethylene glycol antifreeze, and are quite likely to drink any that is left in an uncovered container or in puddles on the ground. This will prove fatal in sufficient quantity. Always*

drain the coolant into a sealable container. Coolant should be reused unless it is contaminated or several years old.

8. Remove the windshield washer reservoir and the air filter housing located on the inner fender panel.

9. Remove the electrical wiring from the engine components. Tag all wires.

10. Disconnect and remove the battery.

11. Remove and tag all vacuum hoses.

NOTE: *Some vacuum hoses are color coded.*

12. Disconnect the throttle linkage.

13. Remove the right kick panel from the passenger compartment, remove the fuel injection control unit wire connector and thread the connector and wire through the hole in the firewall.

14. Attach a lifting sling to the engine. Remove the left and right engine mount retaining nuts and washers. Lift the engine from the engine compartment.

15. To install, reverse the procedures used for removal and lower the engine into the engine compartment. When the engine is positioned, the guide pin must fit in the bore of the axle carrier. Torque the mounting bolts on the front axle carrier (small bolt) to 18-20 ft. lbs.; the larger bolt to 31-35 ft. lbs. The mount-to-bracket bolts are torqued to 31-35 ft. lbs.

16. Connect all of the electrical wiring and all vacuum hoses.

17. Connect the accelerator cable and cruise control cable to the throttle body and adjust the accelerator cable and cruise control cable.

18. Install the air cleaner and reconnect all electrical plugs.

19. Reconnect the wiring to the main control unit.

20. Install the air conditioning compressor and power steering pump, properly route the accessory drive belt. Adjust the belt tension.

21. Install the radiator and connect the hoses.

22. Install the transmission as described in Chapter 7.

23. Install the hood support and lower the hood.

24. Make sure all fluid levels are correct before starting the engine. Bleed the air from the cooling system.

733i and 735i

1983-86 (M30 B34 Engine)

1. Scribe marks for the location of hood hinges on the hood and remove the hood.

2. Disconnect battery positive and negative cables. Unscrew the ground strap at the body. Disconnect the wire that's attached to the positive battery connector at the connector. Remove the battery.

3. Remove the transmission as described later in this section.

4. Drain the coolant, and then remove the fan and radiator (refer to the cooling system section later in this section).

CAUTION: *When draining the coolant, keep in mind that cats and dogs are attracted by the ethylene glycol antifreeze, and are quite likely to drink any that is left in an uncovered container or in puddles on the ground. This will prove fatal in sufficient quantity. Always drain the coolant into a sealable container. Coolant should be reused unless it is contaminated or several years old.*

5. Remove the power steering pump adjusting bolt and hinge nut and bolt. Leave the hoses connected. Suspend the pump while removing the bolts and then wire it in a position that will keep tension off the hoses.

6. In a similar way, loosen and remove the adjusting bolt and the 2 hinge nuts and bolts for the air conditioning compressor. Leave the hoses connected. Suspend the compressor as it is being detached and then wire it in such a position that the hoses will not be stressed.

7. Disconnect the plug (2) and lift out the wiring. Pull off hoses (3 and 4). Loosen the hose clamp (5). Unscrew the air cleaner and airflow sensor.

8. Working under the dash, unscrew the right radio speaker cover. Disconnect the retaining strap for the glovebox. Then, pull off the plug for the idle control unit (located right under the glove-box), and the DME unit plug and 2 other plugs nearby on the right kick panel.

9. Front the front of the cowl in the engine compartment, lift out the master relay (12) and unscrew the socket (13). Take off its rubber ring (14) and lift out the oxygen sensor plug. Disconnect the wire (16). Unstrap the wiring harness. Then, disconnect the heater hose (17).

10. Remove the cover and protective cap from the fusebox. Pull off the connector and the 2 relays nearby. Pull off the wire and hose just below the fusebox. Then, disconnect the wiring harness. Unscrew the fuel line nearby.

11. Working near the air cleaner, remove the windshield washer fluid tank, disconnect the electrical plug at the airflow sensor, and then remove the air cleaner with the airflow sensor attached.

12. Working just in front of the right door, disconnect the additional multiprong connector for the DME control unit. Disconnect the small plug nearby.

13. Working just below the windshield on the right side of the car, lift out the master relay and unscrew the socket nearby. Disconnect the wire at the strut tower. Loosen the firewall

clamps and pull the wiring harness off on this side. Disconnect the other heater hose nearby.

14. Working at the relay box near the coolant reservoir, lift off the cap and disconnect the multiprong wiring connector. Lift the 2 relays from the box. Take the wiring harness out of the clamps.

15. Unscrew the fuel line at the pressure regulator. Disconnect the dipstick tube bracket. Loosen the clamp and unscrew the wiring harness for the oxygen sensor on the floor panel.

16. Disconnect the coil primary and secondary wires and the plug right nearby. Disconnect the air conditioning compressor wires and lift the wires out the holders.

17. Disconnect the throttle and cruise control cables. Pull off the fuel hose nearby. Disconnect the water hoses at the front of the engine.

18. Look around the engine compartment and disconnect any remaining vacuum hoses or wires.

19. Attach lifting hooks to the 2 lift points on the engine. It may be necessary to disconnect a water hose to gain access to one of them. Support the engine with a crane.

20. Unscrew the attaching bolt for the left side engine mount near the steering box. Do the same for the right side mount and ground strap. Unbolt the engine vibration damper. Carefully lift the engine out of the car.

21. To install, reverse the procedures used for removal and lower the engine into the engine compartment. When the engine is positioned, the guide pin must fit in the bore of the axle carrier. Torque the mounting bolts on the front axle carrier (small bolt) to 18-20 ft. lbs.; the larger bolt to 31-35 ft. lbs. The mount-to-bracket bolts are torqued to 31-35 ft. lbs.

22. Connect the fuel lines, use new hose clamps to connect the fuel lines to the fuel filter. Connect all of the multiprong plugs and all vacuum hoses.

23. Connect the accelerator cable and cruise control cable to the throttle body and adjust the accelerator cable and cruise control cable.

24. Install the washer fluid tank, use a new hose clamp on the coolant expansion tank.

25. Install the air cleaner and reconnect all electrical plugs. Connect and install the relays in the relay box.

26. Reconnect the wiring to the main control unit and install the idle control unit.

27. Install the air conditioning compressor and power steering pump, properly route the accessory drive belt. Adjust the belt tension.

28. Install the radiator and connect the hoses.

29. Install the transmission as described in Chapter 7.

30. Install the hood support and lower the hood.

31. Make sure all fluid levels are correct before starting the engine. Bleed air from the cooling system.

1978-88 735i

1. Disconnect first the negative battery cable and then the positive. Remove the transmission as described in Chapter 7. Scribe hinge locations and remove the hood, or remove support struts and prop it securely all the way up.

2. Remove the splash guard from underneath the engine. Then, with the engine cool, remove the drain plugs in the radiator and block and drain the engine coolant.

CAUTION: *When draining the coolant, keep in mind that cats and dogs are attracted by the ethylene glycol antifreeze, and are quite likely to drink any that is left in an uncovered container or in puddles on the ground. This will prove fatal in sufficient quantity. Always drain the coolant into a sealable container. Coolant should be reused unless it is contaminated or several years old.*

3. Loosen the power steering pump bolts from underneath. Turn the adjusting pinion so as to loosen the belt and remove the belt. Then, remove the mounting bolts and remove the power steering pump without disconnecting the hoses. Support the pump out of the way so as to avoid stressing the hoses.

4. Do the same with the air conditioner compressor (this unit does not have the belt adjusting pinion. It is necessary, only to loosen all the bolts and push the compressor toward the engine to remove the belt.

5. Loosen the air intake hose clamp and disconnect the hose. Remove the mounting nut and then remove the air cleaner.

6. The unit on the opposite side of the intake hose from the air cleaner contains the idle speed control valve, which must be removed next. Loosen the hose clamps and pull off the hoses. Disconnect the electrical connector. Remove the mounting nut and then pull the idle speed control out of the air intake hose.

7. Pull off the 3 retainers for the airflow sensor, and then pull the unit off its mountings, disconnecting the vacuum hose from the PCV system at the same time.

8. Working on the coolant expansion tank, disconnect the electrical connector. Remove the nuts on both sides. Loosen their clamps and then disconnect all 3 hoses and remove the tank.

9. Disconnect the heater hoses at both the control valve and at the heater core.

10. Disconnect the throttle and cruise control cables at the throttle lever. Unbolt the cable housing retainer and remove the housing and cables.

11. Pull off the 4 low amperage starter connectors and disconnect the high amperage connector coming from the battery.

12. Loosen its clamp and then disconnect the coolant hose the runs to the alternator.

13. Disconnect the connecting plug for the oxygen sensor, as well as the 2 other plugs nearby.

14. Loosen the clamps and then disconnect the fuel supply and return pipes, draining fuel into a metal container for safe disposal.

15. Disconnect the fuel pipe at the injector supply manifold. Disconnect the plug nearby. Disconnect the electrical connector at the throttle body. Lift off the protective caps and then remove the attaching nuts for the protective cover for the wiring harness for the injectors and remove it.

16. Disconnect the ground strap at the block. Remove the engine mount nut from the top on both sides.

17. Attach a lifting sling to the engine and support the assembly with a crane. Disconnect the ground lead. Carefully lift the engine out of the compartment, tilting the front of the engine upward for clearance.

18. Suspend the engine with a lifting crane via the hooks at the front and rear of the cylinder head. Then, remove the nuts for the engine mounting bolts. The mounts are on the axle carrier and the nut is at the top on the left and on the bottom on the right. Then, carefully lift the engine out of the compartment, avoiding contact between it and the components remaining in the car.

19. Keep these points in mind during installation:

   a. Torque the engine mounting bolts to 32.5 ft. lbs.

   b. Adjust the belt tension for the air conditioning compressor and power steering pump drive belts to give ½-¾" deflection.

   c. Torque the oil cooler line flare nuts to 25 ft. lbs.

   d. When reconnecting the intake manifold to the throttle necks, inspect and, if necessary, replace the O-rings. Torque the mounting nuts to 78 in. lbs.

20. To install, reverse the procedures used for removal and lower the engine into the engine compartment. When the engine is positioned, the guide pin must fit in the bore of the axle carrier. Torque the mounting bolts on the front axle carrier (small bolt) to 18-20 ft. lbs.; the larger bolt to 31-35 ft. lbs. The mount-to-bracket bolts are torqued to 31-35 ft. lbs.

21. Connect the fuel lines, use new hose clamps to connect the fuel lines to the fuel filter. Connect all of the multiprong plugs and all vacuum hoses.

22. Connect the accelerator cable and cruise control cable to the throttle body and adjust the accelerator cable and cruise control cable.

23. Install the coolant recovery tank, use a new hose clamp on the coolant expansion tank.

24. Install the air cleaner and reconnect all electrical plugs. Connect and install the relays in the relay box.

25. Reconnect the wiring to the main control unit and install the idle control unit.

26. Install the air conditioning compressor and power steering pump, properly route the accessory drive belt. Adjust the belt tension.

27. Install the radiator and connect the hoses.

28. Install the transmission as described in Chapter 7.

29. Install the hood support and lower the hood.

30. Make sure all fluid levels are correct before starting the engine. Bleed air from the cooling system.

Cylinder Head (Valve) Cover

REMOVAL AND INSTALLATION

Cylinder head cover removal and installation is basically a straightforward procedure on all

Cylinder head cover bolts/nuts should be removed and installed in a cross-wise pattern—4 cylinder engines

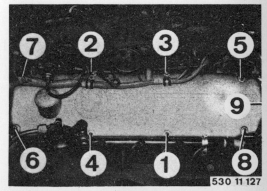

Cylinder head cover bolts/nuts should be removed and installed in a cross-wise pattern—6 cylinder engines

models covered in this book. Simply disconnect any hoses or lines which are in the way, remove the retaining bolts or nuts and lift off the cover. It is always a good idea to remove and install the bolts/nuts in a cross-wise manner starting in the center; snug all bolts/nuts finger tight and then tighten in the same order. Cylinder head cover removal will almost always require the replacement of the gasket upon installation so you may wish to have one on hand before attempting this procedure.

Rocker Arm Shafts/Rocker Arms
REMOVAL AND INSTALLATION
All Models Except 325, 325e, 325i, 325iS, 325ix, 524td, and 528e

1. Remove the cylinder head.
2. Remove the camshaft.
3. On 6-cylinder engines, remove the retaining bolts and remove the end cover from the rear of the cylinder head. Slide the thrust rings and rocker arms rearward and remove the circlips from the rocker arm shafts.

4. On 4-cylinder engines:
   a. Remove the distributor flange from the rear of the cylinder head.
   b. Using a long punch, drive the rocker arm shaft from the rear to the front of the cylinder head.
NOTE: *Be sure all circlips are off the shaft before attempting to drive the shaft from the cylinder head.*

"E" is exhaust side, "A" intake. Order of assembly is: spring (3); washer (4), rocker arm (5), and thrust ring (6)

After pushing the rocker arm back, remove the circlip (1)

On 6 cylinder engines, remove the locking bolts (2) from the cylinder head

Removing the distributor flange—4 cylinder engines

Use a slide hammer to remove the rocker shafts on the 6 cylinder engine

Align the rocker shafts so the head bolts will slide through the indentations in the rocker shafts

c. The intake rocker shaft is not plugged at the rear, while the exhaust rocker shaft must be plugged. Renew the plug if necessary, during the installation.

5. On 6-cylinder engines:

a. Install dowel pins BMW part No. 11 1 063 or equivalent to keep the rocker shafts from turning. Then, remove the rocker shaft retaining plugs from the front of the cylinder head. These require a hex head wrench. Then, push back the rocker arms against spring pressure and remove the circlips retaining the shafts. Remove the dowel pins. If the rocker shafts have welded plugs, the shafts will have to be pressed out of the head with a tool such as 11 3 050 or equivalent. CAUTION: *There is considerable force on the springs positioning the rockers. They may pop out! Be cautious and wear safety glasses.*

b. Install a threaded slide hammer into the ends of the rear rocker shafts and remove.

6. The rocker arms, springs, washers, thrust rings and shafts should be examined and worn parts replaced. Special attention should be given to the rocker arm cam followers. If these are loose, replace the arm assembly. The valves can be removed, repaired or replaced, as necessary, while the shafts and rocker arms are out of the cylinder head.

7. Installation is the reverse of removal. Note the following procedures:

a. Design changes of the rocker arms and shafts have occurred with the installation of a bushing in the rocker arm and the use of 2 horizontal oil flow holes drilled into the rocker shaft for improved oil supply. Do not mix the previously designed parts with the later design.

b. When installing the rocker arms and components to the rocker shafts, install locating pins in the cylinder head bolt bores to properly align the rocker arm shafts. Note that on 6-cylinder engines, the longer rocker

shafts go on the chain end of the engine; the openings face the bores for the cylinder head bolts; and the plug threads face outward. The order of installation is: spring, washer, rocker arm, thrust washer, circlip. Note also that newer, short springs may be used with the older design.

c. Install sealer on the rocker arm shaft retaining plugs and rear cover.

d. On the 4-cylinder engines, position the rocker shafts so that the camshaft retaining plate ends can be engaged in the slots of shafts during camshaft installation.

e. Adjust the valve clearance.

524td

NOTE: *To replace the rocker arms on the 524td, it is necessary to use a special tool which allows the valve involved to be opened and works against the camshaft. Use BMW Tool 11 3 120 or the equivalent. It is also necessary to have a special tool designed to remove the rocker pivots from the head. Because these are retained by an adhesive, it will be necessary to get an adhesive designed to retain the rocker pivots on this engine. It is also necessary, of course, to have the special tools required to adjust the valves after the rockers have been replaced.*

1. Remove the cam cover. Turn the engine over with a wrench on the crankshaft pulley so the cams that drive the vacuum pump (mounted over the camshaft) are pointed downward. Then, remove the attaching nuts and remove the vacuum pump.

2. Pull off the spring clip for each rocker being replaced. Turn the crankshaft so the cams involved are pointing downward.

3. Locate the special valve spring compression tool around the camshaft. Make sure that if the valve will not depress easily, the crankshaft is turned. If the piston is right near top center, the valve may hit it. Also, make sure not to depress the valve spring retainer while the valve remains stationary, which could permit the retaining collets to come loose. When there is sufficient clearance to permit the rocker to clear the ball on the top of the pivot ballstud, remove it by sliding it out from under the camshaft.

4. Remove the ballstud by clamping the special tool on it and pulling it out. Coat a new ballstud with the required adhesive and install it, pressing it in until it hits the stop. Do not replace the rocker arm without also replacing the ballstud. If re-using parts, retain ballstuds and rockers in order so the same parts will be used together.

5. Install the rocker in reverse order. Press the spring clip into the groove in the top of the

ballstud from the outboard side so the end of the clip will retain the rocker. Adjust the valves as described earlier in this section.

6. Install the vacuum pump with the cams that are under it turned downward. Make sure that the vacuum pump pipe is at the rear and that its drive cam will line up with the follower on the pump plunger. Make sure to install the seal on the pipe. Replace the cam cover in reverse or removal.

325, 325e, 325i, 325is, 325ix and 528e

The cylinder head must be removed before the rocker arm shafts can be removed.

1. Remove the cylinder head.

2. Mount the head on BMW stand 11 1 060 and 00 1 490 or equivalent. Secure the head to the stand with one head bolt.

3. Remove the camshaft sprocket bolt and remove the camshaft distributor adapter and sprocket. Reinstall the adapter on the camshaft.

4. Adjust the valve clearance to the maximum allowable on all valves.

5. Remove the front and rear rocker shaft plugs and lift out the thrust plate.

6. Remove the spring-clips from the rocker arms by lifting them off.

7. Remove the exhaust side rocker arm shaft:

a. Set the No. 6 cylinder rocker arms at the valve overlap position (rocker arms parallel), by rotating the camshaft through the firing order.

b. Push in on the front cylinder rocker arm and then turn the camshaft in the direction of the intake rocker shaft, using a ½"

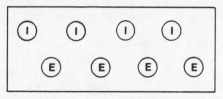

4-cylinder valve location

Installation of locating pins in the cylinder head bolt bores to prevent rocker shafts from turning—six cylinder engines

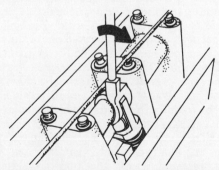

Locate the special valve spring compressing tool around the camshaft, as shown, to force the valve downward. This will give clearance to permit removal of the rocker arm

Removal of camshaft and rocker arm retainer plate from the cylinder head, showing the dowel pin hole on four cylinder engine

Removing the rocker arm shaft with special tool—four cylinder engine

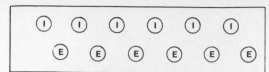

6-cylinder valve location

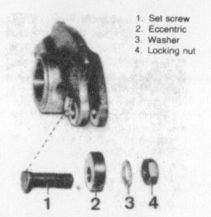

1. Set screw
2. Eccentric
3. Washer
4. Locking nut

Rocker arm valve adjusting mechanism

drive breaker bar and a deep well socket to fit over the camshaft adapter. Slide each rocker arm to one side as it develops sufficient clearance away from its actuating cam and the valve it actuates. Rotate the camshaft until all of the rocker arms are relaxed.

c. Remove the rocker arm shaft.

8. Remove the intake side rocker arm shaft:

a. Turn the camshaft in the direction of the exhaust rocker arm.

b. Use a deep well socket and ½" drive breaker bar on the camshaft adapter to turn the camshaft. Slide each rocker arm to one side as it develops sufficient clearance away from its actuating cam and the valve it actuates. Rotate the camshaft until all of the rocker arms are relaxed.

c. Remove the rocker arm shaft.

9. Install the rocker arm shafts by reversing the removal procedure. Bear the following points in mind:

a. The large oil bores in the rocker shafts must be installed downward (toward the valve guides) and the small oil bores and grooves for the guide plate face inward toward the center of the head.

b. The straight sections of the spring clamps must fit into the grooves in the rocker arm shafts.

c. The guide plate must fit into the grooves in the rocker arm shafts.

d. Adjust the valve clearance.

Thermostat

REMOVAL AND INSTALLATION

The thermostat is located near the water pump, either on the cylinder head or intake manifold on some models and is located between 2 coolant hose sections on other models. On the diesel, it is located right above the water pump. Remove the fan to gain access to it. See the water pump removal procedure for special procedures required to remove the fan.

The removal and installation of the thermostat is accomplished in the conventional manner. Always drain some coolant out and save it in a clean container before removing the thermostat. On the M5, M6 engine, the forward (removable) portion of the housing has a hose connected to it. The hose need not be disconnected to remove the housing. Note that on the 1983-87 3.3 and all 3.5 liter engines and the diesel, there is not only a thermostat housing gasket, but an inner rubber seal to keep the closed thermostat from leaking. On the engine used in the M5, M6, there is a large O-ring seal for the main portion of the housing and a small, O-ring located above it in a small passage. The M20B27 and M20B25 engines also use the large O-ring which must be replaced with the thermostat. Replace both these seals on all models.

CAUTION: *When draining the coolant, keep in mind that cats and dogs are attracted by the ethylene glycol antifreeze, and are quite likely to drink any that is left in an uncovered container or in puddles on the ground. This will prove fatal in sufficient quantity. Always drain the coolant into a sealable container. Coolant should be reused unless it is contaminated or several years old.*

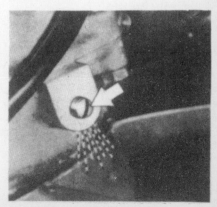

Bleeding of the cooling system with bleeder screw

Note that thermostats for 3.5L engines built in 1986-88 carry an **A** designation. The thermostat for M20B27 and M20B25 engines in 1986-88 models is smaller in diameter. On all models except M3, the thermostat is installed with the thermostatic sensing unit facing inward and the cross-band facing outward. Refill and bleed the cooling system.

On the M3, the thermostat is installed in a coolant lines with a third connection that goes to the block. To replace it, first drain coolant and then note the routing of hoses. Loosen all 3 hose clamps and then replace the unit. Refill and bleed the system.

Bleeding the Cooling System

WITH BLEEDER SCREW ON THERMOSTAT HOUSING

Set the heat valve in the WARM position, start the engine and bring it to normal operating temperature. Run the engine at fast idle and open the venting screw on the thermostat housing until the coolant comes out free of air bubbles. Close the bleeder screw and refill the cooling system.

WITHOUT BLEEDER SCREW

Fill the cooling system, place the heater valve in the WARM position, close the pressure cap to the second (fully closed) position. Start the engine and bring to normal operating temperature. Carefully release the pressure cap to the first position and squeeze the upper and lower radiator hoses in a pumping action to allow trapped air to escape through the radiator. Recheck the coolant level and close the pressure cap to its second position.

Intake Manifold

REMOVAL AND INSTALLATION

1600, 2000, 2002

1. Remove the air cleaner.
2. Remove and tag the fuel lines, vacuum lines and electrical wiring.
3. Drain the cooling system.
CAUTION: *When draining the coolant, keep in mind that cats and dogs are attracted by the ethylene glycol antifreeze, and are quite likely to drink any that is left in an uncovered container or in puddles on the ground. This will prove fatal in sufficient quantity. Always drain the coolant into a sealable container. Coolant should be reused unless it is contaminated or several years old.*
4. Disconnect he manual choke control cable. On the 2002A, disconnect the wire connector to the choke cover.

Removing intake manifold—carbureted models

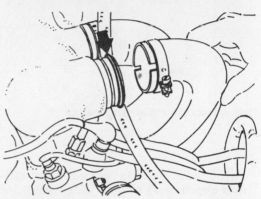

The induction pipes on early 2002tii models were secured with clamps

5. Disconnect the accelerator linkage. On 2002A, disconnect the linkage at the ball socket.
6. Disconnect the coolant lines to the manifold.
7. Disconnect the dipstick support.
8. Remove the intake manifold.
9. Installation is the reverse of removal. Use new gaskets.
NOTE: *The 2 front or rear intake tubes can be removed and installed on the 2002tii engine (4 carburetors), by separating the connecting rod between the middle carburetors and removing the front or rear section as desired by using the above procedure as a guide.*

2002tii

NOTE: *To remove the complete manifold system, first remove the resonator pipes or manifolds; then remove the intake pipe.*

INDUCTION RESONATOR PIPES (SECURED WITH CLAMPS)

1. Remove the air filter.
2. Remove and tag the fuel lines, starter valve cable, vacuum hoses and all induction resonator pipes.
3. Disconnect the throttle return spring and

Most intake tubes were secured with nuts and bolts

remove the injection pipe from No. 1 cylinder. Remove the injector valve.

4. Remove the bracket bolts a the throttle housing.

5. Remove the vacuum hose, auxiliary air hose and injection pipe from the No. 4 cylinder.

6. Remove the air collector from the cylinder head.

7. Installation is the reverse of the removal procedure.

INDUCTION MANIFOLDS (SECURED WITH NUTS AND WASHERS)

1. Remove the air filter.

2. Remove the fuel line, fuel return line starter valve cable and vacuum hose from the air tube assembly.

3. Remove the bracket bolts on the throttle housing.

4. Remove the air collector support bolts at the top engine cover area.

5. Remove the nuts and washers from the bottom of the induction manifold.

6. Remove the air collector together with the induction manifolds and the throttle housing.

7. Installation is the reverse of the removal procedure.

INTAKE PIPE

1. After removing the air collector, induction resonator pipes or the induction manifolds as outlined in the preceding steps, remove all of the remaining injection pipes from the injection valves.

2. Disconnect the coolant hoses and electrical connections at the thermostat housing switches.

3. Remove the retaining nuts and washers from the cylinder head studs and remove the intake pipe. the injector valves can be removed before or after the removal.

4. Installation is the reverse of removal. Use new gaskets and place them on the intake opening properly so as not to interfere with the air flow.

2500, 2800, 3000, Bavaria and 3.0 Carbureted Versions

FRONT INTAKE MANIFOLD

1. Drain the cooling system.

CAUTION: *When draining the coolant, keep in mind that cats and dogs are attracted by the ethylene glycol antifreeze, and are quite likely to drink any that is left in an uncovered container or in puddles on the ground. This will prove fatal in sufficient quantity. Always drain the coolant into a sealable container. Coolant should be reused unless it is contaminated or several years old.*

2. Remove the air filter.

3. Disconnect and tag all fuel and vacuum lines.

4. Disconnect the throttle linkage bar and connecting bar and remove the bearing block.

5. Disconnect the manual choke cable.

6. Remove the coolant hoses to the manifold or carburetor.

7. Remove the dipstick support.

8. Remove the intake manifold with the carburetor attached.

9. Installation is the reverse of the removal procedure. Use new gaskets.

REAR INTAKE MANIFOLD

1. Drain the cooling system.

CAUTION: *When draining the coolant, keep in mind that cats and dogs are attracted by the ethylene glycol antifreeze, and are quite likely to drink any that is left in an uncovered container or in puddles on the ground. This will prove fatal in sufficient quantity. Always drain the coolant into a sealable container. Coolant should be reused unless it is contaminated or several years old.*

2. Disconnect the battery ground cable.

3. Remove the air filter.

Pull off plugs 1, 2, and 3 and unplug or disconnect starter connections 4, 5, and 6. Note that the red cable goes to terminal 50, while the black cable goes to terminal 30

4. Disconnect and tag all fuel and vacuum lines.

5. Disconnect the accelerator thrust bar and bearing block.

6. Disconnect he electrical wire from the choke cover. Remove the choke cover with the coolant lines attached.

7. Disconnect the heater hoses from the manifold base.

8. Remove the intake manifold with the carburetor attached.

9. Installation is the reverse of the removal procedure. Use new gaskets when installing the manifold.

3.0 CSi

NOTE: *Combine the next 2 operations to remove both the front and rear intake manifolds.*

FRONT INTAKE MANIFOLD

1. Remove the air cleaner.
2. Drain the cooling system.
CAUTION: *When draining the coolant, keep in mind that cats and dogs are attracted by the ethylene glycol antifreeze, and are quite likely to drink any that is left in an uncovered container or in puddles on the ground. This will prove fatal in sufficient quantity. Always drain the coolant into a sealable container. Coolant should be reused unless it is contaminated or several years old.*
3. Remove the intake air collector and the 3 front intake pipes.
4. Remove the pressure regulator and support from the intake manifold.
5. Disconnect the coolant hoses from the thermostat housing and the wiring from the coolant switches.
6. Remove the flat plugs from the injection valves by carefully pulling upward.
7. Remove the first 3 injection valves from the manifold.
NOTE: *Leave the circular pipe connected.*
8. Remove the retaining bolts from the intake manifold and remove it from the cylinder head.
9. Installation is the reverse of removal. Use new injection valve sealing rings.

REAR INTAKE MANIFOLD

1. Disconnect the battery ground able.
2. Remove the air cleaner.
3. Remove the intake air collector and the 3 rear intake pipes.
4. Remove the pressure regulator and support from the intake manifold.
5. Remove the flat plugs from the injection valves by carefully pulling upwards.
6. Remove the 3 rear injector valves.

NOTE: *Leave the circular pipe connected.*

7. Remove and tag the electrical flat plugs and connectors from the end of the wire loom, rerouted through the intake manifold.

8. Carefully pull the wire loom upward throught the hole in the intake manifold.

9. Remove the intake manifold from the cylinder head.

10. Installation is the reverse of removal. Always renew the injection valve sealing rings.

318i and 320i

1. Remove the air cleaner and drain the cooling system.
CAUTION: *When draining the coolant, keep in mind that cats and dogs are attracted by the ethylene glycol antifreeze, and are quite likely to drink any that is left in an uncovered container or in puddles on the ground. This will prove fatal in sufficient quantity. Always drain the coolant into a sealable container. Coolant should be reused unless it is contaminated or several years old.*
2. Disconnect the accelerator cable and remove the vacuum hoses from the air collector. Tag the hoses.
3. Remove the injection line holder from No. 4 intake tube.
4. Remove the No. 3 intake tube and disconnect the vacuum and coolant lines from the throttle housing.
5. Disconnect the hoses at the EGR valve and remove the wire plugs at the temperature timing switch.
6. Remove the cold start valve from the air collector.
7. Disconnect the vacuum hose and electrical connections at the timing valve.
8. Disconnect the remaining intake tubes at the collector. Disconnect the collector brackets at the engine and remove the collector.
9. Remove the air intake tubes from the manifold and remove the injector valves.
10. Remove the intake manifold.
11. To install the manifold, use new gaskets and install the manifold to the engine.
12. Install the air intake tubes and the injector valves. Install the collector and bracket.
13. Connect the vacuum line and electrical connections to the timing valve. Install the cold start valve.
14. Connect the line at the EGR valve and the electrical connections at the temperature timing switch.
15. Connect all vacuum, cooling and fuel lines at the throttle housing. Install the accelerator cable and vacuum hoses to the air collector.
16. Install the air cleaner and fill the cooling system. Check all hose connections and fluid levels before operating the engine.

All 6-Cylinder Models Except 524td, M5 and M6

NOTE: *Slight variations may exist among models due to model changes and updating but basic removal and installation remains the same.*

1. Disconnect the battery ground cable and drain the cooling system.

CAUTION: *When draining the coolant, keep in mind that cats and dogs are attracted by the ethylene glycol antifreeze, and are quite likely to drink any that is left in an uncovered container or in puddles on the ground. This will prove fatal in sufficient quantity. Always drain the coolant into a sealable container. Coolant should be reused unless it is contaminated or several years old.*

2. Disconnect the wire harness at the air flow sensor. Remove the air cleaner and sensor as an assembly. Disconnect the air intake hose running from the air cleaner to the manifold.

3. Remove and tag the vacuum hoses and electrical plugs. Disconnect the accelerator linkage (and cruise control linkage, if so-equipped) from the throttle housing.

4. Disconnect the coolant hoses from the throttle housing.

5. Working from the rear of the collector housing, disconnect the vacuum lines, and starting valve connector, fuel line and air line. Tag the hoses and lines for ease of assembly.

6. Remove the EGR valve and line.

7. Remove all intake pipes.

8. Remove the air collector housing from the engine. On later models with a single intake manifold casting, remove the nuts and remove the throttle valve body.

9. Disconnect the plugs at the injector valves and remove the valves.

10. Disconnect the wire plugs at the coolant temperature sensor, the temperature time switch and the temperature switch.

11. Pull the wire loom upward through the opening in the intake manifold neck.

12. Remove the coolant hoses from the intake neck.

NOTE: *Mark the heater hoses for proper reinstallation.*

13. Remove the retaining bolts or nuts and remove either front, rear or both intake manifold necks. On later models, remove the entire assembly.

14. To install the manifold, use new gaskets and install the manifold to the engine.

15. Install the air intake tubes and the injector valves. Install the collector and bracket.

16. Connect the vacuum line and electrical connections to the timing valve. Install the cold start valve.

17. Connect the line at the EGR valve and the electrical connections at the temperature timing switch.

18. Connect all vacuum, cooling and fuel lines at the throttle housing. Install the accelerator cable and vacuum hoses to the air collector.

19. Install the air cleaner and fill the cooling system. Check all hose connections and fluid levels before operating the engine.

524td

1. Loosen the clamps at either end, and remove the air hose linking the turbocharger and intake air box.

2. Using a crowfoot type wrench, disconnect the injection lines at both the pump and injectors, remove the lines as an assembly, and plug all openings.

3. Remove any remaining hoses or wires interfering with manifold removal. Then, remove the retaining nuts and remove the manifold.

4. Clean both gasket surfaces, install a new gasket, and put the manifold into position. Install the retaining nuts. Torque the nuts to the figure shown in the torque chart at the beginning of this section.

5. Reinstall the injection lines, torquing the connections to 14-18 ft. lbs. Bleed the injection system as described under "Injection Pump Removal and Installation" in Chapter 5. Reconnect all hoses and wires that had to be disconnected. Reconnect the hose linking the turbocharger and manifold. Make sure connections are properly positioned and that the clamps are tight.

M5 and M6

The M5 and M6 employ a manifold chamber in combination with 6 throttle necks (one for each cylinder), each of which contains its own throttle. The throttle necks are divided into 3 assemblies each containing the necks for 2 adjacent cylinders.

1. Remove the nuts at the outer ends of the throttle necks (these attach the manifold to the outer ends of the necks). Loosen the hose clamps for the crankcase ventilation hoses-and for the air intake hose. Disconnect the accelerator cable.

2. Pull the intake manifold off the throttle necks. Check O-rings and replace any that are hard or cracked.

3. Disconnect the electrical connectors to the cold start valve, throttle bypass valve, and throttle valve switch. Disconnect all the electrical connections going to the fuel injectors and remove the conduit for the injector wires from the throttle necks.

4. Disconnect the vacuum hoses for the fuel pressure regulator and the heater temperature sensor. Disconnect the fuel return pipe, and col-

lect the fuel in a metal container for safe disposal.

5. Remove the attaching nuts and bolts, and remove the injection pipe and injectors.

NOTE: *Clean the throttle shaft thoroughly and be sure not to use pliers on the shaft surface. Otherwise, needle bearings on which the shaft rides may be damaged.*

6. Using a center punch, drive out the 4 pins locking the throttle shaft in place. Slide the shaft out of the bearings.

7. Unscrew its mounting nuts and remove the throttle bypass valve. Disconnect the air hoses from this valve.

8. Remove the nuts attaching the throttle valve necks to the head and remove them.

9. Remove the connecting pipes that run between the valve neck units. Replace O-rings if necessary. Replace all gaskets and make sure gasket surfaces on the head and inner ends of valve necks are clean.

10. Install in reverse order, providing new pins for the throttle shaft and coating its bearing surfaces with Molykote Longterm® before assembly. Replace the sleeves in the intake manifold, if necessary. Replace the crankcase ventilation hose connecting the intake manifold and crankcase.

M3

NOTE: *A Torx® nut driver is needed to perform this operation.*

1. Remove the capnuts (2 each) at the outer ends of the 4 throttle necks. Then remove the mounting nuts underneath.

2. Make sure the engine has cooled off. Loosen the hose clamps for the air intake lines and for the fuel lines where they connect with the injection pipe. Collect fuel in a metal container.

3. Disconnect the throttle cable.

4. Pull off the intake manifold. Cut off the crankcase ventilation hose running to it from the crankcase. Then, remove the manifold and place it aside. Supply a new crankcase ventilation hose.

5. Pull off the throttle valve switch plug. Carefully pull the injector plug plate evenly off all 4 injectors.

6. Pull the fuel pressure regulator vacuum hose off the pressure regulator.

7. Remove the 2 mounting bolts for the injector pipe. Then, carefully lift off the pipe and injectors.

8. Unscrew the nut attaching the ball joint at the end of the throttle actuating rod to the throttle linkage. Supply a new self-locking nut.

9. Remove the Torx® nuts attaching the throttle necks to the cylinder head. Then, remove the 4 throttle necks as an assembly.

10. Separate the throttle neck assemblies by pulling them apart at the connecting pipe.

11. Inspect the O-rings in the connecting pipe and at the outer ends of the throttle necks. Replace as necessary.

12. Reverse the removal procedure to install. Use the new throttle linkage self-locking nut and the new crankcase ventilation hose. Torque the nuts attaching the throttle necks to the head and the intake manifold to the throttle necks to 78-84 in. lbs. Adjust the throttle cable.

Exhaust Manifold

REMOVAL AND INSTALLATION

1600, 2000, and 2002

1. Loosen the exhaust system supports.

2. Separate the exhaust pipe from the exhaust manifold and remove the hot air guide sleeve.

3. Remove the retaining nuts and washers from the exhaust manifold studs and remove the manifold from the cylinder head.

4. Installation is the reverse of removal. Tighten the clamps holding the exhaust pipes last to avoid having an exhaust system vibration during operation.

2500, 2800, 3000, Bavaria and 3.0 Series

NOTE: *Each exhaust manifold can be removed separately after the exhaust pipes are disconnected.*

1. Remove the air cleaner and manifold cover plate.

2. On automatic tranmission equipped vehicles, detach the oil filler pipe at the rear of the cover plate.

3. On the 528i, disconnect the CO tap connector at the exhaust manifold. Disconnect the exhaust pipe fro the manifold sections.

4. Remove the retaining nuts and washers and remove the exhaust manifolds from the cylinder head.

5. Installation is the reverse of removal.

All 1977-88 Models Except 524td, M3, M5 and M6

The exhaust manifolds are referred to as exhaust gas recirculation reactors. Refer to Chapter 4 for operation.

The removal and installation procedures are basically the same for all models. The 4-cylinder manifold (used on the 320i model), is a one piece, one outlet unit, while the 6-cylinder manifold assembly consists of a 2 piece, double outlet to the exhaust pipe. One piece can be replaced independently of the other.

1. Remove the air volume control and if necessary, air cleaner.

2. Disconnect the exhaust pipe at the reactor outlet(s).

3. Remove the guard plate from the reactor(s).

4. Disconnect the air injection pipe fitting, the EGR counter pressure line, EGR pressure line and any supports.

NOTE: *An exhaust filter is used between the reactor and the EGR valve and must be disconnected. Replace the filter if found to be defective.*

5. Remove the retaining bolts or nuts at the reactor and remove it from the cylinder head.

6. Installation is the reverse of removal. Use new gaskets.

524td

1. Remove the turbocharger, oil lines, and piping as described below.

2. Remove the nuts and disconnect the exhaust pipe at the manifold.

3. Remove the manifold bolts and remove the manifold. Clean both gasket surfaces.

4. Install the gasket, manifold, and attaching nuts. Torque the nuts to the figure shown in the torque chart at the beginning of this section.

5. Install the turbocharger and associated piping as described below.

M5 and M6

1. With the engine cool, remove the drain plug from the block. Remove the 3 electrical connectors from the front of the coolant manifold that runs along the left side of the engine. Disconnect the radiator hose from the front of this pipe. Then, remove all the mounting bolts for this pipe and remove it. Inspect the O-rings (one for each cylinder, located in the block), and replace any that are worn or damaged.

CAUTION: *When draining the coolant, keep in mind that cats and dogs are attracted by the ethylene glycol antifreeze, and are quite likely to drink any that is left in an uncovered container or in puddles on the ground. This will prove fatal in sufficient quantity. Always drain the coolant into a sealable container. Coolant should be reused unless it is contaminated or several years old.*

2. Disconnect the exhaust pipe at the manifold. Remove the heat shields from underneath the engine.

3. Remove the cross brace that runs under the engine by removing the 2 bolts from either end and then removing it.

4. Disconnect the stabilizer bar near both ends where it is bushed to the engine carrier.

5. Attach a lifting sling to the engine. Remove the nut from the right side engine mount and lift the engine slightly for clearance.

6. Remove the mounting bolts and remove the manifold.

7. Clean all gasket material from the surfaces of the manifold and head and replace the gaskets.

8. To install, reverse the removal procedure, torquing the manifold bolts to 36-40 ft. lbs. and the coolant pipe mounting bolts to 7.5-8.5 ft. lbs. Make sure to refill the cooling system with fresh anti-freeze/water mix and bleed it.

M3

1. With the engine cool, remove the drain plug from the block. Remove the 3 electrical connectors from the front of the coolant manifold that runs along the left side of the engine. Disconnect the radiator hose from the front of this pipe. Then, remove all the mounting bolts for this pipe and remove it. Inspect the O-rings (one for each cylinder, located in the block), and replace any that are worn or damaged.

CAUTION: *When draining the coolant, keep in mind that cats and dogs are attracted by the ethylene glycol antifreeze, and are quite likely to drink any that is left in an uncovered container or in puddles on the ground. This will prove fatal in sufficient quantity. Always drain the coolant into a sealable container. Coolant should be reused unless it is contaminated or several years old.*

2. Disconnect the exhaust pipe at the manifold flange. Remove the heat shields from underneath the engine.

3. Remove the mounting nuts at the cylinder head and remove the manifold.

4. Clean all gasket material from the surfaces of the manifold and head and replace the gaskets.

5. To install, reverse the removal procedure, torquing the manifold bolts to 78-84 in. lbs. and the coolant pipe mounting bolts to 90-102 in. lbs. Torque the bolts at the flange attaching manifold and exhaust pipe first to 22-25 ft. lbs. and then to 36-40 ft. lbs. Make sure to refill the cooling system with fresh anti-freeze/water mix and bleed it.

Turbocharger
REMOVAL AND INSTALLATION
524td

1. Disconnect the connecting hoses and remove the air cleaner. Disconnect the turbo inlet and outlet air hoses.

2. Remove the EGR pipe and EGR valve.

3. Unbolt the banjo connector for the oil pressure line going to the turbocharger at the side of the block. Remove the clamps and disconnect the oil drain line from the turbo at the

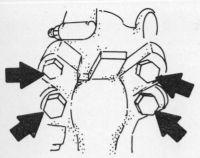

Remove the four arrowed bolts to remove the turbocharger (524 td)

block. Disconnect the exhaust pipe at the turbo exhaust outlet.

4. Remove the 4 bolts attaching the turbocharger to the exhaust manifold, and remove it.

5. Installation is the reverse of removal. Replace gaskets on the EGR valve and seals on the high pressure oil line. Coat EGR valve studs with a copper paste and replace the self-locking nuts.

Air Conditioning Compressor

REMOVAL AND INSTALLATION

All Equipped Models

Before attempting to remove the compressor, the air conditioning system must be discharged. You will find the procedure to do this in Chapter 1. However, if you are not equipped to safely discharge the system, you should have it done by a professional.

1. Discharge the air conditioning system.

2. Remove the splash shield from the compressor. Disconnect the electrical leads from the compressor.

3. Remove the drive belt and disconnect the refrigerant lines from the compressor.

4. Remove the mounting bolts and remove the compressor.

5. Install the compressor and install the drive belt. Check the belt tension.

6. Reconnect the refrigerant lines and charge the system. If you are not equipped to do this have it done by a professional.

7. Connect the electrical leads to the compressor. Check the system operation and check the system for leaks.

Air Conditioning Condenser

REMOVAL AND INSTALLATION

All Equipped Models

Before attempting to remove the condenser, the air conditioning system must be discharged. You will find the procedure to do this in Chap-

ter 1, however, if you are not equipped to safely discharge the system, you should have it done by a professional.

The condenser is located in front of the radiator and has its own cooling fan mounted to it.

1. Discharge the air conditioning system.

2. Disconnect the refrigerant lines to the condenser and plug the openings to prevent dirt from enetering the system.

3. Disconnect the electrical lead from the cooling fan.

4. Remove the mountng bolts and lift the condenser from in front of the radiator.

5. Install the condenser in position, making sure the rubber bottom mounts are in position.

6. Reconnect the refrigerant lines and connect the electrical lead to the cooling fan.

7. Recharge the cooling system, or have it charged by a professional technician. Check for leaks and check the operation of the system.

Radiator

REMOVAL AND INSTALLATION

Remove the radiator as follows:

1. Drain the cooling system. On 1983-88 3.3L and 3.5L engines and on the M3, this requires removing the plug from the bottom radiator tank.

CAUTION: *When draining the coolant, keep in mind that cats and dogs are attracted by the ethylene glycol antifreeze, and are quite likely to drink any that is left in an uncovered container or in puddles on the ground. This will prove fatal in sufficient quantity. Always drain the coolant into a sealable container. Coolant should be reused unless it is contaminated or several years old.*

2. If the car has a coolant expansion tank, re-

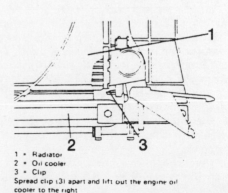

1 = Radiator
2 = Oil cooler
3 = Clip
Spread clip (3) apart and lift out the engine oil cooler to the right
Remove radiator

Late model 5, 6, and 7 Series cars with the M30 B35 engine have an oil cooler that must be removed before removing the radiator (1). To remove the oil cooler (2), remove the clip (3) and then pull the cooler out to the right.

move the cap, disconnect the hose at the radiator, and drain the coolant into a clean container. If the car has a splash guard, remove it.

3. Disconnect and remove the coolant hoses.

4. Disconnect the automatic transmission oil cooler lines and plug their openings as well as the openings in the cooler.

5. Disconnect any of the temperature switch wire connectors (used in many applications, especially if the car has air conditioning).

6. Remove the shroud from the radiator. On some models, this is done by simply pressing plugs toward the rear of the car. On others, there are metal slips that must be pulled upward and off to free the shroud from the radiator. The shroud will remain in the vehicle, resting on the fan on most models. On the 735i, remove the fan and shroud together (make sure to store the fan in a vertical position!). The fan must be held stationary with some sort of flat blade cut to fit over the hub and drilled to fit over 2 of the studs on the front of the pulley (or it is possible to use BMW special tool 11 5 020). Then, unscrew the retaining nut at the center of the fluid drive hub turning it *clockwise* to remove it because it has left hand threads.

• On the 318i, remove the cover from the left side of the radiator.

• On late model cars with the M30 B35 engine, remove the fan and shroud; then, spread the retaining clip and pull the oil cooler out to the right. Remove the radiator retaining bolts (or single bolt on some models) and lift the radiator from the vehicle.

• Note that on the 1983-88 3.3L and 3.5L engines, there are 2 bolts at the top/rear of the radiator and 2 bolts at the bottom rear.

7. The radiator is installed in the reverse order of removal. Fill and bleed the cooling system.

• Note that, on the M3, there are rubber washers that go on either side of the mounting brackets at the top and that the bottom of the unit is suspended by rubber bushings into which prongs located on the bottom tank will fit. Make sure all parts fit right when the unit is installed. On all models, check that rubber mounts are located so as to effectively isolate the radiator from the chassis, as this will help ensure reliable radiator performance and long life. Note that if the car uses plastic upper and lower radiator tanks and has a radiator drain plug, be careful not to over torque the plug. Use only 1.2-2 ft. lbs. Torque engine oil cooler pipes to 18-21 ft. lbs. and transmission cooler pipes to 13-15 ft. lbs. Torque the thermostatic fan hub on the 735i to 29-36 ft. lbs.

Water Pump
REMOVAL AND INSTALLATION
All Models Except 325, 325e, 325i, 325iS, 325iX, M3, 524td and 528e

1. Drain the cooling system and remove the radiator.

CAUTION: *When draining the coolant, keep in mind that cats and dogs are attracted by the ethylene glycol antifreeze, and are quite likely to drink any that is left in an uncovered container or in puddles on the ground. This will prove fatal in sufficient quantity. Always drain the coolant into a sealable container. Coolant should be reused unless it is contaminated or several years old.*

2. Remove the fan blades. Loosen the drive belts and remove as necessary. On the 318i, M3, and 1983-85 733i and the 735i this requires holding the fan pulley via the locating posts (fabricate some sort of flat blade cut to fit over the hub and drilled to fit over 2 of the studs on the front of the pulley, or use BMW special tool 11 5 020. Then turn the coupling nut clockwise (left hand threads) to remove the fan and clutch. Store in a vertical position.

3. On the M3, next loosen the alternator bolts to release belt tension. Then, on all models, unbolt and remove the belt pulley from the pump flange and disconnect the coolant hoses.

Water pump installed—four cylinder engines

Remove the slack adjusting plate (1) from behind the pulley on six cylinder engines

4. On 1983-85 3.3L and all 3.5L engines, remove the lifting hook that's in the way before removing the 2 bolts. In addition, on the M5, M6 models, remove the air cleaner and airflow

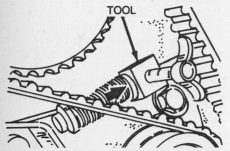

Compress tensioner spring with special tool during water pump removal—528e

When replacing six cylinder thermostats, replace both the gasket (1) and seal (2)

1. Upper radiator hose
2. Lower radiator hose

Removing the water pump retaining bolts—528e

Measuring belt deflection

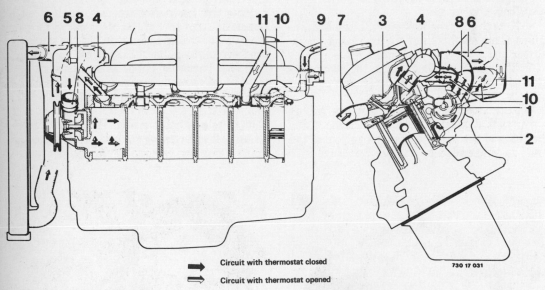

➡ Circuit with thermostat closed
⇉ Circuit with thermostat opened

730 17 031

1. Water pump
2. Crankcase
3. Cylinder head
4. Thermostat housing
5. Thermostat
6. To radiator—thermostat open

7. Radiator outlet
8. To water pump
9. To heat exchanger (car heating)
10. From heat exchanger
11. From expansion tank

Coolant flow circuit—typical 5 series

sensor as an assembly before removing the pump. Remove the retaining bolts and remove the water pump from the engine.

5. The installation is in the reverse of the removal procedure. Use a new gasket and bleed the cooling system.

325, 325e, 325i, 325iS, 325iX, M3, and 528e

1. Drain the cooling system.

CAUTION: *When draining the coolant, keep in mind that cats and dogs are attracted by the ethylene glycol antifreeze, and are quite likely to drink any that is left in an uncovered container or in puddles on the ground. This will prove fatal in sufficient quantity. Always drain the coolant into a sealable container. Coolant should be reused unless it is contaminated or several years old.*

2. Remove the distributor cap and rotor. Remove the inner distributor cap and rubber sealing ring.

3. The fan must be held stationary with some sort of flat blade cut to fit over the hub and drilled to fit over 2 of the studs on the front of the pulley (or use BMW special tool 11 5 030). Remove the fan coupling nut (left hand thread: turn clockwise to remove).

4. Remove the belt and pulley.

5. Remove the rubber guard and distributor and or upper timing belt cover.

6. Compress the timing tensioner spring and clamp pin with BMW special tool 11 5 010 or equivalent.

NOTE: *Observe the installed position of the tensioner spring pin on the water pump housing for reinstallation purposes.*

7. Remove the water hoses, remove the 3 water pump bolts and remove the pump.

8. Clean the gasket surfaces and use a new gasket.

9. Installation is the reverse of the removal procedure.

10. Add coolant and bleed the cooling system.

524td

1. Remove the fan cowl. Hold the fan pulley with the blade of a screwdriver and remove the nut which fastens the fan in place, turning it clockwise because of the use of left hand threads. Drain the cooling system.

CAUTION: *When draining the coolant, keep in mind that cats and dogs are attracted by the ·ethylene glycol antifreeze, and are quite likely to drink any that is left in an uncovered container or in puddles on the ground. This will prove fatal in sufficient quantity. Always drain the coolant into a sealable container. Coolant should be reused unless it is contaminated or several years old.*

2. Remove the front cover as described earli-

er in this section. Unclamp and detach the water pump outlet hose at the pump.

3. Remove the water pump mounting bolts. Remove the pump, pushing the timing belt to one side for clearance.

4. Clean both surfaces of gasket material, and install a new gasket coated with sealer.

5. Install the water pump in the reverse order of the removal procedure. Refill the cooling system and bleed it.

Cylinder Head

REMOVAL AND INSTALLATION

1600, 2000 and 2002

NOTE: *To prevent warpage of the aluminum head, the engine must be cold (coolant temperature less than 96°F [36°C]).*

1. Remove the air cleaner and disconnect the breather tube. On fuel injected engines, remove the intake manifold as detailed earlier.

2. Disconnect the battery ground cable and drain the cooling system.

CAUTION: *When draining the coolant, keep in mind that cats and dogs are attracted by*

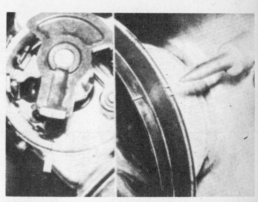

Alignment of the distributor rotor and belt pulley notch

Timing chain tensioner plug removal—typical

the ethylene glycol antifreeze, and are quite likely to drink any that is left in an uncovered container or in puddles on the ground. This will prove fatal in sufficient quantity. Always drain the coolant into a sealable container. Coolant should be reused unless it is contaminated or several years old.

3. Remove the choke cable, if equipped.

4. Disconnect the throttle linkage. On the 2002A, disconnect the downshift linkage. On 1972-74 carbureted models equipped with the Solex 32/32 DIDTA carburetor, disconnect and mark all electrical leads. On the 2002tii, disconnect the throttle butterfly linkage, and all electrical leads (don't forget to tag them!). Pull the torsion shaft towards the firewall until the ball is free of the torsion shaft.

5. Remove and tag the vacuum hoses. On models equipped with the emission control air pump, disconnect the vacuum hose with the non-return valve from its fitting on the intake manifold.

6. Disconnect the coolant hoses from the cyl-

inder head. Disconnect intake manifold water hoses, if so equipped.

7. Tag and disconnect the electrical wiring and connectors from the cylinder head and engine components.

Camshaft notch aligned with raised boss with the No. 1 cylinder at TDC

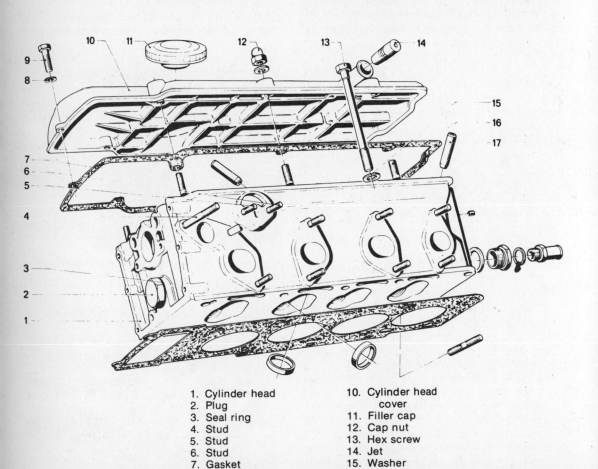

1. Cylinder head
2. Plug
3. Seal ring
4. Stud
5. Stud
6. Stud
7. Gasket
8. Lockwasher
9. Hex screw
10. Cylinder head cover
11. Filler cap
12. Cap nut
13. Hex screw
14. Jet
15. Washer
16. Stud
17. Valve guide

Exploded view of cylinder head components

8. Carbureted models, disconnect and plug the fuel line on the tank side of the fuel pump. On 1975 models, disconnect and plug the fuel and reflow hose. On the fuel injected models, disconnect the fuel line at the injection pump and all lines at the injectors.

9. Remove the cylinder head cover and the front upper timing case cover.

10. Rotate the engine until the distributor rotor points to the notch on the distributor body edge and the timing indicator points to the second notch on the pulley, 2002 models. No. 1 piston should now be at TDC on its firing stroke.

11. Remove the timing chain tensioner piston by removing the plug in the side of the block. CAUTION: *The plug is under heavy spring tension.*

12. Open the lockplates, remove the retaining bolts and remove the timing chain sprocket from the camshaft.

NOTE: *The dowel pin hole on the camshaft flange should be in the 6 o'clock position while the notch at the top for the cam flange should be aligned with the cast projection on the cylinder head and in the 12 o'clock position for proper installation.*

13. Remove the exhaust pipe from the exhaust manifold and remove the dipstick holder.

14. Unscrew the cylinder head bolts in the reverse of the tightening sequence and remove the cylinder head.

15. Installation is the reverse of removal, but note the following points.

a. Tighten the cylinder head bolts in 3 stages, following the illustrated sequence adjust the valves, start the engine and bring to normal operating temperature. Stop the engine and allow it to cool to approximately 95°F (36°C). Retorque the cylinder head bolts to specifications and readjust the valves. NOTE: *The cylinder head bolts should be retorqued after 600 miles (100 km) of driving.*

b. Check the projection of the cylinder head dowel sleeve in the cylinder block mating surface. Maximum height is 5mm.

c. Match the cylinder head gasket to the cylinder block and head to verify coolant flow passages are correct.

d. Adjust timing and idle speed.

e. Bleed the timing chain tensioner, see "Timing Chain Removal and Installation."

f. Bleed the cooling system. Set heater valve to the warm position and fill cooling system. Run the engine to normal temperature and when thermostat has opened, release the pressure cap to the first position. Squeeze the upper and lower radiator hoses in a pumping effect, to allow trapped air to escape through the radiator. Recheck coolant level and close the pressure cap to its second catch position.

2500, 2800, 3000, Bavaria, 3.0 and 630CSi

1. Disconnect the battery ground cable. Drain the cooling system.

CAUTION: *When draining the coolant, keep in mind that cats and dogs are attracted by the ethylene glycol antifreeze, and are quite likely to drink any that is left in an uncovered container or in puddles on the ground. This will prove fatal in sufficient quantity. Always drain the coolant into a sealable container. Coolant should be reused unless it is contaminated or several years old.*

2. Disconnect/remove items for each model of car as described below.

2500, 2800, 3000, BAVARIA AND 3.0 CARBURETED

a. Disconnect throttle linkage rods running between carburetors. Disconnect water temperature sensor at the thermostat and the 2 electrically heated choke connectors.

b. Remove the power brake hose from the base of the front carburetor. Remove the dipstick support.

c. Disconnect heater hoses, water hoses to the intake manifold, and water heated choke hoses.

3.0Si

a. Disconnect and remove the air cleaner and hoses.

b. Remove the igniton high tension wire tube.

c. Disconnect the inductive switch and cable off the coil. Remove the distributor cap and disconnect the primary wire and vacuum line from the distributor.

d. Disconnect the 2 vacuum hoses at the rear of the intake manifold, and the 2 fuel lines at the fuel manifold.

e. Disconnect the water hoses for the heater at the firewall and disconnect the equalizing reservoir hose at the reservoir. Disconnect the oil pressure switch line at the plug.

630CSI

a. Disconnect and remove the air volume control assembly. Disconnect the ignition cable tube and wires and remove it, and disconnect the cam cover vent hose.

FRONT →

Cylinder head torque sequence—2500, 2800, 3000, Bavaria, 3.0, 630CSi and 530i

b. Mark locations and then disconnect the 3 coil connections.

c. Disconnect all 6 injection valve plugs, and the plug at the throttle switch. Disconnect the throttle linkage rod at the top and bottom.

d. Disconnect the vacuum hose from the throttle housing and disconnect the temperature sensor wire at the front of the head.

e. Disconnect the water hose at the throttle housing and the oil pressure switch wire.

f. Disconnect water hoses at the thermostat housing. Disconnect the hose going to the charcoal filter. Disconnect the fuel feed line at the filter.

g. On 530i only, remove the connector from between Nos. 2 and 3 cylinder intake tubes.

h. Disconnect the 4 vacuum sensing hoses from the EGR valve and collector/vacuum valve, noting color coding and locations. Disconnect the brake booster vacuum hoses at the manifold.

i. Disconnect heater hoses at the firewall, noting locations. Disconnect the 2 air hoses at the auxiliary air valve; disconnect the 2 electrical connectors at the auxiliary air valve. Then, remove the auxiliary air valve wiring harness through the opening in the intake manifold.

j. Disconnect and remove the EGR filter.

For each of the vehicles, the remainder of the removal procedure is basically the same. Follow the remaining steps for complete removal.

3. Remove the cylinder head cover.

NOTE: *Do not interchange the heater hoses.*

4. Rotate the engine so that the distributor rotor points to the notch on the distributor body edge and the timing indicator points to the notch on the belt pulley. This will place number one piston at TDC on its firing stroke.

5. Remove the upper timing housing cover after removing the distributor and thermostat housing.

6. Remove the timing chain tensioner piston.

7. Open the camshaft sprocket bolt lockplates and remove the bolts. Remove the sprocket.

NOTE *For installation purposes, the sprocket dowel pin should be located at the lower left, between 7 and 8 o'clock, while the upper bolt bore must align with t the threaded bore of the camshaft and the cylinder head cast tab, visible through the 2 bores, when at the 12 o'clock position.*

8. Disconnect the exhaust line at the exhaust manifold. Remove the exhaust filter (if so equipped).

9. Remove the cylinder head bolts in the reverse order of the tightening sequence and install locating pins in 4 head bolt bores to prevent the rocker shafts from turning.

10. Remove the cylinder head.

11. Installation is the reverse of removal. Note the following points:

a. Tighten the cylinder head bolts in 3 stages, following the illustrated sequence. Make sure bolt holes are free of oil. adjust the valves, start the engine and bring it to normal

Installation of the camshaft sprocket—most models

Open the lock plates and remove the camshaft sprocket bolts—typical

Install locating pins to prevent the camshaft from turning

operating temperature. Stop the engine and allow it to cool to approximately 95°F (35°C). Retorque the cylinder head bolts to specifications and readjust the valves.

NOTE: *the cylinder head bolt on all models should be retorqued after 600 miles (1000 km) of driving.*

b. Check the projection of the cylinder head dowel sleeve in the cylinder block mating surface. Maximum height is 5.0mm.

c. match the cylinder head gasket to the cylinder block and head to verify that the coolant flow passages are correct.

d. Run a straight edge along the head diagonally to check for warpage. Have the head, and the top of the timing cover, machined, as necessary. The head may be machined as much as 0.5mm on 1600, 2002, 2800 and 3.0 models.

e. Apply sealer to the joint between the block and upper timing cover.

f. Bleed the timing chain tensioner.

g. Adjust the timing and idle speeds.

h. When refilling the cooling system, bleed it carefully (see Chapter 1).

318i

NOTE: *In order to perform this procedure, it is necessary to have a special tool (angle gauge) that will accurately measure the angle at which the cylinder head bolts are torqued.*

1. Disconnect exhaust pipes at the exhaust manifold and remove the pipe clamp on the transmission.

2. Disconnect the battery ground cable. Remove the drain plug and drain coolant.

CAUTION: *When draining the coolant, keep in mind that cats and dogs are attracted by the ethylene glycol antifreeze, and are quite likely to drink any that is left in an uncovered container or in puddles on the ground. This will prove fatal in sufficient quantity. Always drain the coolant into a sealable container.*

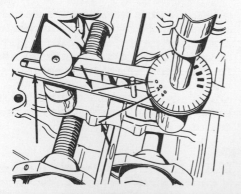

On the final torquing step for 318i cylinder head bolts, tighten head bolts the specified angle, as shown

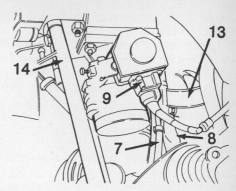

When removing the cylinder head on the 318i, disconnect the coolant hoses (7 and 8), disconnect the plug (9) and vacuum hose (13), and unscrew the support (14)

Coolant should be reused unless it is contaminated or several years old.

3. Disconnect the wire and plug on the air cleaner. Loosen the clamp and disconnect the air intake hose. Then unscrew the nuts and remove the air cleaner.

4. Disconnect the throttle cable. Remove the dipstick tube locating bracket.

5. Disconnect the throttle position electronic plug. Disconnect the coolant and vacuum hoses nearby. Unscrew the support for the throttle body nearby.

6. Detach the fuel supply and return hoses and the hose mounting clamp.

7. Disconnect the intake manifold, distributor, and power brake unit vacuum hoses.

8. Disconnect the diagnosis plug, alternator wiring, and other plugs (2) nearby. Disconnect the coolant hoses at the cylinder head.

9. Disconnect any electrical plugs on the starter and injection system. This includes pulling off each injection plug and opening up the wiring straps.

10. Remove the distributor cap, disconnect distributor wiring plugs, wiring harness, and all plug wires.

11. Disconnect the coolant hoses going into the firewall.

12. Remove the cylinder head cover. Remove the bracket near the upper timing case over. Then, remove bolts and remove the upper timing case cover.

13. Rotate the engine until the TDC mark on the front pulley is aligned with the mark on the front cover and the distributor rotor is aligned with the mark on the side of the distributor (No. 1 cylinder is at TDC). Then, remove the distributor.

14. Remove the timing chain tensioner piston as described below.

15. Remove the retaining bolts and pull off

the upper timing chain sprocket. *Do not rotate crankshaft while the sprocket is off!*

16. Loosen the cylinder head bolts in reverse order of the torquing sequence and remove. Lift off the cylinder head.

17. Install in reverse order, noting these points:

a. Use a new head gasket.

b. Lightly oil all head bolts, keeping oil out of the threaded holes in the block.

c. Torque in the sequence shown in 4 stages:
- 25-29 ft. lbs.
- 42-45 ft. lbs.
- Wait 20 minutes. Adjust the valves during this time
- 56-59 ft. lbs.
- Run the engine until it is warm
- Torque bolts to 25° (on the angle gauge)

d. When installing the timing chain sprocket, first make sure the notch in the camshaft flange is aligned with the cast tab on the cylinder head. The dowel pin will then align with the bore in the sprocket at the 6 o'clock position.

e. When installing the upper timing cover, pack sealer into the crevices between block and the top of lower cover. Install all bolts finger tight. Tighten outer bolts first, from top to bottom on left, and top to bottom on right. Finally, torque the 2 front bolts.
- Sprocket-to-camshaft torque: 5 ft. lbs.
- Chain tensioner plug: 22-29 ft. lbs.
- Timing case cover: 7-8 ft. lbs.

320i

1. Remove the air cleaner and disconnect the breather tube. Remove the intake manifold.

2. Disconnect the battery ground cable and drain the cooling system.

CAUTION: *When draining the coolant, keep in mind that cats and dogs are attracted by the ethylene glycol antifreeze, and are quite likely to drink any that is left in an uncovered container or in puddles on the ground. This will prove fatal in sufficient quantity. Always drain the coolant into a sealable container. Coolant should be reused unless it is contaminated or several years old.*

3. Remove the choke cable, if so equipped.

4. Disconnect the throttle linkage. Pull the torsion shaft towards the firewall until the ball is free of the torsion shaft.

5. Remove and tag the vacuum hoses.

6. Disconnect the coolant hoses from the cylinder head.

7. Disconnect the electrical wiring and connectors from the cylinder head and engine components.

8. Remove the cylinder head cover and the front upper timing case cover.

9. Rotate the engine until the distributor rotor points to the notch on the distributor body edge and the timing indicator points to the first notch on the belt pulley. No. 1 piston should now be at TDC on its firing stroke.

10. Remove the timing chain tensioner piston by removing the plug in the side of the block.

CAUTION: *The plug is under heavy spring tension.*

11. Open the lockplates, remove the retaining bolts and remove the timing chain sprocket from the camshaft.

NOTE: *The dowel pin hole in the camshaft flange should be in the 6 o'clock position while the notch at the top of the cam flange should be aligned with the cast projection on the cylinder head and in the 12 o'clock position for proper installation.*

12. Remove the exhaust pipe from the exhaust manifold and remove the dipstick holder.

13. Unscrew the cylinder head bolts in the reverse of the tightening sequence and remove the cylinder head.

14. Installation is the reverse of removal but note the following points:

a. Tighten the cylinder head bolts in 3 stages, following the illustrated sequence. Adjust the valves, start the engine and bring to normal operating temperature. Stop the engine and allow it to cool to approximately 95°F (35°C). Retorque the cylinder head bolts to specifications and readjust the valves.

NOTE: *The cylinder head bolts should be retorqued after 600 miles (1000 km) of driving.*

b. Check the projection of the cylinder head dowel sleeves in the cylinder block mating surface. Maximum h8 is 5mm.

c. Match the cylinder head gasket to the cylinder block and head to verify coolant flow passages are correct.

d. Adjust timing and idle speed.

e. Bleed the cooling system. Set the heater valve to the warm position and fill the cooling system. Run the engine to normal temperature and when the thermostat has opened, release the pressure cap to the first position. Squeeze the upper and lower radiator hoses in a pumping effect, to allow trapped air to escape through the radiator. Recheck the coolant level and close the pressure cap to its second catch position.

524td

NOTE: *To perform this procedure, a number of special tools will be needed. These include a dial indicator with a bridge that will allow the gauge to measure piston protrusion while*

the edges of the bridge rest on the block deck on either side of the piston; and an angle gauge for measuring turning angle of cylinder head bolts; some means of holding the camshaft in position, such as BMW tool 11 3 090.

1. Disconnect the battery ground cable. Remove the turbocharger as described later in this section.

2. Remove the fan as described under cooling system repair later in this section. Remove the drain plug from the bottom of the radiator and drain the cooling system. Then, remove the 3 coolant hoses connecting to the water pump.

CAUTION: *When draining the coolant, keep in mind that cats and dogs are attracted by the ethylene glycol antifreeze, and are quite likely to drink any that is left in an uncovered container or in puddles on the ground. This will prove fatal in sufficient quantity. Always drain the coolant into a sealable container. Coolant should be reused unless it is contaminated or several years old.*

3. Disconnect the coolant hose located at the front of the intake manifold. Disconnect the electrical plug near this hose connection. Disconnect the injector leakoff line that also connects near these connections.

4. Disconnect the heater hose nearby and under the intake manifold. Remove the bracket next to this hose connection and then disconnect the glow plug wiring.

5. Working inside the glove compartment, disconnect the multi-prong plug on the electronic control unit. Then, disconnect the engine wiring harness at the 2 fasteners on the firewall and pull the harness into the engine compartment.

6. Disconnect the crankcase ventilation hose at the rear of the valve cover. Then, disconnect the 3 electrical plugs right nearby. Disconnect the diagnostic (multi-prong) plug.

7. Disconnect the small coolant hose located to the right of the intake air box. Then, disconnect any remaining flow plug wires nearby. Disconnect the temperature sensor connectors nearby. Then, disconnect the plug at the firewall.

8. Remove the intake air box bracket located near the rear of the intake air box. Then, disconnect the wiring harness from its retaining clips and move it downward and out of the way.

9. Disconnect the transmission dipstick tube bracket at the intake manifold. Disconnect the air hose at the manifold, nearby. Disconnect the wire at the intake pressure relief valve, nearby.

10. Remove the crankcase ventilation system oil trap from the valve cover by first disconnecting the hose and then unbolting it and removing it with its gasket.

Check the height above the block deck of each piston at the locations "A" and "B" shown

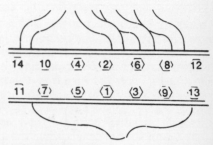

Cylinder head tightening or loosening (14–1) sequence for the 524 td

11. Use a crowfoot wrench to unscrew and remove the injection lines at the pump and injectors. Plug all openings with clean, protective caps.

12. Remove the cam cover. Then, turn the engine until No. 1 cylinder is at TDC (No. 6 cylinder's valves overlap). Either lock the crank in position with a pin such as BMW special tool 11 2 300 or equivalent, or make sure the crankshaft is completely undisturbed until the engine is reassembled.

13. Remove the coolant hose which runs across the front of the timing belt cover and remove the timing belt cover. Then, loosen the camshaft sprocket retaining bolt. Loosen the bolt and nut which position the timing belt tensioner and then remove the timing belt.

14. Remove the cylinder head bolts in the order of 14-1, going in rotation in several stages. Lift the head off the engine.

15. Clean the block deck and cylinder head lower surfaces with a solvent and wooden scraper (to avoid scoring either surface).

16. Set up and zero a dial indicator it will be possible to measure the protrusion of the pistons above the block deck. Measure the protrusion of each piston along the center-line of the block on the flat surface at both the front and rear of the piston. Rock the engine back and

forth for each cylinder until absolute maximum protrusion is obtained. Average the 2 readings for each piston and record the average. Return the crankshaft to No. 6 cylinder overlap position. Note the highest protrusion. Compare it to these figures and select a head gasket of the appropriate thickness from the protrusion figure:

- 0.025-0.030mm 1 hole
- 0.031-0.035mm 2 holes
- 0.036-0.042mm 3 holes

Gaskets have one, 2, or 3 holes along one edge to indicate the thickness classification.

17. Clean all the cylinder head bolts with solvent and give them a very light coating of engine oil. Make sure the bolts are not heavily coated with oil and that the bolt holes do not contain any oil, as this will interfere with torquing and might even crack the cylinder block.

18. Turn the camshaft so that the valves on cylinder No. 6 are at the overlap position. Make sure the camshaft does not turn from this position, or the valves may be bent when the head is installed. Use a jig such as BMW tool 11 3 090 or equivalent. Install the bolts and then torque them in the numbered order shown in the illustration (1-14) to ⅓ the torque figure shown in the chart at the front of this section. Then, retorque them to ⅔ that figure in the numbered order. Finally, retorque them, again in numbered order, to the full torque figure.

19. Install and adjust the timing belt as described later in this section. Adjust the valves and install the cam cover. Then, install the timing belt cover. Install the injection pump lines and torque the fittings to 14-18 ft. lbs. Bleed the fuel system as described under "Injection Pump Removal and Installation" in Chapter 5. Reconnect all electrical lines, hoses, and other fittings so the engine is ready to run. Use a new gasket on the crankcase ventilation system oil trap. Refill the cooling system.

20. Start the engine and run it at about 1000 rpm until it is hot. Then, remove the cam cover and again in numerical order, final-torque the bolts by accurately turning them exactly another 90° tighter. Use a tool designed for angle torquing such as BMW 11 2 110. Replace the cam cover.

633CSi and 733i

NOTE: *Small variations may be encountered among models due to model changes, difference in electrical wiring, vacuum hoses and fuel line routings, but all are basically alike.*

1. Disconnect the battery ground cable.
2. Disconnect the wire-connectors. Loosen the clamps and remove the airflow sensor with the air filter on the fuel injected models, or re-move the air cleaner from carburetor equipped models.

3. Disconnect the rocker cover vent hose, ignition line tube and electrical wiring.
4. Remove the rocker cover.

CAUTION: *When draining the coolant, keep in mind that cats and dogs are attracted by the ethylene glycol antifreeze, and are quite likely to drink any that is left in an uncovered container or in puddles on the ground. This will prove fatal in sufficient quantity. Always drain the coolant into a sealable container. Coolant should be reused unless it is contaminated or several years old.*

5. Drain the cooling system and remove the coolant hoses.

NOTE: *Do not interchange the heater hoses.*

6. Rotate the engine so that the distributor body edge and the timing indicator points to the notch on the belt pulley. This will place number one piston at TDC on its firing stroke.

7. Remove the upper timing housing cover after removing the distributor and thermostat housing.

8. Remove the timing chain tensioner piston.

CAUTION: *The retaining plug is under heavy spring tension.*

9. Open the camshaft sprocket bolt lockplates and remove the bolts. Remove the sprocket.

NOTE: *For installation purposes, the sprocket dowel pin should be located at the lower left, between 7 and 8 o'clock, while the upper bolt bore must align with the threaded bore of the camshaft and the cylinder head cast tab, visible through the 2 bores, when at the 12 o'clock position.*

10. Remove and tag the electrical wiring and connectors.
11. Remove and tag the vacuum lines.
12. Remove the wiring harness by pulling it upward through the opening in the intake neck.
13. Disconnect the fuel lines.
14. Disconnect the exhaust line at the exhaust manifold. Remove the exhaust filter.
15. Remove the cylinder head bolts in the reverse order of the tightening sequence and install locating pins in 4 head bolt bores to prevent the rocker shafts from turning.
16. Remove the cylinder head.
17. Installation is the reverse or removal. Note the following points:

Cylinder head torque sequence—528i, 633CSi and 733i

a. Tighten the cylinder head bolts according to the specifications chart, following the illustrated sequence. Adjust the valves before starting the engine. On those engines not using angle torque as the last torquing step, stop the engine and allow it to cool to approximately 95°F (35°C). Retorque the cylinder head bolts to specifications. Readjust the valves with the engine hot on all engines.

NOTE: *The cylinder head bolts (except those on models using angle torque as the last torquing step) should be retorqued after 600 miles (1000 km) of driving.*

b. Check the projection of the cylinder head dowel sleeve in the cylinder block mating surface. Maximum h8 is 5mm.

c. Match the cylinder head gasket to the cylinder block and head to verify that the coolant flow passages are correct.

d. Adjust the timing and idle speed.

e. Bleed the cooling system. Set the heater valve in the Warm position and fill the cooling system. Start the engine and bring to normal operating temperature. A venting screw is located on the top of the thermostat housing. Run the engine at fast idle and open the venting screw until the coolant comes out free of air bubbles. Close the bleeder screw and refill the reservoir with coolant.

1982-87 325, 325e, 325i, 325iS and 528e

1. Disconnect the battery ground cable. Make sure the engine is cool. Disconnect the exhaust pipes at the manifold and at the transmission clamp. Remove the drain plug at the bottom of the radiator and drain the coolant. Drain the engine oil.

CAUTION: *When draining the coolant, keep in mind that cats and dogs are attracted by the ethylene glycol antifreeze, and are quite likely to drink any that is left in an uncovered container or in puddles on the ground. This will prove fatal in sufficient quantity. Always drain the coolant into a sealable container. Coolant should be reused unless it is contaminated or several years old.*

2. Disconnect the accelerator and cruise control cables. If the car has an automatic transmission, disconnect the throttle cable that goes to the transmission.

3. Working at the front of the block, disconnect the upper radiator hose, the bypass water hose, and several smaller water hoses nearby. Remove the diagnosis plug located at the front corner of the manifold. Remove the bracket located just underneath. Disconnect the fuel line and drain the contents into a metal container for safe disposal.

On the 325, 325i and iS:

a. Working on the air cleaner/airflow sensor, disconnect the vacuum hoses, labeling them if necessary. Disconnect all electrical connectors and unclip and remove the wiring harness. There is a relay located in an L-shaped box near the strut tower. Disconnect and remove it. Unclamp and remove the air hose. Remove the mounting nuts and remove the assembly.

b. Disconnect the hose at the coolant overflow tank. Disconnect the idle speed positioner vacuum hose and then remove the positioner from the manifold.

c. If the car has 4-wheel drive, disconnect the vacuum hose from the servo mounted on the manifold.

d. Place a drain pan underneath and then disconnect the 2 water connections at the front of the intake manifold. Disconnect the electrical connector nearby.

On the 325e and 528e:

a. Working near the air cleaner/air flow sensor unit, disconnect the vacuum hoses at the intake manifold and at the air intake hose. Disconnect the 2 electrical connectors and then remove the wiring harness. Pull off the large hose leading into the unit and loosen the clamp where the air intake hose connects at the intake manifold. Remove the mounting nuts and remove the air cleaner/airflow sensor.

b. Disconnect the water hoses at the throttle body. Disconnect the electrical connector underneath the throttle body. Disconnect the

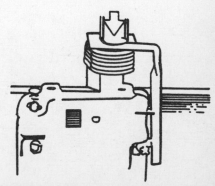

On the 325e and 528e, you'll have to press the vent tube downward (in the direction of the arrow) and then lock the collar in that position with a tool such as 11 1 290. Then, disconnect the tube.

| ⑫ | ⑩ | ④ | ② | ⑥ | ⑧ | ⑭ |
| ⑬ | ⑦ | ⑤ | ① | ③ | ⑨ | ⑪ |

FRONT

Cylinder head torque sequence—528e

bracket under the intake manifold tube nearby.

4. On all models, disconnect the heater water hoses. Press down (in the arrowed direction) on the vent tube collar shown in the illustration and install the special tool or a similar device to retain the collar in the unlocked position. Disconnect the vent tube and inspect its O-ring seal, replacing it if necessary.

5. Unbolt the dipstick tube at the manifold. Remove the fuel hose bracket at the cylinder head. Make sure the engine is cold. Then, place a metal container under the connection and disconnect the fuel hose at the connection nearby.

6. Disconnect the high tension lead from the coil. Put a drain pan nearby and then disconnect and remove the coolant expansion tank.

On the 325, 325i and iS:

a. If the car has 4-wheel drive, disconnect the intake manifold vacuum hose leading the the servo that engages 4-wheel drive.

b. Disconnect the fuel injector electrical connectors at all 6 injectors, as well as the 2 additional electrical connectors to sensors on the head. Disconnect the oil pressure sending unit connector. Then, unfasten the carriers and remove this wiring harness toward the left side of the car.

On 325e and 528e cars:

a. There is a bracket with various vacuum and electrical fittings that runs from the cam cover over toward the intake manifold. Disconnect the electrical connector connected on this bracket and the plug to its left. Remove the nuts fastening the bracket to the cam cover and the gasketed flange on the opposite end and remove the bracket. Inspect the gasket and supply a new one for use in installation, if necessary. Unplug the fuel injectors.

b. Disconnect the Digital Motor Electronics plugs nearby. Disconnect the 4 plugs located near the front 3 fuel injectors and any

remaining injector connectors. Unplug the oil pressure sending unit connector. Then, unfasten the mounting clips and pull the wiring harness out toward the left.

7. Disconnect the coil high tension wire and disconnect the high tension wires at the plugs. Then, disconnect the tube in which the wires run at the cam cover. Disconnect the PCV hose. Then, remove the 8 retaining nuts and remove the cam cover.

8. Turn the crankshaft so that the TDC line is lined up with the indicator and the valves of No. 6 cylinder are in overlapping (slightly open) position.

9. Remove the distributor cap. Then, unscrew and remove the rotor. Unscrew and remove the adapter just underneath the rotor. Remove the cover underneath the adapter. Check its O-ring and replace it if necessary.

10. Remove the distributor mounting bolts and the protective cover.

11. These engines are equipped with a rubber drive and timing belt. Remove the belt covers as described later in this section. To loosen belt tension, loosen the tension roller bracket pivot bolt and adjusting slot bolt. Push the roller and bracket away from the belt to release the tension, hold the bracket in this position, and retighten the adjusting slot bolt to retain the bracket it this position.

12. Remove the timing belt.

NOTE: *Make sure to avoid rotating both the engine and camshaft from this point onward.*

13. Remove the cylinder head mounting bolts in exact reverse order of the tightening sequence shown. Then, remove the cylinder head.

14. Install the head with a new gasket. Check that all passages line up with the gasket holes. Clean the threads on the head bolts and coat with a *very light* coating of oil. Keep oil out of the bolt cavities in the head, or the head could be cracked or proper torquing affected.

15. Install the bolts and torque in stages, with waiting periods, and to the figures as described in specifications. Torque them in the numbered order, as shown in the applicable illustration. Then, adjust the valves.

16. Clean both cylinder head and block sealing surfaces thoroughly with a hardwood scraper. Inspect the surfaces for flatness as described in the Engine Rebuilding section. Note that the M20B25 engine gasket is coded 2.5 and the M20B27 engine gasket is coded 2.7. Complete the installation by reversing all removal procedures. Make sure to refill the engine oil pan and cooling system with proper fluids and to bleed the cooling system. Replace the gaskets for the exhaust system connections, if necessary. Coat the studs with CRC® copper paste or equivalent. Note that the plugs for the DME reference

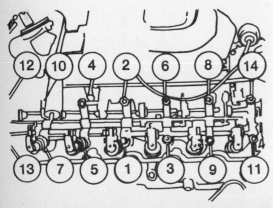

Cylinder head torque sequence for the M20B27 and M20B25 engines

mark and speed signals should be connected so that the gray plug goes to the socket with a ring underneath.

NOTE: *Align the timing marks when installing the timing belt. The crankshaft sprocket mark must point at the notch in the flange of the front engine cover. The camshaft sprocket arrow must point at the alignment mark on the cylinder head. Also, the No. 1 piston must be at TDC of the compression stroke. BMW recommends that the timing belt be replaced every time the cylinder head is removed and the belt is disturbed as a consequence. Tension the belt as described under Timing Belt Removal and Installation.*

16. Start the engine and run it until it is hot. Stop the engine and again remove the cam cover. Using an angle gauge, tighten the head bolts 25° farther in numbered order. Reinstall the cam cover.

1988 325, 325e, 325i, 325iS and 528e

1. Disconnect the battery ground cable. Disconnect the oxygen sensor plug.

2. Remove the bolts attaching the 2 exhaust pipes to the manifold. Then, unfasten the bracket which supports the pipes at the transmission and lower them slightly. Support them from the chassis with wire or another suitable means.

3. Put drain pans underneath and then remove the drain plugs from the radiator and block to drain coolant.

CAUTION: *When draining the coolant, keep in mind that cats and dogs are attracted by the ethylene glycol antifreeze, and are quite likely to drink any that is left in an uncovered container or in puddles on the ground. This will prove fatal in sufficient quantity. Always drain the coolant into a sealable container. Coolant should be reused unless it is contaminated or several years old.*

4. Disconnect the accelerator cable. On cars with cruise control, disconnect the cruise control cable; on cars with automatic transmissions, disconnect the transmission throttle cable.

5. Disconnect the large electrical plug from the airflow sensor unit. Loosen the clamp on the air intake hose. Remove the mounting nuts for the airflow sensor/air cleaner unit and lift it for access. Disconnect the remaining hose and electrical plug and then remove the unit.

6. The diagnosis plug is located on the front of the engine, near the thermostat housing. It is a large, multiprong plug. Disconnect it. Then, disconnect the 5 coolant hoses, 2 of small diameter, and 3 of large diameter, from the thermostat housing and cylinder head.

7. Make sure the engine is cool. With a metal container to collect fuel, carefully and slowly loosen the clamp on the fuel hose where it connects right near the diagnosis plug. When fuel pressure has been relieved, disconnect the hose and collect any remaining fuel in the cup.

8. There is a brace connected to the head at the front. Remove the bolt fastening this brace to the head. Disconnect the 2 electrical connectors nearby. Disconnect the fuel line nearby, draining the fuel into a metal container.

9. Place a drain pan underneath and then disconnect the 2 water connections at the front of the intake manifold. Disconnect the electrical connector nearby.

10. Disconnect the 2 heater hoses at the firewall and drain any coolant into a pan.

11. Press down (in the arrowed direction) on the PCV vent tube collar shown in the illustration above and install the special tool or a similar device to retain the collar in the unlocked position. Disconnect the vent tube and inspect its O-ring seal, replacing it if necessary.

12. Disconnect the electrical leads going to the coil. Unbolt and remove the fan and then store it in an upright position. Unbolt the coolant pipe located near the fan and remove it.

13. Then, remove the 8 retaining nuts and remove the cam cover. Turn the crankshaft so that the TDC line is lined up with the indicator and the valves of No. 6 cylinder are in overlapping (slightly open) position.

14. Remove the distributor cap. Then, unscrew and remove the rotor. Unscrew and remove the adapter just underneath the rotor. Remove the cover underneath the adapter. Check its O-ring and replace it if necessary.

15. Remove the mounting nut and the protective cover. Then, disconnect the wiring clip underneath the distributor and move the leads away, so they are in front of the pulley.

16. These engines are equipped with a rubber drive and timing belt. Remove the belt covers as described later in this section. To loosen belt tension, loosen the tension roller bracket pivot bolt and adjusting slot bolt. Push the roller and bracket away from the belt to release the tension, hold the bracket in this position, and retighten the adjusting slot bolt to retain the bracket it this position.

17. Remove the timing belt.

NOTE: *Make sure to avoid rotating both the engine and camshaft from this point onward.*

18. Remove the cylinder head mounting bolts in exact reverse order of the tightening sequence shown above. Then, remove the cylinder head.

19. Install the head with a new gasket. Check that all passages line up with the gasket holes. Clean the threads on the head bolts and coat with a *very light* coating of oil. Keep oil out of

the bolt cavities in the head, or the head could be cracked or proper torquing affected.

20. Install the bolts and torque in stages, with waiting periods, and to the figures as described in specifications. Torque them in the numbered order, as shown in the applicable illustration. Then, adjust the valves.

21. Clean both cylinder head and block sealing surfaces thoroughly with a hardwood scraper. Inspect the surfaces for flatness as described in the Engine Rebuilding section. Note that the M20B25 engine gasket is coded 2.5 and the M20B27 engine gasket is coded 2.7. Make sure all openings match precisely. Complete the installation by reversing all removal procedures. Make sure to refill the engine oil pan and cooling system with proper fluids and to bleed the cooling system. Replace the gaskets for the exhaust system connections, if necessary. Coat the studs with CRC® copper paste or equivalent. Note that the plugs for the DME reference mark and speed signals should be connected so that the gray plug goes to the socket with a ring underneath.

NOTE: *Align the timing marks when installing the timing belt. The crankshaft sprocket mark must point at the notch in the flange of the front engine cover. The camshaft sprocket arrow must point at the alignment mark on the cylinder head. Also, the No. 1 piston must be at TDC of the compression stroke. BMW recommends that the timing belt be replaced every time the cylinder head is removed and the belt is disturbed as a consequence. Tension the belt as described under Timing Belt Removal & Installation below.*

22. Start the engine and run it until it is hot. Stop the engine and again remove the cam cover. Using an angle gauge, tighten the head bolts 25° farther in numbered order. Reinstall the cam cover.

M3

NOTE: *This is an extremely difficult operation involving the use of a number of special tools. It is necessary to remove both of the camshafts to complete it. Refer to the camshaft removal and installation procedure below for information on those special tools required for that part of the job. It is also necessary to have a set of metric hex wrenches.*

1. Disconnect the negative battery cable. Remove the splash guard from underneath the engine. Put drain pans underneath and then remove the drain plugs from both the radiator and block to drain all coolant.

CAUTION: *When draining the coolant, keep in mind that cats and dogs are attracted by the ethylene glycol antifreeze, and are quite likely to drink any that is left in an uncovered container or in puddles on the ground. This will prove fatal in sufficient quantity. Always drain the coolant into a sealable container. Coolant should be reused unless it is contaminated or several years old.*

2. Loosen the hose clamps for the air intake hose located next to the radiator and then remove the hose. Disconnect the 2 electrical connectors for the airflow sensor. Then, remove the 2 attaching nuts and remove the air cleaner/airflow sensor unit.

3. Disconnect the accelerator and cruise control cables. Unbolt the cable mounting bracket and move the cables and bracket aside.

4. Remove the attaching nut, pull off the clamp, and then detach the vacuum hose from the brake booster.

5. Loosen the hose clamp and remove the air intake hose from the intake manifold. Remove the nut from the manifold brace, nearby.

6. Loosen the clamp and disconnect the other end of the booster vacuum hose at the manifold. Remove the nut from the intake manifold brace.

7. Loosen the hose clamp and disconnect the air intake hose at the manifold. Then, remove all 6 nuts attaching the manifold assembly to the outer ends of the intake throttle necks and remove the assembly.

8. Put a drain pan underneath and then loosen the hose clamps and disconnect the coolant expansion tank hoses. Disconnect the engine ground strap.

9. Disconnect the ignition coil high tension lead. Then, label and then disconnect the 2 plugs on the front of the block, nearby. Remove the nut fastening another lead farther forward of the 2 plugs and move the lead aside so it will not interfere with engine removal.

10. Find the vacuum hose leading to the fuel pressure regulator. Pull it off. Label and then disconnect the 2 plugs nearby. Unscrew the mounting screw for another electrical lead connecting with the top of the block nearby and remove the lead and its carrier.

11. There is a vacuum hose connecting with one of the throttle necks. Disconnect it and pull it out of the intake manifold bracket. Pull off the electrical connector nearby. Pull out the rubber retainer, and then pull the idle speed control out and put it aside. The engine wiring harness is located nearby. Take it out of its carriers.

12. All the fuel injectors are plugged into a common plate. Carefully and evenly pull the plate off the injectors, pull it out past the pressure regulator, and lay it aside.

13. Loosen the clamp and then disconnect the PCV hose. Label and then disconnect the 2 fuel lines connecting with the injector circuit (it's

important to label them so that they can be installed correctly!). Put a drain pan underneath and then disconnect the heater hose from the cylinder head.

14. Loosen the clamp near the throttle necks and then pull the engine wiring harness out and put it aside. Put a drain pan underneath and then disconnect the heater hose that connects to the block.

15. Remove the bolts from the flanges connecting the exhaust pipes to the exhaust manifold. Provide new gaskets and self-locking nuts. Disconnect the oxygen sensor plug.

16. Put a drain pan underneath and then disconnect the 2 radiator hoses from the pipe at the front of the block.

17. See the procedures below for removal of the front timing cover and timing chain. It is not necessary to remove the timing chain completely, but it is necessary to remove the cam cover, front covers (for the camshaft drive sprockets), and the upper guide rail for the timing chain, and then turn the engine to TDC firing position for No. 1. Then, the procedure will be to remove the timing chain tensioner. Note the relationship between the chain and both the crankshaft and camshaft sprockets, and then remove both camshaft drive sprockets. Leave the chain in a position that will not interfere with removal of the head and which will minimize disturbing its routing through the areas on the front of the block.

18. Remove the camshafts as described below.

19. Prepare a clean work area and a way to store the cam followers in order; preferably some sort of rack. Remove the cam followers one at a time, keeping them in exact order for installation in the same positions.

20. Pull off the spark plug connectors. Remove the 2 nuts from the cam cover, located just to one side of the row of spark plugs. Then remove the ignition lead tube. Then, remove the 8 remaining nuts and remove the cam cover. Provide new gaskets.

21. Remove the bolts (some are accessible from below) that retain the timing case to the head at the front (the timing case houses the lifters and the camshaft lower bearing saddles.) Note that one bolt, on the right (passenger's) side of the car, is longer and retains the shaft for the upper timing chain tensioning rail.

22. Remove the coolant pipe that runs along the left rear of the block. Remove one bolt at the left front of the block that is located outside the cam cover. Then, go along in the area under the cam cover and remove all the remaining (42) bolts for the timing case (arrows in the illustration point them out). Remove the timing case.

23. Remove the 2 hex bolts fastening the head to the block at the front. These are located out-

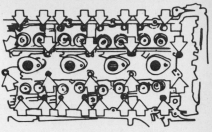

Removing the timing case for the M3. Remove all arrowed bolts

side the cam cover and just behind the water pump drive belt. Then, remove the head bolts located under the cam cover in reverse order of the 4-cylinder engine cylinder head torque sequence (10-1).

24. Make checks of the lower cylinder head and block deck surface to make sure they are true. See the "Engine Rebuilding" section. Clean both cylinder head and block sealing surfaces thoroughly with a hardwood scraper. Lubricate the head bolts with a light coating of engine oil. Make sure there is no oil or dirt in the bolt holes in the block. Install a new head gasket, making sure that all bolt, oil, and coolant holes line up. Install the bolts as follows:

a. Torque them, in the order shown in the illustration for 4-cylinder engines (1-10) to 35-37 ft. lbs.

b. Then, torque them, in order, to 57-59 ft. lbs.

c. Wait 15 minutes.

d. Torque them, in order, to 71-73 ft. lbs.

e. Remember to reinstall the bolts that go outside the cylinder head cover and fasten the front of the head to the block at front and rear.

25. BMW recommends checking the fit of each tappet in the timing case. If the engine is not a high mileage one, has had no lubrication problems, and has exhibited no particular tappet noise, it may be reasonable to skip this step. On the other hand, if the engine exhibits abuse, has been run a great many miles, or has had tappet noise, it is easy to replace worn tappets at this time, and it would be wise to check them. The procedure is as follows:

a. Measure a tappet's outside diameter with a micrometer. Then, zero an inside micrometer at this exact dimension.

b. Then, use the inside micrometer to measure the tappet bore that corresponds to this particular tappet. If the resulting measurement is 0.0025-0.066mm the tappet may be reused. If it is worn past this dimension, replace it with a new one. If the tappet is being replaced, repeat steps a and b to make sure it will now meet specifications. If the

bore were to be worn so much that even a new tappet would not restore clearance to specification, it would be necessary to replace the timing case.

c. Repeat for all the remaining tappets. Make sure to measure each tappet and its *corresponding bore* only!

26. The remaining steps of installation are the reverse of the removal procedure. Note the following specifics, during work:

a. Before remounting the timing case, replace the O-ring in the oil passage located at the left front of the block. Also, check the O-rings in the tops of the spark plug bores and replace these as necessary.

b. Install the timing case and torque the bolts in several stages. The smaller (M7) bolts are torqued to 10-12 ft. lbs.; the larger (M8) bolts are torqued to 14.5-15.5 ft. lbs. Install each tappet back into the same bore.

c. When bolting the exhaust pipes to the flange at the manifold, use new gaskets and self-locking nuts and torque the nuts to 36 ft. lbs.

d. When reinstalling the intake manifold, check and, if necessary, replace the O-rings where the manifold tubes connect to the throttle necks. Torque the nuts to 78 in. lbs.

e. Make sure to refill the radiator and bleed the cooling system.

533i, 535i, 633CSi, 635CSi, 733i and 1983-86 735i (M30 B32 and M30 B34 engines)

1. Unbolt the exhaust pipes at the exhaust manifold. Unclamp the exhaust pipe at the transmission.

2. Disconnect the battery negative and positive cables and drain the coolant by removing the plugs from the radiator and block.

CAUTION: *When draining the coolant, keep in mind that cats and dogs are attracted by the ethylene glycol antifreeze, and are quite likely to drink any that is left in an uncovered container or in puddles on the ground. This will prove fatal in sufficient quantity. Always drain the coolant into a sealable container. Coolant should be reused unless it is contaminated or several years old.*

3. Disconnect the throttle, accelerator, and cruise control cables at the throttle body.

4. These engines are all virtually identical, but wiring harnesses vary from model to model. Systematically disconnect all wiring that goes to the cylinder head or would obstruct its removal. This includes: wiring to the airflow sensor; ignition wiring and, where used, the ignition wiring tube; wires to the fuel injectors; on some models it may be necessary to disconnect the alternator wiring; on many, it will be necessary to disconnect the main harness to the fuse

box. On 535, 635, and 735 Series cars, it is necessary to disconnect the starter wiring.

5. Disconnect fuel lines, vacuum lines, and heater and coolant hoses that are in the way. Disconnect DME plugs on those models so equipped. Note that the gray plug connects to the plug with a ring underneath, for proper installation.

6. Remove the air cleaner and the windshield washer tank.

7. Remove the rocker cover. On 535, 635, and 735 Series cars, disconnect the injector electrical connections, cold start valve, and idle positioner. Disconnect the ground lead on all engines. Then, complete disconnecting the engine wiring harness by disconnecting the oil pressure sending unit and set the harness aside.

8. See the procedures below for removal of the front cover and timing chain and tensioner. Remove the upper timing case cover, tensioner piston, and then open the lockplates and remove the timing chain upper sprocket. Make sure to suspend the sprocket so the timing chain position isn't lost.

9. Loosen the cylinder head bolts following strictly the illustration in reverse order: 14-1. Then, install 4 special pins BMW part No. 11 1 063 or equivalent. This is necessary to keep the rocker arm shafts from moving. Then, lift off the head.

10. Make checks of the lower cylinder head and block deck surface to make sure they are true. See the "Engine Rebuilding" section. Install a new head gasket, making sure that all bolt, oil, and coolant holes line up. Use a gasket marked M 30 B 34 for the larger engine used in 735i. Use a 0.3mm thicker gasket if the head has been machined.

11. Apply a very light coating of oil to the head bolts. Don't let oil get into the bolt holes or apply excessive amounts of oil, or torque could be incorrect and the block could crack. Use the newer type of bolt without a collar. Install the bolts, finger tight.

12. Torque bolts 1-6 in the order shown in the illustration to 42-44 ft. lbs. Remove the 4 pins holding the rocker shafts in place. Now, complete the first stage of torquing by torquing bolts 7-14 in the order shown, to the specifica-

Cylinder head torque sequence for the M30B34 engine until 12/86 and the S38Z engine used in the M5 and M6

tions shown in the Specifications chart for the first stage of torquing. Follow the remaining torquing procedures as described in the Specifications chart. Wait between steps as mentioned. Adjust the valves. Then, reassemble the engine as described below and run it until hot. Then, again remove the valve cover, and either immediately or at any time later (engine temperature isn't critical), turn the head bolts, in order, the number of degrees specified in the specifications chart, using special tool BMW 11 2 110 or equivalent.

13. Reinstall the timing sprocket to the camshaft. Make sure the cam is in proper time, that new lockplates are used, and that nuts are properly torqued. See the procedure for timing chain removal and installation below.

14. When reinstalling the timing cover, make sure to apply a liquid sealer to the joints between upper and lower timing covers. The remainder of installation is the reverse of removal. Note these points.

a. Adjust throttle, speed control, and accelerator cables. Inspect and if necessary replace the exhaust manifold gasket.

b. When reinstalling the cylinder block coolant plug, coat it with sealer. Make sure to refill the cooling system and bleed it (see the Cooling System procedure below).

535i, 635CSi and 1987-88 735i (M30 B35 engine)

1. Unbolt the exhaust pipe connections at the manifold and at the transmission pipe clamp. Disconnect the negative battery cable.

2. Remove the splash shield from under the engine. With the engine cool, remove the drain plugs from the bottom of the radiator and block.

CAUTION: *When draining the coolant, keep in mind that cats and dogs are attracted by the ethylene glycol antifreeze, and are quite likely to drink any that is left in an uncovered container or in puddles on the ground. This will prove fatal in sufficient quantity. Always drain the coolant into a sealable container. Coolant should be reused unless it is contaminated or several years old.*

4. Drain the engine oil.

CAUTION: *The EPA warns that prolonged contact with used engine oil may cause a number of skin disorders, including cancer! You should make every effort to minimize your exposure to used engine oil. Protective gloves should be worn when changing the oil. Wash your hands and any other exposed skin areas as soon as possible after exposure to used engine oil. Soap and water, or waterless hand cleaner should be used.*

5. Remove the fan. Lift out the expansion rivets on either side and remove the fan shroud.

6. Loosen the hose clamp and disconnect the air inlet hose. Remove the mounting nut and remove the air cleaner.

7. The unit on the opposite side of the intake hose from the air cleaner contains the idle speed control valve, which must be removed next. Loosen the hose clamps and pull off the hoses. Disconnect the electrical connector. Remove the mounting nut and then pull the idle speed control out of the air intake hose.

8. Pull off the 3 retainers for the airflow sensor, and then pull the unit off its mountings, disconnecting the vacuum hose from the PCV system at the same time.

9. Working on the coolant expansion tank, disconnect the electrical connector. Remove the nuts on both sides. Loosen their clamps and then disconnect all 3 hoses and remove the tank.

10. Disconnect the heater hoses at both the control valve and at the heater core.

11. Disconnect the throttle and cruise control cables at the throttle lever. Unbolt the cable housing retainer and remove the housing and cables.

12. Disconnect the 4 plugs near the thermostat housing. Loosen the hose clamps and pull off the 2 coolant hoses.

13. Disconnect the plug in the line leading to the oxygen sensor. Disconnect the other 2 plugs nearby.

14. Disconnect the fuel supply and return lines, collecting fuel in a metal container for safe disposal.

15. Disconnect the fuel pipe running along

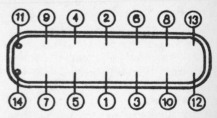

Torque head bolts in the order shown—M30 B35 engine from 12/86 on

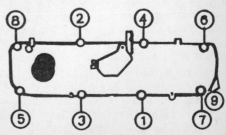

Torque the cam cover bolts on the M30 B34 and B35 engines in the order shown

the cylinder head, near the manifold. Pull off the electrical connector at the throttle body. Remove the caps, then remove the attaching bolts and remove the wiring harness carrier and harness for the fuel injectors.

16. Disconnect the coil high tension lead. Disconnect the high tension wires at the plugs. Then, remove the mounting nuts and remove the carrier for the high tension wires from the head.

17. Remove the attaching nuts for the cam cover and remove it.

18. Turn the engine until the timing marks are at TDC and the No. 6 valves are at overlap (both slightly open) position.

19. Remove the upper timing case cover as described below. Remove the timing chain tensioner piston as also described below.

20. Remove the 4 upper timing chain sprocket bolts and pull the sprocket off, *holding it upward and then supporting it securely so the relationship between the chain and sprockets top and bottom will not be lost* .

21. Disconnect the upper radiator hose at the thermostat housing. Remove the 3 bolts and remove the support for the intake manifold.

22. Remove the cylinder head bolts in the opposite of numbered order. Then, install 4 special pins BMW part No. 11 1 063 or equivalent. This is necessary to keep the rocker arm shafts from moving. Then, lift off the head.

23. Make checks of the lower cylinder head and block deck surface to make sure they are true. See the "Engine Rebuilding" section. Install a new head gasket, making sure that all bolt, oil, and coolant holes line up. Use a gasket marked M30 B35. Use a 0.3mm thicker gasket if the head has been machined.

24. Apply a very light coating of oil to the head bolts. Don't let oil get into the bolt holes or apply excessive amounts of oil, or torque could be incorrect and the block could crack. Use the newer type of bolt without a collar. Install the bolts, finger tight.

25. Torque bolts 1-6 in the order shown in the illustration to 42-44 ft. lbs. Remove the 4 pins holding the rocker shafts in place. Now, complete the first stage of torquing by torquing bolts 7-14 in the order shown, to the same specification. Adjust the valves after a 15 minute wait. Tighten the bolts, in the order shown, with a torque angle gauge 30-36°, using special tool BMW 11 2 110 or equivalent. Then, reassemble the engine as described below and run it until hot (25 minutes). Then, again remove the valve cover, and either immediately or at any time later (engine temperature isn't critical), turn the head bolts, in order, 30-40°.

26. Reinstall the timing sprocket to the camshaft. Make sure the cam is in proper time, that new lockplates are used, and that nuts are properly torqued. See the procedure for timing chain removal and installation below.

27. When reinstalling the timing cover, make sure to apply a liquid sealer to the joints between upper and lower timing covers. The remainder of installation is the reverse of removal. Note these points:

a. Adjust throttle, speed control, and accelerator cables. Inspect and if necessary replace the exhaust manifold gasket.

b. When reinstalling the cylinder block coolant plug, coat it with sealer. Make sure to refill the cooling system and bleed it (see the Cooling System procedure below). Make sure to refill the oil pan with the correct amount of specified oil.

c. Make sure to install the timing chain so that the down pin on the camshaft sprocket is at the lower left (8 o'Clock) when its tapped bores are at right angles to the engine. Torque the sprocket bolts to 6.5-7.5 ft. lbs.

d. Check the cam cover gasket, replacing as necessary. Retighten cam cover bolts in the order shown. Torque the bolts to 6.5-7.5 ft. lbs.

e. When reinstalling the fan shroud, make sure all guides are located properly.

f. Coat the tapered portion of the exhaust pipe connection flange with CRC® Copper Paste or equivalent. Torque the attaching nuts to 4.5 ft. lbs., and then loosen one and a half turns.

M5 and M6

NOTE: *This is an extremely difficult operation involving the use of a number of special tools. It is necessary to remove both of the camshafts to complete it. Refer to the camshaft removal and installation procedure below for information on those special tools.*

1. Disconnect the negative battery cable. Scribe matchmarks where the hood hinges attach to the hood. Then, disconnect the support struts, unbolt the hood at the hinges and remove it.

2. Disconnect the electrical connector at the airflow sensor. Loosen the hose clamp at the air intake hose going to the air cleaner, remove the air cleaner attaching nut, and remove the air cleaner and airflow sensor.

3. Disconnect the large vacuum hose that connects to the bottom of the intake manifold. Disconnect the PCV hoses where they connect to the top of the manifold. Disconnect the throttle cable that runs across the top of the manifold, and the hose running near the front. Remove the bolts fastening the manifold to the outer ends of the intake tubes and remove it.

4. With the engine cool, drain the coolant

from the block. Disconnect the exhaust pipe at the manifold.

CAUTION: *When draining the coolant, keep in mind that cats and dogs are attracted by the ethylene glycol antifreeze, and are quite likely to drink any that is left in an uncovered container or in puddles on the ground. This will prove fatal in sufficient quantity. Always drain the coolant into a sealable container. Coolant should be reused unless it is contaminated or several years old.*

5. Working underneath, remove the heat shields. Remove the cross brace and stabilizer bar where they connect to the engine carrier. Remove the exhaust manifold as described below.

6. Disconnect the upper radiator hose. Pull the 3 plugs off the water manifold that connects with the upper radiator hose. Pull off the plug coming from the same harness and connecting to the top of the engine. Then, unclip this harness and pull it out of the way.

7. Loosen the retaining straps and disconnect the electrical connector that runs directly across the front of the block. Disconnect the fuel pipe on the driver's side of the block, collecting fuel in a metal container for safe disposal.

8. Pull the electrical connector off the throttle bypass valve. Disconnect the water hose and remove the bypass valve. Disconnect the large hose just to the right of the throttle bypass valve. Remove the wiring harness clips just to the right.

9. Going to the rear of the engine, disconnect the fuel return line and collect fuel in a metal container for safe disposal. Disconnect both heater hoses. Remove the conduit for the injector wiring harness from the head. Remove the 2 bolts in the front of the head which run down into the timing cover.

10. See the procedures below for removal of the front timing cover and timing chain. It is not necessary to remove the timing chain completely, but it will be necessary to remove the cam cover, front covers (for the camshaft drive sprockets), and the upper guide rail for the timing chain, and then turn the engine to TDC firing position for No. 1. Then, it will be necessary to remove the timing chain tensioner. Note the relationship between the chain and both the crankshaft and camshaft sprockets, and then remove both camshaft drive sprockets. Leave the chain in a position that will not interfere with removal of the head and which will minimize disturbing its routing through the areas on the front of the block.

11. Remove the camshafts as described below.

12. Prepare a clean work area and a way to store the cam followers in order; preferably some sort of rack. Remove the cam followers one at a time, keeping them in exact order for installation in the same positions.

13. Remove the coolant pipe that runs across the front of the block. Remove the bolts (some are accessible from below) that retain the timing case to the head at the front (the timing case houses the lifters and the camshaft lower bearing saddles.) Then, go along in the area under the cam cover and remove all the remaining bolts for the timing case. Remove the timing case.

14. Loosen the head bolts in reverse of the tightening order shown. Remove the cylinder head.

15. Make checks of the lower cylinder head and block deck surface to make sure they are true. See the "Engine Rebuilding" section. Lubricate the head bolts with a light coating of engine oil. Make sure there is no oil or dirt in the bolt holes in the block. Install a new head gasket, making sure that all bolt, oil, and coolant holes line up. Use a gasket type M6 marked 3.5M 88.3.

16. Replace the O-ring in the head at the right rear where the coolant pipe comes up from the block. Coat the pipe with a Silastic sealer.

17. Install the head onto the block. Install the head bolts and tighten in numbered order according to Specifications.

18. When installing the timing case, replace the O-rings in the 2 small oil passages in the ends of the head. Inspect the 6 O-rings in the center of the block and replace them if necessary. Coat all sealing surfaces with Silastic sealer. Tighten the bolts evenly, torquing the smaller (M7) bolts to 10-12 ft. lbs. and the larger (M8) bolts to 14.5-15.5 ft. lbs. Install all lifters back into the same bores.

19. Install the camshafts as described below.

20. As described under the camshaft and timing chain removal and installation procedures below, reroute the timing chain as necessary and remount the drive sprockets for the camshaft. Install the tensioning rail that goes at the top of the timing chain.

21. Install the front cover according to the procedure below.

22. Continue to reverse the removal procedure. Note these points while working:

a. When reinstalling the intake manifold, inspect the O-rings and replace as necessary.

b. Refill the cooling system with an appropriate antifreeze/water mix for the climate and bleed the cooling system.

CLEANING AND INSPECTION

Chip carbon away from the valve heads, combustion chambers and ports by using a chisel

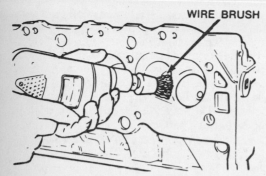

Carbon deposits can be removed from the cylinder head with a wire brush and an electric drill

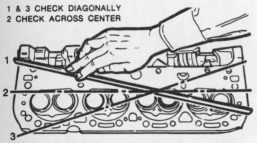

1 & 3 CHECK DIAGONALLY
2 CHECK ACROSS CENTER

Checking for cylinder head warpage with a straight-edge

made of hardwood. Remove the remaining deposits with a stiff wire brush or a wire brush attachment for a hand drill.

NOTE: *Always make sure that the deposits are actually removed, rather than just burnished.*

Clean the remaining cylinder head components in an engine cleaning solvent. Do not remove the protective coating from the valve springs.

CAUTION: *As all BMW cylinder heads are made out of aluminum, NEVER 'hot tank'*

Use a spring compressor to remove the spring collar

the cylinder head as is a common precess with cast iron heads.

Place a straight-edge across the gasket surface of the cylinder head. Using feeler gauges, determine the clearance at the center of the straight-edge. If warpage exceeds 0.08mm in a 152mm span, or 0.15mm over the total length, the cylinder head will require resurfacing.

NOTE: *If warpage exceeds the manufacturer's tolerance for material removal (given previously), the cylinder head must be replaced.*

Cylinder head resurfacing should be performed by a reputable machine shop in your area.

Valves and Springs
REMOVAL AND INSTALLATION

1. Remove the cylinder head and rocker arm shafts as detailed earlier in this chapter.
2. Using a valve spring compressor, compress the springs and remove the spring collar.
3. Lift off the spring retainer and the spring.
4. Pull off the valve seal and the lower spring retainer. Remove the valve through the bottom of the cylinder head.

Removing the valve spring and upper retainer

Install the valve seal (1) over the lower spring retainer (2), BMW special tool 111340 is used to prevent possible seal damage

5. Lubricate the valve stem and guide with engine oil. Install the valve in the head through the bottom and position the lower spring retainer.

6. Lubricate the valve seal with engine oil and then install it into position over the lower spring retainer.

NOTE: *When installing seals, ensier that a small amount of oil is able to pass the seal to lubricate the valve guides; otherwise, excessive wear may result.*

7. Install the valve spring and the upper spring retainer, compress the spring as in Step 2 and install the spring collar.

NOTE: *Valve springs are wound progressively. The end with the tight winding (paint mark) must always be installed facing ghe cylinder head.*

INSPECTION

Inspect the valve faces and seats (in the cylinder head) for pits, burned spots and other evidence of poor seating. If the valve face is in such bad shape that the head of the valve must be ground in order to true up the face, discard the valve because the sharp edge will run too hot. The correct angle for valve faces is given in the specification section at the front of this chapter. It is recommended that any reaming or resurfacing (grinding) be performed by a reputable machine shop.

Check the valve stem for scoring and/or burned spots. If not noticeably scored or damaged, clean the valve stem with a suitable solvent to remove all gum and varnish. Clean the valve guides using a suitable solvent and an expanding wire-type valve guide cleaner (generally available at a local automotive supply store). If you have access to a dial indicator for measuring valve stem-to-guide clearance, mount it so that the stem of the indicator is at a 90° angle to the valve stem and as close to the valve guide as possible. Move the valve off its seat slightly and measure the valve guide-to-stem clearance by rocking the valve back and forth so that the stem actuates the dial indicator. Measure the valve stem using a micrometer, and compare to specifications in order to determine whether the stem or the guide is responsible for the excess clearance. If a dial indicator and a micrometer are not available, take the cylinder head and valves to a reputable machine shop.

Valve Seats
REMOVAL AND INSTALLATION

Valve seats in all BMWs are replaceable in the event that machining fails to restore the seat to proper dimensions. The cylinder head must be heated to 450°F (232°C), while the seat

Valve guide installation (A = .0197 in.)

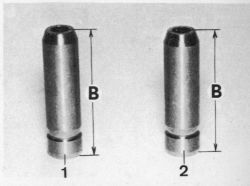
Valve guide 2 is 1.5 mm shorter than valve guide 1, but may be installed in engines originally equipped with the earlier type guide

must be chilled to −94°F (−70°C) for installation. We recommend that this procedure be performed by a reputable machine shop.

Valve Guides
REMOVAL AND INSTALLATION

The valve guides are shrunk-fit into the cylinder head. Therefore, this procedure is best left to a qualified automotive machine shop. The procedure is included here for reference purposes.

1. Remove the cylinder head.

2. Using a suitable valve spring compressor, compress the spring and remove the split keepers. Remove the spring and check it against specifications.

3. Check the valve stem-to-valve clearance by holding the valve about 3mm from the valve seat and rocking it sideways. Movement of the valve head across the seat must not exceed the figure shown in the specifications.

4. If the clearance is excessive, the guide mst be driven out (into the combustion chamber) with a drift of the proper diameter and replaced.

5. To install new valve guide, the cylinder head must be heated to 450°F (232°C) so the new guide can be pressed in without excessive pressure. The guide is then pressed in until it protrudes 15.50-15.51mm. On the 3.3 liter engine, a new type of shorter guide is available, which is pressed in 13.00-14.00mm. BMW special tool 11 1 2o (or the like), incorporates a recess which provides the proper protrusion. With the shorter guide, a washer is used to create the proper dimension. After installation, the guide must be reamed out to the proper dimension.

Oil Pan

REMOVAL AND INSTALLATION

1600, 2000 and 2002

1. Raise and support the vehicle. Drain the engine oil.

CAUTION: *The EPA warns that prolonged contact with used engine oil may cause a number of skin disorders, including cancer! You should make every effort to minimize your exposure to used engine oil. Protective gloves should be worn when changing the oil.*

Sealing application areas—1600, 2000 and 2002

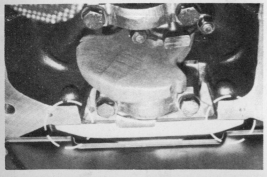

Sealing application areas—1600, 2000 and 2002

Wash your hands and any other exposed skin areas as soon as possible after exposure to used engine oil. Soap and water, or waterless hand cleaner should be used.

2. Remove the front stabilizer bar, if equipped.

3. Remove the oil pan retaining bolts and loosen the pan from the engine block.

4. Disconnect the left and right engine supports.

5. Lower the vehicle and attach a lifting sling and raise the engine slightly.

6. Rotate the crankshaft so the the No. 4 piston is at TDC.

7. Remove the oil pan toward the front.

8. To install the oil pan, use a new gasket. Put sealer on the joints formed where the end cover and timing cover butt up against the block.

9. Slide the oil pan carefully into position and install the retaining bolts. Lower the engine back into position.

10. Connect the left and right engine mounts. Install the front stabilizer bar, if removed.

11. Fill the crankcase to the correct level with clean engine oil.

2500, 2800, Bavaria, 3000, 3.0 Series, 528i and 530i

1. Raise and support the vehicle. Drain the engine oil.

CAUTION: *The EPA warns that prolonged contact with used engine oil may cause a number of skin disorders, including cancer! You should make every effort to minimize your exposure to used engine oil. Protective gloves should be worn when changing the oil. Wash your hands and any other exposed skin areas as soon as possible after exposure to used engine oil. Soap and water, or waterless hand cleaner should be used.*

2. Remove the front lower apron (3.0) and remove the stabilizer bar.

3. Loosen the alternator (remove the alternator on 528i and 530i) and remove the power steering pump, but do not disconnect the hoses.

4. Remove the lower power steering bracket bolt and loosen the remaining bolts (remove the remaining bolts on 528i and 530i) enough to remove the oil pan retaining bolts.

5. Loosen the engine support bracket.

6. Remove the oil pan bolts and loosen the oil pan from the engine block.

7. Rotate the crankshaft until the No. 6 crankpin is above the bottom of the engine block.

8. Lower the front of the oil pan, turn the rear of the pan towards the support bracket and remove the pan.

9. To install the oil pan, use new gaskets. Put

the sealer on the joints formed where the end cover and timing cover butt up against the block.

10. Move the oil pan carefully into position and install the retaining bolts. Reinstall the alternator and power steering pump

10. Connect the left and right engine mounts. Install the front stabilizer bar, and the install the front lower apron.

11. Fill the crankcase to the correct level with clean engine oil.

528e

1. Raise the vehicle and support it. Drain the engine oil.

CAUTION: *The EPA warns that prolonged contact with used engine oil may cause a number of skin disorders, including cancer! You should make every effort to minimize your exposure to used engine oil. Protective gloves should be worn when changing the oil. Wash your hands and any other exposed skin areas as soon as possible after exposure to used engine oil. Soap and water, or waterless hand cleaner should be used.*

2. Remove the front lower splash guard.

3. Disconnect the electrical terminal from the oil sending unit.

4. Remove the flywheel cover.

5. Remove the oil pan bolts and lower the oil pan. Remove the oil pump bolts and take out the oil pump and oil pan.

6. Installation is the reverse of removal. Installation notes:

   a. Clean the gasket surfaces and use a new gasket on the oil pan.

   b. Coat the joints on the ends of the front engine cover with a universal sealing compound.

   c. Install the sending unit wire and the engine oil.

630CSi

1. Raise and support the vehicle. Drain the engine oil.

CAUTION: *The EPA warns that prolonged contact with used engine oil may cause a number of skin disorders, including cancer! You should make every effort to minimize your exposure to used engine oil. Protective gloves should be worn when changing the oil. Wash your hands and any other exposed skin areas as soon as possible after exposure to used engine oil. Soap and water, or waterless hand cleaner should be used.*

2. Remove the front stabilizer bar.

3. Disconnect the wire terminal at he oil level switch.

4. Disconnect the power steering pump, but do not disconnect the hoses. Loosen all the pow-

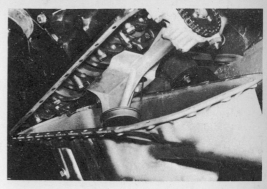

On 600 series cars, rotate the crankshaft until No. 6 connecting rod is above the crankcase sealing surface for clearance at the rear

er steering bracket bolts, and remove the bottom bolt.

5. Remove the engine oil pan bolts, separate the oil pan from the engine block and lower the front of the pan.

6. Rotate the crankshaft until the No. 6 crankpin is above the bottom of the engine block.

7. Lift the engine slightly at the clutch housing while removing the pan to the right side.

8. To install the oil pan, use new gaskets. Put sealer on the joints where the end cover and timing cover butt up against the block.

9. Move the oil pan carefully into position and install the retaining bolts. Reinstall the alternator and power steering pump

10. Connect the left and right engine mounts. Install the front stabilizer bar, and the install the front lower apron.

11. Fill the crankcase to the correct level with clean engine oil.

320i

1. Raise and support the vehicle. Drain the engine oil.

CAUTION: *The EPA warns that prolonged contact with used engine oil may cause a number of skin disorders, including cancer! You should make every effort to minimize your exposure to used engine oil. Protective gloves should be worn when changing the oil. Wash your hands and any other exposed skin areas as soon as possible after exposure to used engine oil. Soap and water, or waterless hand cleaner should be used.*

2. Loosen the steering gear bolts and pull the steering box off the front axle carrier.

3. Remove the oil pan bolts and separate the pan from the engine block.

4. Swing the oil pan downward while rotating the crankshaft to allow the pan to clear the crankpin and remove the pan toward the front.

5. Reverse the procedure to install the oil pan, using new gaskets.

318i

1. Remove the dipstick. Remove the lower pan by draining oil, removing pan bolts, and removing the lower pan.

CAUTION: *The EPA warns that prolonged contact with used engine oil may cause a number of skin disorders, including cancer! You should make every effort to minimize your exposure to used engine oil. Protective gloves should be worn when changing the oil. Wash your hands and any other exposed skin areas as soon as possible after exposure to used engine oil. Soap and water, or waterless hand cleaner should be used.*

2. Remove the oil pump, as described under "Oil Pump Removal and Installation".

3. Unscrew the ground strap, located at the right rear of the upper pan.

4. Remove the bottom 3 flywheel housing bolts, and 2 reinforcement plate bolts, and remove the reinforcement plate.

5. Remove upper pan bolts, and remove the upper pan.

6. Clean all 4 sealing surfaces. Replace both gaskets. Coat the mating surfaces on the timing case and end covers with sealer.

7. Install in reverse order, torquing pan bolts to 7-8 ft. lbs.

524td

1. Drain the oil out of the oil pan. Disconnect the electrical connector for the wire running to the base of the oil pan.

CAUTION: *The EPA warns that prolonged contact with used engine oil may cause a number of skin disorders, including cancer! You should make every effort to minimize your exposure to used engine oil. Protective gloves should be worn when changing the oil. Wash your hands and any other exposed skin*

When removing the upper oil pan on the 318i, remove the arrowed bolts from the bell housing and reinforcing plate, and remove the plate

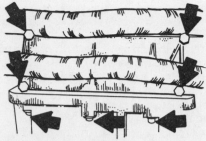

Removing the bolts (arrowed) to remove the flywheel or torque converter cover

areas as soon as possible after exposure to used engine oil. Soap and water, or waterless hand cleaner should be used.

2. Disconnect the turbocharger drain hose running into the side of the oil pan.

3. Remove the flywheel/torque converter cover by removing the 4 bolts from underneath the the 3 from the clutch or converter housing.

4. Remove the oil pan bolts and lower it until it is possible to gain access to the oil pump mounting bolts. Remove those bolts (one on one side of the crankshaft and 2 on the other side) then lower the pan with the pump inside it.

5. Clean all the sealing surfaces. Coat the joints between the block and timing case cover and end cover with a sealing compound. Use a new pan gasket.

6. Guide the oil pump driveshaft into the upper bearing in one side of the block. Guide the pan with the pump inside it upward until it is possible to bolt the oil pump into position. Then, bolt the pan into position. Complete the procedure in reverse order.

533i and 1982 633CSi

1. Raise and support the vehicle. Drain the engine oil.

CAUTION: *The EPA warns that prolonged contact with used engine oil may cause a number of skin disorders, including cancer! You should make every effort to minimize your exposure to used engine oil. Protective gloves should be worn when changing the oil. Wash your hands and any other exposed skin areas as soon as possible after exposure to used engine oil. Soap and water, or waterless hand cleaner should be used.*

2. Remove the front stabilizer bar.

3. Disconnect the wire terminal at the oil level switch.

4. Disconnect the power steering pump, but do not disconnect the hoses. Loosen all the power steering bracket bolts, and remove the bottom bolt.

5. Remove the engine oil pan bolts, separate the oil pan from the engine block and lower the front of the pan.

6. Rotate the crankshaft until the No. 6 crankpin is above the bottom of the engine block.

7. Lift the engine slightly at the clutch housing while removing the pan to the right side.

8. To install the oil pan, use new gaskets. Put the sealer on the joints formed where the end cover and timing cover butt up against the block.

9. Move the oil pan carefully into position and install the retaining bolts. Reinstall the alternator and power steering pump

10. Connect the left and right engine mounts. Install the front stabilizer bar, and the install the front lower apron.

11. Fill the crankcase to the correct level with clean engine oil.

533i and 1983-84 633CSi, 535i, 635CSi, M5 and M6

1. Disconnect the engine ground lead. Disconnect the electrical connector and separate the leads from the air cleaner/air flow sensor. Loosen the hose clamp and disconnect the air intake hose. Remove the mounting nut and remove the air cleaner and the airflow sensor as a unit. Remove the fan shroud.

2. Drain the engine oil.

CAUTION: *The EPA warns that prolonged contact with used engine oil may cause a number of skin disorders, including cancer! You should make every effort to minimize your exposure to used engine oil. Protective gloves should be worn when changing the oil. Wash your hands and any other exposed skin areas as soon as possible after exposure to used engine oil. Soap and water, or waterless hand cleaner should be used.*

3. Loosen the belt tension and remove the alternator drive belt. Loosen the upper front mounting bolt for the alternator and the 2 bolts on the side of the block that mount it at the rear. Remove the lower front mounting bolt. Then, swing the alternator to the side.

4. Loosen the power steering pump mounts and remove the drive belt. Then, remove the mounting bolts and remove the pump and pump mounting bracket. Make sure to retain spacers. If the car has air conditioning, remove the nuts and bolts that fasten the compressor to the hinge type mounting bracket. Make sure the compressor is suspended so there is no tension on the hoses. Unbolt the hinge type mounting bracket and remove it.

5. Remove the brace plate located under the oil pan. Remove those oil pan bolts that can be reached.

6. Remove the engine ground strap. Remove the engine mount through bolts. Attach a lifting sling to the hooks on top of the engine. Lift the engine slightly for clearance.

7. Shift the power steering pump out of the way and support it so no tension will be placed on the hoses.

8. Remove the remaining oil pan mounting bolts. Turn the crankshaft so the rods for cylinders 5 and 6 are as high as possible. Then, remove the pan.

9. Clean all sealing surfaces and supply a new gasket. Apply a liquid sealer to the joints between the block and the timing cover on the front and the rear main seal cover at the rear.

10. Install the oil pan in reverse order. Torque the pan bolts to 6.5-7.5 ft. lbs. Make sure to refill the pan with the required amount of the correct oil. Mount all accessories securely and adjust the drive belts.

1982 733i

1. Raise and support the vehicle. Drain the engine oil.

CAUTION: *The EPA warns that prolonged contact with used engine oil may cause a number of skin disorders, including cancer! You should make every effort to minimize your exposure to used engine oil. Protective gloves should be worn when changing the oil. Wash your hands and any other exposed skin areas as soon as possible after exposure to used engine oil. Soap and water, or waterless hand cleaner should be used.*

2. Remove the power steering pump, but do not disconnect the hoses.

3. Remove the lower power steering bracket bolt. Loosen the upper bracket bolts to move the bracket away from the oil pan.

4. Disconnect the oil level switch wire terminal.

5. Remove the oil pan bolts and separate the oil pan from the engine block.

6. Disconnect the left and right engine mounts.

7. Remove the engine vibration damper.

8. Lower the vehicle and remove the fan housing from the radiator.

9. Attach a lifting sling and raise the engine until the oil pan can be removed.

10. To install the oil pan, use new gaskets. Put the sealer on the joints formed where the end cover and timing cover butt up against the block.

11. Move the oil pan carefully into position and install the retaining bolts. Reinstall the alternator and power steering pump.

12. Connect the left and right engine mounts. Install the front stabilizer bar, and the install the front lower apron.

13. Fill the crankcase to the correct level with clean engine oil.

1983-86 733i and 735i (M30 B34 engine)

1. Remove the alternator drive belt, remove the alternator mounting bolts and move it aside.

2. Loosen the adjusting and mounting bolts and remove the power steering pump belt. Remove the power steering pump hinge bolt and nut. Remove the 2 bolts shown, keeping any shims that may have been used in assembly together with the bolt they were on.

CAUTION: *When draining the coolant, keep in mind that cats and dogs are attracted by the ethylene glycol antifreeze, and are quite likely to drink any that is left in an uncovered container or in puddles on the ground. This will prove fatal in sufficient quantity. Always drain the coolant into a sealable container. Coolant should be reused unless it is contaminated or several years old.*

3. Drain coolant out of the block. Drain the oil pan. Remove the plug from the block and drain the engine of coolant.

CAUTION: *The EPA warns that prolonged contact with used engine oil may cause a number of skin disorders, including cancer! You should make every effort to minimize your exposure to used engine oil. Protective gloves should be worn when changing the oil. Wash your hands and any other exposed skin areas as soon as possible after exposure to used engine oil. Soap and water, or waterless hand cleaner should be used.*

4. Remove the 2 attachments fastening the stabilizer bar to the body.

5. Remove the 2 bolts and nuts shown and move this bracket away from the engine.

6. Remove the bolts and remove the clutch housing cover. Remove all the oil pan bolts that can be reached.

7. Disconnect the oil level sending unit wire. Then, unfasten both engine mounts by removing the nuts from the ends of the bolts.

8. Disconnect the radiator hoses that's near one of the lifting hooks, and securely connect a lifting sling to the engine. Raise the engine.

9. Swing out and tie down the power steering bracket. Then, unscrew the remaining oil pan bolts.

10. Pull the oil pan down. Turn the crankshaft so the rods for cylinders 5 and 6 are in the highest position, pull the stabilizer bar away, and then remove the pan.

11. Install in reverse order, paying attention to these points:

   a. Clean all gasket surfaces thoroughly. Use a new gasket and coat all mating surfaces on the timing cover and clutch housing cover with a liquid sealer.

   b. Torque the stabilizer bar attachment bolts to 16 ft. lbs.

   c. Make sure spacers are used on the power steering pump brace (removed in Step 2) so there will not be any torque on the bracket due to misalignment.

1987-88 735i (M30 B35 engine)

1. Loosen the hose clamp for the air intake hose. Remove the mounting nut for the air cleaner, and remove the air cleaner. Remove the fan and shroud.

2. Disconnect the electrical plug and overflow hose from the coolant expansion tank. Be careful not to kink the hose. Remove the mounting nuts and remove the tank.

3. Remove the splash guard for the power steering pump. Loosen the locknut for the pump adjustment and remove the through bolt that mounts the pump lower bracket (which contains the adjustment mechanism) to the block. Swing the bracket aside. Unscrew the bolt attaching the power steering pump lines to the block and shift them aside too.

4. Disconnect the electrical plug for the suspension leveling switch on the left side engine mounting bracket. Remove the oil pan drain plug and drain the oil.

CAUTION: *The EPA warns that prolonged contact with used engine oil may cause a number of skin disorders, including cancer! You should make every effort to minimize your exposure to used engine oil. Protective gloves should be worn when changing the oil. Wash your hands and any other exposed skin areas as soon as possible after exposure to used engine oil. Soap and water, or waterless hand cleaner should be used.*

5. Remove the bracket for the exhaust pipes located near the oil pan.

6. Disconnect the ground strap from the engine. Remove the nuts and washers attaching the engine to the mounts on both sides.

7. Attach an engine lifting sling to the hooks at either end of the cylinder head. Lift the engine as necessary for clearance.

8. Remove all oil pan mounting bolts and remove the pan. Clean both sealing surfaces and supply a new gasket. Coat the 4 joints (between the block and timing case cover at the front and the block and rear main seal housing cover at the rear) with a sealer such as 3 Bond Silicone Sealer®. Install the oil pan bolts and torque them to 6.5-7.5 ft. lbs.

9. Reverse the remaining procedures to install the oil pan. Torque the engine mount nuts to 31-34 ft. lbs. Refill the oil pan with the required amount and type of oil.

325, 325e, 325i, 325iS and 528e

1. Raise the vehicle and support it. Drain the engine oil.

CAUTION: *The EPA warns that prolonged contact with used engine oil may cause a number of skin disorders, including cancer! You should make every effort to minimize your exposure to used engine oil. Protective gloves should be worn when changing the oil. Wash your hands and any other exposed skin areas as soon as possible after exposure to used engine oil. Soap and water, or waterless hand cleaner should be used.*

2. Remove the front lower splash guard. This may not be necessary for access on 1988 models.

3. Disconnect the electrical terminal from the oil sending unit.

4. On 1987 and earlier models, skip to Step 5. On 1988 models, remove the power steering gear from the front axle carrier as described later in this section.

5. Remove the flywheel cover.

6. Remove the oil pan bolts and lower the oil pan. Remove the oil pump bolts and take out the oil pump and oil pan.

7. Installation is the reverse of removal. Installation notes:

   a. Clean the gasket surfaces and use a new gasket on the oil pan.

   b. Coat the joints on the ends of the front engine cover with a universal sealing compound.

   c. Install the sending unit wire and the engine oil. If the power steering gear was removed, make sure to refill and bleed this system.

M3

1. Remove the dipstick. Remove the splash guard from underneath the engine.

2. Remove the drain plug and drain the oil. Unscrew all the bolts for the lower oil pan and remove it.

CAUTION: *The EPA warns that prolonged contact with used engine oil may cause a number of skin disorders, including cancer! You should make every effort to minimize your exposure to used engine oil. Protective gloves should be worn when changing the oil. Wash your hands and any other exposed skin areas as soon as possible after exposure to used engine oil. Soap and water, or waterless hand cleaner should be used.*

3. Remove the oil pan as described below.

4. Remove the lower flywheel housing cover by removing the 3 bolts at the bottom of the flywheel housing and the 2 bolts in the cover just ahead of the flywheel housing.

5. Disconnect the oil pressure sending unit plug. Unbolt the oil pan bracket. Disconnect the ground lead. Loosen its clamp and disconnect the crankcase ventilation hose.

6. Remove the oil pan bolts and remove the upper oil pan. Clean all sealing surfaces. Supply a new gasket and the coat the joints where the timing case cover and block meet with a brush-on sealant. Install the pan and torque the bolts evenly to 7 ft. lbs.

7. Reverse the remaining removal procedures to install, cleaning all sealing surfaces and using a new gasket on the lower pan, also. Torque the lower pan bolts, also, to 7 ft. lbs.

8. Install the oil pan drain plug, torquing to 24 ft. lbs. Refill the oil pan with the required amount of approved oil. Start the engine and check for leaks.

Oil Pump
REMOVAL AND INSTALLATION

1600, 2000, and 2002

1. Remove the oil pan as outlined under "Oil Pan Removal and Installation".

2. Remove the 3 retaining bolts for the oil pump drive sprocket and pull off the sprocket.

3. Open the lockplates for the pickup tube mounting bolts at the main bearing cap. Remove the 2 bolts for the support mount and the 2 oil pump retaining bolts. Lower the oil pump down and out of the car, taking care not to lose the O-ring in the oil pump housing.

4. Reverse the above procedure to install, observing the following installation notes:

   a. Adjust the oil pump drive chain tension so that the chain may be depressed under light thumb pressure. If the proper tension cannot be achieved with either of the replacement lengths of chain, shims (compensating plates) may be installed between the pump housing and the block to take up the slack. When installing shims, always make sure that the oil hole is not blocked. Use a new-O-ring when possible.

Removing the oil pump assembly—1600, 2000 and 2002

Chain tension adjusting shim installed with oil hole properly positioned

Oil pump mounting shims used on the 600 series cars. Note that both shims must be of the same thickness and that oil holes must be in the proper position

b. After tightening the pump mounting bolts, loosen the pickup tube support bracket and retighten the bracket bolts so that the bracket is tension-free.

All Models Except 325, 325e, 325i, 325iS, 325iX, M3, 524td and 528e

1. Remove the oil pan. On the 318i and M3, only the lower section of the pan need be removed.

2. Remove the bolts retaining the sprocket to the oil pump shaft and remove the sprocket.

3. On 4-cylinder engines:

a. Remove the oil pump retaining bolts and lower the oil pump from the engine block.

b. Check the installed location of the O-ring seal, between the housing and the pressure safety line and make sure it is installed so it will seal properly.

c. Torque the sprocket retaining nut to 18-22 ft. lbs.

d. Be sure that the oil bore in the shim(s) is correctly positioned during the oil pump installation. If there is a lot of play in the drive chain, add one or more shims. The drive

chain should give slightly under light thumb pressure.

4. On 6-cylinder engines:

a. Remove the oil pump retaining bolts and lower the oil pump from the engine block. On 6-cyl. engines other than the M30B35, there are 3 bolts at the front and 2 bolts attaching the rear of the oil pickup to the lower end of a support bracket. It is necessary to remove all 5 bolts. On the M30B35, there are only 3 bolts.

b. Do not loosen the chain adjusting shims from the 2 mounting locations.

c. Add or subtract shims between the oil pump body and the engine block to obtain a slight movement of the chain under light thumb pressure.

5. Install the oil pump in the reverse order of removal.

CAUTION: *When used, the 2 shim thicknesses must be the same. Tighten the pump holder at the pick-up end after shimming is completed to avoid stress on the pump.*

6. On 6-cylinder engines, other than the M30B35, after the main pump mounting bolts are torqued, loosen the bolts at the bracket on the rear of the pick-up, allowing the pick-up to assume its most natural position. This will relieve tension on the bracket. Tighten the bolts. On the M30B35, torque the oil pump mounting bolts to 16 ft. lbs. and the sprocket bolts to 19 ft. lbs.

325, 325e, 325i, 325iS, 325iX, M3, and 528e

1. Raise the vehicle and support it. Drain the engine oil.

CAUTION: *The EPA warns that prolonged contact with used engine oil may cause a number of skin disorders, including cancer! You should make every effort to minimize your exposure to used engine oil. Protective gloves should be worn when changing the oil. Wash your hands and any other exposed skin areas as soon as possible after exposure to used engine oil. Soap and water, or waterless hand cleaner should be used.*

2. Remove the front lower splash guard.

3. Disconnect the electrical terminal from the oil sending unit.

4. Remove the flywheel cover.

5. Remove the 3 oil pan bolts: one on one side and 2 on the other and lower the oil pan. Remove the oil pump bolts and take out the oil pump and oil pan.

6. Installation is the reverse of removal. Installation notes:

a. Clean the gasket surfaces and use a new gasket on the oil pan.

b. Positioning the pump for installation of its mounting bolts, guide the pump drive-

shaft into the hole in the center of the drive gear.

c. Coat the joints on the ends of the front engine cover with a universal sealing compound.

d. Install the sending unit wire and the engine oil.

524td

On the diesel, the pump comes down as the oil pan is removed. Refer to the Oil Pan Removal and Installation procedure which gives complete details.

Timing Chain (Front) Cover
REMOVAL AND INSTALLATION
1600, 2000, 2002, 318i and 320i

There are 2 timing chain covers, one upper and one lower, which must be removed to service the timing chain and sprocket assemblies.

1. Remove the cylinder head cover. Disconnect the negative battery cable. Disconnect the air injection line at the front of the thermal reactor (if so equipped). On the 318i, disconnect the bracket located on the driver's side of the upper cover.

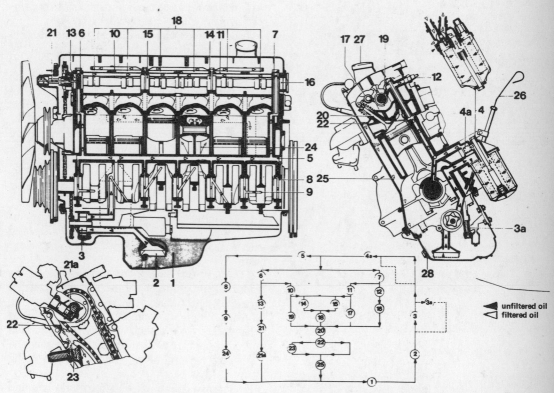

1. Oil pan	15. Camshaft bearing
2. Intake with filter screen	16. Rear camshaft bearing
3. Oil pump	17. Rocker arm bearing (exhaust)
3a. Pressure relief valve	18. Spray jets for cam lubrication
4. Oil filter	19. Rocker arm bearing (intake)
4a. Safety valve (oil filter)	20. Valve guide
5. Main distribution bore	21. Bore in distributor drive
6. Oil bore in cylinder head, front	21a. Spray oil for distributor drive
7. Oil bore in cylinder head, rear	22. Overflow from cylinder head
8. Crankshaft bearing	23. Oil pocket for chain lubrication
9. Connecting rod bearing	24. Spray oil for piston pin
10. Hollow rocker arm shaft, front	25. Oil drain bore
11. Hollow rocker arm shaft, rear	26. Oil dipstick
12. Transmitter for oil pressure indicator lamp	27. Oil filler neck
13. Front camshaft bearing	28. Oil drain plug
14. Camshaft bearing	

Oil flow circuit 528e—others similar

Separating pan gasket from lower timing chain cover with knife

Sealing compound application areas

Sealing compound application areas

Tightening sequence for upper timing chain cover bolts

2. Remove 8 bolts which retain the upper timing gear cover to the cylinder head and lower timing gear cover. remove the upper cover, taking note of the placement of the alternator ground wire.

3. Drain the cooling system and remove the radiator, preheater intake air assembly (carburetor equipped cars only) and radiator hoses as outlined under "Radiator Removal and Installation".

CAUTION: *When draining the coolant, keep in mind that cats and dogs are attracted by the ethylene glycol antifreeze, and are quite likely to drink any that is left in an uncovered container or in puddles on the ground. This will prove fatal in sufficient quantity. Always drain the coolant into a sealable container. Coolant should be reused unless it is contaminated or several years old.*

4. Bend back the lockplates for the fan retaining bolts. Remove the bolts and lift off the fan.

5. Loosen the alternator retaining bolts. Push the alternator toward the engine and remove the fan pulley and the alternator drive (fan) belt. On the 318i, remove the alternator and tensioning bar. remove the 4 mounting bolts from the air pump bracket (where it attaches to the block), and remove the pump and bracket; then remove the bolt attaching the tensioning bar to the block and remove the tensioning bar.

6. Disconnect the coolant hoses from the water pump. Remove the 6 retaining bolts and copper sealing washers and lift off the water pump.

7. Unscrew the plug and remove the spring from the cam chain tensioner assembly, taking care to cushion the sudden release of spring tension. Remove the plunger (piston).

8. On the 320i, disconnect the multiple plug and cable lead from the alternator. Remove the alternator with its bearing block and clamping strap.

9. Remove the flywheel inspection plate and block the ring gear from turning with a small prybar.

10. Unscrew the crankshaft pulley nut and pull off the belt pulley.

11. Remove the bolts which retain the lower cover to the cylinder black and oil pan. On the 318i, remove the bolts retaining the brace plate and remove it. Also on the 318i, loosen the oil pan lower retaining bolts not directly involved with the lower cover. With a sharp knife, carefully separate the lower edge of the timing cover from the upper edge of the oil pan gasket at the front.

12. Remove the lower timing cover. At this time, it is advisable to replace the timing cover

seal (sealing ring) with a new one. The sealing ring is a press fit into the cover.

13. Clean the mating surfaces of the timing covers, oil pan, cylinder head, and cylinder block. Replace all gaskets (except the oil pan gasket), and seal them at the corners with sealing compound such as Permatex® No. 2. If the oil pan gasket has been damaged, remove the oil pan and replace the gasket.

14. Reverse the above procedure to install, taking care to tighten the upper timing gear cover retaining bolts in the following sequence (as per the illustration): hand tighten 1 and 2, then torque 3-8 in numerical order, and finally 1 and 2 to 6.5-7.9 ft. lbs. Note that on the 318i, the mounting web for the tensioning piston must be in the oil pocket. On the 318i, also make sure to pack the bores between the lower cover (at the top) and block with sealer.

6-Cylinder Models Except 325, 325e, 325i, 325iS, 524td, 528e, M5 and M6

NOTE: *On 533, 535, 600CS Series, and 700 Series engines, this procedure requires the use of a special gauge, to be made to a certain dimension, as in Step 16.*

1. Remove the cylinder head cover. Remove the distributor as described earlier in this chapter. On all 3.3 liter models, detach the distributor guard and the air line going to the thermal reactor. On late model cars with Digital Motor Electronics, follow this procedure to remove the distributor:

   a. Remove the distributor cap, which screws onto the cover directly in front of the camshaft.

   b. Then, if the rotor is of the slide-on type, simply pull the rotor off and then remove the cover underneath it.

   c. If the rotor is of the screw-on type, unscrew it from the distributor shaft, then unscrew the adapter underneath and, finally remove the cover underneath the adapter.

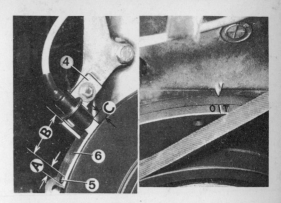

TDC transmitter gauge. A = .197 in., B = 1.398 in., and C = .197 in. Position the gauge on the contact pin (5). Position the transmitter holder (4) on the gauge and tighten

630 11 148

Installing the lower cover; upper arrow shows tensioning piston holding web

2. Drain the coolant to below the level of the thermostat and remove the thermostat housing cover.

CAUTION: *When draining the coolant, keep in mind that cats and dogs are attracted by the ethylene glycol antifreeze, and are quite likely to drink any that is left in an uncovered container or in puddles on the ground. This will prove fatal in sufficient quantity. Always drain the coolant into a sealable container. Coolant should be reused unless it is contaminated or several years old.*

3. Remove the 8 bolts (nine on M30B35MZ) and remove the upper timing case cover with the worm drive which drives the distributor (pre DME cars only).

4. Remove the piston which tensions the timing chain, working carefully because of very high spring pressure.

5. Remove the cooling fan and all drive belts. On late model 600 Series cars, the alternator must be swung aside by loosing the front bolt and removing the 2 side bolts. On all cars with the M30B35MZ engine, remove its attaching

Fill the wells (circled) with sealer on 528i, 630CSi, 633CSi and 733i models

bolts and then remove the drive pulley from the water pump. The power steering pump must be removed, leaving the pump hoses connected and supporting the pump out of the way but so that the hoses are not stressed.

6. Remove the flywheel housing cover and lock the flywheel in position with an appropriate special tool.

7. Unscrew the nut from the center of the pulley and pull the pulley/vibration damper off the crankshaft.

8. Detach the TDC position transmitter on 600CS Series, 700 Series, and certain 528i models.

9. Loosen all the oil pan bolts, and then unscrew all the bolts from the lower timing case cover, noting their lengths for reinstallation in the same positions. Carefully use a knife to separate the gasket at the base of the lower timing cover. Then, remove the cover.

10. To install the lower cover, first coat the surfaces of the oil pan and block with sealer. Put it into position on the block, making sure the tensioning piston holding web (cast into the block) is in the oil pocket. Install all bolts; then tighten the lower front cover bolts evenly; finally, tighten the oil pan bolts evenly.

11. Inspect the hub of the vibration damper. If the hub is scored, install the radial seal so the sealing lip is in front of or to the rear of the scored area. Pack the seal with grease and install it with a sealer installer.

12. Install the pulley/damper and torque the bolt to specifications. When installing, make sure the key and keyway are properly aligned.

13. Remove the flywheel locking tool and reinstall the cover. Reinstall and tension all belts.

14. Before installing the upper cover, use sealer to seal the joint between the back of the lower timing cover and block at the top. On some models, there are sealer wells which are to be filled with sealer. If these are present, fill them carefully. Check the cork seal at the distributor drive coupling, and replace it if necessary.

15. On all but M30B35MZ engines: See the illustration for 4-cylinder engines above, and tighten bolts 1 and 2 (the lower bolts) slightly. Then, tighten bolts 3-8. Finally, fully tighten the lower bolts. On M30B35MZ engines, note that the top bolt on the driver's side and the bottom bolt on the passenger's side are longer. On these engines, tighten the 2 bolts that run down into the lower timing cover first; then tighten the remaining 6 bolts (3 on each side).

16. On the M30B35MZ engine, simply install the TDC transmitter and its mounting bracket. On remaining engines, install the TDC position transmitter loosely, if so equipped. With the engine at exactly 0° Top Center, as shown by the marker on the front cover, adjust the position of the transmitter with a gauge which should be made to conform to the dimensions shown in the illustration: i.e. it must fit the curve on the outside of the balancer, and incorporate a notch (for the pin on the balancer) and a ridge against which the transmitter must rest. The straight line distance between the center of the notch and bottom of the ridge must be exactly 37.5mm. Then, tighten the transmitter mounting screw.

17. Just before installing the upper timing case cover, check the condition of that area of the head gasket. It will usually be in good condition. If it should show damage, it must be replaced.

18. If the car has the DME type distributor, inspect the sealing O-rings and replace as necessary. If it uses the DME distributor with the screw-off type rotor, make sure the bolt at the center of the rotor has its seal in place and that it is installed with a sealer designed to prevent the bolt from backing out.

19. Reverse the remaining portions of the removal procedures, making sure to bleed the cooling system.

524td

1. Disconnect the hoses and remove the air cleaner. Remove the belt driving the alternator and fan. Remove the attaching nuts and remove the fan, keeping it in the vertical position.

2. Remove the air hose running along the top edge of the cover. remove the attaching bolts and remove the cover.

3. If removing the cover to replace the timing belt, proceed further to remove the vibration damper:

   a. Remove the remaining accessory drive belts.

   b. Remove the belts and remove the fan drive pulley.

   c. Remove the center bolt, and pull the pulley and vibration damper off the hub.

4. Install in reverse order, torquing the center bolt for the vibration damper to the specifications shown in the torque specifications chart. Adjust belt tension.

M3

1. Disconnect the negative battery cable. Drain the cooling system through the bottom of the radiator. Remove the radiator and fan as described later in this section.

CAUTION: *When draining the coolant, keep in mind that cats and dogs are attracted by the ethylene glycol antifreeze, and are quite likely to drink any that is left in an uncovered container or in puddles on the ground. This will prove fatal in sufficient quantity. Always*

drain the coolant into a sealable container. Coolant should be reused unless it is contaminated or several years old.

2. Disconnect all electrical plugs, remove the attaching nuts, and remove the air cleaner and airflow sensor.'

3. Note and if necessary mark the wiring connections. Then, disconnect all alternator wiring. Unbolt the alternator and remove it and the drive belt.

4. Unbolt the power steering pump. Remove the belt and then move the pump aside, supporting it out of the way but in a position where the hoses will not be stressed.

5. Remove the 3 bolts from the bottom of the bell housing and the 2 bolts below it which fasten the reinforcement plate in place.

6. Remove the drain plug and drain the oil from the lower oil pan. Then, remove the lower oil pan bolts and remove the lower pan.

CAUTION: *The EPA warns that prolonged contact with used engine oil may cause a number of skin disorders, including cancer! You should make every effort to minimize your exposure to used engine oil. Protective gloves should be worn when changing the oil. Wash your hands and any other exposed skin areas as soon as possible after exposure to used engine oil. Soap and water, or waterless hand cleaner should be used.*

7. Remove the 3 bolts fastening the bottom of the front cover to the front of the oil pan. Loosen all the remaining oil pan bolts so the pan may be shifted downward just slightly to separate the gasket surfaces.

8. Remove the water pump as described below. Remove the center bolt and use a puller to remove the crankshaft pulley.

9. Remove the piston for the timing chain tensioner as described below under Timing Chain and Sprockets Removal and Installation.

10. Remove the 2 bolts attaching the top of the front cover to the cylinder head. Then, remove all the bolts fastening the cover to the block.

11. Run a knife carefully between the upper surface of the oil pan gasket and the lower surface of the front cover to separate them without tearing the gasket. If the gasket is damaged, remove the oil pan and replace it, as described later in this section.

12. Before reinstalling the cover, use a file to break or file off flashing at the top rear of the casting on either side so the corner is smooth. Replace all gaskets, coating them with silicone sealer. Where gasket ends extend too far, trim them off. Apply sealer to the area where the oil pan gasket passes the front of the block.

13. Slide the cover straight on to avoid damaging the seal. Install all bolts in their proper positions. Coat the 3 bolts fastening the front cover to the upper oil pan with a sealer such as Loctite® 270® or equivalent. Tighten the bolts at the top, fastening the lower cover to the upper cover first. Then, tighten the remaining front cover bolts and, finally, the oil pan bolts (to 7 ft. lbs.). If the car has the DME type distributor, inspect the sealing O-rings and replace as necessary. If it uses the DME distributor with the screw-off type rotor, make sure the bolt at the center of the rotor has its seal in place and that it is installed with a sealer designed to prevent the bolt from backing out.

14. Reverse the remaining portions of the removal procedures, making sure to fill and bleed the cooling system and to refill the oil pan with the correct oil. Torque the oil drain plug to 24 ft. lbs. and both upper and lower oil pan bolts to 7 ft. lbs.

M5 and M6

1. Disconnect the battery ground cable. Pull out the plug and remove the wiring leading to the airflow sensor. Loosen the hose clamp and disconnect the air intake hose. Remove the mounting nut and remove the air cleaner and airflow sensor as an assembly.

2. Remove the radiator and fan. See appropriate procedures below. Remove the flywheel housing cover and install a lock to lock the position of the flywheel. Remove the mounting nut for the vibration damper with a deepwell socket. Pull the damper off with a puller.

3. Remove the pipe that runs across in front of the front cover. Remove the mounting bolts and remove the water pump pulley.

4. Loosen the top front mounting bolt for the alternator. Remove the lower front bolt. Loosen the 2 side bolts. Swing the alternator aside.

5. Remove the power steering pump mounting bolts. Make sure to retain the spacer that goes between the pump and oil pan. Swing the pump aside and support it so the hoses will not be under stress.

6. Remove the flywheel housing cover and lock the flywheel in position with an appropriate special tool.

7. Unscrew the nut from the center of the pulley and pull the pulley/vibration damper off the crankshaft.

8. Remove the bolts at the top, fastening the lower front cover to the upper front cover. Remove the bolts at the bottom, fastening the lower cover to the oil pan. Loosen the remaining oil pan mounting bolts.

9. Run a knife carefully between the upper surface of the oil pan gasket and the lower surface of the front cover to separate them without tearing the gasket.

10. Loosen and then remove the remaining

front cover mounting bolts, noting the locations of the TDC sending unit on the upper right side of the engine and the suspension position sending unit on the upper left. Also, keep track of the bolts that mount these accessories, as their lengths are slightly different. If necessary, lay the bolts out in a clean area in a pattern similar to that in which they are positioned on the engine. Remove the timing cover, pulling it off squarely.

11. Before reinstalling the cover, use a file to break or file off flashing at the top rear of the casting on either side so the corner is smooth. Replace all gaskets, coating them with silicone sealer. Where gasket ends extend too far, trim them off. Apply sealer to the area where the oil pan gasket passes the front of the block.

12. Slide the cover straight on to avoid damaging the seal. Install all bolts in their proper positions. Tighten the bolts at the top, fastening the lower cover to the upper cover first. Then, tighten the remaining front cover bolts and, finally, the oil pan bolts. If the car has the DME type distributor, inspect the sealing O-rings and replace as necessary. If it uses the DME distributor with the screw-off type rotor, make sure the bolt at the center of the rotor has its seal in place and that it is installed with a sealer designed to prevent the bolt from backing out.

13. Reverse the remaining portions of the removal procedures, making sure to refill and bleed the cooling system.

Timing Chain Cover Oil Seal

REMOVAL AND INSTALLATION

All Models Except 325, 325e, 325i, 325iS, 524td and 528e

1. Position the No. 1 piston at TDC on the beginning of its compression stroke.
2. Remove the flywheel guard and lock the flywheel with a locking tool.
3. Remove the drive belts and the fan.
4. Remove the retaining nut and remove the vibration damper from the crankshaft.

NOTE: *The Woodruff key should be at the 12 o'clock position on the crankshaft.*

5. Remove the seal from the timing housing cover with a small pry bar.
6. Using a special seal installer or equivalent, lubricate and install the seal in the cover. This tool is used to press the seal into the bore with even pressure around the entire perimeter.

NOTE: *If the balancer hub has serious scoring on the sealing surface, position the seal in the cover so that the sealing lip is in front of or behind the scored groove.*

7. Lubricate the balancer hub and install it

Removing the front cover oil seal with a claw-type puller

Position of crankshaft woodruff key (1)

on the crankshaft, being careful not to damage the seal.

8. Complete the assembly, using the reverse of the removal procedure. Be sure to remove the flywheel locking tool before attempting to start the engine.

325, 325e, 325i, 325iS and 528e

The 325 and 528e have 2 oil seals on the front engine cover. One is on the crankshaft and the other is on the intermediate shaft.

1. Remove the front engine cover (see the "Timing Belt and Front Cover" procedure).
2. Press the 2 radial oil seals out of the front engine cover.
3. Install the oil seals flush with the front engine cover using BMW tools 24 1 050, 33 1 180 and 005 5 500 or equivalents.
4. Install the front engine cover.

524td

NOTE: *A number of special tools are necessary to complete this operation. They include: A wrench designed to hold the vibration*

damper hub BMW 11 2 150 or equivalent; a puller for the vibration damper hub; a pin to hold the vibration damper hub 11 2 040; a puller to remove the timing belt sprocket from the crankshaft such as BMW 00 7 501 and 11 2 131; seal installer 24 1 040 and 24 1 050; and special tools designed to protect the seals when the front engine cover is installed, 11 2 211 and 11 2 212. Equivalents may be available from other sources.

1. Remove the timing belt cover and vibration damper as described above.

2. Remove the radiator. Install the special wrench on the vibration damper hub. Then, unscrew the bolt at the center until it is about 3 turns out. Attach a puller such as 00 7 501 with bolts 11 2 132. The 2 outer bolts screw into holes in the outer rim of the damper hub. Then, turn the center bolt of the puller so it forces the hub off by pressing against the center bolt.

3. Remove the timing belt as described below. Then, use the special tool or another suitable means to hold the intermediate shaft stationary while removing the bolt at the center. Then, remove the intermediate shaft washer and sprocket.

4. Screw the bolt into the center of the crankshaft until it is about 3 turns out. Screw the outer bolts for the puller into the outer edge of the crankshaft sprocket until they are secure. Then, screw in the center bolt of the puller to force the crankshaft sprocket off.

5. Remove the arrowed bolts, and oil pan bolts labeled 4, 5, and 6. Loosen the other pan bolts. Then carefully use a sharp knife to separate the oil pan gasket from the front cover. Remove the cover.

6. From the rear of the cover, press the oil seals outward. Then use tools such as 24 1 040 and 24 1 050 to press in new seals. Replacement seals must be pressed in until 1.00-2.00mm indented. Apply clean engine oil to the sealing lips.

7. Install tools such as 11 2 211 (crankshaft) and 11 2 212 (intermediate shaft) to the ends of these shafts to protect the seals. Then, install the front cover.

8. Installation is the reverse of removal. Keep the following points in mind:

   a. Install the crankshaft sprocket with the woodruff key in the proper position and the step forward.

   b. When installing the intermediate shaft sprocket, make sure the centering pin slides into its bore.

Timing Chain and Tensioner
REMOVAL AND INSTALLATION

All Models Except 325, 325e, 325i, 325iS, 524td, 528e, M3, M5 and M6

1. Rotate the crankshaft to set the No. 1 piston at TDC, at the beginning of its compression stroke.

2. Remove the distributor (6-cylinder engines only).

3. Remove the cylinder head cover, air injection pipe and guard plate.

4. Drain the cooling system and remove the thermostat housing.

CAUTION: *When draining the coolant, keep in mind that cats and dogs are attracted by the ethylene glycol antifreeze, and are quite likely to drink any that is left in an uncovered container or in puddles on the ground. This will prove fatal in sufficient quantity. Always drain the coolant into a sealable container. Coolant should be reused unless it is contaminated or several years old.*

5. Remove the upper timing housing cover. See the "Timing Chain Cover Removal and Installation" procedure above.

Location of upper (4) and lower (3) guide rail retainers

316 11 121

On 4 cylinder engines, the dowel pin bore should be located at the 6 o'clock position and the notch in the top of the flange should align with the tab cast into the cylinder head

Position the camshaft flange so the dowel pin is located as shown and the bore in the sprocket aligns with the threaded bore in the cast tab

6. Remove the timing chain tensioner piston by unscrewing the cap *cautiously*.

NOTE: *The piston is under heavy spring tension.*

7. Remove the drive belts and fan.

8. Remove the flywheel guard and lock the flywheel with a locking tool.

9. Remove the vibration damper assembly.

NOTE: *The crankshaft Woodruff key should be in the 12 o'clock position.*

10. Remove upper and lower timing covers as described above.

11. Turn the crankshaft so that the No. 1 cylinder is at firing position. On the 318i, this will put the top sprocket locating pin at 6 o'clock. Open the camshaft lockplates if so equipped, remove the bolts and remove the camshaft sprocket.

On 4-cylinder engines (except 318i):

a. Remove the bottom circlip holding the chain guide rail to the block. Loosen the upper pivot pin until the guide rail rests against the forward part of the cylinder head gasket.

b. Remove the timing chain from the sprockets and remove the guide rail by pulling downward and swinging the rail to the right.

c. Remove the chain from the guide rail and remove it from the engine.

d. On the 318i engine, take the timing chain off top and bottom sprockets and remove carefully from the guide rail.

12. **On 6-cylinder engines:** Remove the chain from the lower sprocket, swing the chain to the right front and out of the guide rail and remove the chain from the engine.

13. Installation is the reverse of removal, but note the following:

14. Be sure that No. 1 piston remains at the top of its firing stroke and the key on the crankshaft is in the 12 o'clock position.

15. **On 4-cylinder engines:**

a. Position the camshaft flange so that the

dowel pin bore is located at the 6 o'clock position and the notch in the top of the flange aligns with the cast tab on the cylinder head.

b. On all models but the 318i, position the chain in the chain guide rail and move the rail upward and to the left, engaging the lower locating pivot pin and threading the upper pivot pin into the block. Install the circlip on the lower guide pin. On the 318i, simply locate the chain carefully in the guide rail.

c. Engage the chain on the crankshaft sprocket and fit the camshaft sprocket into the chain.

d. Align the gear dowel pin to the camshaft flange and bolt the sprocket into place. Use new lockplates (where so equipped), and secure the bolt heads.

16. **On 6-cylinder engines:**

a. Position the camshaft flange so that the dowel pin bore is between the 7 and 8 o'clock position and the upper flange bolt hole is aligned with the cast tab on the cylinder head.

b. Position the chain on the guide rail and swing the chain inward and to the left.

c. Engage the chain on the crankshaft gear and install the camshaft sprocket into the chain.

d. Align the gear dowel pin to the camshaft flange and bolt and sprocket into place. Torque the sprocket bolts to 5 ft. lbs. (6.5-7.5 on the M30B35 engine).

17. Install the chain tensioner piston, spring and cap plug, but do not tighten.

18. To bleed the chain tensioner, fill the oil pocket, located on the upper timing housing cover, with engine oil and move the tensioner back and forth with a screwdriver until oil is expelled at the cap plug. Tighten the cap plug securely.

19. Complete the assembly in the reverse order of removal. Check the ignition timing and

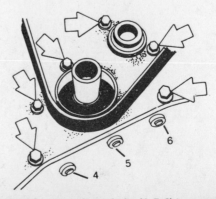

Remove the three oil pan bolts (4, 5, 6) to remove the front cover (524 td). Remove the other arrowed bolts, also

the idle speed. Be sure the flywheel holder is removed before any attempt is made to start the engine.

M3

1. Remove the timing case cover as described above.

2. Refer to the camshaft removal procedure below. Follow the procedure to the point where the 2 camshaft drive sprockets are unbolted and remove them. It is not necessary to remove the cover from the rear of the head.

3. Make sure to catch the washer and lockwashers which will be released at the front as the rest of this step is performed. Now, remove the 2 mounting bolts for the guide rail, which is located on the left (driver's) side of the engine. These are accessible from the rear.

4. Pull the guide rail forward and then turn it clockwise on its axis, looking at it from above, to free it from the chain.

5. Note the relationships between timing chain and sprocket marks. Remove the chain by separating it from the sprockets at top and bottom.

6. Engage the timing chain with the crankshaft sprocket so marks line up. Route the chain up through where the guide rail will go. Install the guide rail in reverse of the removal procedure.

7. Then engage the chain with the driver's side ("E") sprocket with the marks lined up. Bolt this sprocket and the lockplate onto the front end of the intake camshaft. Use the adapter to keep the sprocket from turning, and torque the bolts to 6-7 ft. lbs. Turn this camshaft in the direction opposite to normal rotation to tension the timing chain on that side.

8. Now, engage the timing marks with the mark on the passenger's side ("A") sprocket and then install the sprocket and lockplate onto the front end of the exhaust camshaft. Again, use the adapter to keep the sprocket from turning, and torque the bolts to 6-7 ft. lbs. Make sure the timing chain has stayed in time.

9. Slide the chain tensioner piston into its cylinder. Install a new seal. Now install the spring with the conical end out. Install the cap which retains the spring and torque it to 29 ft. lbs.

10. Turn the engine one revolution in the normal direction of rotation. Recheck the timing. With the crankshaft at TDC, one groove on each camshaft faces inward and another on each faces the cast boss on the nearby bearing cap.

11. Perform the remaining procedures for camshaft installation, including installing and centering the top chain guide rail and centering it.

12. Install the timing case cover as described above.

M5 and M6

1. Remove the fan shroud and the fan. Remove the cylinder head cover. Remove the timing cover as described above.

2. Refer to the camshaft removal procedure below. Follow the procedure to the point where the 2 camshaft drive sprockets are unbolted and remove them. It is not necessary to perform Step 4 to remove the cover from the rear of the head.

3. Refer to the appropriate procedure and remove the water pump.

4. Remove the 2 mounting bolts for the guide rail, which is located on the left (driver's) side of the engine. These are accessible from the rear. Turn the guide rail counterclockwise on its axis, looking at it from above to clear the chain and block and remove it. Be careful to retain all washers.

5. Note the relationships between timing chain and sprocket marks. Remove the timing chain.

6. Install the timing chain with the marks on all 3 sprockets aligned with marked links on the chain. Make sure the chain runs on the inside of the guide sprocket on the left side of the engine and along the groove in the lower tensioning rail. Install the chain onto the camshaft drive sprockets and then install the sprockets onto the camshafts (note that the exhaust side sprocket is marked **A** and the intake sprocket is marked **E**. Then, install the guide rail with all washers and lockwashers by rotating it into position in reverse of the removal procedure.

7. Tighten the camshaft drive sprockets, install the chain tensioner, and install the upper guide rail as described in the camshaft removal and installation procedure. Reverse the remaining removal steps to complete the procedure. Make sure to refill the cooling system with an appropriate antifreeze/water mix and to bleed the cooling system.

Timing Chain Sprocket
REMOVAL AND INSTALLATION

1. Remove the timing chain as described above, remove the oil pan as detailed earlier in this chapter.

2. Remove the 3 oil pump drive sprocket mounting bolts. then, remove the sprocket and oil pump drive chain. Remove the woodruff key from the crankshaft.

3. Pull the sprocket off the crankshaft with a puller.

4. Reverse the removal procedure to install. On 6-cylinder engines, when the oil pump chain

is installed, check play in the oil pump drive chain and, if necessary remove the oil pump and change the thickness of the shims, as detailed in "Oil Pump Removal and Installation" in this chapter.

Timing Belt and Front Cover
REMOVAL AND INSTALLATION
325, 325e, 325i, 325iS and 528e

The 325 and 528e are equipped with a rubber drive and timing belt and the distributor guard plate is actually the upper timing belt cover.

1. Remove the distributor cap and rotor. Remove the inner distributor cover and seal.

2. Remove the 2 distributor guard plate attaching bolts and one nut. Remove the rubber guard and take out the guard plate (upper timing belt cover).

3. Rotate the crankshaft to set No. 1 piston at TDC of its compression stroke.

NOTE: *At TDC of No. 1 piston compression stroke, the camshaft sprocket arrow should align directly with the mark on the cylinder head.*

4. Remove the radiator.

5. Remove the lower splash guard and take off the alternator, power steering and air conditioning belts.

6. Remove the crankshaft pulley and vibration damper.

7. Hold the crankshaft hub from rotating with special BMW tool 11 2 150 or equivalent. Remove the crankshaft hub bolt.

8. Install the hub bolt into the crankshaft about 3 turns and use BMW tools 00 7 501 and 11 2 132 or a gear puller, to remove the crankshaft hub.

9. Remove the bolt from the engine end of the alternator bracket. Loosen the alternator adjusting bolt and swing the bracket out of the way.

10. Lift out the TDC transmitter and set it out of the way.

11. Remove the remaining bolt and lift off the lower timing belt cover.

12. Loosen the 2 tensioner pulley bolts and release the tension on the belt by pushing on the tensioner pulley bracket.

13. Mark the running direction of the timing belt and remove the belt.

14. Remove the 3 bolts across the front of the

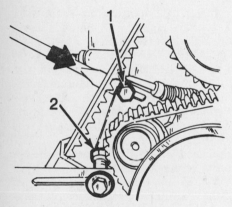

1. Tensioner adjusting slot bolt
2. Tensioner bracket pivot bolt

Releasing the tension on the timing belt—528e

1. Front oil pan bolts

Bolt location for the front engine cover—528e

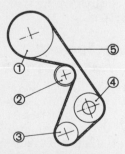

1. Camshaft sprocket
2. Tensioner roller
3. Crankshaft sprocket
4. Intermediate shaft sprocket
5. Timing drive belt

Location of the timing belt sprockets and belt tensioner—528e

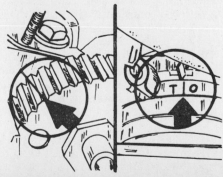

Aligning the marks for timing belt installation—528e

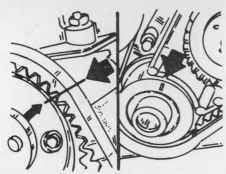

Crankshaft sprocket timing marks aligned for installation of the timing belt—528e

oil pan and loosen the remaining oil pan bolts. Try not to damage the oil pan gasket. Remove the 6 front engine cover bolts and remove the front engine cover.

15. Installation is the reverse of removal. Installation notes:

a. To tighten the timing belt, turn the engine in the direction of normal engine operation, with a ½" drive rachet wrench on the crankshaft bolt. When the timing belt is tight, then torque the 2 tensioner bolts.

b. Align the hub centering pin through the hole in the vibration damper for proper installation.

c. Align the timing marks when installing the timing belt. The crankshaft sprocket mark must point at the notch in the flange of the front engine cover. The camshaft sprocket arrow must point at the alignment mark on the cylinder head. Also, the No. 1 piston must be at TDC of the compression stroke.

d. If the oil pan gasket is damaged, it must be replaced.

e. Check and replace front cover oil seals if needed.

f. Use BMW tools 11 2 211 (crankshaft seal aligner) and 11 2 212 (intermediate shaft seal aligner) or equivalent to install the front engine cover without damaging the oil seals.

g. Check the engine oil level.

h. Install engine coolant and bleed the cooling system. Bring the engine up to operating temperature and loosen the bleed screw on top of the thermostat housing. Continue to bleed until escaping coolant is free of bubbles. Add coolant to the expansion tank if needed.

524td

NOTE: *To perform this procedure, it is necessary to have a means to hold the camshaft stationary such as BMW special tool 11 3 090 and a pin to hold the injection pump gear stationary such as BMW 13 5 340. The engine must be cold.*

1. Turn the engine to No. 1 cylinder at TDC, valves of No. 6 overlapping. Remove the timing belt cover and front pulley as described above. Loosen the camshaft pulley bolt, and the bolt and nut mounting the tensioner.

2. Mark the direction the belt rotates and remove it.

3. Position the camshaft at TDC No. 6 cyl. valves overlapping and lock it there. Lock the injection pump in position with the pin 13 5 340.

4. Install the new belt with the timing marks on the sprockets and belt lined up. Turn the camshaft sprocket so as to begin tensioning the belt and seat it in the grooves. When the belt is in its normal, installed position, remove the pin holding the injection pump sprocket.

5. Insert a 2.5mm thick feeler gauge under the exhaust side of the jig holding the camshaft if the belt is new or had been used less than 10,000 miles.

6. Torque the nut which rotates the tensioner (2) in the direction shown in the illustration. For belts with 10,000 miles or less on them, torque to 30.5-32.5 ft. lbs. For belts with more mileage, torque to 22-25 ft. lbs.

7. Tighten the locknut for the tensioner (3)

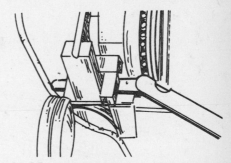

Insert a 2.5mm gauge under the exhaust side of the jig holding the camshaft for new drive belts (524 td)

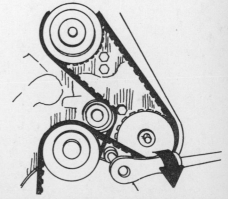

Adjusting the belt tension. Turn the torque wrench in the direction shown to apply the proper tension (see text)

and then tighten (1), the camshaft sprocket bolt, and (2). Remove the camshaft-holding jig.

8. Rotate the engine in the forward direction one full turn and then recheck that timing marks are all lined up.

9. Adjust the static timing of the injection pump as described below. Reinstall the timing belt cover and front pulley in the reverse of removal. Refer to the appropriate procedure above.

Camshaft

REMOVAL AND INSTALLATION

All Models Except 325, 325e, 325i, 325iS, 524td, 528e, M3, M5 and M6

1. Remove the oil line from the top of the cylinder head.

NOTE: *Observe the location of the seals when removing the hollow oil line studs. Install new seals in the same position.*

2. Remove the cylinder head. Support the head in such a way that the valves can be opened during camshaft removal.

3. Adjust the valve clearance to the maximum clearance on all rocker arms.

4. Remove the fuel pump and pushrod on carbureted engines.

5. On 4-cylinder engines: Special tools are used to hold the rocker arms away from the camshaft lobes. On the 320i, use tool 11 1 040; on the 318i, use 11 0 040. Use these numbers to shop for tools from independent sources also.

NOTE: *The proper tool or its equivalent, must be used on fuel injection engines to avoid distorting the valve heads.*

NOTE: *On the 320i and 318i, the clamping bolt for the special tool is off-center. The clamp must be mounted so the shorter end*

Location of seals at hollow oil line stud

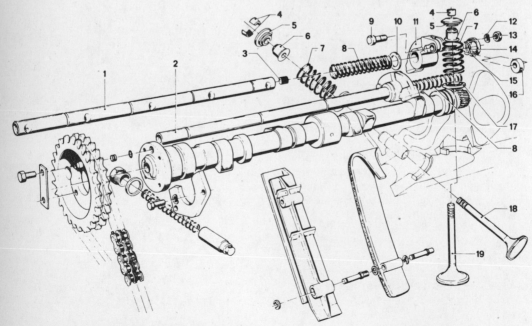

1. Rocker arm shaft, intake	8. Spring	14. Snap ring
2. Rocker arm shaft, exhaust	9. Adjusting screw	15. Washer
3. Plug	10. Washer	16. Cam
4. Valve cone piece	11. Rocker arm with bushing	17. Lower spring plate
5. Upper spring plate	12. Lockwasher	18. Exhaust valve
6. Valve seal ring	13. Hex nut	19. Intake valve
7. Valve spring		

Exploded view of typical BMW camshaft and valve assembly components

faces the exhaust side of the engine, or the valve heads may contact each other. On the 318i, install 2 dowel pins in the head.

6. On 6-cylinder engines: A special tool set (11 1 060 and 00 1 490) or its equivalent, is used to hold the rocker arms away from the camshaft lobes. When installing the tool, move the intake rocker arms of No. 2 and 4 cylinders forward approximately ¼" and tighten the intake side nuts to avoid contact between the valve heads. On the 6, turn the camshaft 15° clockwise to install the tool. On these engines, to avoid contact between the valve heads, first tighten the tool mounting nuts on the exhaust

Removing mechanical fuel pump pushrod

Camshaft designation location—four cylinder

Clamping plate installed on cylinder head to off-load rocker arms

The threaded bore in the camshaft flange must align with the projection cast into the front of the block-six cylinder engines

Removing camshaft guide plate

Checking camshaft axial play

side to the stop and then tighten the intake side nuts slightly. Reverse this exactly during removal.

7. Remove the camshaft.

8. **On 4-cylinder engines:**

a. Turn the camshaft until the flange is aligned with the cylinder head boss. Remove the guide plate retaining bolts and move the plate downward and out of the slots on the rocker arm shafts.

b. Carefully remove the camshaft from the cylinder head.

c. Remove the 2 plugs behind the guide plate (at top), coat with Loctite® No. 270® or equivalent, and replace them.

9. **On 6-cylinder engines:**

a. Rotate the camshaft so that the 2 cutout areas of the camshaft flange are horizontal and remove the retaining plate bolts.

b. Carefully remove the camshaft from the cylinder head.

c. The flange and guide plate can be removed from the camshaft by removing the lockplate and nut from the camshaft end.

10. Install the camshaft and associated components in the reverse order of removal, but observe the following:

a. After installing the camshaft guide plate, the camshaft should turn easily. Measure and correct the camshaft end play.

b. The camshaft flange must be properly aligned with the cylinder head before the sprocket is installed. Refer to the disassembly procedure.

c. Install the oil tube hollow stud washer seals properly, one above and one below the oil pipe. On 6-cyl. engines, the arrow on the oil line must face forward.

d. Install the cylinder head. Adjust the valves.

524td

NOTE: *To complete this procedure, it is necessary to have several special tools to install a new oil seal. Use BMW tools 11 2 212, 11 3 080, and 00 5 500.*

1. Remove the cam cover and vacuum pump as described below.

2. Remove the exhaust side rocker arm of cylinder No. 2 and the intake rocker arm of cylinder No. 3. See the Rocker Arm Removal and Installation procedure above. It is not necessary to disturb the rocker pedestals; keep the rockers in order of reinstallation in the same positions.

3. Turn the crankshaft until it is at TDC with No. 6 cylinder's valves in overlap position.

4. Remove the front cover as described above.

5. Remove the timing belt as described

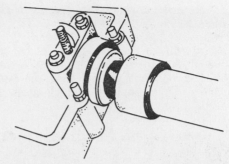

Installing the front camshaft oil seal—524 td

above. Make sure to loosen the camshaft sprocket bolt before releasing belt tension and removing the belt.

6. Once the belt is removed, remove the bolt and washer and remove the camshaft sprocket.

7. Disconnect the oil line that is in the way. Then, remove the camshaft bearing cap bolts and remove the caps, keeping them in order. Remove the oil seal from the front bearing cap. Remove the camshaft.

8. If replacing the camshaft, replace all the rocker arms as described above. Also, transfer the steels ring that drives the vacuum pump to the new camshaft.

9. Oil all bearing surfaces with clean engine oil and install the camshaft. Install the caps and bolts, and torque M6 bolts to 6-7 ft. lbs. M8 bolts should be torqued to 15-17 ft. lbs. The front bearing cap lower surface must be coated with a brush-on universal sealing compound, 3 Bond Silicone 1207 or equivalent.

10. Install a seal installer 11 2 212 or equivalent onto the end of the camshaft. Lubricate the lip of the seal with clean engine oil. Then, press the seal into the bore of the bearing, using a suitable seal installer part no. 11 3 080 and 00 5 500 or equivalent. The seal must be pressed in until it hits the stop.

11. Install the oil line. Check the end play of the camshaft with a dial indicator and compare with specifications. If end play is excessive with a new camshaft, it may be necessary to replace the cylinder head and bearing caps.

12. Install the camshaft sprocket making sure the pin in the camshaft flange fits through the bore in the sprocket and washer. Torque the bolt to 47-51 ft. lbs.

13. Install the timing belt and tension it as described above. Reverse the remaining removal procedures.

325, 325e, 325i, 325iS and 528e

The cylinder head and the rocker arm shafts must be removed before the camshaft can be removed.

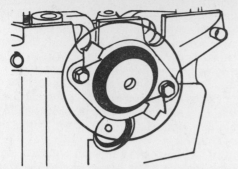

Removing the camshaft thrust bearing cover—528e

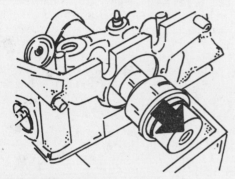

Pulling out the camshaft—528e

1. Remove the cylinder head (see "Cylinder Head Removal and Installation").

2. Mount the head on a stand. Secure the head to the stand with one head bolt.

3. Remove the camshaft sprocket bolt and remove the camshaft distributor adapter and sprocket. Reinstall the distributor adapter on the camshaft.

4. Adjust the valve clearance to the maximum allowable on all valves.

5. Remove the front and rear rocker shaft plugs and lift out the thrust plate.

6. Remove the clips from the rocker arms by lifting them off.

7. Remove the exhaust side rocker arm shaft:

a. Set the No. 6 cylinder rocker arm to the valve overlap position (both rocker arms parallel).

b. Push in on the rocker arm on the front cylinder and turn the camshaft in the direction of the intake rocker shaft, using a ½" breaker bar and a deep well socket to fit over the camshaft adapter. Rotate the camshaft until all of the rocker arms are relaxed.

c. Remove the rocker arm shaft.

8. Remove the intake side rocker arm shaft:

a. Turn the camshaft in the direction of the exhaust valves.

b. Use a deep well socket and ½" drive breaker bar on the camshaft adapter to turn

the camshaft until all of the rocker arms are relaxed.

c. Pull out the rocker arm shaft.

9. Remove the camshaft thrust bearing cover. Check the radial oil seal and round cord seal and replace them if needed.

10. Pull out the camshaft.

11. Installation is the reverse of removal. Installation notes:

a. Use BMW tool 11 2 212 or equivalent over the end of the camshaft during installation of the thrust bearing cover; this will protect the oil seals and guide the cover on.

b. The rocker arm thrust plate must be fit into the grooves in the rocker shafts.

c. The straight side of the springclip must be installed in the groove of the rocker arm shafts.

d. The large oil bores in the rocker shafts must be installed down to the valve guides and the small oil bores must face inward toward the center of the head.

e. Adjust the valve clearance.

M3, M5 and M6

NOTE: *Note that to perform this operation it is necessary to have an expensive jig, special tool No. 11 3 010 or equivalent. This is necessary to permit safe removal of the camshaft bearing caps and then safe release of the tension the valve springs put on the camshafts. The job also requires an adapter to keep the camshaft sprockets from turning while loosening and tightening their mounting bolts.*

1. Remove the cylinder head cover. Remove the fan cowl and the fan.

2. Remove the mounting bolts and remove the distributor cap. Remove the mounting screws and remove the rotor. Unscrew the distributor adapter and the protective cover underneath. Inspect the O-ring that runs around the protective cover and replace it, if necessary.

3. Remove the 2 bolts and remove the protective cover from in front of the right side (intake) camshaft. Remove the bolts and remove the distributor housing from in front of the left (exhaust) side cam. Inspect the O-rings, and replace them if necessary.

4. Remove the 6 mounting bolts from the cover at the rear end of the cylinder head and remove it. Replace the gasket. Note that on the M3, 2 of these bolts are longer. These fit into the 2 holes that are sleeved.

5. Remove the 2 nuts, located at the front of the head, which mount the upper timing chain guide rail. Then, remove the upper guide rail.

6. Turn the crankshaft to set the engine at No. 1 cyl. TDC. On the 6-cylinder engine, valves for No. 6 will be at overlap position: both valves just slightly open with timing marks, of course,

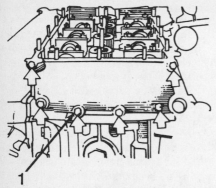

On the rear cover of the M3, install the longer bolts into the two holes marked "1"

at TDC. On the 4-cylinder engine, valves for No. 4 cylinder will be at overlap position: both valves just slightly open with timing marks, of course, at TDC.

7. Remove the cap for the timing chain tensioner, located on the right side of the front timing cover. Then, slide off the damper housing. Remove the seal, discard it, and supply a new one for reassembly.

CAUTION: *The next item to be removed is a plug which keeps the tensioner piston inside its hydraulic cylinder against considerable spring pressure. Use a socket wrench and keep pressure against the outer end of the plug, pushing inward, so that spring pressure can be released very gradually once the plug's threads are free of the block.*

8. Remove the plug as described in the caution, and then release spring tension. Remove the spring and then the piston. Check the length of the spring. It must be 158.5-159.5mm in length; otherwise, replace it to maintain stable timing chain tension.

NOTE: *The timing chain should remain engaged with the crankshaft sprocket while removing the camshafts. Otherwise, it will be necessary to do additional work to restore proper timing. Devise a way to keep the timing chain under slight tension by supporting it at the top while removing the camshaft sprockets in the next step.*

9. Pry open the lockplates for the camshaft sprocket mounting bolts. Install an adapter to hold the sprockets still and remove the mounting bolts.

10. Using an adapter to keep the sprockets from turning and putting tension on the timing chain, loosen and remove the sprocket mounting bolts, keeping the chain supported.

11. Mount the special jig described above on the timing case (which mounts to the top of the head). Then, tighten the jig's shaft to the stop. This will hold both camshafts down against their lower bearings. On the 4-cylinder engine, mark the camshafts as to which side they are on; intake on the driver's side and exhaust on the passenger's side. Also, mark the camshafts as to which end faces forward.

12. Remove the mounting bolts and remove the camshaft bearing caps. It is possible to save time by keeping the caps in order, although they are marked for installation in the same positions.

13. Once all bearing caps are removed, slowly crank backwards on the jig shaft to gradually release the tension on the camshafts. Once all tension is released, remove the camshafts.

14. Carefully remove the camshafts in such a way as to avoid nicking any bearing surfaces or cams.

15. Oil all bearing and cam surfaces with clean engine oil. Carefully install the camshafts (marked **E** for intake and **A** for exhaust) so as to avoid nicking any wear surfaces. The camshafts should be turned so that the groove between the front cam and sprocket mounting flange faces straight up. Install the special jig and tighten down on the shaft to seat the camshafts.

16. Install all bearing caps in order (or as marked). Torque the attaching bolts to 15-17 ft. lbs. Then, release the tension provided by the jig by turning the bolt and remove the jig.

17. Install the intake sprocket (marked **E**), install the lockplate, and install the mounting bolts. Use the adapter to keep the sprocket from turning, and torque the bolts to 6-7 ft. lbs. Do the same for the exhaust side sprocket. Make sure the timing chain stays in time.

18. Now, slide the timing chain tensioner piston into the opening in the cylinder in the block. Install the spring with the conically wound end facing the plug (or outward). Install the plug into the end of the sprocket and then install it over the spring and use the socket wrench to depress the spring until the plug's threads engage with those in the block. Start the threads in carefully and then torque the plug to 27-31 ft. lbs. Install a new seal, connector, damper housing, and the outside cap with a new cap seal. Torque the outside cap to 16-20 ft. lbs. on the engine used in the M5 and M6 and 29 ft. lbs. on the M3 engine.

19. Crank the engine forward just one turn in normal direction of rotation. Now, one camshaft groove on each side should face toward the center of the head and one on each side should face the case boss on the front bearing cap. Lock the sprocket mounting bolts with the tabs on the lockplates.

20. Reverse the remaining removal procedures to complete the installation. Before final tightening of the mounting nuts for the guide

rail for the top of the timing chain, go back and forth, measuring the clearance between the sprockets and the center of the guide rail to center it. Then, tighten the mounting nuts.

CHECKING CAMSHAFT

Camshaft End Play

NOTE: *On engines with an aluminum or nylon camshaft sprocket, prying against the sprocket, with the valve train load on the camshaft, can break or damage the sprocket. Therefore, the rocker arm adjusting nuts must be backed off, or the rocker arm and shaft assembly must be loosened sufficiently to free the camshaft. After checking the camshaft end play, check the valve clearance. Adjust if required. Refer to the procedure in Chapter 2.*

1. Push the camshaft toward the rear of the engine. Install a dial indicator so that the indicator point is on the camshaft sprocket attaching screw.

2. Zero the dial indicator. Position a prybar between the camshaft gear and the engine. Pull the camshaft forward and release it. Compare the dial indicator reading with the specifications.

3. If the end play is excessive, check the spacer for correct installation before it is removed. If the spacer is correctly installed, replace the thrust plate.

4. Remove the dial indicator.

Intermediate Shaft

REMOVAL AND INSTALLATION

325, 325e, 325i, 325iS, 524td and 528e

1. Remove the front cover as detailed previously.

2. Remove the intermediate shaft sprocket.

3. Loosen and remove the 2 retaining screws and then remove the intermediate shaft guide plate.

4. Carefully slide the intermediate shaft out of the block. Turn the crankshaft if necessary to remove it. Inspect the gear on the intermediate shaft, replacing it if necessary.

5. Installation is in the reverse order of removal.

Pistons and Connecting Rods

REMOVAL AND INSTALLATION

Before Removal

Keep all of the following points in mind when rebuilding a BMW engine.

• The pistons and connecting rods may be removed from the engine after the cylinder head, oil pan and oil pump are removed. It may be necessary to first remove a ridge worn into the cylinder above the top ring. See the engine rebuilding section. The connecting rods and caps are marked for each cylinder with No. 1 cylinder at the sprocket end of the engine. Codes pairing the connecting rods with the matching cap are located on the exhaust side of the engine. However, it is a good idea to mark the exact relationship between each rod and the crankshaft to ensure replacement in the exact same position, in case the bearings can be reused.

• On the 524td engine, oil nozzles which are critically aimed must be protected from damage by studs (11 2 050) which screw into the connecting rod cap bolt holes before the rod and piston are shoved upward and out the top of the block. Make sure each crankpin is precisely at BDC prior to removal.

• To disassemble rods and pistons, remove the circlip and press out the piston pin. Note that pistons and piston pins come as a matched set. Do not mix them up.

• A piston pin must always slide through the connecting rod under light pressure.

• If replacing pistons, make sure all are of the same make and weight class (marked + or − on the crown).

• Piston installed clearance must meet specifications. On the 318i, check installed clearance at a point measured up from the lower skirt edge, depending on the piston manufacturer: Mahle − 14mm; KS − 31mm; Alcan − 15.5mm.

• On the M20B27 engine used in 325e and 528e models, check piston diameter according to total height and manufacturer. On pistons 68.7mm high manufactured by Mahle, check the diameter at a point 8mm above the low point on the skirt; on those of this height manufactured by KS, check diameter 14mm above the low point of the skirt. If the total height is 77.7mm, check the diameter of both Mahle and KS pistons 23mm above the low point of the skirt. On the M20B25 engine used in 325i,

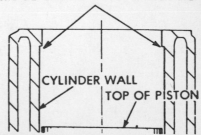

RIDGE CAUSED BY CYLINDER WEAR

CYLINDER WALL
TOP OF PISTON

The cylinder bore ridge must be removed before removing the piston

check the diameter 9mm above the low point of the skirt.

● On the 3.3 liter engine, measure Mahle pistons 26mm up from the lower skirt edge, and KS pistons 34mm up from the skirt edge. On the 3.5 liter engine, measure 14mm up from the skirt edge.

● On the 3.5 liter, M30 B34 engine, measure the Mahle pistons at a point 14mm up from the bottom of the skirt.

● On the 3.5 liter, M30 B35 engine, measure

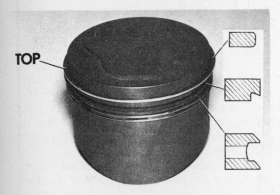

The rings are installed in positions shown. See the text

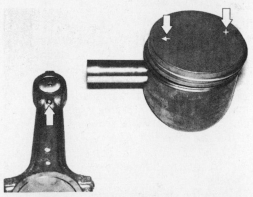

The arrow on top of the piston must face forward and the oil hole in the connecting rod must face the same direction as the arrow on top. See the text for explanation of weight class ("+" or "−" markings)

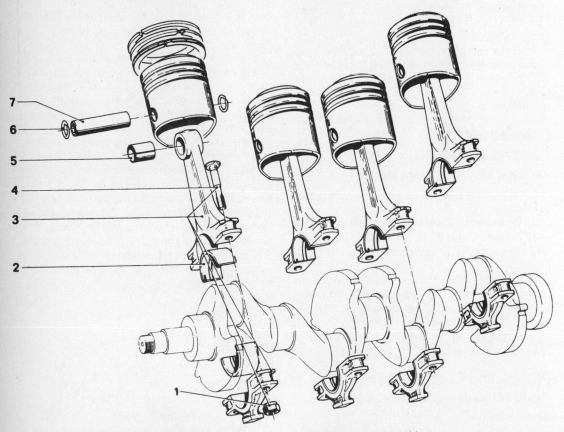

1. Hex nut
2. Bearing shell
3. Connecting rod
4. Connecting rod bolt
5. Connecting rod bushing
6. Circlip
7. Piston pin

Exploded view of piston and connecting rod assemblies—four cylinder engines

Alcan piston diameter at a point 13.5mm from the lowest point of the skirt; measure Mahle pistons at a point 22mm from the lowest point of the skirt.

- On the 524td engine, the dimensions are: Alcan — 15mm; KS — 18mm; Mahle/Konig — 12mm. Measure 14mm up from the skirt edge.
- On the engines used in the M3, M5, and M6, measure the piston at a point 6mm below the deepest part of the skirt.
- Lubricate the piston and rings with engine oil prior to installation. Offset ring gaps 120° apart. Install circlips facing *downward*.
- The side of rings marked **TOP** must face upward. 2.7, 2.5, 3.3 and 3.5 liter engines and the M3 engine use a plain compression ring at top, tapered or beveled second compression ring, and an oil control ring at the bottom. The 524td uses a keystone ring at the top, a taper face lower compression ring, and a beveled oil control ring with a rubber-lined expander at the bottom.

Removal

Before removing the pistons, the top of the cylinder bore must be examined for a ridge. A ridge at the top of the bore is the result of normal cylinder wear; caused by the piston rings only travelling so far up the bore in the cause of the piston stroke. If the ridge can be felt by hand, it must be removed before the pistons are removed.

A ridge reamer is necessary for this operation. Place the piston at the bottom of its stroke, and cover it with a rag. Cut the ridge away with the ridge reamer, using extreme care

to avoid cutting too deeply. Remove the rag, and remove the cuttings that remain on the piston with a magnet and a rag soaked in clean oil. Make sure the piston top and cylinder bore are absolutely clean before moving the piston.

1. Remove engine and cylinder head as detailed previously.
2. Remove oil pan.

Push the piston out with a hammer handle

USE A SHORT PIECE OF 3/8" HOSE AS A GUIDE

Use lengths of vacuum hose or rubber tubing to protect the crankshaft journals and cylinder walls during piston removal and installation

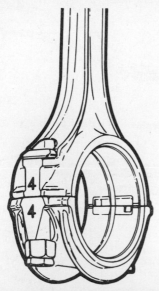

Match the connecting rod to the cylinder with a number stamp

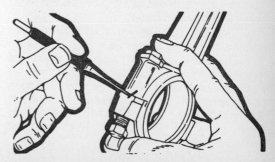

Match the connecting rod and cap with scribe marks

Location of piston in the cylinder bore with ring gaps located 180° apart

3. Remove oil pump assembly if necessary.

4. Matchmark the connecting rod cap to the connecting rod with a scribe; each cap must be reinstalled on its proper rod in the proper direction. Remove the connecting rod bearing cap and the rod bearing. Number the top of each piston with silver paint or a felt-tip pen for later assembly.

5. Cut lengths of ⅜″ diameter rubber hose to use as rod bolt guides. Install the hose over the threads of the rod bolts, to prevent the bolt threads from damaging the crankshaft journals and cylinder walls when the piston is removed.

6. Squirt some clean engine oil onto the cylinder wall from above until the wall is coated. Carefully push the piston and rod assembly up and out of the cylinder by tapping on the bottom of the connecting rod with a wooden hammer handle.

7. Place the rod bearing and cap back on the connecting rod, and install the nuts temporarily. Using a number stamp or punch, stamp the cylinder number on the side of the connecting rod and cap this will help keep the proper piston and rod assembly on the proper cylinder.

NOTE: *On all BMW engines, the cylinders ar numbered 1-4 or 1-6 from front to back.*

8. Remove the remaining pistons in a similar manner.

When ready for reassembly, please not the following:

a. Connecting rods/caps must be reinstalled in the same cylinder and are so marked. Make sure markings on rod and cap are on the same side when reassembling.

b. The piston pins are matched to the pistons and are not interchangeable.

c. The arrow on top of the piston must face forward (toward the timing chain). The oil hole in the connecting rod faces the same direction as the arrow on top of the piston. Pistons are also marked as to manufacturer and weight class † or −). All pistons must be of the same manufacturer and weight class.

d. Offset each ring gap as fas as possible from the next one down, i.e. at 180°.

PISTON RING AND WRIST PIN REMOVAL

All BMW engines covered in this guide utilize pistons with wrist pins that are secured by circlips. To separate the connecting rod from the wrist pin, remove the circlip with a pair of circlip pliers and press out the pin.

A piston ring expander is necessary for removing piston rings without damaging them; any other method (screwdriver blades, pliers, etc.) usually results in the rings being bent, scratched or distorted, or the piston itself being damaged. When the rings are removed, clean the ring grooves using an appropriate ring groove cleaning tool, using care not to cut too deeply. Thoroughly clean all carbon and varnish from the piston with solvent.

CAUTION: *Do not use a wire brush or caustic solvent (acids, etc.) on pistons.*

Inspect the pistons for scuffing, scoring, cracks, pitting or excessive ring groove wear. If these are evident, the piston must be replaced.

Wrist pins are retained with a circlip

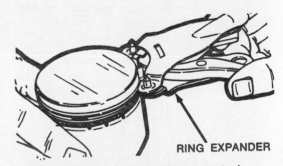

RING EXPANDER

Remove the piston rings with the proper tool

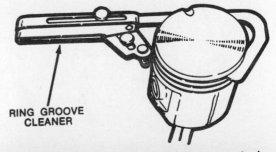

RING GROOVE CLEANER

Clean the piston ring grooves with the proper tool

The piston should also be check in relation to the cylinder diameter. Using a telescoping gauge and micrometer, or a dial gauge, measure the cylinder bore diameter perpendicular (90°)

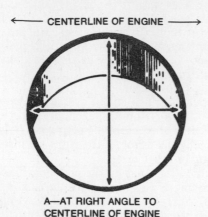

CENTERLINE OF ENGINE

A—AT RIGHT ANGLE TO
CENTERLINE OF ENGINE
B—PARALLEL TO
CENTERLINE OF ENGINE

Cylinder bore measuring points

to the piston pin, 25-30mm below the cylinder block deck (surface where the block mates with the heads). Then, with the micrometer, measure the piston perpendicular to its wrist pin on the skirt. The difference between the 2 measurements is the piston clearance. If the clearance is within specifications or slightly below (after the cylinders have been bored or honed), finish honing is all that is necessary. If the clearance is excessive, try to obtain a slightly larger piston to bring clearance to within specifications. If this is not possible, obtain the first oversize piston and hone (or if necessary, bore) the cylinder to size. Generally, if the cylinder bore is tapered 0.13mm or more, or is out-of-round 0.08mm or more, it is advisable to rebore for the smallest possible oversize piston and rings. After measuring, mark the pistons with a felt-tip pen for reference and assembly.

NOTE: *Cylinder honing and/or boring should be performed by an authorized service technician with the proper equipment. In some cases, "clean-up" honing can be done*

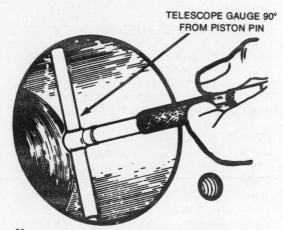

TELESCOPE GAUGE 90°
FROM PISTON PIN

Measure the cylinder bore with a telescoping gauge

Checking cylinder diameter with a dial gauge

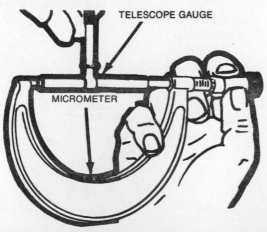

TELESCOPE GAUGE

MICROMETER

Measure the telescoping gauge with a micrometer to determine the cylinder bore

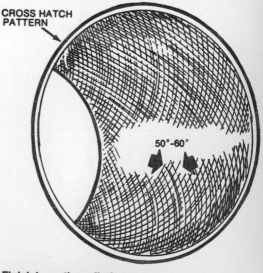

CROSS HATCH
PATTERN

50°-60°

Finish hone the cylinders

with the cylinder block in the car, but most excessive honing and all cylinder boring must be done with the block stripped and removed from the car.

PISTON RING END GAP

Piston ring end gap should be checked while the rings are removed from the pistons. Incorrect end gap indicates that the wrong size rings are being used; ring breakage could occur.

Compress the piston rings to be used in a cylinder, one at a time, into that cylinder. Squirt clean oil into the cylinder, so that the rings and the top 50mm of cylinder wall are coated. Using an inverted piston, press the rings approximately 25mm below the deck of the block. Measure the ring end gap with a feeler gauge, and compare to the specifications chart in this chapter. Carefully pull the ring out of the cylinder and file the ends squarely with a fine file to obtain the proper clearance.

PISTON RING SIDE CLEARANCE CHECK AND INSTALLATION

Check the pistons to see that the ring grooves and oil return holes have been properly cleaned. Slide a piston ring into its groove, and check the side clearance with a feeler gauge. Make sure

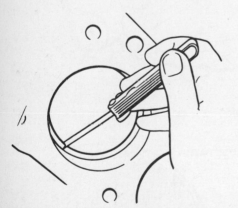

Always check the end gap with the ring in the cylinder

that you insert the gauge between the ring and its lower land (lower edge of the groove), because any wear that occurs, forms a step at the inner portion of the lower land. If the piston grooves have worn to the extent that relatively high steps exist on the lower land, the piston should be replaced, because these will interfere with the operation of the new rings and ring clearances will be excessive. Piston rings are not furnished in oversize widths to compensate for ring groove wear.

Install the rings on the piston, lowest ring first, using a piston ring expander. There is a high risk of breaking or distorting the rings, or scratching the piston, if the rings are installed by hand or other means.

Position the rings on the piston as illustrated; spacing of the various piston ring gaps is crucial to proper oil retention and even cylinder wear. When installing new rings, refer to the installation diagram furnished with new parts.

NOTE: *For piston positioning information, please refer to Step 8 in the "Piston and Connecting Rod Removal" section in this chapter.*

CONNECTING ROD BEARINGS

Connecting rod bearings for the engines covered in this guide consist of 2 halves or shells which are interchangeable in the rod and cap. When the shells are placed in position, the ends extend slightly beyond the rod and cap surfaces so that when the rod bolts are torqued, the shells will be clamped tightly in place to insure positive seating and to prevent turning. A tang holds the shells in place.

NOTE: *The ends of the bearing shells must never be filed flush with the mating surface of the rod and cap.*

If a rod bearing becomes noisy or is worn so that its clearance on the crank journal is sloppy, a new bearing of the correct undersize must be selected and installed since there is no provision for adjustment.

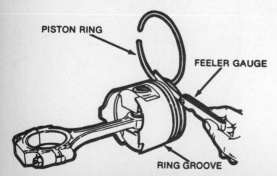

Checking the ring side clearance

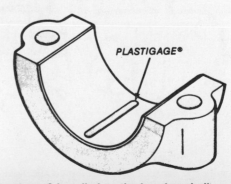

Plastigage® installed on the bearing shell

CAUTION: *Under no circumstances should the rod end or cap be filed to adjust the bearing clearance, nor should shims of any kind be used.*

Inspect the rod bearings while the rod assemblies are out to the engine. If the shells are scored or show flaking, they should be replaced. If they are in good shape check for proper clearance on the crank journal (see below). Any scoring or ridges on the crank journal means the crankshaft must be replaced, or reground and fitted with undersized bearings.

Checking Bearing Clearance and Replacing Bearings

Replacement bearings are available in standard size, and in undersizes for reground crankshafts. Connecting rod-to-crankshaft bearing clearance is checked using Plastigage® has a range of 0.025-0.080mm.

1. Remove the rod cap with the bearing shell. Completely clean the bearing shell and crank journal, and blow any oil from the oil hole in the crankshaft; Plastigage® is soluable in oil.

2. Place a piece of Plastigage® lengthwise along the bottom center of the lower bearing shell, then install the cap with shell and torque the bolt or nuts to specification. DO NOT turn the crankshaft with the Plastigage® in the bearing.

3. Remove the bearing cap with the shell.

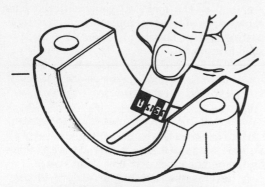

Measure the Plastigage® to determine bearing clearance

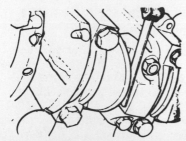

Checking the connecting rod side clearance with a feeler gauge

The flattened Plastigage® will be found sticking to either the bearing shell or crank journal. Do not remove it yet.

4. Use the scale printed on the Plastigage® envelope to measure the flattened material at its widest point. The number within the scale which most closely corresponds to the width of the Plastigage® indicates bearing clearance in thousandths of a millimeter.

5. Check the specifications chart in this chapter for the desired clearance. It is advisable to install a new bearing if clearance exceeds 0.08mm; however, if the bearing is in good condition and is not being checked because of bearing noise, bearing replacement is not necessary.

6. If you are installing new bearings, try a standard size, then each undersize in order until one is found that is with in the specified limits which checked for clearance with Plastigage®. Each undersize shell has its size stamped on it.

7. When the proper size shell is found, clean off the Plastigage®, oil the bearing thoroughly reinstall the cap with its shell and torque the rod bolt nuts to the proper specifications.

NOTE: *With the proper bearing selected and the nuts torqued, it should be possible to move the connecting rod back and forth freely on the crank journal as allowed by the specified connecting rod end clearance. If the rod cannot be moved, either the rod bearing is too far undersize or the rod is misaligned.*

PISTON AND CONNECTING ROD ASSEMBLY AND INSTALLATION

Install the connecting rod to the piston, making sure piston installation notches and any marks on the rod are in proper relation to one another. Lubricate the wrist pin with clean engine oil, and install the pin into the rod and piston assembly, either by hand or by using a wrist pin press as required. Install snap rings if equipped, and rotate them in their grooves to make sure they are seated. To install the piston and connecting rod assembly:

1. Make sure that that the connecting rod big-ends bearings (including end cap) are of the correct size and properly installed.

2. Fit rubber hoses over the connecting rod bolts to protect the crankshaft journals, as in the "Piston Removal" procedure. Coat the rod bearings with clean oil.

3. Using the proper ring compressor, insert the piston assembly into the cylinder so that the word **TOP** faces the front of the engine (this assumes that the dimple(s) or other markings on the connecting rods are in the correct relationship.

4. From beneath the engine, coat each crank journal with clean oil. Pull the connecting rod,

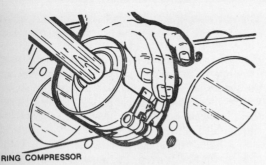

RING COMPRESSOR

Install the pistons with a ring compressor

with the bearing shell in place, into position against the crank journal.

5. Remove the rubber hoses. Install the bearing cap and cap nuts and torque to the proper specifications.

NOTE: *If more than one rod and piston assembly is being installed, the connecting rod cap attaching nuts should only be tightened enough to keep each rod in position until all have been installed. This will ease the installation of the remaining piston assemblies.*

6. Check the clearance between the sides of the connecting rods and the crankshaft using a feeler gauge. Spread the rods slightly with a screwdriver to insert the gauge. If clearance is below the minimum tolerance, the rod ay be machined to provide adequate clearance. If clearance is excessive, substitute an unworn rod, and recheck. If clearance is still outside specifications, the crankshaft must be welded and reground, or replaced.

7. Replace the oil pump if removed and the oil pan.

8. Install the cylinder head.

Rear Main Bearing Oil Seal

REMOVAL AND INSTALLATION

The rear main bearing oil seal can be replaced after the transmission, and clutch/flywheel or the converter/flywheel has been removed from the engine.

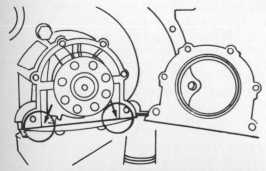

Rear main bearing oil seal and end cover housing showing special sealing locations

Removal and installation, after the seal is exposed, is as follows.

1. Drain the engine oil and loosen the oil pan bolts. Carefully use a knife to separate the oil pan gasket from the lower surface of the end cover housing.

CAUTION: *The EPA warns that prolonged contact with used engine oil may cause a number of skin disorders, including cancer! You should make every effort to minimize your exposure to used engine oil. Protective gloves should be worn when changing the oil. Wash your hands and any other exposed skin areas as soon as possible after exposure to used engine oil. Soap and water, or waterless hand cleaner should be used.*

2. Remove the 2 rear oil pan bolts.

3. Remove the bolts around the outside of the cover housing and remove the end cover housing from the engine block. Remove the gasket from the block surface.

4. Remove the seal from the housing. Coat the sealing lips of the new seal with oil. Install a new seal into the end cover housing with a special seal installer BMW Tool No. 11 1 260 backed up by a mandrel, Tool No. 00 5 500 or equivalent. On 1984-88 3.3 and 3.5L engines, and 1988-88 2.5 and 2.7L engines, press the seal in until it is about 1.00-2.00mm deeper than the standard seal, which was installed flush.

5. While the cover is off, check the plug in the rear end of the main oil gallery. If the plug shows signs of leakage, replace it with another, coating it with Loctite® 270® or equivalent to keep it in place.

NOTE: *Fill the cavity between the sealing lips of the seal with grease before installing. On 1984-86 engines, lubricate the seal with oil.*

6. On all 1983-88 engines, coat the mating surface between the oil pan and end cover with sealer. Using a new gasket, install the end cover on the engine block and bolt it into place.

7. Reverse the removal procedure to complete the installation. If the oil pan gasket has been damaged, replace it.

Crankshaft and Main Bearings

CRANKSHAFT REMOVAL

1. Drain the engine oil and remove the engine from the car. Mount the engine on a workstand in a suitable working area. Invert the engine, so the oil pan is facing up.

CAUTION: *The EPA warns that prolonged contact with used engine oil may cause a number of skin disorders, including cancer! You should make every effort to minimize your exposure to used engine oil. Protective*

gloves should be worn when changing the oil. Wash your hands and any other exposed skin areas as soon as possible after exposure to used engine oil. Soap and water, or waterless hand cleaner should be used.

2. Remove the engine front (timing) cover.

3. Remove the timing chain/belt and gears.

4. Remove the oil pan.

5. Remove the oil pump.

6. Stamp the cylinder number on the machined surfaces of the bolt bosses of the connecting rods and caps for identification when reinstalling. If the pistons are to be removed eventually from the connecting rod, mark the cylinder number on the pistons with silver paint or felt-tip pen for proper cylinder identification and cap-to-rod location.

7. Remove the connecting rod caps. Install lengths of rubber hose on each of the connecting rod bolts, to protect the crank journals when the crank is removed.

8. Mark the main bearings caps with a number punch or punch so that they can be reinstalled in their original positions.

9. Remove all main bearing caps.

10. Note the position of the keyway in the crankshaft so it can be installed in the same position.

NOTE: *To keep the connecting rods from banging against the side of the cylinders while removing the crankshaft, screw 4 oil pan bolts loosely into the block and then stretch a rubber band between a connecting rod bolt and an oil pan bolt.*

11. Carefully lift the crankshaft out of the block. The rods will pivot to the center of the engine when the crank is removed.

MAIN BEARING INSPECTION

Like connecting rod big-end bearings, the crankshaft main bearings are shell-type inserts that do not utilize shims and cannot be adjusted. The bearings are available in various standard and undersizes; if main bearing clearance is found to be too sloppy, a new bearing (both upper and lower halves) is required.

Generally, the lower half of the bearing shell (except No. 1 bearing) shows greater wear and fatigue. If the lower half only shows the effects of normal wear (no heavy scoring or discoloration), it can usually be assumed that the upper half is also in good shape; conversely, if the lower half is heavily worn or damaged, both halves should be replaced. Never replace one bearing half without replacing the other.

Checking Clearance

Main bearing clearance can be checked both with the crankshaft in the car and with the engine out of the car. If the engine block is still in the car, the crankshaft should be supported both from and rear (by the damper and to remove clearance from the upper bearing). Total clearance can then be measured between the lower bearing). Total clearance can then be measured between the lower bearing and journal. If the block has been removed from the car, and is inverted, the crank will rest on the upper bearings and the total clearance can be measured between the lower bearing and journal. Clearance is checked in the same manner as the connecting rod bearings, with Plastigage®.

NOTE: *Crankshaft bearing caps and bearing shells should NEVER be filed flush with the cap-to-block mating surface to adjust for wear in the old bearings. Always install new bearings.*

1. If the crankshaft has been removed, install it (block removed from the car). If the block is still in the car, remove the oil pan and oil pump. Starting with the rear bearing cap and wipe all oil from the crank journal and bearing cap.

2. Place a strip of Plastigage® the full width of the bearing, (parallel to the crankshaft), on the journal.

CAUTION: *Do not rotate the crankshaft while the gaging material is between the bearing and the journal.*

3. Install the bearing cap and evenly torque the cap bolts to specification.

4. Remove the bearing cap. The flattened Plastigage® will be sticking to either the bearing shell or the crank journal.

5. Use the graduated scale on the Plastigage® envelope to measure the material at its widest point.

NOTE: *If the flattened Plastigage® tapers towards the middle or ends, there is a difference in clearance indicating the bearing or journal has a taper, low spot or other irregularity. If this is indicated, measure the crank journal with a micrometer.*

6. If bearing clearance is within specifications, the bearing insert is in good shape. Replace the insert if the clearance is not within specifications. Always replace both upper and lower inserts as a unit.

7. Standard, 0.025mm or 0.050mm undersize bearing should produce the proper clearance. If these sizes still produce a sloppy fit, the crankshaft must be reground for use with the next undersize bearing. Recheck all clearances after installing new bearings.

8. Replace the rest of the bearings in the same manner. After all bearings have been checked, rotate the crankshaft to make sure there is no excessive drag. When checking the No. 1 main bearing, loosen the accessory drive

belts (engine in car) to prevent a tapered reading with the Plastigage®.

MAIN BEARING REPLACEMENT

Engine Out of Car

1. Remove and inspect the crankshaft.
2. Remove the main bearings from the bearing saddles in the cylinder block and main bearing caps.
3. Coat the bearing surfaces of the new, correct size main bearings with clean engine oil and install them in the bearing saddles in the block and in the main bearing caps.
4. Install the crankshaft. See "Crankshaft Installation."

Engine In Car

1. With oil pan, oil pump and spark plugs removed, remove the cap from the main bearing needing replacement and remove the bearing from the cap.

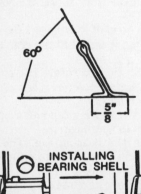

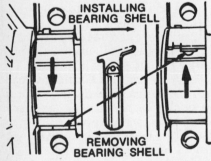

Remove or install the upper bearing insert with a roll-out pin

2. Make a bearing roll-out pin, (using a bent cotter pin) as shown in the illustration. Install the end of the pin in the oil hole in the crankshaft journal.
3. Rotate the crankshaft clockwise as viewed from the front of the engine. This will roll the upper bearing out of the block.
4. Lube the new upper bearing with clean engine oil and insert the plain (unnotched) end between the crankshaft and the indented or notched side of the block. Roll the bearing into place, making sure that the oil holes are aligned. Remove the roll pin from the oil hole.
5. Lube the new lower bearing and install the main bearing cap. Install the main bearing cap, making sure it is positioned in the proper direction with the matchmarks in alignment.
6. Torque the main bearing cap bolts to the proper specification.

NOTE: See "Crankshaft Installation" for that bearing alignment.

CRANKSHAFT END PLAY AND INSTALLATION

When main bearing clearance has been checked, bearings examined and/or replaced, the crankshaft can be installed. Thoroughly clean the upper and lower bearing surfaces, and lube them with clean engine oil. Install the crankshaft and main bearing caps.

Dip all main bearing cap bolts in clean oil, and torque all main bearing caps, excluding the thrust bearing cap, to specifications (see the "Crankshaft and Connecting Rod" chart in this chapter to determine which bearing is the thrust bearing). Tighten the thrust bearing bolts finger tight. To align the thrust bearing, pry the crankshaft to the extent of its axial travel several times, holding the movement toward the front of the engine. Add thrust washers if required for proper alignment. Torque the thrust bearing cap to specifications.

To check crankshaft end-play, pry the crankshaft to the extreme rear of its axial travel, then to the extreme front of its travel. Using a feeler gauge or a dial indicator, measure the end-play

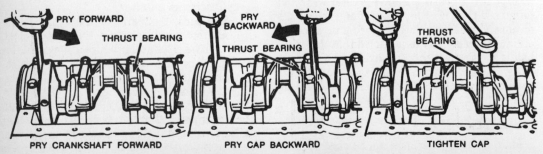

Aligning the thrust bearing

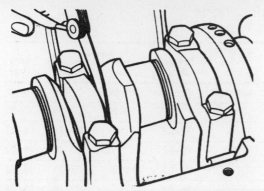

Check the crankshaft end-play with a feeler gauge

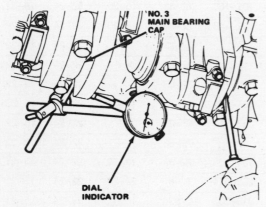

Checking the crankshaft end-play with a dial indicator

at the front of the rear main bearing. End play may also be measured at the thrust bearing. Install a new rear main bearing oil seal in the cylinder block and main bearing cap. Continue to reassemble the engine.

COMPLETING THE REBUILDING PROCESS

Fill the oil pump with oil, to prevent cavitating (sucking air) on initial engine start up. Install the oil pump and the pickup tube on the engine. Coat the oil pan gasket as necessary, and install the gasket and the oil pan. Mount the flywheel and the crankshaft vibration damper or pulley on the crankshaft.

NOTE: *Always use new bolts when installing the flywheel. Inspect the clutch shaft pilot bushing in the crankshaft. If the bushing is excessively worn, remove it with an expanding puller and a slide hammer, and tap a new bushing into place.*

Position the engine, cylinder head side up. Lubricate the lifters, and install them into their bores. Install the cylinder head, and torque it as specified. Insert the pushrods (where applicable), and install the rocker shaft(s) (if so equipped) or position the rocker.

Install the intake and exhaust manifolds, the carburetor(s), the distributor and spark plugs. Mount all accessories and install the engine in the car. Fill the radiator with coolant, and the crankcase with high quality engine oil.

BREAK-IN PROCEDURE

Start the engine, and allow it to run at low speed for a few minutes, while checking for leaks. Stop the engine, check the oil level, and fill as necessary. Restart the engine, and fill the cooling system to capacity. Check and adjust the ignition timing. Run the engine at low to medium speed (800-2,500 rpm) for approximately ½ hour, and retorque the cylinder head bolts. Road test the car, and check again for leaks.

NOTE: *Some gasket manufacturers recommend not retorquing the cylinder head(s) due to the composition of the head gasket. Follow the directions in the gasket set.*

Flywheel/Flex Plate and Ring Gear

NOTE: *Flex plate is the term for a flywheel mated with an automatic transmission.*

REMOVAL AND INSTALLATION

All Engines

NOTE: *The ring gear is replaceable only on engines mated with a manual transmission. Engine with automatic transmissions have ring gears which are welded to the flex plate.*

1. Remove the transmission.
2. Remove the clutch, if equipped, or torque converter from the flywheel. The flywheel bolts should be loosened a little at a time in a cross pattern to avoid warping the flywheel. On cars with manual transmission, replace the pilot bearing in the end of the crankshaft if removing the flywheel.
3. The flywheel should be checked for cracks and glazing. It can be resurfaced by a machine shop.
4. If the ring gear is to be replaced, drill a hole in the gear between two teeth, being careful not to contact the flywheel surface. Using a cold chisel at this point, crack the ring gear and remove it.
6. Polish the inner surface of the new ring gear and heat it in an oven to about 600°F (315°C). Quickly place the ring gear on the flywheel and tap it into place, making sure that it is fully seated.

NOTE: *Never heat the ring gear past 800°F (427°C), or the tempering will be destroyed.*

7. Installation is the reverse of removal. Torque the bolts a little at a time in a cross pattern, to the torque figure shown in the Torque Specifications Chart.

Torque Specifications
All readings in ft. lbs.

Year	Engine Displacement cu. in. (cc)	Cylinder Head Bolts	Main Bearing Bolts	Rod Bearing Bolts	Crankshaft Pulley Bolts	Flywheel Bolts	Manifolds Intake	Manifolds Exhaust	Spark Plugs
1970–72	96 (1573)	[19][20]	42–46	38–41	101–108	72–83	15–20	22–24	18–22
	121 (1990)	[19][20]	42–46	38–41	101–108	72–83	15–20	22–24	18–22
	152.1 (2493)	[19][20]	42–46	38–41	[21]	72–83		22–24	18–22
	170.1 (2788)	[19][20]	42–46	38–41	[21]	72–83		22–24	18–22
1973–76	121 (1990)	[19][20]	42–46	38–41	101–108	72–83	15–20	22–24	18–22
	170.1 (2788)	[19][20]	42–46	38–41	[21]	72–83		22–24	18–22
	182 (2985)	[19][20]	42–46	38–41	[21]	72–83		22–24	18–22
1977–81	121 (1990)	[19][20]	42–46	38–41	101–108	72–83	15–20	22–24	18–22
	107 (1766)	[19][20]	42–46	38–41	101–108	72–83	15–20	22–24	18–22
	182 (2985)	[19][20]	42–46	38–41	[21]	72–83		22–24	18–22
	170.1 (2788)	[19][20]	42–46	38–41	[21]	72–83		22–24	18–22
	196 (3210)	[19][20]	42–46	38–41	[21]	72–83		22–24	18–22
1982	108 (1766)	[1]	42–46	38–41	101–108	72–83	15–20	22–24	18–22
	165 (2693)	[3]	43–48	14	282–311	71–82	—	22–24	18–22
	196 (3210)	[1]	42–46	38–41	[2]	72–83	—	22–24	18–22
1983	108 (1766)	[1]	42–46	38–41	101–108	72–83	15–20	22–24	15–21
	165 (2693)	[5]	42–45[12]	[9]	283–311	71–81	22–24	22–24	15–21
	196 (3210)	[4]	42–46	38–41	318–333	75–83[7]	16–17	22–24	15–21
1984	108 (1766)	[10]	42–46	38–41	130–145	71–81[7]	22–24	22–24	15–21
	165 (2693)	[5]	42–45[12]	[9]	283–311	71–81	22–24	22–24	15–21
	196 (3210)	[4]	42–46	38–41	318–333	75–83[7]	16–17	22–24	15–21
1985	108 (1766)	[10]	42–46	38–41	103–145	71–81[7]	22–24	22–24	15–21
	149 (2443)	[8]	44–49[12]	[9]	283–311	71–81	14–17	14–17	—
	165 (2693)	[5]	42–45[12]	[9]	283–311	71–81	22–24	22–24	15–21
	196 (3210)	[4]	42–46	38–41	318–333	75–83[7]	16–17	22–24	15–21
	209 (3428)	[11]	42–45[12]	38–41	311–325	71–81	22–24	22–24	15–21
1986	149 (2443)	[8]	44–49[12]	[9]	283–311	71–81	14–17	14–17	—
	165 (2693)	[5]	42–45[12]	[9]	283–311	71–81	22–24	22–24	15–21
	209 (3428)	[11]	42–45[12]	38–41	311–325	71–81	22–24	22–24	15–21
1987	152 (2494)	[5]	42–45[12]	[9]	283–311	71–81	22–24	22–24	15–21
	165 (2693)	[5]	42–45[12]	[9]	283–311	71–81	22–24	22–24	15–21
	209 (3428)	[11]	42–45[12]	38–41	311–325	71–81	22–24	22–24	15–21
	210.6 (3453)	[13]	14.5–17.5[12]	[14]	311–325	71–81	14–17	6.5–7	15–21
1988–89	140.4 (2302)	[13]	14.5–17.5[12]	[14]	311–325	75.5–76.5	6.5–7.0	6.5–7.0	15–21
	152 (2494)	[5]	42–45	[9]	283–311	75.5–76.5	22–24	16–18[18]	15–21
	165 (2693)	[5]	42–45	[9]	283–311	75.5–76.5	22–24	16–18[18]	15–21
1988–89	209 (3428)	[11]	42–45	38–41	311–325	75.5–76.5	22–24	16–18[18]	15–21
	210.6 (3453)	[13]	14.5–17.5[12]	[14]	311–325	75.5–76.5	14–17[17]	6.5–7	15–21
	304 (4988)	[15]	[16]	[9]	311–325	74	16–18	16–18	15–21

EXHAUST SYSTEM

Safety Precautions

For a number of reasons, exhaust system work can be the most dangerous type of work you can do on your car. Always observe the following precautions:

• Support the car extra securely. Not only will you often be working directly under it, but you'll frequently be using a lot of force, say, heavy hammer blows, to dislodge rusted parts. This can cause a car that's improperly supported to shift and possibly fall.

• Wear goggles. Exhaust system parts are always rusty. Metal chips can be dislodged, even when you're only turning rusted bolts. Attempting to pry pipes apart with a chisel makes the chips fly even more frequently.

• If you're using a cutting torch, keep it a great distance from either the fuel tank or lines. Stop what you're doing and feel the temperature of the fuel bearing pipes on the tank frequently. Even slight heat can expand and/or vaporize fuel, resulting in accumulated vapor, or even a liquid leak, near your torch.

• Watch where your hammer blows fall and make sure you hit squarely. You could easily tap a brake or fuel line when you hit an exhaust system part with a glancing blow. Inspect all lines and hoses in the area where you've been working.

CAUTION: *Be very careful when working on or near the catalytic converter. External temperatures can reach 1,500°F (816°C) and more, causing severe burns. Removal or installation should be performed only on a cold exhaust system.*

Special Tools

A number of special exhaust system tools can be rented from auto supply houses or local stores that rent special equipment. A common one is a tail pipe expander, designed to enable you to join pipes of identical diameter.

It may also be quite helpful to use solvents designed to loosen rusted bolts or flanges. Soaking rusted parts the night before you do the job can speed the work of freeing rusted parts considerably. Remember that these solvents are often flammable. Apply only to parts after they are cool!

Use this procedure for removing the exhaust

① 320i, 528i, 633CSi & 733i '79–'80
    Step 1—25–32
    Step 2—49–52
    Step 3—56–59
    Step 4—56–59 (after warm-up)
  633CSi & 733i—'81–'82
    Step 1—25–32
    Step 2—49–51
    Step 3—54–59
    Step 4—20–30 degrees (after warm-up)
② Flat hex nut: 174–188
  Shoulder hex nut: 318–333
③ Step 1—22–25
  Step 2—43–47
④ Step 1—25–29
  Step 2—42–45
    Wait 20 minutes
  Step 3—56–59
  Step 4—20°–30°
⑤ Step 1—29–33
    Wait 20 minutes
  Step 2—43–47
    Warm engine fully
  Step 3—20°–30°
⑥   Then turn additional 70°
⑦ First coat w/Loctite® 270 or equivalent
⑧ Step 1—50–60
    Wait 15 minutes
  Step 2—70–76
    Run engine hot—25 minutes
  Step 3—Turn 85°–95° angle torque
    Crossbolts—28–34
⑨ Torque to 14.5 ft. lbs.
  Turn 70° angle torque
⑩ Step 1—42–44
    Wait 15 minutes

  Step 2—30°–36° angle torque
    Run engine warm—25 minutes
  Step 3—20°–30° angle torque
⑪ Step 1—42–44
    Wait 15 minutes
  Step 2—30–36
    Run engine warm—25 minutes
  Step 3—30°–40° angle torque
⑫ Step 1—Torque to figure shown
  Step 2—Turn 47°–53° angle torque
⑬ Step 1—35–37
  Step 2—57–59
    Wait 15 minutes
  Step 3—71–73
⑭ Step 1—7
  Step 2—21.5
  Step 3—60°–62° angle torque
⑮ Step 1—22
    Wait 15 minutes
  Step 2—Turn 120° angle torque
⑯ Step 1—14.5
  Step 2—Turn 70° angle torque
⑰ Applies to (larger) M8 bolts. Torque M6 (smaller) bolts to 6.5–7.0
⑱ Coat the threads of the upper row of bolts with a locking type sealer
⑲ 1600, 2000, 2002, 2500,
  2800, 3000, Bavaria, 3.0: Step 1—25–33
                              2—43–47
                              3—49–52
⑳ 320i, 530i, 538i,
  630CSi, 633CSi, 733i: Step 1—25–32
                            2—49–52
                            3—56–59
                            4—56–59 (after warm-up)
㉑ Flat hex nut: 174–188
  Shoulder hex nut: 318–333

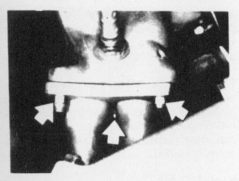

Disconnect the catalytic converter-to-exhaust manifold bolts (arrows)

Disconnect the shield at the final muffler

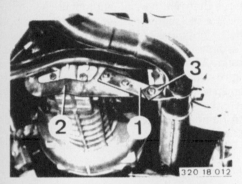

Press the exhaust holder (1) against the pipe to remove tension, bolt the late (2) to the transmission and tighten the bracket (3)

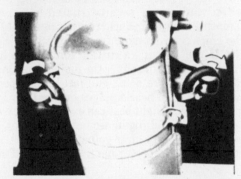

Remove the muffler from the hangers by prying the rubber rings over the hook

Remove the shield from the converter pipe

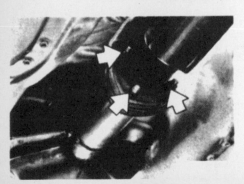

Disconnect the converter at the flange

system to make big repair jobs easier. By removing the exhaust system components, things like transmission removal are much easier. The procedure will vary slightly from model to model and year to year, but the basic procedures are the same. The individual system components can be removed in the same manner as the whole system.

Inspect all of the rubber "donut" exhaust hangers when removing any part of the system. These hangers are the cause of many exhaust system rattles and bangs.

REMOVAL AND INSTALLATION

1970-79 Models

1. Raise and safely support the vehicle. Remove the 3 nuts retaining the header pipe to the exhaust manifold.

2. Loosen the exhaust holder at the rear of the header pipe, then remove the nuts attaching the rear muffler to the intermediate pipe.

3. The rear muffler can be left in place or removed, depending on the repair to be made.

4. Remove the bolt at the exhaust holder, while holding the intermediate and header pipes with your hand. Remove them from the vehicle. On models equipped with a front muf-

fler (resonator), it will come out with the intermediate pipe.

5. To install the exhaust system, reverse the removal procedures noting the following:

a. Coat the header pipe bolts with Molykote® or equivalent and tighten.

b. Align the system correctly before tightening the exhaust holder.

c. Align the tailpipe at the back of the vehicle before tightening the rear muffler-to-intermediate pipe bolts.

1979-89 Models

1. Raise and safely support the vehicle. Disconnect the catalytic converter at the exhaust manifold.

2. Loosen the exhaust holder. Unbolt the catalytic converter shield and disconnect the catalytic converter at the flange.

3. Disconnect the shield from the final muffler and disconnect the final muffler at the flange.

4. Disconnect the final muffler and remove it from its hangers.

5. To install the exhaust system, reverse the removal procedures noting the following:

a. Coat the catalytic converter-to-exhaust manifold bolts with Molykote® or equivalent and tighten.

b. Align the system correctly before tightening the exhaust holder.

c. Align the tailpipe at the back of the vehicle before tightening the rear muffler-to-intermediate pipe bolts.

Emission Controls

4

EMISSION CONTROLS

Crankcase Ventilation System

OPERATION

The BMW crankcase emission control system is considered a sealed system. Rather than purging the crankcase of blow-by vapors with fresh air is done conventionally, the blow-by emissions are routed directly to the air cleaner or air collector with crankcase pressure behind them. Since the purpose of the PCV valve in conventional systems is to regulate the volume of purging air even with varying intake vacuum, this valve and the maintenance associated with it are eliminated.

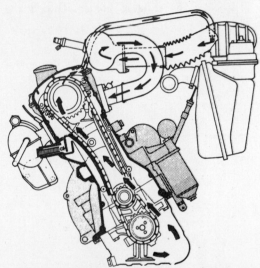

Crankcase emission control system (with Continuous Fuel Injection)

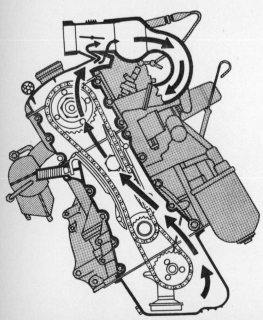

Crankcase emission control system (with Electronic Fuel Injection)

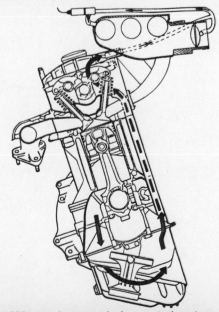

The 528e crankcase emission control system

POSITIVE CRANKCASE VENTILATION SYSTEM
TROUBLE DIAGNOSIS

Symptom	Possible Cause	Repair
Rough engine idle	Defective canister, clogged or leaking vacuum hose.	Replace canister, clean or replace hose.
No PCV flow	Clogged lines or flame trap.	Clean or replace lines and flame trap.
Engine stalls at idle	Saturated carbon canister, clogged breather filter.	Replace canister or filter.
Surging at road speed	Improper PCV flow.	Check PCV system for proper function. Clean all lines and component.

TESTING

The Crankcase Emission Control System is virtually maintenance free. The connecting tube from the top engine cover to the air cleaner or air collector should be inspected during the routine maintenance services and replaced if cracked, distorted or plugged.

With the engine operating and the connect-

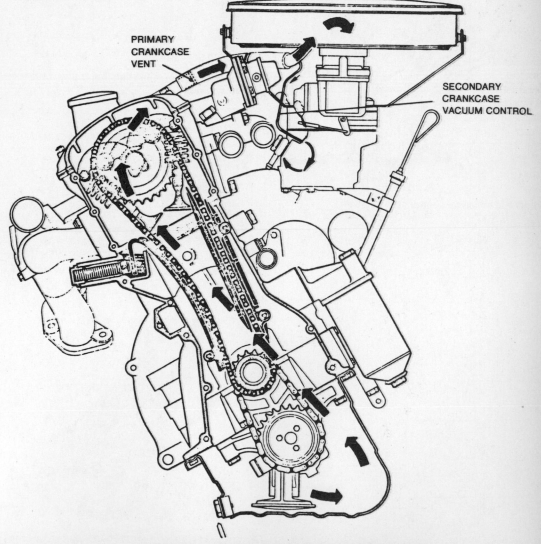

PRIMARY CRANKCASE VENT

SECONDARY CRANKCASE VACUUM CONTROL

Crankcase emission control system—2002 (carburetor)

FUEL EVAPORATIVE SYSTEM DIAGNOSIS

Symptom	Possible Cause	Repair
Noticeable fuel odor or leaks	Damaged or loose lines, defective or saturated canister, broken or leaking vent valve.	Repair lines, replace canister or vent valve
Fuel tank deformed	Canister clogged, tank cap defective, hose clogged.	Replace defective canister or cap, clear vapor lines
Insufficient fuel delivery or vapor lock	Clogged or collapsed vapor lines, vent valve or canister. Clogged fuel feed lines.	Repair as necessary
Tank won't take fuel	Clogged or defective vent valve.	Replace vent valve

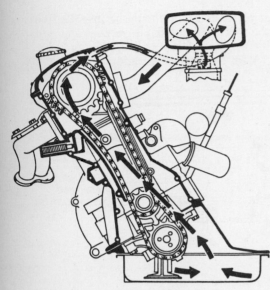

Crankcase emission control system—318i

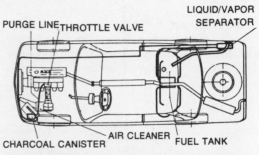

Typical evaporative emission control system—4 cylinder engines

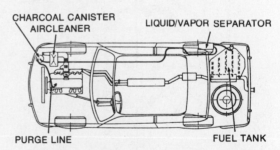

Typical evaporative emission control system—6 cylinder engines

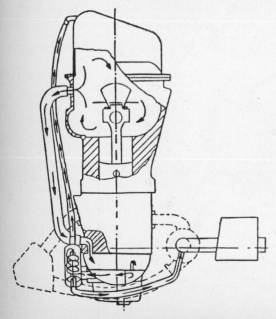

Crankcase emission control system—524td

The tank vent hose is located in the trunk of the 320i

ing tube disconnected, a vacuum should be noted at the air cleaner or air collector side of the hose. If vacuum is not present, an air leak or plugged air induction system may be the cause.

Evaporative Emissions Control System

OPERATION

This system stores gasoline vapors which collect above liquid fuel in the fuel tank and, on carbureted engines, in the float bowl. The system stores the vapors while the engine is off, and then allows the vacuum created in the intake manifold to draw them off and burn them when the engine is started.

Fuel tank vapors are collected by a storage tank located in the trunk. Vapor which cannot be held there, as ell as float bowl vapors, are stored in a charcoal canister located in the front

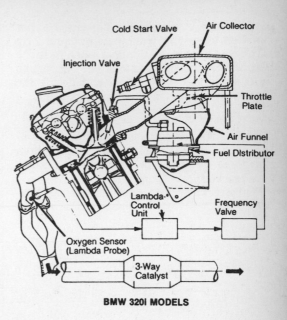

BMW 320i MODELS

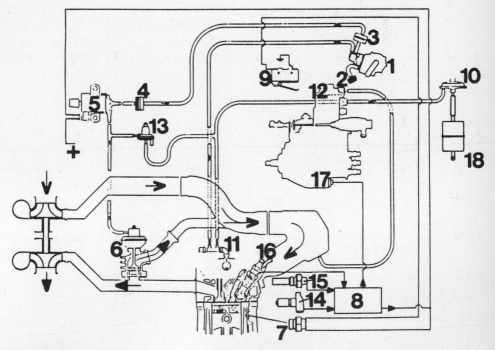

1. Pressure converter
2. Filter
3. Damping container
4. Throttle
5. Electrical switching valve
6. EGR valve
7. Temperature switch
8. Control unit for vp-20 injection pump
9. Idle switch
10. Altitude transmitter for alda
11. Vacuum pump
12. Control box for full stop
13. Venting valve
14. Speed/reference mark sensor
15. Coolant temperature sensor
16. Needle travel sensor in the fuel injector
17. Valve for injection timing control
18. Air cleaner

Emission Control System—524td

of the engine compartment. The charcoal has the effect of keeping the vapors in liquid form so they can be held in a minimal space. As in the case of the crankcase ventilation system, no fresh air is used in purging, eliminating the need to change an air filter in the canister.

MAINTENANCE

Inspect the hoses and hose clamps occasionally or if raw fuel odor is noticed. Tighten clamps as necessary or replace hoses which have cracked.

Under certain operating conditions, contami-

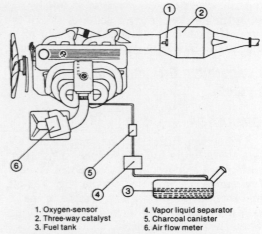

1. Oxygen-sensor
2. Three-way catalyst
3. Fuel tank
4. Vapor liquid separator
5. Charcoal canister
6. Air flow meter

Exhaust emission control system—325e

nation or excessive vapor collection may cause the vapor canister to become saturated with liquid fuel. Under these conditions, the unit should be replaced, even though replacement on a routine basis is not necessary.

Automatic Air Intake Preheating Valve

CHECKING

The automatic air induction pre-heat valve is located in a housing to the right of the radiator,

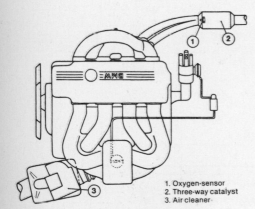

1. Oxygen-sensor
2. Three-way catalyst
3. Air cleaner

Exhaust emission control system—318i

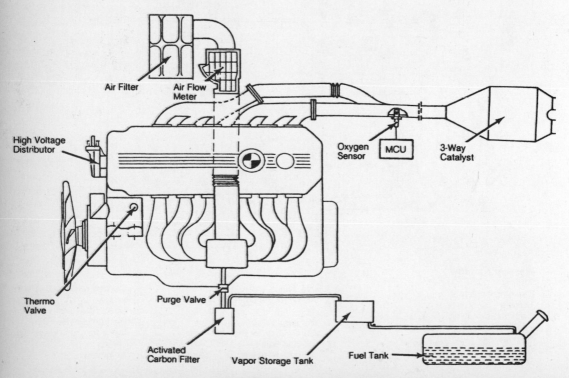

Air Filter

Air Flow Meter

High Voltage Distributor

Oxygen Sensor

MCU

3-Way Catalyst

Thermo Valve

Purge Valve

Activated Carbon Filter

Vapor Storage Tank

Fuel Tank

BMW 533i, 633 CSi and 733i models

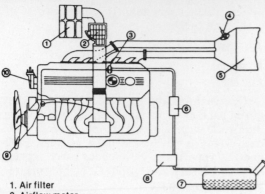

1. Air filter
2. Airflow meter
3. Purge valve
4. Oxygen sensor
5. Three-way catalyst
6. Activated carbon filter
7. Fuel tank
8. Liquid-Vapor separator
9. Thermo switch
10. High voltage distributor

Exhaust emission control system—635CSi 735i 535i

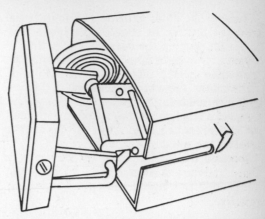

Removing the air intake preheater assembly

on vehicles so equipped. Every 8000 miles, the lever should be placed in the winter (W) position and the valve's freedom of movement checked. If necessary, oil the valve. In the "W" position air drawn in at the front of the car is mixed with air preheated around the exhaust manifold in a ratio dependent on outside and engine temperatures, until it reaches approximately 86°F (30°C). At approximately this same outside temperature, the pre-heat supply hose is completely closed and the car obtains all its induction air supply from the fresh air hose. In summer, the lever should be used to set the valve to the "S" position. The cover plate can be removed for inspection purposes.

ADJUSTMENT

1. Remove the cover.
2. Adjust the butterfly valve by loosening the nuts (1).
3. The butterfly valve is correctly set when the distance (A) is 60mm.

Ignition Timing Controls

A vacuum advance and retard unit is attached to the distributor and is controlled by engine vacuum. The advance can be checked with a strobe light and increasing the engine speed while observing the action of the timing mark during the increase in engine speed. The retard side can be checked at idle by removing the retard vacuum line and noting the increase in engine speed of at least 300 rpm.

NOTE: *Some models built for California and high altitude applications and equipped with manual transmissions, have the vacuum advance in operation only when the high gear is engaged. This controlled by an electrical switch connected to the shifting linkage. Automatic transmission 633CSi for California and high altitude, have the vacuum advance inoperative. Late model 530i and 630CSi vehicles are equipped with a vacuum retard unit only. The 528i has both advance and retard.*

TESTING

Electric Control Valve (Black Cap)
California Equipment Only

This control valve stops the retard distributor control over speeds of 3000rpm.

Preheat valve settings

Adjusting the air intake preheater valve

Remove the outer hose (to distributor) and start the engine. At engine rpm lower than 3000 rpm, vacuum should be present in the distributor retard unit hose and not present when the engine speed is increased above 3000 rpm.

Disconnect the wire terminal end at the control valve and have the engine operating at idle. Connect a test lamp to the terminal and check for the presence of current. If current is present, the speed switch is defective.

Increase the engine speed to 3000 rpm or above, and the test lamp should light. If the test lamp does not light, the speed switch is defective.

Air Injection System

OPERATION

The Air Injection system is used to add oxygen to the hot exhaust gases in the Thermal Reactor or exhaust manifold. The introduction of fresh air (oxygen) aids in more complete combustion of the air/fuel mixture lessening the hydrocarbons and the carbon monoxide emissions. A belt driven air pump is used to force air into the exhaust system, through a series of valves and tubing.

TESTING

Air pump

2002 AND 3.0

Remove the air return pipe and hold the palm of the hand over the pressure regulating valve unit while increasing the engine speed. The excess pressure valve must open between 1700 and 200 rpm. If the valve opens early, replace the valve. If the valve opens at a higher rpm, replace the air pump.

Belt Adjustment

2002 AND 3.0

The air pump drive belt should have a deflection of no more than ⅜″ measured in the middle of its longest span, when properly adjusted.

Control Valve

2002 AND 3.0

The control valve should be replaced if the carburetors are difficult to adjust or if the engine back-fires when the throttle is released.

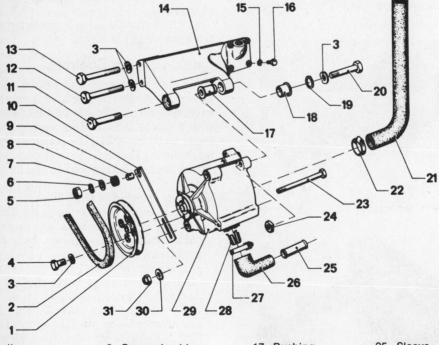

1. Belt pulley	9. Spacer bushing	17. Bushing	25. Sleeve
2. V-belt	10. Tension shackle	18. Bushing	26. Elbow
3. Lockwasher	11. Hex screw	19. Lockring	27. Hose clamp
4. Hex screw	12. Screw	20. Hex screw	28. Pressure regulator
5. Hex nut	13. Screw	21. Hose	29. Air pump
6. Spring ring	14. Bearing bracket	22. Hose clamp	30. Washer
7. Washer	15. Lockwasher	23. Hex screw	31. Hex nut
8. Rubber bushing	16. Screw	24. Square nut	

Exploded view of 2002 recombustion system air pump and related parts

Check Valve
2002 AND 3.0

The check valve should be replaced if air can be blown through the valve in both directions. Air should move towards the manifold only.

Blow-in Pipes
2002 AND 3.0

The exhaust manifold must be removed to expose the blow-in pipes. The pipes can be re-

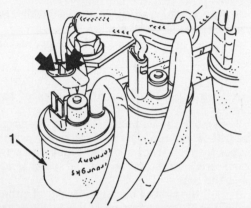

Electronic control valve (1) showing connection test points

Typical air pump control valve

Check valve (2) and air pump line (1)—typical

placed by unscrewing them from the manifold and screwing in new ones.

Air Pump
ALL EQUIPPED 3, 5, 6 AND 7 SERIES VEHICLES

Disconnect the outlet hose and start the engine. The air velocity should increase as the engine speed increases. If not, the air pump drive belt could be slipping, the check valve or the air pump may be defective and would have to be adjusted or replaced.

Blow-off Valve
ALL EQUIPPED 3, 5, 6 AND 7 SERIES VEHICLES

If backfiring occurs when releasing the accelerator or the air pump seems to be overloading, the blow-off valve may be defective.

The valve must release and blow-off during a coasting condition and the internal safety valve must open at 5 psi. The vacuum line must have suction when the engine is running and must allow the air to be blown off when reattached to the valve at idle.

ELECTRIC CONTROL VALVE
WHITE CAP

ALL EQUIPPED 3, 5, 6 AND 7 SERIES VEHICLES

This control valve governs the blow-off valve and must be open at temperatures below 113°F (45°C) and closed above 113°F (45°C) of the coolant.

With the coolant temperatures above 113°F (45°C), the ignition switch on and the engine off, disconnect both vacuum hoses, attach a test hose to one nipple and blow air into the valve. The valve is functioning properly if air cannot flow through the valve. Turn the ignition switch off and blow into the valve again. Air should flow through the valve.

CHECK VALVE

ALL EQUIPPED 3, 5, 6 AND 7 SERIES VEHICLES

The check valve must be replaced if air can be blown through the valve in both directions. Air should move towards the reactors only.

BLOW-IN PIPES

ALL EQUIPPED 3, 5, 6 AND 7 SERIES VEHICLES

The air enters above the reactors, directly into the exhaust ports, behind the exhaust valves. The pipes can be replaced by removing the distribution tube assembly.

THERMAL REACTOR

ALL EQUIPPED 3, 5, 6 AND 7 SERIES VEHICLES

The reactors have a double casing and has internally vented flame deflector plates. Spontaneous combustion, due to high temperatures, and the introduction of oxygen into the exhaust

Blow-in pipes for air pump and EGR valve

Testing the air pump outlet—typical

Thermal reactor—covers removed

gas flow maintains the after-burning of the gases.

A warning light marked "Reactor" alerts the driver to have the unit inspected for external heat damage every 25,000 miles. A triggering device, located behind the dash and operated by the speedometer cable, can be reset to open the electrical contacts and extinguish the warning light.

NOTE: *Two different sized buttons are mounted side by side on the triggering device. The small button is for the reactor and the*

large button is for the EGR valve. Press the button to reset.

REMOVAL AND INSTALLATION
Air Pump
1600, 2002, and 3.0

1. Disconnect inlet and outlet hoses.
2. Remove the adjusting bolt. Then, loosen and remove the front and rear mounting bolts—note that nuts will remain in the grooved portion of the housing.
3. Inspect the rubber bushings inside the mounting bracket and replace if necessary.
4. Install in reverse order; do not pry on the pump when adjusting the belt.

318I AND 320I

1. Disconnect the hose at the back of the pump.
2. Remove the adjusting bolt and disengage the belt. Then, remove the through bolt which passes through front and rear pump brackets, being careful to retain the nut and spacer located at the rear.
3. Pull the rubber bushings (5) out of either end of the air pump mount. If the bushings are worn or cracked replace them. When reinstalling, make sure inside diameters of bushings fit over the inner spacer (6) and outside diameters fit snugly into the mount.
4. Install in reverse order.

ALL EQUIPPED 5, 6 AND 7 SERIES VEHICLES

1. Loosen the adjusting bolt, which is located at the top of the upper pump bracket. Pull off the belt.
2. Loosen the clamp and detach the air hose at the rear.
3. Remove the the mounting bolts from the bracket. Remove the single bolt from the front bracket and remove the pump.
4. Pull the rubber bushings out of the lower pump mount and inspect them. Replace them if they are worn or cracked, making sure the inside diameters fit around the inner (metal) bushing and outside diameters fit inside the mount.
5. Install the pump in reverse order.

Ignition Timing Controls

CAUTION: *Transistorized and CDI ignition systems utilize voltages that can be fatal if accidental contact is made with "live" parts or connections. Whenever working on electronic ignition systems always disconnect the battery and make sure the ignition switch is off before removing or installing any connections at the distributor, coil, spark plugs or control unit.*

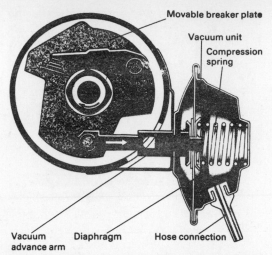

Single diaphragm vacuum advance unit—typical

Black control valve (1) showing collector hose (a) and distributor hose (b)

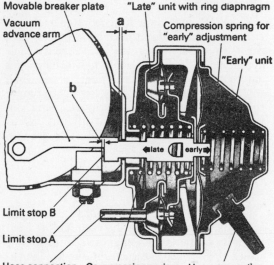

Dual diaphragm vacuum advance/retard unit—typical

Distributor Advance/Retard Units

A vacuum advance and retard unit is attached to the distributor and is controlled by engine vacuum. The advance can be checked with a strobe light by observing the action of the timing mark during the increase in engine speed. The retard side can be checked at idle by removing the retard vacuum line and toting the increase in engine speed of at least 300 rpm.

NOTE: *Some models built for California and high altitude applications and equipped with manual transmissions, have the vacuum advance in operation only when the high gear is engaged. This controlled by an electri-* *cal switch connected to the shifting linkage. Automatic transmission 633CSi for California and high altitude, have the vacuum advance inoperative. Late model 530i and 630CSi vehicles are equipped with a vacuum retard unit only. The 528i has both advance and retard.*

Testing Electric Control Valve (Black Cap)

CALIFORNIA ONLY

This control valve stops the retard distributor control over speeds of 3000 rpm.

Remove the outer hose (to distributor) and start engine. At engine rpm lower than 3000 rpm, vacuum should be present in the distributor retard unit hose and not present when the engine speed is increased above 3000 rpm.

Disconnect the wire terminal end at the control valve and have the engine operating at idle. Connect a test lamp to the terminal and check for the presence of current. If current is present, the speed switch is defective.

Increase the engine speed to 300 rpm or above, and the test lamp should light. If the test lamp does not light, the speed switch is defective.

Testing Timing Valve

The timing valve is shut when the engine is cold or in the warm up phase of operation. Turning on the ignition heats the timing valve continuously. To test the timing valve on a cold engine, detach the hose to the distributor vacuum advance unit and check that no vacuum is felt from the valve connection. When the engine reaches operating temperature, disconnect the hose to the throttle housing and check that the engine speed increases about 200 rpm. Any results other than these, replace the timing valve.

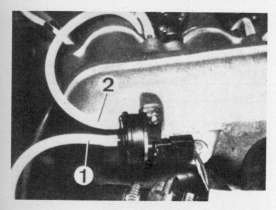

Timing valve assembly with vacuum hoses to throttle housing (2) and distributor advance unit (1)

Speed switch (1) and control valve (2) showing connector

Replacing the timing valve. Remove hoses (1 and 2), bolts and connector (arrows)

Speed Controlled Spark System

The SCS device allows either ignition advance or retard depending on vehicle speed. Generally, this system reduces advance during low speed operation but allows full advance at higher speeds. This system operates on the vacuum advance or retard unit. The SCS vacuum solenoid valve is controlled by a temperature sensor mounted in the intake manifold water passage and by an engine speed switch. When coolant temperature is below 133°F (56°C), or if the engine speed is over 3000 rpm, the solenoid valve closed vacuum flow to vacuum control valve and to first stage of the EGR valve. This prevents the EGR system from operating when the engine is cold, improving driveability and cold response.

TESTING SPEED SWITCH

With the engine running and at operating temperature, connect a test lamp to the disconnected plug of the solenoid valve. The test lamp should be on at engine speeds over 3000 rpm. If not, replace the speed switch.

Exhaust Gas Recirculating System

OPERATION

The EGR valve is vacuum operated by the position of the carburetor or injection system throttle plate in the throttle bore during vehicle operation. A metered amount of exhaust gas enters the combustion chamber to be mixed with the air/fuel blend. The effect is to reduce the peak combustion temperatures, which in turn reduces the amount of nitrous oxides (NO_2), formed during the combustion process.

TESTING

EGR Valve

2002 AND 3.0

Remove the air filter and adjust the engine idle to 900 rpm. Remove the vacuum line from the valve and using an engine vacuum source, attach the hose to the vacuum nipple. The engine speed should drop 500-600 rpm if the valve is operating properly. If little or no change of engine speed is noted, the recirculation pipes, the cyclone filter or the EGR valve may be plugged or defective.

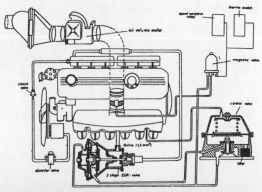

EGR system on 6 cylinder engines—typical

EGR SYSTEM DIAGNOSIS

Symptom	Possible Cause	Repair
EGR valve does not move during test.	Leaking or clogged vacuum line or hose connection. Defective EGR valve.	Repair vacuum line or replace valve.
Engine won't idle or dies on return to idle.	EGR control system blocked or inoperative.	Check all vacuum connections and control valve. Replace defective control valve.
EGR valve leaks in closed position. Poor wide-open throttle performance.	EGR valve defective or clogged with carbon. Defective EGR control valve.	Clean or replace EGR valve. Replace control valve.
EGR warning light on.	Normal service due.	Service EGR system and reset counter.
Excessive HC and CO levels in exhaust.	Air injection system inoperative.	Check all components for proper operation. Check all hoses for unrestricted flow.

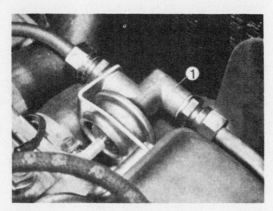

EGR valve (1)—2002 and 3.0 models

1. Blue hose 2. Red hose to throttle housing 3. Black hose at header

Electronic control valves—black (1), red (2) and blue (3)

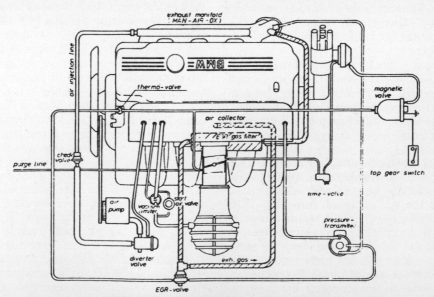

EGR system on 4 cylinder engines—typical

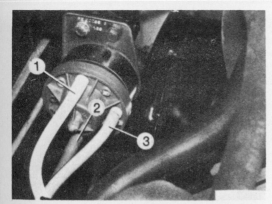

Pressure converter with white (1), red (2) and blue (3) hoses

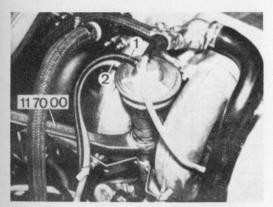

Removing the EGR valve with the special tool

318I AND 320I

1. Start the engine and let it idle. Disconnect the blue hose at the EGR valve, and leave both ends open. The engine speed should remain the same. If the engine speed changes, the throttle blade opens too far at idle or the EGR valve is sticking open.

2. Leave the blue hose detached and disconnect the black hose at the intake header. Detach the red hose at the throttle housing and connect it to the open port on the intake header. The engine speed should drop considerably, or the EGR valve is defective and must be replaced.

3. Detach the black hose the header. Detach the red hose at the temperature sensing valve and connect it to the open port on the intake header. If the engine speed drops, the EGR valve is sticking open or the pressure converter is defective. To check the pressure converter, detach red and blue hoses and check for vacuum at the open converter ports (engine running). If there is no vacuum at the ports, but the white hose to the converter has vacuum, the converter is defective.

ALL 5 SERIES

1. With the engine idling and hot, disconnect the black hose at the tee leading into the vacuum control valve.

2. Disconnect the hose at the vacuum limiter, and connect its open end with the open end of the black hose. The engine speed should drop about 100 rpm. Reconnect the black hose to the tee.

3. Disconnect the blue hose at the vacuum control valve and connect its open end to the open end of the hose disconnected from the vacuum limiter in Step 2. The engine speed should now drop about 200 rpm. If either test is failed, replace the EGR valve.

ALL 6 AND 7 SERIES

1. Bring the engine to operating temperature at idle speed. Detach the blue hose at the EGR valve – do not plug either the open end or the hose or the fitting on the valve. The engine speed should stay the same. If the engine speed should stay the same. If the engine speed drops, check the red hose from the throttle housing for vacuum. If there is vacuum there, adjust the idle position of the throttle. If there is no vacuum, the EGR valve is defective.

2. Detach the blue hose at the EGR valve. On 600 Series cars, remove the plug from the intake collector, On the 733i, disconnect the white hose at the collector. Pull the red hose off the throttle housing and attach it to the open fitting on the intake collector. If the engine speed does not drop considerably, the EGR valve, coolant temperature switch, or red electric switching valve is defective. If the engine speed does drop, go to step 5.

3. To test the coolant temperature switch, turn on the engine with the engine stopped and cold − temperature below 113°F (45°C). Pull the connector plug off the red magnetic valve and connect the test lamp between the 2 open terminals on the valve. The test lamp should not come on. If the test lamp does come on, test the speed switch as described in the next step.

4. To test speed switch, remove the electrical connector from the blue switching valve with the engine idling. Connect a test lamp between the 2 leads. If not, make sure the valve is properly grounded and, if so, replace the speed switch. If the engine speed did not drop in Step 2, and you have made tests described in Steps 3 and 4, test the red cap electric control valve (see below) before condemning the EGR valve.

5. Connect the blue hose back to the EGR valve. Leave the red hose connected as in Step 2. Engine sped should have dropped slightly from normal idle. If the idle speed drops considerably from the normal idle, there are leaking hoses, a defective pressure converter, or a bad

EGR valve. Restore all hoses to their normal positions. Check for leaks. If there are no leaks, detach the red hose at the pressure converter with the engine idling and hot. There should be back pressure. Then, detach the white hose to make sure there is intake vacuum. Repair broken or loose red or white hoses, if necessary. Then, reinstall the white hose, pull off the blue hose, and check for vacuum at the blue pressure converter connection. If there is no vacuum, replace the pressure converter; otherwise, replace the EGR valve.

Testing the electronic control valve (1), coolant temperature switch (2), and the speed switch (3). Tests are similar for remaining switches

REMOVAL AND INSTALLATION
EGR Valve

1. Note color coding of vacuum hoses and disconnect them.
2. On 320i, loosen the clamp and disconnect the hose running into the side of the valve.
3. Unscrew the nut at the bottom of the valve with a spanner wrench. On 6 cylinder engines, remove the 2 mounting bolts for the EGR valve holding bracket, from the intake pipes, and pull the valve free of the recirculation hose.
4. Install the valve to the hose and install the retaining bolts.
5. Screw in the nut at the bottom of the valve and connect the vacuum hoses. On 320i models, connect the hose to the side of the valve and tighten the clamp.

Electric Control Valve — Red Cap

ALL 5, 6 AND 7 SERIES

On models so equipped, the electric control valve should stop the EGR valve operation at coolant temperatures below 113°F (45°C), and speeds above 3000 rpm. Tag and disconnect both vacuum hoses at the control valve with the engine off and the coolant temperature below 113°F (45°C). Connect a test hose to one of the nipples and blow through the hose. The valve is functioning properly when there is air flowing through the valve with the ignition **OFF** and no air flow through the valve with the ignition **ON**.

Connect the vacuum hoses to the valve and operate the engine until the coolant is heated over 113°F (45°C). Disconnect the hoses and check for air flow through the valve. Air should now flow through the valve.

Coolant Temperature Switch and Control Relay

1. With the coolant temperature below 113°F (45°C), turn the ignition **ON**, bit do not start the engine. Remove the wire plug at the control valve and connect a test lamp to the plug.
    a. The test lamp should light. If the test lamp does not light, connect the test lamp to ground. If the lamp now operates, the ground wire to the control valve has an open circuit.
    b. If the test lamp still does not light, disconnect the wire terminal at the coolant temperature switch and connect it to ground. If the test lamp still does not light, replace the control valve.
2. With the coolant temperature above 113°F (45°C), turn the ignition switch ON but do not start the engine. Disconnect the wire terminal plug at the control valve and connect a test lamp. The lamp should be off. If the lamp is on, the coolant temperature switch or control relay is defective.
3. With the engine running at temperatures above 113°F (45°C), connect the test light to the disconnected plug of the control light to the disconnected plug of the control valve. The test lamp should be on over an engine speed of 3000 rpm. If the test lamp does not light, the speed switch is defective.

REMOVAL AND INSTALLATION

Exhaust Gas Filter

NOTE: *The EGR filter should be replaced every 25,000 miles. Exhaust system should be cool before replacing.*

Electronic control valves—Black (1), Red (2), and Blue (3)

Typical EGR filter

1. Detach all lines.
2. Loosen hold down bolts.
3. Remove bolts and filter.
4. Installation is the reverse of removal.

EGR Warning Light

A warning light marked EGR is triggered at 25,000 miles, to alert the driver to service the exhaust gas recirculation system filter.

A triggering device, located under the dash and driven by the speedometer cable, can be reset to open the electrical contracts and extinguish the EGR warning light.

NOTE: *Two different sized buttons are mounted side by side on the triggering device. The small button is for the reactor light and the large button is for the EGR light. Press the button to reset.*

Thermal Reactor System

The thermal reactor system is used on all models except Federal (49 States) versions of 4 cylinder engines. The reactor allows additional burning of exhaust gases, thus reducing HC and CO emissions. The reactor depends on a

Triggering device showing reactor (1) and EGR (2) resetting devices

Removing bolts for heat shields

Thermal reactors showing attaching bolts

supply of fresh air supplied by the air injection system to operate.

MAINTENANCE

After 25,000 miles, a warning light will indicate that the thermal reactor should be inspected for cracks or other damage. Other than this inspection, the thermal reactor is maintenance free. After inspection, the mileage interval switch must be reset. The switch is connected to the speedometer cable on the inside of the left side engine carrier. 2 buttons are located on the switch. Push the button marked REAC to reset the switch for the thermal reactor.

CHECKING THE THERMAL REACTOR

1. Remove the air cleaner with air flow sensor.
2. Remove the heat guards.
3. Check both reactors for cracks and heat damage, replacing if necessary.
4. Reinstall heat shields and air cleaner assembly.

Oxygen Sensor System

An oxygen (lambda) sensor system is used on all models equipped with a 3-way catalyst. No

CATALYTIC CONVERTER DIAGNOSIS

Symptom	Possible Cause	Repair
Leaking exhaust gases	Leaks at pipe joints, damaged gaskets or rusted exhaust pipes	Tighten clamps, repair exhaust system as necessary
Loss of engine power, internal rattles in exhaust system	Dislodged baffles in muffler, broken ceramic insert in converter	Replace muffler or converter
Excessive CO	Contaminated catalyst	Replace converter
Excessive catalyst temperature	Mixture set too rich, oxygen sensor malfunction	Reset mixture, check oxygen sensor system
Catalyst warning light on	Normal service due	Replace converter and reset warning light

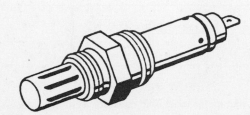

Typical oxygen sensor

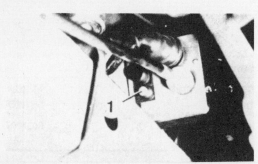

Resetting the oxygen sensor interval switch—push button (1)

exhaust gas recirculation is required. In completely burned fuel in the form of carbon monoxide is used, within the catalyst, to remove oxygen from the nitrogen oxide emissions, leaving them in their normal state as nitrogen. This process can only be accomplished if the fuel/air ratio is kept precisely at the optimum level with no excess air or oxygen. A sensor located in the exhaust gas stream constantly regulates the fuel/air mixture provided by the injection system according to the amount of air (oxygen) in the exhaust.

MAINTENANCE

Every 30,000 miles an oxygen sensor warning light will indicate the need to change the oxygen sensor. The warning light must be reset when the sensor is replaced by pushing the reset button on the mileage switch under the hood.

REMOVAL AND INSTALLATION

1. Disconnect the electrical sensor lead.
2. Unscrew the oxygen sensor from the exhaust manifold. Coat the replacement sensor threads with anti-seize.
CAUTION: *Do not get any anti-seize on the sensor body or it will ruin it. This operation should be carried out with the exhaust system cold.*
3. Thread the new sensor into the exhaust manifold and torque to 3.5 ft. lbs.
4. Reset service interval switch and make sure the dash warning light is out.
5. Reset CO level with exhaust analyzer with the oxygen sensor disconnected. If the CO level fails to drop when the sensor is reconnected, there is a fault in the system.

Catalytic Converter System

A 3-way catalyst is installed in the exhaust system to reduce HC and CO emissions by a chemical reaction which finishes the combustion process on fuel that is not completely burned. The catalyst turns HC and CO emissions into Carbon Dioxide and water vapor (steam).

MAINTENANCE

The 3-way catalyst does not require any servicing, aside from periodic inspection for cracks, damage or rattles. If the car has been driven with leaded gasoline, it will be necessary to replace both the converter and the oxygen sensor.

REMOVAL AND INSTALLATION

1. Detach the exhaust pipe at the exhaust manifold.
2. Detach the brace and heat shield.
3. Disconnect the converter from the exhaust pipe and remove the converter.
4. Installation is the reverse of removal. Re-

place all gaskets and self-locking nuts. Make sure the mounting brace is not under excessive stress or exhaust system noises may be caused.

Motronic Emission Control System

NOTE: *The Motronic engine control system is an extremely complex, electrical control system. Most testing and repair on the system requires the use of very expensive, factory only, test equipment. The test procedures and explanations explained here, are to be used ONLY as a guide to basic system operation and testing. For any major problems, you should take the vehicle to an authorized factory shop for repair.*

The Motronic Emission Control system is an electronically controlled, computerized engine system which controls the fuel injection and ignition timing as well as air/fuel ratio.

The system uses this information to determine engine operating conditions, and adjusts timing and fuel ratio accordingly. The Motronic control unit is located behind the speaker in the right kick panel of 635Csi and 735i models and in the glove compartment of the 3 and 5 series vehicles.

The Motronic control unit is the brain of the system. Various engine sensors supply the unit

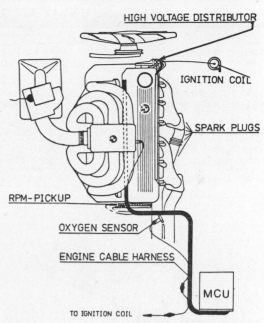

Digital motor electronic emission control system— 528e

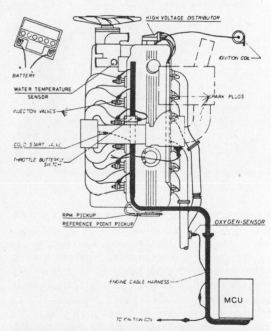

Digital motor electronic emission control system— 535i

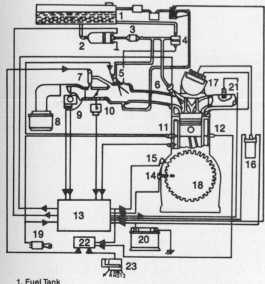

1. Fuel Tank
2. Fuel Pump
3. Fuel Filter
4. Regulator
5. Cold Start Valve
6. Injector
7. Idle Control Valve
8. Air Filter
9. Air Flow Sensor
10. Throttle Position Sensor
11. Thermo Timer
12. Coolant Temp. Sensor
13. Motronic Control Unit
14. Reference-Point Pickup
15. Engine Speed Sensor
16. Coil
17. Distributor
18. Starter Ring Gear
19. Ignition Switch
20. Battery
21. Oxygen Sensor
22. Idle Control Unit
23. Coolant Temp. Switch

Typical motronic emission control system

with operating information air flow, air temperature, throttle position, coolant temperature, engine speed, piston position and oxegyn content of exhaust gases.

The system receives electronic input signals from several engine sensors. Information supplied by these sensors is used to determine opti-

mum ignition and fuel injection timing under various engine operating conditions.

An ideal air/fuel ratio of 14:1 is maintained under most driving conditions. This is the ratio at which the catalytic converter operates most efficiently to reduce exhaust emissions.

The main components that make up the Motronic control system are: oxegyn sensor, air flow sensor, 3 coolant temperature sensors, reference point pickup, engine speed sensor and the throttle position sensor.

SYSTEM SENSORS

Coolant Temperature Sensor

There are 3 components that supply temperature information to the Motronic control unit. They are the coolant temperature sensor, coolant temperature switch and the thermo timer. All 3 devices are located in the water jacket of the engine block. They supply the temperature information to the control unit in the form of electrical signals.

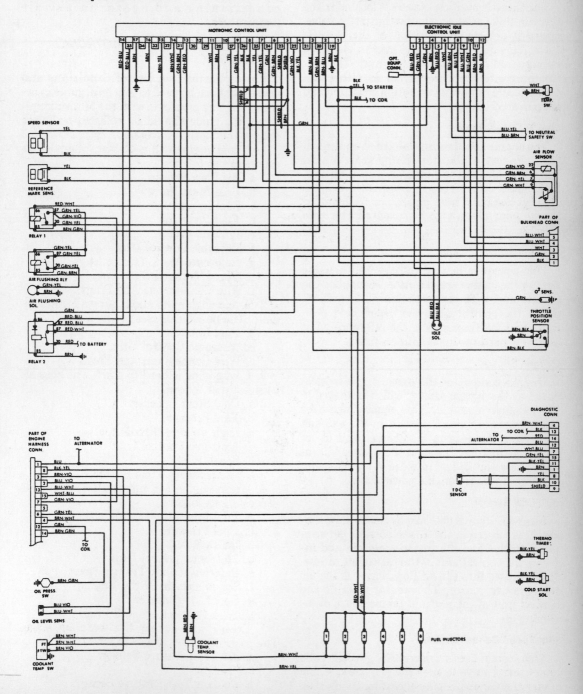

The system interprets these signals as cold or normal operating temperatures. During cold operating conditions, the air/fuel mixture is enriched by the cold start valve. This valve is located in the intake manifold, downstream from the butterfly valve. It supplies additional fuel to the inlet charge when signaled by the control unit. Extra rich conditions are maintane until the normal operating temperature is reached.

Throttle Position Sensor

The throttle position sensors is located in the throttle linkage at the intake butterfly valve, where it detects the position of the throttle valve. This data is converted into an electrical impulse and sent to the control unit. The control unit interprets the signal as either full throttle, idle or normal operating condition and adjusts accordingly.

Engine Speed Sensor

The engine speed sensor is located on the bell housing, next to the starter ring gear. A steel ball, embedded in the ring gear, causes an electronic pulse in the speed sensor, with each engine revolution. These pulses are transmitted to the control unit to be used as the rpm reading.

Reference-Point Pickup

This sensor is located ihn the bell housing next to the engine speed sensor. It supplies the control unit with piston position information. When the control unit has determined optimum ignition timing data, the reference-point pickup is used to signal ignition firing.

Oxygen Sensor

Oxygen content of the exhaust gas is measured by the oxygen sensor, which is located in the exhaust manifold. This sensor measures the amount of oxygen present in the exhaust and sends the data to the control unit as an electrical impulse. The control unit uses this input to keep the air/fuel mixture at the optimum ratio for optimum engine performance.

Air FLow Sensor

Intake air flow is detected by the air flow sensor. It is located in the intake passage between the air filter and the intake manifold and informs the control unit of the rate of air intake. Incorporated into the air flow sensor is the air temperature sensor. This sensor informs the control unit of the ambient temperature of incoming air.

Idle Speed Control System

This system uses an electrically governed idle rpm control valve to keep the idle speed stable under the various engine operating conditions.

Measured intake air from the air flow sensor by-passes the throttle plate through the idle rpm control valve and subsequently calls for additional fuel injection. The amount of by-passed air is determined by the variable orifice of the control valve.

An additional electronic control unit, the Idle Speed Control Unit, controls the orifice opening according to the engine speed and the engine operating conditions as related to the engine coolant temperature, transmission, air conditioning and heater intake air temperature.

TROUBLESHOOTING THE MOTRONIC SYSTEM

The following is a list of conditions and causes that can be used as a helpful guide in determining any problems with the Motronic system. This guide should be referred to before testing the Motronic system.

1. A cold engine will not start. The possible causes are as follows:
    a. Air Flow Sensor.
    b. Cold Start Valve.
    c. Fuel Injector.
    d. Fuel Pressure.
    e. Ignition Coil.
    f. Motronic Control Unit.
    g. Reference Mark Transmitter.
    h. Speed Transmitter.
    i. Wire Connections And Plugs.

2. A cold engine will start, but stalls immediately. The possible causes are as follows:
    a. Fuel Injector.
    b. Motronic Control Unit.
    c. Wire Connections and Plugs.

3. Cold engine is hard to start. The possible causes are as follows:
    a. Cold Start Injector.
    b. Fuel Pressure.
    c. High Voltage Distributor.
    d. Motronic Control Unit.
    e. Spark Plugs.
    f. Temperature Time Switch.

4. Warm engine will not start. The possible causes are as follows:
    a. Fuel Injector.
    b. Fuel Pressure.
    c. Ignition Coil.
    d. Motronic Control Unit.
    e. Reference Mark Transmitter.
    f. Secondary Air Of the Engine.
    g. Speed Transmitter.
    h. Wire Connections and Plugs.

5. Erratic idle during the warm-up stage. The possible causes are as follows:
    a. Air Temperature Sensor.
    b. Coolant.
    c. Coolant Temperature Sensor.

d. High Voltage Distributor.
e. Idle Control Unit.
f. Idle Valve.
g. Ignition Circuit.
h. Ignition System.
i. Motronic Control Unit.
j. Spark Plugs.
k. Temperature Switch (112°F [44°C]).
l. Throttle Switch.
m. Wire Connections and Plugs.

6. The engine is backfiring. The possible causes are as follows:
a. Exhaust System.
b. Fuel Injector.
c. High Voltage Distributor.
d. Ignition Circuit.
e. Motronic Control Unit.
f. Spark Plugs.

7. The engine idle speed is incorrect. The possible causes are as follows:
a. Cold Start Injector.
b. Coolant Temperature Switch.
c. Fuel Injector.
d. High Voltage Distributor.
e. Intake System.
f. Motronic Control Unit.
g. Temperature Switch.
h. Throttle Switch.

8. The engine has a hesitation during acceleration. The possible causes are as follows:
a. Fuel Injector.
b. High Voltage Distributor.
c. Ignition Circuit.
d. Motronic Control Unit.
e. Spark Plugs.
f. Wire Connections and Plugs.

9. The engine is knocking during acceleration. The possible causes are as follows:
a. Ignition Circuit.
b. Motronic Control Unit.
c. Spark Plugs.
d. Wire Connections and Plugs.

10. The engine has a coasting hesitation. The possible causes are as follows:
a. Fuel Injector.
b. Motronic Control Unit.
c. Wire Connections and Plugs.

11. The engine is misfiring under all conditions. The possible causes are as follows:
a. Air Flow Sensor.
b. Air Temperature Sensor.
c. Coolant.
d. Coolant Temperature Switch.
e. Exhaust System.
f. Fuel Injector.
g. Fuel Pressure.
h. Ignition Circuit.
i. Intake System.
j. Insufficient Engine Power.
k. Motronic Control Unit.
l. Secondary Air Of the Engine.
m. Throttle Switch.
n. Wire Connections and Plugs.

12. The engine has a fuel high fuel consumptions. The possible causes are as follows:
a. Air Temperature Sensor.
b. Cold Start Injector.
c. Coolant Temperature Sensor.
d. Fuel Injector.
e. Motronic Control Unit.
f. Temperature Time Switch.
g. Throttle Switch.

13. The engine CO level is incorrect. The possible causes are as follows:
a. Cold Start Injector.
b. Intake System.
c. Oxygen Sensor.
d. Secondary Air of the Engine.
e. Wire Connections and Plugs.

14. The HC and NOx levels are too excessive. The possible causes are as follows:
a. Cold Start Injector.
b. Fuel Injector.
c. Intake System.
d. Motronic Control Unit.
e. Oxygen Sensor.
f. Secondary Air Of the Engine.
g. Wire Connections and Plugs.

DIAGNOSING THE MOTRONIC SYSTEM

NOTE: *The Motronic engine control system is an extremely complex, electrical control system. Most testing and repair on the system requires the use of very expensive, factory only, test equipment. The test procedures and explanations explained here, are to be used ONLY as a guide to basic system operation and testing. For any major problems, you should take the vehicle to an authorized factory shop for repair.*

Before suspecting the Motronic control system to be at fault, be sure that all other systems are in proper working order. Any engine system that would normally be checked in a vehicle not equipped with the Motronic control system, should be checked first.

If the Motronic control unit has been found to be causing the problem, determined which component or area is the most probable source of performance difficulty and begin testing there. Many component failures may be traced to faults in the wiring circuit. Before beginning other diagnostic procedures, check the appropriate circuit for breaks or shorts and be sure that all electrical connections are clean and tight.

Required Testing Equipment

In order to properly diagnose and repair any defects in the Motronic control system the fol-

lowing test equipment will be necessary. The BMW service test kit, Bosch L-Jetronic fuel injection test kit and service procedures, BMW test meter 22-13-100 and a standard volt/ohm meter. Failure to use the proper test equipment may result in unnecessary replacement of good components or damage to the system. These special tools are expensive and designed for factory authorized and trained technicians. They are listed here only to give you a reference to the tools used.

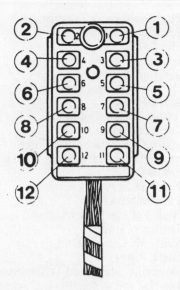

COLD START VALVE

Testing

COLD START VALVE DOES NOT OPEN

1. Remove valve, leaving fuel lines connected. Supply battery voltage to valve with jumper wire and be sure valve is properly grounded. Pull off relay 1. Apply batter voltage to connecter 87 in relay plug and check that fuel pump runs. Cold start valve should deliver fuel. If not, replace valve.

2. If valve functions properly, check power supply to valve: Pull plug off valve and connect voltmeter between wires of plug. Start engine. Meter should read battery voltage while cranking engine. If not, trace circuit and repair wiring.

3. Check thermo timer and replace if resistance values are not correct.

COLD START VALVE LEAKS

Check valve operation as in first cold start valve test. If valve operates properly (fuel is delivered), remove jumper wire to battery voltage and check that fuel delivery stops. If fuel is still delivered, or leaks, or seeps out, replace valve.

Multiple Pin Plug Connections:

No.	mm²	Color	Connection To
1	0.5	BLRT	Idle control valve A
2	0.5	GNGE	Terminal 15
3	1.0	GN	DME contr. unit (pin 8)
4	0.5	BR	Terminal 31
5	0.5	BLSW	Idle control valve B
6	0.5	WS	Temp.switch 45°C/113°F
7	0.5	BLBR	Conn. transm. P
8	0.5	BLGE	Conn. transm. N
9	0.5	BLWS	Air conditioner
10	0.5	BLGN	Air temp. switch
11	0.5	BRRT	DME contr. unit (pin 13)
12	0.5	BRBL	DME contr. unit (pin 2)

Wire Colors:

BL = Blue
BR = Brown
GE = Yellow
GN = Green
RT = Red
SW = Black
WS = White

Typical idle control valve control unit multiple pin plug connector

IDLE CONTROL VALVE

Testing

1. Valve should be open when vehicle is at rest (no voltage to valve). When voltage is applied to valve (engine on), valve should close. Remove 2 valve hoses and observe valve operation. If valve does not operate as described, replace valve.

2. If valve operates properly, pull of connector plug and connect voltmeter between the 2 wires in plug. Start engine and turn A/C **ON**. Voltmeter should read battery voltage. If it does not, see idle control diagnosis test.

COOLANT TEMPERATURE SENSOR

Testing

Check that sensor is properly installed and firmly seated. Check that cooling system is full. Bleed system. Check resistance between switch connections. If resistance is incorrect, replace sensor. If resistance is correct, trace sensor circuit and repair wiring.

COOLANT TEMPERATURE SWITCH

Testing

Switch must be tightly installed. Check that cooling system is full. Bleed system. Check resistance between switch contacts. Resistance below 106°F (41°C) should be zero. At higher temperatures, resistance should be infinite. If values are correct, trace circuit and repair wiring. If values are incorrect, replace switch.

THERMO TIMER

Testing

1. Check that timer is properly installed and firmly seated. Check radiator for correct coolant level. Bleed cooling system.

2. Disconnect timer and check resistance values between plug terminals G and W, G and ground, and W and ground. If values are correct, trace timer circuit and repair wiring. If values are incorrect, replace timer. The specifications are as follows:

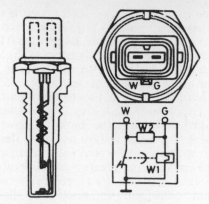

Typical thermo time switch schematic

a. G to ground is 40-70Ω.

b. G to W & W to ground is infinite when the temperature is above 60°F (15°C).

c. G to W & W to ground is zero when the temperature is below 60°F (15°C).

OXYGEN SENSOR

The oxygen sensor light on the dash will light the first time the mileage reaches 30,000. Replace the oxygen sensor and remove the light bulb from the dash. The bulb lights the first time only. However, the sensor must be changed every 30,000 miles.

1. Disconnect the oxygen sensor wire connector and remove the wires from the clip.

2. Pull off the sensor protective plate.

3. Unscrew the oxygen sensor.

4. Before installation, coat the threads of the new sensor with CRC copper paste.

5. Install the sensor unit.

6. Remove the call unit from the dash by unscrewing the bolt, push the unit to the right and remove the oxygen sensor display bulb. On some models, the bulb must be broken to remove it.

ALL 1985-88 Models

This heated type oxygen sensor needs to be replaced only at 50,000 mile intervals. The sensor is located on the engine exhaust pipe, just in front of the catalytic convertor.

To replace it, unscrew the protective plate and disconnect the plus in wire leading to the sensor. Then, unscrew the oxygen sensor. Replace in reverse order, coating the threads of the new sensor with an anti-seize compound.

NOTE: *A special tool (Special Service Indicator Resetter 62-1-100), only available through BMW sources, must be used to reset certain electronic type emission or oxygen sensor indicator light controls.*

Digital Motor Electronics (DME)
OPERATION

Some BMW models are equipped with the Bosch Digital Motor Electronics (DME). This system incorporates various data sensors that monitor the air intake volume, engine speed, crank-shaft position, coolant temperature, intake air temperature and throttle position. Signals from these sensors as well as the oxygen sensor signal and the start sensor signal are sent to the electronic control unit. The electronic control unit is a micro-computer and the brain of the DME system. It uses the information obtained from the data sensors in order to determine the correct amount of fuel and the optimum ignition timing.

The DME system also has the capability of switching from an open loop system to a closed loop system when the coolant temperature is above 113°F (45°C) and when the oxygen sensor temperature is above 480°F (249°C). The digital engine control system consists of 4 main sub systems; electronic control unit, fuel control, spark timing, and various data sensors.

SPARK CONTROL

The spark control system allows the electronic control unit to determine the exact instant that ignition is required to operate the vehicle properly, based upon the information provided from the data sensors. At the proper time the electronic control unit breaks the primary circuit of the ignition coil and this in turn produces a high voltage spark at the coil center tower. This voltage surge fires the spark plug at the proper time for most efficient combustion, eliminating the need for vacuum and/or centrifugal advance.

FUEL CONTROL

The vehicle is equipped with the Bosch air flow controlled fuel injection system. The system is electronically controlled by the electronic control unit, which is programmed to regulate fuel injection based upon data received from the various data sensors. The electronic control unit generates control signals for the fuel pump relay, auxiliary air valve, cold start injector coil and the cylinder port injector coils. These components control the curb idle speed and mixture, cold idle, air/fuel ratio and the fuel supply.

ELECTRONIC CONTROL UNIT

The electronic control unit monitors and controls all digital engine control functions. The electronic control unit consists of input and output devices, a central processing unit, a power supply and various memory banks. The input and output devices of the electronic control

unit convert electrical signals received by the data sensors and switches to the digital signals that are used by the central processing unit. The central processing unit receives digital signals that are used to perform all mathematical computations and logic functions necessary to deliver proper air/fuel mixture. The central processing unit is also responsible for calculating spark timing information. The main source of power that allows the electronic control unit to function is generated from the battery of the vehicle and transported through the ignition system. The memory bank of the electronic control unit is programmed with exact information that is used by the electronic control unit during the open loop mode. This data is also used when a sensor of other component fails, allowing the vehicle to be driven to a repair facility.

DATA SENSORS

The digital engine control system consists of 6 data sensors. They are an oxygen sensor, reference mark sensor, speed sensor, coolant temperature sensor, air intake temperature sensor and the air flow sensor. Each sensor supplies electronic data to the electronic control unit, which in turn computes spark timing and the correct amount of fuel that is necessary to maintain proper engine operation. The system also uses a throttle switch, a high altitude switch, an auxiliary air valve, a fuel pressure regulator and a pressure damper.

The oxygen sensor is mounted in line with the exhaust system directly in front of the catalytic converter. The oxygen sensor supplies voltage under one half volt when the fuel mixture is lean and up to one volt when the fuel mixture is rich. The sensor must be hot to function properly and to allow the electronic control unit to accept its power signals. The function of the oxygen sensor measures the amount of oxygen. Most vehicles are equipped with a special electrically heated oxygen sensor which aids the system so that it will begin to function earlier. The heated oxygen sensor has 3 wires, 2 for the heater element and one for the sensor signal. The heating function begins as soon as the ignition is turned on. The plugs from the sensor to the wiring harness are located near the flywheel sensor plugs.

NOTE: *No attempt should be made to measure oxygen sensor voltage output. Current drain on the voltmeter could permanently damage the sensor, shift sensor calibration range and/or render sensor unusable. Do not connect jumper wire, test leads or other electrical connectors to sensor. Use these devices only on the electronic control unit side of the harness after disconnecting sensor.*

The reference mark sensor is located on the engine crankcase flange. Its function is to detect crankshaft position in relation to top dead center and then to send the proper signal to the electronic control unit. It is triggered by a bolt which is fastened to the engine flywheel.

The speed sensor is mounted on an adjustable bracket along with the reference mark sensor. This sensor measures engine speed by counting the teeth on the starter ring gear. The speed sensor sends voltage surges to the electronic control unit for each tooth that passes.

The coolant temperature sensor is located on the intake manifold. Its function is to supply coolant temperature information to the electronic control unit. This generated data effects the air/fuel ratio, the spark timing and the engine temperature light.

The air intake temperature sensor is located in the air stream of the air flow meter. The main function of this sensor is to supply incoming air temperature information to the electronic control unit. The electronic control unit uses this data along with other important data to regulate the fuel injection rate.

The air flow sensor functions the same as the air intake temperature sensor, except that the air flow sensor incorporates a measuring flap that opens against the pressure of a spiral spring which is connected to a potentiometer. The potentiometer transmits an electrical signal which is determined by a position on the measuring flap to tell the electronic control unit the vehicle engine load.

A contact type throttle link switch, which is located on the throttle body, convert throttle position into electrical signals. These signals are used to inform the electronic control unit of throttle position. The potentiometer within the air flow meter prevents the loss of engine power during sudden acceleration or deceleration by signaling the electronic control unit for the necessary fuel requirements.

The high altitude switch is mounted under the dashboard on the driver's side of the vehicle. In altitudes higher than 3300 feet the switch closes, signaling the electronic control unit to lean out the fuel mixture so that the vehicle will continue to function properly.

The function of the auxiliary air valve is to provide additional air during engine warm up. The valve is located next to the throttle body. It consists of an electrically heated bi-metallic strip, a movable disc and an air by-pass channel. The heating coil on the bi-metallic strip is energized by the fuel pump relay.

Control of the auxiliary valve is governed by engine temperature. The air by-pass channel is open when the engine is cold and gradually closes as the engine warms up. At predetermined temperature the air by-pass channel in

the valve is blocked and additional air flow is cut off.

The fuel pressure regulator is located at the end of the fuel injection collection line. The function of the pressure regulator is to maintain constant fuel pressure to the fuel injectors.

The pressure damper is located at the inlet of the fuel injection collector tube. The pressure damper absorbs fuel pressure oscillation caused by the fuel injection cycle.

DIGITAL MOTOR ELECTRONICS (DME) CONTROL UNIT

Testing

1. Check the electrical power supply. Turn the ignition switch on and disconnect the DME control unit electrical connector.

2. With a suitable voltmeter, check connection 18 and 35 of the DME control unit. There should be approximately 12 volts.

3. Connections 5, 16, 17 and 19 are all connected in with the ground.

4. Pull off relay number 2 and jump terminals 87 and 30. This will supply voltage to the control unit.

5. If necessary, check activation or replace relay number 2. Turn on the ignition and check the voltage on terminals 85 and 86. There should be 12 volts present.

6. To be sure that the source of defect is only in the control unit, it is recommended to replace the DME unit for comparison.

7. In addition, carry out the various L-Jetronic test with a suitable BMW service test unit first, depending on the type of complaint.

ADAPTIVE PILOT CONTROL

Test

ALL MODELS EQUIPPED WITH DME

The adaptive pilot control has been integrated in the DME control unit since 1985.

1. Remove the adaptive pilot control screw from the exhaust manifold and mount exhaust tester 13-0-090 or equivalent with adapter 13-0-100 or equivalent into the exhaust manifold.

2. Connect the BMW service test unit or equivalent. Remove the anti-tamper lock.

3. Remove the air cleaner assembly and the air flow sensor.

4. Drill a hole in the anti-tamper lock with special tool 13-1-092 or equivalent.

5. Knock the tool with the anti-tamper lock out of the air flow sensor with suitable impact. Re-install the air flow sensor and air cleaner assembly.

6. Start the engine and let it run at idle to reach normal operating temperature. Pull off and plug the vacuum hose on the fuel pressure regulator.

7. The oxygen sensor must regulate the CO level back to nominal valve after a brief rise.

8. Tighten the air control screw in the air flow sensor completely with special tool 13-1-100 or equivalent for a richer mixture.

9. Run the engine at idle speed and the CO level will be regulated back to its nominal value.

10. Disconnect the oxygen sensor plug. The CO level will rise approximately 2.0% by volume. Also not the instantaneous actual value.

11. Stop the engine. Disconnect the negative battery so as to cancel the value stored in the memory of the DME control unit.

12. Start the engine. If the actual CO level value is considerably higher, the adaptive control pilot is working. Reconnect the vacuum hose.

13. Adjust the CO level to its nominal value (0.2-2.0%) with tool 13-1-100 or equivalent.

14. Connect the oxygen sensor plug and remove the exhaust tester. Remove the air cleaner and the air flow sensor (if necessary). Install a new anti-tamper lock in the air-flow sensor.

15. Reinstall the air flow sensor and air cleaner assembly. Remove all test equipment.

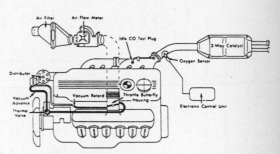

528i, 633CSi and 733i vacuum circuits—all models with catalytic converter

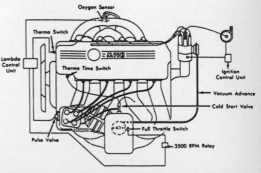

320i vacuum circuits—all models with catalytic converter

Fault descriptions (columns):

2.) Engine does not start or hard to start (coolant temp. < 35° C/95° F)
3.) Engine hard to start (coolant temp. > 35° C/95° F)
5.) "Injection" warning lamp on (check control)
7.) Insufficient power/smoke (no warning lamp)
9.) Insufficient power in cold running phase
10.) Unsatisfactory idling
12.) Erratic engine running/black smoke
13.) Foggy type smoke
15.) Engine power output not reached

Test Position	1	2	3	4	5	6	7	8	9	10	11	12	13	14	15	16	17	18	19	20
1 Heating system	X																			
2 Fuel feed/filter/shutoff valve		X	X						X	X					X					
3 Air in fuel system		X	X						X	X										
4 Accel. pedal/linkage/cable adjustments					X				X						X					
5																				
6																				
7 Injection begin - static/dynamic		X	X		X		X					X			X					
8 Injection pump internal pressure		X	X		X		X					X								
9 Fuel return / OUT bolt															X					
10 Injection pump		X	X				X		X	X		X								
11 Pressure valve/injection nozzles		X	X				X		X	X		X	X		X					
12																				
13 Power supply to control unit/relay VP-20												X	X							
14 Speed sensor					X							X								
15 Injection durration nozzle					X							X								
16 Coolant temperature sensor VP-20					X				X	X		X								
17 Timing valve in injection pump					X							X	X							
18 Control unit							X					X	X							
19																				
20 ALDA/altitude compensator							X		X						X					
21 EGR control/EGR valve							X		X											
22																				
23																				
24																				
25																				
26																				
27																				
28																				
29																				
30																				

Trobleshooting chart for the engine electrical and fuel injection systems for the 524 turbo diesel engine

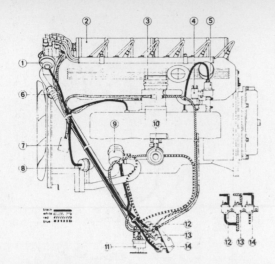

Hose Routing Plan

1 Distributor vacuum box
2 Reactor
3 Throttle housing
4 Throttle bypass valve
5 Vacuum control
6 Check valve
7 Active carbon filter
8 Pressure regulator
9 Blowoff valve
10 EGR valve
11 Pressure converter
12 Black electric valve
13 Red electric valve
14 Blue electric valve

733i vacuum circuits—California version

1 Distributor vacuum box
2 Reactor
3 Throttle housing
4 Throttle bypass valve
5 Vacuum control
6 Check valve
7 Active carbon filter
8 Pressure regulator
9 Blowoff valve
10 EGR valve
11 Pressure converter
12 Black electric switching valve
13 Red electric switching valve
14 Blue electric switching valve

633CSi vacuum circuits—California version

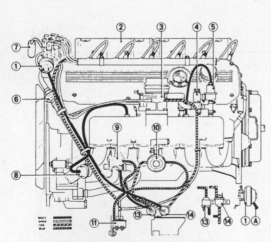

Hose (S) is omitted and connection (A) is plugged on
California and 49 State High Altitude models with an
automatic transmission.

1 Distributor vacuum box
2 Reactor
3 Throttle housing
4 Throttle bypass valve
5 Vacuum control
6 Check valve
7 Active carbon filter
8 Pressure regulator
9 Blowoff valve
10 EGR valve
11 Pressure converter
13 Red electric valve
14 Blue electric valve

633CSi vacuum circuits—49 states version

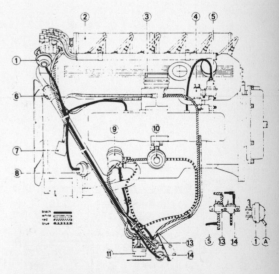

Hose (S) is omitted and connection (A) is
plugged on California and 49 State High
Altitude models with an automatic transmission.

Hose Routing Plan

1 Distributor vacuum box
2 Reactor
3 Throttle housing
4 Throttle bypass valve
5 Vacuum control
6 Check valve
7 Active carbon filter
8 Pressure regulator
9 Blowoff valve
10 EGR valve
11 Pressure converter
13 Red electric valve
14 Blue electric valve

733i vacuum circuits—49 states version

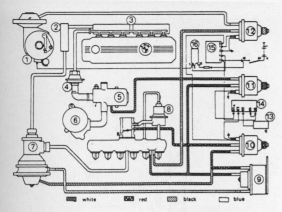

white　　red　　black　　blue

1.	Distributor	9.	Vacuum control valve
2.	Cyclone exhaust gas filter	10.	Electric control valve
3.	Reactor	11.	Electric control valve
4.	Check valve	12.	Electric control valve
5.	Blow-off valve	13.	Coolant temperature switch
6.	Air pump	14.	Control relay
7.	EGR valve	15.	Speed switch
8.	Vacuum control	16.	Ignition coil

528i vacuum circuits—Catalytic converter version

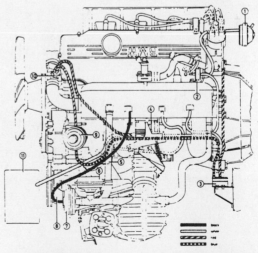

1	Distributor vacuum box	7	Carbon filter
2	Reactor	8	Booster blowoff valve
3	Throttle housing	9	EGR valve
4	Auxiliary air valve	10	Pressure converter
	(n/a to 1977 models)	11	Black electric switching valve
5	Vacuum control	12	Red electric switching valve
6	Check valve	13	White electric switching valve

630CSi vacuum circuits

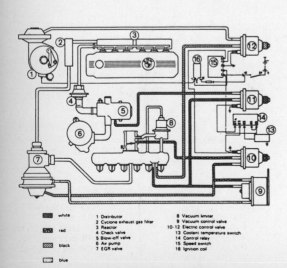

white
red
black
blue

1 Distributor
2 Cyclone exhaust gas filter
3 Reactor
4 Check valve
5 Blow-off valve
6 Air pump
7 EGR valve
8 Vacuum limiter
9 Vacuum control valve
10-12 Electric control valve
13 Coolant temperature switch
14 Control relay
15 Speed switch
16 Ignition coil

530i vacuum circuits—California version

1.	Vacuum box/distributor	7.	Vacuum control
2.	Thermo timing valve	8.	Air pump
3.	Pressure converter	9.	EGR valve
4.	Throttle housing	10.	Thermo valve
5.	Blowoff coasting valve	11.	Charcoal filter
6.	Bypass throttle valve		

320i vacuum circuits—all models with automatic transmission

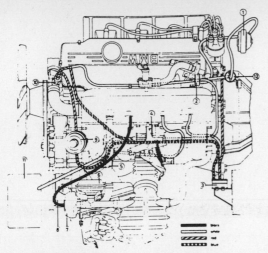

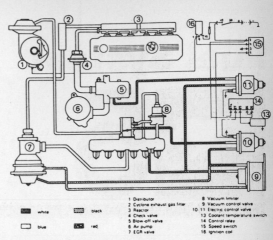

1. Distributor
2. Cyclone exhaust gas filter
3. Reactor
4. Check valve
5. Blow-off valve
6. Air pump
7. EGR valve

8. Vacuum limiter
9. Vacuum control valve
10-11. Electric control valve
13. Coolant temperature switch
14. Control relay
15. Speed switch
16. Ignition coil

530i vacuum circuits—49 states version

1. Vacuum box/distributor
2. Thermo timing valve
3. Pressure converter
4. Throttle housing
5. Blowoff coasting valve
6. Bypass throttle valve
7. Vacuum control
8. Air pump
9. EGR valve
10. Thermo valve
11. Charcoal filter
12. Electric switching valve

320i vacuum circuits—all models with manual transmission

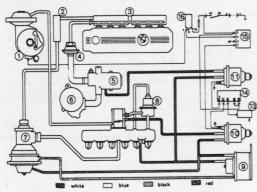

1. Distributor
2. Cyclone exhaust gas filter
3. Reactor
4. Check valve
5. Blow-off valve
6. Air pump
7. EGR valve
8. Vacuum control
9. Vacuum control valve
10. Electric control valve
11. Electric control valve
13. Coolant temperature switch
14. Control relay
15. Speed switch
16. Ignition coil

528i vacuum circuits—49 states version

Fuel System

GENERAL FUEL SYSTEM SERVICE

This chapter will cover fuel system component repair and replacement, as well as carburetor adjustment. The fuel injection systems discussed later in this chapter are very complex and require the use of specialized equipment for extensive repair.

SERVICE PRECAUTIONS

When working with any of the fuel system components it is essential to follow very strict safety precautions. Since fuel is so volatile, it is very dangerous to work around. The best protection against accidents when working with fuel, is to use common sense.

The following precautions should be adhered to very closely:

• Never work on the fuel system when the engine is hot. Fuel can be ignited by hot engine components, such as exhaust manifolds. Fuel in fuel injection systems is under pressure and when it is released it sprays in a very fine vapor that is easily ignited.

• Never work with fuel around an open flame. This includes cigarettes, matches, kerosene heaters and torches, etc.

• Always store fuel in an approved container. NOT in plastic milk jugs or similar containers. Always dispose of fuel in a safe manner.

• Fuel is not a cleaning solvent and should not be used as such. It will damage painted and unprotected surfaces.

• ALWAYS relieve the fuel system pressure before working on fuel injection systems as the fuel is under pressure, even when the engine is off.

• Use extreme care when handling fuel, it can cause burns to the skin in some cases, as well as severe damage to the eyes. Always keep out of the reach of children.

Fuel Tank

REMOVAL AND INSTALLATION

1600-2, 2002 and 2002A

1. Disconnect the negative battery cable.
2. Drain the fuel from the fuel tank.
CAUTION: *Never smoke when working around gasoline! Avoid all sources of sparks or ignition. Gasoline vapors are EXTREMELY volatile!*
3. Remove the fiber floor panel from the trunk. Disconnect the positive lead (2), lead (3), and ground wire (1).
4. Disconnect the fuel feed hose from the immersion tube transmitter.
5. Label and disconnect all evaporative control vapor lines.
6. Disconnect the hose clamp from the bottom of the filler neck and push up on the rubber sleeve.
7. Remove the tank retaining bolts and carefully lift out the tank.
8. Reverse the above procedure to install.

2002tii

1. Disconnect the negative battery cable.
2. Drain the fuel from the tank.

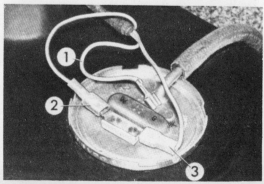

Disconnecting fuel tank leads

2002tii fuel tank hose connections

To remove the 320i fuel tank, disconnect the suction line (1), return line (2), plug (3), and vent line (4)

CAUTION: *Never smoke when working around gasoline! Avoid all sources of sparks or ignition. Gasoline vapors are EXTREMELY volatile!*

3. Remove the fiber floor panels from the trunk. Disconnect the leads from the fuel gauge sending unit. Disconnect the fuel feed (2) and return (3) lines from the suction unit.

4. Label and disconnect all evaporative control vapor lines.

5. Disconnect the hose clamp from the filler neck.

6. Remove the tank retaining bolts, separate the filler neck sections and carefully lift out the tank.

7. Reverse the above procedure to install.

2500, 2800, Bavaria, 3000 and 3.0

1. Drain the fuel and disconnect the negative battery terminal.

CAUTION: *Never smoke when working around gasoline! Avoid all sources of sparks or ignition. Gasoline vapors are EXTREMELY volatile!*

2. Remove the luggage compartment mat and the lining which rests against the right side quarter panel.

3. Remove the fuel hose from the tank sending unit. Pull the 3 electrical connections off, noting that the ground wire (Brown) goes to the rounded connector, the Brown/Yellow wire to the **G** connector, and the Brown Black wire to the **W** connector.

4. Remove the filler cap and slip he rubber ring off the filler neck.

5. Detach the tank from the luggage compartment floor, tilt upwards at the front, and remove it.

6. Install in reverse order. Before putting the tank into position, check the foam gasket supporting the tank and replace it if necessary. Make sure to install the sealing ring onto the filler neck before the tank goes into final position.

318i and 320i

1. Disconnect the battery negative terminal and drain the fuel.

CAUTION: *Never smoke when working around gasoline! Avoid all sources of sparks or ignition. Gasoline vapors are EXTREMELY volatile!*

2. Remove the rear seat. Remove the black guard plate to gain access to fuel lines and the sending unit.

3. Disconnect the electrical connector and the suction and return lines at the sending unit. Disconnect the vent line at the tank.

4. Disconnect the filler neck at the lower end.

5. Remove the mounting screw and remove the guard from behind the connecting hose (which goes to the left side tank).

6. Disconnect the connecting hose. Then, remove the 2 mounting screws on the inboard side of the tank at the bottom, and lower the tank out of the car.

7. For the tank on the left side, perform Steps 5 and 6 in a similar way, but before lifting the tank out of the car, disconnect the small vent line from the top of the tank. If this line should have to be replaced, limit the length of the replacement hose section to 600mm.

8. Install the fuel tanks in reverse order.

524td

1. Open the tank cap, lift off the rubber cover and disconnect the 3 vent hoses. Drain the fuel.

CAUTION: *Never smoke when working around gasoline! Avoid all sources of sparks or ignition. Gasoline vapors are EXTREMELY volatile!*

2. Remove the trunk mat and unscrew the tank cover.

3. Disconnect the 2 electrical plugs and the 2 hoses.

4. Unscrew the bolts and disconnect the exhaust suspension parts on the rear axle carrier. Position the exhaust assembly out of the way and secure it with wire.

5. Unscrew the retaining strap mounting bolt, remove the liner and then remove the strap.

6. Unscrew the mounting bolt and remove the fuel tank.

7. Installation is in the reverse order of removal.

All 5 Series

1. Disconnect the battery ground cable. Siphon the fuel out of the tank.

2. Fold the floor mat out of the way for access. Remove the 3 screws and remove the round black cover which permit access to the sending unit

3. Disconnect the wires at the sending unit (Brown-ground, Brown/Yellow -G, Brown/Black-W). Detach the unclamped vent line.

4. Detach the feed and return lines at the filter and return pipe (both under the car).

5. Detach the front and rear mounting bushings of the rear-most muffler, and then remove the rear bracket from the body.

6. Loosen the tank mounting bolts at the front and right sides, remove the filler cap, and remove the tank.

7. Install in reverse order.

All 6 Series

1. Disconnect the negative battery cable, and siphon fuel from the tank. Lift the rear compartment rug out of the way. Remove the round access cover.

2. Disconnect the electrical plug and the 2 fuel lines from the top of the sending unit.

3. Remove the fuel tank filler cap and the rubber seal which surrounds the filler neck. Then, disconnect the 4 vent hoses.

4. Remove the bushings from the rear muffler at front and rear, and then remove the mounting bracket at the rear.

5. Bend the tabs down, remove the mounting bolts, and remove the heat shield. Remove the nut and bolt, and remove the stone guard.

6. Remove the 3 mounting bolts from the right side panel, and lower the tank, right side

Remove the arrowed bolts and remove the rear mounting bracket—600 series cars

first, and then remove it, being careful to avoid pinching any of the hoses.

7. Install in reverse order, making sure the rubber bumpers against which the tank is held by the mounting straps are in good shape, or replace them, as necessary.

All 7 Series

1. Unscrew the filler cap and siphon out the tank.

2. Disconnect the negative battery cable. Fold the rug in the rear compartment out of the way, and remove the round access panel.

3. Disconnect inlet and outlet hoses at the sending unit.

4. Disconnect the sending unit electrical connector at the plug, located near the wiring harness in the trunk.

5. Remove the mounting bolts from the straps and lower the tank slightly and support it. Pull off the (4) vent hoses. Then, lower the tank out of the car.

6. Install in reverse order, making sure the rubber bumpers against which the tank is held by the mounting straps are in good shape, or replace them, as necessary.

CARBURETED FUEL SYSTEM

Mechanical Fuel Pump

REMOVAL AND INSTALLATION

1. Remove the air cleaner. Disconnect and plug the 2 fuel lines.

2. Remove the 2 retaining nuts and pull the pump off the cylinder head. Pull the insulator block off and the pushrod out.

3. If there is much evidence of wear, check the length of the pushrod. It should be 88mm on 4-cylinder cars and 119.5mm on 6-cylinder cars.

4. Install in reverse order. Do not use sealer on the insulator block, as this will change the effective length of the pushrod.

TESTING

Insert a tee in the fuel pump discharge line where it enters the carburetor. Connect a gauge rated at about 10 psi to the open end of the tee. Run the engine at 4,000 rpm. The pressure should be 2.99-3.56 psi.

Carburetor

APPLICATIONS

The 1970-71 1600-2 uses a single barrel downdraft Solex 38 PDSI carburetor. This unit has a manual choke. The 1970-71 2002, up to chassis no. 2 583 405 uses a Solex 40 PDSI,

which also uses a manual choke. The 1970-71 2002A (up to chassis no. 2 532 752 uses a Solex 40PDSIT unit with a water heated automatic choke.

Later 2002 and 2002A models use a Solex 32/32 DIDTA carburetor with the water heated choke, to which was added an electric heating element in 1974. Later models also incorporate a float bowl return valve to reduce vapor lock. The 2002ti uses 2 separate Solex 40 PHH carburetors, which have 2 progressively activated barrels each.

Removing mechanical fuel pump

The 2500, 2800, Bavaria, 3000 and 3.0 use 2 Zenith 35.40 2 stage carburetors.

REMOVAL AND INSTALLATION
1600-2 and 2002 w/Manual Choke

1. Remove the air cleaner assembly, marking the vacuum lines, breather hoses, and air intake hose for reassembly.
2. Disconnect the fuel feed line at the carburetor.
3. Loosen the clamp screw (1) and clamp (2), and disconnect the choke cable.
4. Lever off the clamp spring connecting the accelerator rod to the carburetor and disconnect the throttle linkage.
5. Label and remove the vacuum line(s) from the carburetor.
6. Remove the 2 carburetor attaching nuts, and lift the carburetor from the manifold. Remove the flange gaskets and carburetor spacer, taking note of their placement.
7. Install the carburetor to the manifold using new gaskets and installing the spacer.
8. Reconnect all fuel and vacuum lines. Install the air cleaner and breather hose. Connect the throttle linkage.
9. Adjust the choke cable in the following

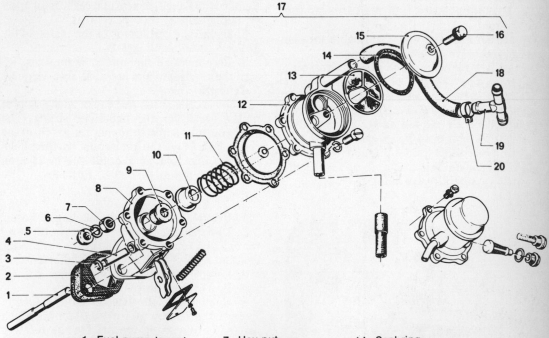

1. Fuel pump tappet
2. Insulating flange with gaskets
3. Circlip for axle
4. Axle
5. Insulating bushing
6. Lockwasher
7. Hex nut
8. Pump lower part
9. Collar
10. Hold-down
11. Diaphragm spring
12. Pump upper part
13. Fuel strainer
14. Seal ring
15. Cap
16. Screw with gasket
17. Fuel pump
18. Fuel hose
19. Distributing piece
20. Hose clamp

Exploded view of a typical mechanical fuel pump

Proper choke cable installation—1600, 2002

Automatic choke adjustment

manner: push the choke knob on the dash into the bottom notch. Press the fast idle cam (3) against its stop so that the outer choke cable projects 15mm (distance A) in front of the cable clamp, and tighten the clamp screw (2) in this position. Adjust the idle speed. Tighten the attaching nuts to 7.23-10.12 ft. lbs.

2002-A and 2002 w/Automatic Choke

1. Remove the air cleaner assembly, marking the vacuum lines, breather hoses, and air intake hose for reassembly.
2. Disconnect the fuel feed line at the carburetor.
3. Disconnect the electrical cable for the thermostat valve. Drain the radiator.
   CAUTION: *When draining the coolant, keep in mind that cats and dogs are attracted by the ethylene glycol antifreeze, and are quite likely to drink any that is left in an uncovered container or in puddles on the ground. This will prove fatal in sufficient quantity. Always drain the coolant into a sealable container. Coolant should be reused unless it is contaminated or several years old.*

Disconnecting throttle linkage—Solex 40 PDSIT

4. Remove the 3 retaining screws and lift the choke mechanism cover from the carburetor body.
5. Remove the safety clip (1) from the ball socket at the throttle linkage connection to the carburetor. Press the throttle and down-shift rotary shaft downward and rearward and disconnect the throttle linkage.
6. Label and remove the vacuum line(s) from the carburetor.
7. Remove the 2 carburetor attaching nuts, and lift off the carburetor from the manifold. Remove the flange gaskets and carburetor spacer, taking note of their placement.
8. Install the carburetor to the manifold using new gaskets and installing the spacer.
9. Reconnect all fuel and vacuum lines. Install the air cleaner and breather hose. Connect the throttle linkage.
10. Insert the automatic choke engaging arm in the eyelet for the bimetallic spring. The choke must be adjusted so that the notch on the choke cover and the projection on the choke housing align. Adjust the idle speed. Tighten the attaching nuts to 7.23-10.12 ft. lbs.

2002Ti

1. Remove the air cleaner, labeling all hoses.
2. Disconnect the choke cable at the carburetor end and remove the cable at the carburetor end and remove the cable from the bracket.
3. Loosen the dipstick retainer clip.
4. Pull off fuel hoses.
5. Remove the throttle tensioning spring. Remove the 2 carburetor mounting nuts which fasten the mounting bracket for the rotating shaft, and pull the bracket off the manifold studs. Disconnect the rod from the rotating shaft.
6. Remove the remaining mounting nuts and remove the carburetors. Remove all gaskets.
7. To install, reverse the removal procedure, bearing the following points in mind:

On the 2002ti, make sure the torsion spring is in the proper position. See text

Dimension "A" should be 1.57 in. on Zenith 35/40 units

a. Before installing the carburetor on the right side, position the prong on the choke butterfly lever so it engages with the hole in the linkage of the left hand carburetor by rotating the linkage on the left hand carburetor as necessary.

b. Make sure the torsion spring on the carburetor synchronizing portion of the throttle mechanism is in the proper position.

c. Push the choke knob in to the first notch. Open the choke mechanism on the carburetors all the way. Then, clamp the choke cable snugly in place, making sure the cable sheath does not protrude more than 15mm.

2500, 2800, Bavaria, 3000 and 3.0

1. Drain the radiator, and remove the air cleaner.

CAUTION: *When draining the coolant, keep in mind that cats and dogs are attracted by the ethylene glycol antifreeze, and are quite likely to drink any that is left in an uncovered container or in puddles on the ground. This will prove fatal in sufficient quantity. Always drain the coolant into a sealable container. Coolant should be reused unless it is contaminated or several years old.*

2. Disconnect fuel, vacuum, and water lines.

3. Disconnect and remove the choke cables. Disconnect the fuel return hose at the carburetor, on cars so equipped.

4. Disconnect throttle rod at the carburetor. Remove the carburetor mounting nuts from the studs, and remove the carburetor.

5. Install in reverse order, noting that the flange gasket must be in position so the smaller opening is situated toward the cylinder head, and the coated side faces down. Synchronize the carburetors and bleed the cooling system when filling it.

THROTTLE LINKAGE ADJUSTMENT

Throttle linkage adjustments are generally not necessary except that, if synchronization of the Zenith 35/40 units proves difficult, the adjustable link connecting the 2 throttle linkages should be adjusted to a center-to-center length of 40mm.

FLOAT LEVEL ADJUSTMENT

38 PDSI, 40 PDSI and 40 PDSIT

1. Run the engine until it reaches operating temperature. Shut the engine off.

2. Disconnect the fuel feed line from the carburetor.

3. Remove the carburetor top cover and seal.

4. Using a depth gauge, the level of fuel in the bowl must be 18-19mm.

5. Adjust, as necessary, by varying the number of or thickness of the seals underneath the float needle valve.

Solex 38 PDSI and Solex 32/32 DIDTA

The float level cannot be adjusted without the carburetor completely assembled, and, therefore, this adjustment cannot be accomplished without a special sightglass and equipment for adjusting the amount of fuel in the bowl.Zenith 35/40

The float level is not adjustable, but depends upon the condition of various parts only, especially the gasket used under the float valve, which must be 1mm thick.

FAST IDLE ADJUSTMENT

2002,2002A w/Automatic Choke

1. Start the engine and bring it to operating temperature.

2. Operate the accelerator rod until the choke plate can be closed by hand. Then, close

Adjusting the fast idle (40 PDSIT)

the choke plate until only 0.25 in (6.5 mm) clearance exists between the plate and the carburetor air horn. This will bring the stop lever into the fast idling speed position. Once this clearance is set, do not disturb the accelerator rod.

3. Using the adjusting nuts (1 and 2) at the choke connector rod, adjust the fast idle speed to 2100 rpm. To increase engine speed, increase the rod length. To decrease engine speed, decrease rod length.

2500, 2800, Bavaria, 3000 and 3.0

1. Make sure the engine is hot, the air cleaner is removed, the carburetors are synchronized, and that the idle speed is 900 rpm.

2. Where the distributor has 2 hoses going to the diaphragm (both advance and retard), remove the retard hose (connected on the distributor side of the diaphragm).

3. Switch off the engine and disconnect the choke rod at the rear carburetor.

4. Get a drill bit with 2.4mm diameter and insert it between the lower edge of the choke

butterfly and the throttle bore. Open the throttle slightly and then close the choke to touch the drill, and pin it against the throttle bore. This will set the fast idle mechanism on the second step. Then, release the choke.

5. Without touching the throttle linkage, start the engine. If the rpm is not 1,400, note exactly how far off and which direction from the speed.

6. If the speed must be readjusted, stop the engine, open the throttle all the way, and adjust the screw on the choke housing inward to speed the idle up or outward to slow it down, about 1 turn for each 300 rpm.

7. Repeat 4-6 until idle speed is at 1,400.

8. Open the throttle to open the rear choke. Then repeat Steps 4-6 for the front carburetor.

9. Finally, repeat Step 4 for both front and rear chokes. Both chokes must be set to the proper position while the throttle is held open. Then, both chokes must be held there as the throttle is released. Remove the drills, release the chokes, and start the engine. RPM must be 1,800-2000.

AUTOMATIC CHOKE AND CHOKE UNLOADER ADJUSTMENT

2002 and 2002A

1. Be sure the choke valve shaft will rotate freely in its bore and that the choke cap aligning notch is aligned with the lug on the choke valve housing.

2. Depress the accelerator to allow the choke valve to close under spring tension.

NOTE: *The choke valve should close if the ambient temperature is below 68°F. (20°C).*

3. If adjustment is needed, remove the choke cap with the water hoses attached.

4. Depress the choke rod (the vertical shaft inside choke housing) downward to its stop and

6,5mm ø

Checking pulldown clearance

Pressing choke rod down to stop—2002

Adjusting clearance "1"

check the choke valve clearance between the choke valve and the throttle bore. The gap should be 6.3-6.8mm.

5. An adjusting screw and locknut (1) is located under the choke housing and controls the height of the choke rod. Loosen the locknut and move the screw (arrowed) in or out to change the choke valve gap.

6. Reposition of the choke cover on the carburetor. Be sure the choke arm engages the coil spring loop in the choke cover. Align the notch on the cover with the lug on the choke housing.

7. Connect the heating coil wire terminal to the housing.

8. Adjust the fast idle speed to 2000-2200 rpm with the engine at normal operating temperature.

9. With the choke valve set at a gap of 6mm, adjust the choke connector rod nuts to set the fast idle. Shorten the rod to reduce the rpm.

2500, 2800, Bavaria, 3000 and 3.0

1. Remove the choke cover, leaving water hoses attached.

2. Open the throttle and close the choke butterfly.

3. Loosen the lockscrew on the pivot unit at the top of the choke rod. Make sure the adjusting screw inside the choke housing points to the high step of the actuating cam.

4. Raise and lower the rod until the gap between the lower end of the rod until the gap between the lower end of the rod and the actuating cam is 1.5mm. Then, tighten the lockscrew and press the clamping ring on the rod up against the pivot unit.

5. Then, push the rod upward and push the actuating cam against the rod.

6. Check the gap between the lower edge of the choke butterfly and the throttle bore. It should be 3mm. If not, loosen the locknut and turn the adjusting screw on the choke unloader

until the dimension is correct. Tighten the locknut and apply sealer.

ACCELERATOR PUMP ADJUSTMENT

A special metering cup is used to measure accelerator pump stroke and performance. If this is not available, the pump stroke (and fuel delivery) can be adjusted: on the 2002 Series by adjusting the position of the locknuts on the pump lever; on the 2500, 2800, Bavaria, 3000 and 3.0 Series by bending the plunger lever (located under the float bowl cover) at the pivot point. Make sure, before making adjustment, that idle mixture and ignition timing are correct, that the carburetor is clean, and that the plunger and check valves in the accelerator pump system are in good condition.

IDLE STOP SOLENOID

The idle stop solenoid prevents any tendency for the engine to run on after the ignition is switched off. To check operation, pull off the electrical connector when the engine is running. The solenoid is working properly if the engine shuts down. When the connector is replaced, a slight click should be heard. To replace the idle stop solenoid, remove the connector and unscrew the valve assembly from the carburetor. When installing the new solenoid valve, make sure there is a good seal at the taper.

WARNING: *Tightening torque for the solenoid is only 1.8 ft. lbs.*

CARBURETOR DASHPOT

Operation

A dashpot is used to slow the carburetor throttle return while the vehicle engine is above 1800 rpm on carbureted engines. An eletrically

On the 2800 and 3.0, adjust the accelerator pump at the arrowed bending point. A special metering cup ("7040") is available for checking pump performance

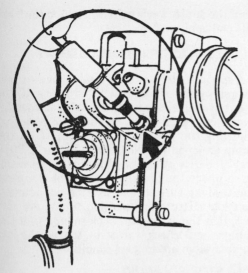

Replacing the idle stop solenoid

Magnetic valve (1), connector (2) and speed sensitive relay (3)

| 1. Vacuum line | 2. Plunger | 3. Dashpot |

Dashpot

controlled set of relays and magnetic switches are used to direct engine speeds under a certain rpm.

Testing

Operate the engine at 2500 rpm and slowly decrease the speed to approximately 1800 rpm. The dashpot plunger should contact the throttle linkage at the 1700-1900 rpm mark (2002-1500 minimum). Adjust the dashpot plunger if necessary.

The plunger must be free of the throttle linkage under 1700 rpm minimum (2002-1550 minimum) when the engine vacuum is directed through the magnetic valve to the dashpot.

If no vacuum is present at the dashpot hose under 1700 rpm, check the engine speed relay connector. Remove the terminal end from the magnetic valve and increase the engine speed to 2000 rpm. If voltage is present at the terminal, the magnetic valve to the dashpot.

If no vacuum is present at the dashpot hose

under 1700 rpm, check the engine speed relay connector. Remove the terminal end from the magnetic valve and increase the engine speed to 2000 rpm. If voltage is present at the terminal, the magnetic switch is defective and if no voltage is present, the speed sensitive relay must be replaced.

COMPENSATION SPEED DASHPOT

Adjustment

1. Pull off vacuum hose (6).
2. Increase engine speed to approximately 2000 rpm, then slowly decrease.
3. At 1800 ± 100 rpm, dashpot plunger (7) must touch carburetor linkage (8).
4. Correct if necessary by turning dashpot (9) after loosening locknut (10).
5. Reconnect vacuum hose.

NOTE: *If the engine speed is lower then 1700 rpm, but the dashpot plunger does not free the carburetor linkage, check that there is vacuum to the dashpot. If vacuum is present in the signal line, the dashpot must be replaced.*

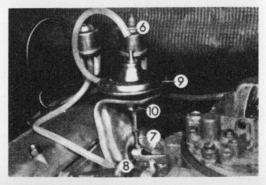

Adjusting the dashpot

Carburetor Overhaul

REPAIR KITS

Carburetor repair kits are recommended for each overhaul. Kits contain a complete set of gaskets and new parts to replace those that generally deteriorate most rapidly. Not substituting all of the new parts supplied in the kits can result in poor performance later.

Zenith/Solex carburetor repair kits are of their basic types-repair, Vit, and gasket. The following summarizes the parts in each type:

VIT KITS
- All gaskets
- Float needle
- Volume control screw
- All diaphragms
- Spring

REPAIR KITS
- All jets and gaskets
- All diaphragms

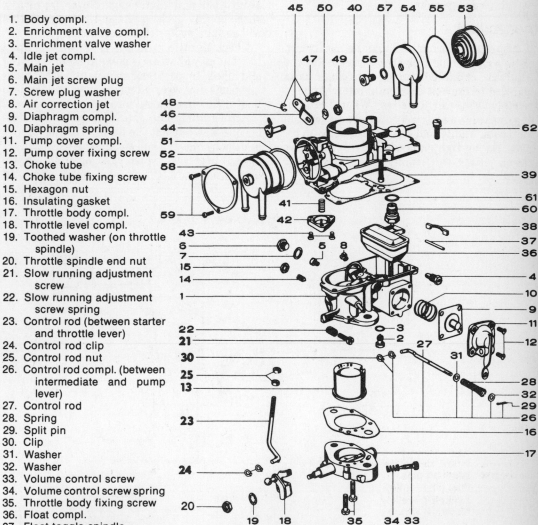

1. Body compl.
2. Enrichment valve compl.
3. Enrichment valve washer
4. Idle jet compl.
5. Main jet
6. Main jet screw plug
7. Screw plug washer
8. Air correction jet
9. Diaphragm compl.
10. Diaphragm spring
11. Pump cover compl.
12. Pump cover fixing screw
13. Choke tube
14. Choke tube fixing screw
15. Hexagon nut
16. Insulating gasket
17. Throttle body compl.
18. Throttle level compl.
19. Toothed washer (on throttle spindle)
20. Throttle spindle end nut
21. Slow running adjustment screw
22. Slow running adjustment screw spring
23. Control rod (between starter and throttle lever)
24. Control rod clip
25. Control rod nut
26. Control rod compl. (between intermediate and pump lever)
27. Control rod
28. Spring
29. Split pin
30. Clip
31. Washer
32. Washer
33. Volume control screw
34. Volume control screw spring
35. Throttle body fixing screw
36. Float compl.
37. Float toggle spindle
38. Float toggle spindle holder
39. Float chamber cover gasket
40. Float chamber cover compl.
41. Spring (for starter diaphragm)
42. Valve cover (for starter diaphragm)
43. Valve cover fixing screw
44. Spindle with abutment lever compl.

45. Strangler lever compl.
46. Strangler lever
47. Clamp roller
48. Clip
49. Hexagon nut
50. Clip
51. Insulating washer
52. Starter cover compl.
53. Starter cover compl.
54. Water connection
55. O-ring
56. Cylindrical screw (with internal hexagon)
57. Washer
58. Retaining screw
59. Fixing screw (for retaining ring)
60. Float needle valve compl.
61. Float needle valve washer
62. Assembly screw

Exploded view of Solex 40 PDSIT carburetor

- Float needle valve
- Volume control screw
- Spring for pump diaphragm
- Spring for pump diaphragm
- Pump ball valve
- Main jet carrier
- Float
- Complete intermediate rod
- Intermediate pump lever
- Complete injector tube
- Some cover holddown screws and washers

GASKET KITS
- All needed gaskets

PROCEDURES

Carburetor overhaul should be performed only in a clean, dust-free area. Disassemble the carburetor carefully keeping look-alike parts separated to prevent accidental interchange at assembly. Note all jet sizes. When reassembling, make sure all screws and jets are tight in their seats. Tighten all screws gradually, in rotation. Do not tighten needle valves into seats. Uneven jetting will result. Use a new flange gasket.

Wash carburetor parts—except diaphragm and electric choke units, in a carburetor cleaner, rinse in solvent, and blow dry with compressed air.

Carburetors have numerous small passages that can be fouled by carbon and gummy deposits. Soak metal parts in carburetor solvent until thoroughly clean. The solvent will weaken or destroy cork, plastic, and leather components. These parts should be wiped with a clean, lint-free cloth. Clean all fuel channels in float bowl and cover. Clean jets and valves separately to avoid accidental interchange. Never use wire or sharp objects to clean jets and passages as this will seriously alter their calibration.

Check throttle valve shafts for wear or scoring that may allow air leakage affecting starting and idling. Inspect float spindle and other moving parts for wear. Replace if worn. Replace float if fuel has leaked into it.

Accelerator pump check valves should pass air one way but not the other. Test for proper seating by blowing and sucking on valve and replace if necessary. Wash valve again to remove breath moisture. Check bowl cover with with

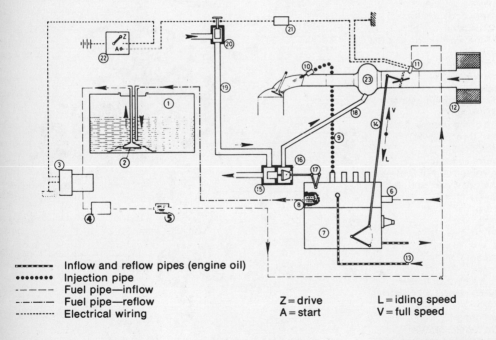

-----------	Inflow and reflow pipes (engine oil)	
•••••••	Injection pipe	
— — —	Fuel pipe—inflow	
—·—·—	Fuel pipe—reflow	
----------	Electrical wiring	

Z = drive   L = idling speed
A = start   V = full speed

1. Fuel tank with induction unit
2. Fine-mesh filter
3. Fuel pump
4. Pressure regulator
5. Main fuel filter
6. Fine-mesh filter—fuel intake
7. Injection pump
8. Fuel return line with pressure valve
9. Injection pipe
10. Injection valve
11. Starter valve
12. Air cleaner
13. Engine oil line
14. Adjustment of engine idling and top speed (by accelerator pedal)
15. Warmup runner with expansion element
16. Air adjustment cone
17. Lever for eccentric shaft
18. Intake pipe for additional air
19. Coolant line
20. Temperature switch
21. Retard Switch
22. Ignition switch
23. Plenum chamber

Schematic diagram of the Kugelfischer fuel injection system used on the 2002tii

straight edge for warped surfaces. Closely inspect valves and seats valves and seats for wear and damage.

Rebuild kits contain complete, step by step disassembly and assembly instructions, for each specific type of carburetor, so they are not included here.

FUEL INJECTION GENERAL SERVICE

NOTE: *This book contains testing and service procedures for your vehicles fuel injection system. More comprehensive testing and diagnosis procedures may be found in CHILTON'S GUIDE TO FUEL INJECTION AND FEEDBACK CARBURETORS, available at your local retailer.*

System Operation

BMW 2002tii models use the Kugelfischer mechanical fuel injection system, in which fuel and air are inducted separately through the injection pump and the throttle manifold butter-

fly. Fuel and air are mixed in the intake manifold. Fuel is injected into the intake manifold behind the open intake valve under high pressure.

The electric fuel pump pumps fuel from the tank through a fine-mesh filter in the tank and a filter in the fuel line. The fuel flows through the expansion container, the main fuel fuel flows through the expansion container, the main fuel filter, and into the injector pump at 21.7-36.2 psi. Excess fuel and any air bubbles are routed back to the tank via a return line. This ensures that the fuel is always kept cool and free of bubbles.

The injection pump camshaft is belt-driven from the engine crankshaft. 4 pumping pistons, operating in firing order sequence, inject the required amount of fuel. The amount of fuel injected depends on engine load and speed.

Fuel injection volume is regulated by engine load. The accelerator pedal is connected with throttle butterfly and the lever on the injection pump. When the pedal is depressed, the throttle butterfly moves and the stroke length of the pump piston is governed by the regulating cam, depending on throttle opening. Fuel injection

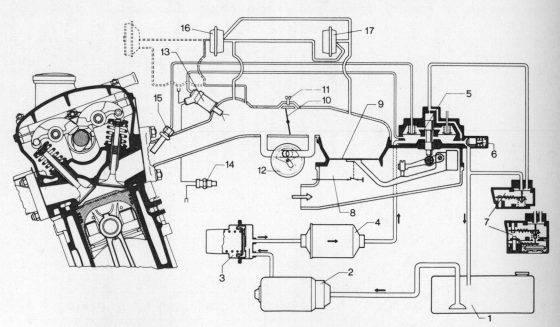

1. Fuel tank with pre-fuel pump	9. Sensor plate
2. Fuel delivery pump	10. Throttle butterfly
3. Fuel accumulator	11. Idle adjustment screw
4. Fuel filter	12. Aux. air device
5. Fuel distributor	13. Electric starting valve
6. System pressure regulator and topping point valve	14. Thermo-time switch
	15. Injectors
7. Warming-up regulator	16. Vacuum limiter
8. Airflow meter	17. Start air valve

Schematic diagram of the K–Jetronic fuel injection system used on the 320i

Troubleshooting—L-Jetronic

Cause	Correction	Engine cranks but does not start	Engine starts but then dies	Rough or unstable idle	Idle speed incorrect	CO value incorrect	Erratic running	Engine misses when driving	Fuel consumption too high	No maximum power
Defect in ignition system	Check battery, distributor, plugs, coil and timing	●	●	●		●	●	●		●
Mechanical defect in engine	Check compression, valve adj. and oil pressure	●	●	●		●	●	●		●
Leaks in air intake system (false air)	Check all hoses and connections; eliminate leaks	●	●	●		●	●			●
Blockage in fuel system	Check fuel tank, filter and lines for free flow	●	●	●						●
Relay defective; wire to injector open	Test relay; check wiring harness	●								
Fuel pump not operating	Check pump fuse, pump relay and pump	●	●							
Fuel system pressure incorrect	Check pressure regulator	●	●	●		●		●		●
Cold start valve not operating	Test for spray; check wiring and thermo-time switch	●								
Cold start valve leaking	Check valve for leakage	●	●	●			●			
Thermo-time switch defective	Test for resistance readings vs. temperature	●								
Auxiliary air valve not operating correctly	Must be open with cold engine; closed with warm	●	●	●						
Temperature sensor defective	Test for 2-3 kΩ at 68° F.	●	●	●			●			
Air flow meter defective	Check pump contacts; test flap for free movement	●	●				●	●		
Throttle butterfly does not completely close or open	Readjust throttle stops			●	●					
Throttle valve switch defective	Check with ohmmeter and adjust									
Idle speed incorrectly adjusted	Adjust idle speed with bypass screw			●	●					
Defective injection valve	Check valves individually for spray	●	●	●		●				●
CO concentration incorrectly set	Readjust CO with screw on air flow meter			●		●			●	
Loose connection in wiring harness or system ground	Check and clean all connections	●	●	●	●	●			●	
Control unit defective	Use known good unit to confirm defect	●	●	●		●			●	

Symptom key:

1. Engine does not start in cold condition
2. Engine starts, but fails to keep running (engine cold)
3. Engine does not start in warm condition
4. Engine starts poorly in cold condition
5. Engine starts poorly in warm condition
6. Irregular idling during warm-up
7. Engine starts, but fails to keep running (engine warm)
8. Idle deviates from specification
9. Engine backfires into intake manifold
10. Hesitation during acceleration
11. Engine misfires
12. Poor performance — reduced power
13. Fuel consumption too high
14. Idle CO level deviates from specification
15. Pinging during acceleration
16. HC and/or NOx emissions too high

Possible Cause	1	2	3	4	5	6	7	8	9	10	11	12	13	14	15	16	What to do . . . .
No fuel in the tank	X		X														Refill fuel (unleaded 87 AKI at least)
Electric fuel pump not operating	X		X														Check current / replace fuel pump(s)
Fuel filter/fine mesh filter clogged	X		X	X	X					X	X	X					Replace fuel filter/clean fine mesh filter
Fuel return line kinked or pinched				X	X					X		X					Check routing of fuel lines
Fuel system pressure too high						X	X	X					X	X			Check pressure regulator
Fuel system pressure too low	X			X	X					X		X					Check pressure regulator
Control pressure too high	X			X				X		X							Check warm-up regulator
Control pressure too low						X		X					X	X		X	Check/replace warm-up regulator
Fuel injection lines clogged								X		X	X	X					Replace injection lines
Fuel injection valves leaking								X	X		X			X		X	Replace injection valves
Fuel injection valves have reduced fuel flow					X					X	X	X					Replace injection valves
Cold start valve does not inject	X	X		X													Check cold start valve and valve control
Cold start valve leaking			X				X	X						X			Replace cold start valve
Thermo time switch defective	X			X													Replace thermo time switch
Temperature sensor "engine" defective/unactive	X		X	X	X			X						X		X	Reconnect/replace temperature sensor
Throttle valve not correctly adjusted						X		X									Readjust throttle valve
Auxiliary air valve does not close								X						X		X	Check/replace auxiliary valve
Intake system not tight, airflow meter								X						X		X	Check/reseal intake system

Fuel system troubleshooting—318i and 320i

volume is also regulated by engine speed. The stroke of the pump piston is governed by the injection pump governor.

During cold engine operation, the air/fuel mixture is enriched until the engine temperature reaches 140-149°F ((60-65°C). A temperature switch in the coolant also regulates the piston pump stroke. Additional air, which does not pass through the throttle butterfly, is metered into the manifold plenum chamber.

When the engine is started, fuel is injected into the intake manifold by a solenoid valve. The duration time of injection depends on the coolant temperature.

When the injection pump pressure reaches 435-551 psi, each injection valve opens. Intake air flows through the air cleaner and the throttle manifold butterfly to the manifold plenum chamber, and from there through the 4 manifold branches to the combustion chambers.

The 320i models up to 1982, are equipped with a continuous injection system called the Bosch K-Jetronic. All the air drawn through the intake passes through a very large venturi which moves up or down as airflow (and therefore the pressure on it) increases or decreases.

This motion is mechanically transferred to a piston located in the fuel distributor, nearby. The electric fuel pump supplies fuel to the distributor via a warm up regulator. Pressure to the warm up regulator is regulated to a constant pressure by the system pressure in the base of the distributor. Then, the warm up regulator receives signals indicating outside air and engine water temperatures and further regulates the pressure accordingly. The distrib-

To remove the pressure regulator, remove the air hose (1) and disconnect the fuel line (2)

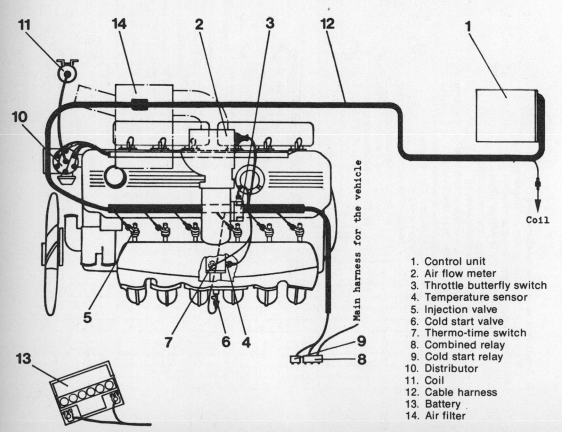

1. Control unit
2. Air flow meter
3. Throttle butterfly switch
4. Temperature sensor
5. Injection valve
6. Cold start valve
7. Thermo-time switch
8. Combined relay
9. Cold start relay
10. Distributor
11. Coil
12. Cable harness
13. Battery
14. Air filter

The L-Jetronic fuel injection system used on six cylinder engines

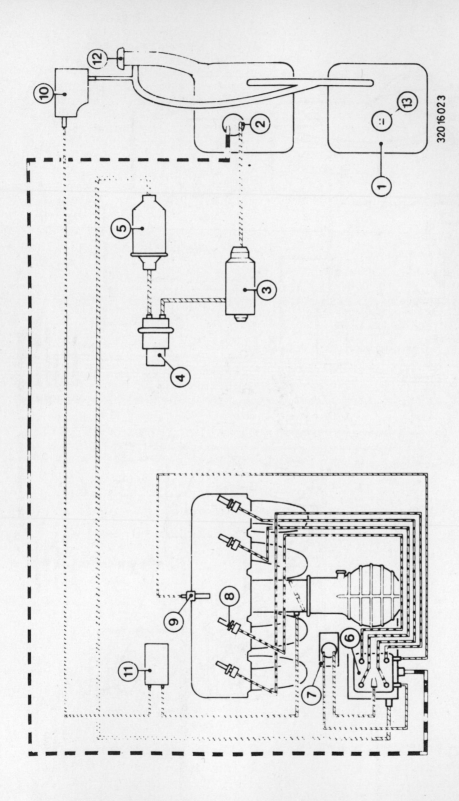

32016023

Early 320i fuel system layout

1 Fuel tank
2 Fuel suction unit[1])
3 Fuel pump
4 Pressure reservoir
5 Fuel filter

6 Fuel distributor
7 Warm-up regulator
8 Fuel injector
9 Cold start valve

10 Expansion tank
11 Activated carbon filter
12 Tank cap without vent
13 Suction unit/level transmitter
     (1978 models)

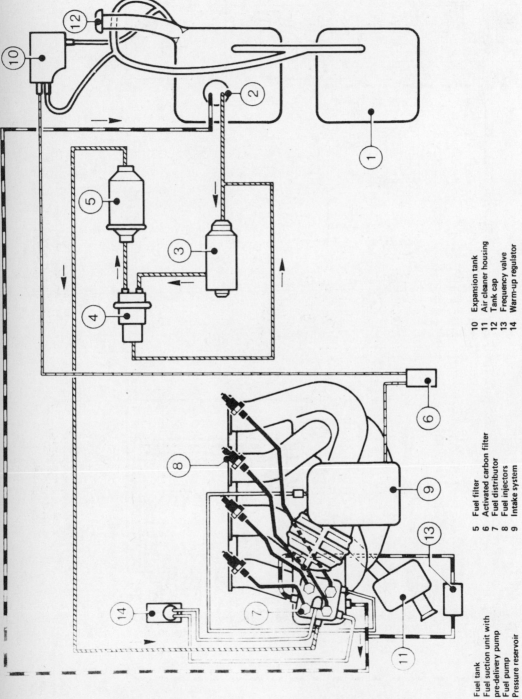

Fuel system layout—4 cylinder engines

1 Fuel tank
2 Fuel suction unit with pre-delivery pump
3 Fuel pump
4 Pressure reservoir
5 Fuel filter
6 Activated carbon filter
7 Fuel distributor
8 Fuel injectors
9 Intake system
10 Expansion tank
11 Air cleaner housing
12 Tank cap
13 Frequency valve
14 Warm-up regulator

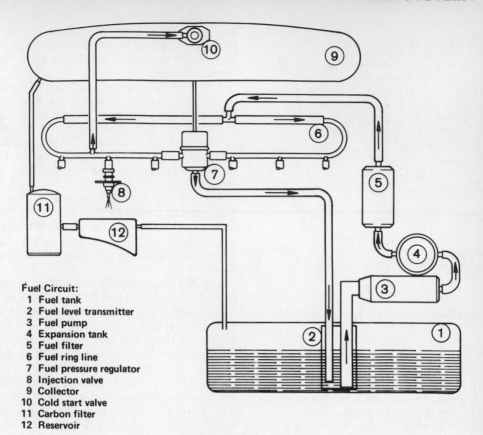

Fuel Circuit:
1 Fuel tank
2 Fuel level transmitter
3 Fuel pump
4 Expansion tank
5 Fuel filter
6 Fuel ring line
7 Fuel pressure regulator
8 Injection valve
9 Collector
10 Cold start valve
11 Carbon filter
12 Reservoir

Fuel flow circuit—630i

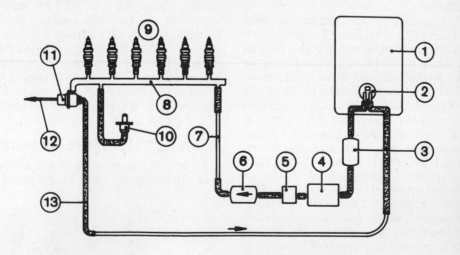

Fuel Circuit:

1 Tank	7 Supply line
2 Fuel level transmitter	8 Injection line
3 Expansion tank	9 Fuel injectors
4 Fuel pump	10 Cold start valve
5 Damper tank	11 Pressure regulator
6 Fuel filter	12 Vacuum hose
	13 Return line

Fuel flow circuit—633CSi

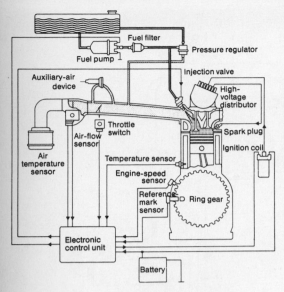

Schematic of Motronic fuel injection system

utor also divides the fuel flow 4 ways to deliver it in equal amounts to the injectors, which will not open until there is at least 47 psi, thus ensuring delivery of a constant flow of properly atomized fuel to the intake ports.

A thermo-time switch also measures water temperature and opens the cold start valve, located on the intake header, a varying amount each time the engine is started, depending on the conditions.

The fuel injection system used on 6-cylinder engines from 1977-1983, Bosch L-Jetronic, employs a pressure regulator (adjustable only on the 3.0) which maintains a constant pressure above the level of vacuum in the intake manifold. 6 fuel injectors are located at the intake ports and inject fuel simultaneously, once each engine revolution. Readings of temperature from the air intake and engine water jacket compensate for temperature changes. An intake throttle housing contains a flapper valve working against a spring which, through a slight venturi action, shifts its position as flow through the engine changes. This operates a "potentiometer" which generates an electric signal representing total airflow. On the 3.0, this unit is replaced by a pressure sensor. The system receives a signal from the primary side of the distributor (2.8 and 3 liter engines) or a timing TDC Position transmitter (3.3 liter engines), thus enabling total airflow to be divided up into an appropriate number of individual "shots" of fuel required, which depends upon engine rpm. Fuel is injected simultaneously once each engine revolution. If air flow is lower, as when the throttle is nearly closed, the system's computer opens the injector valve for a

shorter length of time at a given rpm; if air flow is higher, injection time is increase proportionately. Cold starting is aided just as in the K-Jetronic system.

The 1979 528i, and all models, 1980 and later, which must run at a mixture ratio which gives only the amount of air required to fully burn the fuel, an oxygen sensor located in the exhaust pipe also influenced the time signal the computer sends to the injection valves. If too much air is present, the fuel amount is increased, and vice-versa.

The fuel injection system used in almost all BMW vehicles from 1983 to the present is the Motronic injection system. The Motronic injection system is an integral part of the Digital Motor Electronics system (described in Chapter 4).

The Motronic fuel injection system combines the digital control of individual systems such as fuel injection and ignition into a single unit. The heart of the Motronic system is a microcomputer that is programmed according to dynomometer data on a specific engines characteristics. In operation, various engine sensors deliver data on engine speed (rpm), crankshaft position and temperature (engine and ambient air). From this input, the control unit determines the the ideal spark advance and fuel quantity, up to 400 times a second. In this manner spark advance and fuel quantity are tailored exactly to the engine operating conditions such as idling, part load, full load, warmup, deceleration and transient modes. Optimal fuel injection and ignition settings improve the engines overall performance, while reducing fuel consumption and emissions. The components and operation of the Motronic system are very similar to the L-Jetronic, and in fact the Motronic system is actually the next generation of L-Jetronic in BMW vehicles.

Relieving Fuel System Pressure

To relieve the pressure in the system, first find the fuel pump relay plug, located on the

Most electronic fuel pumps are mounted under the right, rear side of the car

cowl, as specified in applicable the Electric Fuel Pump Pressure Checking procedure below. Unplug the relay, leaving it in a safe position where the connections cannot ground. If necessary, tape the plug in place or tape over the connector prongs with electrical tape. Then, start the engine and operate it until it stalls. Crank the engine for 10 seconds after it stalls to remove any residual pressure.

Electric Fuel Pump

REMOVAL AND INSTALLATION

All Equipped Models Until 1981

On all electric pump (fuel injection) equipped cars the fuel pump is mounted together with the expansion tank for the evaporative emissions control system. The pumps which are mounted together with the expansion tank are located under the rear of the car.

1. To replace the pump, first disconnect the battery and then the electrical connector(s) at the pump.

2. Disconnect both hoses, one at the pump, and one at the expansion tank and plug the openings.

3. Remove the attaching nuts for the mounting bracket. Loosen the clamp bolt, and separate the pump from the pump/expansion tank mounting bracket.

4. To install the pump, position it in the mounting bracket and tighten the clamp bolt.

5. Connect both hoses and the electrical connector at the pump. Connect the negative battery cable and run the engine. Check for fuel leaks.

All 1982-88 except Those Listed Below

The fuel pump is an electrical unit, delivering fuel through a pressure regulator, to a fuel distributor or a ring-line for the injection valves. The fuel pump is mounted under the vehicle, near the fuel tank, or in the engine compartment.

1. Relieve fuel system pressure, as described above. Disconnect the negative battery connector. Push back any protective caps and disconnect the electrical connector(s).

2. If the fuel lines are flexible, pinch them closed with an appropriate tool. Disconnect the fuel lines and plug the ends.

3. Remove the retaining bolts and remove the pump and expansion tank as an assembly. On the 318i, the pump and mounting bracket come off together. On the 1983-85 733i and 1986 735i, remove the clamp bolt, bend the clamp open, and remove the pump.

4. The pump can be separated from the expansion tank after removal. On the 318i, separate the pump from the mounting bracket and slide the rubber mounting ring from the pump.

5. To install the pump, position the pump in its mounting bracket, sliding the rubber ring around it.

6. Install the pump to the expansion tank and mount them both as an assembly, connecting the fuel lines.

7. Connect the electrical leads and the negative battery cable. Run the engine and check for leaks.

1987-88 325, 325e, 325i, 325IS, 325IX and M3

1. Relieve fuel system pressure. Disconnect the negative battery connector. Going to the pump, which is under the car and near the fuel tank, push back any protective caps, note the routing and disconnect the electrical connector(s).

2. Securely clamp the suction hose (coming from the tank) and plug the discharge hose so no fuel can escape.

3. Open the hose clamp connecting the suction hose to the pump and disconnect it.

4. Remove the 3 attaching nuts which mount the pump and bracket to the floor pan and remove both as an assembly.

5. Remove the bolt passing through the 2 parts of the bracket and also mounting the hose attaching strap to the bracket. Then, pull the pump out of the bracket.

6. Loosen the hose clamp for the discharge hose and disconnect it at the pump. Pull the rubber ring off the pump.

7. Note the code number on the pump and make sure to replace it with one of the same number. Inspect all the rubber mounts on the pump mounting bracket and replace any that are cracked or crushed.

8. Install the pump in the mounting bracket and install the bolt passing through the bracket.

9. Attach the pump and bracket assembly to the floor pan and secure with the 3 attaching nuts.

Electric fuel pump assembly—typical

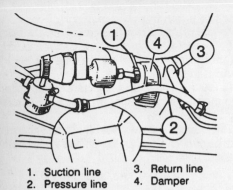

1. Suction line   3. Return line
2. Pressure line   4. Damper

Note the arrangement of the fuel pump, lines, and damper on the 1987–89 325 series cars

10. Attach all hoses to the pump assembly, make sure to correctly route them. Reconnect the electrical leads.

11. Run the engine and check all hose connections for leaks.

633CSi, M5 and M6

1. Relieve fuel system pressure, as described above. Disconnect the battery cables. Working under the fuel tank, pull back the protective caps and then unscrew the attaching nuts and pull off the electrical connections for the fuel pump.

2. Pinch off the inlet line to the fuel pump and the outlet from the filter. Then, loosen the clamps and disconnect these 2 hoses.

3. Remove the nut that clamps the fuel line near the pump. Then, remove the 3 bolts which mount the pump and filter to the bottom of the body and remove the assembly.

4. Remove the bolt fastening the halves of the bracket together and remove the filter from the bracket. Loosen the clamp on the outlet side of the fuel pump and disconnect the line. Then, slide off the rubber bushing in which the pump is mounted.

5. Check the code number on the side of the pump and make sure the replacement unit carries the same code.

6. Install the pump in the mounting bracket and install the bolt passing through the bracket.

7. Attach the pump and bracket assembly to the floor pan and secure with the 3 attaching nuts.

8. Attach all hoses to the pump assembly, make sure to correctly route them. Reconnect the electrical leads.

9. Run the engine and check all hose connections for leaks.

1987-88 735i

The pump on this car is mounted in the top of the tank along with the fuel level sending unit.

1. If the fuel pump is working well enough to drive the car, run it until the fuel level is as low as possible. If the car cannot be run, devise a safe way to draw fuel out of the tank until the level is low. The best means is some sort of pump and container system designed for this purpose, as siphoning is no longer considered safe *because gasoline is a deadly poison*.

2. Relieve fuel system pressure, as described above. Remove the trim panels from the trunk. Then, remove the screws from the cover for the pump/sending unit assembly.

3. Label the 3 fuel hoses connecting at the top of the pump/sending unit assembly. Unclamp and disconnect the fuel hoses and then plug them.

4. Slide the collar for the electrical connector to one side and then unplug the connector.

5. Remove the eight attaching screws and remove the pump/sending unit assembly. Replace the gasket.

6. Press the 2 retaining locks for the pump unit inward and slide the pump out of the pump/sending unit assembly.

7. Note the routing of the fuel and electrical lines to the pump from the top of the pump/sending unit assembly. Loosen the 2 hose clamp screws and the screws attaching the electrical connectors to the pump. Disconnect the hose and connector.

8. Unscrew the pressure regulator from the top of the check valve. Then, unscrew the check valve from the top of the pump.

9. Pull the insulating sleeve off the pump. Then, loosen the retaining screw and slide the filter off the pump.

10. To install the pump, first position the filter on the pump and install the retaining screw.

11. Install the insulating sleeve to the pump. Screw the check valve into the top of the pump and attach the pressure regulator to the pump.

12. Connect the hose and the electrical leads to the pump. slide the pump into the pump/sending unit assembly. Position the sending unit assembly in the tank, using a new gasket, and install the 8 retaining screws.

13. Connect the plug to the top of the sending unit and connect the fuel hoses.

14. Install the trim panels in the trunk and install the pump/sending unit cover. Connect the negative battery cable and run the engine. Check for fuel leaks.

PRESSURE TESTING

2002tii

Connect a pressure gauge to the union at the front of the injection pump. Idle the engine. The pressure should be 28.5 psi. If pressure is low, check the pump ground. If that is ok and pressure is still low, replace the pump.

CHILTON'S
FUEL ECONOMY
& TUNE-UP TIPS

Tune-up • Spark Plug Diagnosis • Emission Controls

Fuel System • Cooling System • Tires and Wheels

General Maintenance

CHILTON'S FUEL ECONOMY & TUNE-UP TIPS

Fuel economy is important to everyone, no matter what kind of vehicle you drive. The maintenance-minded motorist can save both money and fuel using these tips and the periodic maintenance and tune-up procedures in this Repair and Tune-Up Guide.

There are more than 130,000,000 cars and trucks registered for private use in the United States. Each travels an average of 10-12,000 miles per year, and, and in total they consume close to 70 billion gallons of fuel each year. This represents nearly ⅔ of the oil imported by the United States each year. The Federal government's goal is to reduce consumption 10% by 1985. A variety of methods are either already in use or under serious consideration, and they all affect you driving and the cars you will drive. In addition to "down-sizing", the auto industry is using or investigating the use of electronic fuel delivery, electronic engine controls and alternative engines for use in smaller and lighter vehicles, among other alternatives to meet the federally mandated Corporate Average Fuel Economy (CAFE) of 27.5 mpg by 1985. The government, for its part, is considering rationing, mandatory driving curtailments and tax increases on motor vehicle fuel in an effort to reduce consumption. The government's goal of a 10% reduction could be realized — and further government regulation avoided — if every private vehicle could use just 1 less gallon of fuel per week.

How Much Can You Save?

Tests have proven that almost anyone can make at least a 10% reduction in fuel consumption through regular maintenance and tune-ups. When a major manufacturer of spark plugs sur-

TUNE-UP

1. Check the cylinder compression to be sure the engine will really benefit from a tune-up and that it is capable of producing good fuel economy. A tune-up will be wasted on an engine in poor mechanical condition.

2. Replace spark plugs regularly. New spark plugs alone can increase fuel economy 3%.

3. Be sure the spark plugs are the correct type (heat range) for your vehicle. See the Tune-Up Specifications.

Heat range refers to the spark plug's ability to conduct heat away from the firing end. It must conduct the heat away in an even pattern to avoid becoming a source of pre-ignition, yet it must also operate hot enough to burn off conductive deposits that could cause misfiring.

The heat range is usually indicated by a number on the spark plug, part of the manufacturer's designation for each individual spark plug. The numbers in bold-face indicate the heat range in each manufacturer's identification system.

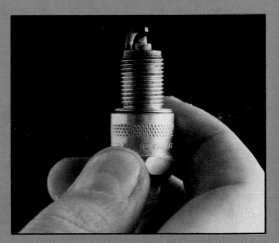

Periodically, check the spark plugs to be sure they are firing efficiently. They are excellent indicators of the internal condition of your engine.

Manufacturer	Typical Designation
AC	R **45** TS
Bosch (old)	WA **145** T30
Bosch (new)	HR **8** Y
Champion	RBL **15** Y
Fram/Autolite	**415**
Mopar	P-**62** PR
Motorcraft	BRF-**42**
NGK	BP **5** ES-15
Nippondenso	W **16** EP
Prestolite	14GR **5** 2A

On AC, Bosch (new), Champion, Fram/Autolite, Mopar, Motorcraft and Prestolite, a higher number indicates a hotter plug. On Bosch (old), NGK and Nippondenso, a higher number indicates a colder plug.

4. Make sure the spark plugs are properly gapped. See the Tune-Up Specifications in this book.

5. Be sure the spark plugs are firing efficiently. The illustrations on the next 2 pages show you how to "read" the firing end of the spark plug.

6. Check the ignition timing and set it to specifications. Tests show that almost all cars have incorrect ignition timing by more than 2°.

veyed over 6,000 cars nationwide, they found that a tune-up, on cars that needed one, increased fuel economy over 11%. Replacing worn plugs alone, accounted for a 3% increase. The same test also revealed that 8 out of every 10 vehicles will have some maintenance deficiency that will directly affect fuel economy, emissions or performance. Most of this mileage-robbing neglect could be prevented with regular maintenance.

Modern engines require that all of the functioning systems operate properly for maximum efficiency. A malfunction anywhere wastes fuel. You can keep your vehicle running as efficiently and economically as possible, by being aware of your vehicle's operating and performance characteristics. If your vehicle suddenly develops performance or fuel economy problems it could be due to one or more of the following:

PROBLEM	POSSIBLE CAUSE
Engine Idles Rough	Ignition timing, idle mixture, vacuum leak or something amiss in the emission control system.
Hesitates on Acceleration	Dirty carburetor or fuel filter, improper accelerator pump setting, ignition timing or fouled spark plugs.
Starts Hard or Fails to Start	Worn spark plugs, improperly set automatic choke, ice (or water) in fuel system.
Stalls Frequently	Automatic choke improperly adjusted and possible dirty air filter or fuel filter.
Performs Sluggishly	Worn spark plugs, dirty fuel or air filter, ignition timing or automatic choke out of adjustment.

Check spark plug wires on conventional point type ignition for cracks by bending them in a loop around your finger.

Be sure that spark plug wires leading to adjacent cylinders do not run too close together. (Photo courtesy Champion Spark Plug Co.)

7. If your vehicle does not have electronic ignition, check the points, rotor and cap as specified.

8. Check the spark plug wires (used with conventional point-type ignitions) for cracks and burned or broken insulation by bending them in a loop around your finger. Cracked wires decrease fuel efficiency by failing to deliver full voltage to the spark plugs. One misfiring spark plug can cost you as much as 2 mpg.

9. Check the routing of the plug wires. Misfiring can be the result of spark plug leads to adjacent cylinders running parallel to each other and too close together. One wire tends to pick up voltage from the other causing it to fire "out of time".

10. Check all electrical and ignition circuits for voltage drop and resistance.

11. Check the distributor mechanical and/or vacuum advance mechanisms for proper functioning. The vacuum advance can be checked by twisting the distributor plate in the opposite direction of rotation. It should spring back when released.

12. Check and adjust the valve clearance on engines with mechanical lifters. The clearance should be slightly loose rather than too tight.

SPARK PLUG DIAGNOSIS

Normal

APPEARANCE: This plug is typical of one operating normally. The insulator nose varies from a light tan to grayish color with slight electrode wear. The presence of slight deposits is normal on used plugs and will have no adverse effect on engine performance. The spark plug heat range is correct for the engine and the engine is running normally.

CAUSE: Properly running engine.

RECOMMENDATION: Before reinstalling this plug, the electrodes should be cleaned and filed square. Set the gap to specifications. If the plug has been in service for more than 10-12,000 miles, the entire set should probably be replaced with a fresh set of the same heat range.

Oil Deposits

APPEARANCE: The firing end of the plug is covered with a wet, oily coating.

CAUSE: The problem is poor oil control. On high mileage engines, oil is leaking past the rings or valve guides into the combustion chamber. A common cause is also a plugged PCV valve, and a ruptured fuel pump diaphragm can also cause this condition. Oil fouled plugs such as these are often found in new or recently overhauled engines, before normal oil control is achieved, and can be cleaned and reinstalled.

RECOMMENDATION: A hotter spark plug may temporarily relieve the problem, but the engine is probably in need of work.

Incorrect Heat Range

APPEARANCE: The effects of high temperature on a spark plug are indicated by clean white, often blistered insulator. This can also be accompanied by excessive wear of the electrode, and the absence of deposits.

CAUSE: Check for the correct spark plug heat range. A plug which is too hot for the engine can result in overheating. A car operated mostly at high speeds can require a colder plug. Also check ignition timing, cooling system level, fuel mixture and leaking intake manifold.

RECOMMENDATION: If all ignition and engine adjustments are known to be correct, and no other malfunction exists, install spark plugs one heat range colder.

Carbon Deposits

APPEARANCE: Carbon fouling is easily identified by the presence of dry, soft, black, sooty deposits.

CAUSE: Changing the heat range can often lead to carbon fouling, as can prolonged slow, stop-and-start driving. If the heat range is correct, carbon fouling can be attributed to a rich fuel mixture, sticking choke, clogged air cleaner, worn breaker points, retarded timing or low compression. If only one or two plugs are carbon fouled, check for corroded or cracked wires on the affected plugs. Also look for cracks in the distributor cap between the towers of affected cylinders.

RECOMMENDATION: After the problem is corrected, these plugs can be cleaned and reinstalled if not worn severely.

MMT Fouled

APPEARANCE: Spark plugs fouled by MMT (Methycyclopentadienyl Maganese Tricarbonyl) have reddish, rusty appearance on the insulator and side electrode.

CAUSE: MMT is an anti-knock additive in gasoline used to replace lead. During the combustion process, the MMT leaves a reddish deposit on the insulator and side electrode.

RECOMMENDATION: No engine malfunction is indicated and the deposits will not affect plug performance any more than lead deposits (see Ash Deposits). MMT fouled plugs can be cleaned, regapped and reinstalled.

High Speed Glazing

APPEARANCE: Glazing appears as shiny coating on the plug, either yellow or tan in color.

CAUSE: During hard, fast acceleration, plug temperatures rise suddenly. Deposits from normal combustion have no chance to fluff-off; instead, they melt on the insulator forming an electrically conductive coating which causes misfiring.

RECOMMENDATION: Glazed plugs are not easily cleaned. They should be replaced with a fresh set of plugs of the correct heat range. If the condition recurs, using plugs with a heat range one step colder may cure the problem.

Ash (Lead) Deposits

APPEARANCE: Ash deposits are characterized by light brown or white colored deposits crusted on the side or center electrodes. In some cases it may give the plug a rusty appearance.

CAUSE: Ash deposits are normally derived from oil or fuel additives burned during normal combustion. Normally they are harmless, though excessive amounts can cause misfiring. If deposits are excessive in short mileage, the valve guides may be worn.

RECOMMENDATION: Ash-fouled plugs can be cleaned, gapped and reinstalled.

Detonation

APPEARANCE: Detonation is usually characterized by a broken plug insulator.

CAUSE: A portion of the fuel charge will begin to burn spontaneously, from the increased heat following ignition. The explosion that results applies extreme pressure to engine components, frequently damaging spark plugs and pistons.

Detonation can result by over-advanced ignition timing, inferior gasoline (low octane) lean air/fuel mixture, poor carburetion, engine lugging or an increase in compression ratio due to combustion chamber deposits or engine modification.

RECOMMENDATION: Replace the plugs after correcting the problem.

Photos Courtesy Champion Spark Plug Co.

EMISSION CONTROLS

13. Be aware of the general condition of the emission control system. It contributes to reduced pollution and should be serviced regularly to maintain efficient engine operation.

14. Check all vacuum lines for dried, cracked or brittle conditions. Something as simple as a leaking vacuum hose can cause poor performance and loss of economy.

15. Avoid tampering with the emission control system. Attempting to improve fuel econ-

FUEL SYSTEM

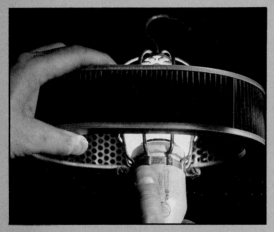

Check the air filter with a light behind it. If you can see light through the filter it can be reused.

Extremely clogged filters should be discarded and replaced with a new one.

18. Replace the air filter regularly. A dirty air filter richens the air/fuel mixture and can increase fuel consumption as much as 10%. Tests show that ⅓ of all vehicles have air filters in need of replacement.

19. Replace the fuel filter at least as often as recommended.

20. Set the idle speed and carburetor mixture to specifications.

21. Check the automatic choke. A sticking or malfunctioning choke wastes gas.

22. During the summer months, adjust the automatic choke for a leaner mixture which will produce faster engine warm-ups.

COOLING SYSTEM

29. Be sure all accessory drive belts are in good condition. Check for cracks or wear.

30. Adjust all accessory drive belts to proper tension.

31. Check all hoses for swollen areas, worn spots, or loose clamps.

32. Check coolant level in the radiator or expansion tank.

33. Be sure the thermostat is operating properly. A stuck thermostat delays engine warm-up and a cold engine uses nearly twice as much fuel as a warm engine.

34. Drain and replace the engine coolant at least as often as recommended. Rust and scale

TIRES & WHEELS

38. Check the tire pressure often with a pencil type gauge. Tests by a major tire manufacturer show that 90% of all vehicles have at least 1 tire improperly inflated. Better mileage can be achieved by over-inflating tires, but never exceed the maximum inflation pressure on the side of the tire.

39. If possible, install radial tires. Radial tires deliver as much as ½ mpg more than bias belted tires.

40. Avoid installing super-wide tires. They only create extra rolling resistance and decrease fuel mileage. Stick to the manufacturer's recommendations.

41. Have the wheels properly balanced.

omy by tampering with emission controls is more likely to worsen fuel economy than improve it. Emission control changes on modern engines are not readily reversible.

16. Clean (or replace) the EGR valve and lines as recommended.

17. Be sure that all vacuum lines and hoses are reconnected properly after working under the hood. An unconnected or misrouted vacuum line can wreak havoc with engine performance.

---

23. Check for fuel leaks at the carburetor, fuel pump, fuel lines and fuel tank. Be sure all lines and connections are tight.

24. Periodically check the tightness of the carburetor and intake manifold attaching nuts and bolts. These are a common place for vacuum leaks to occur.

25. Clean the carburetor periodically and lubricate the linkage.

26. The condition of the tailpipe can be an excellent indicator of proper engine combustion. After a long drive at highway speeds, the inside of the tailpipe should be a light grey in color. Black or soot on the insides indicates an overly rich mixture.

27. Check the fuel pump pressure. The fuel pump may be supplying more fuel than the engine needs.

28. Use the proper grade of gasoline for your engine. Don't try to compensate for knocking or "pinging" by advancing the ignition timing. This practice will only increase plug temperature and the chances of detonation or pre-ignition with relatively little performance gain.

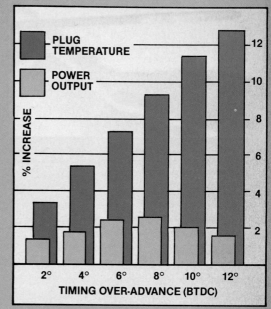

Increasing ignition timing past the specified setting results in a drastic increase in spark plug temperature with increased chance of detonation or preignition. Performance increase is considerably less. (Photo courtesy Champion Spark Plug Co.)

---

that form in the engine should be flushed out to allow the engine to operate at peak efficiency.

35. Clean the radiator of debris that can decrease cooling efficiency.

36. Install a flex-type or electric cooling fan, if you don't have a clutch type fan. Flex fans use curved plastic blades to push more air at low speeds when more cooling is needed; at high speeds the blades flatten out for less resistance. Electric fans only run when the engine temperature reaches a predetermined level.

37. Check the radiator cap for a worn or cracked gasket. If the cap does not seal properly, the cooling system will not function properly.

---

42. Be sure the front end is correctly aligned. A misaligned front end actually has wheels going in differed directions. The increased drag can reduce fuel economy by .3 mpg.

43. Correctly adjust the wheel bearings. Wheel bearings that are adjusted too tight increase rolling resistance.

Check tire pressures regularly with a reliable pocket type gauge. Be sure to check the pressure on a cold tire.

GENERAL MAINTENANCE

Check the fluid levels (particularly engine oil) on a regular basis. Be sure to check the oil for grit, water or other contamination.

A vacuum gauge is another excellent indicator of internal engine condition and can also be installed in the dash as a mileage indicator.

44. Periodically check the fluid levels in the engine, power steering pump, master cylinder, automatic transmission and drive axle.

45. Change the oil at the recommended interval and change the filter at every oil change. Dirty oil is thick and causes extra friction between moving parts, cutting efficiency and increasing wear. A worn engine requires more frequent tune-ups and gets progressively worse fuel economy. In general, use the lightest viscosity oil for the driving conditions you will encounter.

46. Use the recommended viscosity fluids in the transmission and axle.

47. Be sure the battery is fully charged for fast starts. A slow starting engine wastes fuel.

48. Be sure battery terminals are clean and tight.

49. Check the battery electrolyte level and add distilled water if necessary.

50. Check the exhaust system for crushed pipes, blockages and leaks.

51. Adjust the brakes. Dragging brakes or brakes that are not releasing create increased drag on the engine.

52. Install a vacuum gauge or miles-per-gallon gauge. These gauges visually indicate engine vacuum in the intake manifold. High vacuum = good mileage and low vacuum = poorer mileage. The gauge can also be an excellent indicator of internal engine conditions.

53. Be sure the clutch is properly adjusted. A slipping clutch wastes fuel.

54. Check and periodically lubricate the heat control valve in the exhaust manifold. A sticking or inoperative valve prevents engine warm-up and wastes gas.

55. Keep accurate records to check fuel economy over a period of time. A sudden drop in fuel economy may signal a need for tune-up or other maintenance.

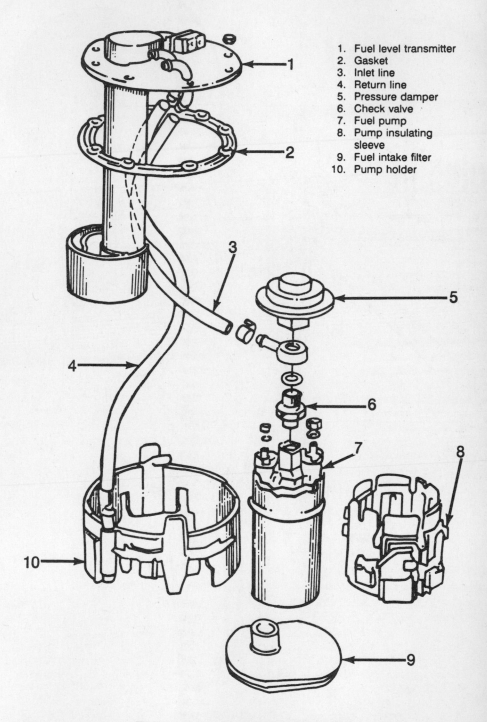

1. Fuel level transmitter
2. Gasket
3. Inlet line
4. Return line
5. Pressure damper
6. Check valve
7. Fuel pump
8. Pump insulating sleeve
9. Fuel intake filter
10. Pump holder

The in-tank fuel pump used in 1987–89 735i

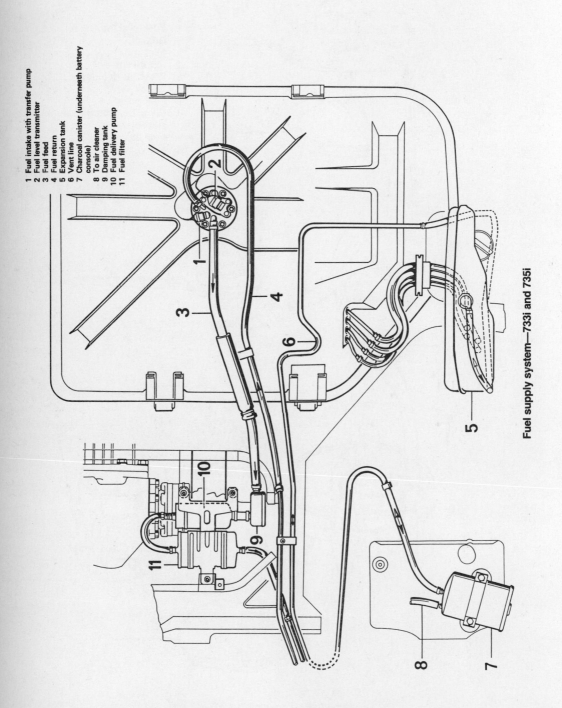

1 Fuel intake with transfer pump
2 Fuel level transmitter
3 Fuel feed
4 Fuel return
5 Expansion tank
6 Vent line
7 Charcoal canister (underneath battery console)
8 To air cleaner
9 Damping tank
10 Fuel delivery pump
11 Fuel filter

Fuel supply system—733i and 735i

3.0Si

Install a pressure gauge in the line between the fuel filter and the injector feed circuit. The pressure must be 31.2. If not, adjust the pressure. If that will not correct low pressure, replace the pump.

The fuel pressure regulator is located in the circuit which feeds all the injectors between 2 of the injectors. An adjusting bolt and locknut protrude from the top. To adjust it, connect a pressure gauge and idle the engine as described in the pressure check above, loosen the locknut, turn the bolt in or out until the pressure is correct, and then retighten the locknut.

318i and 320i

1. Relieve fuel system pressure, as described above. Connect a pressure gauge in the line leading from the fuel distributor on top of the injector pump to the warm-up regulator. Plug the open end of the line leading to the warm-up regulator, and make sure the gauge will read the pressure coming from the distributor.

2. Disconnect the wire plug on the mixture control unit, and turn on the ignition. The pres-

Checking pump delivery pressure on the 320i. Valve (12) must be closed or line plugged, and electrical plug (15) must be disconnected

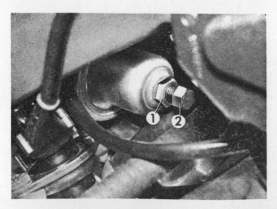

Loosen the locknut (1) and adjust the pressure (2) on the 3.0 pressure regulator

sure should read 64-74 psi, or the fuel pump will have to be replaced.

1982-86 325e, 528e, 533i, 633CSi and 1982 733i

Relieve fuel system pressure, as described above. Connect a pressure gauge in the line leading to the cold start valve from the injector feed circuit. With the engine idling, the pressure must be 33-38 psi, or the fuel pump (or filter) is defective.

1987-88 325e, 325, 325i, 325iS and 325iX

1. Relieve fuel system pressure, as described above. Tee a pressure gauge into the fuel feed line in front of the pressure regulator.

2. Disconnect the fuel pump relay. Connect a remote starter switch between terminals KL30 and KL87 of the relay. Close the switch and check the pressure. It should be 43 psi. If not, the filter is severely clogged or the fuel pump is defective.

M3

1. Relieve fuel system pressure, as described above. Tee a pressure gauge into the fuel return line at the pressure regulator. Then, clamp off the return line so pressure builds up to the maximum level the pump can produce.

2. Remove the trim from the cowl on the right (passenger's side). Then, unplug the fuel pump relay. Connect a remote starter switch between terminals 30 and 87 (left side and top holding the male side of the connector). Energize the switch and check the pressure. It must be 43 psi. Check the filter for excessive clogging. If it is okay, the pump is defective.

1983-88 533i, 535i, 633CSi, 635CSi, 733i, 735i, M5 and M6

1. Relieve fuel system pressure, as described above. Tee a pressure gauge into the fuel feed line in front of the pressure regulator (on M5, M6, tee in between the cold start valve and the fuel rail). Plug the fuel return hose.

2. Pull off the pump relay. Jumper terminals 87 and 30. Measure the delivery pressure. It should be 43 psi on these models except the 1987-89 735i and 750iL. On these models, it should be 48 psi.

Fuel Pressure Regulator

REMOVAL AND INSTALLATION

1982 633CSi

1. Remove No. 4 intake tube. Pull off the vacuum hose located on one end of the regulator. Loosen the fuel line hose clamp and pull off the fuel return line that attaches to the opposite end.

2. Using a backup wrench on the flats that

are an integral part of the regulator body, loosen the coupling nut and then disconnect the fuel supply line.

3. The fitting that the fuel return line connects to is screwed into the pressure regulator and also mounts the regulator. Unscrew this fitting using an open-end wrench and remove the regulator.

4. To install the regulator, first position it so the return line connection fitting will pass through the hole in the mounting bracket, and then install that fitting. Make the other connections in reverse order. Make all connections tight and then run the engine while checking for leaks.

1982-83 733i

Follow the procedure just above for 1982 633CSi models, but note these differences: The regulator connections are identical with those on the unit described above. However, the mounting bracket that fits under the return line connection is bolted together. Once the lines have been disconnected, remove this bolt and remove the unit. Now, remove the return line connection and bracket parts and transfer them to the replacement unit before mounting the unit on the car. Make sure to run the engine and check for leaks.

318i, 325, 325e, 325i, 325iS, 325iX, 528e
1983-84 533i
All 535i
1983-84 633CSi
All 635CSi
1984 733i
All 735i, M5 and M6

1. Remove the vacuum hose from the unit.
2. Loosen the clamp and pull off the fuel hose.
3. Remove the 2 bolts and pull the unit from the injection tube (318i, 325, M3, all models with M30 B35 engine), or from the body (other models).
4. Inspect the seal that seals the connection

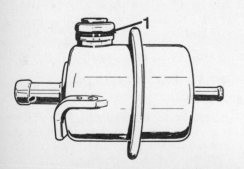

On the 318i fuel pressure regulator, check the seal (1) and replace it if necessary

with the injection tube and replace it, if necessary.

5. Install a new seal on the unit and install it into the injection tube. Install the 2 bolts that retain the unit and install the fuel and vacuum hoses.

6. Run the engine and check for leaks.

KUGELFISCHER FUEL INJECTION SYSTEM

The Kugelfischer injection system consists basically of mechanical type fuel injectors, engine driven injection pump, cold start valve and electrically controlled switches and sensors. This system was used in the 2002tii models.

Air Container and Throttle Valve Stub Assembly
REMOVAL AND INSTALLATION

1. Label and disconnect all hoses from the air cleaner. Remove the air cleaner.
2. Disconnect the fuel hose (1) and cable for the start (2) from the throttle valve stub. Disconnect the vacuum hose (3) from the air container.
3. Loosen all hose clamps and remove the 4 induction pipes.
4. Unhook the return spring from the throttle valve stub linkage. Disconnect the retaining screw for the linkage bracket.
5. Taking care to support the pipe connection while loosening, disconnect the injection pipe at No. 1 cylinder. Remove the injection valve.
6. Remove the 2 retaining bolts (7,8) for the throttle valve stub support bracket. Disconnect the vacuum hose (9) from the valve stub and the auxiliary air hose (10) from the air container.
7. Again taking care to support the pipe connection while loosening, disconnect the injection pipe (11) from no. 4 cylinder.
8. Remove the 6 nuts retaining the air container to the cylinder head and lift off the air container and throttle valve stub assembly.
9. To install, install new gaskets at the cylinder head flange and new cord rings at the induction pipes, if necessary.
10. Install the air container to the cylinder head and install the 6 nuts that retain it.
11. Install the valve stub support bracket and retaining bolts.
12. Install the No. 1 injection pipe and connect all 4 induction pipes. Connect the fuel lines and vacuum hose. Reconnect the cable to valve stub.

Air container and throttle valve stub assembly installed with air cleaner removed

1. Plate nut
2. Special tool to lift air regulator cone
A. Clearance between grub screw and stop screw

Warm-up sensor adjustment—2002tii

Disconnecting hoses and bracket from throttle valve stub assembly

1. Grub screw   2. Stop screw
A. Projection of air regulator come above the valve body
B. Projection of plate washer above lever

Checking the warm–up sensor when the engine is at normal operating temperature

Removing air container and throttle valve stub assembly

13. Install the air cleaner and connect all hoses.

14. Check the tightness of the induction pipes by spraying water at the pipe connections. If there is an air leak, the engine will idle unevenly.

Warm-up Sensor

Adjustment

NOTE: *The warm-up sensor adjustment must be made before the engine is warmed up.*
1. Remove the air filter housing.

2. Press out the air regulator cone with a screwdriver until special tool 6073 or the equivalent can be inserted into the groove of the air regulator cone.

3. A distance of 2.5-3.0mm should exist between the grub screw and the stop screw (distance A). Adjustments can be made at the plate nut (1).

4. After the engine is at normal operating temperature, the air regulator valve cone must project 9-10mm (distance A). The plate washer must project above the lever by 4mm (distance B) and the grub screw must be in full contact with the stop screw.

5. If these specifications are not obtained, the warm up sensor must be replaced.

REMOVAL AND INSTALLATION

1. Drain the coolant and remove the air filter.

CAUTION: *When draining the coolant, keep in mind that cats and dogs are attracted by the ethylene glycol antifreeze, and are quite*

likely to drink any that is left in an uncovered container or in puddles on the ground. This will prove fatal in sufficient quantity. Always drain the coolant into a sealable container. Coolant should be reused unless it is contaminated or several years old.

2. Disconnect the coolant hoses and the auxiliary air hose.

3. Disconnect the return spring and remove the warm-up sensor while disconnecting the accelerator linkage.

4. After installation, adjust the sensor as previously outlined and adjust the idle speed.

Cold Start Valve

TESTING

1. Remove the start valve from the throttle valve section.

2. Turn the ignition switch to ON to obtain fuel pressure from the pump, but do not start the engine.

3. Connect a positive current jumper wire to the **SV** connection of the time switch.

4. If fuel is ejected from the start valve, the valve and the feed pipe are considered to be good.

NOTE: *The valve must not drip fuel with the current OFF.*

REMOVAL AND INSTALLATION

1. Remove the electrical connector and the fuel line to the valve.

2. Remove the retaining bolts and pull the valve assembly from the air collector.

3. Replace the rubber sealing ring during installation.

Thermo-time Switch

TESTING

1. Remove the wire terminal from the thermo-time switch.

2. Connect a test lamp to a positive terminal and the **W** terminal of the thermo-time switch.

3. The lamp should light at coolant temperature below 95°F (35°C).

4. Leave the test lamp attached to the **W** terminal and connect a positive jumper wire to terminal **G**.

5. The internal bi-metal control should open after a short time and the light should then go out. If not, replace the thermo-time switch.

Time Switch

TESTING

1. Remove the time switch from the firewall.

2. Connect a test lamp between ground and the **SV** terminal of the time switch.

3. Remove the No. 4 wire from the ignition

coil and actuate the starter. The test lamp should go out after a short time.

NOTE: *The injection time period of start valve is as follows:*

At 4°F (–15°C) – 9-15 seconds
At 32°F (0°C) – 4-10 seconds
At 95°F (35°C) – 1 second

4. Remove the terminal plug from the thermo-time switch. Actuate the starter; the light should go on for one second and then go out.

5. Connect a test lamp between the **TH** terminal and ground. The test lamp must light up as long as the starter is actuated.

Injection Pump

REMOVAL AND INSTALLATION

1. Drain the cooling system.

CAUTION: *When draining the coolant, keep in mind that cats and dogs are attracted by the ethylene glycol antifreeze, and are quite likely to drink any that is left in an uncovered container or in puddles on the ground. This will prove fatal in sufficient quantity. Always drain the coolant into a sealable container. Coolant should be reused unless it is contaminated or several years old.*

2. Label and disconnect all hoses from the air cleaner. Remove the air cleaner.

3. Disconnect the 4 injection lines and fitting rings at the pump, noting their placement for installation. Plug the pressure valve with dust caps.

4. Disconnect the fuel return hose, oil feed hose, water inflow hose and the oil dipstick support bracket from the pump.

5. Disconnect the coolant return hose (4), oil return hose (5) and the hose for the auxiliary air (6) from the warm-up runner. Loosen screw (7).

6. Disconnect the connecting link from the pump lever.

Disconnecting hoses and loosening screw (7) from rear of pump housing

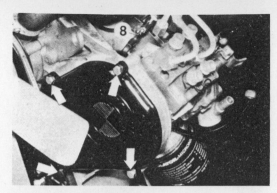

Disconnecting connecting rod (8) and removing dust cover retaining bolts

Aligning pump and pulleys at top dead center

Injector lines-to-cylinder numbering sequence from the fuel distributor head. Location of the fuel filter (S) is in the hollow fuel line bolt

7. Remove the 4 retaining bolts for the injection pump drive belt dust cover and remove the cover.

8. Rotate the engine until the No. 1 cylinder is at Top Dead Center. At this point, the notch in the drive belt pulley is aligned with the projection on the lower section of the drive belt dust cover, and the distributor rotor is pointing to the spark plug wire connection for the No. 1 cylinder (cap removed). Also, the notch in the

cogged belt pulley is aligned with the cast-in projection on the pump housing. With the engine at TDC, remove the pump drive pulley retaining nut.

9. Using a puller, remove the pump drive pulley, taking care not to misplace the woodruff key. Remove the cogged belt.

10. Remove the 2 bolts retaining the injection pump to the timing case cover. The, pull out the pump to the rear so that the intermediate shaft may be lifted out at the warm-up sensor housing. Lift out the injection pump.

11. Install the injection pump to the timing case cover. Using a pulley puller/installer, install the pump drive pulley and install the pump drive pulley retaining nut.

12. Using the procedure outlined below, install the cogged belt. Install the belt cover. Connect the connecting link to the pump lever.

13. Connect the coolant return hose, oil return hose and the hose for the auxiliary air to the warm-up runner.

14. Connect the fuel return hose, oil feed hose, water inflow hose and the oil dipstick support to the pump bracket.

15. Reconnect the injection lines at their fittings at the pump. Install the air cleaner and reconnect all hoses.

Cogged Belt
REMOVAL AND INSTALLATION

1. Remove the front air filter hood and the upper dust cover on the pump assembly.

2. Rotate the engine so that the No. 1 piston is at TDC on its compression stroke. The crankshaft pulley must point to the mark on the dust cap and the pump pulley must align with the casting mark on the pump body.

3. Loosen the alternator and remove the belt.

4. Mark the V-pulley on the crankshaft and remove the retaining bolts from the pulley.

Removal of the cogged belt through the lower front dust cover

5. Remove the pulley and do not turn the engine, due to the pulley fitting at 180°.

6. Loosen the upper dust cover bolt, remove all other retaining bolts for the lower dust cover and remove the cogged belt by pulling the dust cover to the front and pulling the cogged belt out between the hub and the front dust cover.

7. Be sure of the pulley alignment for both the crankshaft and the injection pump and reverse the removal procedure to install the cogged belt.

Injection Valve

REMOVAL AND INSTALLATION

1. Disconnect the feed line to the injector with fitting wrenches to avoid damage to the threaded areas.

2. Unscrew the injector valve from the induction sleeve.

3. During installation, use new sealing rings.

SYNCHRONIZING THROTTLE VALVE WITH INJECTION PUMP

1. Make sure that the connecting rod (linkage) between the pump and the throttle valve is adjusted to 85mm. The length of the connecting rod is measured from the centers of the ball sockets of the connecting rod.

2. Remove the 2 screws for the throttle valve cover and lift off the cover. Rotate the idling speed screw (1) until it is not in contact with the eccentric. Loosen the 2 clamping screws (2).

3. Using a 100mm long piece of metal rod (approximately 4mm thick in diameter), bent at a 90° angle at the end (such as BMW special tool 6075), insert the rod through the upper slotted hole of the regulating lever so that the rod seats in the bore of the injection pump housing (see the illustration).

4. Insert a 4mm diameter drift pin (such as

Inserting drift pin (BMW 6077) into hole in throttle valve section (left); loosening clamping screws (2) (right)

Correct synchronization shown by eccentric partially overlapping bore (B) of throttle valve

Using metal rod (such as BMW 6075) to align lowest hole of regulator lever with pump housing hole to adjust full load setting clearance with stop screw (3)

BMW 6077) into the bore of the throttle valve section (see illustration). Then, with the regulating lever set in position with the metal rod and the throttle valve eccentric pressed against the drift pin, tighten the 2 clamping screws (2).

Using metal rod (such as BMW 6075) to align top hole of regulating lever with pump housing hole

5. Remove the drift pin and metal rod and check the synchronization. The synchronization is correct when the eccentric partially overlaps the bore (B) in the throttle valve section.

6. Finally, adjust the idle speed using screw (1) to 900 rpm plus or minus 50 rpm.

7. Check the synchronization at full load setting. Disconnect the induction pipe from the No. 1 cylinder. Using the metal rod, insert the rod through the lowest slotted hole of the regulator lever so that the rod seats in the bore of the injection pump housing. Then, adjust the stop screw (3) so that the pump lever is barely contacted.

BOSCH K-JETRONIC (CIS) FUEL INJECTION

The Bosch Continuous Fuel Injection System (K-Jetronic) consists of mechanical type fuel injectors, a fuel distributor unit, operated by a sensor plate, and control valve. Electrical and vacuum operated regulators and switches complete the assembly. An electrical control box is not used.

BASIC THROTTLE SETTING

1. Disconnect the accelerator cable and loosen the throttle stop screw.

2. Adjust the distance between the throttle lever and the stop screw to 1.0-1.5mm clearance.

3. Loosen the throttle lever clamping screw and position the throttle valve in the housing to zero play. Tighten the clamping screw.

4. Tighten the throttle stop screw one complete turn and lock it in place.

5. Adjust the accelerator cable to the throttle lever and attach.

AUXILIARY AIR REGULATOR

TESTING

1. Disconnect the electrical terminal plug and the 2 air hoses at the auxiliary air regulator.

2. Voltage must be present at the terminal plug with the ignition switch ON.

3. Check the air bore of the regulator. With the engine temperature approximately 68°F (20°C), the bore should be half open.

4. Connect the terminal plug and the 2 air hoses tot he auxiliary air regulator.

5. Start the engine and the auxiliary air regulator bore should close within 5 minutes of engine operation by the cut-off valve.

Mixture Control Unit and Sensor Plate

REMOVAL AND INSTALLATION

1. Disconnect the large intake pipe (made of rubber) from the unit by loosening the clamp and pulling it off.

2. Loosen the 3 screws in the top of the fuel distributor. Open the clips holding the fuel line to the extreme control unit, and remove the clamp linking the 4 fuel lines together.

3. Lift the distributor off the control unit,

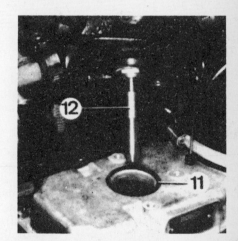
Fuel distributor control valve (12) and seal (11)

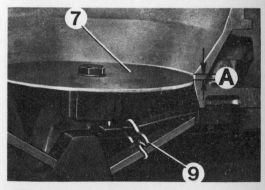
Sensor plate (7) positioning in venturi with adjusting spring (9). "A" is clearance allowable between the top of the venturi and surface of sensor plate

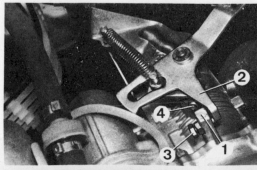
Adjusting 320i basic throttle setting

using tape to hold the piston up inside the unit, and move it aside.

4. Disconnect the electrical plug at the air horn, and the small vacuum hose and large air line connected to the vacuum regulator, mounted near the rear of the mixture control unit.

5. Loosen the 2 mounting nuts located on the wheel well side of the unit and lift it out.

6. Remove the bolts in the flange holding upper (10) and lower (11) sections of the unit together. Then remove the 6 bolts (3 located inside the lower housing) which retain the air cleaner housing to the mixture control unit.

7. Replace the mixture control unit lower and upper housings together with an entire new unit. The new unit will have to be split (top and bottom sections separate at the flange). This will permit the air cleaner bolts to be attached from inside. Use a new gasket, and reassemble the upper and lower sections of the new mixture control unit after the air cleaner housing is attached; then, reverse the remaining procedures to install it, using a new seal under the fuel distributor.

ADJUSTMENT

NOTE: *49 state and California control units are not interchangeable.*

1. Remove the air intake cowl at the mixture control unit and throttle housing.

2. Turn the ignition ON for approximately 5 seconds, and during this time, slowly raise the sensor plate with a magnet. Turn the ignition switch OFF.

NOTE: *The amount of resistance should be constant when raising the sensor and no resistance should be felt when pushing the sensor plate down quickly.*

3. The sensor plate should be flush or 0.5mm below the beginning of the venturi taper. If necessary to adjust, remove the mixture control from the intermediate housing and bend the spring accordingly. Center the sensor plate in the bore by loosening the center plate screw. Tighten when aligned.

NOTE: *With the sensor plate too high, the engine will run on and with the sensor plate too low, poor cold and warm engine start-up will result.*

4. If the sensor plate movement is erratic, the control piston can be sticking. Remove the fuel distributor and inspect the control piston for damage and replace as necessary.

CAUTION: *Do not drop the control valve.*

SYSTEM PRESSURE TESTING

Install a shut-off valve and an oil pressure gauge between the control pressure line and the fuel distributor, with the pressure gauge next to the fuel distributor.

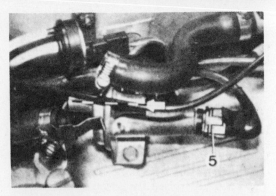

Installation of the shut-off valve (12) and pressure gauge (13-3-060) on the fuel distributor pressure line (11)

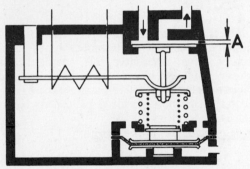

Cross-section of the warm-up valve. "A" represents opening of the valve—large opening on cold engine and small opening on hot engine

COLD ENGINE PRESSURE TEST

1. Disconnect the terminal plug at the mixture control unit to avoid excessive heat.

2. Open the valve for oil flow and turn on the ignition switch to operate the fuel pump, but do not start the engine.

3. Control pressures depend upon the engine coolant temperature. At a temperature of 50°F (10°C), oil pressure should be 10-11 psi and at 77°F (25°C), oil pressure should be 22.0 psi. At coolant temperature of 104°F (40°C), the pressure should be over 29.4 psi.

NOTE: *Oil pressure too low warm-up regulator defective. Oil pressure too high-fuel return flow insufficient or defective warm-up regulator.*

4. Turn the ignition OFF.

WARM ENGINE CONTROL PRESSURE

1. Open the shut-off valve for oil flow. Disconnect the mixture control terminal plug and turn the ignition ON to start the fuel pump. Do not start the engine.

2. The control pressure should be 48-54 psi after 3 minutes, with the engine coolant at operating temperature. If the control pressure

does not rise, check the wire plug terminal for current at the warm-up regulator. If current is present, the heating coil may be defective and would necessitate the replacement of the warm-up regulator.

TEST WITH ENGINE OPERATING

1. Connect the wire plugs to the auxiliary air regulator and to the mixture control unit. Install the air intake cowl.
2. With the engine running at idle speed, the control pressure should be 48-54 psi.

COLD OR WARM ENGINE SYSTEM PRESSURE

1. Close the pressure shut-off valve with the engine stopped and disconnect the mixture control unit terminal plug.
2. Turn the ignition ON, but do not start the engine.
3. The speed control pressure must be 64-74 psi.
4. Turn the ignition OFF and if the pressure is not within specifications, one of the following defects may be the cause:
   a. Leakage at the fuel lines or connections.
   b. Fuel filter clogged.
   c. Engine overruns.
   d. Defective fuel pump.
   e. Pressure adjustment incorrect.

If the pressure is too high:
   a. Fuel return flow is restricted.
   b. Incorrect pressure regulator setting.
   c. Control piston stuck.

NOTE: *Shims may be used to change the pressure. Shim thickness changes will vary the pressure as follows:*
   0.01mm − 0.85 psi
   0.50mm − 4.3 psi

5. The transfer valve of pressure regulator must open at 50-57 psi.

CUT-OFF PRESSURE CHECKING FOR LEAKAGE

1. Open the pressure shut-off valve and turn the ignition ON.
2. Disconnect the wire plug at the mixture control unit and then reconnect the plug. Turn the ignition OFF.
3. Cut-off pressure must not drop below 24 psi after several minutes.
4. If the pressure drops too early, one of the following may be leaking.
   a. Pressure regulator O-ring.
   b. Warm-up regulator or supply line.
   c. Fuel pump check valve.
   d. Pressure reservoir.
5. Remove the pressure gauge and shut-off valve and reconnect the pressure line.

Location of vacuum regulator (1), vacuum control line (2) and auxiliary air valve (3)

Vacuum Regulator

TESTING

The coasting vacuum regulator must be open to supply air behind the throttle valve, through the by-pass bore, when the vehicle is coasting.
1. Disconnect the vacuum hose and plug the end.
2. Increase the engine speed to 3000 rpm and release the throttle. The engine speed should drop quickly.
3. Connect the vacuum hose to the regulator valve and again increase the engine speed.
4. Release the throttle. The engine speed should drop slowly if the regulator is functioning properly.

Auxiliary Air Valve

TESTING

The auxiliary air valve is good, if after starting the engine, the rpm is higher than normal idle, for a brief period of time.

Temperature Timing Switch

The purpose of the timing switch is to control the cold start valve during the initial start-up of

Disconnecting the air hose and electrical connection (5) from the auxiliary air regulator

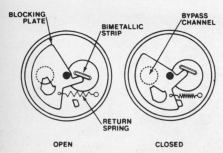

Internal components of the auxilliary air regulator showing cold (open) and warm (closed) positions

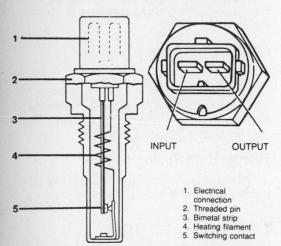

Testing the temperature timing switch (19) with terminals G and W shown

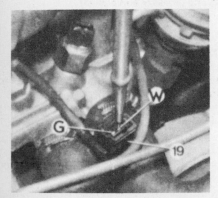

1. Electrical connection
2. Threaded pin
3. Bimetal strip
4. Heating filament
5. Switching contact

Typical thermo-time switch showing construction and terminal location

the engine, in the relationship to the coolant temperature of $-4°F$ ($-20°C$). The off temperature is $95°F$ ($35°C$).

TESTING

1. Disconnect the terminal plug from the switch.

2. Connect a test lamp from the positive battery terminal to the **W** post on the temperature timing switch.

3. The test lamp should be on at coolant temperatures below $95°F$ ($35°C$) and go out above temperatures of $95°F$ ($35°C$).

Cold Start Valve

The purpose of the cold start valve is to inject added fuel into the induction system as dictated by the temperature timing switch.

REMOVAL AND INSTALLATION

1. Remove the electrical connector and the fuel line to the valve.

2. Remove the retaining bolts and pull the valve assembly from the air collector.

3. Replace the rubber seal ring during installation.

TESTING

Remove the colt start valve from the induction header. Connect the relay terminal C87 to a positive battery connector. The cold start valve should eject fuel. If not, it should be replaced.

CAUTION: *When testing the cold start valve, eject the fuel into a safe container as fuel is extremely hazardous.*

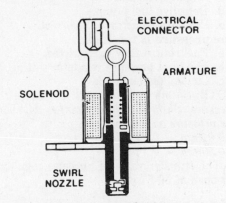

Sectional view of cold start valve

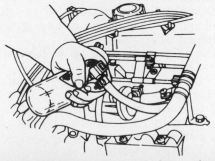

Place the cold start valve nozzle into a clear container when testing

Numbered locations of fuel distributor lines for the 320i. See text

Detach upper housing (10). Remove the bolts (arrowed). Make sure to replace the gasket (11) in reassembly

Fuel Distributor

REMOVAL AND INSTALLATION

1. Remove the 4 nuts attaching the fuel lines leading to the injectors to the top of the distributor (1 through 4). Unscrew the union nut and disconnect the line leading to the warm-up regulator (5) (at the front).

2. Disconnect the 2, large low pressure fuel lines coming from the fuel filter (6 and 9) (at the front) and going back to the tank (at the wheel well side), by removing the attaching bolts. Also disconnect the 2 high pressure (small) lines (7 and 8) from the side of the unit (front to warm up regulator, and the rear line going to the start valve) in a similar manner.

3. Remove the 3 screws from the top of the distributor unit. Then, lift the unit off the top of the mixture control.

4. Install in reverse order. Clean the control piston in a suitable solvent and replace it, if it is damaged. Use a new gasket where the distributor fits onto the top of the mixture control unit.

Injection Valves

The injection valves must open at a minimum fuel pressure of 47 psi.

TESTING

1. Connect a pressure valve and shut-off valve in the pressure line to the fuel distributor, with the pressure gauge on the fuel distributor side of the shut-off valve.

2. Open the shut-off valve, remove the injec-

Use of special tool (13–5–030) to measure fuel discharge to determine a good injector valve

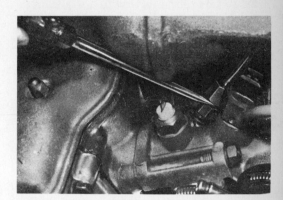

Using a screwdriver to remove 320i injection valves

Pulling the sensor plate (7) upward to test the injector valves

tors from the intake manifold and turn the ignition switch ON.

3. Disconnect the terminal plug from the mixture control unit.

4. Lift the sensor plate for a maximum of 4 seconds.

5. The pressure should not drop more than 4 psi. If the pressure drops more than the specifications, the fuel filter is clogged, fuel pump rate is inadequate or the fuel tank is empty.

REMOVAL AND INSTALLATION

1. Remove the rubber intake hose leading from the mixture control unit to the throttle unit. Remove the 4 retaining nuts for each, and then remove No. 2 and No. 3 (the 2 center cylinders) intake pipes.

2. The injector valves incorporate union nuts and flatted section on each valve to permit the lines to be attached to the valves. However, the injection lines need not be disconnected to remove the valves, which are simply pressed into the intake ports. To remove each valve, simply pass a small pry-bar downward between the intake header and the cam cover, insert the blade into the groove between the fuel line nut and flatted portion of the injection valve, and pry out. After the valve is out of the port, hold the flatted section of the valve with a wrench, use another wrench to unscrew the union nut, and disconnect the fuel line.

3. On installation, first press the white insulating bushing back into the intake port, if it came out with the valve. Then, press the rubber seal into the grove. Finally, snugly press in the injection valve. Reinstall the intake pipes, using new gaskets.

INJECTOR VALVE COMPARISON

When the engine is operating erratically, with the compression and the air induction systems good, the injector valves should be tested with the use of a special tool (13-5-030) or equivalent.

Testing

1. The tool consists of scaled measuring tubes. Insert each injector valve into one of the tubes and secure. Disconnect the wire terminal plug from the mixture control valve, turn the ignition switch ON. Lift the sensor plate so that the injectors will fill the tubes with fuel.

2. Empty the tubes and again fill the tubes with fuel until the 15cc mark is reached on one tube. Compare the difference between the tubes for the fuel levels. The difference should not be over 15%.

3. If the fuel level difference is over 15% between tubes, exchange a good injector valve with a questionable one and repeat the test.

4. If the questionable injector valve flow rate remains the same, the valve is defective and must be replaced. If the injector valve flow rate is normal, the fuel distributor unit is defective and must be replaced.

BOSCH L-JETRONIC AND MOTRONIC FUEL INJECTION SYSTEMS

The Bosch L-Jetronic fuel injection system is electronically controlled to regulate the fuel supply in relation to the air flow. An air flow meter, located in the air intake chamber, converts angular movement of an air baffle plate

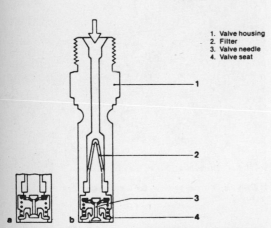

1. Valve housing
2. Filter
3. Valve needle
4. Valve seat

Cross section of typical K-Jetronic fuel injector showing closed (a) and open (b) positions

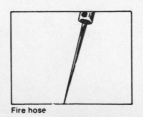
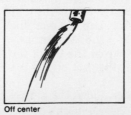
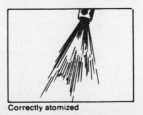

Uneven spray   Fire hose   Off center   Correctly atomized

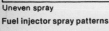
Fuel injector spray patterns

Fuel injector spray patterns

into a voltage signal, which is sent to the control unit.

As the engine begins its revolution, twin contacts, located 180° apart in the base of the distributor, trigger current impulses to the control unit at one impulse per crankshaft rotation.

After computation of the signals, a command signal is sent from the control unit to the electromagnetic injector valve, which are wired in a parallel circuit, causing them to open simultaneously. To obtain smooth combustion, half the total fuel volume necessary for the engine cycle, is injected per half rotation of the camshaft, which corresponds to each rotation of the crankshaft.

Automatic cold start and warm-up devices are incorporated in the system to give better driveability and engine operation during the initial start and warm-up period, when added fuel is needed.

Control Unit

REMOVAL AND INSTALLATION

3.0Si

1. Remove the rear seat and remove the control unit from the floor panel.

2. Open the wire connector clamp and pull out the cover slide.

3. Carefully remove the connector from the control unit.

4. During the installation, a matched pressure sensor should be replaced also. Random pairing can result in excessive fuel consumption and poor engine operation.

All Other Models

1. The control unit is located behind the glove box on all models but the 733i where it is behind the right side cowl cover.

2. Push the lock lug towards the wire loom or press the circlip rearward and pull the multiple terminal plug to the right. Disconnect the individual plug, if connected.

3. Remove the control unit from the body.

4. When installing the control box, connect the individual connector if the vehicle is to be used in high altitude operation.

NOTE: *When the individual connector circuit is complete, the fuel injection time is reduced, resulting in a 6% leaner air/fuel mixture necessary for high altitude operation.*

Pressure Sensor

REMOVAL AND INSTALLATION

3.0Si

1. The pressure sensor is located near the firewall on the left side of the engine compartment.

2. Remove the vacuum hose from the pressure sensor.

3. Remove the base plate from the bearing block and if equipped with automatic transmission, remove the starter locking relay.

4. Invert the base plate and remove the pressure sensor retaining bolts.

5. Install the pressure sensor in the reverse order.

NOTE: *Refer to steps 4 and 5 under the 3.0Si control unit removal and installation for proper part replacement.*

All Other Models

The pressure sensor is an integral part of the air flow sensor unit and cannot be replaced separately.

Mixture control unit upper section (10) separated from the lower section (11). Arrows indicate bolts to remove to separate the lower section from the air filter housing

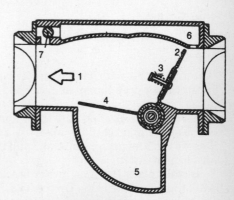

1. Air direction
2. Baffle plate
3. Check valve
4. Compensation valve
5. Damper valve chamber
6. By-pass circuit
7. By-pass adjusting screw

Cross–section of the air flow sensor

Remove the three (arrowed) nuts attaching the airflow sensor to the base of the air filter

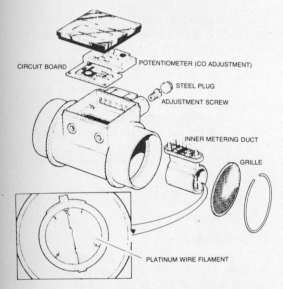

Exploded view of air mass sensor systems

Air Flow Sensor

REMOVAL AND INSTALLATION

528e AND 530i

1. Disconnect the multiple connector and then loosen the air hose clamps at either end of the unit.

2. Remove the air cleaner. Lift the volume control out of the bracket (530i only).

3. Remove the 3 mounting bolts, and pull the unit out of the bracket.

4. To install, place the unit in the bracket and install the mounting bolts. On the 530i, install the volume control unit. Install the air cleaner and connect the hoses to either end.

All Other Models

1. Disconnect the multiple connector. Loosen the air hose clamps at either end of the unit, and detach the hose on the engine side.

2. Remove the 2 air cleaner mounting nuts and remove the air cleaner and air flow sensor. Then, remove the 3 nuts attaching the air flow sensor to the base of the air filter, detach the hose from the air cleaner, and remove the unit. Install in reverse order.

Throttle Valve

ADJUSTMENT

3.0Si

1. Loosen the locknut and loosen the adjusting screw until there is play between the stop and the screw.

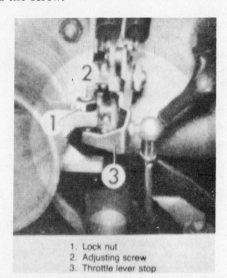

1. Lock nut
2. Adjusting screw
3. Throttle lever stop

Throttle valve adjustment—3.0Si

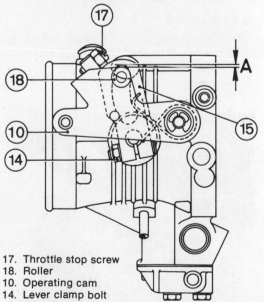

17. Throttle stop screw
18. Roller
10. Operating cam
14. Lever clamp bolt
15. Throttle lever
A. Clearance between roller and gate

Throttle lever adjustment—528i, 530i, 600 series, and 733i

2. Tighten the adjusting screw until the stop is just contacted. Operate the throttle lever several times and allow to snap back against the stop by spring pressure.

3. Tighten the adjusting screw one full turn and lock the screw with the locknut.

All Other Models

1. Loosen the throttle lever clamp screw and the throttle stop screw.

2. Press the throttle valve closed and tighten the throttle stop screw until the clearance between the roller and the gate is approximately 0.5-1.0mm (clearance A).

3. Tighten the throttle lever clamp screw. Tighten the throttle stop screw one complete turn and lock with the locknut.

4. Adjust the throttle switch and the idle speed.

Throttle Valve Switch

The throttle valve switch cuts off the fuel supply to avoid engine overrunning. This is done by switch contacts, which are closed when the throttle valve is in the idling position.

When the throttle valve is moved 2°, the throttle valve switch movement opens the cutoff contacts and closes the acceleration enrichment control. Electrical impulses sent to the control unit determine the fuel quantity required for acceleration. A second switch closes

Throttle switch—528e

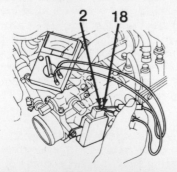

Checking the throttle switch adjustment with an ohmmeter

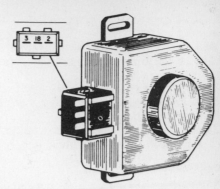

Typical throttle switch showing pin numbers

the acceleration enrichment circuit only when the fuel cut-off switch is open.

REMOVAL AND INSTALLATION

All Models except 528e

1. Remove the terminal plug from the throttle valve switch.

2. Remove the switch retaining screws and remove the switch from the throttle shaft.

3. To install the switch, engage the throttle shaft into the switch orifice. Install the retaining screws and terminal plug.

528e

1. Unscrew the hose clamp (1) and push back the air hose.

2. Disconnect the accelerator cables (2 and 3).

3. On models with automatic transmissions, disconnect the accelerator cable for the automatic transmission.

4. Disconnect the electrical connector, unscrew the mounting screws and remove the throttle housing.

5. Installation is in the reverse order of removal. Always replace the gasket and adjust the accelerator cable setting.

ADJUSTMENT

3.0Si

1. Disconnect the electrical terminal plug from the throttle valve switch and loosen the switch retaining screws.

2. Connect the leads of a calibrated ohmmeter to terminals #17 and #45 of the throttle valve switch.

3. Rotate the switch until the meter needle shows infinity. Rotate the switch in the opposite direction until the meter needle moves to 0 resistance.

4. Mark the housing opposite the center indicator on the switch scale.

5. Rotate the switch clockwise 2° as indicated on the scale.

NOTE: *The scale is graduated in ½° increments.*

6. As the switch is rotated, the meter needle should move to infinity as the switch contacts open.

7. Rotate the switch counterclockwise to the original scale to housing mark. The meter needle should return to 0 resistance.

8. Lock the switch in place with the retaining screws and attach the wire terminal plug.

All Other Models

1. Connect an ohmmeter lead to terminals #18 and #2 of the throttle switch, after removing the terminal plug.

2. At idle position of the throttle, the meter needle should read 0 resistance.

3. Connect the meter leads to terminals #2 and #3.

4. With the throttle wide open, the meter needle should read 0 resistance.

5. The switch can be moved for small adjustments. If adjustments are unattainable, replace the switch.

Air Intake Temperature Sensor
REMOVAL AND INSTALLATION
3.0Si

The temperature sensor can be unscrewed from the air collector after disconnecting the electrical plug.

Testing

The desired resistance is listed in the following chart depending on temperature readings.

Degrees F (C)	Resistance (Ohms)
14 (−10)	9.6
32 (0)	6.4
50 (+10)	4.3
68 (20)	3.0
86 (30)	2.1
104 (40)	1.5
122 (50)	1.0
140 (60)	0.79

Coolant Temperature Sensor
REMOVAL AND INSTALLATION
All Models

Disconnect the electrical terminal plug and unscrew the coolant temperature sensor.

Testing
3.0Si

The desired resistance is noted in the chart depending on the temperature reading

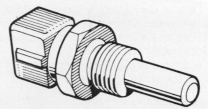

Typical coolant temperature sensor used on L-Jetronic systems

Degrees F (C)	Resistance (Ohms)
14 (−10)	9.2
32 (0)	5.9
50 (+10)	3.7
68 (20)	2.5
86 (30)	1.7
104 (40)	1.2
122 (50)	0.84
140 (60)	0.60
158 (70)	0.43
176 (80)	0.32
194 (90)	0.25
212 (100)	0.20

All Other Models

The coolant temperature sensor can be checked with a test lamp. The circuit should open at temperatures above 113°F (45°C) and closed below 113°F (45°C).

Temperature Timing Switch
REMOVAL AND INSTALLATION
All Models except 3.0Si

Partially drain the coolant and disconnect the electrical connector plug. Pull off plug (if so equipped) and unscrew the temperature timing switch. After installation, bleed the cooling system.

CAUTION: *When draining the coolant, keep in mind that cats and dogs are attracted by the ethylene glycol antifreeze, and are quite likely to drink any that is left in an uncovered container or in puddles on the ground. This will prove fatal in sufficient quantity. Always drain the coolant into a sealable container. Coolant should be reused unless it is contaminated or several years old.*

TESTING

With the use of a test lamp, the switch can be tested at various temperatures for continuity. The operating time is eight seconds at −4°F (−20°C) and declines to 0 seconds at +59°F (−15°C).

Cold Start Valve
REMOVAL AND INSTALLATION
All Models

1. Remove the electrical connector and the fuel line to the valve.
2. Remove the retaining bolts and pull the valve assembly from the air collector.
3. Replace the rubber sealing ring during installation.

TESTING
3.0Si

The cold start valve should only receive current when the starter or the timer switch is in operation. The use of a test lamp on the terminal end of the starter valve and to ground, will indicate current presence to the switch when starting. The current should stop flowing no longer than eight seconds after the starter is stopped. The temperature timing switch is operable under temperatures of 41°F (5°C).

All Other Models

1. Remove the cold start valve from the air collector but do not remove the fuel hose or the electrical connector.
2. Remove the connector plug from the air flow sensor.
3. Install a jumper wire between plug #36 and #39 on the air flow sensor connector.
4. Remove the connector from the cold start relay.
5. Connect a jumper wire from terminal #87 to #30 of the cold start relay connector.
6. Turn the ignition switch ON. The cold start valve should eject fuel.

Cold Start Relay
TESTING

All Models

1. Connect a ground wire to terminal #85.
2. Connect a positive lead to terminal #30 and #86 C.
3. The relay is good when the test lamp operates when probed to terminals #87 and #86.

Injection Valves
REMOVAL AND INSTALLATION
3.0Si

1. Remove the electrical plug from the injection valves.
2. Loosen and remove the injection valve from the ring line.
3. Remove the retaining bolts and pull the injector from the manifold.

Cold start relay contact points

4. To install, replace the rubber ring and do not damage the nozzle jet during the installation.

530i, 630CSi, and 633i

1. With the air collector removed, disconnect the electrical connector plugs from the 6 injection valves.
2. Remove the valve retaining bolts and remove the injector tube with all the valves attached.
3. Remove the retaining clamps and remove the valves from the injector tube.
4. To install, reverse the removal procedure.

All Other Models

1. With the injector tube and injector valves removed from the engine, cut the metal hose clamp sleeve and remove the sleeve.

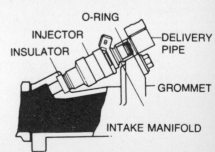

L-Jetronic fuel injector installation showing position of nozzle in the intake port

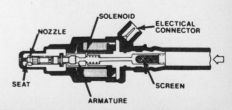

Cross section of a typical L-Jetronic fuel injector

2. Heat the hose with a soldering iron and remove the injector hose from the tube.

3. To install the injector valve assembly on the tube, clean the tube adapter and coat the inside of the hose with fuel.

4. Install the fuel injector hose with the hose sleeve on the injector tube and push against the stop, with the electrical terminal facing up.

5. Complete the installation in the reverse of the removal procedure.

DIESEL FUEL SYSTEM
Fuel Filter
REPLACEMENT

1. Loosen the bleeder screw located on top of the filter mounting fitting with a regular screwdriver. Place a container under the filter and loosen the drain cock to drain a small amount of fuel (this will keep fuel from spilling when the filter is removed).

CAUTION: *Never smoke when working around diesel fuel! Avoid all sources of sparks or ignition. Fuel vapors are EXTREMELY volatile!*

2. Disconnect the plug on the water level sensor. Unscrew the filter with a standard oil filter strap wrench.

3. Remove the water level sensor from the old filter and move it over to the new one.

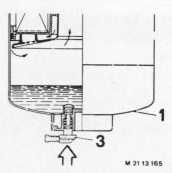

Drain the water from the filter (1) through the drain valve (3)

M 21 13 165

4. Thoroughly coat the seal on top of the new filter with clean fuel. Start the filter onto the threads, turn it until the gasket touches, and then turn it just one half turn more by hand.

5. Disconnect the plug for the fuel transfer pump. Open the bleeder screw. Jumper terminals 30 and 87. When fuel that is bubble-free runs out of the bleed screw, tighten it. Remove the jumper and reconnect the plug.

6. Start the engine and operate it to check for leaks. Tighten the filter just a bit further, if necessary.

DRAINING WATER FROM THE SYSTEM

Hold a half pint container under the bleeder screw and open the drain cock. See Step 5 of the

1 – Fuel tank
2 – Fuel feed line
3 – Fuel filter with water trap
4 – Distributor-pattern injection pump
    with integral fuel pump
5 – Fuel injection pipe
6 – Injector
7 – Fuel return line

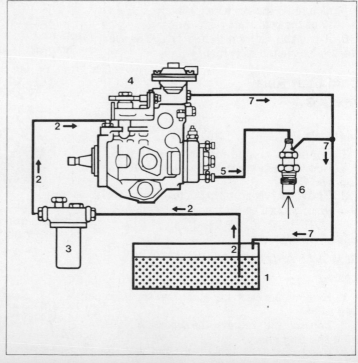

524 Turbo Diesel—fuel supply system

procedure above for fuel filter replacement, and activate the fuel transfer pump as described there. Then, press the drain adapter in to open it. Drain until pure fuel runs out.

Diesel Injection Pump

REMOVAL AND INSTALLATION

NOTE: *This is a complex operation requiring several special tools. Use 13 5 020 or equivalent to remove injection lines. Use 13 5 010 and 13 5 061 or equivalent to press the injection pump off its sprocket. Also required are 2 M6 × 20mm bolts and plastic caps to seal openings.*

1. Remove the drain plugs from both the block and the radiator to completely drain coolant. Remove the fan cowl and fan as described earlier in this section.

CAUTION: *When draining the coolant, keep in mind that cats and dogs are attracted by the ethylene glycol antifreeze, and are quite likely to drink any that is left in an uncovered container or in puddles on the ground. This will prove fatal in sufficient quantity. Always drain the coolant into a sealable container. Coolant should be reused unless it is contaminated or several years old.*

2. Remove the oil filler cap to watch the valves. Turn the crankshaft with a socket

Remove the nut on the cogged pulley

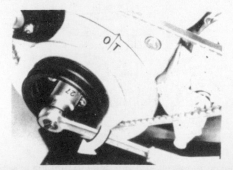

Turn the crankshaft to T.D.C.

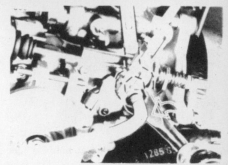

Unscrew the line and hold it with the special wrench

wrench so tha No. 1 cylinder is at TDC firing position (No. 6 valves overlapping).

3. Disconnect and remove the upper and lower radiator hoses. Remove the alternator drive belt. Remove the timing belt cover, as described earlier in this section.

4. Using a backup wrench, use the special injection line wrench to disconnect the inlet line at the injection pump. Plug the opening.

5. Disconnect the fuel return line at the connector below the pump. Remove the wiring harness clamp nearby.

6. Remove the clamp for the oil dipstick tube. Disconnect the hoses on the timing advance unit. Remove the air collector bracket near the rear of the injection pump. Remove the popoff valve air connection.

7. Disconnect the hoses for boost pressure, injection pump oil drain, vacuum, and the altitude compensator.

8. Remove the line running from the turbo to the intake manifold. Remove the oil trap from the valve cover. Then pull off the 3 plugs nearby.

9. Disconnect the fuel shutoff and idle switch connectors.

10. Disconnect the throttle cables at the cam and remove the cable housings from the bracket.

11. Disconnect all the coupling nuts at the injection nozzles with the special wrench, being careful not to bend the injection lines. Do the same with the lines at the injection pump end. Plug all openings and then pull the lines out of the way.

12. Remove the nut attaching the injection pump sprocket to the pump. Then, bolt the special tools for pressing the pump off the sprocket to the sprocket. Turn the crankshaft as necessary to line the boltholes up so the bolts fastening the tool to the block on either side can be installed and then install them.

13. Remove the 2 nuts situated directly behind the front cover. Then, remove the 3 bolts that fasten the pump at the rear.

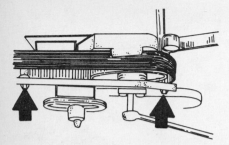

Install bolts at the arrowed point to hold the injection pump installation

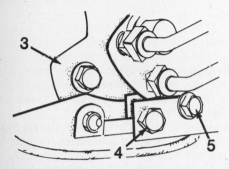

Loosen the bolts shown (3–5) before starting injection pump installation

14. Turn the large bolt at the center of the special tool and press the pump out of the sprocket.

15. Pull off the EGR pressure converter hoses at the converter. Remove the wiring harness for the pump out of the clips. Remove the pump. Be careful not to disturb the pump shaft. The key must remain at the top (don't lose it).

16. Install the pump so the key fits through the slot in the sprocket. Then, install and tighten the 2 nuts situated directly behind the front cover. Make sure the pump rests tightly against its mounting on the front cover.

17. Remove the special tool used to press the pump out of the sprocket. Then, install the sprocket bolt and torque it to 33-35 ft. lbs.

18. Adjust the static timing as described below.

19. Perform the remaining procedures in reverse order. Install the injection lines as described above under Injector Nozzle Replacement. Bleed the fuel system as described above.

INJECTION TIMING

NOTE: *To perform this procedure, a special dial indicator gauge and a timing pin, BMW tools 13 5 330 and 11 2 300 or equivalent are needed.*

1. Make sure the coolant temperature is above 68xF so the throttle lever will rest against the idle stop—not in the cold fast idle position.

2. Unfasten the coolant overflow tank and move it out of the way. Disconnect and plug the overflow hose.

3. Remove the plug in the injection pump head (between 2 of the lines going to the injectors). Install 13 5 330 or equivalent and hand tighten it. Remove the fan as described in the cooling system section. Turn the crankshaft, watching the dial gauge, in the forward direction until the gauge reaches its maximum value. Then, zero the gauge. Continue turning the engine toward TDC as while pressing the timing pin into the timing hole in the flywheel housing. The pin will lock into a hole in the flywheel, keeping the engine at TDC. Check that No. 6 valves are overlapping by removing the oil filler cap. Repeat the procedure, to set the engine at TDC firing position for No. 1, if the valves of No. 6 are not overlapping. Make sure to zero the gauge in the same way.

4. The reading should be 0.65-0.67mm. If it is within these limits, remove the gauges and replace the plug with a new gasket, restoring other parts disturbed to their normal condition. If the reading is incorrect, follow the rest of the steps.

5. Remove the bracket for the air collector that is near the injection pump. Remove the wiring harness from its clamps.

6. Remove the bolts 3, 4 and 5 at the rear of the pump (see the illustration).

7. Loosen the hose clamp that's in the way at the front of the pump. Loosen the 2 nuts behind the front cover just enough to permit turning the pump. To increase the reading or advance the timing, turn the pump toward the engine. When the figure is within tolerance, tighten the 2 nuts on the front cover and then tighten 3-5 in numerical order at the rear. Reverse the remaining procedures.

Injection Nozzle

REMOVAL AND INSTALLATION

NOTE: *To remove these injection nozzles, a special tool BMW 13 5 020 or equivalent will*

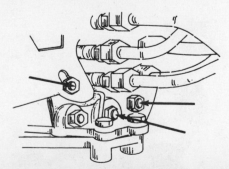

Loosen the three arrowed bolts to turn the injection pump for timing it. These are at the rear of the pump

be required. Also needed are caps to prevent the entry of dirt.

1. Remove the oil trap located on the valve cover. Loosen the mounting clamps for the injection lines.

2. Disconnect the plugs associated with the injection system. There are a diagnostic plug and 2 others nearby.

3. Pull off the leakoff hoses for the injectors with a pair of pliers. Then, unscrew the coupling nuts on the injectors with the special tool 13 5 020 or equivalent.

4. Use the same tool to unscrew the coupling nuts on the injection pump. Make sure not to hit the lines with the tool handle and bend them.

5. Unscrew the injectors using the special tool. For No. 1 injector with the wire, run the plug through the tool to protect it. Make sure it is as close as possible to the middle.

6. Install in reverse order. Coat the threads of each injector with CRC® and torque each injector to 25-33 ft. lbs.

7. When tightening injection lines to the pump, tighten No.4 cylinder's line first. All injection line fittings (both ends) are torqued to 10-18 ft. lbs. Leave the injector ends loose for bleeding.

8. Bleed the fuel system as follows:

a. Disconnect the electrical plug for the fuel transfer pump relay. Jumper the terminals numbered 30 and 87 to operate the fuel transfer pump. Then, loosen the banjo fitting for the inlet fuel line on the injection pump until pure fuel runs out. Tighten the fitting. Remove the jumper wire and reconnect the plug.

b. Loosen the bleed plug on the injection pump 2 turns. Then, crank the engine until air-free fuel runs out. Torque the plug to 10.5-14.5 ft. lbs.

c. With the injection lines still loose at the nozzles, crank the engine. When fuel that is free of bubbles runs out of each line at the nozzle, stop cranking the engine. Torque the nozzles with the special tool to 10-18 ft. lbs.

Chassis Electrical

UNDERSTANDING AND TROUBLESHOOTING ELECTRICAL SYSTEMS

With the rate at which both import and domestic manufacturers are incorporating electronic control systems into their production lines, it won't be long before every new vehicle is equipped with one or more on-board computer, like the EEC-IV unit installed on the truck. These electronic components (with no moving parts) should theoretically last the life of the vehicle, provided nothing external happens to damage the circuits or memory chips.

While it is true that electronic components should never wear out, in the real world malfunctions do occur. It is also true that any computer-based system is extremely sensitive to electrical voltages and cannot tolerate careless or haphazard testing or service procedures. An inexperienced individual can literally do major damage looking for a minor problem by using the wrong kind of test equipment or connecting test leads or connectors with the ignition switch ON. When selecting test equipment, make sure the manufacturers instructions state that the tester is compatible with whatever type of electronic control system is being serviced. Read all instructions carefully and double check all test points before installing probes or making any test connections.

The following section outlines basic diagnosis techniques for dealing with computerized automotive control systems. Along with a general explanation of the various types of test equipment available to aid in servicing modern electronic automotive systems, basic repair techniques for wiring harnesses and connectors is given. Read the basic information before attempting any repairs or testing on any computerized system, to provide the background of information necessary to avoid the most common and obvious mistakes that can cost both time and money. Although the replacement and testing procedures are simple in themselves, the systems are not, and unless one has a thorough understanding of all components and their function within a particular computerized control system, the logical test sequence these systems demand cannot be followed. Minor malfunctions can make a big difference, so it is important to know how each component affects the operation of the overall electronic system to find the ultimate cause of a problem without replacing good components unnecessarily. It is not enough to use the correct test equipment; the test equipment must be used correctly.

Safety Precautions

CAUTION: *Whenever working on or around any computer based microprocessor control system, always observe these general precautions to prevent the possibility of personal injury or damage to electronic components.*

• Never install or remove battery cables with the key ON or the engine running. Jumper cables should be connected with the key OFF to avoid power surges that can damage electronic control units. Engines equipped with computer controlled systems should avoid both giving and getting jump starts due to the possibility of serious damage to components from arcing in the engine compartment when connections are made with the ignition ON.

• Always remove the battery cables before charging the battery. Never use a high output charger on an installed battery or attempt to use any type of "hot shot" (24 volt) starting aid.

• Exercise care when inserting test probes into connectors to insure good connections without damaging the connector or spreading the pins. Always probe connectors from the rear (wire) side, NOT the pin side, to avoid accidental shorting of terminals during test procedures.

• Never remove or attach wiring harness connectors with the ignition switch ON, especially to an electronic control unit.

• Do not drop any components during service procedures and never apply 12 volts directly to any component (like a solenoid or relay) unless instructed specifically to do so. Some component electrical windings are designed to safely handle only 4 or 5 volts and can be destroyed in seconds if 12 volts are applied directly to the connector.

• Remove the electronic control unit if the vehicle is to be placed in an environment where temperatures exceed approximately 176°F (80°C), such as a paint spray booth or when arc or gas welding near the control unit location in the car.

ORGANIZED TROUBLESHOOTING

When diagnosing a specific problem, organized troubleshooting is a must. The complexity of a modern automobile demands that you approach any problem in a logical, organized manner. There are certain troubleshooting techniques that are standard:

1. Establish when the problem occurs. Does the problem appear only under certain conditions? Were there any noises, odors, or other unusual symptoms?

2. Isolate the problem area. To do this, make some simple tests and observations; then eliminate the systems that are working properly. Check for obvious problems such as broken wires, dirty connections or split or disconnected vacuum hoses. Always check the obvious before assuming something complicated is the cause.

3. Test for problems systematically to determine the cause once the problem area is isolated. Are all the components functioning properly? Is there power going to electrical switches and motors? Is there vacuum at vacuum switches and/or actuators? Is there a mechanical problem such as bent linkage or loose mounting screws? Doing careful, systematic checks will often turn up most causes on the first inspection without wasting time checking components that have little or no relationship to the problem.

4. Test all repairs after the work is done to make sure that the problem is fixed. Some causes can be traced to more than one component, so a careful verification of repair work is important to pick up additional malfunctions that may cause a problem to reappear or a different problem to arise. A blown fuse, for example, is a simple problem that may require more than another fuse to repair. If you don't look for a problem that caused a fuse to blow, for example, a shorted wire may go undetected.

Experience has shown that most problems tend to be the result of a fairly simple and obvious cause, such as loose or corroded connectors or air leaks in the intake system; making careful inspection of components during testing essential to quick and accurate troubleshooting. Special, hand held computerized testers designed specifically for diagnosing the EEC-IV system are available from a variety of aftermarket sources, as well as from the vehicle manufacturer, but care should be taken that any test equipment being used is designed to diagnose that particular computer controlled system accurately without damaging the control unit (ECU) or components being tested.

NOTE: *Pinpointing the exact cause of trouble in an electrical system can sometimes only be accomplished by the use of special test equipment. The following describes commonly used test equipment and explains how to put it to best use in diagnosis. In addition to the information covered below, the manufacturer's instructions booklet provided with the tester should be read and clearly understood before attempting any test procedures.*

TEST EQUIPMENT
Jumper Wires

Jumper wires are simple, yet extremely valuable, pieces of test equipment. Jumper wires are merely wires that are used to bypass sections of a circuit. The simplest type of jumper wire is merely a length of multistrand wire with an alligator clip at each end. Jumper wires are usually fabricated from lengths of standard automotive wire and whatever type of connector (alligator clip, spade connector or pin connector) that is required for the particular vehicle being tested. The well equipped tool box will have several different styles of jumper wires in several different lengths. Some jumper wires are made with three or more terminals coming from a common splice for special purpose testing. In cramped, hard-to-reach areas it is advisable to have insulated boots over the jumper wire terminals in order to prevent accidental grounding, sparks, and possible fire, especially when testing fuel system components.

Jumper wires are used primarily to locate open electrical circuits, on either the ground (-) side of the circuit or on the hot (+) side. If an electrical component fails to operate, connect the jumper wire between the component and a good ground. If the component operates only with the jumper installed, the ground circuit is open. If the ground circuit is good, but the component does not operate, the circuit between the power feed and component is open. You can sometimes connect the jumper wire directly from the battery to the hot terminal of the com-

ponent, but first make sure the component uses 12 volts in operation. Some electrical components, such as fuel injectors, are designed to operate on about 4 volts and running 12 volts directly to the injector terminals can burn out the wiring. By inserting an inline fuseholder between a set of test leads, a fused jumper wire can be used for bypassing open circuits. Use a 5 amp fuse to provide protection against voltage spikes. When in doubt, use a voltmeter to check the voltage input to the component and measure how much voltage is being applied normally. By moving the jumper wire successively back from the lamp toward the power source, you can isolate the area of the circuit where the open is located. When the component stops functioning, or the power is cut off, the open is in the segment of wire between the jumper and the point previously tested.

CAUTION: *Never use jumpers made from wire that is of lighter gauge than used in the circuit under test. If the jumper wire is of too small gauge, it may overheat and possibly melt. Never use jumpers to bypass high resistance loads (such as motors) in a circuit. Bypassing resistances, in effect, creates a short circuit which may, in turn, cause damage and fire. Never use a jumper for anything other than temporary bypassing of components in a circuit.*

12 Volt Test Light

The 12 volt test light is used to check circuits and components while electrical current is flowing through them. It is used for voltage and ground tests. Twelve volt test lights come in different styles but all have three main parts; a ground clip, a probe, and a light. The most commonly used 12 volt test lights have pick-type probes. To use a 12 volt test light, connect the ground clip to a good ground and probe wherever necessary with the pick. The pick should be sharp so that it can penetrate wire insulation to make contact with the wire, without making a large hole in the insulation. The wrap-around light is handy in hard to reach areas or where it is difficult to support a wire to push a probe pick into it. To use the wrap around light, hook the wire to probed with the hook and pull the trigger. A small pick will be forced through the wire insulation into the wire core.

CAUTION: *Do not use a test light to probe electronic ignition spark plug or coil wires. Never use a pick-type test light to probe wiring on computer controlled systems unless specifically instructed to do so. Any wire insulation that is pierced by the test light probe should be taped and sealed with silicone after testing.*

Like the jumper wire, the 12 volt test light is used to isolate opens in circuits. But, whereas the jumper wire is used to bypass the open to operate the load, the 12 volt test light is used to locate the presence of voltage in a circuit. If the test light glows, you know that there is power up to that point; if the 12 volt test light does not glow when its probe is inserted into the wire or connector, you know that there is an open circuit (no power). Move the test light in successive steps back toward the power source until the light in the handle does glow. When it does glow, the open is between the probe and point previously probed.

NOTE: *The test light does not detect that 12 volts (or any particular amount of voltage) is present; it only detects that some voltage is present. It is advisable before using the test light to touch its terminals across the battery posts to make sure the light is operating properly.*

Self-Powered Test Light

The self-powered test light usually contains a 1.5 volt penlight battery. One type of self-powered test light is similar in design to the 12 volt test light. This type has both the battery and the light in the handle and pick-type probe tip. The second type has the light toward the open tip, so that the light illuminates the contact point. The self-powered test light is dual purpose piece of test equipment. It can be used to test for either open or short circuits when power is isolated from the circuit (continuity test). A powered test light should not be used on any computer controlled system or component unless specifically instructed to do so. Many engine sensors can be destroyed by even this small amount of voltage applied directly to the terminals.

Open Circuit Testing

To use the self-powered test light to check for open circuits, first isolate the circuit from the vehicle's 12 volt power source by disconnecting the battery or wiring harness connector. Connect the test light ground clip to a good ground and probe sections of the circuit sequentially with the test light. (start from either end of the circuit). If the light is out, the open is between the probe and the circuit ground. If the light is on, the open is between the probe and end of the circuit toward the power source.

Short Circuit Testing

By isolating the circuit both from power and from ground, and using a self-powered test light, you can check for shorts to ground in the circuit. Isolate the circuit from power and ground. Connect the test light ground clip to a

good ground and probe any easy-to-reach test point in the circuit. If the light comes on, there is a short somewhere in the circuit. To isolate the short, probe a test point at either end of the isolated circuit (the light should be on). Leave the test light probe connected and open connectors, switches, remove parts, etc., sequentially, until the light goes out. When the light goes out, the short is between the last circuit component opened and the previous circuit opened.

NOTE: *The 1.5 volt battery in the test light does not provide much current. A weak battery may not provide enough power to illuminate the test light even when a complete circuit is made (especially if there are high resistances in the circuit). Always make sure that the test battery is strong. To check the battery, briefly touch the ground clip to the probe; if the light glows brightly the battery is strong enough for testing. Never use a self-powered test light to perform checks for opens or shorts when power is applied to the electrical system under test. The 12 volt vehicle power will quickly burn out the 1.5 volt light bulb in the test light.*

Voltmeter

A voltmeter is used to measure voltage at any point in a circuit, or to measure the voltage drop across any part of a circuit. It can also be used to check continuity in a wire or circuit by indicating current flow from one end to the other. Voltmeters usually have various scales on the meter dial and a selector switch to allow the selection of different voltages. The voltmeter has a positive and a negative lead. To avoid damage to the meter, always connect the negative lead to the negative (-) side of circuit (to ground or nearest the ground side of the circuit) and connect the positive lead to the positive (+) side of the circuit (to the power source or the nearest power source). Note that the negative voltmeter lead will always be black and that the positive voltmeter will always be some color other than black (usually red). Depending on how the voltmeter is connected into the circuit, it has several uses.

A voltmeter can be connected either in parallel or in series with a circuit and it has a very high resistance to current flow. When connected in parallel, only a small amount of current will flow through the voltmeter current path; the rest will flow through the normal circuit current path and the circuit will work normally. When the voltmeter is connected in series with a circuit, only a small amount of current can flow through the circuit. The circuit will not work properly, but the voltmeter reading will show if the circuit is complete or not.

Available Voltage Measurement

Set the voltmeter selector switch to the 20V position and connect the meter negative lead to the negative post of the battery. Connect the positive meter lead to the positive post of the battery and turn the ignition switch ON to provide a load. Read the voltage on the meter or digital display. A well charged battery should register over 12 volts. If the meter reads below 11.5 volts, the battery power may be insufficient to operate the electrical system properly. This test determines voltage available from the battery and should be the first step in any electrical trouble diagnosis procedure. Many electrical problems, especially on computer controlled systems, can be caused by a low state of charge in the battery. Excessive corrosion at the battery cable terminals can cause a poor contact that will prevent proper charging and full battery current flow.

Normal battery voltage is 12 volts when fully charged. When the battery is supplying current to one or more circuits it is said to be "under load". When everything is off the electrical system is under a "no-load" condition. A fully charged battery may show about 12.5 volts at no load; will drop to 12 volts under medium load; and will drop even lower under heavy load. If the battery is partially discharged the voltage decrease under heavy load may be excessive, even though the battery shows 12 volts or more at no load. When allowed to discharge further, the battery's available voltage under load will decrease more severely. For this reason, it is important that the battery be fully charged during all testing procedures to avoid errors in diagnosis and incorrect test results.

Voltage Drop

When current flows through a resistance, the voltage beyond the resistance is reduced (the larger the current, the greater the reduction in voltage). When no current is flowing, there is no voltage drop because there is no current flow. All points in the circuit which are connected to the power source are at the same voltage as the power source. The total voltage drop always equals the total source voltage. In a long circuit with many connectors, a series of small, unwanted voltage drops due to corrosion at the connectors can add up to a total loss of voltage which impairs the operation of the normal loads in the circuit.

INDIRECT COMPUTATION OF VOLTAGE DROPS

1. Set the voltmeter selector switch to the 20 volt position.
2. Connect the meter negative lead to a good ground.

3. Probe all resistances in the circuit with the positive meter lead.

4. Operate the circuit in all modes and observe the voltage readings.

DIRECT MEASUREMENT OF VOLTAGE DROPS

1. Set the voltmeter switch to the 20 volt position.

2. Connect the voltmeter negative lead to the ground side of the resistance load to be measured.

3. Connect the positive lead to the positive side of the resistance or load to be measured.

4. Read the voltage drop directly on the 20 volt scale.

Too high a voltage indicates too high a resistance. If, for example, a blower motor runs too slowly, you can determine if there is too high a resistance in the resistor pack. By taking voltage drop readings in all parts of the circuit, you can isolate the problem. Too low a voltage drop indicates too low a resistance. If, for example, a blower motor runs too fast in the MED and/or LOW position, the problem can be isolated in the resistor pack by taking voltage drop readings in all parts of the circuit to locate a possibly shorted resistor. The maximum allowable voltage drop under load is critical, especially if there is more than one high resistance problem in a circuit because all voltage drops are cumulative. A small drop is normal due to the resistance of the conductors.

HIGH RESISTANCE TESTING

1. Set the voltmeter selector switch to the 4 volt position.

2. Connect the voltmeter positive lead to the positive post of the battery.

3. Turn on the headlights and heater blower to provide a load.

4. Probe various points in the circuit with the negative voltmeter lead.

5. Read the voltage drop on the 4 volt scale. Some average maximum allowable voltage drops are:

FUSE PANEL — 7 volts
IGNITION SWITCH — 5volts
HEADLIGHT SWITCH — 7 volts
IGNITION COIL (+) — 5 volts
ANY OTHER LOAD — 1.3 volts
NOTE: *Voltage drops are all measured while a load is operating; without current flow, there will be no voltage drop.*

Ohmmeter

The ohmmeter is designed to read resistance (ohms) in a circuit or component. Although there are several different styles of ohmmeters, all will usually have a selector switch which permits the measurement of different ranges of resistance (usually the selector switch allows the multiplication of the meter reading by 10, 100, 1000, and 10,000). A calibration knob allows the meter to be set at zero for accurate measurement. Since all ohmmeters are powered by an internal battery (usually 9 volts), the ohmmeter can be used as a self-powered test light. When the ohmmeter is connected, current from the ohmmeter flows through the circuit or component being tested. Since the ohmmeter's internal resistance and voltage are known values, the amount of current flow through the meter depends on the resistance of the circuit or component being tested.

The ohmmeter can be used to perform continuity test for opens or shorts (either by observation of the meter needle or as a self-powered test light), and to read actual resistance in a circuit. It should be noted that the ohmmeter is used to check the resistance of a component or wire while there is no voltage applied to the circuit. Current flow from an outside voltage source (such as the vehicle battery) can damage the ohmmeter, so the circuit or component should be isolated from the vehicle electrical system before any testing is done. Since the ohmmeter uses its own voltage source, either lead can be connected to any test point.

NOTE: *When checking diodes or other solid state components, the ohmmeter leads can only be connected one way in order to measure current flow in a single direction. Make sure the positive (+) and negative (-) terminal connections are as described in the test procedures to verify the one-way diode operation.*

In using the meter for making continuity checks, do not be concerned with the actual resistance readings. Zero resistance, or any resistance readings, indicate continuity in the circuit. Infinite resistance indicates an open in the circuit. A high resistance reading where there should be none indicates a problem in the circuit. Checks for short circuits are made in the same manner as checks for open circuits except that the circuit must be isolated from both power and normal ground. Infinite resistance indicates no continuity to ground, while zero resistance indicates a dead short to ground.

RESISTANCE MEASUREMENT

The batteries in an ohmmeter will weaken with age and temperature, so the ohmmeter must be calibrated or "zeroed" before taking measurements. To zero the meter, place the selector switch in its lowest range and touch the two ohmmeter leads together. Turn the calibration knob until the meter needle is exactly on zero.

NOTE: *All analog (needle) type ohmmeters*

must be zeroed before use, but some digital ohmmeter models are automatically calibrated when the switch is turned on. Self-calibrating digital ohmmeters do not have an adjusting knob, but its a good idea to check for a zero readout before use by touching the leads together. All computer controlled systems require the use of a digital ohmmeter with at least 10 meagohms impedance for testing. Before any test procedures are attempted, make sure the ohmmeter used is compatible with the electrical system or damage to the on-board computer could result.

To measure resistance, first isolate the circuit from the vehicle power source by disconnecting the battery cables or the harness connector. Make sure the key is OFF when disconnecting any components or the battery. Where necessary, also isolate at least one side of the circuit to be checked to avoid reading parallel resistances. Parallel circuit resistances will always give a lower reading than the actual resistance of either of the branches. When measuring the resistance of parallel circuits, the total resistance will always be lower than the smallest resistance in the circuit. Connect the meter leads to both sides of the circuit (wire or component) and read the actual measured ohms on the meter scale. Make sure the selector switch is set to the proper ohm scale for the circuit being tested to avoid misreading the ohmmeter test value.

CAUTION: *Never use an ohmmeter with power applied to the circuit. Like the self-powered test light, the ohmmeter is designed to operate on its own power supply. The normal 12 volt automotive electrical system current could damage the meter.*

Ammeters

An ammeter measures the amount of current flowing through a circuit in units called amperes or amps. Amperes are units of electron flow which indicate how fast the electrons are flowing through the circuit. Since Ohms Law dictates that current flow in a circuit is equal to the circuit voltage divided by the total circuit resistance, increasing voltage also increases the current level (amps). Likewise, any decrease in resistance will increase the amount of amps in a circuit. At normal operating voltage, most circuits have a characteristic amount of amperes, called "current draw" which can be measured using an ammeter. By referring to a specified current draw rating, measuring the amperes, and comparing the two values, one can determine what is happening within the circuit to aid in diagnosis. An open circuit, for example, will not allow any current to flow so the ammeter reading will be zero. More current flows through a heavily loaded circuit or when the charging system is operating.

An ammeter is always connected in series with the circuit being tested. All of the current that normally flows through the circuit must also flow through the ammeter; if there is any other path for the current to follow, the ammeter reading will not be accurate. The ammeter itself has very little resistance to current flow and therefore will not affect the circuit, but it will measure current draw only when the circuit is closed and electricity is flowing. Excessive current draw can blow fuses and drain the battery, while a reduced current draw can cause motors to run slowly, lights to dim and other components to not operate properly. The ammeter can help diagnose these conditions by locating the cause of the high or low reading.

Multimeters

Different combinations of test meters can be built into a single unit designed for specific tests. Some of the more common combination test devices are known as Volt/Amp testers, Tach/Dwell meters, or Digital Multimeters. The Volt/Amp tester is used for charging system, starting system or battery tests and consists of a voltmeter, an ammeter and a variable resistance carbon pile. The voltmeter will usually have at least two ranges for use with 6, 12 and 24 volt systems. The ammeter also has more than one range for testing various levels of battery loads and starter current draw and the carbon pile can be adjusted to offer different amounts of resistance. The Volt/Amp tester has heavy leads to carry large amounts of current and many later models have an inductive ammeter pickup that clamps around the wire to simplify test connections. On some models, the ammeter also has a zero-center scale to allow testing of charging and starting systems without switching leads or polarity. A digital multimeter is a voltmeter, ammeter and ohmmeter combined in an instrument which gives a digital readout. These are often used when testing solid state circuits because of their high input impedance (usually 10 megohms or more).

The tach/dwell meter combines a tachometer and a dwell (cam angle) meter and is a specialized kind of voltmeter. The tachometer scale is marked to show engine speed in rpm and the dwell scale is marked to show degrees of distributor shaft rotation. In most electronic ignition systems, dwell is determined by the control unit, but the dwell meter can also be used to check the duty cycle (operation) of some electronic engine control systems. Some tach/dwell meters are powered by an internal battery, while others take their power from the car bat-

tery in use. The battery powered testers usually require calibration much like an ohmmeter before testing.

Special Test Equipment

A variety of diagnostic tools are available to help troubleshoot and repair computerized engine control systems. The most sophisticated of these devices are the console type engine analyzers that usually occupy a garage service bay, but there are several types of aftermarket electronic testers available that will allow quick circuit tests of the engine control system by plugging directly into a special connector located in the engine compartment or under the dashboard. Several tool and equipment manufacturers offer simple, hand held testers that measure various circuit voltage levels on command to check all system components for proper operation. Although these testers usually cost about $300-$500, consider that the average computer control unit (or ECM) can cost just as much and the money saved by not replacing perfectly good sensors or components in an attempt to correct a problem could justify the purchase price of a special diagnostic tester the first time it's used.

These computerized testers can allow quick and easy test measurements while the engine is operating or while the car is being driven. In addition, the on-board computer memory can be read to access any stored trouble codes; in effect allowing the computer to tell you where it hurts and aid trouble diagnosis by pinpointing exactly which circuit or component is malfunctioning. In the same manner, repairs can be tested to make sure the problem has been corrected. The biggest advantage these special testers have is their relatively easy hookups that minimize or eliminate the chances of making the wrong connections and getting false voltage readings or damaging the computer accidentally.

NOTE: *It should be remembered that these testers check voltage levels in circuits; they don't detect mechanical problems or failed components if the circuit voltage falls within the preprogrammed limits stored in the tester PROM unit. Also, most of the hand held testes are designed to work only on one or two systems made by a specific manufacturer.*

A variety of aftermarket testers are available to help diagnose different computerized control systems. Owatonna Tool Company (OTC), for example, markets a device called the OTC Monitor which plugs directly into the assembly line diagnostic link (ALDL). The OTC tester makes diagnosis a simple matter of pressing the correct buttons and, by changing the internal PROM or inserting a different diagnosis cartridge, it will work on any model from full size to subcompact, over a wide range of years. An adapter is supplied with the tester to allow connection to all types of ALDL links, regardless of the number of pin terminals used. By inserting an updated PROM into the OTC tester, it can be easily updated to diagnose any new modifications of computerized control systems.

Wiring Harnesses

The average automobile contains about ½ mile of wiring, with hundreds of individual connections. To protect the many wires from damage and to keep them from becoming a confusing tangle, they are organized into bundles, enclosed in plastic or taped together and called wire harnesses. Different wiring harnesses serve different parts of the vehicle. Individual wires are color coded to help trace them through a harness where sections are hidden from view.

A loose or corroded connection or a replacement wire that is too small for the circuit will add extra resistance and an additional voltage drop to the circuit. A ten percent voltage drop can result in slow or erratic motor operation, for example, even though the circuit is complete. Automotive wiring or circuit conductors can be in any one of three forms:

1. Single strand wire
2. Multistrand wire
3. Printed circuitry

Single strand wire has a solid metal core and is usually used inside such components as alternators, motors, relays and other devices. Multistrand wire has a core made of many small strands of wire twisted together into a single conductor. Most of the wiring in an automotive electrical system is made up of multistrand wire, either as a single conductor or grouped together in a harness. All wiring is color coded on the insulator, either as a solid color or as a colored wire with an identification stripe. A printed circuit is a thin film of copper or other conductor that is printed on an insulator backing. Occasionally, a printed circuit is sandwiched between two sheets of plastic for more protection and flexibility. A complete printed circuit, consisting of conductors, insulating material and connectors for lamps or other components is called a printed circuit board. Printed circuitry is used in place of individual wires or harnesses in places where space is limited, such as behind instrument panels.

Wire Gauge

Since computer controlled automotive electrical systems are very sensitive to changes in resistance, the selection of properly sized wires is critical when systems are repaired. The wire gauge number is an expression of the cross section area of the conductor. The most common

system for expressing wire size is the American Wire Gauge (AWG) system.

Wire cross section area is measured in circular mils. A mil is $\frac{1}{1000}''$ (0.001″); a circular mil is the area of a circle one mil in diameter. For example, a conductor ¼″ in diameter is 0.250 in. or 250 mils. The circular mil cross section area of the wire is 250 squared (250^2) or 62,500 circular mils. Imported car models usually use metric wire gauge designations, which is simply the cross section area of the conductor in square millimeters (mm^2).

Gauge numbers are assigned to conductors of various cross section areas. As gauge number increases, area decreases and the conductor becomes smaller. A 5 gauge conductor is smaller than a 1 gauge conductor and a 10 gauge is smaller than a 5 gauge. As the cross section area of a conductor decreases, resistance increases and so does the gauge number. A conductor with a higher gauge number will carry less current than a conductor with a lower gauge number.

NOTE: *Gauge wire size refers to the size of the conductor, not the size of the complete wire. It is possible to have two wires of the same gauge with different diameters because one may have thicker insulation than the other.*

12 volt automotive electrical systems generally use 10, 12, 14, 16 and 18 gauge wire. Main power distribution circuits and larger accessories usually use 10 and 12 gauge wire. Battery cables are usually 4 or 6 gauge, although 1 and 2 gauge wires are occasionally used. Wire length must also be considered when making repairs to a circuit. As conductor length increases, so does resistance. An 18 gauge wire, for example, can carry a 10 amp load for 10 feet without excessive voltage drop; however if a 15 foot wire is required for the same 10 amp load, it must be a 16 gauge wire.

An electrical schematic shows the electrical current paths when a circuit is operating properly. It is essential to understand how a circuit works before trying to figure out why it doesn't. Schematics break the entire electrical system down into individual circuits and show only one particular circuit. In a schematic, no attempt is made to represent wiring and components as they physically appear on the vehicle; switches and other components are shown as simply as possible. Face views of harness connectors show the cavity or terminal locations in all multi-pin connectors to help locate test points.

If you need to backprobe a connector while it is on the component, the order of the terminals must be mentally reversed. The wire color code can help in this situation, as well as a keyway, lock tab or other reference mark.

NOTE: *Wiring diagrams are not included in this book. As trucks have become more complex and available with longer option lists, wiring diagrams have grown in size and complexity. It has become almost impossible to provide a readable reproduction of a wiring diagram in a book this size. Information on ordering wiring diagrams from the vehicle manufacturer can be found in the owner's manual.*

WIRING REPAIR

Soldering is a quick, efficient method of joining metals permanently. Everyone who has the occasion to make wiring repairs should know how to solder. Electrical connections that are soldered are far less likely to come apart and will conduct electricity much better than connections that are only "pig-tailed" together. The most popular (and preferred) method of soldering is with an electrical soldering gun. Soldering irons are available in many sizes and wattage ratings. Irons with higher wattage ratings deliver higher temperatures and recover lost heat faster. A small soldering iron rated for no more than 50 watts is recommended, especially on electrical systems where excess heat can damage the components being soldered.

There are three ingredients necessary for successful soldering; proper flux, good solder and sufficient heat. A soldering flux is necessary to clean the metal of tarnish, prepare it for soldering and to enable the solder to spread into tiny crevices. When soldering, always use a resin flux or resin core solder which is non-corrosive and will not attract moisture once the job is finished. Other types of flux (acid core) will leave a residue that will attract moisture and cause the wires to corrode. Tin is a unique metal with a low melting point. In a molten state, it dissolves and alloys easily with many metals. Solder is made by mixing tin with lead. The most common proportions are 40/60, 50/50 and 60/40, with the percentage of tin listed first. Low priced solders usually contain less tin, making them very difficult for a beginner to use because more heat is required to melt the solder. A common solder is 40/60 which is well suited for all-around general use, but 60/40 melts easier, has more tin for a better joint and is preferred for electrical work.

Soldering Techniques

Successful soldering requires that the metals to be joined be heated to a temperature that will melt the solder — usually 360-460°F (182-238°C). Contrary to popular belief, the purpose of the soldering iron is not to melt the solder itself, but to heat the parts being soldered to a temperature high enough to melt the solder

when it is touched to the work. Melting flux-cored solder on the soldering iron will usually destroy the effectiveness of the flux.

NOTE: *Soldering tips are made of copper for good heat conductivity, but must be "tinned" regularly for quick transference of heat to the project and to prevent the solder from sticking to the iron. To "tin" the iron, simply heat it and touch the flux-cored solder to the tip; the solder will flow over the hot tip. Wipe the excess off with a clean rag, but be careful as the iron will be hot.*

After some use, the tip may become pitted. If so, simply dress the tip smooth with a smooth file and "tin" the tip again. An old saying holds that "metals well cleaned are half soldered." Flux-cored solder will remove oxides but rust, bits of insulation and oil or grease must be removed with a wire brush or emery cloth. For maximum strength in soldered parts, the joint must start off clean and tight. Weak joints will result in gaps too wide for the solder to bridge.

If a separate soldering flux is used, it should be brushed or swabbed on only those areas that are to be soldered. Most solders contain a core of flux and separate fluxing is unnecessary. Hold the work to be soldered firmly. It is best to solder on a wooden board, because a metal vise will only rob the piece to be soldered of heat and make it difficult to melt the solder. Hold the soldering tip with the broadest face against the work to be soldered. Apply solder under the tip close to the work, using enough solder to give a heavy film between the iron and the piece being soldered, while moving slowly and making sure the solder melts properly. Keep the work level or the solder will run to the lowest part and favor the thicker parts, because these require more heat to melt the solder. If the soldering tip overheats (the solder coating on the face of the tip burns up), it should be retinned. Once the soldering is completed, let the soldered joint stand until cool. Tape and seal all soldered wire splices after the repair has cooled.

Wire Harness and Connectors

The on-board computer (ECM) wire harness electrically connects the control unit to the various solenoids, switches and sensors used by the control system. Most connectors in the engine compartment or otherwise exposed to the elements are protected against moisture and dirt which could create oxidation and deposits on the terminals. This protection is important because of the very low voltage and current levels used by the computer and sensors. All connectors have a lock which secures the male and female terminals together, with a secondary lock holding the seal and terminal into the connector. Both terminal locks must be released when disconnecting ECM connectors.

These special connectors are weather-proof and all repairs require the use of a special terminal and the tool required to service it. This tool is used to remove the pin and sleeve terminals. If removal is attempted with an ordinary pick, there is a good chance that the terminal will be bent or deformed. Unlike standard blade type terminals, these terminals cannot be straightened once they are bent. Make certain that the connectors are properly seated and all of the sealing rings in place when connecting leads. On some models, a hinge-type flap provides a backup or secondary locking feature for the terminals. Most secondary locks are used to improve the connector reliability by retaining the terminals if the small terminal lock tangs are not positioned properly.

Molded-on connectors require complete replacement of the connection. This means splicing a new connector assembly into the harness. All splices in on-board computer systems should be soldered to insure proper contact. Use care when probing the connections or replacing terminals in them as it is possible to short between opposite terminals. If this happens to the wrong terminal pair, it is possible to damage certain components. Always use jumper wires between connectors for circuit checking and never probe through weather-proof seals.

Open circuits are often difficult to locate by sight because corrosion or terminal misalignment are hidden by the connectors. Merely wiggling a connector on a sensor or in the wiring harness may correct the open circuit condition. This should always be considered when an open circuit or a failed sensor is indicated. Intermittent problems may also be caused by oxidized or loose connections. When using a circuit tester for diagnosis, always probe connections from the wire side. Be careful not to damage sealed connectors with test probes.

All wiring harnesses should be replaced with identical parts, using the same gauge wire and connectors. When signal wires are spliced into a harness, use wire with high temperature insulation only. With the low voltage and current levels found in the system, it is important that the best possible connection at all wire splices be made by soldering the splices together. It is seldom necessary to replace a complete harness. If replacement is necessary, pay close attention to insure proper harness routing. Secure the harness with suitable plastic wire clamps to prevent vibrations from causing the harness to wear in spots or contact any hot components.

NOTE: *Weatherproof connectors cannot be replaced with standard connectors. Instructions are provided with replacement connector and terminal packages. Some wire har-*

nesses have mounting indicators (usually pieces of colored tape) to mark where the harness is to be secured.

In making wiring repairs, it's important that you always replace damaged wires with wires that are the same gauge as the wire being replaced. The heavier the wire, the smaller the gauge number. Wires are color-coded to aid in identification and whenever possible the same color coded wire should be used for replacement. A wire stripping and crimping tool is necessary to install solderless terminal connectors. Test all crimps by pulling on the wires; it should not be possible to pull the wires out of a good crimp.

Wires which are open, exposed or otherwise damaged are repaired by simple splicing. Where possible, if the wiring harness is accessible and the damaged place in the wire can be located, it is best to open the harness and check for all possible damage. In an inaccessible harness, the wire must be bypassed with a new insert, usually taped to the outside of the old harness.

When replacing fusible links, be sure to use fusible link wire, NOT ordinary automotive wire. Make sure the fusible segment is of the same gauge and construction as the one being replaced and double the stripped end when crimping the terminal connector for a good contact. The melted (open) fusible link segment of the wiring harness should be cut off as close to the harness as possible, then a new segment spliced in as described. In the case of a damaged fusible link that feeds two harness wires, the harness connections should be replaced with two fusible link wires so that each circuit will have its own separate protection.

NOTE: *Most of the problems caused in the wiring harness are due to bad ground connections. Always check all vehicle ground connections for corrosion or looseness before performing any power feed checks to eliminate the chance of a bad ground affecting the circuit.*

Repairing Hard Shell Connectors

Unlike molded connectors, the terminal contacts in hard shell connectors can be replaced. Weatherproof hard-shell connectors with the leads molded into the shell have non-replaceable terminal ends. Replacement usually involves the use of a special terminal removal tool that depress the locking tangs (barbs) on the connector terminal and allow the connector to be removed from the rear of the shell. The connector shell should be replaced if it shows any evidence of burning, melting, cracks, or breaks. Replace individual terminals that are burnt, corroded, distorted or loose.

NOTE: *The insulation crimp must be tight to prevent the insulation from sliding back on the wire when the wire is pulled. The insulation must be visibly compressed under the crimp tabs, and the ends of the crimp should be turned in for a firm grip on the insulation.*

The wire crimp must be made with all wire strands inside the crimp. The terminal must be fully compressed on the wire strands with the ends of the crimp tabs turned in to make a firm grip on the wire. Check all connections with an ohmmeter to insure a good contact. There should be no measurable resistance between the wire and the terminal when connected.

Mechanical Test Equipment

Vacuum Gauge

Most gauges are graduated in inches of mercury (in.Hg), although a device called a manometer reads vacuum in inches of water (in. H_2O). The normal vacuum reading usually varies between 18 and 22 in.Hg at sea level. To test engine vacuum, the vacuum gauge must be connected to a source of manifold vacuum. Many engines have a plug in the intake manifold which can be removed and replaced with an adapter fitting. Connect the vacuum gauge to the fitting with a suitable rubber hose or, if no manifold plug is available, connect the vacuum gauge to any device using manifold vacuum, such as EGR valves, etc. The vacuum gauge can be used to determine if enough vacuum is reaching a component to allow its actuation.

Hand Vacuum Pump

Small, hand-held vacuum pumps come in a variety of designs. Most have a built-in vacuum gauge and allow the component to be tested without removing it from the vehicle. Operate the pump lever or plunger to apply the correct amount of vacuum required for the test specified in the diagnosis routines. The level of vacuum in inches of Mercury (in.Hg) is indicated on the pump gauge. For some testing, an additional vacuum gauge may be necessary.

Intake manifold vacuum is used to operate various systems and devices on late model vehicles. To correctly diagnose and solve problems in vacuum control systems, a vacuum source is necessary for testing. In some cases, vacuum can be taken from the intake manifold when the engine is running, but vacuum is normally provided by a hand vacuum pump. These hand vacuum pumps have a built-in vacuum gauge that allow testing while the device is still attached to the component. For some tests, an additional vacuum gauge may be necessary.

Supplementary Restraint System (SRS)

Certain late model BMW vehicles are equipped with the SRS system, more commonly known as an air bag system. The SRS system requires no owner service, however it is important to know that the system is there. Improper electrical testing or repair procedures inside of your car could activate the system and deploy the air bag. Once the air bag is deployed it must be replaced, this could be a costly repair, especially if it is done by accident.

The most important thing to remember is to disconnect the battery cables WHENEVER you are going to be working on the electrical system. Also, never use a self powered test light on any of the SRS system components. Finally, never strike the steering column with any amount of force. The air bag deploys rapidly, faster then you can blink, and it does so with great force. In an accident this will save your life, but with your head next to the steering wheel, it could be very painful. So, just follow these very simple precautions and you will have no problems.

A brief explanation of the system operation and components, as well as a functional test, follow for your reference.

SRS OPERATION

The SRS system consists of an air bag (located in the center of the steering wheel), the gas generator (located beneath the air bag), the crash sensors (located in the front of the car) and the control unit (located in the front of car).

The SRS system is designed to deploy the air bag in the case of a frontal collision at speeds of approximately 12 mph into a solid barrier or higher speeds for a flexible barrier (another vehicle for example). The basic operation is simple; sensors at the front of the vehicle, detect sudden deceleration which then sends a signal to the control unit which in turn, ignites the propellent that inflates the air bag. This all takes place in a few mili-seconds. The air bag is deflated by the impact of the body hitting it and forcing the air through vents around the perimeter of the bag. In the event of an electrical system failure at or before impact there is a capacitor that stores enough electricity to operate the system.

It should be noted that the SRS system will not be activated in the event of a side impact collision or a rear impact collision.

The SRS can be activated only one time, after which the entire air bag unit (the center pad of the steering wheel) must be replaced and the control unit checked. This can only be done by an authorized dealer.

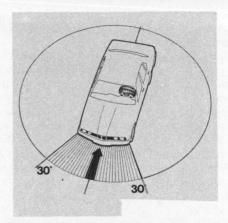

Angles at which the SRS system reads vehicle impact

Functional Test

The SRS system is continually monitored by a diagnostic system that monitors the control unit, sensors and the wiring integrity of the system. Monitoring begins when the ignition key is turned to position 1 and beyond, and while the car is being driven.

If the key is turned to position 1 and left there, the SRS telltale light will appear in the Check-Control panel and stay lit for approximately 6 seconds and then go out. The SRS indicator should also illuminate for about 6 seconds after the engine is started.

If the telltale light does not come on or if it does not go out after 6 seconds or comes on while driving, the system is not ready to operate during a collision. Also if the light flutters, it means there is a problem in the system. If any of these occur the system should be checked by an authorized BMW dealer as soon as possible.

In the event of the air bag being deployed in a non-accident situation, it will deflate quickly

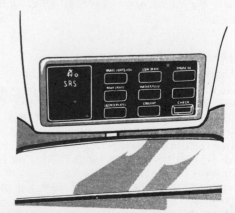

The SRS indicator will appear in the check-control panel, it should remain lit for approximately 6 seconds

and should not obstruct your view while driving. Also, a small amount of smoke and a very loud inflation noise will be heard.

HEATING AND AIR CONDITIONING

Refer to Chapter 1 for A/C system discharging, evacuation and charging procedures. Observe all cautions pertaining to exsposure to refrigerant.

Heater/Air Conditioner Assembly, Core and Blower

REMOVAL AND INSTALLATION

16002 and 2002

The entire heater assembly must be removed from the car to replace either the blower motor or the heater core.

1. Disconnect the negative battery cable.
2. Move the heater control lever on the dash all the way to the **WARM** position. Remove the

radiator and engine drain cocks and drain the cooling system.

CAUTION: *When draining the coolant, keep in mind that cats and dogs are attracted by the ethylene glycol antifreeze, and are quite likely to drink any that is left in an uncovered container or in puddles on the ground. This will prove fatal in sufficient quantity. Always drain the coolant into a sealable container. Coolant should be reused unless it is contaminated or several years old.*

3. Loosen the hose clamp and disconnect the heater return hose from its fitting on the engine side of the firewall. Also, loosen the clamps and disconnect the heater feed hose (1) from the heater control valve (2) at the firewall. Remove the valve and check that it is not blocked with cooling system deposits. Replace it, as necessary.

4. On 1970 models, remove the retaining screws and pull the storage tray to the rear. On 1971 and later models, with a full-length console, unscrew the shift knob, pull off the rubber boot, unscrew the phillips head screws for the

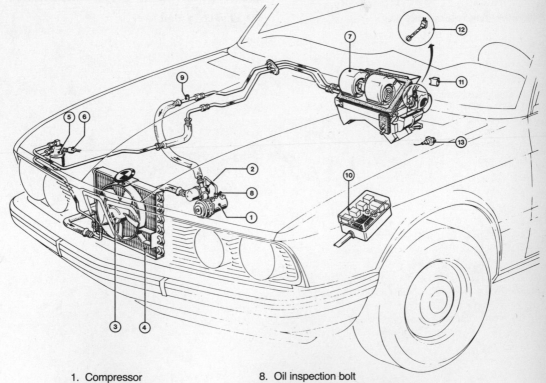

1. Compressor	8. Oil inspection bolt
2. Stabilizer	9. Schrader valve
3. Auxiliary fan	10. Central electric board
4. Condenser	11. Evaporator temperature regulator
5. Drier	12. Temperature sensor—heater
6. Safety pressure switch	13. Temperature sensor—passenger compartment
7. Blower	

Air conditioning and heater system components—6 and 7 series

side and center sections, life out the center section, disconnect the electrical connections for the hazard flasher and radio (if so equipped), and lift out the remaining sections of the console.

5. Remove the phillips head retaining screws and remove the following dashboard finish panels: the lower steering column casing, the lower center trim panel, the outer left-hand trim pan-

el, and the bottom half of the upper steering column casing.

6. Pull off the black knobs for the air control and heater temperature controls. On 1970 models, remove the inner knurled nuts and the phillips head screw for the air control outer finish panel and lift off the panel. Then remove the 2 phillips head screws securing the air controls to the dash. Finally, pull out the ashtray, and

Disconnecting return hose

Disconnecting feed hose

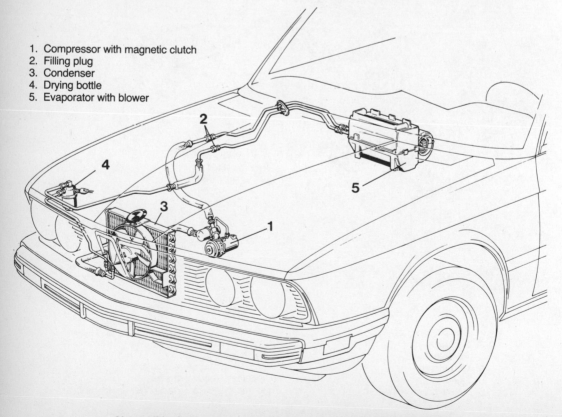

1. Compressor with magnetic clutch
2. Filling plug
3. Condenser
4. Drying bottle
5. Evaporator with blower

Air conditioning system component layout—typical of 3 and 5 series

Heater assembly removed showing positioning of foam rubber gaskets

remove the 2 phillips head screws retaining the heater temperature control to the dash. On 1971 and later models, lever out the snap-fit clear plastic covers for both the air control and the heater temperature controls. Then, remove the phillips head screws retaining the controls to the dash (2 each), and pull the levers downward and out.

7. Label and disconnect the electrical leads for the heater (3 wires for 2-speed blower; 4 wires for 3-speed blower) underneath the dash. Remove the nut and disconnect the heater ground wire.

8. Pull off the left-hand hot air hose and slightly turn the retaining bracket for the steer-

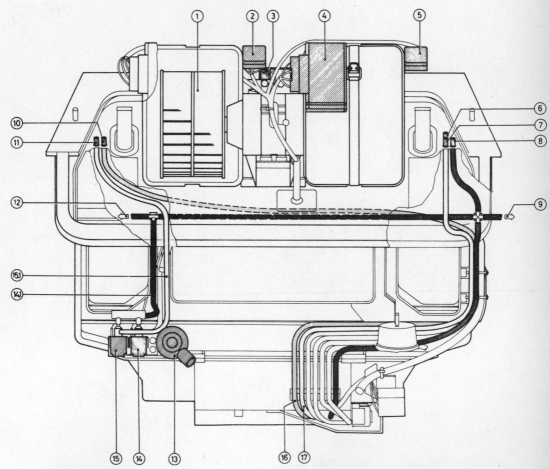

1. Blower motor	10. Connecting pipe, violet (fresh air, left, stage 1)
2. Compressor relay	11. Connecting pipe, brown (fresh air, left, stage 2)
3. Temperature switch	12. To solenoids (defroster flap)
4. Final stage	13. Airflow pump
5. Blower relay	14. Solenoid valve (recirculating air flaps)
6. Connecting pipe, grey (fresh air, right, stage 3)	14.1 Green supply line (vacuum)
7. Connecting pipe, red (water valve)	15. Solenoid valve (fresh air flap, left, stage 2)
8. Connecting pipe, green (vacuum)	15.1 Brown supply line (fresh air flap, left, stage 2)
9. (To water valve solenoid)—on right of heater casing	16. To solenoid valve for left fresh air flap, stage 1
	17. To solenoid valve for right fresh air flap

Air conditioning and heater case components and vacuum hose routing and layout—7 series

ing column. Loosen the right-hand trim panel and pull off the right-hand hot air hose.

9. Open the glove compartment. Remove the left and right-hand side heater retaining nuts (one on each side). Carefully pull out the heater unit.

10. Drill out the rivets retaining the heater cover. Unsnap the clasps at the rear of the heater housing. Separate the housing valves.

11. Loosen the hose clamp for the heater valve. Loosen the cable clamp screw, and remove the lever pivot screw and the 2 control mounting screws.

12. Remove the rubber sleeves at either side of the blower.

13. Label and disconnect the electrical leads from the blower motor.

14. Disconnect the cable for the heater regulator.

15. Label and disconnect the leads from the heater housing.

16. Unsnap the clips and pull the motor and blower wheel assembly downward.

NOTE: *The motor and blower wheel are balanced as an assembly. If the motor is burned out, or if the blower wheel is damaged, the motor and blower wheel should be replaced as a unit., otherwise the blower will vibrate excessively during operation.*

17. To install, install the blower motor in the

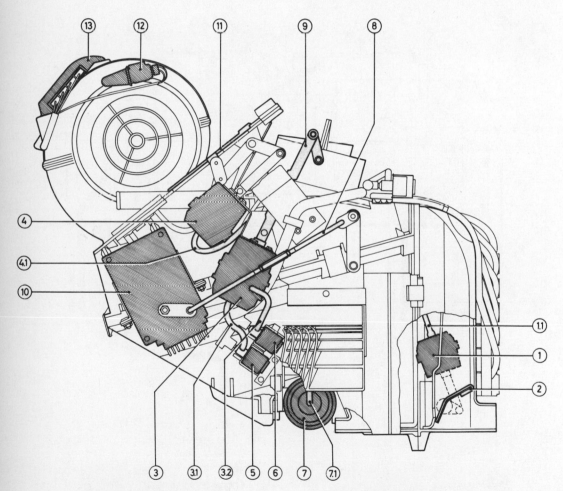

1. Rear seat area servo	6. Solenoid valve (defroster flap, stage 2)
1.1 Vacuum connection (black)	7. Footwell servo
2. Rear seat area flap	7.1 Vacuum connection (dark blue)
3. Defroster flap servo	8. Actuating linkage with adjusting nut
3.1 Vacuum line, stge 2 (light blue)	9. Vent flap
3.2 Vacuum line, stage 1 (white)	10. Control unit
4. Recirculating air flap servo	11. Recirculating air flap
4.1 Vacuum connection (pink)	12. External sensor
5. Solenoid valve (defroster flap, stage 1)	13. Final stage

Air conditioning and heater case components and location—7 series

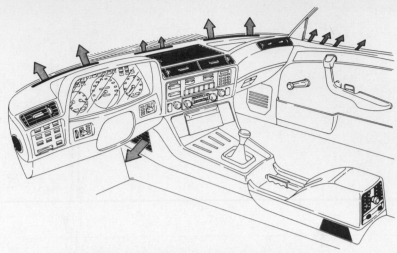

Air conditioning and heater airflow points—7 series

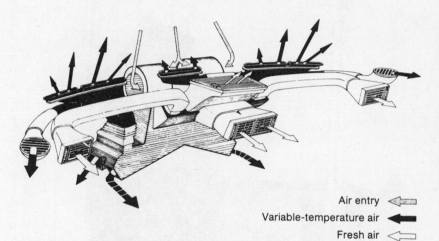

Air entry
Variable-temperature air
Fresh air

Air conditioning and heater airflow points—5 and 6 series

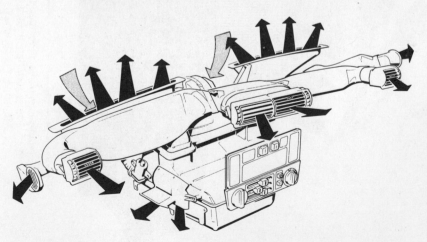

Air entry
Variable-temperature air

Air conditioning and heater airflow points—3 series

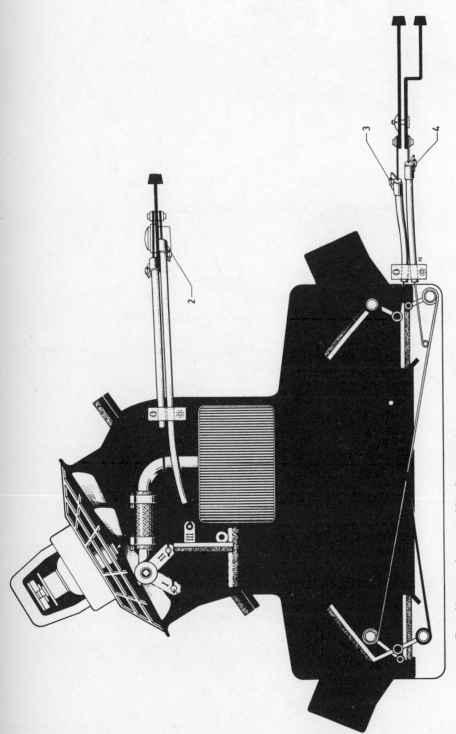

Test: Heater valve at position I = warm.
The mixing flap III must be closed in this position.
Adjustment is effected with the clamp screw (1) at the swinging arm of the heater valve.
Position II = cold.
Adjustment of air mixing, demister and footwell flaps is effected at the Bowden cable retaining screws 2, 3 and 4.
The flaps are lubricated with Ecubsol at the bearing points.

Cross section of heater unit showing proper adjustment procedure for the control cable

assembly and install the retaining clips. Connect the cable for the heater regulator and install the leads on the heater housing.

18. Connect the leads at the blower and install the sleeves at the sides of the blower. Install the heater valve and connect the lever. Attach the halves of the heater case and install retaining screws where the rivets were drilled out.

19. Install the heater unit in the vehicle and install the retaining nuts. Reconnect the hot air hoses and install the trim panels.

20. Reconnect the heater electrical leads under the dash. Install all the air controls to the dash. Install all removed dash panels.

21. Reinstall all console components. Attach all heater hoses and fill the cooling system to the correct level.

22. Run the engine to normal operating temperature and check the operation of the heater. Be sure to bleed the cooling system, also, check for leaks.

2500, 2800, Bavaria, 3000 and 3.0

1. Open the hood and remove the cover plate from the top of the cowl.

2. Remove the metal grid from the top of the blower. Disconnect the electrical connectors.

3. Unscrew the motor mount where it attaches to the heater housing., tilt the forward part up, and remove the unit from the cowl.

4. Release the 4 retaining clips, and then pull the motor off the motor mount.

5. Install in reverse order. Make sure the shorter ends of the remaining clips go over the motor mount.

528i, 530i and 630CSi

1. Open the hold and remove the black access cover from the upper portion of the cowl.

2. On the 600 Series, remove the 2 screws on the windshield side, and the 3 screws on the front of the cowl, and remove the blower cover.

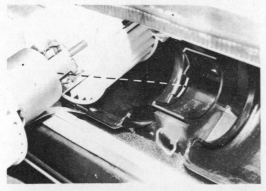

On the 530i, make sure the part of the motor between the wiring connectors fits into the notch. See text

3. Open the 3 fasteners on the retaining straps, and then pull off the 2 upper halves of the blower cages.

4. Lift out the motor with wheels attached, and disconnect the wiring; the whole assembly may then be removed.

5. If the motor if faulty, the entire unit must be replaced. Install the unit in reverse order, positioning the flat surfaces on the intake ducts downward. On the 530i, make sure the area of the motor between the 2 wiring connectors fits into the notch on the passenger's side of the mounting bracket.

320i

1. Disconnect the battery ground.

2. Move the selector lever to the WARM position.

3. Drain the cooling system.

CAUTION: *When draining the coolant, keep in mind that cats and dogs are attracted by the ethylene glycol antifreeze, and are quite likely to drink any that is left in an uncovered container or in puddles on the ground. This will prove fatal in sufficient quantity. Always drain the coolant into a sealable container. Coolant should be reused unless it is contaminated or several years old.*

4. Loosen the hose clamp, and remove the heater core return hose.

5. Disconnect the heater hose between the hot water control valve and the engine.

6. Remove the package tray.

7. Remove outer tube casing.

8. Remove the lower center trim panel.

9. Remove the left side outer trim panel.

10. Remove the upper section of the steering tube casing.

11. Remove the heater control knobs.

12. Remove the heater control trim panel.

13. Remove the right side trim panel.

14. Disconnect the heater electrical lead.

15. Remove the heater housing retaining nuts.

16. Disconnect the left side distribution duct, and move the steering tube outer casing retaining bracket out of the way.

17. Remove the glove box lower trim panel.

18. Disconnect the left side distribution duct, and lift out the heater housing.

19. Remove the housing rivets.

20. Remove the housing clamps, and separate the housing halves.

21. Disconnect the bowden cable from the hot water control valve.

22. Remove the hot water control valve and hose from the water valve bracket on the heater housing.

23. Remove the rubber sleeves from the heater core inlet and outlet tubes.

24. Disconnect the electrical leads at the blower motor.

25. Disconnect the electrical leads at the blower resistor in the heater housing.

26. Open the blower motor support clamps, and remove the blower motor and fan as an assembly.

27. To install, install the blower motor in the assembly and install the retaining clips. Connect the cable for the heater regulator and install the leads on the heater housing.

28. Connect the leads at the blower and install the sleeves at the sides of the blower. Install the heater valve and connect the lever. Attach the halves of the heater case and install retaining screws where the rivets were drilled out.

29. Install the heater unit in the vehicle and install the retaining nuts. Reconnect the hot air hoses and install the trim panels.

30. Reconnect the heater electrical leads under the dash. Install all the air controls to the dash. Install all removed dash panels.

31. Reinstall all console components. Attach all heater hoses and fill the cooling system to the correct level.

32. Run the engine to normal operating temperature and check the operation of the heater. Be sure to bleed the cooling system, also, check for leaks.

528e, 533i and 1982 633CSi

1. Remove the center tray. Remove the instrument panel trim to bottom right of tray.

2. Remove the glove box and remove heater controls at water valve and at air doors. Remove center console if equipped.

3. Disconnect the battery ground.

4. Push the selector lever to the WARM position.

5. Drain the coolant and remove the air conditioning evaporator:

CAUTION: *When draining the coolant, keep in mind that cats and dogs are attracted by the ethylene glycol antifreeze, and are quite likely to drink any that is left in an uncovered container or in puddles on the ground. This will prove fatal in sufficient quantity. Always drain the coolant into a sealable container. Coolant should be reused unless it is contaminated or several years old.*

a. Drain the refrigerant slowly out of the low side Schrader® valve. If not trained and experienced in refrigeration work, leave this to a specialist.

b. Take off the no-drip tape type insulation and disconnect both refrigerant lines from the evaporator.

NOTE: *Plug the refrigerant lines immedi-*

ately to prevent moisture and contaminants from entering the system.

c. Pull the temperature sensor out of the evaporator housing.

d. Disconnect the evaporator/heater control electrical connector.

e. Remove the right and left screw from the housing (from area where the housing meets the passenger compartment carpeting).

f. Remove the floor pan to evaporator housing bracket. Lift the housing slightly and pull it from under the dash.

WARNING: *Do not bend the temperature sensor or it will have to be replaced!*

g. Disconnect the blower wires and the blower resistor wire. Lift the evaporator slightly and pull the adapter and evaporator from under the dash.

6. Disconnect the heater hoses from the heater core, and remove the rubber seal.

7. Remove the lower instrument panel center trim.

8. Disconnect the heater controls at the instrument panel.

9. Disconnect the control shafts at the joints.

10. Disconnect the multiple electrical connector at the heater.

11. Remove the instrument panel center cover.

12. Working from inside the engine compartment, remove the upper section of the fire shield.

13. Remove the heater assembly retaining nuts, and lift out the heater.

14. Open the heater housing clips, and separate the housing halves and remove the heater core.

15. Disconnect the electrical leads at the blower motor, and remove the motor.

16. To install, install the blower motor and connect the electrical leads. install the heater and clip the housing halves together. Install the heater and install the mounting nuts.

17. Install the upper section of fire shield under the hood.

18. Install the instrument panel center cover. Connect the electrical connector at the heater and connect the control shafts at the joints.

19. Connect the heater controls at the instrument panel. Install the lower instrument panel trim.

20. Reconnect the heater hoses at the heater core. Install the blower wires and install the evaporator. Install the evaporator bracket.

21. Connect both refrigerant lines to the evaporator. Install all heater controls and connect the heater hoses.

22. Install the glove box. Install the center tray and instrument panel lower trim.

23. Fill the cooling system and recharge the A/C system.

CAUTION: *If you are not experienced with air conditioning repair, have the system charged by a professional.*

24. Run the engine and check for leaks. Check the operation of the heating and A/C systems.

1982-86 733i and 735i

1. Drain the coolant from the system.

CAUTION: *When draining the coolant, keep in mind that cats and dogs are attracted by the ethylene glycol antifreeze, and are quite likely to drink any that is left in an uncovered container or in puddles on the ground. This will prove fatal in sufficient quantity. Always drain the coolant into a sealable container. Coolant should be reused unless it is contaminated or several years old.*

2. Discharge the refrigerant from the air conditioner or have this done by someone trained in this type of work if not familiar with it.

3. Remove the instrument trim panel.

4. Remove the cowl fresh air grille.

5. Remove the heater assembly cover attaching screws, and remove the cover.

6. Disconnect the heater hoses at the heater core.

7. Disconnect the vacuum lines at the heater.

8. Bend open the heater duct mounting clamp.

9. Disconnect the central electrical lead.

10. Pull the duct cover downward, and remove it.

11. Remove the center strut attaching bolts (4).

12. Remove the insulation from the refrigerant lines.

13. Disconnect the refrigerant lines from the evaporator.

14. Disconnect the evaporator drain tube.

15. Remove the heater assembly retaining bolts, remove the heater and the heater core.

16. Install the heater and heater core. Install the heater assembly and connect the evaporator drain tube.

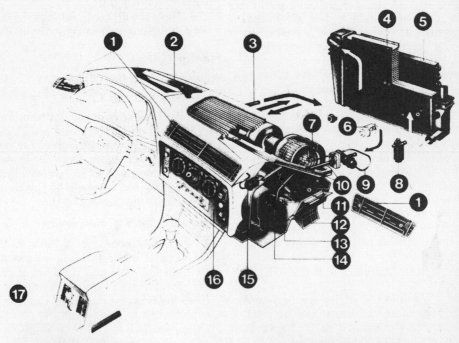

1. Summer air grill
2. Fresh air flap
3. Heat exchanger outlet
4. Engine radiator
5. Condenser and extra fan
6. Swash plate compressor
7. Blower
8. Drier
9. Water valve
10. Heat exchanger inlet
11. Evaporator
12. Footwell grill
13. Temperature control flap
14. Heat exchanger
15. Servo for summer air flap
16. Heater and air conditioner controls
17. Rear compartment grill and tray

Integral heating and air conditioning system components—7 series

17. Connect the refrigerant lines to the evaporator. Install the center strut and install the duct cover.

18. Connect the electrical lead and connect the vacuum lines at the heater.

19. Connect the heater hoses at the heater core.Install the heater assembly cover. Install the cowl fresh air grille. Install the instrument trim panel.

20. Charge the A/C system and fill the cooling system.

CAUTION: *If you are not familiar with air conditioning system service, have the system charged professionally.*

21. Run the engine and check all connections for leaks. Check the operation of the blower.

Heater/Air Conditioner Assembly and Core

REMOVAL AND INSTALLATION

524td, 528e, 533i and 633CSi from 1983, 535i, 635CSi, M5 and M6

1. Disconnect the battery ground. Remove the instrument panel trim at bottom left. Remove the package tray.

2. If not trained in air conditioning work, have the air conditioning system discharged professionally. Otherwise, discharge it carefully through the Schrader® valve, and then cap the valve off.

3. Remove the 2 bolts and remove the trim panel underneath the evaporator unit.

4. Remove the tape type insulation. Get caps for the refrigerant lines. *Using a backup wrench*, disconnect the low and high pressure lines and cap them.

5. Disconnect the electrical connector for the evaporator. Disconnect the temperature sensor plug, accessible from the outside of the evaporator housing.

6. Remove the 2 bolts and then remove the bracket that braces the housing at the firewall. Remove the mounting bolt from either side of the housing.

7. Unclip both fasteners and remove the housing.

8. Now, move into the engine compartment and remove the rubber insulator from the cowl.

9. Remove the mounting bolts for the cover which is located under the windshield.

10. Remove the mounting nuts for the heater housing located on either side of the blower.

11. Drain the cooling system and disconnect the 2 hoses at the core.

CAUTION: *When draining the coolant, keep in mind that cats and dogs are attracted by the ethylene glycol antifreeze, and are quite likely to drink any that is left in an uncovered container or in puddles on the ground. This will prove fatal in sufficient quantity. Always drain the coolant into a sealable container. Coolant should be reused unless it is contaminated or several years old.*

12. Working inside the car, remove the 3 electrical connectors for the heater housing. Pull off the 2 air ducts.

13. Remove the 2 mounting nuts and remove the heater unit.

14. Remove the 4 air duct connections from the housing. Push the retaining bar back and then split and remove the 2 blower shells.

15. Remove the 13 retaining clips from the housing halves and split the housing. Then, remove the core.

16. To install, reverse the removal procedure, noting the following points:

a. Cement a new rubber seal on the core.

b. Make sure that when reassembling the halves of the housing, all the distributor door flap shafts pass through the holes in the housing.

c. Before reconnecting the refrigerant lines, coat the threads with clean refrigerant oil.

d. Refill the cooling system with clean coolant and bleed it.

e. Have the air conditioning system evacuated and recharged or do so if qualified.

Heater Core

REMOVAL AND INSTALLATION

1600, 2000, 2002 and 320i

In order to remove the heater core, it is necessary to first remove the entire heater assembly from the car. See the procedure for removing the blower motor, above. Once the heater is out of the car, the core may be removed by drilling out the rivets and unsnapping the clips which hold the housing halves together.

2500, 28000, Bavaria, 3000 and 3.0

1. Drain the coolant from the system.

CAUTION: *When draining the coolant, keep in mind that cats and dogs are attracted by the ethylene glycol antifreeze, and are quite likely to drink any that is left in an uncovered container or in puddles on the ground. This will prove fatal in sufficient quantity. Always drain the coolant into a sealable container. Coolant should be reused unless it is contaminated or several years old.*

2. Disconnect the heater hoses from the heater core, and remove the rubber seal.

3. Remove the fresh air outlet grille cover. Coupe only:

a. Remove the heater control cover.

b. Disconnect the air distribution hoses from the discharge nozzles.

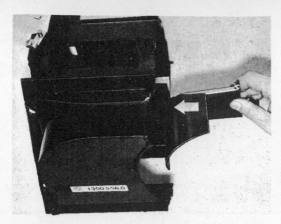

Slide the air guide baffle in as shown (2500, 2800, etc.)

Disconnect the ducts by pulling outward to pull the connector pins out of the bushings. See text

c. Remove the intermediate distribution duct.

4. Remove the buttons from the control levers.

5. Remove the threaded knobs for the left instrument panel trim strip.

6. Remove the rear switch plate.

7. Remove the front switch plate.

8. Remove the heater retaining nuts.

9. Tilt the heater and switch plate inwards, and remove the heater.

10. Detach the cable going to the defroster flap.

11. Pull off the retaining clips, remove the seals, and pull apart the halves of the heater housing (the core will stay in the left side of the housing).

12. Slide the core out of the housing, pulling the outer end toward you to permit the hose connections to clear the housing.

13.To install, reverse the removal procedure, noting the following points:

a. Slide the air guide baffle in as shown.

b. First insert the switch plate into the dash and then insert the heater. Tighten attaching nuts firmly. Check the foam rubber seal between the heater and dash panel and replace, if necessary.

c. When installing the front switch plate, make sure the control levers do not scrape against the trim.

d. Replace the sealing gasket which goes under the cowl cover.

528i and 530i

1. Remove the center tray.

2. Remove the glove bos.

3. Disconnect the battery ground.

4. Push the selector lever to the **WARM** position.

5. Drain the coolant.

Meshing the damper gears—528i and 530i

CAUTION: *When draining the coolant, keep in mind that cats and dogs are attracted by the ethylene glycol antifreeze, and are quite likely to drink any that is left in an uncovered container or in puddles on the ground. This will prove fatal in sufficient quantity. Always drain the coolant into a sealable container. Coolant should be reused unless it is contaminated or several years old.*

6. Disconnect the heater hoses from the heater core, and remove the rubber seal.

7. Remove the lower instrument panel center trim.

8. Disconnect the heater controls at the instrument panel.

9. Disconnect the control shafts at the joints. To do this, press in locking prongs with needle nose pliers.

10. Disconnect the multiple electrical connector at the heater.

11. Remove the instrument panel center cover.

12. Working from inside the engine compart-

ment, remove the upper section of the fire shield.

13. Disconnect ducts by pulling outward to pull connector pins out of bushings which are in the ducts.

14. Remove clips and remove the outer portion of the lower blower housing. Pull out the motor/blower unit, disconnect wires, and remove it.

15. Pull the foam rubber seal about halfway off and fold it back.

16. Remove the clamp from the pipe leading to the water valve, disconnect the water valve and remove the valve and pipe as an assembly.

17. Remove clips and detach the right side housing (this housing covers ears which operate the heater damper).

18. Remove the attaching circlip and remove the smaller gear. Then, pull out the shaft to which the smaller gear was mounted.

19. Remove the housing clips and separate the housing halves.

20. Press out the grommet and pull wires out from between core pipes and the core. Remove the core from the heater assembly.

21. To install, reverse the above, keeping the following points in mind:

a. Glue new rubber seals onto the outside of the core before installing it into the heater.

b. When reassembling halves of the heater, first position the sleeve on the air flap and position the flap carefully and guide it into the bore on the opposite side of the heater housing.

c. When reinstalling damper gears, mesh the gears so the timing marks line up.

d. Replace the water valve seals.

e. When remounting the lower blower motor, make sure the portion of the motor between the 2 electrical connectors engages with the slot in the heater housing. Then, when reinstalling the blower housing, make sure the flat surface on either side of the intake duct faces down.

f. Secure the cables so that air flaps are closed when the control switch is at **OFF**.

g. Turn the fan switch and water valve and air distribution flaps left to the stop for each when reconnecting the control shafts.

1987-88 735i

1. Drain coolant from the cooling system (engine cooled off). Remove the center console.

CAUTION: *When draining the coolant, keep in mind that cats and dogs are attracted by the ethylene glycol antifreeze, and are quite likely to drink any that is left in an uncovered container or in puddles on the ground. This will prove fatal in sufficient quantity. Always drain the coolant into a sealable container.*

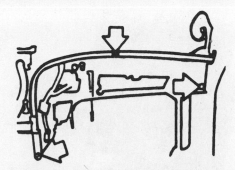

Remove the two arrowed screws to remove the heater core on 1987–88 735i

Coolant should be reused unless it is contaminated or several years old.

2. Remove the 2 bolts and remove the right core mounting bracket. Lift out the front blower motor.

3. Remove the core cover screws. Loosen the wire straps and clips and remove the cover.

4. Unscrew the 6 mounting bolts and lift out the 3 heater pipes. Replace the O-rings. Then, lift out the core from the right side.

5. Install core by reversing the above procedures. Check all connections for leaks and check the system for correct operation.

318i, 325, 325e, 325i, 325iS, 325iX and M3

1. Disconnect the negative battery cable. Remove the package tray. Remove bolts and remove the left lower dash trim panel.

2. Drain the coolant, loosen the bolt and remove the clamp bracing the 2 lines going to the heater core.

CAUTION: *When draining the coolant, keep in mind that cats and dogs are attracted by the ethylene glycol antifreeze, and are quite likely to drink any that is left in an uncovered container or in puddles on the ground. This will prove fatal in sufficient quantity. Always drain the coolant into a sealable container. Coolant should be reused unless it is contaminated or several years old.*

3. Remove the left side duct carrying air from the heater to the rear seat duct.

4. Unscrew the bolts and remove the lower heater discharge duct.

5. Unscrew the bolts fastening the water lines from the engine compartment to the lines coming down from the heater core. Remove and discard the O-ring seals.

6. Unscrew the bolts, separate the halves of the core housing, and pull the core out of the housing.

7. Install the core into the housing and connect the halves. Reconnect the lines coming from the engine compartment to the heater core install new O-rings.

8. Install the lower heater duct and the left side rear heater duct.

9. Install the Package tray and the left lower dash trim panel.

10. Fill the cooling system and check all connections for leaks. Check the operation of the system.

Blower Motor
REMOVAL AND INSTALLATION
318i, 325, 325e, 325i, 325iS, 325iX and M3

1. Disconnect the negative battery cable. The blower is accessible by removing the cover at the top of the firewall in the engine compartment. To remove the cover, pull off the rubber strip, cut off the wire that runs diagonally across the cover, unscrew and remove the bolts, and pull the cover aside.

2. Open the retaining straps, swing them aside, and then remove the blower cover.

3. Pull off both connectors. Disengage the clamp that fastens the assembly in place by pulling the bottom in the direction of the operator. Now, lift out the motor/fan assembly, being careful not to damage the air damper underneath.

524td, 528e, 533i and 633CSi from 1983, 535i, 635CSi, M5 and M6

1. Disconnect the battery ground cable.

2. Remove the rubber insulator from the cowl. Remove the mounting bolts for the cover which is located under the windshield.

3. Push back the 3 retaining tabs and remove the 2 shells that cover the blower wheels.

4. Disconnect the electrical connector for the motor. Unclip the retaining strap for the motor and remove the motor and blower wheels.

5. Replace the motor and blower wheels as an assembly (prebalanced). The motor will fit into the housing only one way. Reverse all procedures to install, making sure the flat surface on the inlet cowls face the body.

1987–88 735i

1. Disconnect the battery ground cable. Pull the rubber cover off the overflow tank for the cooling system. Disconnect the electrical connector and overflow hose from the overflow tank. Then, remove the mounting nuts and put the tank aside without damaging the hose leading to the radiator.

2. Cut the straps for the wiring harness running across the cowl.

3. Remove the 5 attaching screws and remove the blower cover from the cowl.

4. Disconnect the cable and unclip it where it is clipped to the blower cover. Then, open the plastic retainer and take off the cover.

5. Disconnect the electrical connector. Lift off the metal retainer for the blower motor and remove the blower motor.

6. Install a new, prebalanced motor and blower assembly. Install in reverse order.

Heater and Air Conditioning Control Panel
REMOVAL AND INSTALLATION
Early Models With Cable Control

1. Disconnect the negative battery cable.

2. Remove the Radio as outlined in this chapter.

3. Remove the control panel retaining screws and pull the panel forward.

4. Disconnect the electrical wires from the rear of the panel.

5. Loosen the tang that holds the cable in position and remove the cable from the control head, by tilting the control head up slighlty.

6. Install the control head in position, first connecting the actuating cable to it.

7. Reconnect the electrical leads and install the panel retaining screws.

8. Reconnect the battery and check the operation of the system and check the levers for freedom of movement.

Late Models with Vacuum Control

1. Disconnect the negative battery cable.

2. Remove the radio and surrounding trim panel.

3. Remove the screws along the top edge of the control panel and pull the panel out slightly.

4. Disconnect the electrical leads from the back of the panel.

5. Unplug the vacuum line connector, note the position of the connector for installation.

6. Remove the panel from the dash.

7. Install the control panel in position and reconnect the vacuum connector, note the color coding of the hoses for correct installation, they should match.

8. Reconnect the electrical leads and screw the panel into position.

9. Connect the negative battery cable. Check the operation of the system and check for any vacuum leaks.

RADIO
REMOVAL AND INSTALLATION
1600–2, 2002, and 320i

1. Disconnect the negative battery cable.

2. Unscrew the shift lever and lift off the boot.

3. Remove the phillips head screws which retain the console to the dash and transmission tunnel.

4. Remove the phillips head screws which retain the left and right-hand side panels of the console to the radio mounting bracket. Remove the side panels, exposing the radio mounting bracket. (The radio mounting bracket houses the speaker.)

5. Disconnect the antenna cable from the radio. Disconnect the radio ground cable (if so equipped) from the left-hand heater mounting bolt. Disconnect the power lead for the radio from the existing plug location inline to the hazard warning switch.

6. Lift the radio mounting bracket forward. The radio may now be disconnected from the speaker by removing the speaker multiple plug from the back of the radio.

7. Pry off the radio control knobs exposing the mounting nuts. Unscrew the mounting nuts and remove the radio from its bracket.

8. Install the radio in its mounting bracket and install the mounting nuts.

9. Install the radio control knobs. Connect the speaker plug to the radio and connect the power and ground leads to the radio.

10. Install the side console panels and install the console retaining screws.

11. Install the shift lever boot, if equipped. Connect the negative battery cable and check the operation of the radio.

2500, 2800, Bavaria, 3000 and 3.0

1. Disconnect the negative battery cable. Remove the 4 screws from the outside of the underdash console while supporting the radio

from underneath. Pull the unit out and lay it on the console.

2. Disconnect the aerial cable (large plug), the negative cable ("B-"), the speaker plugs (from the back of the unit) and the positive cable ("B +"-violet in color).

3. Connect the wires to the radio and connect the antenna lead.

4. Slide the unit into position and install the retaining screws.

5. Connect the negative battery cable and check the operation of the radio.

528e, 530i and 630CSi

1. Disconnect the negative battery cable. Pull off the radio knobs and ornamental rings.

2. Push up on spring catches and remove them from the control shafts. Remove the radio mask.

3. Remove the bolts from supports on both sides of the radio.

4. Disconnect the automatic antenna lead, the antenna, the right and left speaker wires and the power supply.

5. Connect the power, speaker and antenna leads to the radio and install it in the dash.

6. Install the radio mask, ornamental rings, face plate and control knobs to the radio.

7. Connect the negative battery cable and check the radio for proper operation.

All Models Equipped with Electronically Tuned Radio (ETR)

Most models after 1984 are equipped with an electronically tuned stereo system, this system uses push buttons instead of knobs for radio control.

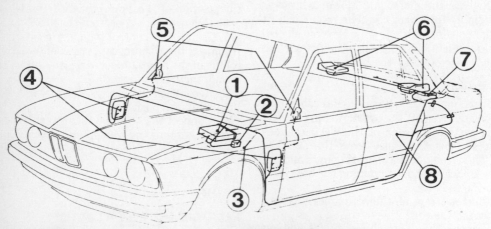

1. Radio
2. Speaker balance control
3. Special equipment plug
4. Front speaker in footwell
5. High tuner in mirror triangle
6. Rear speaker on hatrack incl. high tuner
7. Amplifier underneath hatrack, accessible from trunk
8. Ground point underneath rear seat cushion

Typical sound system layout for late model vehicles

Typical radio mounting—late model vehicles with ETR

To remove the ETR radio receiver, first disconnect the negative battery cable then, remove the screws retaining the trim around the radio (and the A/C and heating control panel). Remove the screws retaining the radio. Slide it out of the dash and disconnect the wiring.

The radio is installed by simply connecting the wiring and sliding it back into place in the dash and securing it with the screws. Reinstall the trim around the radio and connect the battery cable. Check the radio operation.

WINDSHIELD WIPERS

Blade and Arm

Blade and arm removal and installation are described in Chapter 1.

Windshield Wiper Motor

The electric wiper motor assembly is located under the engine hood, at the top of the cowl panel. A few models have covers over the wiper motor assembly, while others have the motors exposed. Link rods operate the left and right wiper pivot assemblies from a drive crank bolted to the wiper motor output shaft.

REMOVAL AND INSTALLATION

1600–2 and 2002

NOTE: *The motor is accessible from the engine side of the firewall.*

1. Disconnect the negative batter cable.
2. Remove the nut which retains the drive crank linkage to the motor, and disconnect the drive crank.
3. Remove the 3 mounting bolts for the motor.
4. Label and disconnect the 3 electrical leads from the clear plastic socket connection. Loosen

the retaining screw for the ground wire and disconnect the ground wire from the body.

5. Lift out the wiper motor.
6. Install the wiper motor in position and install the 3 retaining bolts.
7. Connect the electrical leads and attach the ground wire.
8. Connect the drive crank. Reconnect the

Disconnecting the wiper drive crank—1600, 2000 and 2002

Removing motor retaining bolts

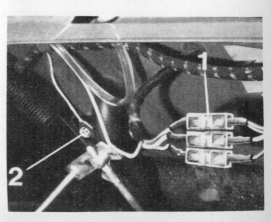

Disconnecting multiple plug (1) and ground (2)

battery cable and check the operation of the wipers.

2500, 2800, Bavaria, 3000 and 3.0

1. Remove the cover for the heater unit on the cowl panel (except coupes).
2. Remove the crank arm retaining nut and washer.
3. Remove the wiper motor retaining screws, tilt the motor downward and remove.
4. Disconnect the electrical contact plug from the wiper motor.
5. Connect the electrical contact plug to the wiper motor and install the motor.
6. Install the crank arm retaining nut and washer.

NOTE: *The complete wiper motor, pivot assemblies and linkage can be removed as a unit, if necessary.*

320i, 524td, 528e, 528i, 533i, 535i, 633CSi, 635CSi, M5 and M6

1. Remove the cowl cover to expose the wiper motor (320i and 530i and all 5 and 6 Series cars after 1983).
2. Disconnect the wiper motor crank arm from the motor output shaft by removing the nut and pulling off the crank arm.
3. Remove the motor retaining screws and disconnect the electrical connector.
4. Remove the wiper motor from the vehicle.
5. Reverse the procedure to install the motor.

318i, 325, 325e, 325i 325iS, 325iX, and M3

1. Disconnect the negative battery cable. Remove the heater motor, as described above. Remove the bracket bracing the windshield wiper motor, which is now visible.
2. Disconnect the electrical connector for the motor.
3. Lift out the grille located at the top of the cowl and disconnect the linkages to both wiper arms at the left side shaft mounts.
4. Disconnect both wiper arms from their shafts by lifting the cover, unscrewing the nut, and pulling the arm off. Then, remove the cover, nut and washer surrounding the shafts and holding the console in place. Now remove the entire console.
5. With the motor still mounted, remove the nut retaining the linkage to the motor shaft. Then, unbolt and remove the motor from the console.
6. Install the motor in the console and connect the linkage to the motor shaft. Install the console and install the cover, nut and washers on the shafts.
7. Install both wiper arms on their shafts. Install the grille on the cowl and connect both wiper linkages.
8. Connect the electrical leads to the motor. and install the bracket bracing the wiper motor.
9. Install the heater motor, as described earlier in this chapter. Connect the negative battery cable.

1982 733i

1. Remove the cowl fresh air intake grille and tilt rearward.
2. Remove the cover from the windshield wiper motor and remove the electrical plugs.
3. Remove the left and right wiper arms. Loosen the left and right pivot bearings.
4. Turn the rubber pad at the motor, counterclockwise and disconnect the right wiper linkage.
5. Remove the motor bracket retaining screws. Separate the spacers and remove the wiper motor assembly.

NOTE: *Do not lose the shims.*

6. The wiper motor can be removed from the bracket after the removal.
7. Install the wiper motor assembly and install the retaining screws.
8. Connect the right wiper linkage and install the left and right wiper arms.

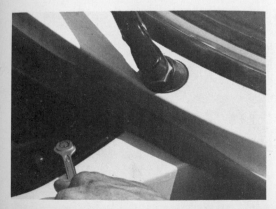

Removing the Cowl cover for access to the wiper motor—320i

When reinstalling the 733i motor, make sure it is in park position—with the arm positioned as shown (1)

9. Connect the electrical leads and install the cover on the wiper motor. Install the cowl fresh air intake grille.

1983–84 733i and 1985–86 735i

1. Remove the mounting screws and remove the grille from the cowl.

2. The wiper motor is located under a cover located in front of the windshield on the left side of the car. Unscrew the 2 mounting screws on the firewall and the 2 directly in front of the windshield. Pull the rubber seal out part way and move the cover slightly away from its normal position. Disconnect the hose from the cover and then tilt the cover forward.

3. Remove the wiper motor cover and unplug the electrical connector.

4. Remove both wiper arms. Unscrew the collar nuts and disconnect both wiper shaft mounts. Turn back the rubber pad and disconnect the linkage for the right wiper. Unscrew and remove the 2 mounting bolts and pull the spacer tube apart; remove the motor. Note the exact position of the motor crank.

5. Disconnect the linkage and pull the crank off the motor. The motor may be removed from the bracket after removing the 3 mounting bolts.

6. Install in reverse order, noting these points:

   a. Install the crank in the position shown to get proper parking of the wipers.

   b. When remounting the motor, make sure the bumpers that rest against the firewall are properly positioned.

   c. Situate the rubber pad so the motor has proper support.

   d. When reassembling the wiper shaft mounts, install the diaphragm spring and then the ring and torque to only 9 ft. lbs.

   e. When reinstalling the outer cover, take care not to pinch any vacuum hoses.

1987–88 735i

1. Make sure the wipers are in the parked position. Remove the heater blower as described above. Take off the cover near the blower.

2. Disconnect the heater cable and lift out the linkage. Disconnect the temperature sensor.

3. Disconnect the clips, lift the cowl cover slightly and then remove the fresh air inlet cowls on either side. Then, remove the cover.

4. Unscrew bolts and remove the mounting bracket for the wiper housing. Remove the left wiper arm by pulling up the cover, loosening the pinch bolt, and removing it. Remove the right wiper by pulling up the cover, removing the through bolt and then pulling it off.

5. Lift out the clips and remove the cover for the linkage.

6. Unscrew and remove the nuts fastening the linkage to the cowl. Pull the linkage arms downward and out of the cowl.

7. Mark the relationship between the linkage lever and the motor. Remove the nut and disconnect the linkage at the motor shaft. Disconnect the electrical connector and remove the linkage.

8. Remove the 3 mounting bolts and remove the wiper motor. If installing a new motor, connect the motor and operate it until it reaches parked position; then install the linkage so that the shaft lever and linkage link are in a straight line.

9. Perform the remaining portions of the installation in reverse order, noting these points:

   a. Make sure the wiper arms are pressed all the way onto the linkage shafts so the contact pressure control will work.

   b. Make sure the inlet cowling is installed in proper relation to the blower housing and fresh air flap.

Windshield Wiper Linkage
REMOVAL AND INSTALLATION
1600, 2000, 2002, 2500, 2800, Bavaria, 3000 and 3.0

1. Remove the cover plate from the top of the cowl.

2. Pull off the wiper arms.

3. Loosen the nuts retaining both wiper pivot bearings (the bearing located where the drive passes through the cowl).

4. Swing out the wiper motor complete with linkage.

5. Unplug the multiple connector and remove it with its rubber grommet.

6. Disconnect the connecting link and drive rod by pressing off.

7. Completely unscrew the retaining nuts from the wiper pivot bearings and remove them.

8. Install the wiper pivot bearings and install the wiper connecting link, and drive rod.

9. Reconnect the electrical lead and install the wiper motor and linkage.

10. Install the wiper arms and the cover plate on the cowl.

11. Adjust the wiper arms so the clearance between blades and the bottom of the windshield is 10-20mm. Put a new sealing strip between the cowl cover and the gutter.

5 and 6 Series Vehicles

1. Open the hood, loosen the mounting screws, and remove the cover from the top of the firewall.

2. Remove both wiper arms. Press off both the connecting rod and the drive arm at the drive bushings. Disconnect the drive arm and detach the motor crank.

3. Remove the knurled cap from both arm drive shafts, and remove the nut above the cowl. Then, loosen the nut located below the cowl, and remove the assembly.

4. Install the assembly into the vehicle and tighten the nut located below the cowl.

5. Install the knurled cap on both arm drive shafts and install the nut above the cowl.

6. Attach the motor crank and drive arm. Press the connecting rod back into position.

7. Install both wiper arms and install the cover on the top of the fire wall.

Removing lower section of steering column shroud—1600, 2002

7 Series

1. Remove the wiper motor and linkage assembly as described above.

2. Unscrew the nut on the motor crank, and remove the crank from the motor.

3. Install in reverse order, noting the following points:

  a. Make sure to install the unit with the motor in park position. At this position, the crank covers the bolt on the motor side of the crank halfway.

  b. Make sure the motor mounting shims fit properly.

  c. Turn the rubber mounting pad under the motor to a position which supports the motor securely.

  d. Be careful not to pinch vacuum hoses.

Removing lower center instrument panel trim—1600, 2002

INSTRUMENTS AND SWITCHES

Instrument Cluster

REMOVAL AND INSTALLATION

1600-2 and 2002

1. Disconnect the negative battery cable.

2. Remove the lower section of the steering column shroud. Remove the lower center instrument panel trim.

3. Disconnect the speedometer cable at the speedometer.

4. Unscrew the knurled nuts at the rear of the speedometer housing.

5. On 1970 models, unscrew the cluster hood retaining screws.

6. Push the instrument cluster out the front of the dash. Disconnect the central plug (12-pronged) at the rear of the cluster.

7. Lift out the instrument cluster, containing the fuel gauge, warning lights, speedometer, and tachometer or clock.

8. To install, install the instrument cluster

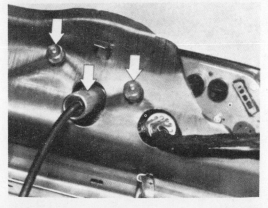

Disconnecting speedometer cable and knurled nuts

and connect the central plug to the rear of the cluster.

9. Connect the speedometer cable to the speedometer and install the knurled nuts.

10. Install the steering column shroud and the instrument panel trim.

11. Connect the negative battery cable.

2500, 2800, Bavaria, 3000 and 3.0

1. Disconnect the negative battery cable. Remove the 2 screws attaching the upper instrument panel housing—one at either side, accessible through the hole at the bottom corner of the lower housing.

2. Pull off the upper section of the housing until the speaker wires can be disconnected. Then, disconnect the speaker wires and remove the upper housing.

3. Pull off the 2 multiple connectors, unscrew the speedometer cable, and remove the cluster.

4. Install the cluster in position and connect the electrical connectors.

5. Connect the speedometer cable. Connect the speaker wires and install the upper instrument panel housing.

6. Connect the negative battery cable.

318i, 325, 325e, 325i 325iS, 325iX, and M3

1. Disconnect the negative battery cable. Remove the attaching screws and remove the lower instrument panel trim from under the steering column.

2. Remove the mounting nuts for the trim just under the instrument carrier, and remove it.

3. Unscrew the 4 screws underneath and 2 above the instrument carrier, and remove trim that surrounds the instrument carrier.

4. Remove the 2 screws at the top of the carrier, lift it out of the instrument panel, and then disconnect the plugs. To disconnect the combination plug, first pull the sliding clamp off the center.

5. Install the instrument panel and connect the electrical leads. Install the trim around the instrument cluster.

6. Install the trim under the instrument carrier and the trim under the steering column. Connect the negative battery cable.

320i

1. Disconnect the negative battery cable.
2. Remove the steering wheel assembly.
3. Remove the bottom center instrument trim panel.
4. Disconnect the speedometer cable, loosen the knurled nut and pull the instrument assembly outward.
5. Remove the electrical plugs and wires.
6. Remove the instrument cluster from the dash.
7. Install the instrument cluster into the dash and connect the electrical leads.
8. Connect the speedometer cable. Install the bottom center instrument trim panel.
9. Install the steering wheel. Connect the negative battery cable.

528e

1. Remove the negative battery cable.
2. Remove the lower instrument trim panel.
3. Disconnect the speedometer cable.
4. Loosen the knurled nuts on the cluster back.
5. Loosen the steering column to dash screws.
6. Pull the instrument cluster outward and remove the electrical wires and connectors.
7. Remove the cluster from the dash panel.
8. Install the instrument cluster into the dash and connect the electrical leads.
9. Connect the speedometer cable. Install the bottom center instrument trim panel.
10. Tighten the steering column screws. Connect the negative battery cable.

533i and 535i through 1985, 633CSi to 1983

1. Disconnect the negative battery cable.
2. Remove the steering wheel assembly.
3. Remove the bottom center instrument trim panel.
4. Remove the cover from the "INQUIRY" unit.
5. Remove the 3 retaining screws and remove the "INQUIRY" printed circuit board.
6. Remove the light switch, leaving the wiring connected.
7. Remove the left air control knob and remove the bezel cover.
8. Remove the fog lamp switch and leave the wiring attached.
9. Remove the screws from the instrument cluster and loosen the steering column control base screws.
10. Disconnect the speedometer cable.
11. Push downward on the upper section casing and the steering column, so that the instrument cluster can be removed at an angle. Disconnect the electrical wiring and connectors.
12. To install the instrument cluster, connect the electrical leads and install the cluster in the dash.
13. Connect the speedometer cable. Install the retaining screws to the cluster and tighten the steering column base screws.
14. Install the fog lamp switch and the air control bezel and knob.
15. Install the "INQUIRY" unit printed circuit board and cover. Install the bottom instrument panel trim.
16. Install the steering wheel assembly. Connect the negative battery cable.

524td, 528e, 1986-88 535i and M5

1. Disconnect the negative battery cable. Unscrew the 2 retaining screws in the hood above the instrument carrier.
2. Lift the carrier out far enough to unplug

Tilt the instrument cluster forward to remove it

all the plugs and remove it. Before pulling off the combination plug, pull the sliding clip off the side of the plug.

3. Install the carrier by, first connecting all of the electrical leads and then positioning it in the dash.

4. Reconnect the negative battery cable.

1983–84 633CSi, 1985–88 635CSi and M6

1. Disconnect the battery ground cable. Remove the steering wheel as described earlier.

2. Lift the glass cover off the check control, located to the left of the instrument cluster. Unscrew the 3 mounting screws, lift off the housing, and pull off the plugs while removing it.

3. Remove the fog light switch from the dash without disconnecting the wiring.

4. Lift off the plate covering mounting screws located to the right of the cluster by pulling up on the right side. Then, remove the screws located underneath.

5. Remove the mounting screws for the trim panel under the steering wheel and remove it (it can be stored in the footwell).

6. Remove the 2 large mounting bolts located under the dash at the front and just on either side of the steering column.

7. Lift the cluster out of the dash and disconnect the plugs. When pulling the large combination plug off the carrier, first push the clip off the plug.

Removing the instrument cluster retaining screws

8. To install, install the cluster in position and connect the electrical leads.

9. Install the 2 steering column bolts and install the trim under the steering wheel. Install the cluster retaining screws and the garnish plate over the screws.

10. Install the fog light switch. Install the check control and cover with the 3 mounting screws.

11. Install the steering wheel and connect the negative battery cable.

1982 733i

1. Remove the negative battery cable from the battery post.

2. Remove the instrument panel trim section at the left bottom of the dash.

3. Remove the upper bezel retaining screws.

4. Loosen the steering column control and pull the steering housing all the way out.

5. Pull the instrument cluster outward, remove the electrical wires and plugs, after removal of the speedometer cable.

6. Turn the cluster assembly towards the right rear and pull it away from the dash.

7. Install the cluster in the dash connecting all electrical leads.

8. Connect the speedometer cable. Slide the steering housing in and install the retaining screws.

9. Install the bezel retaining screws and install the lower trim panel. Connect the negative battery cable.

1983–84 733i
1985–86 735i

1. Disconnect the negative battery cable. Remove the 3 bolts from the top of the instrument cluster.

2. Lift the instrument cluster out of the dash. Disconnect all electrical connectors. Note that the combination plugs have a slide clamp that must be removed before they can be pulled apart.

3. Install the instrument cluster into the dash and connect the electrical leads.

4. Install the cluster retaining bolts and connect the negative battery cable.

1987–88 735i

1. Remove the steering wheel as described earlier. Remove the 2 large screws located under the cluster hood.

2. Pry the cluster out slightly from the top and pull it forward and down until it touches the steering column.

3. Press the levers next to the electrical connector plugs upward and then pull the plugs off the cluster. Remove the cluster.

4. The cluster may be further disassembled by turning the toggle screws 90 degrees.

5. Install the instrument cluster into the dash and connect the electrical leads. Make sure the levers that lock the electrical connector plugs are upward before trying to connect them.

6. Install the cluster retaining bolts and connect the negative battery cable.

Windshield Wiper Switch

REMOVAL AND INSTALLATION

NOTE: *On many models, this switch is a combination unit which also controls the direction signals and headlight dimming. Refer to the procedure below and then refer to "Turn Signal/Dimmer Switch and Wiper Switch" in Chapter 8, for more specific information on those models where these functions are combined. On 325, 325e, 325i, 325iS, 325iX and M3, this switch is mounted right next to the turn signal switch and its removal is covered specifically under that procedure.*

All Models Except 1987-88 735i

The wiper switch is located on the steering column and in most cases the steering wheel will have to be removed, along with the lower steering column trim panels, to gain access to the switch.

After the retaining screws and electrical connectors are removed, the switch can be lifted from the plate of the steering column.

CAUTION: *To avoid possible electrical short-circuits, the negative battery cable should be removed before the repairs are attempted.*

1987-88 735i

1. Disconnect the negative battery cable. Remove the steering wheel. Remove the lower left instrument panel trim.

2. Remove the screws and remove the lower steering column cover.

3. Push the locking hook for the flasher back and remove the relay, socket facing downward.

4. Take off the upper steering column cover. If the car has airbags, drive out the pins and lift out the expansion rivet first.

CAUTION: *On vehicles equipped with air bags, DO NOT bang on the steering column very hard or the air bag may be discharged!*

5. Press the retaining hooks inward on both sides, pull the switch out, and then disconnect the electrical connector.

6. Reinstall the switch then install the electrical connectors. Install the column cover and lower instrument panel trim.

7. Install the steering wheel and connect the negative battery cable.

Headlight Switch

REMOVAL AND INSTALLATION

1600, 2002, 2500, 2800, Bavaria, 3000, 3.0 and All 3 Series

1. Disconnect the battery ground cable. Remove the lower left trim panel screws and remove the panel.

2. Unscrew the knob from the switch.

3. Pull off the connector plug from behind the dash panel. Pull out the switch from behind and remove it.

4. Install the switch back into position and connect the electrical lead.

5. Screw the knob back onto the switch and install the lower trim panel. Connect the negative battery cable.

524td, 528e, 535i, M5, 733i, 735i

1. Disconnect the negative battery cable. The switch is pressed into the left side of the dash. Pry the switch out using a small screwdriver top and bottom.

2. Unplug the switch.

3. Connect the switch to the electrical lead and push it into the dash.

1983-84 633CSi, 635CSi, M6

1. Disconnect the battery ground. Remove the lower left instrument panel trim.

2. Unscrew and remove the light switch knob.

3. Remove the 4 bolts and remove the brace located under the instrument panel.

4. Pull off the switch plug. Then, pull the switch out of the dash from behind.

5. Install the switch into the dash and plug it in.

6. Install the brace under the instrument panel.

7. Screw in the switch control knob. Install the trim panel and connect the negative battery cable.

Clock

REMOVAL AND INSTALLATION

On vehicles equipped with a clock, it is removed by simply pulling the trim from around it, and using a small screwdriver, remove the 4 phillips head screws retaining it and then carefully pry it from the instrument panel. Disconnect the electrical lead from it and remove it from the dash. It can be installed by just firmly pushing it back into position, installing the 4 screws and installing the trim panel.

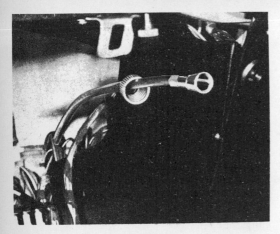

Removing the speedometer cable—2500, 2800, etc.

Speedometer Cable

REMOVAL AND INSTALLATION

1600, 2000, and 2002

1. Unscrew the cable fastening bolt on the transmission and pull the cable out.
2. Pull the cable out of the clamp under the car.
3. Remove the cable cover from under the steering column.
4. Reach up behind the instrument cluster and unscrew the cable retaining nut. The cable may now be pulled from the firewall together with the rubber grommet.
5. Install the cable through the firewall with the grommet and install it into the speedometer.
6. Install the cable cover. Attach the cable to the transmission. Check the operation of the speedometer, if it sticks or makes a clicking noise, check that the cable is correctly routed.

2500, 2800, Bavaria, 3000, 3.0
320i
5 Series Vehicles Through 1984
633Csi
1982 733i

1. Unscrew the retaining bolt, and pull the cable out of the transmission. Pull the cable off the retaining clips under the car.
2. Open the glove compartment on the left side. Reach up behind the instrument cluster and unscrew the cable retaining nut behind the speedometer.
3. Detach the hazard flasher relay, and move it aside. Then, pull the cable and the rubber grommet out of the firewall.
5. Install the cable through the firewall with the grommet and install it into the speedometer. Reposition the hazard flasher relay.
6. Attach the cable to the transmission.

Check the operation of the speedometer, if it sticks or makes a clicking noise, check that the cable is correctly routed.

All Other Models

All of the remaining models not listed above, are equipped with an electronic speedometer. This speedometer has no mechanical connection to the transmission, instead, a sensor in the transmission sends electronic signals to the speedometer which are then translated into the motion of the needle. The only service for any problems with this system is replacement of the speed sensor in the transmission or replacement of the speedometer or circuit board.

Ignition Switch

NOTE: *Removal and installation procedures for the steering column-mounted switch are found in Chapter 8.*

LIGHTING

Headlights

AIMING

Headlights should be precision aimed using special equipment; however, as a temporary measure, you might wish to re-aim your lights to an approximately correct position.

Most of the BMW models covered by this book employ large, knurled knobs, located behind the headlights, for aiming purposes. The horizontal adjustment is located on the right (driver's) side of the light, and the vertical adjustment above the light. Screw the vertical adjustment inward (clockwise) to lower the beam; screw the horizontal adjustment in (clockwise) to turn the beam to left, and vice-versa.

The lights may be aimed against a wall. High beams should point just slightly below straight ahead and horizontal. Low beams should point

Adjust the headlights at the large knurled knobs. Knobs (1) are for vertical adjustment, knobs (2) for horizontal—320i

somewhat downward, with the left side beam pointing slightly to the right.

REPLACEMENT

1600, 2000 and 2002

1. Remove the 4 phillips head screws from the front of the radiator gille.

2. Open the hood. Remove the weather-proof cover, if so equipped. Unscrew the knurled nut which retains the outside edge of the grille to the front panel. Lift off the grille.

3. Disconnect the electrical connector from the back of the sealed beam.

4. Remove the 3 screws which retain the headlight outer ring to the headlight, taking care not to drop the sealed beam.

5. Lift out the headlight.

6. Reverse the above procedure to install. Have the headlights adjusted at a garage with the proper equipment. If this is not possible, park the car on a level surface about 25 feet from a light colored wall. With the tires properly inflated and a friend sitting in the from seat, adjust the beams to the proper height using the black knurled knobs located inside the fender well. The upper knob controls the vertical setting and the knob at the side controls the horizontal setting.

2500, 2800, Bavaria, 3000 and 3.0

1. Open the hood and pull the cover off the rear of the headlight. Detach the electrical connector.

2. The bulb is retained by a spring clip—turn the clip back and pull the bulb out to the rear.

3. Installation is the reverse of the removal procedure. Make sure to properly align the reflector.

320i

1. First, remove the top and bottom screws from the parking light. Pull the parking light lens off. Then, open the hood, disconnect the electrical connector for the parking light, and pull the rubber grommet out of the engine compartment wall. Now pull the entire parking light assembly out of the grille.

2. Remove the attaching screws and remove the grille.

3. Loosen the 3 screws on the trim ring (don't let the headlight fall) and then pull the lamp out. Disconnect the connector and remove the lamp.

4. Install the new lamp in reverse order, making sure the tab on the rear of the lamp is aligned with the notch in the reflector so that the lamp cannot be turned once it is in position.

3, 5, 6 and 7 Series Vehicles to 1986

1. On the 7 series vehicles, disconnect the wiring connector going to the turn indicator light and push the rubber grommet through the engine compartment wall. Then, remove the indicator assembly. Then, on all other models listed, remove the attaching screws and remove the grille.

2. Remove the 3 screws which secure the clamping ring to the reflector, pull the lamp out far enough to remove the plug from the back, remove the plug and remove the lamp.

3. Replace the lamp in reverse order, making sure to fit the tab on the lamp into the notch in the reflector so that the lamp cannot be turned once it is in position.

1987-88 All Models

Almost all new models use halogen headlamps, these lamps provide brighter and longer lasting light. The bulbs for the headlight are separate from the reflector, where as conventional bulbs are part of the reflector.

NOTE: *Halogen bulbs are very sensitive and must be nadled carefully. They must not be touched with bare hands. Always use a clean, soft cloth to change the bulbs.*

1. Open the hood and disconnect the negative battery cable.

2. Remove the cover from the rear of the headlight assembly.

3. Turn the headlight holder counterclockwise and remove the light assembly.

4. Replace the bulb. Install a new bulb, making sure not to handle it with your bare hands.

Marker Lights and Front Turn Signal Lamps

REMOVAL AND INSTALLATION

All Models except 1987-88 6 and 7 Series

The front turn signal and all 4 marker lamp bulbs can easily be replaced. To replace the marker lamp bulbs, just remove the plastic lens

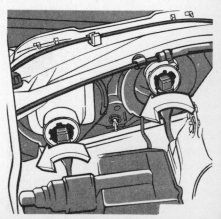

Changing the headlight bulbs on most late model vehicles

Remove the plastic lens to replace the front marker light

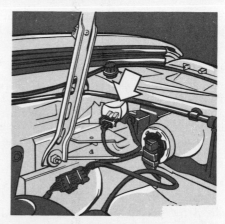

Replacing the front turn signal and marker lamp bulbs—1987–88 6 and 7 series

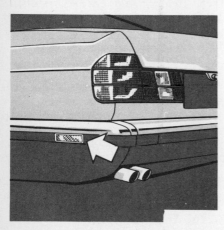

Remove the plastic lens to replace the rear marker light

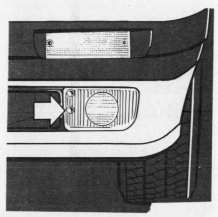

Remove the retaining screws to remove the fog light lens

and change the bulb. Most of the vehicles are equipped with a 4 watt bulb. On some of the older models the plastic lens will be retained with screws and on the newer models it can be popped out.

The turn signal bulbs in most of the vehicle slisted are in the same housing as the marker lamps.

1987-88 6 and 7 Series

The front marker and turn signal lamps on these models are replaced in the same manner as the headlamps. The bulbs are acessible under the hood and are removed by grasping the housing and turning it slightly. The bulbs can then be replaced.

The rear marker lamps are replaced by removing the plastic cover and replacing the bulb.

Fog Lamps

REMOVAL AND INSTALLATION

All Equipped Models

To replace the fog lamp bulbs on models so equipped, remove the screws that retain the fog lamp cover. Remove the cover and the rubber seal and replace the bulb. On newer models the bulb is an halogen bulb and should be handled carefully. Replace the cover, making sure the rubber seal is properly seated.

Rear Signal, Brake Lamps and Reverse Lights

REMOVAL AND INSTALLATION

All except 1986-88 6 and 7 Series

1. Open the trunk and remove the rear lining cover.

2. Remove the wing nuts or screws that retain the tail lamp lens and remove the lens.

Replacing the rear turn, brake and backup light bulbs—all models except 1986–88 6 and 7 series

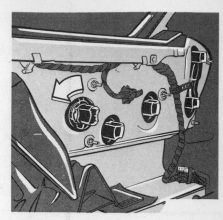

Replacing the rear light bulbs on 1986—88 7 series

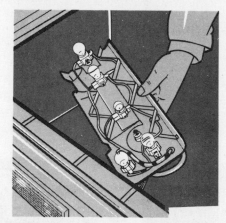

Replacing the rear light bulbs on 1986–88 6 series

High mount brake lamp bulb replacement

3. Replace the defective bulb and reinstall the lens assembly.

NOTE: *On some of the earlier models, the rear lens assembly was attached by screws on the outside instead of in the trunk.*

1986-88 6 Series

On these vehicles, remove the defective bulb by first, removing the rear trunk liner and then removing the assembly that the bulbs are housed in. Replace the defective bulb and reinstall.

1986-88 7 Series

To replace any of the rear bulbs on these models, open the trunk and pull back the rear liner. The defective bulb can be removed by rotating the socket counterclockwise and removing it. Replace the bulb and turn the socket clockwise to lock into position.

High Mount Brake Light
REMOVAL AND INSTALLATION
All Equipped Models

From inside the vehicle remove the screws that retain the lamp cover. Remove the lamp cover and then pull the reflector assembly out. Replace the bulb and reinstall the reflector assembly.

CIRCUIT PROTECTION
Fuses

The fuse box is located under the hood on the right or left fender well, except on the 3.0 series. On that series it is behind the left glove box door.

The transparent cover lists acessoroes served by each circuit, except on the 1600, 2000 and 2002 series, which are simply coded. Codes are explained in the chart.

Some of the newer model have a solid cover

Typical late model fusebox. Circuits are labeled on the cover

that lists the fuses and their respective circuits on the inside. A removal tool is also inside the cover.

Flashers

REMOVAL AND INSTALLATION

3, 5, 6 and 7 Series

1. Remove the screws and remove the bottom center instrument panel trim. Disconnect the negative battery cable.

2. Detach the flasher from the mounting bracket. Unplug the electrical connector and remove the flasher.

3. Install in the reverse order.

1600, 2000, 2500, 2800, Bavaria, 3000 and 3.0

1. Open the glovebox at the left side. Pull the relay hanger off the panel on which it is hung.

2. Disconnect the electrical connector. Install in the reverse order.

Fuse Specifications—
1600, 2000 and 2002

Fuse Location	Capacity (amps)	Circuits Protected
	1970	
1	8	Front parking lights (right and left)
2	8	Right taillight and license plate lights
3	8	Left taillight and instrument illumination
4	8	Interior light, clock, cigar lighter and buzzer
5	8	Stop and turn lights, back-up lights
6	16	Heater blower, horn, windshield wiper and washer, fuel and temperature gauges, oil pressure and brake warning lights

Fuse Location	Capacity (amps)	Circuits Protected
	1971 and Later	
1	5	Taillights and left parking light
2	5	Taillights, right parking light, license plate and instrument illum., side marker lights, fog light relay
3	8	Left low beam
4	8	Right low beam
5	5	Left turn signal
6	5	Right turn signal
7	16	Cigar lighter
8	8	Clock, interior light, ignition buzzer, hazard warning flashers, trailer flashers system
9	16	Heater blower
10	16	Rear window defroster
11	8	Automatic choke, electric fuel pump, oil pressure warning, fuel and temperature indicators, brake fluid warning, and tachometer
12	16	Stoplights, turn signals, horn, windshield wiper/washer, back-up lights

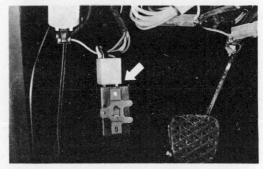

Removing the hazard flasher—733i

Relay	Description
1	High beams
2	Low beams
3	Fog lamps
4	Two-tone horns
5	Power saving relay
6	Wipe/wash intermittent action control unit (intensive cleaning)

Fuse box and fuse identification—typical 5 series

Fuse No.	Current (A)	Description
1	16	Electric fuel pump
2	8	Low beam right
3	8	Low beam left
4	25	Cigar lighter, automatic antenna, seat control, seat heating
5	8	Hazard lights, passenger compartment light, luggage compartment light, reading lamp, clock, central locks, on-board computer, burglar alarm, service indicator, door lock heating, check control
6	8	Indicator lamps, tachometer, mirror, on-board computer, central warning lamp, fuel consumption, service indicator, check control, window regulators, reversing, cruise control, backup lights
7	8	High beam right
8	8	High beam left
9	8	Park/side marker and tail lights right, instrument and license plate lights
10	8	Park/side marker and tail lights left
11	16	Turn signal indicators, windshield wipers and washer, horn relay, headlights
12	8	Stop lights, radio
13	16 (25)	Rear window defogger, electric sun roof
14	25	Heater blower, air conditioner
15	8	Front fog lamp right
16	8	Front fog lamp left
17	25	Supplementary fan

Fuse box and fuse identification—typical 7 series

Relay	Description
K 1	Auxiliary fan—speed 1
K 2	Two-tone horn
K 3	High beams
K 4	Low beams
K 5	Heater blower
K 6	Auxiliary fan—speed 2
K 7	Rear window defogger, power sliding roof, heated seat
K 8	Front fog lamps
K 9	—
K10	Control unit for wipe/wash and intensive cleaning system

Fuse No.	Current (A)	Description
1	15	Left high beam, right low beam
2	15	Right high beam, left low beam
3	15	Auxiliary fan 91°C (196°F)
4	15	Turn signal
5	30	Windshield wipers and washer
6	7.5	Brake light, cruise control
7	15	Horn

Fuse No.	Current (A)	Description
8	—	Without connection
9	15	Engine electrical equipment
10	7.5	Instruments
11	15	Main and aux. fuel pump
12	7.5	Radio, check control, instruments, on-board computer
13	7.5	Left low beam
14	7.5	Right low beam
15	—	Without connection
16	30	Heater blower, air conditioner
17	15	Backup light, power outside mirrors, mirror heating, fasten seat belt sign, washer jet heating
18	30	Auxiliary fan 99°C (210°F)
19	30	Power sliding roof, heated seat
20	30	Rear window defogger
21	7.5	Interior lights, radio, glove box, luggage compartment light, rechargeable flashlight, seat belt buzzer, on-board computer, radio memory, clock
22	7.5	Left side lights
23	7.5	Right side lights, engine compartment light, license plate lights, instrument panel lights, make-up mirror light
24	15	Hazard warning lights, open door buzzer
25	—	Without connection
26	30	Seat adjustment, electric window lifts
27	30	Central locking system, door lock heating, burglar alarm, on-board computer
28	30	Cigar lighters, power antenna
29	7.5	Left fog light
30	7.5	Right fog light

Troubleshooting Basic Turn Signal and Flasher Problems

Most problems in the turn signals or flasher system, can be reduced to defective flashers or bulbs, which are easily replaced. Occasionally, problems in the turn signals are traced to the switch in the steering column, which will require professional service.

F = Front   R = Rear   ● = Lights off   o = Lights on

Problem		Solution
Turn signals light, but do not flash		• Replace the flasher
No turn signals light on either side		• Check the fuse. Replace if defective. • Check the flasher by substitution • Check for open circuit, short circuit or poor ground
Both turn signals on one side don't work		• Check for bad bulbs • Check for bad ground in both housings
One turn signal light on one side doesn't work		• Check and/or replace bulb • Check for corrosion in socket. Clean contacts. • Check for poor ground at socket
Turn signal flashes too fast or too slow		• Check any bulb on the side flashing too fast. A heavy-duty bulb is probably installed in place of a regular bulb. • Check the bulb flashing too slow. A standard bulb was probably installed in place of a heavy-duty bulb. • Check for loose connections or corrosion at the bulb socket
Indicator lights don't work in either direction		• Check if the turn signals are working • Check the dash indicator lights • Check the flasher by substitution
One indicator light doesn't light		• On systems with 1 dash indicator: See if the lights work on the same side. Often the filaments have been reversed in systems combining stoplights with taillights and turn signals. Check the flasher by substitution • On systems with 2 indicators: Check the bulbs on the same side Check the indicator light bulb Check the flasher by substitution

Troubleshooting Basic Dash Gauge Problems

Problem	Cause	Solution
Coolant Temperature Gauge		
Gauge reads erratically or not at all	• Loose or dirty connections • Defective sending unit • Defective gauge	• Clean/tighten connections • Bi-metal gauge: remove the wire from the sending unit. Ground the wire for an instant. If the gauge registers, replace the sending unit. • Magnetic gauge: disconnect the wire at the sending unit. With ignition ON gauge should register COLD. Ground the wire; gauge should register HOT.
Ammeter Gauge—Turn Headlights ON (do not start engine). Note reaction		
Ammeter shows charge Ammeter shows discharge Ammeter does not move	• Connections reversed on gauge • Ammeter is OK • Loose connections or faulty wiring • Defective gauge	• Reinstall connections • Nothing • Check/correct wiring • Replace gauge
Oil Pressure Gauge		
Gauge does not register or is inaccurate	• On mechanical gauge, Bourdon tube may be bent or kinked • Low oil pressure • Defective gauge • Defective wiring • Defective sending unit	• Check tube for kinks or bends preventing oil from reaching the gauge • Remove sending unit. Idle the engine briefly. If no oil flows from sending unit hole, problem is in engine. • Remove the wire from the sending unit and ground it for an instant with the ignition ON. A good gauge will go to the top of the scale. • Check the wiring to the gauge. If it's OK and the gauge doesn't register when grounded, replace the gauge. • If the wiring is OK and the gauge functions when grounded, replace the sending unit
All Gauges		
All gauges do not operate All gauges read low or erratically All gauges pegged	• Blown fuse • Defective instrument regulator • Defective or dirty instrument voltage regulator • Loss of ground between instrument voltage regulator and car • Defective instrument regulator	• Replace fuse • Replace instrument voltage regulator • Clean contacts or replace • Check ground • Replace regulator
Warning Lights		
Light(s) do not come on when ignition is ON, but engine is not started Light comes on with engine running	• Defective bulb • Defective wire • Defective sending unit • Problem in individual system • Defective sending unit	• Replace bulb • Check wire from light to sending unit • Disconnect the wire from the sending unit and ground it. Replace the sending unit if the light comes on with the ignition ON. • Check system • Check sending unit (see above)

Troubleshooting Basic Lighting Problems

Problem	Cause	Solution
Lights		
One or more lights don't work, but others do	· Defective bulb(s) · Blown fuse(s) · Dirty fuse clips or light sockets · Poor ground circuit	· Replace bulb(s) · Replace fuse(s) · Clean connections · Run ground wire from light socket housing to car frame
Lights burn out quickly	· Incorrect voltage regulator setting or defective regulator · Poor battery/alternator connections	· Replace voltage regulator · Check battery/alternator connections
Lights go dim	· Low/discharged battery · Alternator not charging · Corroded sockets or connections · Low voltage output	· Check battery · Check drive belt tension; repair or replace alternator · Clean bulb and socket contacts and connections · Replace voltage regulator
Lights flicker	· Loose connection · Poor ground · Circuit breaker operating (short circuit)	· Tighten all connections · Run ground wire from light housing to car frame · Check connections and look for bare wires
Lights "flare"—Some flare is normal on acceleration—if excessive, see "Lights Burn Out Quickly"	· High voltage setting	· Replace voltage regulator
Lights glare—approaching drivers are blinded	· Lights adjusted too high · Rear springs or shocks sagging · Rear tires soft	· Have headlights aimed · Check rear springs/shocks · Check/correct rear tire pressure
Turn Signals		
Turn signals don't work in either direction	· Blown fuse · Defective flasher · Loose connection	· Replace fuse · Replace flasher · Check/tighten all connections
Right (or left) turn signal only won't work	· Bulb burned out · Right (or left) indicator bulb burned out · Short circuit	· Replace bulb · Check/replace indicator bulb · Check/repair wiring
Flasher rate too slow or too fast	· Incorrect wattage bulb · Incorrect flasher	· Flasher bulb · Replace flasher (use a variable load flasher if you pull a trailer)
Indicator lights do not flash (burn steadily)	· Burned out bulb · Defective flasher	· Replace bulb · Replace flasher
Indicator lights do not light at all	· Burned out indicator bulb · Defective flasher	· Replace indicator bulb · Replace flasher

Troubleshooting the Heater

Problem	Cause	Solution
Blower motor will not turn at any speed	• Blown fuse • Loose connection • Defective ground • Faulty switch • Faulty motor • Faulty resistor	• Replace fuse • Inspect and tighten • Clean and tighten • Replace switch • Replace motor • Replace resistor
Blower motor turns at one speed only	• Faulty switch • Faulty resistor	• Replace switch • Replace resistor
Blower motor turns but does not circulate air	• Intake blocked • Fan not secured to the motor shaft	• Clean intake • Tighten security
Heater will not heat	• Coolant does not reach proper temperature • Heater core blocked internally • Heater core air-bound • Blend-air door not in proper position	• Check and replace thermostat if necessary • Flush or replace core if necessary • Purge air from core • Adjust cable
Heater will not defrost	• Control cable adjustment incorrect • Defroster hose damaged	• Adjust control cable • Replace defroster hose

Troubleshooting Basic Windshield Wiper Problems

Problem	Cause	Solution
Electric Wipers		
Wipers do not operate— Wiper motor heats up or hums	• Internal motor defect • Bent or damaged linkage • Arms improperly installed on linking pivots	• Replace motor • Repair or replace linkage • Position linkage in park and reinstall wiper arms
Wipers do not operate— No current to motor	• Fuse or circuit breaker blown • Loose, open or broken wiring • Defective switch • Defective or corroded terminals • No ground circuit for motor or switch	• Replace fuse or circuit breaker • Repair wiring and connections • Replace switch • Replace or clean terminals • Repair ground circuits
Wipers do not operate— Motor runs	• Linkage disconnected or broken	• Connect wiper linkage or replace broken linkage
Vacuum Wipers		
Wipers do not operate	• Control switch or cable inoperative • Loss of engine vacuum to wiper motor (broken hoses, low engine vacuum, defective vacuum/fuel pump) • Linkage broken or disconnected • Defective wiper motor	• Repair or replace switch or cable • Check vacuum lines, engine vacuum and fuel pump • Repair linkage • Replace wiper motor
Wipers stop on engine acceleration	• Leaking vacuum hoses • Dry windshield • Oversize wiper blades • Defective vacuum/fuel pump	• Repair or replace hoses • Wet windshield with washers • Replace with proper size wiper blades • Replace pump

Drive Train

7

UNDERSTANDING THE MANUAL TRANSMISSION

Because of the way an internal combustion engine breathes, it can produce torque, or twisting force, only within a narrow speed range. Most modern, overhead valve engines must turn at about 2,500 rpm to produce their peak torque. By 4,500 rpm they are producing so little torque that continued increases in engine speed produce no power increases.

The manual transmission and clutch are employed to vary the relationship between engine speed and the speed of the wheels so that adequate engine power can be produced under all circumstances. The clutch allows engine torque to be applied to the transmission input shaft gradually, due to mechanical slippage. The car can, consequently, be started smoothly from a full stop.

The transmission changes the ratio between the rotating speeds of the engine and the wheels by the use of gears. On trucks, three-speed or four-speed transmissions are most common. The lower gears allow full engine power to be applied to the rear wheels during acceleration at low speeds.

The transmission contains a mainshaft which passes all the way through the transmission, from the clutch to the driveshaft. This shaft is separated at one point, so that front and rear portions can turn at different speeds.

Power is transmitted by a countershaft in the lower gears and reverse. The gears of the countershaft mesh with gears on the mainshaft, allowing power to be carried from one to the other. All the countershaft gears are integral with that shaft, while several of the mainshaft gears can either rotate independently of the shaft or be locked to it. Shifting from one gear to the next causes one of the gears to be freed from rotating with the shaft and locks another to it. Gears are locked and unlocked by internal dog clutches which slide between the center of the gear and the shaft. The forward gears usually employ synchronizers; friction members which smoothly bring gear and shaft to the same speed before the toothed dog clutches are engaged.

The clutch is operating properly if:

1. It will stall the engine when released with the vehicle held stationary.

2. The shift lever can be moved freely between 1st and reverse gears when the vehicle is stationary and the clutch disengaged.

MANUAL TRANSMISSION

Identification

Transmission

REMOVAL AND INSTALLATION

1600-2 and 2002

1. From inside the car, lift up the rubber boot to the shift lever. Raise the foam rubber ring and unsnap the circlip (1). Then, pull out the shifter from its socket. Take care not to lose the shims which take up the clearance in the shifter socket under the circlip.

2. Raise the hood. Remove all of the transmission-to-engine retaining bolts within reach.

3. Jack up the front of the car and place jackstands beneath the front jacking points or beneath the lower suspensions arms. Place blocks behind the rear wheels and make sure that the parking brake is firmly applied.

CAUTION: *Test the stability of the supports by rocking the car sideways and forward and backward. Before climbing under the car, make sure that it will stay up there.*

4. Remove the drain plug from the transmission and drain the contents into a drain pan for

Troubleshooting the Manual Transmission and Transfer Case

Problem	Cause	Solution
Transmission shifts hard	• Clutch adjustment incorrect • Clutch linkage or cable binding • Shift rail binding	• Adjust clutch • Lubricate or repair as necessary • Check for mispositioned selector arm roll pin, loose cover bolts, worn shift rail bores, worn shift rail, distorted oil seal, or extension housing not aligned with case. Repair as necessary.
	• Internal bind in transmission caused by shift forks, selector plates, or synchronizer assemblies • Clutch housing misalignment • Incorrect lubricant • Block rings and/or cone seats worn	• Remove, dissemble and inspect transmission. Replace worn or damaged components as necessary. • Check runout at rear face of clutch housing • Drain and refill transmission • Blocking ring to gear clutch tooth face clearance must be 0.030 inch or greater. If clearance is correct it may still be necessary to inspect blocking rings and cone seats for excessive wear. Repair as necessary.
Gear clash when shifting from one gear to another	• Clutch adjustment incorrect • Clutch linkage or cable binding • Clutch housing misalignment • Lubricant level low or incorrect lubricant • Gearshift components, or synchronizer assemblies worn or damaged	• Adjust clutch • Lubricate or repair as necessary • Check runout at rear of clutch housing • Drain and refill transmission and check for lubricant leaks if level was low. Repair as necessary. • Remove, disassemble and inspect transmission. Replace worn or damaged components as necessary.
Transmission noisy	• Lubricant level low or incorrect lubricant • Clutch housing-to-engine, or transmission-to-clutch housing bolts loose • Dirt, chips, foreign material in transmission • Gearshift mechanism, transmission gears, or bearing components worn or damaged • Clutch housing misalignment	• Drain and refill transmission. If lubricant level was low, check for leaks and repair as necessary. • Check and correct bolt torque as necessary • Drain, flush, and refill transmission • Remove, disassemble and inspect transmission. Replace worn or damaged components as necessary. • Check runout at rear face of clutch housing
Jumps out of gear	• Clutch housing misalignment • Gearshift lever loose • Offset lever nylon insert worn or lever attaching nut loose • Gearshift mechanism, shift forks, selector plates, interlock plate, selector arm, shift rail, detent plugs, springs or shift cover worn or damaged • Clutch shaft or roller bearings worn or damaged	• Check runout at rear face of clutch housing • Check lever for worn fork. Tighten loose attaching bolts. • Remove gearshift lever and check for loose offset lever nut or worn insert. Repair or replace as necessary. • Remove, disassemble and inspect transmission cover assembly. Replace worn or damaged components as necessary. • Replace clutch shaft or roller bearings as necessary

Troubleshooting the Manual Transmission and Transfer Case (cont.)

Problem	Cause	Solution
Jumps out of gear (cont.)	• Gear teeth worn or tapered, synchronizer assemblies worn or damaged, excessive end play caused by worn thrust washers or output shaft gears • Pilot bushing worn	• Remove, disassemble, and inspect transmission. Replace worn or damaged components as necessary. • Replace pilot bushing
Will not shift into one gear	• Gearshift selector plates, interlock plate, or selector arm, worn, damaged, or incorrectly assembled • Shift rail detent plunger worn, spring broken, or plug loose • Gearshift lever worn or damaged • Synchronizer sleeves or hubs, damaged or worn	• Remove, disassemble, and inspect transmission cover assembly. Repair or replace components as necessary. • Tighten plug or replace worn or damaged components as necessary • Replace gearshift lever • Remove, disassemble and inspect transmission. Replace worn or damaged components.
Locked in one gear—cannot be shifted out	• Shift rail(s) worn or broken, shifter fork bent, setscrew loose, center detent plug missing or worn • Broken gear teeth on countershaft gear, clutch shaft, or reverse idler gear Gearshift lever broken or worn, shift mechanism in cover incorrectly assembled or broken, worn damaged gear train components	• Inspect and replace worn or damaged parts • Inspect and replace damaged part • Disassemble transmission. Replace damaged parts or assemble correctly.
Transfer case difficult to shift or will not shift into desired range	• Vehicle speed too great to permit shifting • If vehicle was operated for extended period in 4H mode on dry paved surface, driveline torque load may cause difficult shifting • Transfer case external shift linkage binding • Insufficient or incorrect lubricant • Internal components binding, worn, or damaged	• Stop vehicle and shift into desired range. Or reduce speed to 3–4 km/h (2–3 mph) before attempting to shift. • Stop vehicle, shift transmission to neutral, shift transfer case to 2H mode and operate vehicle in 2H on dry paved surfaces • Lubricate or repair or replace linkage, or tighten loose components as necessary • Drain and refill to edge of fill hole with SAE 85W-90 gear lubricant only • Disassemble unit and replace worn or damaged components as necessary
Transfer case noisy in all drive modes	• Insufficient or incorrect lubricant	• Drain and refill to edge of fill hole with SAE 85W-90 gear lubricant only. Check for leaks and repair if necessary. Note: If unit is still noisy after drain and refill, disassembly and inspection may be required to locate source of noise.
Noisy in—or jumps out of four wheel drive low range	• Transfer case not completely engaged in 4L position • Shift linkage loose or binding • Shift fork cracked, inserts worn, or fork is binding on shift rail	• Stop vehicle, shift transfer case in Neutral, then shift back into 4L position • Tighten, lubricate, or repair linkage as necessary • Disassemble unit and repair as necessary
Lubricant leaking from output shaft seals or from vent	• Transfer case overfilled • Vent closed or restricted	• Drain to correct level • Clear or replace vent if necessary

Troubleshooting the Manual Transmission and Transfer Case (cont.)

Problem	Cause	Solution
Lubricant leaking from output shaft seals or from vent (cont.)	• Output shaft seals damaged or installed incorrectly	• Replace seals. Be sure seal lip faces interior of case when installed. Also be sure yoke seal surfaces are not scored or nicked. Remove scores, nicks with fine sandpaper or replace yoke(s) if necessary.
Abnormal tire wear	• Extended operation on dry hard surface (paved) roads in 4H range	• Operate in 2H on hard surface (paved) roads

inspection. Check the fluid for metal particles. Clean and replace the drain plug.

5. Disconnect the exhaust pipe bracket from the back of the transmission. Disconnect the head pipe from the exhaust manifold.

6. Disconnect the driveshaft from the transmission at the flexible coupling (doughnut)

leaving the coupling attached to the driveshaft. Discard the old locknuts.

7. Remove the 2 bolts which retain the driveshaft center support bearing housing to the underbody. Push the driveshaft downward and away from the centering pin.

8. Using an allen wrench, loosen the set

Manual Transmission Application Chart

Vehicle	Transmission	
Model	Model	Speeds
1600	232/6	4
2002	242/6	4
2002Tii	242/4	4
	235/5	5
2500,2800,Bavaria 3000	262/8 ①	4
3.0	ZF-S4-18/3	4
320i	242/9	4
	242/18	4
	242/18.5	4
	265/6	5
528i,6 series,M6,L6	262/9	4
	265/6	5
528e,533i,525i,535i	265/6	5
318i,325e,325is,325ix	265/OD	5
M3,M5	260/5	5
	260/OD	5
	240(ZF-S5-16)	5
733i,735i	262/9.10	4
	262/9.30	4
	265/6	5

① Getrag

Removing flexible coupling from transmission

Disconnecting shifter linkage

Disconnecting 1600-2 clutch linkage

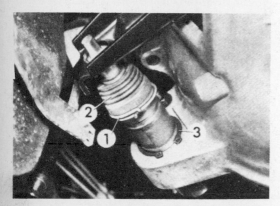

Disconnecting 2002 series slave cylinder

screw (2) and drive out the retaining pin (1) from the shift linkage.

9. On 1600-2 models, detach the clutch linkage return spring. Push the retainer downward and remove the pushrod (2) to the front.

10. On 2002 and 200tii models, disconnect the slave cylinder from the throwout lever by lifting out the retaining ring (1), slipping off the rubber collar (2), unsnapping the circlip (3), and withdrawing the cylinder forward.

NOTE: *Mark the position of the torsional retainer.*

11. Loosen the bolts for the transmission support bracket. Remove the bolts which retain the flywheel inspection cover to the transmission and remove the cover.

12. Place a wooden block beneath the oil pan between the pan and front crossmember to support the engine. Support the weight of the transmission with a hydraulic floor jack.

13. Loosen the speedometer cable set bolt (1) and disconnect the speedometer. Disconnect the back-up light leads (2). Remove the transmission support crossmember.

14. Turn the front wheels to the full right hand lock position. The transmission may now be removed by pulling it out straight to the rear. When the transmission is clear of the pressure plate, carefully lower the jack and transmission to the ground.

15. Reverse the above procedure to install, using the following installation notes:

a. When hooking up the clutch linkage on 1600-2 models, adjust the linkage as outlined under "Clutch Linkage Adjustment."

b. When hooking up the shift linkage, first drive in the retaining pin and then secure it with the allen head setscrew.

c. When hooking up the driveshaft, check the freeness of the centering bearing and pack it with chassis grease, as necessary. Use new locknuts for the flexible coupling.

d. When installing the center support for the driveshaft, preload the bearing housing 2mm (distance A) to the front. The bolts are tightened after the transmission is installed.

e. When connecting the exhaust pipe support bracket (2), the bracket must lie tension-free against the head pipe (3), or severe engine vibration may result.

f. When installing the shift lever, fill the ball socket with chassis grease. Use shims beneath the circlip to obtain a tight fit.

g. The transmission-to-engine bolts are torqued to 18.1 ft. lbs. (small bolts) and 34.0 ft. lbs. (large bolts).

h. Remember to fill the transmission to the bottom of the filler plug hole with SAE 80 gearbox oil before road testing.

320i and 318i

1. Drain the transmission. On 320i only, unscrew all transmission mounting bolts (4) accessible from above. Swing up the bracket mounted to the top left bolt.

2. Disconnect the exhaust system support at the rear of the transmission.

3. Detach the exhaust pipe at the manifold.

4. Detach the driveshaft at the transmission by pulling out bolts from the rear of the coupling (the coupling remains attached to the driveshaft).

5. Remove the heat shield. Remove the bolts for the center bearing bracket, and pull the bracket downward. Bend the driveshaft downward and pull it out of the bearing journal.

6. Remove the bolt and disconnect the speedometer drive cable. Disconnect the back-up light switch wire, and pull the wire out of the clips on the transmission.

7. Remove the 2 Allen bolts at the top and pull the console off the transmission.

8. Disconnect the gearshift selector rod by pulling off the circlip, removing the washer and pulling the rod off the pin.

9. Detach the clutch slave cylinder line bracket at the front of the transmission, re-

move the mounting bolts from the slave cylinder mounting, and remove the slave cylinder.

10. Remove the flywheel housing cover.

11. Support the transmission securely at the center with a floor jack and wooden block.

12. Detach the crossmember by removing the nuts attaching it to the body at either end. On 318i, remove all front mounting bolts. Remove the 3 remaining front mounting bolts on the 320i, and pull the transmission out toward the rear.

Remove the arrowed bolts from the driveshaft coupling—320i

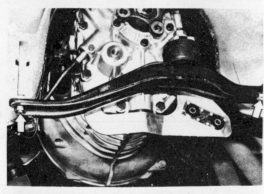

Detach the crossmember at the body by removing the two arrowed nuts

Install the clutch slave cylinder in the position shown

13. To install, install the transmission under the vehicle and align it into position. Install the crossmember.

14. Install the flywheel cover. Install 2 of the top transmission-to-engine bolts to retain the transmission.

15. Attach the clutch slave cylinder and mounting bracket. Install the gear selector rod and install the retaining circlip.

16. Connect the speedometer drive cable and then continue the installation in reverse order, noting the following points:

   a. Front mounting bolts are torqued to 18-19 ft. lbs. on the M8 transmissions; 34-37 ft. lbs. on the M10 transmissions. Torque the crossmember rubber mounts to 31-35 ft. lbs.

   b. On the 318i, the console has self-locking bolts which must be replaced for reassembly.

   c. When reinstalling the clutch slave cylinder, make sure the bleeder screw faces downward.

   d. When installing the driveshaft center support bearing, preload it forward 2mm on 320i; 2-4mm on 318i.

   e. Replace the locknuts on the driveshaft coupling and tighten the nuts only, not the bolts, to 31-35 ft. lbs.

   f. Inspect the gasket at the joint between the exhaust manifold and pipe and replace it if necessary.

   g. When reattaching exhaust system support at the rear, leave the attaching nut/bolt slightly loose; loosen the 2 nuts/bolts attaching the support via slots to the transmission; push the support toward the exhaust pipe until all tension is removed and then secure nuts and bolts.

All 6-Cylinder Models Except All 3 Series
1982 733i
1983-84 533i
535i
M5
1983-84 633CSi
635CSi
M6
1983-84 733i
735i

1. Remove the complete exhaust system. Drain the transmission.

2. Remove the circlip and washer at the selector rod and disengage the rod at the transmission.

3. Unzip the leather boot surrounding the gearshift lever. With a pointed object such as an ice pick, release the circlip at the bottom of the gearshift lever and then pull the lever upward and out of the transmission. Lubricate the nylon bushings at the bottom of the lever mecha-

nism with a permanent lubricant for reassembly.

4. Remove the 3 bolts from the coupling at the front of the driveshaft out through the rear of the coupling, leaving the nuts/bolts attaching the driveshaft to the coupling in place.

5. Remove the heat shield. Remove the mounting bolts and remove the center bearing support bracket. Bend the driveshaft downward at the front and slide the spline out of the center bearing.

6. Support the transmission securely between the front axle carrier and oil pan with a floorjack and wooden block.

7. Remove the attaching bolt and pull out the speedometer cable. Disconnect the back-up light wiring electrical connectors and pull the wire out of the clips on the transmission.

8. Loosen the connection to the rubber bushing at the transmission, remove the mounting nuts at either end, and remove the crossmember. On the 633CSi, lower the transmission to the front axle carrier.

9. On the 633CSi, disconnect the mount for the clutch hydraulic line at the front of the transmission. Then, on all models, unscrew the mounting nuts and detach the clutch slave cylinder (with the line connected).

10. Remove the mounting nuts at the clutch housing and separate the transmission and clutch housing.

11. Pull the gearbox to the rear and out of the car.

12. To install the transmission, position the gearbox under the vehicle and move it into position. Install the mounting nuts at the clutch housing.

13. Attach the clutch slave cylinder to the transmission.

14. Install the crossmember and rubber mounts. Install the speedometer cable and connect the wire to the backup light switch.

15. Install the heat shield and the mounting nuts for the center bearing carrier.

16. Complete the installation, keeping the following points in mind:

    a. Use a slave cylinder to move the clutch throw-out arm to the correct position. Align the throw-out bearing. Grease the guide sleeve and groove in the throw-out bearing with a permanent lubricant.

    b. Put the transmission into gear before installing.

    c. Make sure, when installing the clutch slave cylinder, make sure that the hose connection faces downward.

    d. Preload the center bearing 2mm toward the front.

    e. When tightening the coupling, hold the bolt heads and torque only the nuts only to 75

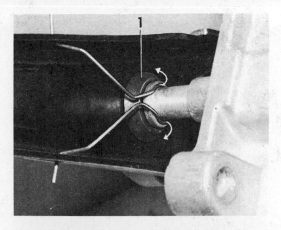

On the 2800 and 3.0, lift both sides of the spring at the pivot point of the throwout arm over the collar (1) to prevent breaking it

Preload the bearing .08 in. (A) in the forward direction

ft. lbs. Use new nuts. Torque the transmission-to-engine bolts to 16-17 ft. lbs. (M8 transmission) or 31-35 ft. lbs. (M10 transmission); torque the bolt for the rubber bushing on the crossmember to 18 ft. lbs.

325, 325e, 325i, 325iS, 325iX, and M3

1. Raise the car and support it securely. Remove the exhaust system. Remove the cross brace and heat shield. On the 325iX, remove the transfer case as described later in this section.

2. Hold the nuts on the front with one wrench, and remove bolts from the rear with another to disconnect the flexible coupling at the front of the driveshaft. Some models have a vibration damper at this point in the drivetrain. This damper is mounted on the transmission output flange with bolts that are pressed into the damper. On these models, unscrew and remove the nuts located behind the damper.

3. Loosen the threaded sleeve on the drive-

shaft. Get a special tool such as BMW 261040 to hold the splined portion of the shaft while turning the sleeve.

4. Remove its mounting bolts and remove the center driveshaft mount. Then, bend the driveshaft down at the center and pull it off the transmission output flange. Keep the sections of the driveshaft from pulling apart and suspend it from the car with wire.

5. Remove the retainer and washer, and pull out the shift selector rod.

6. Use a hex-head wrench to remove the 2 self-locking bolts that retain the shift rod bracket at the rear of the transmission and then remove the bracket. If the car has a shift arm, use a screwdriver to pry the spring clip up off the boss on the transmission case and swing it upward. Then, pull out the shift shaft pin.

7. Unscrew and remove the clutch slave cylinder and support it so the hydraulic line can remain connected.

8. The transmission incorporates sending units for flywheel rotating speed and position. Remove the heat shield that protects these from exhaust heat and then remove the retaining bolt for each sending unit. Note that the speed sending unit, which has *no* identifying ring goes in the bore on the right, and that the reference mark sending unit, which has a marking ring, goes in the bore on the left. If the sending units are installed in reverse positions, the engine will not run at all. Pull these units out of the flywheel housing.

9. Disconnect the wiring connector going to the backup light switch and pull the wires out of the harness.

10. *Support the transmission from underneath in a secure manner.* Remove mounting bolts and remove the crossmember holding the rear of the transmission to the body. Then, lower the transmission onto the front axle carrier.

11. Using a Torx® socket, remove the Torx® bolts holding the transmission flywheel housing to the engine at the front. Make sure to retain the washers with the bolts. Pull the transmission rearward to slide the input shaft out of the clutch disc and then lower the transmission and remove it from the car.

12. Install the transmission in position under the car and install the retaining bolts.

13. Install the crossmember. Connect the wiring to to the backup light switch.

14. Install the sending units into the transmission keeping in mind to install them in their correct position.

15. Install the clutch slave cylinder and install the shift shaft and bracket.

16. Install the center driveshaft mount and complete the installation, keeping the following points in mind:

a. Coat the input shaft splines and flywheel housing guide pins with a light coating of a grease such as Microlube GL 261®.

b. Make sure the front mounting bolts are installed with their washers. Torque them to 46-58 ft. lbs.

c. Before reinstalling the 2 sending units for flywheel position and speed, make sure their faces are free of either grease or dirt and then coat them with a light coating of Molykote Longterm 2®. Inspect the O-rings and replace them if they are cut, cracked, crushed, or stretched.

d. When installing the shift rod bracket at the rear of the transmission, use new self-locking bolts and make sure the bracket is level before tightening them. Torque the shift rod bracket bolts to 16.5 ft. lbs. except on the M3, which uses an aluminum bracket. On the M3, torque these bolts to 8 ft. lbs.

e. Install the clutch slave cylinder with the bleed screw downward.

f. When installing the driveshaft center bearing, preload it forward 4-6mm. Check the driveshaft alignment with an appropriate tool such as BMW 26 1 030. Replace the nuts and then torque the center mount bolts to 16-17 ft. lb.

g. Torque the flexible coupling bolts to 83-94 ft. lb.

1982 733i

NOTE: *This procedure requires a special tool for clamping the flexible drive coupling.*

1. Remove the circlip and washer from the front end of the selector rod, and disconnect it from the lower end of the shift lever.

2. Push up the dust cover, and with needle nose pliers, remove the circlip which holds the gearshift lever in place. Lubricate the nylon bushing surrounding the socket with a permanent lubricant for reassembly.

Using special tool 26 1 011 to aid removal of coupling bolts—733i

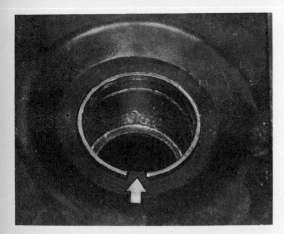

The opening in the shift arm is arrowed

3. Disconnect the back-up light plug near the gearshift lever. Remove the large circlip which surrounds the gearshift mount.

4. Drain the transmission. Raise the car and support it. Install the special tool (BMW 26 1 011 or equivalent) which clamps around the flexible coupling. Then, unscrew the 3 nuts on the forward side of the coupling, withdraw the bolts out the rear. This requires tightening the clamping tool until the bolts can be pulled out by hand.

5. Remove the web type crossmember located under the driveshaft. Then, loosen the mounting nuts for the center bearing bracket and detach it. Bend the driveshaft downward and pull it off the centering pin.

6. Support the transmission securely with a floor jack working through a wooden block. Then, remove the mounting nut from the crossmember rubber bushing, the nuts and bolts from either end of the crossmember where it bolts to the body, and remove the crossmember.

7. Detach the exhaust system bracket both at the transmission and at the exhaust pipes and remove it.

8. Detach the mounting bracket for the clutch slave cylinder hydraulic line at the transmission and then remove the 2 mounting bolts and remove the slave cylinder. Detach the 4th gear switch wires, if so equipped.

9. Detach the transmission at the clutch housing and remove it toward the rear.

10. Install the transmission in position under the vehicle and align into the clutch housing. Install the mounting bolts. Attach the mounting bracket for the clutch slave cylinder and attach the slave cylinder.

11. Install the crossmember and reattach the exhaust system at the transmission.

12. Install the driveshaft into position. Complete the installation, keeping the following points in mind:

a. Use the clutch slave cylinder to put the release lever in position for transmission installation. Align the clutch bearing and lubricate the lubrication groove inside it with Molykote® BR2-750 or its equivalent.

b. Put the transmission into gear prior to installation.

c. Install the guide sleeve of the transmission into the bearing carefully, then turn the output flange until the driveshaft slides into the drive plate. Then, remove the slave cylinder while mounting the transmission. Torque transmission-to-clutch housing bolts to 54-59 ft. lbs.

d. When installing the clutch slave cylinder, make sure the bleeder screw faces downward.

e. When remounting the exhaust system bracket, make sure there is no torsional strain on the system.

f. Preload the center driveshaft bearing toward the front of the car 2mm.

g. When reassembling the flexible drive coupling, use new self-locking nuts. Leave the special tool in the compression while installing the bolts, and then install the nuts, holding the bolts in position and turning only the nuts.

h. Torque the transmission mount-to-crossmember bolt to 36-40 ft. lbs., and the crossmember-to-body nuts to 16-17 ft. lbs.

i. When install the shift lever, note that the tab on the damper plate nuts engage in the opening in the shift arm.

1983-84 533i, 633CSi, and 733i
All 535i, 635CSi, M5 and M6

1. Raise the car and support it securely. Disconnect and lower the exhaust system to provide clearance for transmission removal. Remove the heat shield brace and transmission heat shield.

2. Support the driveshaft and then unscrew the driveshaft coupling at the rear of the transmission. Use a wrench on both the nut and the bolt.

3. Working at the front of the driveshaft center bearing, unscrew the screw-on type ring type connector which attaches the driveshaft to the center bearing. Then, unbolt the center bearing mount. Bend the driveshaft down and pull it off the centering pin. If the car has a vibration damper, turn it and pull it back over the output flange before pulling the driveshaft off the guide pin. Suspend it from the car.

4. Pull off the wires for the backup light switch. Unscrew the passenger compartment console to disconnect it from the top of the transmission by removing the 2 self-locking

bolts. Discard these and purchase replacements.

5. Pull out the locking clip, and disconnect the shift rod at the rear of the transmission. Take care to keep all the washers.

6. If the transmission is linked to the shift lever with an arm, use a screwdriver to lift the spring out of the holder on the bracket and then raise the arm. Pull out the shift shaft bolt.

7. If the car has a flywheel housing cover (semi-circular in shape), remove the mounting bolts and remove the cover.

8. If the car has Digital Motor Electronics, the speed sensor and reference mark sensor on the flywheel housing must be disconnected. Note their locations. The speed sensor goes in the upper bore, marked **D**. The reference mark sensor, which has a ring, goes in the lower bore, marked **B**. Check the O-rings for the sensors and install new ones if they are damaged.

9. Support the transmission securely. Then, unbolt and remove the rear transmission crossmember.

10. Remove the upper and lower attaching nuts and remove the clutch slave cylinder, supporting it so the hydraulic line need not be disconnected. Disconnect the reverse gear backup light switch nearby, and pull the wires out of the holders.

11. Unscrew the bolts fastening the transmission to the bell housing, using an angled box wrench. On late model cars there are some Torx® bolts; use a special Torx® wrench for these. Pull the transmission rearward until the input shaft has disengaged from the clutch disc and then lower and remove it.

12. To install the transmission, first put it in gear. Insert the guide sleeve of the input shaft into the clutch pilot bearing carefully. Turn the output shaft to rotate the front of the input shaft until the splines line up and it engages the clutch disc.

Perform the remaining portions of the procedure in reverse of removal, observing the following points:

a. Make sure the arrows on the rear crossmember point forward.

b. Preload the center bearing mount forward of its most natural position 2-4mm. On 7 Series cars with the M30 B35 engine only, and 6 Series cars with the 265/6 transmission (no integral clutch housing), preload the bearing 4-6mm.

c. In tightening the driveshaft screw on ring, use special Tool No. 26 1 040 or equivalent.

d. When reconnecting the nuts and bolt at the transmission coupling, replace the nuts with new ones and turn only the nut, holding the bolts stationary.

e. Make sure DME sensor faces are clean. Coat the sensor outside diameters with Molykote Longterm 2® or equivalent.

f. If the car has a shift arm (Step 6), lubricate the bolt with a light layer of Molykote Longterm 2® or equivalent.

g. Observe these torque figures in ft. lbs:
- Transmission to bell housing: 52-58 ft. lbs.
- Rear top transmission Torx® bolts: 46-58 ft. lbs.
- Center mount to body: 16-17 ft. lbs.
- Front joint-to-transmission: 83-94 ft. lbs.

735i

1. Disconnect the negative battery cable. Remove the exhaust system. Remove the attaching bolts and remove the heat shield mounted just to the rear of the transmission on the floorpan.

2. Support the transmission securely from underneath. Then, remove the crossmember that supports it at the rear from the body by removing the mounting bolts on both sides.

3. Using wrenches on both the bolt heads and on the nuts, remove the bolts passing through the vibration damper and front universal joint at the front of the driveshaft.

4. Remove its mounting bolts and remove the center driveshaft mount. Then, bend the driveshaft down at the center and pull it off the transmission output flange. Keep the sections of the driveshaft from pulling apart and suspend it from the car with wire.

5. Pull out the circlip, slide off the washer, and then pull the shift selector rod off the transmission shift shaft. Disconnect the backup light switch, nearby.

6. Lower the transmission slightly for access. Then, use a screwdriver to lift the spring out of the holder on the bracket and then raise the arm. Pull out the shift shaft bolt.

7. Remove the upper and lower attaching nuts and remove the clutch slave cylinder, sup-

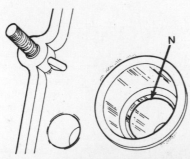

Pack the groove ("N") with Molykote® Longterm 2 or equivalent before installing the transmission used on the 733i/735i, and 633CSi/35CSi/M6

porting it so the hydraulic line need not be disconnected.

8. Unscrew the bolts fastening the transmission to the bell housing. Since these are Torx® bolts; use a special Torx® wrench. Make sure to retain the washer with each bolt to ensure that they can be readily removed later, if necessary. Pull the transmission rearward until the input shaft has disengaged from the clutch disc and then lower and remove it.

9. Install the transmission in position under the car and install the retaining bolts.

10. Install the crossmember. Connect the wiring to to the backup light switch.

11. Install the clutch slave cylinder and install the shift shaft and bracket.

12. Install the center driveshaft mount and complete the installation, keeping the following points in mind:

a. Preload the center bearing mount forward of its most natural position 4-6mm.

b. When reconnecting the nuts and bolt at the transmission coupling, replace the nuts with new ones and turn only the nut, holding the bolts stationary.

c. When reconnecting the shift arm (Step 6), lubricate the bolt with a light layer of Molykote Longterm 2® or equivalent and check the O-ring for crushing, cracks or cuts, replacing it if it is damaged.

d. When installing the clutch slave cylinder, make sure the bleeder screw faces downward.

e. Observe these torque figures:
● Center mount to body: 16-17 ft. lbs.
● Front joint-to-transmission: 58.5 ft. lbs.

4-speed Models 242/9, 242/18, 242/18.50
Overhaul

DISASSEMBLY

1. Remove the crossmember and exhaust system bracket from the rear of the transmission.

2. Mount the transmission securely and drain the lubricating oil from the unit. Remove the console from the transmission.

3. Remove the clutch release bearing assembly and release lever from the front of the transmission.

4. Remove the front guide sleeve and retaining bolts. Do not lose the shims.

5. Remove the circlip and shim from the input shaft.

6. Remove the case cover mounting bolts and drive the 2 dowel pins from the case cover.

7. Using a special case puller or equivalent, remove the case cover from the transmission.

NOTE: *The input shaft bearing will remain with the case cover as the cover is removed from the transmission case.*

8. Remove the front bearing from the case cover by driving it from the rear to the front. Do not lose the accompanying shim.

9. Remove the lockpin and spring from the case.

NOTE: *The lockpin maintains the selector shaft positioning.*

10. Move the 3rd/4th selector lever and rod to the 3rd speed position. Drive the fork retaining

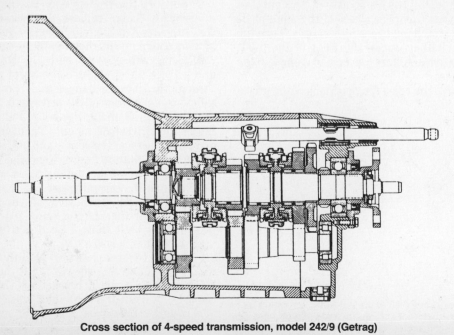

Cross section of 4-speed transmission, model 242/9 (Getrag)

pin downward very carefully until rod can be pulled out.

NOTE: *The fork retaining pin must be driven downward between the teeth of the synchronizer body. The pin should remain in the lower part of the selector fork.*

11. Slide the locking sleeve away from the pin of the selector shaft coupler and drive the pin from the coupler.

12. Remove the selector rod by pulling it forward and out of the shifting fork.

13. Move the gear sleeve back to the neutral position and remove the selector fork.

14. Remove the bushing and the speedometer driven gear.

15. Straighten the bend in the lockplate on the output flange retaining nut. Install a flange holding tool and remove the locknut. Pull the flange from the output shaft.

16. Remove the rear bearing support ring and shims.

17. Using a special bearing puller or equivalent, remove the rear bearing from the transmission cover.

NOTE: *A 2mm metal strip must be placed between the 2nd and 3rd gears to prevent the pressing off of the 2nd gear synchronizer body during the removal of the rear bearing from the shaft and cover.*

18. Lift the input and output shaft assemblies slightly and remove the countergear assembly from the end bearing and out of the cover.

19. Pull the selector fork, the reverse gear and the selector rod from the transmission cover. Do not lose the detent balls.

20. Remove the input and output shaft assemblies, align with the 1st/2nd selector rod and fork, from the transmission cover. Do not lose the detent balls.

21. Remove the back-up lamp switch and the end cap for the 1st/2nd selector shaft.

22. Remove the input shaft from the output shaft and remove the 4th speed synchronizer (baulk) ring.

23. Remove the circlip from the front of the output shaft and remove the support disc, synchronizer body assembly, 3rd gear synchronizer (baulk) ring, needle bearing race and the 3rd gear from the shaft.

24. Place the output shaft into a press or equivalent and remove the speedometer drive gear, washer, reverse gear, spacer, needle bearing race, 1st gear, synchronizer (baulk) ring, synchronizer body with the sliding sleeve, synchronizer (baulk) ring, needle bearing race and the 2nd speed gear from the shaft.

25. The 3rd and 4th gears can be pressed from the countershaft gear assembly, along with the roller bearing.

26. The pilot bearing can be removed from the bore of the input shaft.

27. The synchronizer unit can be disassembled by sliding the sleeve off the hub. The pressure pads will drop from the unit as the sleeve is removed.

28. Replace all worn, damaged or broken parts, along with new gaskets and seals.

ASSEMBLY

1. Install the synchronizer springs onto the hub with the hooked ends of the springs in different pressure pads.

2. Install the pressure pads in place slide the

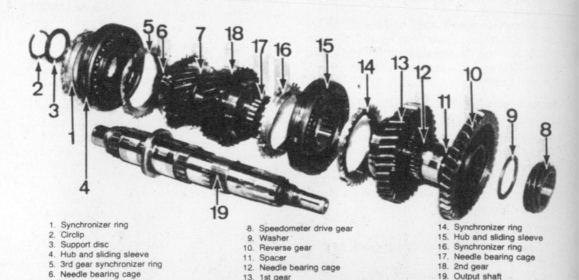

1. Synchronizer ring	8. Speedometer drive gear
2. Circlip	9. Washer
3. Support disc	10. Reverse gear
4. Hub and sliding sleeve	11. Spacer
5. 3rd gear synchronizer ring	12. Needle bearing cage
6. Needle bearing cage	13. 1st gear
7. 3rd gear	

14. Synchronizer ring
15. Hub and sliding sleeve
16. Synchronizer ring
17. Needle bearing cage
18. 2nd gear
19. Output shaft

Output shaft components

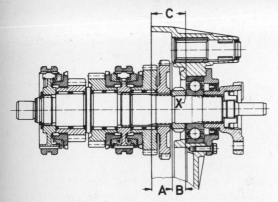

Measurement of extension case and gear assembly to determine shim "X" thickness

sleeve, with the flat teeth locations, over the pressure pads.

3. If the 3rd and 4th gears have been removed from the countershaft, reinstall or replace the gears back on to the shaft. Heat the gears to 250-300°F (120-150°C) and install. The high collar on the bore of the 3rd and 4th gears should face the 2nd gear. Install the bearing and race onto the shaft.

4. Place the output shaft in an upright position with the rear of the shaft up. Place the 2nd speed gear and needle bearing assembly onto the shaft. Install the 1st/2nd synchronizer assembly with the 2 synchronizer (baulk rings onto the shaft, followed by the 1st speed gear, needle bearing, spacer, reverse gear wheel, washer and complete the assembly by pressing the speedometer gear onto the shaft.

NOTE: *The end-play of the gear train should be 0.08mm. Adjust by changing the selective washer between the speedometer gear and the reverse gear.*

5. Invert the output shaft and install the 3rd gear onto the shaft. Install the synchronizer assembly less the 4th speed synchronizer (baulk) ring onto the shaft and retain with the support disc and circlip.

Measurements Prior to Transmission Assembly

Washer type shims are used to control the end play of the shafts and gears, while maintaining gear positioning, so that tooth contact is in proper relationship with each other. It is most important to inspect, measure and correct the shim packs to obtain the necessary preloads and clearances.

INPUT SHAFT

1. Install a 1mm shim and the ball bearing into the case bore.

2. With a depth gauge, measure the distance **A**, from the sealing surface of the case to the surface of the bearing race.

3. A numerical figure is electrically engraved on the input shaft and represents column **B** in the accompanying chart.

4. The thickness of the shim **X**, needed on the input shaft can be determined by corresponding the measurements **A** and **B** to the chart and locating the proper shim from column **X**.

COUNTERSHAFT ASSEMBLY

1. Measure the distance **A**, from the sealing surface of the case housing to the circlip in the bottom of the housing.

2. Install the countershaft into the transmission case bearing and measure the distance **B**, from the top of the large bearing race to the sealing surface of the case, with the gasket installed.

3. Determine the thickness of the shim **C**, by subtracting distance **B** from distance **A**. The result is shim **C**.

NOTE: *The "C" shims can be used to change tooth engagement.*

SPEEDOMETER GEAR-TO-TRANSMISSION CASE

1. Measure the thickness **B**, of the speedometer gear.

2. Press the ball bearing into the transmission case and measure the distance **C**, from the sealing surface of the case to the race of the bearing, without the gasket installed.

3. The nominal distance **A**, is predetermined distance and is used to arrive at the proper sized shim.

4. Subtract distance **B** from the nominal dis-

"A"	"B"	"X"
153.9 mm 6.059"	45 . . . 50 mm 1.772 . . . 1.968"	0.5 mm / 0.020"
	35 . . . 40 mm 1.378 . . . 1.575"	0.6 mm / 0.024"
	25 . . . 30 mm 0.984 . . . 1.181"	0.7 mm / 0.027"
153.8 mm 6.055"	45 . . . 50 mm 1.772 . . . 1.968"	0.4 mm / 0.016"
	35 . . . 40 mm 1.378 . . . 1.575"	0.5 mm / 0.020"
	25 . . . 30 mm 0.984 . . . 1.181"	0.6 mm / 0.024"
153.7 mm 6.051"	45 . . . 50 mm 1.772 . . . 1.968"	0.3 mm / 0.012"
	35 . . . 40 mm 1.378 . . . 1.575"	0.4 mm / 0.016"
	25 . . . 30 mm 0.984 . . . 1.181"	0.5 mm / 0.020"
153.6 mm 6.047"	45 . . . 50 mm 1.722 . . . 1.968"	0.2 mm / 0.008"
	35 . . . 40 mm 1.378 . . . 1.575"	0.3 mm / 0.012"
	25 . . . 30 mm 0.984 . . . 1.181"	0.4 mm / 0.016"

Example: A   22.0mm (0.866 in.)
                    nominal distance
        + B   14.8mm (0.582 in.)
        ─────────────────────────
              36.8mm (1.488 in.)
          C   37.0mm (1.456 in.)
          −   36.8mm (1.448 in.)
        ─────────────────────────
          X   0.2mm (0.008 in.)

Measurement of distance between extension case edge and ball bearing. "C" equals distance.

tance **A**. Subtract the result of **A** minus **B** from distance **C**, which is the proper sized shim **X**, to be used between the speedometer gear and the ball bearing of the case.

5. An example is as follows:
Example:

Transmission Assembly After Basic Measurements

1. Have the transmission case in a secure support.
2. Insert the selector rod detent balls and springs. Install the reverse gear selector rod with the reverse gear, into the case until the 1st lock is engaged.
3. Install the countershaft into the roller bearing, mounted in the case.
4. Install the input shaft on the output shaft and install the assembly into its position on the transmission case.
5. Install the predetermined shim between the speedometer gear and the ball bearing. Install the bearing into the case, but do not seat completely.
6. Using a special bearing installer tool or equivalent, seat the bearing on the output shaft and into the transmission case.
7. Check the tooth engagement of the input, output and countergear assemblies. Tooth engagement can be changed by movement of shims.
8. Install the speedometer bushing and driven gear.
9. Set the transmission assembly in the upright position with the output shaft pointing upward. Measure the distance A, from the case to the ball bearing race.
10. Measure the distance B, from the shoulder height of the sealing cover, to the surface of the gasket on the cover.
11. Subtract distance B from distance A and the result is the thickness of the needed shim between the ball bearing and the sealing cover.
CAUTION: *There should be no end-play between the ball bearing race and the sealing cover. Remeasure and remove play with shims.*
12. Secure the sealing cover and install the output flange. Install the locknut and washer. Place the lockplate washer into the groove of the flange.

Measurement of case edge to ball bearing ... "A" equals distance.

Location of shim "X" and engraved measurement "B".

13. Install the 1st/2nd gear selector rod and fork into place. Insert the locking detent balls and springs. Secure the fork to the rod with the rolled pin.
14. Install the 3rd/4th selector fork into place on the sliding sleeve. Install the main selector rod. Install the lockpin and spring into the ta-

pered bushing. Install the locking detent balls and springs.

15. Install the 3rd/4th gear selector rod and secure to the fork with the rolled pin. Remove pin and reinstall from the top of the fork.

16. Install the back-up lamp switch and the selector rod cap.

17. Install the gasket on the mating surfaces of the transmission case and housing. Install the predetermined shims on their respective locations and install the transmission housing over the gear assembly.

18. Bolt the housing to the case securely.

NOTE: *It may be necessary to heat the transmission area of the input shaft to install the front bearing.*

19. Install the shim and bearing onto the input shaft and housing. Install washer and circlip.

20. Install the clutch release guide sleeve and install a shim to eliminate any existing play between the guide and the bearing.

21. Measure the distance between the case and the ball bearing. This distance is A. Measure the distance from the top of the shoulder of the guide sleeve to the mating surface, with the gasket installed. This distance is B.

22. Subtract distance B from distance A and the result is the thickness of shim needed to remove the existing play between the guide and the bearing.

23. Install the selector rod coupler and secure with the pin. Slide the sleeve over the pin location.

24. Install the console onto the transmission case.

25. Fill the unit with the proper level of lubricating oil.

26. Install the clutch release bearing assembly and the operating lever.

27. Install the crossmember and the exhaust system bracket.

5-speed Models 265/6, 265/OD, 260/5, 260/OD, 240 (ZF-S5-16) Overhaul

DISASSEMBLY

1. Remove the transmission from the vehicle and mount it on a transmission stand.

2. Drain the lubricant and remove the console.

3. Engage 3rd gear, pull back on the spring

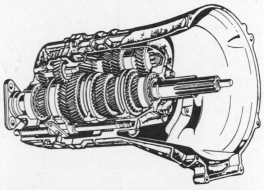

Phantom view of ZE S5-16 ZF synchromesh five speed transmission

Removing the lockpin

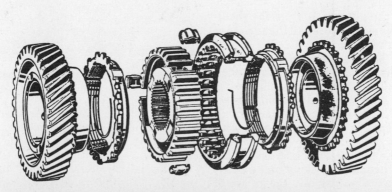

Exploded view of synchronizer assembly, ZF S5-16 five speed transmission

sleeve and knock out the dowel pin. Pull off the selector rod.

4. Disconnect the extension bracket and the crossmember (with the rubber mount). Unscrew the back-up light switch.

5. Unscrew the 7 mounting bolts and remove the guide flange.

NOTE: *Be careful not to lose any shims upon removal of the guide flange.*

6. Remove the circlip and slotted washer from around the input shaft.

7. Remove the cover, spring and lockpin.

8. Knock out the guide pin aligning the front case and then unscrew the mounting bolts.

9. Separate the front case from the transmission.

10. Remove the lock plate from the rear case.

11. While holding the output flange with the special tool, remove the collar nut. Pull off the output flange.

12. Swing the selector shaft against its left stop and push forward; this will engage 2nd gear.

13. Unscrew the rear mounting bolts and pull off the rear case.

CAUTION: *Always make sure that 2nd gear is engaged before removing the rear transmission case.*

14. Remove the radial oil seal.

15. Swing down the output shaft and pull 5th gear off the layshaft with a gear puller.

NOTE: *The bearing inner race will be removed with the gear.*

CAUTION: *To avoid damage to 3rd gear when removing 5th , make sure that there is always play between 3rd gear and the layshaft. If possible, push up on the output shaft.*

16. Using a puller, remove the bearing inner race from the output shaft.

17. Remove the washer and ball and then pull off 5th gear with the synchromesh ring and split needle bearing.

18. Remove the needle bearings from the selector shaft.

Remove the bearing inner race

19. Knock the centerhold pin out of the selector shaft, pull the shaft backward and remove the selector arm.

20. Engage 2nd gear and knock out the centerhold pin.

21. Pull off and remove the rotary lock on the reversing lever, pull the selector rail forward and out and then take out 2nd gear again.

22. With the selector fork operating sleeve toward the rear, pull out the 5th gear selector rod far enough so the centerhold pin can be knocked out.

23. Pull off the sliding sleeve and the 5th gear selector fork. Pull out the selector rod forward.

24. Pull the guide sleeve and bearing inner race off of the output shaft.

25. Remove the synchromesh ring. Pull off the reverse gear and needle bearing.

26. Engage 3rd gear and then knock out the pin.

NOTE: *Knock the pin onto the tooth of 3rd gear until the selector rod can be pulled out forward. Remove the 3rd/4th gear selector rod.*

27. Pull the output shaft toward the rear far enough so that the bearing inner race can be pulled off. Remove the shim.

28. Pull the input shaft, output shaft, layshaft and 1st/2nd gear selector rod out of the intermediate case.

29. Disconnect the holder and remove the reverse gear.

30. Unscrew the bolt and thrust washer holding the front end of the reverse gear shaft and remove the shaft.

ASSEMBLY

1. Install the reverse gear and holder.

NOTE: *The shouldered collar of the reverse gear faces the holder.*

2. Install the input/output shaft assembly into the intermediate case.

3. Install the output shaft shim. Heat the bearing bushing to about 175°F and press onto the shaft.

4. Position the needle bearing and reverse gear and then mount the synchromesh ring.

5. Knock the pin out of the 1st/2nd gear selector rod. Install the 1st/2nd gear selector fork. Push the 1st/2nd gear selector rod in against the spring. Insert the detent ball and while pushing down, push the selector rod in against the stop. Install a new centerhold pin.

6. Install the 3rd/4th gear selector fork and then repeat Step 5.

7. Insert the guide sleeve in the sliding sleeve so that the tab on the locking lever aligns with the opening in the sliding sleeve. Push the balls in far enough so that the guide sleeve slides into the sliding sleeve.

NOTE: *The shouldered end of the sliding sleeve must be opposite the centering pin.*

8. Install the guide sleeve so that the centering pin faces 5th gear.

9. Install the 5th/reverse gear selector fork. Insert the locking ball and push the selector rod in against the spring. Insert the detent ball and while pushing down, turn the selector rod while pushing in so that the openings are opposite the detent balls.

10. Push the selector rod in far enough so that a new centerhold pin can be pressed in. Push the rod and guide sleeve in against the stop.

11. Install the reverse lever with the smooth sides facing down.

12. Install the selector rail, push on the rotary lock and then press in a new pin.

13. Place a small rod in the centering pin, heat the bearing bushing to about 175°F (79°C) and then press it onto the output shaft.

14. Install the split needle bearing, synchromesh ring and 5th gear.

15. Mount the transmission on a press and lubricate the contact surface on the layshaft with oil. Heat 5th gear to about 300°F (149°C), mount it on the layshaft and then press it on.

NOTE: *Lift and turn 5th gear until the teeth mesh.*

16. Knock the bearing inner race onto the layshaft so that the collar faces the gear.

17. Insert the ball with grease and press on the washer.

18. Heat the ball bearing inner race to about 175°F (79TC) and then press it onto the output shaft.

NOTE: *The opening in the inner race (rotary lock) must engage with the ball in the output shaft. Make a reference line to facilitate installation of the bearing race.*

19. Install the selector shaft while pushing on the selector arm with the long arm facing the 3rd/4th gear selector rod. Install a new centerhold pin.

NOTE: *The stop on the selector shaft must face the selector rail.*

20. Hold the 4 needles on the selector shaft with grease.

21. Swing up the output shaft so that 2nd gear is engaged. Slide the 5th/reverse gear selector rod in until the opening is aligned with the end of the 1st/2nd gear selector rod.

22. Clean the sealing surfaces of the rear and intermediate cases thoroughly and then apply Loctite.

NOTE: *The lockpin must move easily and touch bottom.*

23. Hold the needles with grease. Position the rear transmission case making sure that the spring of the selector arm engages on the lever.

24. Using an awl, push the lockpin into the opening of the 1st/2nd gear selector rod.

25. Hold down the rear transmission case and then press on the bearing inner race.

26. Install the space over the output shaft and then press in the radial oil seal.

27. Clean the sealing surfaces of the front and intermediate cases, coat with Loctite and then attach the front case.

28. Install the back-up light switch and the lockpin.

29. Heat the bearing inner race to 175°F (79°C), pull out the input shaft and press on the bearing race.

30. Install the slotted washer and circlip on the input shaft.

NOTE: *Play between the washer and circlip should be 0-0.09mm. Adjustment is made with different thickness circlips.*

31. Check that the grooved ball bearing play of the input shaft and layshaft to the guide flange is 7.8mm (input shaft) and 4.3mm (layshaft).

32. Position the shims and install the guide flange.

33. Installation of the remaining components is in the reverse order of removal.

Make a reference line to facilitate installation of the bearing race

CLUTCH

CAUTION: *The clutch driven disc contains asbestos, which has been determined to be a cancer causing agent. Never clean clutch surfaces with compressed air! Avoid inhaling any dust from the clutch surface. When cleaning clutch surfaces use a commercially available brake cleaning solvent.*

The purpose of the clutch is to disconnect and connect engine power at the transmission. A car at rest requires a lot of engine torque to get all that weight moving. An internal combustion engine does not develop a high starting torque

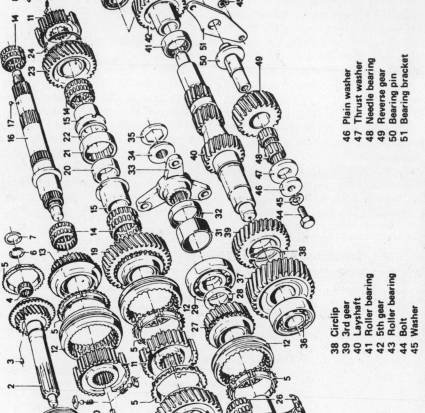

Exploded view of the gear and shaft assembly

1 Ball bearing
2 Input shaft with 4th gear
3 Rotary lock
4 Needle bearing
5 Synchromesh ring
6 Circlip
7 Washer
8 Pressure piece
9 Ball
10 Spring
11 Guide sleeve
12 Sliding sleeve
13 3rd gear
14 Needle bearing
15 Bearing bush
16 Output shaft
17 Ball
18 2nd gear
19 1st gear
20 Bearing race
21 Roller bearing
22 Shim X
23 Reverse gear
24 Circlip
25 Bearing bush
26 Split needle bearing
27 5th gear
28 Washer
29 Ball bearing
31 Spacer
32 Radial oil seal
33 Output flange
34 Collar nut
35 Lockplate
36 Roller bearing
37 4th gear
38 Circlip
39 3rd gear
40 Layshaft
41 Roller bearing
42 5th gear
43 Roller bearing
44 Bolt
45 Washer
46 Plain washer
47 Thrust washer
48 Needle bearing
49 Reverse gear
50 Bearing pin
51 Bearing bracket

(unlike steam engines), so it must be allowed to operate without any load until it builds up enough torque to move the car. Torque increases with engine rpm. The clutch allows the engine to build up torque by physically disconnecting the engine from the transmission, relieving the engine of any load or resistance. The transfer of engine power to the transmission (the load) must be smooth and gradual; if it weren't, drive line components would wear out or break quickly. This gradual power transfer is made possible by gradually releasing the clutch pedal. The clutch disc and pressure plate are the connecting link between the engine and transmission. When the clutch pedal is released, the disc and plate contact each other (clutch engagement), physically joining the engine and transmission. When the pedal is pushed in, the disc and plate separate (the clutch is disengaged), disconnecting the engine from the transmission.

The clutch assembly consists of the flywheel, the clutch disc, the clutch pressure plate, the throwout bearing and fork, the actuating linkage and the pedal. The flywheel and clutch pressure plate (driving members) are connected to the engine crankshaft and rotate with it. The clutch disc is located between the flywheel and pressure plate, and splined to the transmission shaft. A driving member is one that is attached to the engine and transfers engine power to a driven member (clutch disc) on the transmission shaft. A driving member (pressure plate) rotates (drives) a driven member (clutch disc) on contact and, in so doing, turns the transmission shaft. There is a circular diaphragm spring within the pressure plate cover (transmission side). In a relaxed state (when the clutch pedal is fully released), this spring is convex; that is, it is dished outward toward the transmission. Pushing in the clutch pedal actuates an attached linkage rod. Connected to the other end of this rod is the throwout bearing fork. The throwout bearing is attached to the fork. When the clutch pedal is depressed, the clutch linkage pushes the fork and bearing forward to contact the diaphragm spring of the pressure plate. The outer edges of the spring are secured to the pressure plate and are pivoted on rings so that when the center of the spring is compressed by

Troubleshooting Basic Clutch Problems

Problem	Cause
Excessive clutch noise	Throwout bearing noises are more audible at the lower end of pedal travel. The usual causes are: • Riding the clutch • Too little pedal free-play • Lack of bearing lubrication A bad clutch shaft pilot bearing will make a high pitched squeal, when the clutch is disengaged and the transmission is in gear or within the first 2″ of pedal travel. The bearing must be replaced. Noise from the clutch linkage is a clicking or snapping that can be heard or felt as the pedal is moved completely up or down. This usually requires lubrication. Transmitted engine noises are amplified by the clutch housing and heard in the passenger compartment. They are usually the result of insufficient pedal free-play and can be changed by manipulating the clutch pedal.
Clutch slips (the car does not move as it should when the clutch is engaged)	This is usually most noticeable when pulling away from a standing start. A severe test is to start the engine, apply the brakes, shift into high gear and SLOWLY release the clutch pedal. A healthy clutch will stall the engine. If it slips it may be due to: • A worn pressure plate or clutch plate • Oil soaked clutch plate • Insufficient pedal free-play
Clutch drags or fails to release	The clutch disc and some transmission gears spin briefly after clutch disengagement. Under normal conditions in average temperatures, 3 seconds is maximum spin-time. Failure to release properly can be caused by: • Too light transmission lubricant or low lubricant level • Improperly adjusted clutch linkage
Low clutch life	Low clutch life is usually a result of poor driving habits or heavy duty use. Riding the clutch, pulling heavy loads, holding the car on a grade with the clutch instead of the brakes and rapid clutch engagement all contribute to low clutch life.

the throwout bearing, the outer edges bow outward and, by so doing, pull the pressure plate in the same direction - away from the clutch disc. This action separates the disc from the plate, disengaging the clutch and allowing the transmission to be shifted into another gear. A coil type clutch return spring attached to the clutch pedal arm permits full release of the pedal. Releasing the pedal pulls the throwout bearing away from the diaphragm spring resulting in a reversal of spring position. As bearing pressure is gradually released from the spring center, the outer edges of the spring bow outward, pushing the pressure plate into closer contact with the clutch disc. As the disc and plate move closer together, friction between the two increases and slippage is reduced until, when full spring pressure is applied (by fully releasing the pedal), The speed of the disc and plate are the same. This stops all slipping, creating a direct connection between the plate and disc which results in the transfer of power from the engine to the transmission. The clutch disc is now rotating with the pressure plate at engine speed and, because it is splined to the transmission shaft, the shaft now turns at the same engine speed. Understanding clutch operation can be rather difficult at first; if you're still confused after reading this, consider the following analogy. The action of the diaphragm spring can be compared to that of an oil can bottom. The bottom of an oil can is shaped very much like the clutch diaphragm spring and pushing in on the can bottom and then releasing it produces a similar effect. As mentioned earlier, the clutch pedal return spring permits full release of the pedal and reduces linkage slack due to wear. As the linkage wears, clutch free-pedal travel will increase and free-travel will decrease as the clutch wears. Free-travel is actually throwout bearing lash.

The diaphragm spring type clutches used are available in two different designs: flat diaphragm springs or bent spring. The bent fingers are bent back to create a centrifugal boost ensuring quick re-engagement at higher engine speeds. This design enables pressure plate load to increase as the clutch disc wears and makes low pedal effort possible even with a heavy-duty clutch. The throwout bearing used with the bent finger design is 1¼" long and is shorter than the bearing used with the flat finger design. These bearings are not interchangeable. If the longer bearing is used with the bent finger clutch, free-pedal travel will not exist. This results in clutch slippage and rapid wear.

The transmission varies the gear ratio between the engine and rear wheels. It can be shifted to change engine speed as driving conditions and loads change. The transmission allows disengaging and reversing power from the engine to the wheels.

ADJUSTMENTS

Pedal Height and Overcenter Spring

ALL 6-CYLINDER MODELS EXCEPT 325, 325e, 325i, 325is

Measure the length of the over-center spring (Dimension **A**) and, if necessary, loosen the locknut and rotate the shafts as necessary to get the proper clearance. Measure the distance (Dimension **B**) from the firewall to the tip of the clutch pedal and move the pedal in or out, if necessary, by loosening the locknut and rotating the shaft. Specifications for the various models are shown below:

ALL 4-CYLINDER MODELS AND 325, 325e, 325i, 325IS AND 325IX

Measure the distance between the bottom edge of the clutch pedal and the firewall (A). It should be 252-259mm except on 325 models built in years up to 1986. On 325 up to 1986 — 253-264mm. 1987-88 325 models and M3 do not require clutch pedal adjustment. If out of specification, loosen the locknut and rotate the piston rod (1) to correct it.

1600-2 AND 2002

Measure the length of the clutch tension spring (hook-to-hook). Specified length is 92mm. If the dimension is incorrect, unlock the 2 nuts, rotate them together as necessary to get the right dimension, and then relock them.

Clutch Pedal Free Play

1600-2

On 1600-2 models, the free-play of the thrust rod at the release lever is adjusted at 8,000 mile intervals. Loosen the locknut (1) and turn the nut (2) until 3.0-3.5mm clearance exist between the release lever and the adjustment nut on the thrust rod. Tighten the locknut.

Driven Disc and Pressure Plate

REMOVAL AND INSTALLATION

1. On cars with Digital Motor Electronics, remove the heat shield and then the 2 attaching

	Dimension "A"	Dimension "B"
733i 630CSi,	1.338 in.	10.472–10.787 in.
633CSi 528i,	1.138–1.358 in.	9.644–9.960 in.
530i 2800,	1.283–1.302 in.	10.078–9.764 in.
3.0	1.34–1.36	10.35–10.63 in.

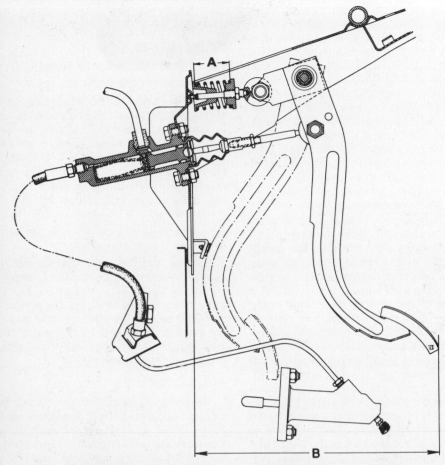

Adjusting pedal height and overcenter spring—six cylinder models

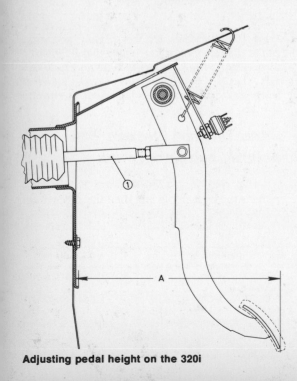

Adjusting pedal height on the 320i

bolts; disconnect the speed and reference mark sensors at the flywheel housing. Mark the plugs for reinstallation.

2. Remove the transmission and clutch housing as described earlier in this chapter.

3. On late model 6-cylinder cars, a Torx® socket is required. If the car has a 265/6 transmission (without an integral clutch housing), remove the clutch housing.

4. Prevent the flywheel from turning, using a locking tool.

1982 Models	Dimension "A" (in.)	Dimension "B" (in.)
733i	1.338	10.472–10.787
633CSi	1.138–1.358	10.472–10.787
528e, 528i	1.283–1.302	10.078–9.764

Clutch pedal height and over center adjustment dimensions—1982 models

1983–88 Models	Dimension "A" (in.)	Dimension "B" (in.)
733i,	1.358	10.472–10.787
735i,	—	10.433–10.827
633CSi, 635CSi, M6	1.358	10.669–11.102
528e, 524td, 533i, 535i	1.358	9.843–10.276

Clutch pedal height and over center adjustment dimensions—1983–88 models

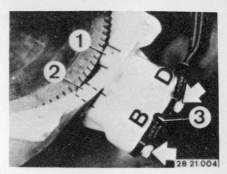

Speed transmitter (1), reference mark transmitter (2) and grey ring on the 528e

Adjusting clutch free-play—1600-2

Checking pressure plate for warpage

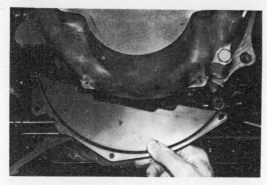

On some six cylinder models, remove the black cover plate from the front of the clutch housing

Install the clutch assembly over the three dowel pins, as shown. Then, insert a centering tool, as shown

5. Loosen the mounting bolts one after another gradually (1-1½ turns at a time) to relieve tension from the clutch.

6. Remove the mounting bolts, clutch, and drive plate. Coat the splines of the transmission input shaft with Molykote® Longterm 2, Microlube® GL 2611, or equivalent. Make sure the clutch pilot bearing, located in the center of the crankshaft, turns easily.

7. Check the clutch driven disc for excess wear or cracks. Check the integral torsional damping springs (used with lighter flywheels only) for tight fit (so they cannot rattle or become dislocated). Inspect the rivets to make sure they are all tight. Check the flywheel to make sure it is not scored, cracked, or burned, even at a small spot. Use a straight edge to make sure the contact surface is true. Replace any defective parts.

8. To install, fit the new clutch plate and disc in place and install the mounting bolts.

9. When installing the clutch retaining bolts turn them in gradually to evenly tighten the clutch disc and to prevent warpage.

10. Install the transmission and the clutch housing.

11. On vehicles equipped, install the speed and reference mark sensors. Install the heat shield.

12. Note that on late model 6-cylinder engines, the clutch pressure plate must fit over dowel pins. Torque the clutch mounting bolts to 16-17 ft. lbs. (17-19 for 1983-88 3.3L and 3.5L engines).

Clutch Master Cylinder
REMOVAL AND INSTALLATION

1. Remove the necessary trim panel or carpet.

2. On the 320i, disconnect the accelerator cable and pull it forward out of the engine firewall.

3. Disconnect the pushrod at the clutch pedal.

4. Remove the cap on the reservoir tank. On some models, there is a clutch master cylinder reservoir, while on others there is a common reservoir shared with the brake master cylinder. Remove the float container (if equipped). Remove the screen (if equipped) and remove enough brake fluid from the tank until the level drops below the refill line or the connection for the filler pipe, if there is one.

5. Disconnect the coolant expansion tank without removing the hoses on models 733i and 735i (latest models with the M30 B35 engine do not require this).

6. Remove the lower left instrument panel trim. Then, remove the retaining nut from the end of the master cylinder actuating rod where the bolt passes through the pedal mechanism.

7. Disconnect the line to the slave cylinder and the fluid fill line going to the top of the master cylinder. Remove the retaining bolts and remove the master cylinder from the firewall.

8. Installation is the reverse of removal. On all 1983-88 models the piston rod bolt should be coated with Molykote® Longterm 2 or equivalent. Make sure all bushings remain in position. Bleed the system and adjust the pedal travel with the pushrod to 152mm.

Clutch Slave Cylinder
REMOVAL AND INSTALLATION

1. Remove enough brake fluid from the reservoir until the level drops below the refill line connection.

2. Remove the circlip or retaining bolts depending on the model and pull the unit down.

3. Disconnect the line and remove the slave cylinder.

4. Installation is the reverse or removal. On the 325 Series and M3, if the engine uses the 2-section flywheel, make sure a larger cylinder

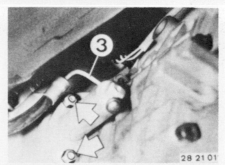

The slave cylinder is on the left side of the transmission. Remove the hydraulic line (3) and then the retaining bolts (arrows)

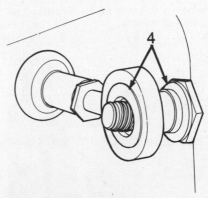

On 733i and 735i models, make sure the bushings (4) on the clutch master cylinder linkage are still in position.

with a diameter of 22mm is used instead of the usual cylinder diameter of 20.5mm. Make sure to install the cylinder with the bleed screw facing downward. When installing the front pushrod, coat it with Molykote® Longterm 2 or equivalent anti-seize compound. Bleed the system.

CLUTCH MASTER AND SLAVE CYLINDER OVERHAUL

1. Remove the master cylinder and slave cylinder as described above.

2. Remove rubber boots or seals, pull the pistons out, and clean all parts in alcohol.

3. Inspect cylinder bores for corrosion or scoring; replace parts as necessary.

4. Install overhaul kits, consisting of the parts listed below:
Master Cylinder:
1. Rubber boot
2. Circlip
3. Grooved piston ring seals
4. Sealing plug (fits into the top of the unit)
5. Washer (situated under the sealing plug)
Slave Cylinder:

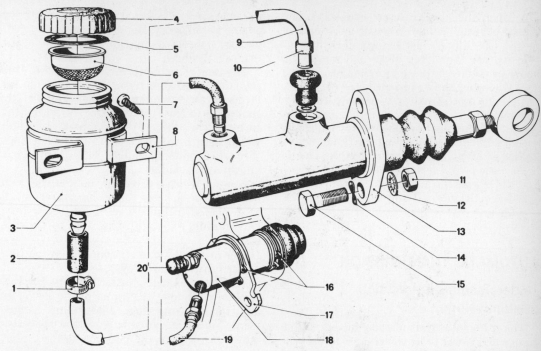

1. Hose clamp
2. Connection hose
3. Brake fluid tank
4. Filler cap
5. Gasket

6. Strainer
7. Sheet metal screw
8. Support
9. Tube
10. Rubber sleeve

11. Hex nut
12. Internal star washer
13. Transmitting cylinder
14. Lockwasher
15. Screw

16. Lockring
17. Support plate
18. Transmitting cylinder
19. Hose line
20. Dust cap

Clutch hydraulic system components—2002 series

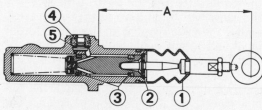

Cross section of the clutch master cylinder. See the text for key to numbers

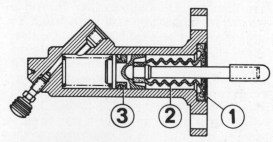

Cross section of the clutch slave cylinder. See the text for key to numbers

1. Ring type retainer (retains the part below).

2. Remove rubber boots or seals, pull the pistons out, and clean all parts in alcohol.

3. Inspect cylinder bores for corrosion or scoring; replace parts as necessary.

BLEEDING THE HYDRAULIC CLUTCH SYSTEM

1. Fill the reservoir.

2. Connect a bleeder hose from the bleeder screw to a container filled with brake fluid so that air cannot be drawn in during bleeding procedures.

3. Pump the clutch pedal about 10 times and then hold it down.

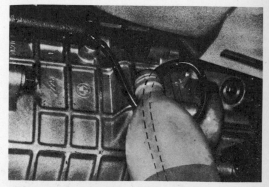

Bleeding the clutch hydraulic system with a special bleeder. To bleed using ordinary equipment, simply force the upper end of a hose tightly over the end of the bleeder screw, rigging the lower end as shown here. See text

4. Open the bleeder screw and watch the stream of escaping fluid. When no more bubbles escape, close the bleeder screw and tighten it.

5. Release the clutch pedal and repeat the above procedure until no more bubbles can be seen when the screw is opened.

6. If this procedure fails to produce a bubble-free stream:

a. Pull the slave cylinder off the transmission without disconnecting the fluid line. NOTE: *Do not depress the clutch pedal while the slave cylinder is dismounted.*

b. Depress the pushrod in the cylinder until it hits the internal stop. Then, reinstall the cylinder.

AUTOMATIC TRANSMISSION

Understanding Automatic Transmissions

The automatic transmission allows engine torque and power to be transmitted to the rear wheels within a narrow range of engine operating speeds. The transmission will allow the engine to turn fast enough to produce plenty of power and torque at very low speeds, while keeping it at a sensible rpm at high vehicle speeds. The transmission performs this job entirely without driver assistance. The transmission uses a light fluid as the medium for the transmission of power. This fluid also works in the operation of various hydraulic control circuits and as a lubricant. Because the transmission fluid performs all of these three functions, trouble within the unit can easily travel from one part to another. For this reason, and because of the complexity and unusual operating principles of the transmission, a very sound understanding of the basic principles of operation will simplify troubleshooting.

THE TORQUE CONVERTER

The torque converter replaces the conventional clutch. It has three functions:

1. It allows the engine to idle with the vehicle at a standstill, even with the transmission in gear.

2. It allows the transmission to shift from range to range smoothly, without requiring that the driver close the throttle during the shift.

3. It multiplies engine torque to an increasing extent as vehicle speed drops and throttle opening is increased. This has the effect of making the transmission more responsive and reduces the amount of shifting required.

The torque converter is a metal case which is shaped lika sphere that has been flattened on opposite sides. It is bolted to the rear end of the engine's crankshaft. Generally, the entire metal case rotates at engine speed and serves as the engine's flywheel.

The case contains three sets of blades. One set is attached directly to the case. This set forms the torus or pump. Another set is directly connected to the output shaft, and forms the turbine. The third set is mounted on a hub which, in turn, is mounted on a stationary shaft through a one-way clutch. This third set is known as the stator.

A pump, which is driven by the covnerter hub at engine speed, keeps the torque converter full of transmission fluid at all times. Fluid flows continuously through the unit to provide cooling.

Under low-speed acceleration, the torque converter functions as follows:

The torus is turning faster than the turbine. It picks up fluid at the center of the converter and, through centrifugal force, slings it outward. Since the outer edge of the converter moves faster than the portions at the center, the fluid picks up speed.

The fluid then enters the outer edge of the turbine blades. It then travels back toward the center of the converter case along the turbine blades. In impinging upon the turbine blades, the fluid loses the energy picked up in the torus.

If the fluid were now to immediately be returned directly into the torus, both halves of the converter would have to turn at approximately the same speed at all times, and torque input and output would both be the same.

In flowing through the torus and turbine, the fluid picks up two types of flow, or flow in two spearate directions. It flows through the turbine blades, and it spins with the engine. The stator, whose blades are stationary when the vehicle is being accelerated at low speeds, converts one type of flow into another. Instead of allowing the fluid to flow straight back into the torus, the stator's curved blades turn the fluid almost 90 degrees toward the direction of rotation of the engine. Thus the fluid does not flow as fast toward the torus, but is already spinning when the torus picks it up. This has the effect of allowing the torus to turn much faster than the turbine. This difference in speed may be compared to the difference in speed between the smaller and larger gears in any gear train. The result is that engine power output is higher, and engine torque is multiplied.

As the speed of the turbine increases, the fluid spins faster and faster in the direction of engine rotation. As a result, the ability of the stator to redirect the fluid flow is reduced. Under cruising conditions, the stator is eventually forced to rotate on its one-way clutch in the di-

rection of engine rotation. Under these conditions, the torque converter begins to behave almost like a solid shaft, with the torus and turbine speeds being almost equal.

THE PLANETARY GEARBOX

The ability of the torque converter to multiply engine torque is limited. Also, the unit tends to be more efficient when the turine is rotating at relatively high speeds. Therefore, a planetary gearbox is used to carry the power output of the turbine to the driveshaft.

Planetary gears function very similarly to conventional transmission gears. However, their construction is different in that three elements make up one gear system, and, in that all three elements are different from one another. The three elements are: an outer gear that is shaped like a hoop, with teeth cut into the inner surface; a sun gear, mounted on a shaft and located at the very center of the outer gear; and a set of three planet gears, held by pins in a ring-like planet carrier, meshing with both the sun gear and the outer gear. Either the outer gear or the sun gear may be held stationary, providing more than one possible torque multiplication factor for each set of gears. Also, if all three gears are forced to rotate at the same speed, the gearset forms, in effect, a solid shaft.

Most modern automatics use the planetary gears to provide either a single reduction ratio of about 1.8:1, or two reduction gears: a low of about 2.5:1, and an intermediate of about 1.5:1. Bands and clutches are used to hold various portions of the gearsets to the transmission case or to the shaft on which they are mounted. Shifting is accomplished, then, by changing the portion of each planetary gearset which is held to the tranmission case or to the shaft.

THE SERVOS AND ACCUMULATORS

The servos are hydraulic pistons and cylinders. They resemble the hydraulic actuators used on many familiar machines, such as bulldozers. Hydraulic fluid enters the cylinder, under pressure, and forces the piston to move to engage the band or clutches.

The accumulators are used to cushion the engagement of the servos. The transmission fluid must pass through the accumulator on the way to the servo. The accumulator housing contains a thin piston which is sprung away from the discharge passage of the accumulator. When fluid passes through the accumulator on the way to the servo, it must move the piston against spring pressure, and this action smooths out the action of the servo.

THE HYDRAULIC CONTROL SYSTEM

The hydraulic pressure used to operate the servos comes from the main transmission oil pump. This fluid is channeled to the various servos through the shift valves. There is generally a manual shift valve which is operated by the tranmission selector lever and an automatic shift valvee for each automatic upshift the transmission provides: i.e., two-speed automatics have a low-high shift valve, while three-speeds have a 1-2 valve, and a 2-3 vavle.

There are two pressures which effect the operation of these valves. One is the governor pressure which is affected by vehicle speed. The other is the modulator pressure which is affected by intake manifold vacuum or throttle position. Governor pressure rises with an increase in vehicle speed, and modulator pressure rises as the throttle is opened wider. By responding to these two pressures, the shift valves cause the upshift points to be delayed with increased throttle opening to make the best use of the engine's power output.

Most transmissions also make use of an auxiliary circuit for downshifting. This circuit may be actuated by the throttle linkage or the vacuum line which actuates the modulator, or by a cable or solenoid. It applies pressure to a special downshift surface on the shift valve or valves.

The transmission modulator also governs the line pressure, used to actuate the servos. In this way, the clutches and bands will be actuated with a force matching the torque output of the engine.

Identification

The transmission identification chart shows the transmissions used from 1970-82, from 1982 on BMW used the same ZF transmission as well as a newer model. The new model is identified as the ZF/4HP-22. The 2 transmissions are almost identical, except that the new one is a 4-speed unit instead of a 3 speed.

Vehicle	Transmission	Cover Designation
2002A	ZF/3HP-12	028
2500, 2800	ZF/3HP-20	1019
3000, Bavaria, 3.0	ZF/BW-65	—
320i ('77–'79)	ZF/3HP-22	A ①, Red ②
('80–'82)	ZF/3HP-22	T ①
538e	ZF/3HP-22	RB
528i	ZF/3HP-22	N ①
530i ('75–'76)	ZF/BW-65	—
('77–'78)	ZF/3HP-22	Silver/Black ②, N ①
630CSi	ZF/3HP-22	Silver/Black ②, N ①
633CSi	ZF/3HP-22	Q ①
733i ('78–'80)	ZF/3HP-22	J
('81–'82)	ZF/3HP-22	AG

ZF: Zahnradfabrik Friedrichshafen AG
BW: Borg Warner
① With deep oil pan
② With flat oil pan

Troubleshooting Basic Automatic Transmission Problems

Problem	Cause	Solution
Fluid leakage	• Defective pan gasket	• Replace gasket or tighten pan bolts
	• Loose filler tube	• Tighten tube nut
	• Loose extension housing to transmission case	• Tighten bolts
	• Converter housing area leakage	• Have transmission checked professionally
Fluid flows out the oil filler tube	• High fluid level	• Check and correct fluid level
	• Breather vent clogged	• Open breather vent
	• Clogged oil filter or screen	• Replace filter or clean screen (change fluid also)
	• Internal fluid leakage	• Have transmission checked professionally
Transmission overheats (this is usually accompanied by a strong burned odor to the fluid)	• Low fluid level	• Check and correct fluid level
	• Fluid cooler lines clogged	• Drain and refill transmission. If this doesn't cure the problem, have cooler lines cleared or replaced.
	• Heavy pulling or hauling with insufficient cooling	• Install a transmission oil cooler
	• Faulty oil pump, internal slippage	• Have transmission checked professionally
Buzzing or whining noise	• Low fluid level	• Check and correct fluid level
	• Defective torque converter, scored gears	• Have transmission checked professionally
No forward or reverse gears or slippage in one or more gears	• Low fluid level	• Check and correct fluid level
	• Defective vacuum or linkage controls, internal clutch or band failure	• Have unit checked professionally
Delayed or erratic shift	• Low fluid level	• Check and correct fluid level
	• Broken vacuum lines	• Repair or replace lines
	• Internal malfunction	• Have transmission checked professionally

Transmission Fluid Indications

The appearance and odor of the transmission fluid can give valuable clues to the overall condition of the transmission. Always note the appearance of the fluid when you check the fluid level or change the fluid. Rub a small amount of fluid between your fingers to feel for grit and smell the fluid on the dipstick.

If the fluid appears:	It indicates:
Clear and red colored	• Normal operation
Discolored (extremely dark red or brownish) or smells burned	• Band or clutch pack failure, usually caused by an overheated transmission. Hauling very heavy loads with insufficient power or failure to change the fluid, often result in overheating. Do not confuse this appearance with newer fluids that have a darker red color and a strong odor (though not a burned odor).
Foamy or aerated (light in color and full of bubbles)	• The level is too high (gear train is churning oil)
	• An internal air leak (air is mixing with the fluid). Have the transmission checked professionally.
Solid residue in the fluid	• Defective bands, clutch pack or bearings. Bits of band material or metal abrasives are clinging to the dipstick. Have the transmission checked professionally.
Varnish coating on the dipstick	• The transmission fluid is overheating

Lockup Torque Converter Service Diagnosis

Problem	Cause	Solution

No lockup	• Faulty oil pump
	• Sticking governor valve
	• Valve body malfunction
	  (a) Stuck switch valve
	  (b) Stuck lockup valve
	  (c) Stuck fail-safe valve
	• Failed locking clutch
	• Leaking turbine hub seal
	• Faulty input shaft or seal ring
		• Replace oil pump
		• Repair or replace as necessary
		• Repair or replace valve body or its internal components as necessary
		
		• Replace torque converter
		• Replace torque converter
		• Repair or replace as necessary

Will not unlock	• Sticking governor valve
	• Valve body malfunction
	  (a) Stuck switch valve
	  (b) Stuck lockup valve
	  (c) Stuck fail-safe valve
		• Repair or replace as necessary
		• Repair or replace valve body or its internal components as necessary

Stays locked up at too low a speed in direct	• Sticking governor valve
	• Valve body malfunction
	  (a) Stuck switch valve
	  (b) Stuck lockup valve
	  (c) Stuck fail-safe valve
		• Repair or replace as necessary
		• Repair or replace valve body or its internal components as necessary

Locks up or drags in low or second	• Faulty oil pump
	• Valve body malfunction
	  (a) Stuck switch valve
	  (b) Stuck fail-safe valve
		• Replace oil pump
		• Repair or replace valve body or its internal components as necessary

Sluggish or stalls in reverse	• Faulty oil pump
	• Plugged cooler, cooler lines or fittings
	• Valve body malfunction
	  (a) Stuck switch valve
	  (b) Faulty input shaft or seal ring
		• Replace oil pump as necessary
		• Flush or replace cooler and flush lines and fittings
		• Repair or replace valve body or its internal components as necessary

Loud chatter during lockup engagement (cold)	• Faulty torque converter • Failed locking clutch • Leaking turbine hub seal	• Replace torque converter • Replace torque converter • Replace torque converter
Vibration or shudder during lockup engagement	• Faulty oil pump • Valve body malfunction • Faulty torque converter • Engine needs tune-up	• Repair or replace oil pump as necessary • Repair or replace valve body or its internal components as necessary • Replace torque converter • Tune engine
Vibration after lockup engagement	• Faulty torque converter • Exhaust system strikes underbody • Engine needs tune-up • Throttle linkage misadjusted	• Replace torque converter • Align exhaust system • Tune engine • Adjust throttle linkage
Vibration when revved in neutral Overheating: oil blows out of dip stick tube or pump seal	• Torque converter out of balance • Plugged cooler, cooler lines or fittings • Stuck switch valve	• Replace torque converter • Flush or replace cooler and flush lines and fittings • Repair switch valve in valve body or replace valve body
Shudder after lockup engagement	• Faulty oil pump • Plugged cooler, cooler lines or fittings • Valve body malfunction • Faulty torque converter • Fail locking clutch • Exhaust system strikes underbody • Engine needs tune-up • Throttle linkage misadjusted	• Replace oil pump • Flush or replace cooler and flush lines and fittings • Repair or replace valve body or its internal components as necessary • Replace torque converter • Replace torque converter • Align exhaust system • Tune engine • Adjust throttle linkage

Fluid Pan

REMOVAL AND INSTALLATION

Normally, it is not required to remove the oil pan from the transmission. The transmission oil may be drained and refilled at the required intervals using the oil pan drain plug. However, if the pan is leaking and a damaged pan gasket is suspected, or if the transmission fluid appears brownish in color on the dipstick, or if a clogged transmission oil filter is suspected, the pan should be removed. The procedure for removing the pan is as follows:

1. If the car is running, drive the car for 3-5 miles to warm up the transmission. Park the car on a level surface. Shut off the engine.

2. Place a drip pan (minimum 2 quart capacity) beneath the oil pan. Unscrew and remove the transmission oil drain plug, taking care not to get scalded by the hot fluid.

3. Inspect the drained oil. If the oil has a "burned" smell or is dark brown in color, the transmission should be disassembled and rebuilt. Also, if the oil contains tiny iron or aluminum particles (fluid is gray in color), the transmission will be needing service.

4. On the ZF 22 type transmission, disconnect the oil filler neck at the oil pan. On ZF 12 and ZF 20 transmission, remove the pan mounting bolts, noting the location of the 2 clips on one side, and remove the pan and gasket. On ZF 22 transmission, remove the retaining bolt and bracket at each corner and remove the pan and gasket.

5. If desired, service the strainer, as described below.

6. Clean the gasket surfaces. Replacing the gasket, reinstall the pan. On ZF 22 transmissions, place the magnetic disc next to the oil filter screen in the oil pan, and make sure the retaining brackets are installed with the shorter leg going inside the groove on the pan. Torque the bolts alternately and in small steps to the following values:

7. With the car parked on a level surface, and the selector lever in Park, fill the transmission slowly until the fluid level is ¼" above the minimum mark on the dipstick. Consult Chapter 1 for the type of fluid to use and approximate quantities.

8. Start the engine and let it warm up to normal operating temperature. Recheck the fluid level with the selector lever in park. If the level

ZF/3HP–22 transmission oil pan with the magnetic discs in position

is not between the 2 marks on the dipstick (slightly more than a pint from one to the other), or drain fluid as required.

FILTER SERVICE

1. Drain and remove the oil pan as described above.

2. Remove the bolts retaining the strainer to the valve body, remove the strainer, and clean it in trichloroethylene. Allow to dry.

3. Install the strainer and gently retighten the mounting bolts or screws alternately and evenly. On the 22 type transmission, the valve body to transmission bolts should be torqued to 7-8 ft. lbs. (some of these retain the strainer); the phillips screws which retain the strainer should be torqued to 3.6-4.3 ft. lbs. on all 22 type transmission except those designated "J" (733i). On "J" type transmission, the figure is 4.3-5.0 ft. lbs.

4. Replace the oil pan as described above.

Removing the transmission oil strainer—2800 (others similar)

Transmission	Oil Pan	Filler Neck
ZF3HP12	7 ft. lbs.	—
ZF3HP20	7.2 ft. lbs.	—
ZF3HP22	6–6.5 ft. lbs.	74–84 ft. lbs.

Adjustments
NEUTRAL SAFETY SWITCH

The neutral safety switch (starter lock switch) used in the ZF automatic transmission is combined with the back-up light switch. Therefore, if you are having problems with the back-up lights going on or staying on when they are not supposed to, chances are that you might have difficulty starting the car with the selector lever in Park or Neutral.

1. Check the operation of the switch by disconnecting the 2 leads at terminals 50. Ground one terminal tag. Connect a 12 volt test lamp to the positive terminal and the second terminal tag. The test lamp should light when the selector lever is placed on **P** (Park) or **N** (Neutral), if the switch is properly adjusted.

2. If the switch is in need of adjustment, unscrew the switch and place correspondingly thicker seals (shims) behind the switch and the transmission housing.

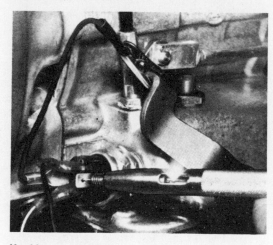

Hooking up test light

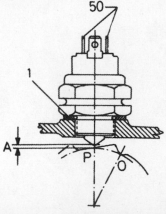

Cross-section of neutral start safety switch showing terminals 50 and shims (1). Distance "A" inside the transmission is .02 in.

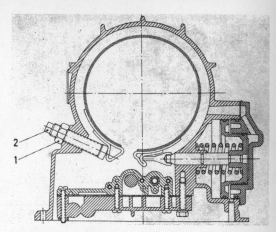

Adjusting the transmission band. See text for key to numbers

BRAKE BANDS

These adjustments are made externally. Each is made in a square headed bolt retained by a hex type locknut. Adjustment is required after 600 miles and every 15,000 miles thereafter.

1. Loosen the locknut (1) about 1 turn (an offset hex wrench will be helpful). Tighten the adjusting (square) bolt (2) to 50-51 ft. lbs.

2. Note the exact position of the adjusting bolts, and loosen it exactly ¾ of a turn. Then, tighten the locknut.

SELECTOR LEVER ADJUSTMENT
All Models Except 1983-84 633CSi, 635CSi, 733i, 735i, M5 and M6

1. Detach the selector rod (1) at the selector lever lower section (2).

2. Move the selector lever (3) on the transmission to position O or N.

3. Press the selector lever (4) against the stop (5) on the shift gate.

4. Adjust the length of the selector rod (1)

Loosen the locknut (1) and adjust via the bolt (2)

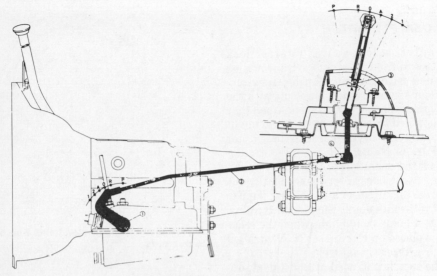

Selector lever adjustment—typical

until the pin (6) aligns with the bore in the selector lever lower section (2). Shorten the selector rod length by:

- 1 turn — 320i
- 1-2 turns — 318i, 325e, 325i, 325iX, 524td, 535, 633CSi and 733i
- 2-2½ turns — 530i

NOTE: *If equipped with air conditioning on the 4-cylinder models, plates (7) must be installed between the bearing bracket and float plate and selector rod (1) must be attached in bore (K) of selector lever (3).*

1983-84 633CSi, 635CSi and 735i
All 735, M5 and M6

1. Move the selector lever (1) to PARK position. Loosen the nut (2).

2. Push the transmission lever (3) to the forward or park position. Then push the cable rod (4) in the opposite direction; tighten the nut (2) to 7.0-8.5 ft. lbs.

ACCELERATOR LINKAGE ADJUSTMENT

2002A

1. Remove the air cleaner.
2. Remove the accelerator cable.
3. Press the accelerator pedal down to the kick down stop into the full acceleration position. In this position the throttle valve must be fully open and not extend beyond the vertical position. When adjusting, bend the stop.

4. Adjust the length of the accelerator linkage using the eye bolt.

3.0, 528i, 530i

1. Synchronize the idle speed with the engine at operating temperature.

2. Detach linkage (1).
3. Detach the accelerator cable at the operating lever (2).
4. Adjust linkage (1) so that the operating lever (2) rests on stop (3).
NOTE: *Make sure that linkage (1) is not pulled down into the kickdown position.*
5. The swivel joint (5) must align with the hole in the operating lever (2) leaving a play of 0.23-0.48mm between nipple (4) and the end of the cable sleeve.
6. The accelerator must not sag. Press lever (6) against the acceleration stop (7) and adjust linkage (8) until the distance between nipple (4) and the end of the cable sleeve is 37mm. When in kickdown, the nipple (4) must be at least 43mm from the end of the cable sleeve.
NOTE: *If the idle speed is altered, repeat the above procedure.*

Inserting bearing pin for accelerator cable— 2002A

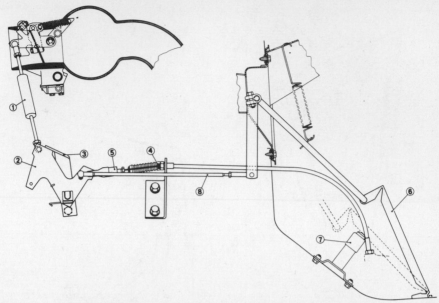

Accelerator linkage and cable adjustment—528i, 530i, 2800, 3.0

ACCELERATOR CABLE ADJUSTMENT

2002A

1. Remove the accelerator cable from the rotary shaft.

2. Press down the accelerator linkage to the full acceleration position.

3. Pull the accelerator cable to determine the full acceleration position. The holes in the fork head must not coincide with the hole in the rotary selector so that the bearing pin can be inserted with correct alignment.

4. Turn the fork head to adjust the cable length.

1982 533i, 633CSi and 733i

1. Adjust play (S) to 0.25-0.75mm with the nuts when in Neutral.

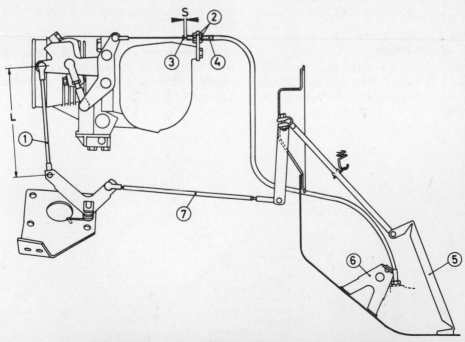

Accelerator cable adjustment—600 and 700 series

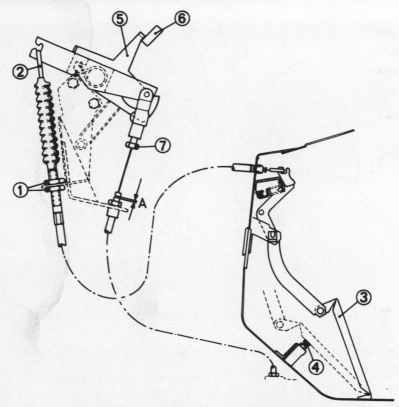

Accelerator and transmission cable adjustments—320i

2. Press the accelerator pedal against the stop.

3. Adjust the pressure rod (7) until the distance from the seal (3) to the end of the cable (4) is 633CSi — 44-51mm; 733i — 43.75-52.25mm.

**1983-84 533i, 535i, 633CSi and 733i
All 635CSi, 735, M5 and M6**

1. On the injection system throttle body, loosen the 2 locknuts at the end of the throttle cable and adjust the cable until there is a play of 0.25-0.75mm.

2. Loosen the locknut and lower the kickdown stop under the accelerator pedal. Have someone depress the accelerator pedal until he can feel the transmission detent. Then, back the kickdown stop back out until it just touches the pedal.

3. Check that the distance from the seal at the throttle body end of the cable housing is at least 44mm from the rear end of the threaded sleeve. If this dimension checks out, tighten all the locknuts.

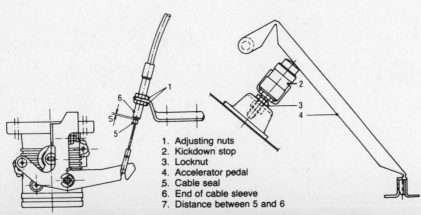

1. Adjusting nuts
2. Kickdown stop
3. Locknut
4. Accelerator pedal
5. Cable seal
6. End of cable sleeve
7. Distance between 5 and 6

Automatic transmission accelerator cable adjustment—528e

524td

NOTE: *For diesels, see "Idle Speed Diesel Engines", covered earlier in this section.*

320i

1. Adjust the accelerator cable at nuts (1) until the accelerator cable eye (2) has a play of 0.2-0.3mm.

2. Depress the accelerator pedal (3) to the full throttle stop screw (4).

3. There must be 0.5mm play between the operating lever (5) and stop nut (6).

4. Adjust by the full throttle stop screw (4).

318i, 325, 325e, 325i and 325iS, 325iX and M3

1. Adjust the cable for zero tension with the throttle closed and accelerator pedal released.

2. Loosen the locknut on the throttle stop bolt. Now adjust the bolt inward just until it suspends the accelerator pedal at the point where the throttle just reaches wide open position. On automatic transmission equipped cars, make sure the throttle is in full detent position. Now, turn the stop screw 1½ turns lower to get a clearance of 0.5mm between the accelerator pedal and stop bolt at full throttle. Tighten the locknut.

528e

1. Adjust the freeplay (s) of the cable in N position to 0.25-0.75mm. Use cable adjuster nuts (1) to adjust the freeplay.

2. In the passenger compartment, loosen the kickdown switch. Screw in the kickdown stop (2) all the way in the direction of the floor pan.

3. Press down on the accelerator pedal (4) to the transmission pressure point. Unscrew the kickdown stop (2) until it contacts the accelerator pedal.

4. Press the accelerator to the kickdown (wide open throttle position.

5. In kickdown position, the distance (s) must be 44mm. The distance (s) equals the distance from the cable seal (5) to the end of the cable sleeve (6).

TRANSMISSION CABLE ADJUSTMENT

320i

NOTE: *The accelerator cable must be correctly adjusted.*

1. With the transmission in the Neutral position, adjust play to 0.25-0.75mm with the screw.

2. Depress the accelerator pedal to kickdown stop; play must now be 43.5-51.5mm. Make corrections with screw (4).

318i, 325, 325e, 325i, 325iS and M3

1. Adjust the play in the cable **S** to 0.25-0.75mm. Make sure both cable locknuts are loose.

Adjusting cable length by rotating fork head

2. Back off the accelerator pedal kickdown stop and then depress the accelerator pedal until the transmission just reaches the detent and some resistance is felt.

3. Run the kickdown stop out until it just touches the bottom of the pedal.

4. Depress the accelerator through the detent and hold while measuring distance **S** from the lead seal to the end of the sleeve. It must be at least 44mm. Adjust further, if necessary.

5. Tighten all locknuts.

524td

1. The engine must be at normal operating temperature so the operating lever on the injection pump rests on the idle stop. Adjust the play between the throttle cable stop and the end of the threads on the cable jacket to 0.25-0.75mm.

2. Then, loosen the nut that locks the accelerator pedal kickdown stop. Press the pedal down until it reaches the transmission detent. Screw the kickdown stop back out until it just touches the lower side of the accelerator pedal.

3. Press the accelerator pedal down until it has kicked down (extreme position). Make sure the distance measured above is at least 44mm. Readjust to obtain this figure, if necessary.

Transmission

REMOVAL AND INSTALLATION

3-Speed Automatic

1. Disconnect the accelerator cable.

2. On the 4-cylinder engine remove all of the transmission mounting bolts which are accessible from above.

3. Detach the oil filler neck and drain the oil.

4. On 4-cylinder engines remove the exhaust pipe support bracket and separate the pipe from the exhaust manifold. On the 318i and 325, remove the exhaust system and detach the heat shield.

5. On all 6-cylinder engines except model 733i, remove the entire exhaust system.

6. Detach the oil cooler lines from the transmission and drain fluid.

7. Disconnect the driveshaft at the transmis-

Remove the 4 torque convertor retaining bolts

sion, On model 733i, use special clamping tool. On the 318i and 325, disconnect the selector rod.

8. Disconnect the speedometer cable.

9. Remove the heat guard and center bearing and bend down and pull off the driveshaft.

10. Remove the torque converter cover and remove the 4 bolts that attach the torque converter to the drive plate. Turn the engine for this procedure, using the vibration damper.

NOTE: *On 1982-88 6-cylinder models, the speed transmitter and reference transmitter must be unbolted and removed from the flywheel housing. For installation, the speed transmitter faces the gear ring. The reference transmitter has a plug with a grey ring and faces the flywheel. The engine will not start if the plugs are mixed up. Coat both with anti-seize compound before installing. Make sure their tips are clean.*

11. Support the transmission and disconnect the crossmember at the body.

12. Remove the remaining transmission mounting bolts.

13. Separate the transmission from the engine and take off the torque converter at the same time. On 1983-88 733i and 735i models, this is done by removing the protective grill on the side of the converter housing and gently

prying it toward the transmission as the transmission is pulled rearward. On the 318i, lower the transmission onto the front axle carrier. Remove the grill from the torque converter housing and gently pry the torque converter backwards as the transmission is pulled off.

14. Install the transmission into the vehicle and push the torque converter back against the stop on the main transmission and rotate it to align bolt holes with the drive plate holes before installing.

15. On 1983-88 733i and 735i models, drive connections on the front of the converter must be indented inside the converter housing at least 9mm.

16. Use new nuts on the driveshaft flexible coupling. Torque drive plate bolts to 16-17 ft. lb.

17. Install the exhaust suspension without twisting. When installing the driveshaft preload the center bearing by 2mm in the forward direction.

18. Make sure the torque converter is positioned correctly before installing. Replenish drained fluid with new fluid, only.

4-Speed Automatic Except 325e, 325i, and 325iX

NOTE: *To perform this operation, a support for the transmission, BMW tool 24 0 120 and 00 2 020 or equivalent and a tool for tightening the driveshaft locking ring, BMW tool 26 1 040 or equivalent are required. If the car has the M30 B35 type engine, a special socket (that retains bolts) 24 1 110 or equivalent will be needed.*

1. Disconnect the battery ground cable. On both gas and diesel engines, loosen the throttle cable adjusting nuts, release the cable tension, and disconnect the cable at the throttle lever. Then, remove (and retain) the nuts, and pull the cable housing out of the bracket.

2. Disconnect the exhaust system at the manifold and hangers, and lower it out of the way. Remove the hanger that runs across under the driveshaft. Remove the exhaust heat shield from under the center of the car.

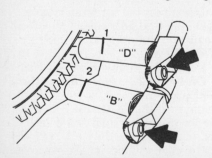

Note that the speed sensor (1) is installed into bore "D" and that the reference mark sensor (2) goes into bore "B"

The torque converter is installed correctly if the drive shell mounting parts are located underneath the converter housing

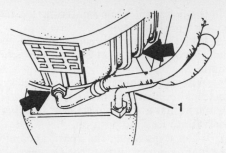

Remove the oil filler neck (1) and disconnect the arrowed hoses to drain fluid from the 4HP-22 transmission

3. Support the transmission via a floorjack and the special tools. 24 0 120 goes under the transmission oil pan and 00 2 020 supports it via the jack. Then, remove the crossmember that supports the transmission at the rear.

4. Remove the driveshaft coupling through bolts and nuts or the CV-joint through bolts and nuts. Either type is located right at the rear of the transmission. Discard used self-locking coupling nuts. Keep the CV-joint clean, and replace its gasket.

5. Unscrew the transmission locking ring at the center mount (if equipped). Then, remove the bolts and remove the center mount. Bend the propshaft downward and pull it off the centering pin. Suspend it with wire from the underside of the car.

6. Drain the transmission oil and discard it. Remove the oil filler neck. Disconnect the oil cooler lines at the transmission by unscrewing the flare nuts and plug the open connections.

7. On most models, remove the converter cover by removing 3 Torx® bolts with a Torx® screwdriver from behind and the 4 regular bolts from underneath. On cars with the M30 B35 type engine pull the cover out of the bottom of the transmission housing, just behind the oil pan.

8. Remove the 3 bolts fastening the torque converter to the drive plate, turning the flywheel as necessary to gain access from below. Use a special socket (that retains the bolts) 24 1 110 or equivalent on cars with the M30 B35 type engine.

9. On cars so-equipped, remove the guard for the speed and reference mark sensors. Remove the attaching bolt for each and remove each sensor (the diesel only has a reference mark sensor). Keep the sensors clean.

10. Disconnect the shift cable by loosening the locknut fastening it to the shift lever and disconnecting the cable at the cable housing bracket.

11. If the transmission has an electrical connection, turn the bayonet fastener to the left to release the connection, disconnect it, and pull the wire out of the ties.

12. Lower the transmission as far as possible. Then, remove all the Torx® or standard type bolts attaching the transmission to the engine.

13. Remove the small grill from the bottom of the transmission. Then press the converter off with a large screwdriver passing through this opening while sliding the transmission out.

14. Install the transmission and observe the following points:

a. Make sure the converter is fully installed onto the transmission, so the ring on the front is inside the edge of the case.

b. When reinstalling the driveshaft, tighten the lockring with a special tool such as 26 1 040.

c. If the driveshaft has a simple coupling (524td), rather than a CV-joint, make sure to replace the self-locking nuts and to hold the bolts still while tightening the nuts to keep from distorting the coupling.

d. When installing the center mount, preload it forward from its most natural position 4-6mm.

e. Adjust the throttle cables.

325e, 325i, and 325iX
4-Speed Automatic

NOTE: *To perform this operation, a support for the transmission, BMW tool 24 0 120 and 00 2 020 or equivalent and a tool for tightening the driveshaft locking ring, BMW tool 26 1 040 or equivalent, are required. If the car has the M30 B35 type engine, a special socket (that retains bolts) 24 1 110 or equivalent will also be needed.*

1. Disconnect the battery ground cable. Loosen the throttle cable adjusting nuts, release the cable tension, and disconnect the cable at the throttle lever. Then, remove (and retain) the nuts, and pull the cable housing out of the bracket.

2. Disconnect the exhaust system at the manifold and hangers, and lower it out of the way. Remove the hanger that runs across under the driveshaft. Remove the exhaust heat shield from under the center of the car.

3. On the 325iX with 4-wheel drive, remove the transfer case from the rear of the transmission as described later in this chapter.

4. Drain the transmission oil and discard it. Remove the oil filler neck. Disconnect the oil cooler lines at the transmission by unscrewing the flare nuts and plug the open connections.

5. Support the transmission via a floorjack and the special tools. 24 0 120 goes under the transmission oil pan and 00 2 020 supports it via the jack. Separate the torque converter housing from the transmission by removing 3

Torx® bolts with a Torx® screwdriver from behind and the 4 regular bolts from underneath. Retain the washers used with the Torx® bolts.

6. On the 325iX, disconnect the front driveshaft as described below under the procedure for removing the transfer case.

7. Remove bolts attaching the torque converter housing to the engine, making sure to retain the spacer used behind one of the bolts. Then, loosen the 2 mounting bolts for the oil level switch just enough so that the plate can be removed while pushing the switch mounting bracket to one side.

8. Remove the 3 bolts attaching the torque converter to the drive plate. Turn the flywheel as necessary to gain access to each of the 3 bolts, which are spaced at equal intervals around it. Make sure to re-use the same bolts and retain the washers.

9. To remove the speed and reference mark sensors, remove the attaching bolt for each and remove each sensor. Keep the sensors clean.

10. Turn the bayonet type electrical connector counterclockwise and then pull the plug out of the socket. Then, lift the wiring harness out of the harness bails.

11. Support the transmission via a floorjack and the special tools. 24 0 120 goes under the transmission oil pan and 00 2 020 supports it via the jack. Then, remove the crossmember that supports the transmission at the rear.

12. Disconnect the transmission shift rod. Then, remove the nuts and then the through bolts from the damper-type U-joint at the front of the transmission.

13. Unscrew the transmission locking ring at the center mount (if equipped), using the special tool designed for this purpose 26 1 040 or equivalent). Then, remove the bolts and remove the center mount. Bend the propshaft downward and pull it off the centering pin. Suspend it with wire from the underside of the car.

14. Lower the transmission as far as possible. Then, remove all the Torx® or standard type bolts attaching the transmission to the engine.

15. Remove the small grill from the bottom of the transmission. Then press the converter off with a large screwdriver passing through this opening while sliding the transmission out.

16. Install the transmission into the vehicle and observe the following points:

a. Make sure the converter is fully installed onto the transmission, so the ring on the front is inside the edge of the case.

b. When reinstalling the driveshaft, tighten the lockring with a special tool such as 26 1 040.

c. Make sure to replace the self-locking nuts on the driveshaft flexible joint and to

hold the bolts still while tightening the nuts to keep from distorting it.

d. When installing the center mount, pre-load it forward from its most natural position 4-6mm.

e. When reconnecting the bayonet type electrical connector, make sure that the alignment marks are aligned after the plug it twisted into its final position.

f. When reinstalling the speed and reference mark sensors, inspect the O- rings used on the sensors and install new ones, if necessary. Make sure to install the speed sensor into the bore marked **D** and the reference mark sensor, which is marked with a ring, into the bore marked **B**.

g. Torque the crossmember mounting bolts to 16-17 ft. lbs.

h. If O-rings are used with the transmission oil cooler connections, replace them.

i. Adjust the throttle cables.

TRANSFER CASE

Currently BMW only offers one 4-wheel drive model, the 325iX. This vehicle is equipped with full-time 4-wheel drive, this means that the car is always driving with 4 wheels in operation.

REMOVAL AND INSTALLATION

Cars with Manual Transmission

NOTE: *To perform this procedure, a special, large wrench that locks onto flats on alternate sides of a section of the rear driveshaft is required. Use BMW special tool No. 26 1 060 or an equivalent that is available in the aftermarket.*

1. Raise the car and support it securely at the 4 corners so it is possible to work underneath it safely. Remove the exhaust system. Unbolt and remove the exhaust system heat shields located behind and below the transfer case.

2. Unscrew the rear section of the driveshaft at the sliding joint located behind the output flange of the transfer case.

3. Hold the through-bolts stationary and remove the self-locking nuts from in front of the flexible coupling at the transfer case output flange. Discard all the self-locking nuts and replace them.

CAUTION: *During the next step, be careful not to let the driveshaft rest on the metal fuel line that crosses underneath it, or the line could be damaged!*

4. Slide the sections of the driveshaft together at the sliding joint and then pull the front of

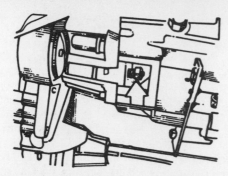

The arrow shows the location of the flexible coupling linking the transmission output flange with the input flange of the transfer case.

the driveshaft off the centering pin at the transmission output shaft.

5. Remove the nuts and through bolts from the flexible coupling linking the transmission output flange with the short driveshaft linking the transmission and the transfer case.

6. Support the transmission from underneath in a secure manner (supported squarely with a floorjack). Then, mark each of the 4 bolts fastening the crossmember that supports the transmission at the rear to the body (bolts are of different lengths). Remove the crossmember.

7. Lower the transmission/transfer case unit just enough to gain access to the bolts linking the 2 boxes together. Remove the 2 lower and 2 upper bolts. It is possible to gain access to the upper bolts using a socket wrench with a U-joint and extension.

8. There is a protective cap on the forward driveshaft where it links up with the transfer case. The cap is made of a brittle material, so it *must be handled carefully*. Gently slide the cap forward until is free of the transfer case.

CAUTION: *The transfer case weighs about 55 lbs. If necessary, to handle this much weight, get a helper or another floorjack.*

9. Now, slide the transfer case to the rear so it can be separated from both the transmission and the forward driveshaft. When it is free, remove it.

10. Install the transfer case in the vehicle, bearing the following points in mind:

a. Inspect the dowel holes locating the transfer case with the transmission and the guide hole for the output shaft where it slides into the transfer case to make sure these parts will be properly located. Lubricate the guide pin and the splines of the front driveshaft section with grease.

b. When fitting the transfer case onto the transmission, check to make sure the output flange of the transmission is properly aligned with the flexible coupling. Put the through-

bolts through the flexible coupling and then install and torque the nuts to 65 ft. lbs. while holding the bolts stationary, rather than turning them.

c. When reconnecting the transfer case to the gearbox, torque the bolts to 30 ft. lbs.

d. Before fitting the driveshaft back onto the rear of the transmission, retain the seal in the protective cap by applying grease to it.

e. Torque the transmission crossmember bolts to 17 ft. lbs.

f. Check the fluid level and fill with the recommended lubricant.

Cars with Automatic Transmission

NOTE: *To perform this procedure, a special, large wrench that locks onto flats on alternate sides of a section of the rear driveshaft is required. Use BMW special tool No. 26 1 060 or an equivalent that is available in the aftermarket.*

1. Raise the car and support it securely at the 4 corners so it will be possible to work underneath it safely. Remove the exhaust system. Unbolt and remove the exhaust system heat shields located behind and below the transfer case.

2. Unscrew the rear section of the driveshaft at the sliding joint located behind the output flange of the transfer case.

3. Hold the through-bolts stationary and remove the self-locking nuts from in front of the flexible coupling at the transfer case output flange. Discard all the self-locking nuts and replace them.

CAUTION: *During the next step, be careful not to let the driveshaft rest on the metal fuel line that crosses underneath it, or the line could be damaged!*

4. Slide the sections of the driveshaft together at the sliding joint and then pull the front of the driveshaft off the centering pin at the transmission output shaft.

5. Remove the nuts and through bolts from the flexible coupling linking the transmission output flange with the short driveshaft linking the transmission and the transfer case.

6. Note the locations of all the washers and then loosen the retaining nut and disconnect the range selector lever cable at the transmission by pulling out the pin. Be careful not to bend the cable in doing this. Then, loosen the nuts that position the cable housing onto the transmission and slide the cable housing backward so it can be separated from the bracket on the transmission housing.

7. There is a protective cap on the forward driveshaft where it links up with the transfer case. The cap is made of a brittle material, so it

must be handled carefully. Gently slide the cap forward until is free of the transfer case.

8. Remove the drain plug in the bottom of the pan and drain the transmission fluid.

9. Support the transmission from underneath in a secure manner (supported squarely with a floorjack). Then, mark each of the 4 bolts fastening the crossmember that supports the transmission at the rear to the body (bolts are of different lengths). Remove the crossmember.

CAUTION: *The transfer case weighs about 55 lbs. If necessary to handle this much weight, get a helper or another floorjack.*

10. Remove the nine nuts fastening the transfer case to the transmission housing. Note the location of the wiring holder so it will be possible to reinstall it on the same bolt.

11. Slide the transfer case to the rear and off the transmission.

12. Install the transfer case in the vehicle, bearing the following points in mind:

  a. Inspect the sealing surfaces as well as the dowel holes in the transfer case to make sure they will seal and locate properly. Clean the sealing surfaces and replace the gasket.

  b. When sliding the transfer case back onto the transmission, turn the front driveshaft section slightly to help make the splines mesh.

  c. When reconnecting the shift cable, inspect the rubber mounts and replace any that are cut, crushed, or cracked. Adjust the shift cable.

  d. Before fitting the driveshaft back onto the rear of the transmission, retain the seal in the protective cap by applying grease to it.

  e. When fitting the transfer case onto the transmission, check to make sure the output flange of the transmission is properly aligned with the flexible coupling. Put the through-bolts through the flexible coupling and then install and torque the nuts to 65 ft. lbs. while holding the bolts stationary, rather than turning them.

  f. Torque the bolts holding the transfer case to the transmission to 65 ft. lbs.

  g. Torque the transmission crossmember bolts to 17 ft. lbs.

  h. Check the fluid level and fill with the recommended lubricant.

DRIVELINE

Driveshaft and U-Joints

BMW U-joints are not serviced. If U-joint bearings are worn or defective, the entire driveshaft must be replaced.

REMOVAL AND INSTALLATION

Except Below

1. On the 5 and 6 series cars, remove the entire exhaust system. On the 1984-86 733i and 735i remove just the muffler.

2. On the 320i, detach the outer pipe at the manifold and support it at the transmission.

3. Remove the heat shield near the fuel tank, if so equipped. On 1984-88 733i, 735i, this requires loosening the automatic transmission rear crossmember bolts slightly on the right side for clearance. On 6 and 7 Series models now also use BMW Special Tool 26 1 040 or

Special clamping tool installed on the flexible coupling

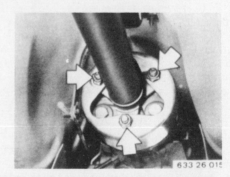

Some models have a guard over the flexible coupling

Checking driveshaft alignment

equivalent to loosen the threaded sleeve attaching the rear of the driveshaft to the front of the center bearing.

4. Disconnect the driveshaft at the transmission by removing the nuts and bolts from the flexible coupling. If the car has a vibration damper where the shaft connects to the transmission, turn the damper 60° counterclockwise and remove it with the rubber coupling.

NOTE: *On 1982 733i, install a special clamping tool (BMW-261011) or equivalent around the coupling and remove the bolts.*

5. Loosen the center bearing bolts and remove them.

Troubleshooting Basic Driveshaft and Rear Axle Problems

When abnormal vibrations or noises are detected in the driveshaft area, this chart can be used to help diagnose possible causes. Remember that other components such as wheels, tires, rear axle and suspension can also produce similar conditions.

BASIC DRIVESHAFT PROBLEMS

Problem	Cause	Solution
Shudder as car accelerates from stop or low speed	• Loose U-joint • Defective center bearing	• Replace U-joint • Replace center bearing
Loud clunk in driveshaft when shifting gears	• Worn U-joints	• Replace U-joints
Roughness or vibration at any speed	• Out-of-balance, bent or dented driveshaft • Worn U-joints • U-joint clamp bolts loose	• Balance or replace driveshaft • Replace U-joints • Tighten U-joint clamp bolts
Squeaking noise at low speeds	• Lack of U-joint lubrication	• Lubricate U-joint; if problem persists, replace U-joint
Knock or clicking noise	• U-joint or driveshaft hitting frame tunnel • Worn CV joint	• Correct overloaded condition • Replace CV joint

BASIC REAR AXLE PROBLEMS

First, determine when the noise is most noticeable.

Drive Noise: Produced under vehicle acceleration.

Coast Noise: Produced while the car coasts with a closed throttle.

Float Noise: Occurs while maintaining constant car speed (just enough to keep speed constant) on a level road.

Road Noise

Brick or rough surfaced concrete roads produce noises that seem to come from the rear axle. Road noise is usually identical in Drive or Coast and driving on a different type of road will tell whether the road is the problem.

Tire Noise

Tire noises are often mistaken for rear axle problems. Snow treads or unevenly worn tires produce vibrations seeming to originate elsewhere. **Temporarily** inflating the tires to 40 lbs will significantly alter tire noise, but will have no effect on rear axle noises (which normally cease below about 30 mph).

Engine/Transmission Noise

Determine at what speed the noise is most pronounced, then stop the car in a quiet place. With the transmission in Neutral, run the engine through speeds corresponding to road speeds where the noise was noticed. Noises produced with the car standing still are coming from the engine or transmission.

Front Wheel Bearings

While holding the car speed steady, lightly apply the footbrake; this will often decease bearing noise, as some of the load is taken from the bearing.

Rear Axle Noises

Eliminating other possible sources can narrow the cause to the rear axle, which normally produces noise from worn gears or bearings. Gear noises tend to peak in a narrow speed range, while bearing noises will usually vary in pitch with engine speeds.

NOISE DIAGNOSIS

The Noise Is	Most Probably Produced By
• Identical under Drive or Coast	• Road surface, tires or front wheel bearings
• Different depending on road surface	• Road surface or tires
• Lower as the car speed is lowered	• Tires
• Similar with car standing or moving	• Engine or transmission
• A vibration	• Unbalanced tires, rear wheel bearing, unbalanced driveshaft or worn U-joint
• A knock or click about every 2 tire revolutions	• Rear wheel bearing
• Most pronounced on turns	• Damaged differential gears
• A steady low-pitched whirring or scraping, starting at low speeds	• Damaged or worn pinion bearing
• A chattering vibration on turns	• Wrong differential lubricant or worn clutch plates (limited slip rear axle)
• Noticed only in Drive, Coast or Float conditions	• Worn ring gear and/or pinion gear

6. On 1982 733i, with manual transmission, loosen the crossmember and push the left end forward.

7. Disconnect the driveshaft at the final drive. Bend the driveshaft down and pull out.

8. Installation is the reverse of removal.

9. The driveshaft is balanced as an assembly and must only be renewed as a complete assembly.

10. Align the driveshaft with a gauge (BMW-21-1-000) (use 26 1 000 on 1984-86 733i, 735i) or equivalent by moving the center bearing sideways or by placing washers underneath the center bearing (this is not required on 6 Series cars).

11. On the 1982-83 733i, remove the special coupling tool only after the nuts have been tightened to prevent stress on the coupling.

12. Preload the center bearing by 2mm in the forward direction (4-6mm on 6 Series cars).

13. Wherever self-locking nuts are used, replace them. Hold the nut or bolt in place where is runs through a U-joint, and torque at the opposite end; where the driveshaft flange is located. Check the center bearing for lubrication and if it's dry, lubricate with Molykote® Longterm 2 or equivalent.

325iX (Front Wheel Drive)

CAUTION: *Never drive the car using front wheel drive when the rear driveshaft is removed, or the lockup system in the transfer case may be damaged.*

1. Remove the exhaust system. Remove both exhaust system heat shields.

2. Loosen the threaded sleeve near the front of the driveshaft with 26 2 060 oor 26 1 040 or the equivalent. Turn the sleeve several turns outward, but do not disconnect it entirely.

3. Disconnect the driveshaft at the output flange of the transfer case by removing the nuts and through bolts.

4. Disconnect the driveshaft at the final drive by removing the nuts and through bolts.

CAUTION: *Make sure the drive axle does not rest on the fuel line that runs across under it.*

5. Slide the sections of the driveshaft together and then slide it out of the centering pin on the output flange of the transfer case. Remove it from the car.

6. Install the driveshaft in reverse order, bearing these points in mind:

  a. Wherever self-locking nuts are used, replace them.

  b. Hold the nut or bolt in place where is runs through a U-joint, and torque at the opposite end; where the driveshaft flange is located.

  c. Check the center bearing for lubrication and if it's dry, lubricate with Molykote® Longterm 2 or equivalent.

1987-88 735i

NOTE: *If the car has a front universal joint, use special tools 24 0 120 and 00 2 020 to support the transmission during this operation.*

1. Remove the exhaust system. Remove the heat shield from the floorpan. Remove the nuts and bolts fastening the driveshaft to the transmission at the flexible coupling. Replace the self-locking nuts.

2. If the car has a front U-joint, support the transmission from underneath with tools 24 0 120 or the equivalent. When the transmission is securely supported, remove the 6 bolts and remove the rear transmission mounting crossmember.

3. Remove the self-locking nuts and then the bolts fastening the driveshaft to the final drive. Replace the self-locking nuts. Remove the driveshaft, taking care to keep it protected from dirt.

4. Remove the bolts from the crossbrace underneath and remove the center propshaft mount. Then, bend the shaft at the middle and remove it from the car by pulling it off the centering pin on the forward end.

5. Install in reverse order, keeing the following points in mind:

a. Repack the CV joining with approved grease and replace the gasket, if necessary.

b. Check the center bearing for lubrication and if it's dry, lubricate with Molykote® Longterm 2 or equivalent.

c. If the vibration damper at the forward end of the driveshaft must be replaced, turn it 60° to remove it.

d. When remounting the center mount, preload it forward from its most natural position 4-6mm.

e. Torque U-joint bolts to 52 ft. lbs. and CV-joint bolts to 51 ft. lbs.

528e, 535i and 633CSi with CV-Joint

NOTE: *To perform this procedure, procure a set of tools designed to support the transmission via the pan BMW tools 24 0 120 and 00 2 020 or equivalent.*

1. Support the transmission from underneath with the special tools and a floorjack. Remove the nuts and washers from the transmission mounts on top of the rear transmission mounting crossmember. Loosen but do not remove the nuts located underneath which fasten the crossmember to the body. Then, slide this crossmember as far to the rear as it will go.

2. Unscrew the fastening nuts on the forward end of the CV-joint and then discard them.

3. Using a prybar to keep the driveshaft from turning, remove the self locking nuts and bolts fastening the rear of the driveshaft to the final drive.

4. Remove the bolts fastening the center mount to the body. Bend the propshaft down and pull the CV-joint off the transmission flange. Cover the joint to keep it clean.

5. Replace the gasket that fits between the joint bolts. Install in reverse order, keeping these points in mind:

a. Replace the self-locking nuts used at either end of the shaft.

b. Preload the center mount forward by forcing the bracket 4-5mm forward from the neutral position on 5 Series cars and 4-6mm forward on 6 Series cars.

318i, 325, 325e, 325i, 325iS and M3

1. Remove the mufflers. Unscrew and remove the exhaust system heat shield near the fuel tank.

2. Unbolt and remove the cross brace that runs under the driveshaft.

3. Support the transmission. The automatic transmission must be supported by the case and not the pan. BMW makes a jig and support (No. 24 0 120 and 00 2 020) for this. Loosen all transmission support bolts and remove. Remove the transmission rear support crossmember.

4. Lower the manual transmission for clearance. Remove the driveshaft bolts from the front coupling.

CAUTION: *Make sure the drive axle does not rest on the fuel line that runs across under it!*

5. Unscrew and remove bolts at the coupling near the final drive.

6. Loosen the threaded sleeve on the driveshaft with a tool such as BMW 26 1 040. Unbolt and remove the center mount.

7. Bend the driveshaft downward and remove it, being careful not to allow it to rest on the connecting line on the fuel tank.

8. Upon installation:

a. Mount the holder for the oxygen sensor plug.

b. Make sure the heat shield clears the fuel tank.

c. Wherever self-locking nuts are used, replace them. On the transmission-end flange, tighten the nuts/bolts only on the flange side, holding the other end stationary.

d. Preload the center mount to 2-4mm in the forward direction on the 318i and 4-6mm on other models before tightening the bolts. Torque the mounting bolts to 16 ft. lbs.

Remove circlip (2) and dust guard (3)

Drive center bearing onto grooved ball bearing

e. Lubricate the center bearing with Molykote® Longterm 2 or equivalent if it is dry.

f. Make sure to reinstall the bracket for the oxygen sensor plug.

g. Make sure that there is sufficient clearance between the rear heat shield and fuel tank.

Front Driveshaft and U-Joints

REMOVAL AND INSTALLATION

325iX (Front Wheel Drive)

CAUTION: *Never drive the car with either driveshaft disconnected. This could damage the lockup mechanism in the transfer case.*

1. Remove the nuts at the front drive axle input flange. Discard the nuts and replace them with new self-locking nuts. Remove the 6 through-bolts.

2. Gently push the driveshaft to the rear. Then, remove the coupling and centering disc from the front drive axle.

3. Pull the driveshaft and protective cap out of the front of the transfer case and remove it.

4. To install, reverse the removal procedure, bearing the following points in mind:

a. Inspect the cap and seal for the area of the transfer case where the driveshaft engages. Replace parts, if necessary. After engaging the shaft with the transfer case, slide the protective cap back over the front of the transfer case.

b. Inspect the seal on the output flange for the front drive axle and replace it if necessary.

c. When reinstalling the coupling at the rear of the front drive axle, make sure the 3 arrows line up with the 3 flange arms.

d. When installing the bolts and nuts for the front driveshaft coupling, install the bolts and then hold them stationary with a wrench while installing new self locking nuts.

Center Driveshaft Bearing

REMOVAL AND INSTALLATION

1600, 2000 and 2002

1. With the driveshaft removed, remove the coupling nut.

2. Using a standard puller, pull off the center bearing without the dust guard plate.

3. Remove the grooved ball bearing with a puller.

4. Using a standard puller, install the ball bearing and install the driveshaft.

All 5, 6, and 7 Series Cars Except 528e, 535i, 633CSi, M5 and M6 Without Splines,

1. Bend down the driveshaft and pull it out of the centering pin on the transmission (refer to "Driveshaft Removal and Installation").

Remove the circlip and dust cap—six cylinder models

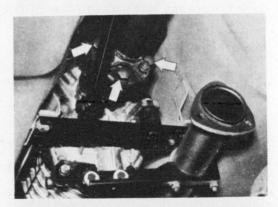

Disconnecting front rubber coupling from transmission flange

Disconnecting driveshaft from differential flange

2. Loosen the threaded bushing. On 1983-86 733, 735, also remove the felt ring.

3. Mark the driveshaft position on slide with a punch mark and pull the front half of the driveshaft out of the slide.

4. Remove the circlip and dust guard.

5. Using a standard puller remove the center bearing without the dust guard.

6. Use a puller and remove the grooved ball bearing in the center bearing. On 1983-88 733i and 735i, press the grooved ball bearing into the center mount.

7. Installation is the reverse of removal. Lubricate the splines with Molykote® Longterm 2 or equivalent. Drive the center bearing onto the grooved ball bearing with tool (BMW-24-1-050) or equivalent. On 1983-88 733i and 735i, check the installed position of the dust guard. It must be flush with the center mount.

1987-88 M5 and M6
528e, 535i and 633CSi
Without Splines

NOTE: *This type of propshaft has the 2 sections bolted together just behind the center bearing. Use a press and a puller to complete this operation.*

1. Remove the driveshaft as described above. Matchmark the relationship between the forward and rear sections of the shaft at the center bearing.

2. Remove the bolt that fastens the forward U-joint section to the center mount.

3. Using a standard puller remove the center mount and bearing without the dust guard.

4. Press the old bearing out of the mount and press a new one in. Then, use a mandrel 24 1 040 or equivalent to drive the bearing center race onto the driveshaft.

5. Assemble the driveshaft in reverse order, lining up its halves with the matchmarks. Install the bolt fastening the shaft sections together with a locking type of sealer, torquing to 72 ft. lbs.

320i

1. With the driveshaft removed, mark the shaft's location to the coupling.

2. Remove the circlip and pull out the driveshaft.

3. Using a standard puller remove the center bearing without its dust cover.

4. Drive the grooved ball bearing out of the center bearing.

5. Installation is the reverse of removal.

318i, 325, 325e, 325i, 325iS, 325iX and M3

1. Remove the driveshaft as described above. Since the shaft is a balanced assembly, matchmark both halves so it can be reassembled in the same position.

2. Unscrew the threaded sleeve (1), and remove the front propshaft section. Remove the washer (2) and rubber ring (3). A BMW special tool is shown, but it is possible to loosen the sleeve with an ordinary wrench, provided a way is carefully devised to hold the propshaft against the torque required to loosen the sleeve without damaging it.

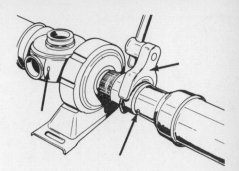

In replacing the center mount on the driveshaft on the 318i, unscrew the threaded sleeve as shown. Matchmark the assembly prior to taking it apart as shown by the arrows.

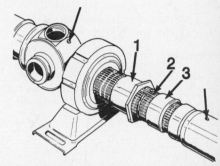

When assembling the driveshaft on the 318i, push on the threaded sleeve (1), washer (2), and rubber ring (3)

3. Lift out the circlip and remove the dustguard behind it.

4. Pull out the center mount and ball bearing with a puller.

5. Lay the center mount on a flat plate and press the new ball bearing in with even pressure all around the outer race.

6. Install the dust guard and then drive the center mount onto the splined portion of the shaft. Make sure the dust guard is installed flush with the center mount and that the center mount will operate with adequate clearance.

7. Assemble the shaft with matchmarks aligned. Push on the threaded sleeve, washer, and rubber ring (do not tighten the threaded sleeve yet).

8. Install the driveshaft as described above. Then, tighten the threaded sleeve.

Flexible Coupling Centering Ring
REMOVAL AND INSTALLATION

1600, 2000, 2002, 2500, 2800, Bavaria, 3000 and 3.0

1. Press off the sealing cap.

2. Lift out the circlip.

3. Take out the ball cup, centering ring, disc and spring.

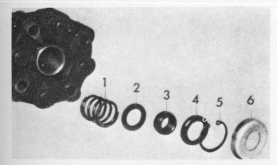

Centering ring components: spring (1); washer (2); centering ring (3); ball socket (4); retaining ring (5); and sealing cap (6)

4. Fill the centering assembly with approximately 6g (0.2 oz.) of grease and install the ball cup, centering ring, disc and spring. Install the circlip. Install the sealing cap.

All Other Models

1. Fill the center with grease and using a 14mm (0.551") dia. mandrel, drive out the ring.
2. Installation is the reverse of removal.
NOTE: *The shaft ring faces out.*

DRIVE AXLE

Understanding Rear Axles

The rear axle is a special type of transmission that reduces the speed of the drive from the engine and transmission and divides the power to the rear wheels. Power enters the rear axle from the driveshaft via the companion flange.The flange is mounted on the drive pinion shaft. The drive pinion shaft and gear which carry the power into the differential turn at engine speed. The gear on the end of the pinion shaft drives a large ring gear the axis of rotation of which is 90 degrees away from the of the pinion. The pinion and gear reduce the gear ratio of the axle, and change the direction of rotation to turn the axle shafts which drive both wheels. The rear axle gear ratio is found by dividing the number of pinion gear teeth into the number of ring gear teeth.

The ring gear drives the differential case. The case provides the two mounting points for the ends of a pinion shaft on which are mounted two pinion gears. The pinion gears drive the two side gears, one of which is located on the inner end of each axle shaft.

By driving the axle shafts through the arrangement, the differential allows the outer drive wheel to turn faster than the inner drive wheel in a turn.

The main drive pinion and the side bearings, which bear the weight of the differential case, are shimmed to provide proper bearing preload, and to position the pinion and ring gears properly.

NOTE: *The proper adjustment of the relationship of the ring and pinion gears is critical. It should be attempted only by those with extensive equipment and/or experience.*

Limited-slip differentials include clutches which tend to link each axle shaft to the differential case. Clutches may be engaged either by spring action or by pressure produced by the torque on the axles during a turn. During turning on a dry pavement, the effects of the clutches are overcome, and each wheel turns at the required speed. When slippage occurs at either wheel, however, the clutches will transmit some of the power to the wheel which has the greater amount of traction. Because of the presence of clutches, limited-slip units require a special lubricant.

Determining Axle Ratio

The drive axle is said to have a certain axle ratio. This number (usually a whole number and a decimal fraction) is actually a comparison of the number of gear teeth on the ring gear and the pinion gear. For example, a 4.11 rear means that theoretically, there are 4.11 teeth on the ring gear and one tooth on the pinion gear or, put another way, the driveshaft must turn 4.11 times to turn the wheels once. Actually, on a 4.11 rear, there might be 37 teeth on the ring gear and 9 teeth on the pinion gear. By dividing the number of teeth on the pinion gear into the number of teeth on the ring gear, the numerical axle ratio (4.11) is obtained. This also provides a good method of ascertaining exactly what axle ratio one is dealing with.

Another method of determining gear ratio is to jack up and support the car so that both rear wheels are off the ground. Make a chalk mark on the rear wheel and the driveshaft. Put the transmission in neutral. Turn the rear wheel one complete turn and count the number of turns that the driveshaft makes. The number of turns that the driveshaft makes in one complete revolution of the rear wheel is an approximation of the rear axle ratio.

Identification

Generally, BMW axle ratios do not vary with options (such as automatic transmission), but only with engine size. The axle ratio, as well as an alpha-numerical identification code required in ordering parts, are displayed on the outside of the housing.

Output Shaft
REMOVAL AND INSTALLATION

Except 325iX (Front Wheel Drive Front Axle)

1. Detach the output shaft at the final drive and drive flange.

2. On the 1982 733i, support the control arm as the spring strut and shock absorber are detached.

3. The spring strut serves as a retaining strap and the trailing arm must be supported if the spring strut is detached.

4. Replace the bellows as follows:

   a. Take off the sealing cover.

   b. Remove the circlip.

   c. Unscrew the clamp on the dust cover. Take off the dust cover.

   d. Press off the inner cover.

   e. Press the output shaft out of the constant velocity joint. Make sure in doing this that the bearing inner race is supported.

   f. Place the dust cover and inside cover on the output shaft.

   g. Coat the splined threads with Loctite® 270 or equivalent. Keep the compound out of ball races.

   h. Press the joint and cap on and install the circlip.

Constant velocity type output shaft

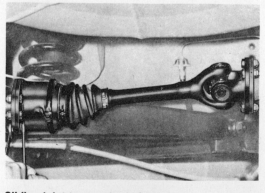

Sliding joint type output shaft

   i. Pack the joint and bellows with CV-joint grease. Clean the sealing surfaces to remove grease. Then, coat the larger diameter end of the bellows with an adhesive and secure with new clamps. Seal the cover with Curil or equivalent and install it.

325iX (Front Wheel Drive)

NOTE: *A number of special tools are required to perform this operation. Use the BMW factory numbers given to shop for these from factory sources, or to cross-reference similar tools that may be available in the aftermarket. Use 33 4 050 and 00 5 500 to drive in a new lockplate for the brake disc. The tie rod must be pressed off with 342 2 070. Control arms are pressed off with 31 2 160. Use 33 2 112 and 33 2 113 to press the output shafts out of the brake discs and 33 2 112, 33 2 124 and 33 4 042 to press them back in. On the left side, the output shaft is pulled out of the drive axle with 31 5 011 and 30 31 581. On the right side, 31 5 011 and 31 5 012 are used to pull the output shaft out of the axle.*

1. Raise the car and support it securely. Remove the front wheels. Remove the drain plug and drain the lube oil from the front axle.

2. Lift out the lockplate in the center of the brake disc with a screwdriver. Then, unscrew the collar nut.

3. Remove the attaching nut from each tie rod and then press the rod off the steering knuckle with 33 2 070.

4. Remove the retaining nut and then press the control arm off the steering knuckle on either side.

5. Mount 33 2 112 and 33 2 113 to the brake disc with 2 wheel bolts. Press the output shaft out of the center of the steering knuckle on that side. Repeat on the other side.

6. To remove the drive axle from the differential on the left side: Install special tool 31 5 011 by bolting it together around the axle so that the ring on its inner diameter fits into the groove on the shaft. Install 30 31 581 onto the shaft so it will rest against the housing ang the bolt heads of 31 5 011 will rest against it. Screw the 2 bolts in alternately in small increments to get even pressure on the shaft, pulling it out of the differential.

7. To remove the drive axle on the right side: Install 31 5 012 on the diameter of the shaft directly against the housing. Install 31 5 011 by bolting it together around the axle so that the ring on its inner diameter fits into the groove on the shaft. Screw the 2 bolts in alternately in small increments to get even pressure on the shaft, pulling it out of the differential.

8. Install the halfshafts, bearing the following points in mind:

a. Install the shafts into the housing until the circlip inside engages in the groove of the shaft. It may be necessary to install the removal tool and tap against it with a plastic-headed hammer to drive the shaft far enough into the housing.

b. Before installing the shafts into the steering knuckle, coat the spline with light oil.

c. When installing the control arms onto the steering knuckle, torque the nut to 61.5 ft. lbs. and use a new cotter pin. When installing the tie rod onto the steering knuckle, torque to 61.5 ft. lbs. and use a new self-locking nut.

d. Drive a new lockplate into the brake disc with 33 4 050 and 00 5 500. Torque the nut to 181 ft. lbs.

e. Replace the drain plug and refill the final drive unit with the required lubricant.

Rear Axle Shaft, Wheel Bearings, and Seals

REMOVAL AND INSTALLATION

6-Cylinder Models Except 325, 325e, 325i, 325iS, 325iX, 1983-84 733i and 735i

1. Remove the wheel.
2. Loosen the brake caliper and leave the brake line connected.
3. Remove the brake disc.
4. Remove the driving flange as follows:
   a. Disconnect the output shaft.
   b. Remove the lockplate.
   c. Loosen the collared nut and pull off the drive flange.
5. Tighten the collared nut and drive off the rear axle shaft.
6. Drive off the wheel bearings and seals toward the outside.
7. Install the wheel bearings and seals. Install the drive flange and lockplate. Install the brake disc and caliper. Install the wheel.

Lock the collared nut in the drive flange groove (arrowed)

Axle bearing components—four cylinder models

Removing the output shaft on the 318i. Use two wheel bolts to fasten the bridge (33 2 112), and then press the shaft out as shown.

320i

1. Remove the wheel.
2. Remove the cotter pin from the castellated nut.
3. Apply the handbrake.
4. Loosen the castellated nut.
5. Release the handbrake.
6. Remove the brake drum.

Check the spacer (arrowed) and radial oil seals, and replace the drive flange and seals, as necessary

Determine installation play:

A = 64.0 mm (2.5197")
−B = 61.0 mm (2.4016")

3.0 mm (0.1181")
−0.1 mm (0.0039") play

C 2.9 mm (0.1142")
shim thickness

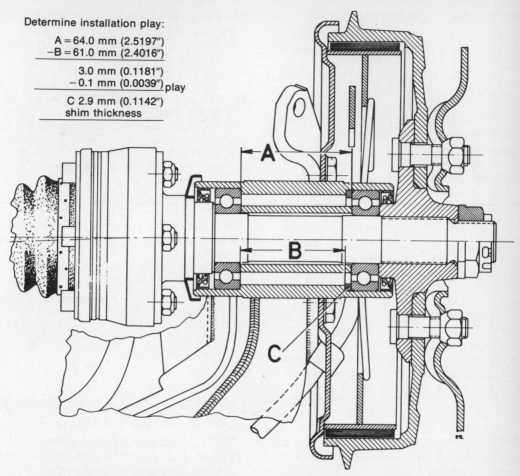

Cross-section of the rear axle hub showing bearing adjustment lengths—typical

7. Pull off the drive flange with a puller.
8. Disconnect the output shaft and tie it up.
9. Drive out the halfshaft with a plastic hammer using the castellated nut to protect the end of the shaft.
10. Drive out the bearing and sealing ring.

11. Take out the spacer sleeve and shim.
12. Install bearing and seal ring, install the drive flange and connect the output shaft.
13. Install the brake drum and tighten the castellated nut, use a new cotter pin.
14. Install the wheel.

Driving out rear axle shaft—4 cylinder models

Wheel bearing with rear axle shaft removed—6 cylinder models

318i, 325, 325e, 325i, 325iS, 325iX and M3

1. Lift out the lockplate and remove the retaining nut from the output flange. Remove the flange.

2. Disconnect the output shaft from the final drive and suspend it.

3. Press out the output shaft with a special tool set 33 2 110 or equivalent. Bolt the bridge to the brake drum (or disc on 325e) with 2 wheel bolts and hold it with an open-end wrench. Force the output shaft toward the center of the car via the spindle by turning the threaded portion of the tool.

4. Drive out the rear axle shaft with tool 33 4 010 or equivalent.

5. Lift out the circlip. Then, pull out the wheel bearings with special tool 33 4 040 or equivalent. On the 325e (with disc brakes and larger bearings), use 33 4 031.

6. Pull out the seal with a tool such as 33 4 045.

7. If the inner bearing shell is damaged, pull it off with a puller and thrust pad.

8. To install, pull in the wheel bearing assembly, pull in the seal, insert the circlip and then pull in the rear axle shaft, all in reverse of steps above. Use 33 4 040 except on 325e; on that model, use 33 4 049. Install the axle shaft seal with a tool such as 33 4 045.

9. To install the output shaft, screw the threaded spindle into the shaft all the way, and then use the nut and washer against the outside of the bridge.

10. Reconnect the output shaft to the final drive.

11. Lubricate the bearing surface of the outer nut with oil. Then install and torque the nut.

12. Using installers 33 4 050 and 00 5 000 or equivalent, knock in the lockplate. Use the following torque figures:

Output shaft to drive flange — 42-46 ft. lb.
Drive flange hub to output shaft — 140-152 ft. lb.

1982-83 528e, 535i and 633CSi
1983-84 M5, M6 and 733i
All 735i

1. Remove the rear wheel. Disconnect the output shaft at the outer flange and suspend it with wire.

2. Unbolt the caliper and suspend it with the brake line connected. Unbolt and remove the rear disc.

3. Remove the large nut and remove the lockplate. If the car has ABS, disconnect and then remove the ABS speed sensor by unscrewing it.

4. Use a special tool BMW 33 4 000 or equivalent and 2 M10 x 30 bolts to unscrew the collar nut. Then, pull off the drive flange with tools 00 7 501 and 00 7 502.

5. Screw on the collar nut until it is just flush with the end of the shaft and use a soft (nylon) hammer to knock out the shaft.

6. Remove the circlip. Then, use special tools 33 4 031, 33 4 032 and 33 4 038 or equivalent to pull off the wheel bearings.

7. Pull the inner bearing race off the axle shaft with special tool 00 7 500 or equivalent.

8. Pull the new bearing assembly in with special tools 33 4 036, 33 4 032, and 33 4 038 or equivalent.

9. Install special tool 33 4 037 or equivalent. Then, reinstall the circlip.

10. Pull the rear axle shaft through with special tools 23 1 300, 33 4 080 and 33 4 020 or equivalent.

11. Use special tool 33 4 000 or equivalent to tighten the collar nut.

12. Fit special tool 33 4 060 or equivalent into the lockplate and top it in with a slide hammer 00 5 000 or equivalent.

13. Reconnect the output shaft. Remount the brake disc and caliper.

Front Wheel Drive Hub and Bearings
REMOVAL AND INSTALLATION

NOTE: *A number of special tools are required to perform this operation. Read through the procedure and procure these before attempting to start work. Factory part numbers for tools are given, but it is possible to shop for equivalent tools, using these part numbers, in the aftermarket.*

1. Raise the car and support it securely. Remove the output halfshaft as described above. Then, remount the control arm with nuts just finger tight, to keep the spring strut in position.

2. Remove the upper and lower attaching bolts and remove the brake caliper, suspending it nearby with wire so that there is no tension on the brake hose.

3. Remove the allen bolt and remove the brake disc.

4. Bolt special tool 31 2 090 or equivalent to the knuckle with its 3 bolts. Then, mount 33 1 307 hooked around the tie rod arm and press the drive flange off. If it is scored, pull the bearing's inner race out of the drive flange with 33 1 307 and 00 7 500 or equivalent.

5. Compress the snapring with snapring pliers and remove it.

6. Remove 31 2 090 or the equivalent and replace 33 1 307 or its equivalent with a tool such as 31 2 070. Again install and use the combination, this time to press out the bearing.

7. Screw out the spindle of 31 2 090 and install 33 4 032 or equivalent so it is flush with the surface of 31 2 090. Use 33 4 034 and 33 4 038 to pull in the new bearing. Then, remove 31 2 090.

8. Install the circlip again, with snapring pliers, *making sure the open end faces downward.*

9. Pull the drive flange into place with 33 4 032 or equivalent, 33 4 038 or equivalent, 33 4 045 or equivalent, and 33 4 048 or equivalent.

10. Install the brake disc and caliper and the wheel in reverse order.

Suspension and Steering

FRONT SUSPENSION

The front suspension on all BMWs is fully independent, utilizing MacPherson type struts with integral coil springs (the springs surround the structure of the strut, which contains the shock absorber). Transverse mounted wishbones are used at the bottom to locate the lower end of the strut laterally as it moves up and down in relation to the body. A stabilizer bar is mounted between the front crossmember and the lower wishbones. All suspension mounts are rubber cushioned.

CAUTION: *When removing front suspension components, be sure to support the car securely via the reinforced boxmember area adjacent to the front jacking points.*

MacPherson Strut Assembly

REMOVAL AND INSTALLATION

NOTE: *Not too much in the way of special tools and equipment is required to remove the struts from the front of your BMW, although care should be taken in ensuring proper torquing of the fasteners during reassembly. However, once the strut is off the car, special equipment is required to disassemble it safely. You will either have to purchase a special spring compressor or take the strut to a qualified repair shop. Rebuilding the shock absorbers contained within the body of the strut requires a good deal of specialized equipment and knowledge. By removing the strut and, if you're equipped to handle it, removing the spring, you could, however, substantially reduce the cost of doing the work.*

1600, 2000 and 2002

1. Raise the vehicle and support it safely. Remove the wheel.
2. Disconnect the angle bracket from the strut assembly.
3. Disconnect the caliper, leaving the brake line attached. Tie the caliper to the vehicle body so that the weight is not supported by the brake hose.
4. Disconnect the lower arm from the axle beam.
5. Remove the lockwire and disconnect the track rod arm from the strut assembly.
6. Remove the 3 retaining nuts and detach the strut assembly at the wheelhouse.
7. Install the strut assembly at the wheelhouse.
8. When reattaching the wishbone at the front axle beam, use a new self-locking nut and make sure the spacer touches the axle beam.
9. Torque specifications are as follows:
- Strut thrust bearing at wheelhouse: 16-17.4 ft. lbs.
- Lower arm-to-axle: 123-137 ft. lbs. – this should be finalized after the vehicle has been lowered to the ground.
- Track rod arm from strut: 18-24 ft. lbs.
- Caliper-to-strut: 58-69 ft. lbs.

2500, 2800, Bavaria, 3000 and 3.0

1. Raise the vehicle and support it safely. Remove the wheel.
2. Disconnect the brake caliper and suspend it from the vehicle body with a wire. Do not remove the brake hose.
3. Disconnect the angle bracket from the strut assembly.
4. Remove the lock wire and disconnect the track rod arm from the strut assembly.
5. Remove the 3 retaining nuts and detach the strut assembly at the wheel house.
6. Install the strut assembly at the wheel house and connect the track rod.
7. Complete the installation and use the following torque figures:
- Brake caliper-to-strut: 59-70 ft. lbs.
- Track rod-to-strut: 33-44 ft. lbs.
- Bearing-to-wheelhouse: 16-18 ft. lbs.

318i, 325, 325e, 325i, 325iS and M3

1. Remove the front wheel. Disconnect the brake pad wear indicator plug and ground wire. Pull the wires out of the holder on the strut.

2. Unbolt the caliper and pull it away from the strut, suspending it with a piece of wore from the body. Do not disconnect the brake line.

3. Remove the attaching nut and then detach the push rod on the stabilizer bar at the strut.

4. Unscrew the attaching nut and press off the guide joint. Use special tool 31 1 110 or

Removing safety wiring from strut assembly— 1600, 2002

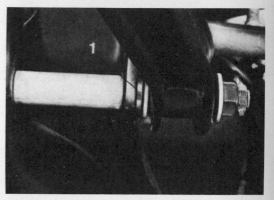

Proper installation of wishbone to front axle carrier with spacer ring (1) facing carrier

Troubleshooting Basic Steering and Suspension Problems

Problem	Cause	Solution
Hard steering (steering wheel is hard to turn)	• Low or uneven tire pressure • Loose power steering pump drive belt • Low or incorrect power steering fluid • Incorrect front end alignment • Defective power steering pump • Bent or poorly lubricated front end parts	• Inflate tires to correct pressure • Adjust belt • Add fluid as necessary • Have front end alignment checked/adjusted • Check pump • Lubricate and/or replace defective parts
Loose steering (too much play in the steering wheel)	• Loose wheel bearings • Loose or worn steering linkage • Faulty shocks • Worn ball joints	• Adjust wheel bearings • Replace worn parts • Replace shocks • Replace ball joints
Car veers or wanders (car pulls to one side with hands off the steering wheel)	• Incorrect tire pressure • Improper front end alignment • Loose wheel bearings • Loose or bent front end components • Faulty shocks	• Inflate tires to correct pressure • Have front end alignment checked/adjusted • Adjust wheel bearings • Replace worn components • Replace shocks
Wheel oscillation or vibration transmitted through steering wheel	• Improper tire pressures • Tires out of balance • Loose wheel bearings • Improper front end alignment • Worn or bent front end components	• Inflate tires to correct pressure • Have tires balanced • Adjust wheel bearings • Have front end alignment checked/adjusted • Replace worn parts
Uneven tire wear	• Incorrect tire pressure • Front end out of alignment • Tires out of balance	• Inflate tires to correct pressure • Have front end alignment checked/adjusted • Have tires balanced

Press the tie rod off the steering knuckle with a tool such as the BMW special tool pictured

Remove the three retaining nuts from the top of the strut housing—320i

equivalent except for M3; on M3, use 31 2 160 or equivalent.

5. Unscrew the nut and press off the tie rod joint.

6. Press the bottom of the strut outward and push it over the guide joint pin. Use 32 2 070 or equivalent for all but M3; for M3, use 31 2 160 or equivalent. Support the bottom of the strut.

7. Unscrew the nuts at the top of the strut (from inside the engine compartment) and then remove the strut.

8. Install the strut into position, keeping the following points in mind:

a. Replace the self-locking nuts that fasten the top of the strut.

b. Tie rod and guide joints must have both

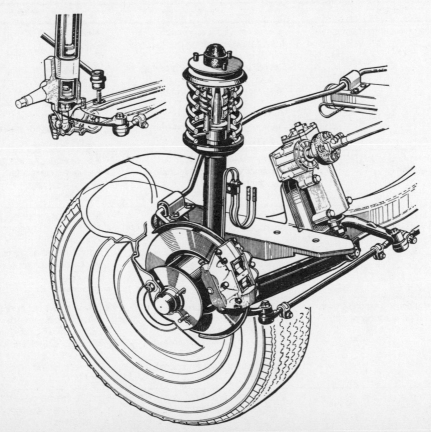

Front suspension and steering system—2002

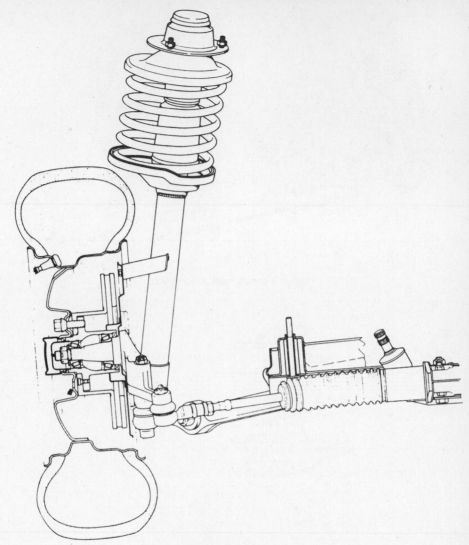

320i front suspension

The wheelhouse strut mounting nuts on 500 and 600 series cars

Tie rod arm-to-shock absorber retaining bolts—733i

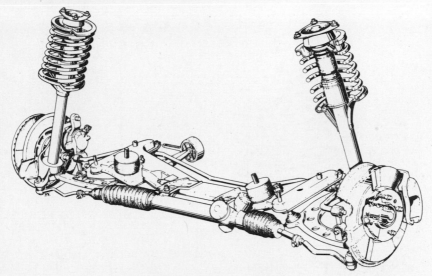

Typical 3 series front suspension

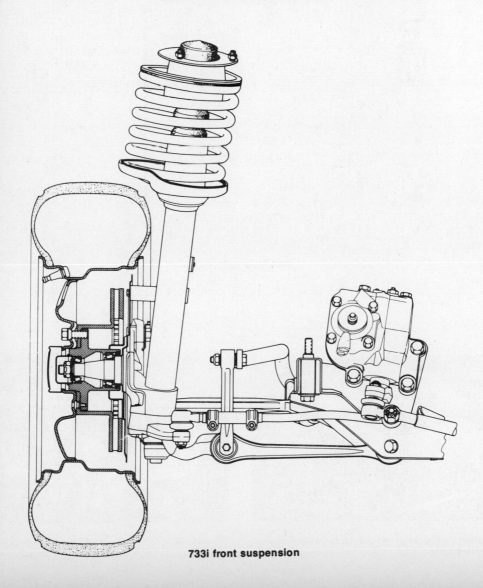

733i front suspension

pins and both bores clean for reassembly. Replace both self-locking nuts.

c. Torque the control arm to spring strut attaching nut to 43-51 ft. lbs. Torque the spring strut to wheel well nuts to 16-17 ft. lbs.

325iX

NOTE: *A number of special tools are required to perform this operation. Read through the procedure and procure these before attempting to start work. Factory part numbers for tools are given, but it is possible to shop for equivalent tools, using these part numbers, in the aftermarket.*

1. Raise the vehicle and support it securely by the chassis. Remove the front wheel. Unplug the ABS pulse transmitter.

2. Lift out the lockplate at the center of the brake disc with a screwdriver. Unscrew the collar nut.

3. Disconnect the brake pad wear indicator plug and the ground wire. Pull the wires and brake hose out of the clip on the spring strut. Then, disconnect the small rod at the strut.

4. Remove the brake caliper mounting bolts and support the assembly nearby with a piece of wire, keeping stress off the brake hose.

5. Remove the attaching nut from the tie rod end. Then press the stud off the knuckle with a tool such as 32 2 070.

6. Remove the attaching nut for the control arm and then press the stud off the knuckle with a tool such as 31 2 160.

7. Mount a tool such as 33 2 112 and 33 2 113 to the brake disc with 2 of the wheel bolts. Then, press the output shaft out of the center of the knuckle.

8. Support the spring strut from underneath. Remove the cap from the center of the wheel house. Remove the 3 bolts from the upper mount near the wheel housing. Remove the strut.

9. Install the strut into the vehicle, keeping these points in mind:

a. Torque the nuts attaching the strut to the wheel house to 16 ft. lbs.

b. Lubricate the splines of the output shaft with oil before pressing it back into the center of the knuckle. Use tools 33 2 112, 332 114, and 33 4 038 or equivalent.

c. Keep grease off the studs for the control arm and tie rod end. Replace the cotter pin on the control arm and the self-locking nut on the tie rod end. Torque the control arm stud nut to 61.5 ft. lbs. Torque the tie rod nut to 61.5 ft. lbs. and then tighten it further to install the cotter pin, if necessary.

d. Replace the lockplate in the center of the disc with tools such as 005 500 and 33 4 050.

e. Torque the bolts attaching the caliper to the steering knuckle to 63-79 ft. lbs.

320i

1. Raise the vehicle and support safely. Remove the wheel.

2. Detach the bracket at the strut assembly.

3. Disconnect and suspend the bake caliper

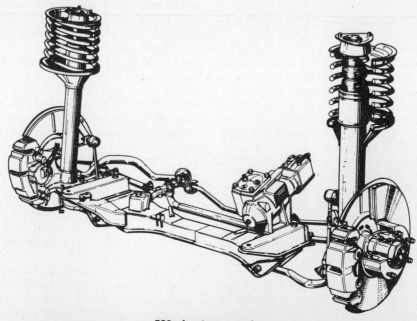

528e front suspension

with a wire from the vehicle body. Do not disconnect the brake line.

4. Remove the cotter pin and castle nut. Press the tie rod off the steering knuckle.

5. Remove the 3 retaining nuts and detach the strut assembly at the wheel house.

6. Install the strut assembly into the vehicle and attach it at the wheel house.

7. Install the cotter pin and castle nut and install the tie rod.

8. Connect the brake caliper and install the wheel.

1982 533i and 633CSi

1. Raise the vehicle and support safely. Remove the wheel.

2. Disconnect the bracket at the strut assembly.

3. Disconnect the brake caliper and suspend from the vehicle body with wire. Do not remove the brake hose.

4. Remove the lock wire and disconnect the tie rod arm at the strut assembly.

5. Remove the 3 retaining nuts and detach the strut assembly at the wheelhouse.

6. Install the strut assembly into the vehicle and attach it at the wheel house.

7. Install the cotter pin and castle nut and install the tie rod.

8. Connect the brake caliper and install the wheel.

524td, 528e
1983-84 533i 535i
1983-84 633CSi
635CSi, M5, M6
1987-88 735i

1. Raise the vehicle and support it securely. Remove the front wheel.

2. Disconnect the brake caliper and suspend it with a piece of wire so there is no tension on the brake hose (do not disconnect the hose).

3. If removing the left side strut, lift the electrical plug out of the clip on the strut, disconnect the ground wire, and disconnect the plug.

4. On cars with ABS, disconnect the ABS pulse transmitter at the strut.

5. Disconnect the stabilizer push rod at the bracket on the side of the strut; To do this, use a wrench to hold the rod end on the flats just outside the bracket and unscrew the nut from the inside of the bracket.

6. Remove the bolts from the underside of the tie rod arm that attach the bottom of the strut to the arm. Then, move the strut outward.

7. On the 735i, remove the cap. Support the bottom of the strut and then remove the 3 nuts attaching the strut to the top of the fender well.

8. Install the strut in position on the vehicle.

9. Use new self-locking nuts on the studs that pass through the fender well. Align the bottom of the strut with the tie rod arm so the tab on the arm fits into the notch on the bottom of the strut.

1982 733i

1. Raise the vehicle and support safely. Remove the wheel.

2. Disconnect the vibration strut from the control arm.

3. Disconnect the bracket and clamps from the strut assembly.

4. Disconnect the wire connection and press out the wire from the clamp on the spring strut tube.

5. Remove the brake caliper and suspend it from the vehicle body with a wire. Do not remove the brake hose.

6. Disconnect the tie rod from the shock absorber.

7. Remove the 3 retaining nuts and disconnect the strut assembly from the wheelhouse.

8. Install the strut assembly into the vehicle and attach it at the wheel house.

9. Install the cotter pin and castle nut and install the tie rod.

10. Connect the brake caliper and install the wheel.

1983-84 733i
1985-86 735i

1. Raise the vehicle and support it safely by the body. Remove the front wheel. Detach the brake line bracket and clamp from the strut.

2. Pull off the rubber cover, and then use an Allen type wrench to unbolt the antilock sensor at the rear of the caliper. Remove it.

3. Pull the antilock sensor electrical connector out of the holder and unplug it. Disconnect the ground wire.

4. Detach the caliper and suspend it from the body without disconnecting the brake line.

5. Support the strut in a secure manner at the bottom. Remove the self-locking nut and through bolt connecting the lower end of the vibration strut where it connects to the control arm.

6. Then, remove the 3 self-locking nuts from the top of the strut housing in the engine compartment, and remove the strut.

7. Install the strut in position on the vehicle, noting the following points:

a. Use new self-locking nuts on the top of the strut housing and at the connection to the control arm.

b. When reconnecting the lower strut to the track arm, clean the bolt threads and bolt holes and install the bolts with a special bolt tightener HWB No. 81 22 9 400 086 or equivalent.

Strut assembly mounted in spring compressor tool BMW 6035—1600, 2002

Removing telescopic leg support bearing assembly

Proper order of assembly of telescopic leg support bearing components

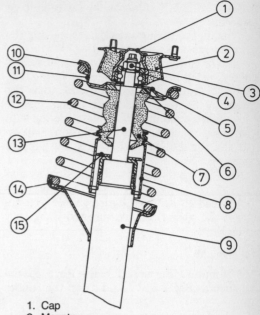

1. Cap
2. Mount
3. Self-locking nut
4. Washer
5. Insulator
6. Washer
7. Rubber damper
8. Protective tube
9. Shock absorber
10. Upper rubber ring
11. Upper spring retainer
12. Coil spring
13. Shock absorber piston rod
14. Lower rubber ring
15. Screw-on ring

Typical strut-spring components

Strut Spring

REMOVAL AND INSTALLATION (STRUT REMOVED)

1600, 2000 and 2002

CAUTION: *In order to disassemble the spring and shock absorber strut assembly, it is necessary to use a special spring compressor. It is extremely dangerous to use any other method of compressing the spring, as the spring could slip while compressed, possibly striking you and causing serious injury. For this reason, if a spring compressor of the proper type is not available, this procedure is best left to your dealer or a qualified repair shop.*

NOTE: *If a spring is determined to be worn out or broken, it is necessary also to replace the other spring on the same axle.*

1. Install the special spring compressor on the strut assembly and compress the spring.

2. Lift off the plastic sealing cap from the top of the strut. Unscrew the elastic locknut (1), while holding the shock absorber piston rod (2) steady. Lift out the telescopic leg support bearing assembly from the top of the strut.

3. Remove the upper spring cup and support.

4. Slowly release the compressor tool until the spring is completely tension-free. Remove the coil spring, and lower spring cup.

5. Check the condition of the upper and lower spring cups (collars), and the inner rubber auxiliary buffer spring. Replace them if they are cracked, dry-rotted or otherwise damaged.

6. Inspect the coil spring and shock absorber. Coil spring free length is 333mm. If the spring is sagged much beyond this, it should be replaced, of course along with the other front spring as they are a matched pair.

7. If the shock absorber is leaking excessively or it displays weak damping action, it and the

one on the other side should be rebuilt or replaced.

8. Install the spring onto the strut using the following assembly notes:

    a. The conical end of the inner rubber auxiliary spring must face the lower spring cup.

    b. The coil spring ends must locate on the stops in the upper and lower spring cups.

    c. When installing the telescopic leg support bearing, make sure that the inner curvature of the sealing washer faces the support bearing.

    d. Tighten the locknut for the strut assembly to 52 ft. lbs. Only after the locknut is tightened to its final figure should you release the spring compressor, and then, very slowly.

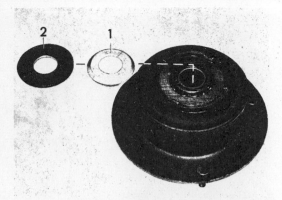

The internal dish of the sealing washer should face toward the thrust bearing—2800, 3.0

318i and 320i

1. Compress the spring coil with a special tool such as BMW 313 110. Lift off the rubber cap.

2. Hold the piston rod with one wrench while removing the self-locking nut with another.

3. Release the spring and remove the strut support bearing.

4. Install the spring on the strut assembly, keeping the following points in mind:

    a. A tapered special tool is available to facilitate installation of the support bearing over the shock absorber piston rod.

    b. Check mounting rings for the spring, auxiliary spring (which fits over the piston rod) and outer tube, and replace any which are faulty.

    c. Make sure the spring ends rest on the locating shoulders in both upper and lower spring retainers before compressing the spring and support bearing. Replace the self locking nut which goes on the piston rod, and torque to 57-62 ft. lbs.

    d. Sequence of installation above spring itself is: large washer (1) sealing washer (2), support bearing (3), concave washer (4), self locking nut (5).

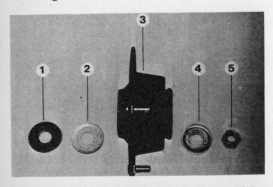

Sequence of installation of parts at the top of the strut—320i

2500, 2800, Bavaria, 3000 and 3.0

1. Compress the coil spring with a spring compressor.

2. Remove the rubber cap, lock the piston rod with one wrench, and use another wrench to remove the locknut.

3. Remove the strut thrust bearing from the top of the strut.

4. Gradually loosen the spring compressors and remove the spring plate and spring.

5. Check the rubber bushings above and below the spring and replace if necessary.

6. Wind the spring into the spring plates to spring ends rest against stops, and then reverse the remaining procedures to install, keeping the following points in mind:

    a. The internal dish of the sealing washer (1) that goes right above the thrust bearing should face the spring. Another washer (2) goes on top of that.

    b. Torque the retaining nut to 53-59 ft. lbs.

All 1983-88 3, 5, 6 and 7 Series

1. Compress the coil spring with a tool such as BMW 31 3 100 (on 733i use a tool which works on the strut and support bearing, surrounding the whole assembly, such as BMW 31 1 111).

2. Lift off the rubber cap. Holding the piston rod with one wrench, use another to remove the locknut.

3. Then, release the spring and remove the mount, washers, and spring.

4. Check the rubber damper rings at either end of the spring and at the ends of the auxiliary spring (which surrounds the piston rod) and the outer tube below it, and replace any which are defective.

5. Align the spring before starting the compression process, winding it against the stops on the strut and upper retainer.

A special tool such as BMW 31 3 113 may ease the insertion of the piston rod into the strut mount. Make sure to install the disc (1) on the 733i

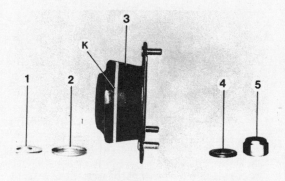

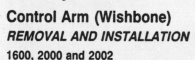

Order of installation of upper strut mounting parts—see text

6. A special tool (such as BMW 31 3 113) may be screwed onto the top of the piston rod to ease inserting it into the thrust bearing. Pull the piston rod all the way up. Install parts above the spring upper retainer as follows:

    a. Large diameter washer (1)

    b. Seal (2)

    c. Thrust bearing (3)

    d. Small diameter washer (4)

    e. Self-locking nut (5) (use a new nut only!)

7. Torque the self-locking nut to 52-58 ft. lbs. except on 733i; on the 733i, the torque is 57-63 ft. lbs.

Shock Absorbers

TESTING

The basic test for shock absorber performance is the vehicle's behavior on the road. Shock absorbers have the job of eliminating spring bounce shortly after the car hits a bump. If the car tends to lose control over washboard surfaces or if there is any sign of fluid leakage, shock absorber work is required.

If you're uncertain about shock performance,

you can jounce test the car. To do this, rest your weight on the front bumper or hood and release it repeatedly, in sympathy with the natural rhythm of the springs until the car is bouncing up and down as fast as you can make it. Then release it, and carefully observe its behavior. The car should move upward, then return to its normal riding height and virtually stop. Several bounces after release indicates worn shock absorbers.

REMOVAL AND INSTALLATION

With the MacPherson strut type front suspension used on BMWs, the shock absorber is an integral part of the strut. Since the strut and associated parts are a very expensive assembly, the shock absorbers in front are rebuilt. This is an extremely difficult job requiring a good deal of specialized mechanical skill and a number of special tools. The work is best left up to a qualified repair shop, but you can reduce the cost by removing the strut and, if you're equipped, removing the spring from it, and taking the strut to the shop to be rebuilt.

Control Arm (Wishbone)

REMOVAL AND INSTALLATION

1600, 2000 and 2002

1. Raise the vehicle and support it safely. Remove the wheel.

2. Disconnect the trailing link at the lower arm.

3. Disconnect the lower arm from the front axle beam and push off at the trailing link.

4. Remove the cotter pin and castle nut. Press off the track rod at the track rod arm with special tool such as BMW 00 7 500 or equivalent.

5. Remove the lockwire and nuts. Remove the track rod arm with the lower arm.

6. Remove the cotter pin and nut. Press off the track rod arm from the guide joint with a special tool such as BMW 00 7 500 or equivalent.

7. Install the track rod arm and lower arm into position. Note the following points:

    a. Use a new self-locking nut where the trailing link connects to the wishbone, and torque to 51-65 ft. lbs. Also, make sure the convex faces of both washers face the wishbone.

    b. Use a new self-locking nut where the wishbone attaches to the front axle beam. Also make sure the spacer is on the axle beam side and that you install washers on either side of the wishbone.

    c. Torque the track rod-to-track arm castlellated nut to 25-29 ft. lbs.

    d. Torque the nuts attaching the track rod

Make sure the convex faces of both washers face the wishbone—1600, 2002

Proper installation of wishbone to front axle carrier with spacer ring (1) facing carrier—1600, 2002

arm and wishbone to the bottom of the strut to 18-24 ft. lbs. Replace the lockwire.

e. Torque the castlellated nut attaching the track rod arm to the wishbone to 43-50 ft. lbs.

f. Check the guide (ball) joint end play and if it exceeds 2.4mm, replace the guide joint.

2500, 2800, Bavaria, 3000 and 3.0

1. Raise the vehicle and support it safely. Remove the wheel.

2. Remove the lockwire and disconnect the track rod arm from the strut assembly.

3. Press the guide (ball) joint out of the track rod arm with an extractor.

4. Disconnect the lower arm from the axle carrier.

5. Disconnect the trailing link from the lower arm.

6. Connect the trailing link tp the lower arm and connect the lower arm to the axle carrier. Note the following points during installation:

a. Torque the bolts fastening the track rod arm to the strut to 33-44 ft. lbs. Use new lockwire.

b. When attaching the wishbone to the

front axle carrier, tighten it snugly, complete assembly of the front suspension, and then lower the vehicle and allow it to sit at its normal ride height. Torque the stop nut to 60-66 ft. lbs.

c. Make sure, when reattaching the trailing link to the wishbone that the convex faces of the washers are outward. Check the play of the guide (ball) joint and replace it if the play is greater than 2.4mm.

d. Some wishbones and some track rods have metal stops cast integrally into the structure. A wishbone with a stop may be used in conjunction with a track rod arm without a stop, but if the track rod arm has a stop, the wishbone must also have a stop.

e. Torque the nut attaching the trailing link to the wishbone to 52-66 ft. lbs.

Control Arm

REMOVAL AND INSTALLATION

528e, 533i and 1982 633CSi

1. Raise the vehicle and support safely. Remove the wheel.

2. Disconnect the stabilizer at the control arm.

3. Remove the tension strut nut on the control arm.

4. Disconnect the control arm at the front axle support and remove it from the tension strut.

5. Remove the lock wire, remove the bolts and take the control arm off the spring strut.

6. Remove the cotter pin and nut.

7. Using special tool BMW 00-7-500 or equivalent, pull the guide joint from the tie rod arm.

8. Install the guide joint to the tie rod with the special tool.

9. Install the control arm to the spring strut and connect it to front axle support. Install the stabilizer to the control arm.

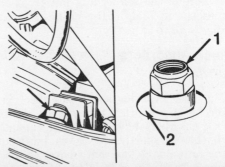

In replacing the nut located in the center of the control arm, use a replacement nut (1) and washer (2) of the type shown

Vibration strut attaching bolt—733i

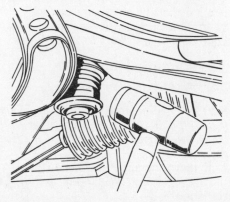

On the 318i, knock the pin loose with a soft hammer, as shown

524td, 1982-84 533i, 535i, 1983-84 633CSi, 635i, M5, M6 and 1987-88 735i

1. Raise and support the vehicle securely. Remove the wheel.

2. Remove the 3 bolts that fasten the bottom of the strut to the steering knuckle.

3. Remove the cotter pin and castlellated nut. Use a ball joint remover (BMW 31 1 110 or equivalent) to press the ball joint end of the control arm off the steering knuckle.

4. Remove the self locking nut. Then, remove the through bolt and the 2 washers, slide the inner end of the strut and bushing out of the front suspension crossmember.

5. Install the control arm to the vehicle, noting the following points:

a. Make sure both washers are replaced to cushion the bushing where it contacts the suspension crossmember.

b. Replace the bushing if it is worn or cracked.

c. Use a new self-locking nut on the bolt fastening the inner end of the strut.

d. Align the bottom of the strut with the steering knuckle so the tab on the arm fits into the notch on the bottom of the strut. Install the bolts with a locking type sealer.

e. When installing the arm ball joint onto the steering knuckle, tighten the nut until a castlellation lines up with the cotter pin hole and then use a new cotter pin in the nut.

f. Final tighten the through bolt for the inner end of the arm after the car is on the ground and at normal ride height.

318i, 325, 325e, 325i, 325iS and M3

1. Remove the front wheel. Disconnect the rear control arm bracket where it connects to the body by removing the 2 bolts.

2. Remove the nut and disconnect the thrust rod on the front stabilizer bar where it connects to the center of the control arm.

3. Unscrew the nut which attaches the front of the stabilizer bar to the crossmember and remove the nut from above the crossmember. Then, use a plastic hammer to knock this support pin out of the crossmember.

4. Unscrew the nut and press off the guide joint where the control arm attaches to the lower end of the strut. To do this, use a special tool such as 31 1 110 (31 2 160 for the M3) or equivalent.

5. Install the control arm on the vehicle, keeping these points in mind:

a. Replace the self-locking nut that fastens the guide joint to the control arm.

b. Make sure the support pin and the bore in the crossmember are clean before inserting the pin through the crossmember. Replace the original nut with a replacement nut and washer equivalent to those shown in the illustration.

c. Torque the control arm-to-spring strut nut to 43-51 ft. lbs. Torque the control arm support to crossmember nut to 29-34 ft. lbs. Torque the push rod on the stabilizer bar to 29-34 ft. lbs.

325iX

1. Remove the front wheel. Disconnect the rear control arm bracket where it connects to the body by removing the 2 bolts.

2. Remove the nut from the top of the stud that attaches to one corner of the control arm and runs through the crossmember.

3. Remove the cotter pin and then remove the nut from the balljoint stud where it passes through the steering knuckle. Then, press the balljoint stud out of the knuckle with a tool such as 31 2 160. Make sure to keep the stud and bore free of grease.

4. Install the control arm to the vehicle keeping these points in mind:

a. Make sure the support pin and the bore in the crossmember are clean before inserting the pin through the crossmember. Replace the original nut with a replacement nut

and washer equivalent to those shown in the illustration.

b. Torque the control arm-to-spring strut nut to 61.5 ft. lbs. Turn the nut farther, as necessary to align the castlellations with the cotter pin hole and install a new cotter pin. Torque the control arm support to cross-member nut to 30 ft. lbs.

320i

1. Raise the vehicle and support it safely, remove the wheel. Disconnect the stabilizer at the control arm.
2. Disconnect the control arm at the front axle support.
3. Remove the cotter pin and castlellated nut.
4. Press the control arm off the steering knuckle with special tool BMW 31-1-100 or equivalent.
5. Install the control arm to the steering knuckle using the special tool.
6. Install the castle nut and cotter pin. Connect the control arm at the front axle and connect the stabilizer bar.

733i and 1985-86 735i

1. Raise the vehicle and support safely. Remove the wheel.
2. Disconnect the vibration strut from the control arm.
3. Disconnect the control arm from the axle carrier.
4. Disconnect the tie rod arm from the front strut.
5. Remove the cotter pin and castlellated nut. Press off the control arm with special tool BMW 31-1-110 or equivalent.
6. Install the control arm onto the vehicle. Connect the tie rod to the front strut and connect the control arm to the axle carrier.
7. Use new self-locking nuts on the connections at the vibration strut and axle carrier. On 1983-88 models, when reconnecting the arm to the tie rod arm, use a bolt tightener HBW No. 81 22 9 400 086 and make sure the threads and bolt holes are clean.

Stabilizer Bar
REMOVAL AND INSTALLATION

1. Raise and support the front end on jackstands.
2a. On the 320, 528e, 533i and 1982 633CSi: Disconnect the stabilizer bar at the control arms.
2b. On the 318i, 325, 325e, 325i, 325iS and M3: Remove the attaching nut and then detach the push rod on the stabilizer bar at the strut.
2c. On the 524td, 528e, 1983-84 533i, 535i,

1983-84 633CSi, 635CSi, M5, M6, 1987-88 735i: Disconnect the stabilizer push rod at the bracket on the side of the strut. To do this, use a wrench to hold the rod end on the flats just outside the bracket and unscrew the nut from the inside of the bracket.
2d. On the 318i, 325, 325e, 325i, 325iS and M3: Remove the nut and disconnect the thrust rod on the front stabilizer bar where it connects to the center of the control arm.
2e. On the 318i, 325, 325e, 325i, 325iS and M3: Unscrew the nut which attaches the front of the stabilizer bar to the crossmember and remove the nut from above the crossmember. Then, use a plastic hammer to knock this support pin out of the crossmember.
3. Installation is the reverse of removal. Torque the pushrod nuts to 24-34 ft. lbs.

Guide Joint (Ball Joint)
REMOVAL AND INSTALLATION

NOTE: *These joints are replaceable only on the 1600 and 2002 Series. On other models, the entire control arm must be if the joint is defective.*

1. Remove the lower wishbone from the car as outlined under "Wishbone Removal and Installation".

Drilling out guide joint attaching rivets—1600, 2002

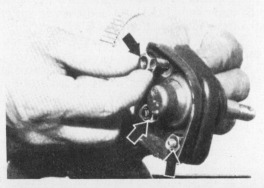

Attaching guide joint to wishbone with nuts and bolts

2. Clamp the wishbone in a vise.

3. Drill out the rivets which retain the guide joint to the wishbone.

4. Install a new guide joint using M8 × 20 hex bolts and M8 hex nuts.

5. Install the lower wishbone as outlined under "Wishbone Removal and Installation".

Front Wheel Bearings
ADJUSTMENT

NOTE: *The wheel bearings for 318i and 325, 5 and 6 Series for 1983-88, and 7 Series for 1987-88 cannot be adjusted.*

320i, 533i, 633CSi, 733i and 735i

1. Raise the vehicle, support it and remove the front wheel.

2. Remove the end cap, and then straighten the cotter pin and remove it. Loosen the castlellated nut.

3. While continuously spinning the brake disc, torque the castlellated nut down to 22-24 ft. lbs. Keep turning the disc throughout this and make sure it turns at least 2 turns after the nut is torqued and held.

4. Loosen the nut until there is end play and the hub rotates with the nut.

5. Torque the nut to no more than 2 ft. lbs. Finally, loosen slowly just until castlellations and the nearest cotter pin hole line up and insert a new cotter pin.

6. Make sure the slotted washer is free to turn without noticeable resistance; otherwise, there is no end play and the bearings will wear excessively.

528i

1. Remove the wheel. Remove the locking cap from the hub by gripping it carefully on both sides with a pair of pliers.

2. Remove the cotter pin from the castlellated nut, and loosen the nut.

3. Spin the disc constantly while torquing the nut to 7 ft. lbs. Continue spinning the disc a couple of turns after the nut is torqued and held.

4. Loosen the castlellated nut ¼-⅓ turn until the slotted washer can be turned readily.

5. Fasten a dial indicator to the front suspension and rest the pin against the wheel hub. Preload the meter about 1mm to remove any play.

6. Adjust the position of the castlellated nut while reading the play on the indicator. Make the play as small as possible while backing off the castlellated nut just until a new cotter pin can be inserted. The permissible range is 0.02-0.10mm.

7. Install the new cotter pin, locking cap, and the wheel.

REMOVAL AND INSTALLATION (PACKING)

NOTE: *Wheel bearings on 318i, 325, 5 and 6 Series for 1983-88 and 7 Series for 1987-88 are permanently sealed bearings and do not require periodic disassembly and packing.*

1. Remove the wheel. Unbolt and remove the caliper. Hang it from the body. Do not disconnect or stress the hose. On models with a separate disc, remove the locking cap by gripping carefully on both sides with a pair of pliers, remove the cotter pin from the castlellated nut, and remove the nut and, where equipped, the slotted washer. Then, remove the entire hub and bearing.

2. Remove the shaft sealing ring and take out the roller bearing.

3. On most models, the outer bearing race may be forced out through the recesses in the wheel hub. A BMW puller 00 8 550 or the equivalent may also be used. On the 733i, the recesses are not provided and a puller is necessary.

4. Clean all bearings and races and the interior of the hub with alcohol, and allow to air dry.

NOTE: *Do not dry with compressed air as this can damage the bearings by rolling them over one another unlubricated or force one loose from the cage causing injury. Replace all bearings and races if there is any sign of scoring or galling.*

6. Press in the outer races with a suitable sleeve. Pack a new shaft seal with graphite grease and refill the hub with fresh grease.

7. Assemble in this order: outer race; inner race; outer race; inner race; shaft seal.

8. If necessary, adjust the wheel bearing play as described above.

318i, 325, 325e, 325i, 325iS and M3

NOTE: *The bearings on the 318i and 325 are only removed if they are worn. They cannot be removed without destroying them (due to side thrust created by the bearing puller). They are not periodically disassembled, repacked and adjusted.*

1. Remove the front wheel and support the car. Remove the attaching bolts and remove and suspend the brake caliper, hanging it from the body so as to avoid putting stress on the brake line.

2. Remove the setscrew with an Allen wrench. Pull off the brake disc and pry off the dust cover with a small prybar.

3. Using a chisel, knock the tab on the collar nut away from the shaft. Unscrew and discard the nut.

4. Pull off the bearing with a puller set such as 31 2 101/102/104 and discard it. On the M3, use a puller set such as 31 2 102/105/106. On

the M3, install the main bracket of the puller with 3 wheel bolts.

5. If the inside bearing inner race remains on the stub axle, unbolt and remove the dust guard. Bend back the inner dust guard and pull the inner race off with a special tool capable of getting under the race (BMW 00 7 500 and 33 1 309 or equivalent). Reinstall the dust guard.

6. If the dust guard has been removed, install a new one. Install a special tool (BMW 31 2 120 or equivalent; on M3, use 31 2 110 or equivalent) over the stub axle and screw it in for the entire length of the guide sleeve's threads. Press the bearing on.

7. Reverse the remaining removal procedures to install the disc and caliper. Torque the wheel hub collar nut to 188 ft. lbs. Lock the collar nut by bending over the tab.

325iX

NOTE: *Refer to "Front Wheel Drive Hub and Bearings, Removal and Installation" in Chapter 7.*

1982-86 733i and 735i

1. Remove the front wheel. Detach the brake line clamp and bracket on the strut. On cars with ABS, remove the rubber boot and unbolt and remove the anti-lock sensor.

2. Detach the caliper without disconnecting the brake line and suspend it.

3. Use a tool such as 21 2 000 to remove the end cap. Remove the cotter pin and unscrew the castlellated nut. Then, remove the stepped washer, brake disc, and wheel hub.

4. Use an Allen type wrench to unscrew the bolt and separate the disc from the wheel hub.

5. Lift out the shaft seal. Remove the tapered roller bearings. Knock out the outer races if they show scoring with a punch by tapping all around.

6. Press in new outer races with special tools such as 31 2 061 for the inside bearings and 31 2 062 for the outside bearings. Pack the 2 inner races with wheel bearing grease. The order of

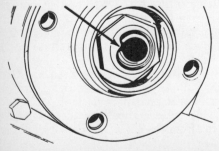

On 318i, unlock the collar nut as shown with a chisel, by applying force in the direction shown by the arrow

installation is: outer race, inner race, outer race, inner race, shaft seal. To install the seal, lubricate the sealing lip of the shaft seal with grease and install the seal with a tool such as 31 2 040. Repack all bearings thoroughly with wheel bearing grease before installation.

7. Adjust the wheel bearings as described above.

524td, 528e, 535i
1983-84 633CSi, 635CSi, M5 and M6

1. Raise the vehicle and support it securely. Unbolt and remove the caliper, suspending it so the brake line will not be stressed. Remove the Allen bolt and remove the brake disc.

2. Remove the grease cap. Use a flat punch and hammer to push the punched-in area of the retaining nut away from the groove in the axle. If necessary, chisel the nut off. Then, use a socket 31 2 080 or equivalent to unscrew the bearing retaining nut.

3. Install a puller 31 2 100 or equivalent. Screw the tool's bolt inward to pull the bearing housing out of the axle.

4. Install a new bearing assembly cover on the stub axle. Use special tool set 31 2 110 to pull the new bearing assembly into the axle.

5. Install a washer and a new retaining nut. Torque the nut to 210 ft. lbs. Use a center punch and hammer to punch the inner edge of the nut into the indentation on the axle shaft. Install a new grease cap coated with a sealer such as HWB 88 228 407 420.

1987-88 735i

1. Remove the front wheel and support the car. Remove the attaching bolts and remove and suspend the brake caliper, hanging it from the body so as to avoid putting stress on the brake line.

2. Remove the setscrew with an Allen wrench. Pull off the brake disc and pry off the dust cover with a small prybar.

3. Using a chisel, knock the tab on the collar nut away from the shaft. Unscrew and discard the nut.

4. Install a puller collar such as 31 2 105 to the bearing housing with 3 bolts. Install a puller such as 31 2 102 and 312 2 106 and pull off the bearing and discard it.

5. If the inside bearing inner race remains on the stub axle, unscrew and remove the dust guard, using a socket extension. Bend back the inner dust guard and pull the inner race off with a special tool capable of getting under the race (BMW 31 2 100 and 31 2 102 or equivalent). Reinstall the dust guard and install a new dust cover.

6. Then install a special tool (BMW 31 2 110 or equivalent) over the stub axle and screw it in

for the entire length of the guide sleeve's threads. Slide the bearing on and follow it with 31 2 100 or equivalent, and use this tool to press the bearing on.

7. Reverse the remaining removal procedures to install the disc and caliper. Torque the wheel hub collar nut to 210 ft. lbs. Lock the collar nut by bending over the tab.

8. Install a new grease cap coated with a sealer such as HWB 88 228 407 420.

Front Wheel Alignment

Caster and Camber

Caster and camber are not adjustable, except for replacement of bent or worn parts.

On the 1983-88 models, camber that is out of specification because of excessive tolerances can be corrected by installing eccentric mounts. This cannot be done to correct misalignment caused by a collision, however.

Toe-in Adjustment

Toe-in is adjusted by changing the length of the tie rod and tie rod end assembly. Center the steering by aligning marks on the steering shaft and the steering housing. Then, loosen the clamp bolt on either end of each tie rod and turn the tie rod, using a wrench on the flats. When adjusting the tie rod ends, adjust each by equal amount (by turning in the opposite direction) to increase or decrease the toe-in measurement.

REAR SUSPENSION

BMW rear suspension incorporates semi trailing arms pivoting on maintenance-free rubber bushings. Springs are coil type, and the spring strut incorporates the double acting shock absorber on later models. Some models include a rear stabilizer bar. All are fully independent for maximum ride comfort and control.

MacPherson Strut Assembly
REMOVAL AND INSTALLATION
All Models except 1600, 2000 and 2002

CAUTION: *MacPherson strut springs are under tremendous pressure and any attempt to remove them without proper tools could result in serious personal injury!*

1. On model 1981-82 733i and on 1987-88 735i, remove the rear seat and back rest. On 1983-86 733i and 735i, remove the trim from over the wheel well in the trunk.

2. Jack up the car and support the control arms.

CAUTION: *The coil spring, shock absorber assembly acts as a strap so the control arm should always be supported!*

3. On 1987-88 735i if the car has automatic ride control (for other models skip to Step 4):

a. Pull off and bridge (electrically) the low pressure switch electrical connection and turn on the ignition.

Wheel Alignment

Year	Model		Caster Range (deg.)	Caster Preferred Setting (deg.)	Camber Range (deg.)	Camber Preferred Setting (deg.)	Toe-in (in.)	Steering Axis Inclination (deg.)
1970–76	1600,2000,2002	Front	—	4P	—	½P	.07	8½P
		Rear	—	2N	—	—	—	—
1970–76	2500,Bavaria	Front	—	9⅔P	—	½P	.07	8½P
	2800,3.0	Rear	—	2N	—	—	—	—
1977–81	320i	Front	—	8⅓P	—	0	.07	10½P
		Rear	—	2N	—	—	—	—
1977–78	530i	Front	—	7⅔P	—	½P	.07	8½P
		Rear	—	2N	—	—	—	—
1979–81	528i	Front	—	7⅔P	—	0	.06	8½P
		Rear	—	2N	—	—	—	—
1978–81	633CSi	Front	—	7⅔P	—	0	.06	8P
		Rear	—	2N	—	—	—	—
1978–79	733i	Front	—	9P	—	0	.03	11½P
		Rear	—	1½N	—	—	—	—

Wheel Alignment (cont.)

Year	Model		Caster Range (deg.)	Caster Preferred Setting (deg.)	Camber Range (deg.)	Camber Preferred Setting (deg.)	Toe-in (in.)	Steering Axis Inclination (deg.)
1982	320i	Front	—	8⁵⁄₁₆P	—	0	¹⁄₁₆	10⁵⁄₁₆P
		Rear	—	8⁵⁄₁₆P	—	0	¹⁄₁₆	10⁵⁄₁₆P
	633CSi	Front	—	7²⁄₃P	—	0	.060	8P
		Rear	—	—	—	2N	.080	—
	733i	Front	—	9P	—	0	³⁄₆₄P	11⁹⁄₁₆
		Rear	—	—	—	1½N	³⁄₁₆P	—
1983	320i	Front	—	8⁵⁄₁₆P	—	0	¹⁄₁₆	10⁵⁄₁₆P
		Rear	—	—	—	2N	¹⁄₃₂P	—
	63CSi	Front	—	8¼P	—	⁵⁄₁₆N	⁵⁄₆₄P	12³⁄₁₆P
		Rear	—	—	—	2⁵⁄₁₆N	⁵⁄₆₄P	—
	733i	Front	—	8¼P	—	⅓N	.078	12³⁄₁₆P
		Rear	—	—	—	2N	.08	—
1984	318i	Front	8¼P–9¼P	8¾P	1¹⁄₁₀N–¹⁄₁₀N	⅔N	0.079①	13⅔P
		Rear	—	—	—	1¹³⁄₁₆N	0.079①	—
	528e	Front	7¾P–8¾P	8¼P	½N–¹⁄₁₀P	¹⁄₁₃N	³⁄₃₂P	12³⁄₁₀P
		Rear	—	—	—	2N	³⁄₃₂P	—
	533i	Front	7¾P–8¾P	8¼P	½N–¹⁄₁₀P	¹⁄₁₃N	³⁄₃₂P	12³⁄₁₆P
		Rear	—	—	—	2N	³⁄₃₂P	—
	633CSi	Front	—	8¼P	—	⁵⁄₁₆N	⁵⁄₆₄P	12³⁄₁₆P
		Rear	—	—	—	2⁵⁄₁₆N	⁵⁄₆₄P	—
	733i	Front	9P–10P	9½P	½N–¹⁄₁₂P	0	½	11⅓P
		Rear	—	—	—	2N	³⁄₃₂P	—
1985	318i	Front	8¼P–9¼P	8¾P	1¹⁄₁₀N–¹⁄₁₀N	⅔N	0.079①	13⅔P
		Rear	—	—	—	1¹³⁄₁₆N	0.079①	—
	325e	Front	8¼P–9¼P	8¾P	1¹⁄₁₀N–¹⁄₁₀N	⅔N	0.079①	13⅔P
		Rear	—	—	—	1¹³⁄₁₆N	0.079①	—
	528e	Front	7¾P–8¾P	8¼P	½N–¹⁄₁₀P	⅓N	³⁄₃₂P	12¹³⁄₁₆P
		Rear	—	—	—	2N	³⁄₃₂P	—
	533i	Front	7¾P–8¾P	8¼P	½N–¹⁄₁₀P	⅓N	³⁄₃₂P	12¹³⁄₁₆P
		Rear	—	—	—	2N	³⁄₃₂P	—
	635CSi	Front	7¾P–8¾P	8¼P	½N–¹⁄₁₀P	⅓N	0.079①	12³⁄₁₆P
		Rear	—	—	—	2⅓N	0.079①	—
	735i	Front	9P–10P	9½P	½N–½P	0	0.020②	11⅓P
		Rear	—	—	—	2⅓N	0.079①	—
1986	325e	Front	8¼P–9½P	8¾P	1¹⁄₁₀N–¹⁄₁₀N	⅔N	0.079①	13⅔P
		Rear	—	—	—	1¹³⁄₁₆N	0.079①	—
	528e	Front	7¾P–8¾P	8¼P	½N–¹⁄₁₀P	⅓N	0.079①	12¹³⁄₁₆P
		Rear	—	—	—	2⅓N	0.079①	—

Wheel Alignment (cont.)

Year	Model		Caster Range (deg.)	Caster Preferred Setting (deg.)	Camber Range (deg.)	Camber Preferred Setting (deg.)	Toe-in (in.)	Steering Axis Inclination (deg.)
1986	535i	Front	7¾P–8¾P	8¼P	½N–⅒P	⅓N	0.079 ①	12 13/16P
		Rear	—	—	—	2⅓N	0.079 ①	—
	635CSi	Front	7¾P–8¾P	8¼P	½N–⅒P	⅓N	0.079 ①	12 13/16P
		Rear	—	—	—	2⅓N	0.079 ①	—
	735i	Front	9P–10P	9½P	½N–½P	0	0.020 ②	11⅓P
		Rear	—	—	—	2⅓N	0.079 ①	—
1987	325e	Front	8¼P–9¼P	8¾P	1⅒N–⅒N	⅔N	0.079 ①	13⅔P
		Rear	—	—	1½N–2⅓N	1⅚N	0.079 ①	—
	528e	Front	7¾P–8¾P	8¼P	½N–⅒P	⅓N	0.079 ①	12 13/16P
		Rear	—	—	—	2⅓N	0.079 ①	—
	535i	Front	7¾P–8¾P	8¼P	½N–⅒P	⅓N	0.079 ①	12 13/16P
		Rear	—	—	—	2⅓N	0.079 ①	—
	325	Front	8P–9P	8½P	1⅒N–⅙P	⅔N	0.079	13 5/16P
		Rear	—	—	1⅓N–2⅓P	1 5/16N	0.079	—
	325 ③	Front	8¼P–8¾P	8¾P	1⅔N–⅔N	1⅙N	0.079	14⅓P
		Rear	—	—	1⅓N–2⅓P	1 5/16N	0.079	—
	325iX	Front	1P–1⅓P	1⅓	1½P–½N	1N	0.024	12⅔P
		Rear	—	—	1¾N–2¾N	2¼N	0.102	—
	635CSi	Front	7½P–8½P	8P	⅚N–⅙P	⅓N	0.079	12P
		Rear	—	—	2⅚N–1⅚N	2⅓N	0.079 ⑤	—
	M6	Front	7½P–8½P	8¼P	⅚N–⅙P	⅓N	0.079	12P
		Rear	—	—	2⅚N–1⅚N	2⅓N	0.079 ①	—
	528e	Front	7½P–8½P	8P	⅚N–⅙P	⅓N	0.079 ⑤	12P
		Rear	—	—	1⅚N–2⅚N	2⅓N	0.079 ⑤	—
	535i	Front	7½P–8½P	8P	⅚N–⅙P	⅓N	0.079 ⑤	12P
		Rear	—	—	1⅚N–2⅚N	2⅓N	0.079 ⑤	—
	M5	Front	7½P–8½P	8P	⅚N–⅙P	⅓N	0.098 ①	12P
		Rear	—	—	1⅚N–2⅚N	2⅓N	0.098 ①	—
	735i	Front	7½P–8½P	8P	¾N–¼P	¼N	0.087 ⑥	12P
		Rear	—	—	—	2⅓N	0.079 ①	—
1988–89	325e	Front	8P–9P	8½P	1⅒N–⅒N	⅔N	0.079	13⅚P
		Rear	—	—	1⅓N–2⅓N	1 5/16N	0.079	—
	325	Front	8P–9P	8½P	1⅒N–⅙N	⅔N	0.079	13 5/16P
		Rear	—	—	1⅓N–2⅓P	1 5/16N	0.079	—
	325 ③	Front	8¼P–8¾P	8¾P	1⅔N–⅔N	1⅙N	0.079	14⅓P
		Rear	—	—	1⅓N–2⅓P	1 5/16N	0.079	—
	326iX	Front	1P–1⅔P	1⅓P	1½N–½N	1N	0.024	12⅔P
		Rear	—	—	1¾N–2⅓P	1 5/16N	0.079	—

Wheel Alignment (cont.)

Year	Model		Caster Range (deg.)	Caster Preferred Setting (deg.)	Camber Range (deg.)	Camber Preferred Setting (deg.)	Toe-in (in.)	Steering Axis Inclination (deg.)
1988–89	325iX ③	Front	1P–1⅔P	1⅓P	$1\frac{15}{16}$N–$\frac{5}{16}$N	1⅓N	0.024	12⅔P
		Rear	—	—	1¾N–2⅓P	$1\frac{5}{16}$N	0.079	—
1988	325 Convertible	Front	8P–9P	8½P	1⅒N–⅙N	⅔N	0.079	$13\frac{5}{16}$P
		Rear	—	—	1⅓N–2⅓N	1⅚N	0.079	—
	528e	Front	7¾P–8¾P	8¼P	½N–⅒P	⅓N	0.079 ①	$12\frac{13}{16}$P
		Rear	—	—	—	2⅓N	0.079 ①	—
	535i	Front	7¾P–8¾P	8¼P	½N–⅒P	⅓N	0.079 ①	$12\frac{13}{16}$P
		Rear	—	—	—	2⅓N	0.079 ①	—
	635CSi	Front	7½P–8½P	8P	⅚N–⅙P	⅓N	0.079 ⑤	12P
		Rear	—	—	2⅚N–1⅚N	2⅓N	0.079 ⑤	—
	M6	Front	7¾P–8¾P	8P	⅚N–⅙P	⅓N	0.079 ⑤	12P
		Rear	—	—	2⅚N–1⅚N	2⅓N	0.079 ⑤	—
	528e	Front	7½P–8½P	8P	⅚N–⅙P	⅓N	0.079 ⑤	12P
		Rear	—	—	1⅚N–2⅚N	2⅓N	0.079 ⑤	—
	535i	Front	7½P–8½P	8P	⅚N–⅙P	⅓N	0.079 ⑤	12P
		Rear	—	—	1⅚N–2⅚N	2⅓N	0.079 ⑤	—
	M5	Front	7½P–8½P	8P	⅚N–⅙P	⅓N	0.098	12P
		Rear	—	—	1⅚N–2⅚N	2⅓N	0.098	—
	735i	Front	7½P–8½P	8P	¾N–¼P	¼N	0.087 ⑥	12P
		Rear	—	—	2⅚N–1⅚N	2⅓N	0.087	—
	750iL	Front	7½P–8½P	8P	¾N–¼P	¼N	0.087 ⑥	12P
		Rear	—	—	2⅚N–1⅚N	2⅓N	0.087	—

All 300, 500 and 700 series models aligned with 150 lbs. in each front seat, 150 lbs. in rear seat and 46 lbs. in trunk.
All 600 series models aligned with 150 lbs. in each front seat and 30 lbs. in trunk on left side
① 14P—1986 and later models
F Front
R Rear
N Negative
P Positive

① .083 with TRX tires
② .024 with TRX tires
③ With "M" suspension
④ .122 with 16 in. rims
⑤ .083 with TRX 390 rims
⑥ .094 with TRX 415 rims

b. Disconnect the control rod nut, holding the collar with an 8mm wrench against torque. Don't disconnect the rod at the ball joint.

c. Operate the lever on the control switch in the **discharge** direction for about 20 seconds to discharge fluid from the lines.

d. Disconnect the hydraulic line on the shock absorber.

4. Remove the lower shock retaining bolt.
5. Remove trim if necessary and disconnect the upper strut retaining nuts at the wheel arch and remove the assembly.
6. Install the assembly back into position, using new gaskets between the unit and the wheel arch, and new self-locking nuts on top of the strut.
7. Torque the shock-to-body nuts to 16-17 ft.

lbs.; spring retainer-to-wheel house nuts (6 cyl.) to 16-17 ft. lbs.; lower bolt to 52-63 ft. lbs. (4 cyl.), 90-103 ft. lbs. (6 cyl.).

8. On 1983-88 733i, 735i, replace the gasket that goes between the top of the strut and the lower surface of the wheel well. Final torquing of the lower strut bolt should be done with the car in the normal riding position.

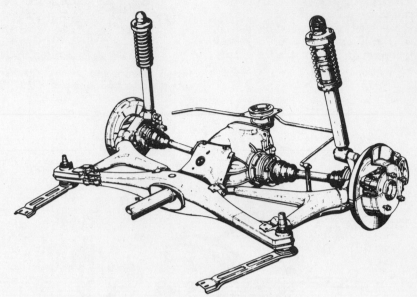

Rear suspension—528e

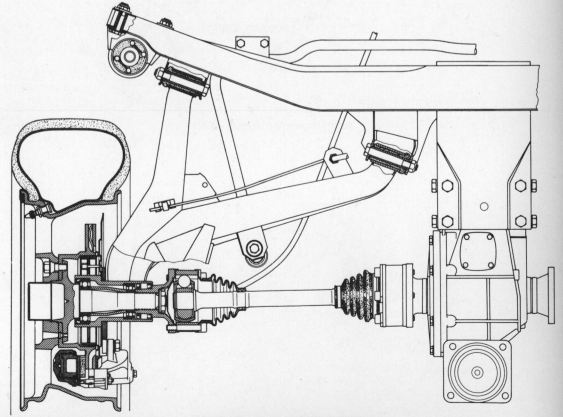

600 series rear suspension layout

318i and 325

1. Jack up the car and support the control arms.

CAUTION: *On the 318i and 325, the spring and shock absorber are separate. The control arm must be securely supported throughout this procedure!*

2. Remove the lower shock retaining bolt.

3. Remove trim if necessary and disconnect the upper strut retaining nuts at the wheel arch and remove the assembly.

Install spacers and position the damper ring (3) with the tabs front and rear—2800, 3.0, 530i

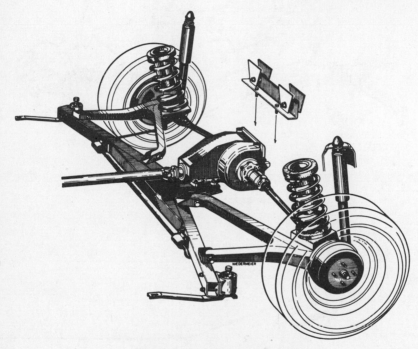

Rear suspension system—2002

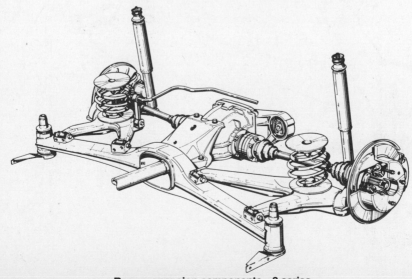

Rear suspension components—3 series

NOTE: *On the 318i and 325, this is located behind the trim panel in the trunk. The shock absorber, because it is separate from the spring, may now be replaced.*

6. Install the shock into position, using new gaskets between the unit and the wheel arch, and new self-locking nuts on top of the strut.

7. Torque the fasteners as follows:
- shock-to-body nuts: 16-17 ft. lbs.
- spring retainer-to-wheel house nuts (6 cyl.): 16-17 ft. lbs.
- lower bolt (4-cyl.): 52-63 ft. lbs.
- lower bolt (6-cyl.): 90-103 ft. lbs.

8. Final torquing of the lower strut bolt should be done with the car in the normal riding position.

Rear Springs

REMOVAL AND INSTALLATION

1600, 2000 AND 2002

CAUTION: *Make sure that the car is firmly supported with jackstands.*

1. Remove the shock absorber as outlined under "Shock Absorber Removal and Installation". Make sure that the trailing arm is securely supported with a jack.

2. Remove the rear wheel and tire assembly.

3. On 2002 models, disconnect the stabilizer bar from its mount on the trailing arm.

4. Disconnect the output shaft at the halfshaft flange and tie the output shaft up to an underbody component so that it does not hang down.

5. Safety wire or chain the bottom coil of the spring to an underbody component to protect yourself from injury should the spring slip off its lower mount during removal.

6. Slowly lower the jack supporting the trailing arm and carefully release the spring.

7. Inspect the condition of the rubber damp-

Locating recess in lower damping ring into projection on lower mounting plate

ing rings. Replace them if they are damaged or dry-rotted. Make sure that the lower ring's locating recess fits into the projection on the lower mounting plate. If the spring is broken, it is recommended that both springs be removed and replaced with new ones of the same size, diameter, free length, and color coding (spring rate).

8. Install the spring into position, using new bushings on the mounting plate.

9. Reconnect the output shaft at the half shaft. Reconnect the stabilizer bar.

10. Install the wheel and tire and install the shock absorber.

NOTE: *Take care to rotate the coil spring so that the spring ends locate on the stop (projection) of the upper and lower damping rings.*

318i, 325, 325e, 325i, 325iS, 318iX, and M3

1. Disconnect the rear portion of the exhaust system and hang it from the body.

2. Disconnect the final drive rubber mount, push it down, and hold it down with a wedge.

3. Remove the bolt that connects the rear stabilizer bar to the strut on the side being worked on. Be careful not to damage the brake line.

NOTE: *Support the lower control arm securely with a jack or other device that will permit it to be lowered gradually, while maintaining secure support.*

4. Then, to prevent damage to the output shaft joints, lower the control arm only enough to slip the coil spring off the retainer.

5. Make sure, in replacing the spring, that the same part number, color code, and proper rubber ring are used. Reverse all removal procedures to install, making sure that the spring is in proper position, keeping the control arm securely supported until the shock bolt is replaced, and tightening stabilizer bar and lower

Disconnecting and hanging up the output shaft—1600, 2002

shock mount bolts with the control arm in the normal ride position.

6. Torque the stabilizer bolt to 22-24 ft. lbs., and the shock bolt to 52-63 ft. lbs.

Shock Absorbers

TESTING

The basic test for shock absorber performance is the vehicle's behavior on the road. shock absorbers have the job of eliminating spring bounce shortly after the car hits a bump. If the car tends to lose control over washboard surfaces or if there is any sign of fluid leakage, shock absorber work is required.

If you're uncertain about shock absorber performance, you can jounce test the car. To do this, rest your weight on the rear bumper or hood and release it repeatedly, in sympathy with the natural rhythm of the springs until the car is bouncing up and down as fast as you can make it. Then release it, carefully observe its behavior. the car should move upward, and then return to its normal riding height and virtually stop. Several bounces after release indicates worn shock absorbers.

REMOVAL AND INSTALLATION

All Equipped Models Except 1600, 2000 and 2002

1. On the 2500, 2800, Bavaria and 3.0, remove the sleeve which surrounds the shock ab-

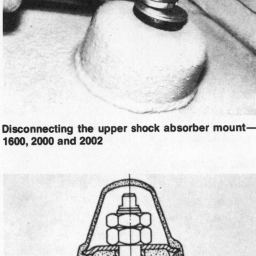

Disconnecting the upper shock absorber mount—1600, 2000 and 2002

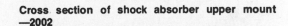

Cross section of shock absorber upper mount—2002

sorber and the auxiliary spring as well as: the rubber washer; large metal washer; spacer tube; and the fastening plate.

2. On the other models (except 1600, 2000 and 2002), remove the support disc, auxiliary spring (which fits around the shock absorber piston rod), and the outer tube. Remove both upper and lower lines, and inspect them, replacing if necessary.

3. Install in reverse order. In case you are replacing a shock absorber which has failed prematurely (especially due to leakage), it may be possible to avoid the cost of replacing the unit located on the opposite side. BMW dealers and some other shops are equipped with a machine designed for testing the shocks. You might be able to remove both shocks and have the performance of a new shock compared with that of the apparently effective old shock. If machine testing proves the performance of a new shock and slightly used shock to be sufficiently similar, re-use is possible. However, it is dangerous to risk replacing the only one rear shock without machine testing!

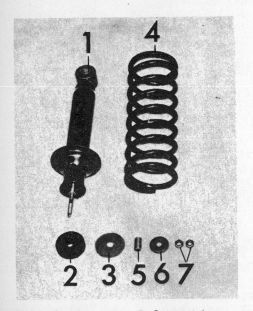

1. Shock absorber
2. Rubber washer
3. Large metal washer
4. Spring
5. Spacer tube
6. Fastening plate
7. Mounting nuts

Identification of shock absorber mounting parts for the 2800 and 3.0

1600, 2000,and 2002

1. Place blocks in front of the front wheels. jack up the rear of the car and place jackstands beneath the reinforced boxmember area adjacent to the rear jacking points.

CAUTION: *Make sure that the car is firmly supported with jackstands before climbing under it. Never rely on the car jack alone.*

2. Support the trailing arm with a jack. The shock absorber is used to limit the downward travel of the suspension. If the trailing arm is not supported, the output shafts may swivel downward beyond their design limit when the shock absorber lower mount is released, possibly damaging the output shaft joints.

3. Open the trunk and remove the protective cap covering the shock absorber upper mount. Disconnect the shock absorber upper mount from the body.

4. Disconnect the shock absorber from its lower mount at the brake backing plate. Fully compress the shock absorber and remove it from the vehicle.

5. Inspect the condition of the bushing at the upper mount. Replace it if it is damaged or dry-rotted, by pressing it out of the body cavity. When replacing the mount, insert the small end facing down and replace the spacing sleeve. If the damping action of the shock absorber is insufficient, replace both rear shock absorbers as a matched pair.

Stabilizer Bar

REMOVAL AND INSTALLATION

1. Disconnect the stabilizer from the trailing arm on either side by removing the connecting bolt from the lower end of the link.

2. Disconnect the stabilizer on the crossmember.

3. Check the rubber bushings for wear and replace as necessary.

4. Installation is the reverse of removal.

Rear Control Arm

REMOVAL AND INSTALLATION

524td, 528e, 535i and M5

1. Apply the parking brake and then remove the rear wheel. Disconnect the driveshaft at the outer flange by removing the bolts.

2. Remove the parking brake lever.

3. Plug the front hose to prevent loss of brake fluid in the reservoir.

4. Support the body.

5. Disconnect the brake line at the brake hose.

6. Disconnect the stabilizer and coil spring at the control arm.

7. Disconnect the control arm at the axle carrier.

8. Reconnect the control arm, stabilizer bar and coil spring. Reconnect the brake line.

9. Install the parking brake lever and install the rear wheel.

10. Bleed the brake system.

733i and 735i

1. Remove the rear wheel.

2. Apply the parking brake to hold the driveshaft stationary. Disconnect the output shaft at the drive flange. Hang the shaft from the body by a piece of wire.

3. Disconnect the parking brake cable at the lever.

4. Remove the float housing from the brake fluid reservoir and then remove as much fluid as possible from the reservoir, using a syringe used only for brake fluid (or a new one).

5. Pull the brake cable housing out of the mounting bracket near the control arm. Disconnect the brake line.

6. On 735i models with ABS: *Carefully, to avoid damaging the rubber grommet in which*

1. Spacer ring 2. Washer 3. Wishbone

Detaching the lower arm at front axle beam

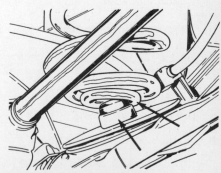

On the 318i, lower the trailing arm just enough to get the spring off the locating tang

it is mounted, pull the wiring for the pulse transmitter out of its mount so it will be possible to unplug it. Then, do so.

7. Support the trailing arm from underneath in a secure manner.

8. Remove the nuts and then remove the 2 through bolts to disconnect the control arm from the rear axle carrier.

9. If the car has a stabilizer bar, remove the bolts and remove the attaching bracket for the stabilizer bar.

10. Disconnect the shock absorber and remove the control arm.

11. Install the shock absorber in position under the vehicle. When reattaching the control arm, insert the bolt on the inner bracket first. Final tighten all mounting bolts with the car resting on its wheels. Torque the bolts attaching the control arm to the axle carrier to 49-54 ft. lbs. Refill and bleed the brake system.

Trailing Arm

REMOVAL AND INSTALLATION

1982 528e, 533i, 633CSi

1. Raise the vehicle and remove the rear wheel. Apply the parking brake and disconnect the output shaft at the rear axle shaft. Then, disconnect the parking brake cable at the handbrake. Remove the parking brake lever.

2. Remove the rear wheel.

3. Using vise grips, clamp the front hose to prevent loss of fluid.

4. Support the body.

5. Pull the parking brake cable out of the pipe.

6. Disconnect the stabilizer and spring strut at the trailing arm.

7. Disconnect the brake line at the brake hose.

8. Disconnect the driveshaft at the outboard flange.

9. Disconnect the brake pad wear indicator wire at the right trailing arm and take the wire out of the clamps.

10. Disconnect the trailing arm at the rear axle support.

11. Install the trailing arm at the rear axle support.

12. Reconnect the brake pad wear indicator. Connect the stabilizer and spring to the trailing arm.

13. Reconnect the driveshaft at the outboard flange. Reattach the parking brake cable and lever.

14. Refill and bleed the brake system.

318i, 320i, 325, 325e, 325i, 325iS, 325iX and M3

1. Raise the vehicle and remove the rear wheel. Apply the parking brake and disconnect the output shaft at the rear axle shaft. Then, on the 320i, disconnect the parking brake cable at the handbrake. On the 318i and 325, remove the parking brake lever.

2. Remove the brake fluid from the master cylinder reservoir on the 318i and 325. To do this, it will be necessary to remove the strainer at the top of the reservoir and use a new syringe or one used only with brake fluid. Disconnect the brake line connection on the rear control arm on both types of car. Plug the openings.

3. Support the control arm securely. Disconnect the shock absorber at the control arm. On 318i and 325, lower the control arm slowly and remove the spring. On the 320i, the control arm need not be lowered slowly because the spring is integral with the strut.

4. Remove the nuts and then slide the bolts out of the mounts where the control arm is mounted to the axle carrier.

5. Install the trailing arm into position. Install the bolt that goes into the inner bracket first.

6. Torque the bolts holding the trailing arm to the axle carrier to 48-54 ft. lbs.

7. On the 318i and 325, make sure the spring is positioned properly top and bottom. Torque the strut bolt to 52-63 ft. lbs.

8. Reinstall the handbrake or reconnect the cable and adjust. Then apply the brake and reconnect the output shaft.

9. Reconnect the brake line, replenish with the proper brake fluid, and bleed the system.

Rear Suspension Alignment

The rear suspension of the BMW is not adjustable. However, the rear wheel alignment can be checked using the figures in the "Wheel Alignment Specifications" chart to check for bent components. The trailing arm, if suspected of causing improper rear wheel alignment, can be checked with a special jig. If bent but not cracked or dented, it may be possible to straighten it with special equipment. This is best left to a trained technician.

STEERING

CAUTION: *On models equipped with air bags, extreme caution must be used so as not to accidentally discharge the air bag. DO NOT hammer on the steering wheel.*

Steering Wheel

REMOVAL AND INSTALLATION

NOTE: *Remove and install steering wheel in straight ahead position. Mark the relationship between the wheel and spindle.*

Troubleshooting the Power Steering Gear

Problem	Cause	Solution
Hissing noise in steering gear	• There is some noise in all power steering systems. One of the most common is a hissing sound most evident at standstill parking. There is no relationship between this noise and performance of the steering. Hiss may be expected when steering wheel is at end of travel or when slowly turning at standstill.	• Slight hiss is normal and in no way affects steering. Do not replace valve unless hiss is extremely objectionable. A replacement valve will also exhibit slight noise and is not always a cure. Investigate clearance around flexible coupling rivets. Be sure steering shaft and gear are aligned so flexible coupling rotates in a flat plane and is not distorted as shaft rotates. Any metal-to-metal contacts through flexible coupling will transmit valve hiss into passenger compartment through the steering column.
Rattle or chuckle noise in steering gear	• Gear loose on frame • Steering linkage looseness • Pressure hose touching other parts of car • Loose pitman shaft over center adjustment NOTE: A slight rattle may occur on turns because of increased clearance off the "high point." This is normal and clearance must not be reduced below specified limits to eliminate this slight rattle. • Loose pitman arm	• Check gear-to-frame mounting screws. Tighten screws to 88 N·m (65 foot pounds) torque. • Check linkage pivot points for wear. Replace if necessary. • Adjust hose position. Do not bend tubing by hand. • Adjust to specifications • Tighten pitman arm nut to specifications
Squawk noise in steering gear when turning or recovering from a turn	• Damper O-ring on valve spool cut	• Replace damper O-ring
Poor return of steering wheel to center	• Tires not properly inflated • Lack of lubrication in linkage and ball joints • Lower coupling flange rubbing against steering gear adjuster plug • Steering gear to column misalignment • Improper front wheel alignment • Steering linkage binding • Ball joints binding • Steering wheel rubbing against housing • Tight or frozen steering shaft bearings • Sticking or plugged valve spool • Steering gear adjustments over specifications • Kink in return hose	• Inflate to specified pressure • Lube linkage and ball joints • Loosen pinch bolt and assemble properly • Align steering column • Check and adjust as necessary • Replace pivots • Replace ball joints • Align housing • Replace bearings • Remove and clean or replace valve • Check adjustment with gear out of car. Adjust as required. • Replace hose
Car leads to one side or the other (keep in mind road condition and wind. Test car in both directions on flat road)	• Front end misaligned • Unbalanced steering gear valve NOTE: If this is cause, steering effort will be very light in direction of lead and normal or heavier in opposite direction	• Adjust to specifications • Replace valve

Troubleshooting the Power Steering Gear (cont.)

Problem	Cause	Solution
Momentary increase in effort when turning wheel fast to right or left	• Low oil level • Pump belt slipping • High internal leakage	• Add power steering fluid as required • Tighten or replace belt • Check pump pressure. (See pressure test)
Steering wheel surges or jerks when turning with engine running especially during parking	• Low oil level • Loose pump belt • Steering linkage hitting engine oil pan at full turn • Insufficient pump pressure • Pump flow control valve sticking	• Fill as required • Adjust tension to specification • Correct clearance • Check pump pressure. (See pressure test). Replace relief valve if defective. • Inspect for varnish or damage, replace if necessary
Excessive wheel kickback or loose steering	• Air in system • Steering gear loose on frame • Steering linkage joints worn enough to be loose • Worn poppet valve • Loose thrust bearing preload adjustment • Excessive overcenter lash	• Add oil to pump reservoir and bleed by operating steering. Check hose connectors for proper torque and adjust as required. • Tighten attaching screws to specified torque • Replace loose pivots • Replace poppet valve • Adjust to specification with gear out of vehicle • Adjust to specification with gear out of car
Hard steering or lack of assist	• Loose pump belt • Low oil level **NOTE:** Low oil level will also result in excessive pump noise • Steering gear to column misalignment • Lower coupling flange rubbing against steering gear adjuster plug • Tires not properly inflated	• Adjust belt tension to specification • Fill to proper level. If excessively low, check all lines and joints for evidence of external leakage. Tighten loose connectors. • Align steering column • Loosen pinch bolt and assemble properly • Inflate to recommended pressure
Foamy milky power steering fluid, low fluid level and possible low pressure	• Air in the fluid, and loss of fluid due to internal pump leakage causing overflow	• Check for leak and correct. Bleed system. Extremely cold temperatures will cause system aeriation should the oil level be low. If oil level is correct and pump still foams, remove pump from vehicle and separate reservoir from housing. Check welsh plug and housing for cracks. If plug is loose or housing is cracked, replace housing.
Low pressure due to steering pump	• Flow control valve stuck or inoperative • Pressure plate not flat against cam ring	• Remove burrs or dirt or replace. Flush system. • Correct
Low pressure due to steering gear	• Pressure loss in cylinder due to worn piston ring or badly worn housing bore • Leakage at valve rings, valve body-to-worm seal	• Remove gear from car for disassembly and inspection of ring and housing bore • Remove gear from car for disassembly and replace seals

Troubleshooting the Manual Steering Gear

Problem	Cause	Solution
Hard or erratic steering	• Incorrect tire pressure	• Inflate tires to recommended pressures
	• Insufficient or incorrect lubrication	• Lubricate as required (refer to Maintenance Section)
	• Suspension, or steering linkage parts damaged or misaligned	• Repair or replace parts as necessary
	• Improper front wheel alignment	• Adjust incorrect wheel alignment angles
	• Incorrect steering gear adjustment	• Adjust steering gear
	• Sagging springs	• Replace springs
Play or looseness in steering	• Steering wheel loose	• Inspect shaft spines and repair as necessary. Tighten attaching nut and stake in place.
	• Steering linkage or attaching parts loose or worn	• Tighten, adjust, or replace faulty components
	• Pitman arm loose	• Inspect shaft splines and repair as necessary. Tighten attaching nut and stake in place
	• Steering gear attaching bolts loose	• Tighten bolts
	• Loose or worn wheel bearings	• Adjust or replace bearings
	• Steering gear adjustment incorrect or parts badly worn	• Adjust gear or replace defective parts
Wheel shimmy or tramp	• Improper tire pressure	• Inflate tires to recommended pressures
	• Wheels, tires, or brake rotors out-of-balance or out-of-round	• Inspect and replace or balance parts
	• Inoperative, worn, or loose shock absorbers or mounting parts	• Repair or replace shocks or mountings
	• Loose or worn steering or suspension parts	• Tighten or replace as necessary
	• Loose or worn wheel bearings	• Adjust or replace bearings
	• Incorrect steering gear adjustments	• Adjust steering gear
	• Incorrect front wheel alignment	• Correct front wheel alignment
Tire wear	• Improper tire pressure	• Inflate tires to recommended pressures
	• Failure to rotate tires	• Rotate tires
	• Brakes grabbing	• Adjust or repair brakes
	• Incorrect front wheel alignment	• Align incorrect angles
	• Broken or damaged steering and suspension parts	• Repair or replace defective parts
	• Wheel runout	• Replace faulty wheel
	• Excessive speed on turns	• Make driver aware of conditions
Vehicle leads to one side	• Improper tire pressures	• Inflate tires to recommended pressures
	• Front tires with uneven tread depth, wear pattern, or different cord design (i.e., one bias ply and one belted or radial tire on front wheels)	• Install tires of same cord construction and reasonably even tread depth, design, and wear pattern
	• Incorrect front wheel alignment	• Align incorrect angles
	• Brakes dragging	• Adjust or repair brakes
	• Pulling due to uneven tire construction	• Replace faulty tire

Troubleshooting the Steering Column

Problem	Cause	Solution
Will not lock	• Lockbolt spring broken or defective	• Replace lock bolt spring
High effort (required to turn ignition key and lock cylinder)	• Lock cylinder defective	• Replace lock cylinder
	• Ignition switch defective	• Replace ignition switch
	• Rack preload spring broken or deformed	• Replace preload spring
	• Burr on lock sector, lock rack, housing, support or remote rod coupling	• Remove burr
	• Bent sector shaft	• Replace shaft
	• Defective lock rack	• Replace lock rack
	• Remote rod bent, deformed	• Replace rod
	• Ignition switch mounting bracket bent	• Straighten or replace
	• Distorted coupling slot in lock rack (tilt column)	• Replace lock rack
Will stick in "start"	• Remote rod deformed	• Straighten or replace
	• Ignition switch mounting bracket bent	• Straighten or replace
Key cannot be removed in "off-lock"	• Ignition switch is not adjusted correctly	• Adjust switch
	• Defective lock cylinder	• Replace lock cylinder
Lock cylinder can be removed without depressing retainer	• Lock cylinder with defective retainer	• Replace lock cylinder
	• Burr over retainer slot in housing cover or on cylinder retainer	• Remove burr
High effort on lock cylinder between "off" and "off-lock"	• Distorted lock rack	• Replace lock rack
	• Burr on tang of shift gate (automatic column)	• Remove burr
	• Gearshift linkage not adjusted	• Adjust linkage
Noise in column	• One click when in "off-lock" position and the steering wheel is moved (all except automatic column)	• Normal—lock bolt is seating
	• Coupling bolts not tightened	• Tighten pinch bolts
	• Lack of grease on bearings or bearing surfaces	• Lubricate with chassis grease
	• Upper shaft bearing worn or broken	• Replace bearing assembly
	• Lower shaft bearing worn or broken	• Replace bearing. Check shaft and replace if scored.
	• Column not correctly aligned	• Align column
	• Coupling pulled apart	• Replace coupling
	• Broken coupling lower joint	• Repair or replace joint and align column
	• Steering shaft snap ring not seated	• Replace ring. Check for proper seating in groove.
	• Shroud loose on shift bowl. Housing loose on jacket—will be noticed with ignition in "off-lock" and when torque is applied to steering wheel.	• Position shroud over lugs on shift bowl. Tighten mounting screws.
High steering shaft effort	• Column misaligned	• Align column
	• Defective upper or lower bearing	• Replace as required
	• Tight steering shaft universal joint	• Repair or replace
	• Flash on I.D. of shift tube at plastic joint (tilt column only)	• Replace shift tube
	• Upper or lower bearing seized	• Replace bearings
Lash in mounted column assembly	• Column mounting bracket bolts loose	• Tighten bolts
	• Broken weld nuts on column jacket	• Replace column jacket
	• Column capsule bracket sheared	• Replace bracket assembly

Troubleshooting the Steering Column (cont.)

Problem	Cause	Solution
Lash in mounted column assembly (cont.)	• Column bracket to column jacket mounting bolts loose • Loose lock shoes in housing (tilt column only) • Loose pivot pins (tilt column only) • Loose lock shoe pin (tilt column only) • Loose support screws (tilt column only)	• Tighten to specified torque • Replace shoes • Replace pivot pins and support • Replace pin and housing • Tighten screws
Housing loose (tilt column only)	• Excessive clearance between holes in support or housing and pivot pin diameters • Housing support-screws loose	• Replace pivot pins and support • Tighten screws
Steering wheel loose—every other tilt position (tilt column only)	• Loose fit between lock shoe and lock shoe pivot pin	• Replace lock shoes and pivot pin
Steering column not locking in any tilt position (tilt column only)	• Lock shoe seized on pivot pin • Lock shoe grooves have burrs or are filled with foreign material • Lock shoe springs weak or broken	• Replace lock shoes and pin • Clean or replace lock shoes • Replace springs
Noise when tilting column (tilt column only)	• Upper tilt bumpers worn • Tilt spring rubbing in housing	• Replace tilt bumper • Lubricate with chassis grease
One click when in "off-lock" position and the steering wheel is moved	• Seating of lock bolt	• None. Click is normal characteristic sound produced by lock bolt as it seats.
High shift effort (automatic and tilt column only)	• Column not correctly aligned • Lower bearing not aligned correctly • Lack of grease on seal or lower bearing areas	• Align column • Assemble correctly • Lubricate with chassis grease
Improper transmission shifting—automatic and tilt column only	• Sheared shift tube joint • Improper transmission gearshift linkage adjustment • Loose lower shift lever	• Replace shift tube • Adjust linkage • Replace shift tube

Troubleshooting the Ignition Switch

Problem	Cause	Solution
Ignition switch electrically inoperative	• Loose or defective switch connector • Feed wire open (fusible link) • Defective ignition switch	• Tighten or replace connector • Repair or replace • Replace ignition switch
Engine will not crank	• Ignition switch not adjusted properly	• Adjust switch
Ignition switch wil not actuate mechanically	• Defective ignition switch • Defective lock sector • Defective remote rod	• Replace switch • Replace lock sector • Replace remote rod
Ignition switch cannot be adjusted correctly	• Remote rod deformed	• Repair, straighten or replace

Troubleshooting the Turn Signal Switch

Problem	Cause	Solution
Turn signal will not cancel	• Loose switch mounting screws • Switch or anchor bosses broken • Broken, missing or out of position detent, or cancelling spring	• Tighten screws • Replace switch • Reposition springs or replace switch as required
Turn signal difficult to operate	• Turn signal lever loose • Switch yoke broken or distorted • Loose or misplaced springs • Foreign parts and/or materials in switch • Switch mounted loosely	• Tighten mounting screws • Replace switch • Reposition springs or replace switch • Remove foreign parts and/or material • Tighten mounting screws
Turn signal will not indicate lane change	• Broken lane change pressure pad or spring hanger • Broken, missing or misplaced lane change spring • Jammed wires	• Replace switch • Replace or reposition as required • Loosen mounting screws, reposition wires and retighten screws
Turn signal will not stay in turn position	• Foreign material or loose parts impeding movement of switch yoke • Defective switch	• Remove material and/or parts • Replace switch
Hazard switch cannot be pulled out	• Foreign material between hazard support cancelling leg and yoke	• Remove foreign material. No foreign material impeding function of hazard switch—replace turn signal switch.
No turn signal lights	• Inoperative turn signal flasher • Defective or blown fuse • Loose chassis to column harness connector • Disconnect column to chassis connector. Connect new switch to chassis and operate switch by hand. If vehicle lights now operate normally, signal switch is inoperative • If vehicle lights do not operate, check chassis wiring for opens, grounds, etc.	• Replace turn signal flasher • Replace fuse • Connect securely • Replace signal switch • Repair chassis wiring as required
Instrument panel turn indicator lights on but not flashing	• Burned out or damaged front or rear turn signal bulb • If vehicle lights do not operate, check light sockets for high resistance connections, the chassis wiring for opens, grounds, etc. • Inoperative flasher • Loose chassis to column harness connection • Inoperative turn signal switch • To determine if turn signal switch is defective, substitute new switch into circuit and operate switch by hand. If the vehicle's lights operate normally, signal switch is inoperative.	• Replace bulb • Repair chassis wiring as required • Replace flasher • Connect securely • Replace turn signal switch • Replace turn signal switch
Stop light not on when turn indicated	• Loose column to chassis connection • Disconnect column to chassis connector. Connect new switch into system without removing old.	• Connect securely • Replace signal switch

Troubleshooting the Turn Signal Switch (cont.)

Problem	Cause	Solution
Stop light not on when turn indicated (cont.)	Operate switch by hand. If brake lights work with switch in the turn position, signal switch is defective. • If brake lights do not work, check connector to stop light sockets for grounds, opens, etc.	• Repair connector to stop light circuits using service manual as guide
Turn indicator panel lights not flashing	• Burned out bulbs • High resistance to ground at bulb socket • Opens, ground in wiring harness from front turn signal bulb socket to indicator lights	• Replace bulbs • Replace socket • Locate and repair as required
Turn signal lights flash very slowly	• High resistance ground at light sockets • Incorrect capacity turn signal flasher or bulb • If flashing rate is still extremely slow, check chassis wiring harness from the connector to light sockets for high resistance • Loose chassis to column harness connection • Disconnect column to chassis connector. Connect new switch into system without removing old. Operate switch by hand. If flashing occurs at normal rate, the signal switch is defective.	• Repair high resistance grounds at light sockets • Replace turn signal flasher or bulb • Locate and repair as required • Connect securely • Replace turn signal switch
Hazard signal lights will not flash—turn signal functions normally	• Blow fuse • Inoperative hazard warning flasher • Loose chassis-to-column harness connection • Disconnect column to chassis connector. Connect new switch into system without removing old. Depress the hazard warning lights. If they now work normally, turn signal switch is defective. • If lights do not flash, check wiring harness "K" lead for open between hazard flasher and connector. If open, fuse block is defective	• Replace fuse • Replace hazard warning flasher in fuse panel • Conect securely • Replace turn signal switch • Repair or replace brown wire or connector as required

Troubleshooting the Power Steering Pump

Problem	Cause	Solution
Chirp noise in steering pump	• Loose belt	• Adjust belt tension to specification
Belt squeal (particularly noticeable at full wheel travel and stand still parking)	• Loose belt	• Adjust belt tension to specification
Growl noise in steering pump	• Excessive back pressure in hoses or steering gear caused by restriction	• Locate restriction and correct. Replace part if necessary.

Troubleshooting the Power Steering Pump (cont.)

Problem	Cause	Solution
Growl noise in steering pump (particularly noticeable at stand still parking)	• Scored pressure plates, thrust plate or rotor • Extreme wear of cam ring	• Replace parts and flush system • Replace parts
Groan noise in steering pump	• Low oil level • Air in the oil. Poor pressure hose connection.	• Fill reservoir to proper level • Tighten connector to specified torque. Bleed system by operating steering from right to left—full turn.
Rattle noise in steering pump	• Vanes not installed properly • Vanes sticking in rotor slots	• Install properly • Free up by removing burrs, varnish, or dirt
Swish noise in steering pump	• Defective flow control valve	• Replace part
Whine noise in steering pump	• Pump shaft bearing scored	• Replace housing and shaft. Flush system.
Hard steering or lack of assist	• Loose pump belt • Low oil level in reservoir **NOTE:** Low oil level will also result in excessive pump noise • Steering gear to column misalignment • Lower coupling flange rubbing against steering gear adjuster plug • Tires not properly inflated	• Adjust belt tension to specification • Fill to proper level. If excessively low, check all lines and joints for evidence of external leakage. Tighten loose connectors. • Align steering column • Loosen pinch bolt and assemble properly • Inflate to recommended pressure
Foaming milky power steering fluid, low fluid level and possible low pressure	• Air in the fluid, and loss of fluid due to internal pump leakage causing overflow	• Check for leaks and correct. Bleed system. Extremely cold temperatures will cause system aeration should the oil level be low. If oil level is correct and pump still foams, remove pump from vehicle and separate reservoir from body. Check welsh plug and body for cracks. If plug is loose or body is cracked, replace body.
Low pump pressure	• Flow control valve stuck or inoperative • Pressure plate not flat against cam ring	• Remove burrs or dirt or replace. Flush system. • Correct
Momentary increase in effort when turning wheel fast to right or left	• Low oil level in pump • Pump belt slipping • High internal leakage	• Add power steering fluid as required • Tighten or replace belt • Check pump pressure. (See pressure test)
Steering wheel surges or jerks when turning with engine running especially during parking	• Low oil level • Loose pump belt • Steering linkage hitting engine oil pan at full turn • Insufficient pump pressure	• Fill as required • Adjust tension to specification • Correct clearance • Check pump pressure. (See pressure test). Replace flow control valve if defective.
Steering wheel surges or jerks when turning with engine running especially during parking (cont.)	• Sticking flow control valve	• Inspect for varnish or damage, replace if necessary
Excessive wheel kickback or loose steering	• Air in system	• Add oil to pump reservoir and bleed by operating steering. Check hose connectors for proper torque and adjust as required.

Troubleshooting the Power Steering Pump (cont.)

Problem	Cause	Solution
Low pump pressure	• Extreme wear of cam ring • Scored pressure plate, thrust plate, or rotor • Vanes not installed properly • Vanes sticking in rotor slots • Cracked or broken thrust or pressure plate	• Replace parts. Flush system. • Replace parts. Flush system. • Install properly • Freeup by removing burrs, varnish, or dirt • Replace part

1. Remove steering wheel pad or BMW emblem. Mark the relationship between the steering wheel and shaft for installation in the same position. On 1986-89 models, unlock the steering wheel lock with the key. Otherwise, the wheel cannot be removed.

2. Unscrew retaining nut and remove the wheel.

CAUTION: *Be careful not to damage the direction signal cancelling cam, which is right under the steering wheel, in performing this operation.*

3. Install the steering wheel on the shaft, making sure to align the marks made earlier. Lubricate the direction signal cancelling cam. Replace the self-locking nut on all 1983-88 models, and torque it to 58 ft. lbs.

4. On the 1600, 2000 and 2002, torque the 12mm nut to 40 ft. lbs., the 14mm nut to 61 ft. lbs. On the 2800, Bavaria and 3.0, torque the nut to 69 ft. lbs.

Turn Signal Switch (Combination Switch)

REMOVAL AND INSTALLATION

1600, 2000, and 2002

1. Remove the steering wheel. Unscrew and remove the padded trim surrounding the column.

2. Unscrew the choke knob, and the retaining nut behind it. Unscrew the mounting screws and remove the steering column lower surround.

3. Mark the position of the turn signal switch; then, remove the attaching screws and remove the switch.

4. During installation, note that the switch is mounted via slots and, before tightening the mounting screws, slide the switch back and forth until the gap between the canceling cam and the actuating dog on the switch is 0.3mm.

5. Connect wiring to the switch as follows:
   a. Gray-P
   b. Green/Yellow-54
   c. Blue/Black-R
   d. Blue/Red-L
   e. Brown/Black-H
   f. Gray/Green-PR
   g. Gray/Black-Pl

2500, 2800, Bavaria, 3000 and 3.0

1. Put the steering wheel in the straight ahead position. Remove the lower steering col-

1600, 2002 turn signal switch (right side of the steering column). Dimension "A" is the gap between the canceling cam and the actuating dog (see text)

"A" represents the gap between the cancelling cam and the switch cam follower. The mounting screws are arrowed

On the 500 series, disconnect the parking light connector near the column

Disconnect the main supply plug (arrowed)

umn housing and the lower center instrument panel trim on the left side.

2. Remove the steering wheel.

3. Remove the attaching screws and remove the turn signal switch.

4. Extract the cable harness from the retaining clips. Pull out the control lever light, detach the plug, and separate the cable connector.

5. Pull off the black multiple connector and the gray/blue cable.

6. Install the switch, with the switch in the center position, the actuating peg pointing toward the center of the canceling cam, and the clearance between the canceling cam and switch cam follower, **A**, at 0.3mm the switch is slotted at the mounting points to allow for this adjustment before the mounting screws receive final tightening.

318i, 320i

1. Turn the steering wheel to the straight ahead position. Remove the steering wheel and the lower steering column cover.

2. Disconnect the (–) cable from the battery. Disconnect the direction signal switch multiple

connector from under the dash by squeezing in the locks on either side and pulling it off.

3. Remove the cable straps from the column.

4. Loosen the mounting screws and remove the switch and harness.

5. Install the switch in position, noting the following points:

a. Make sure to mount the ground wire.

b. Make sure the switch is in the middle position and that the follower faces the center of the cancelling cam on the steering column shaft. Then, before finally tightening the switch mounting screws, adjust the switch on slotted mounting holes so the gap between the cam and follower is 3mm.

325, 325e, 325i, 325iS, 325iX and M3

1. Turn the steering wheel to the straight ahead position. Remove the steering wheel and the lower steering column cover. Remove the 5 retaining screws and remove the lower left instrument panel cover.

2. Disconnect the (–) cable from the battery. If the turn signal switch is to be replaced, remove the screw at top left and the ground wire attaching screw at the bottom left. If the wiper switch is to be replaced, remove the 2 similar screws on the right side.

3. To disconnect the turn signal/dimmer switch wiring:

a. Lift the plug and flasher relay out of the clip on the left side of the steering column and unplug the relay. Unplug the horn lead just above.

b. Cut the straps retaining the wiring and then disconnect the plug the turn signal/dimmer switch wiring goes to just below.

4. To disconnect the wiper switch wiring, cut the 2 wire straps and disconnect the plug the wiper switch wiring connects with the the lower left column.

5. Install the switch into position and reinstall all of the components removed. Make sure to inspect the ground wires carefully for any breaks in insulation or other problems (if the switch is being re-used) and ensure that they are properly connected.

533i and 633CSi

Follow the procedure for 318i and 320i above exactly; when adjusting the gap between the cancelling cam and the switch follower, use the dimension 3mm.

524td, 528e, 535i, 635CSi, M5 and M6

1. Disconnect the battery ground cable. Remove the steering wheel as described above.

2. Remove the instrument panel trim which

Turn signal switch adjustment

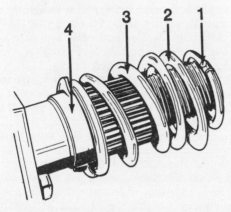

When removing the 318i steering lock, remove the snap ring (1), washer (2), spring (3), and seating ring (4)

is near the bottom of the steering wheel on the left side.

3. Remove the 2 screws from underneath and remove the steering column lower cover.

4. Disconnect the electrical connectors near the bottom of the column and at the area just under the front of the dash.

5. Unscrew the 2 screws fastening the switch and one ground wire to the column just to the left of the steering shaft. Pull off the plug connecting the switch to the relay on the right side of the column. Remove the switch.

6. Install the switch in position and connect the wiring. Install the steering column covers and the lower instrument panel trim.

7. Install the steering wheel and connect the negative battery cable.

1982 733i

1. Remove the steering wheel and disconnect the battery ground cable.

2. Remove the trim from below the steering column. Remove the mounting screws and detach the switch from the switch plate.

3. Loosen the straps holding the switch cable to the steering column. Pull the center plug out of the panel on the cowl and remove the switch.

4. Install the switch in position and connect the wiring. Install the steering column covers and the lower instrument panel trim.

5. Install the steering wheel and connect the negative battery cable.

1983-85 733i
1985-86 735i

1. Disconnect the negative battery cable. Remove the steering wheel as described above.

2. Remove the lower steering column cover.

3. Remove the 2 Phillips type screws located to the left of the steering shaft (the lower screw mounts a ground wire).

4. Disconnect the electrical connector for the switch and the flasher relay, located along the front of the column. Pull the flasher relay out of the holder.

5. Follow the wiring to the area under the dash. Open ties and unplug the electrical connector. Remove the switch.

6. Install the switch into position, making sure to retie electrical wiring going under the dash and to reconnect the ground wire to the lower switch mounting screw.

1987-88 735i

1. Disconnect the battery ground. Remove the steering wheel as described above.

2. Remove the instrument panel trim below and to the left of the steering wheel.

3. Remove the lower steering column cover.

4. Compress its retaining hook and then pull off the flasher relay socket facing downward.

5. On cars with airbags, drive out the pin and pry out the expansion rivet. Then, on all cars, remove the upper steering column cover.

On the 2800 and 3.0, also remove screws numbered 2, 3, and 4 to remove the lower center, left section of the instrument panel

On the 2800 and 3.0, remove the screw shown (1) to remove the lower, center left section of the instrument panel housing

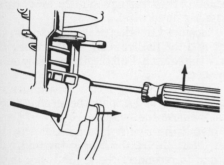

On the 318i, press down the locking hook with a screwdriver, as shown, and remove the ignition switch

6. Pull off the connector plug. This is located between the column and the dash in front of and just above where the steering wheel is normally located.

7. Compress the retaining hooks and remove the switch (located to the left of the steering shaft). Disconnect all electrical plugs and remove the switch.

8. Install the switch in position and connect the wiring. Reinstall all other components that were removed. Install the steering column covers and the lower instrument panel trim.

9. Install the steering wheel and connect the negative battery cable.

Ignition Switch
REMOVAL AND INSTALLATION

Except Below

1. Disconnect negative battery terminal.
2. Remove lower steering column casing.
3. On 320i, 633CSi, 733i and 528e models, shear off the 4 tamper-proof screws with a chisel or other tool.
4. Unscrew the set screw and remove the switch.
5. Disconnect the central fuse/relay plate plug.

6. Installation is the reverse of removal.
NOTE: *Turn ignition key all the way back and set the switch at the "0" position before installing. Marks on the switch must be opposite each other.*

318i, 325, 325e, 325i, 325iS and M3

1. Disconnect the battery ground cable. Remove the steering wheel.
2. Remove the 4 screws, and remove the lower steering column cover.
3. Disconnect the turn signal/wiper switch by removing the 4 screws and disconnecting the wires.
4. Remove the collar from the steering column shaft. Then, remove the snapring (1), washer (2), spring (3) and seating ring (4).
CAUTION: *In the next step, pry carefully. Don't use too much force, because a screwdriver can slip and cause injury!*
5. Pry off the steering spindle bearings with 2 screwdrivers. Pry by the *inner race only*
6. Disconnect the main electrical plug at the bottom of the steering column.
7. Use a chisel to remove the tamper proof screw. Pull the lock assembly with the upper section of the casting off the outer column.
8. With a suitable tool, press downward on the lock and then slide the switch off, noting the switch position and that of the lock assembly.
9. To install, locate the switch in the correct position and install it, noting these points:
   a. When installing the switch, make sure its position is the same in relationship with the lock, so the actions of the 2 will be synchronized.
   b. Use a Torx® screwdriver for the tamper proof screw.
   c. Drive the steering spindle bearings back on by the inner races only.
   d. When installing the seating ring that goes on the shaft, make sure the spring seat faces outward. Use a piece of pipe slightly larger than the shaft and tap it with a hammer to install the snapring. Then, make sure the collar that goes on next locks the snapring in place.

1985-86 524td, 528e, 535i and 635i

1. Disconnect the battery ground cable. Remove the steering wheel as described above.
2. Remove the instrument panel lower trim and the steering column lower cover.
3. Unplug the flasher relay and then pull the relay and holder off the front of the column. Then, remove the 4 Phillips screws retaining the headlight dimmer and wiper combination switch.

4. Use a hammer and chisel to shear off the 5 screws mounting the switch.

5. Remove the setscrew. Then, press downward on the steering column and pull the steering lock out.

6. Install the position in the correct position, using new shear-off type screws to mount the switch. Make sure to install the switch so it is properly positioned in relation to the steering lock.

7. Apply paint to the setscrew to lock it in position after it has been installed and tightened.

524td, 1987-88 528e, 535i, M5, 635i and M6

NOTE: *To perform this operation, use special tools 32 3 052 and 32 3 050 or equivalent. These are a sleeve, tapered at the outer end, which permits mounting a snapring over the threaded end of the steering shaft without damaging those threads. There is also a pipe which fits over the sleeve and permits the snapring to be forced down the sleeve while being kept square.*

1. Disconnect the battery ground cable. Remove the steering wheel as described above.

2. Remove the steering column lower cover.

3. Unplug the flasher relay and then pull the relay and holder off the front of the column. Pull the plug off the horn contact.

4. Note the location of the 2 ground wires. Then, remove the 4 Phillips screws and remove the headlight/wiper switch.

5. Pull the collar off the steering shaft. Then, remove, in order, the snapring, washer, spring, and seating ring.

6. Press downward on the locking hook and pull the ignition switch off the column.

7. Install the switch in position. Install the seating ring with the flat side outward. Use the special tools to fit the snapring on as described in the note above.

8. Mount the collar with the recess downward. Make sure to reconnect the ground wires to the bottom left Phillips screw.

1983-84 733i

1. Remove the outer steering column cover.

2. Lift the flasher relay out of its holding clamp. Unscrew the attaching screw and pull out the switch.

3. Open the wire strap and pull off the plug.

4. Install the switch into position, noting these points:

   a. With the ignition key in the new switch, turn the key slowly back and forth while sliding in the switch until it engages. Apply a new coating of locking sealer.

   b. Connect the black wire from the ignition switch to the black wire coming from the

power saving relay. Use new straps to tie the wiring harness back in place.

1985-86 735i

1. Disconnect the battery ground cable. Remove the steering wheel as described above.

2. Remove the steering column lower cover.

3. Then, remove the 4 Phillips screws retaining the headlight dimmer and wiper switches.

4. Use a hammer and chisel to shear off the 4 screws mounting the switch to the switch plate.

5. Remove the setscrew. Then, pull the ignition switch out.

6. To synchronize the positions of the ignition lock and switch, use the key to turn the ignition lock as far back from the on position as it will go, and set the ignition switch to the **O** position. Complete the installation in reverse order, using new shear-off type screws to mount the switch. Make sure to install the switch so it is properly positioned in relation to the steering lock.

7. Apply clear lacquer to the setscrew to lock it in position after it has been installed and tightened.

1987-88 735i

1. Disconnect the battery ground cable. Remove the steering wheel as described above. Remove the instrument panel trim located just below the steering column.

2. Remove the steering column cover casing by removing the 2 screws from underneath and the 2 from the front of the column.

3. Remove the bolt and nut fastening the lower end of the steering spindle (the bolt passes through a groove in the spindle). Mark alignment of the steering shaft splines with a spot of paint on each side.

4. Remove the bolts and nuts at the forked lower end of the steering column. Replace the nuts, which are self-locking.

5. Remove the 2 bolts fastening the upper column to the dash. Remove the column by pressing it downward.

6. Pull off the ignition switch connector. Then, compress the locking hooks and pull off the combination switch.

7. Turn the ignition switch to **R** position. Use a center punch to press the retainer into the locking bore in the case and then pull the ignition switch out of the case.

8. Install the switch into position, noting the following points:

   a. Make sure to remount the spacer sleeve that goes in the column mounting bracket.

   b. After realigning the splines of the steering shaft and lower column, tighten the adjusting nut so the sliding force of the column is about 10 lbs.

c. Make sure the bolt which fastens the steering spindle in place passes through the groove in the spindle.

d. Check the position of the concave collar located just under the steering wheel. It must fit over the snapring.

e. Double check to make sure to replace all self-locking nuts.

Steering Column

REMOVAL AND INSTALLATION

NOTE: *On models with SRS, observe all safety precautions. Special care should be taken when handling the column, so as not to damage the shear pins. Damage to the shear pins could cause the column not to collapse in the event of an accident.*

1. Disconnect the negative battery cable.
2. Remove the steering wheel and surrounding trim, as outlined earlier in this chapter.
3. Remove the turn signal/combination switch as outlined in Chapter 6.
4. Remove the ignition switch and remove the warning buzzer from the steering column.
5. Remove the bolts that hold the lower and upper halves of the steering column together.
6. Unscrew the left and right column mounting bolts. Remove the 2 mounting bolts at the pedal assembly bracket.

7. Unscrew the bolt at the bottom of the column upper casing and remove the casing.
8. Under the hood disconnect the lower column coupling and pull the column from the vehicle.
9. Install the column in position and connect the lower coupling, to steering gear bolts to 18-20 ft. lbs.
10. Install the column-to-bracket mounting bolts and tighten to 15-16 ft. lbs. Install the lower coupling bolts and tighten to 15-17 ft. lbs.
11. Install the trim panels and the buzzer. Install the steering wheel.

NOTE: *Do not bang on the steering column as column damage may result.*

Steering Linkage

REMOVAL AND INSTALLATION

Tie Rod Arm

1. Raise and safely support the front of the vehicle. Remove the front wheel.
2. On the 2002, detach the stabilizer wishbone. Detach the wishbone at the front axle

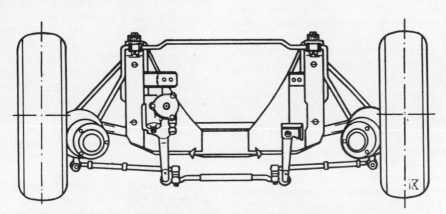

Typical steering linkage—all models except 320i

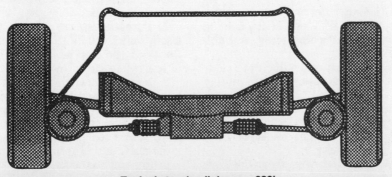

Typical steering linkage—320i

beam. Detach the trailing link from the wishbone.

3. Remove the cotter pin and castle.

4. Press the outer tie rod off the tie rod arm, and press the stabilizer off the control arm.

5. Remove the lockwire and detach the tie rod arm at the shock absorber.

6. Press the tie rod arm off the control arm.

7. Install the tie rod into the control arm.and attach the tie rod at the shock.

8. Press on the outer tie rod and press the stabilizer onto the control arm.

9. Install the trailing link to the wishbone and install the castle nut and cotter pin. Install the front wheel.

Outer Tie Rod

1. Remove the cotter pin, castle nut and press the outer tie rod off the center tie rod.

2. Remove the cotter pin, loosen the castle nut and press the outer tie rod off the tie rod arm.

Disconnecting outer tie-rod from spindle lever

Tie rod arm-to-shock absorber retaining bolts—733i

3. Install the outer tie rod to the tie rod arm and install the castle nuts.

4. Align the front axle.

Center Tie Rod

1. On the 733i, remove the heat guard.

2. Remove the cotter pins, loosen the castle nuts and press the left and right tie rods off the center tie rod.

3. Press the center tie rod off of the steering control arm.

4. Attach the center tie rod to the steering control arm and install the left and right tie rods.

5. Align the front axle.

Left and Right Tie Rods

1. Loosen the wheel.

2. Remove the cotter pin and loosen the castle nut.

3. Press the tie rod off the steering knuckle.

4. Detach the strap, slide back the bellows and bend open the lock plate.

5. Detach the tie rod at the rack.

6. Attach the tie rod at the steering rack and install the bellows in position.

7. Install the tie rod to the steering knuckle and install the castle nut.

Manual Steering Gear

REMOVAL AND INSTALLATION

320i

1. Loosen the front wheels.

2. Remove the cotter pin and castle nut.

3. Press the tie rods off of the steering knuckles.

4. Detach the steering gear at the front axle support.

5. Pull the steering gear off of the steering spindle.

6. Install the steering gear on the steering spindle. Attach the steering gear at the front axle support.

7. Attach the tie rods to the steering knuckles. Install the castle nuts and cotter pins to the tie rods. Install the front wheel

NOTE: *Turn the steering wheel until the wheels point straight ahead. The mark on the dust seal must be between the marks on the gear box.*

2002, 2500, 2800, Bavaria, 3000 and 3.0

1. Loosen the bolt connecting the coupling flange to the steering column, remove the bolt attaching the flange to the steering box.

NOTE: *On the 2002, do not reuse self-locking nuts.*

2. Remove the castle nut and press off the left track rod from the center track rod.

Pressure pad adjustment—320i

Steering adjustment 320i

Turning torque adjustment—320i

3. Press the center track rod from the steering drop arm.

4. Detach and remove the steering box from the front axle beam.

5. Install the steering box to the front axle beam and attach the drop arm to the track rod. Connect the left track rod to the center track rod.

6. Connect the steering column coupling to the steering box flange.

NOTE: *The steering wheel must be in the straight ahead position and the markings on*

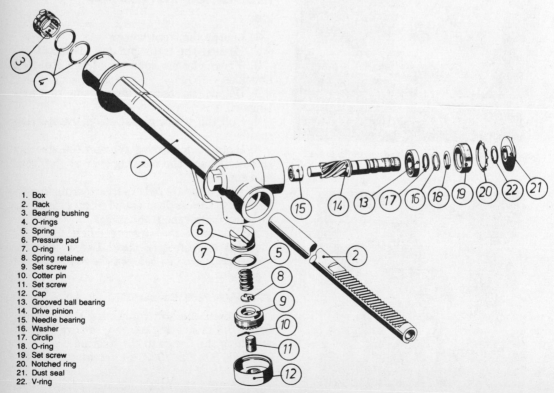

1. Box
2. Rack
3. Bearing bushing
4. O-rings
5. Spring
6. Pressure pad
7. O-ring
8. Spring retainer
9. Set screw
10. Cotter pin
11. Set screw
12. Cap
13. Grooved ball bearing
14. Drive pinion
15. Needle bearing
16. Washer
17. Circlip
18. O-ring
19. Set screw
20. Notched ring
21. Dust seal
22. V-ring

Typical steering gear

the steering box and the pitman shaft must align.

ADJUSTMENT

320i

1. Remove the steering gear from the car.
2. Clamp the special tool 32-1-100, or equivalent, in a vise and place the steering gear assembly into the tool.
3. Unscrew the nut on the steering damper and slide it back.
4. Remove the cap and unscrew the socket head cap about 12mm.
5. Pressure pad adjustment:

   a. Remove the cotter pin. Tighten the set screw with special 32-1-100, or equivalent, and a torque wrench, to 4 ft. lbs. Loosen the set screw by one full castle slot to align the cotter pin bore.

   b. Use special tools 32-1-00 and 00-2-000 or equivalent to move rack to the left and right over the entire stroke and check for sticking and hooking. If this is the case, loosen the set screw by one more castle slot and insert the cotter pin.

   c. Repeat test. If there is still sticking or hooking, replace rack, drive pinion or the entire steering gear. Never loosen the screw by 2 castle slots regardless of circumstances.
6. Turning torque adjustment:

   a. Move rack to the center position. Place special tools 00-2-000 and 32-1-000 or equivalent on the drive pinion, check the turning torque. If it is not between 7.8 and 11.2 ft. lbs., adjust the set screw.

   b. Turn to the right to increase friction, and turn to the left to decrease friction.

   c. Install cap.

2002, 2500, 2800, Bavaria, 3000 and 3.0

1. Remove the air intake filter on the 2002.
2. Position the front wheels straight ahead.
3. The marking on the worm shaft must be in alignment with the marking on the steering box.
4. Remove the castle nut and press the left hand tie rod from the center tie rod.
5. Remove the castle nut and press the center tie rod from the drop arm with special tool 7009, or the equivalent.
6. Remove the steering wheel center and install a friction gauge.
7. Turn the steering wheel one turn to the left from the straight ahead position. In this position the worm cannot be pressed one-sided into its bearing by the steering roller shaft, which might indicate absence of play.
8. Turn the adjustment screw until the specified friction coefficient is reached when passing through the straight ahead position.

Power Steering Gear

REMOVAL AND INSTALLATION

All Except Below

1. Turn the steering to left lock.
2. On 1985-89 models, which share the hydraulic system with the power brakes, discharge pressure from the system by operating the brake pedal hard about 20 times. Then, drain brake fluid out of the reservoir. Remove the 2 mounting nuts/bolts and remove the pipe connecting the steering unit and the rest of the system.
3. On all other systems, drain the steering fluid at this point.
4. Remove the cotter pin and loosen the castlellated nut. Then, press the center tie rod off the steering drop arm.
5. Remove the screw or nut(s) and bolt(s) and slide the U-joint off the steering box or slide the flange coupling the steering column and steering gear upward. Replace all self-locking nuts.
6. Disconnect the hoses at the steering gear and plug the openings.
7. Detach and remove the steering gear mounting bolts at the front axle carrier, working below it. Be careful to retain all washers. They are used on both side of the front axle carrier members.
8. Install the steering gear into position. Use new seals on the hydraulic lines.
9. The U-joint bolts must pass through the locking grooves on the steering shaft and steering unit shaft.
10. When reinstalling the gearbox on 1983-88 6 and 7 Series cars, line up marks on the steering shaft and gearbox so the steering wheel will be in the straight ahead position.
11. Use a new cotter pin on the castlellated nut. Replace all self-locking nuts. A new, self locking nut is available to replace the castlellated nut on the steering drop arm. Use new hydraulic fluid.

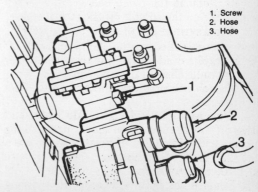

1. Screw
2. Hose
3. Hose

Coupling flange and steering box

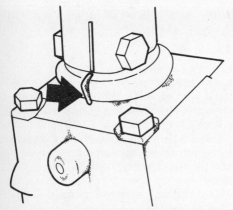

On late model 733i and 735is, line up the marks on the steering shaft and gearbox to put the steering wheel in the straight ahead position.

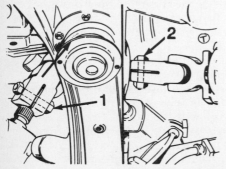

On the 318i, remove the pinch bolt (1), and through bolt (2)

NOTE: *System must be bled and the front wheels must be in the straight ahead position. Marks on the housing and propeller shaft must align. Use new self locking nuts on all models.*

318i, 325, 325e, 325i, 325iS and M3

1. Support the car securely and remove front wheels. Remove the pinch bolt (1) and loosen bolt (2). Press the spindle off the steering gear.

2. Use a syringe to empty the power steering fluid reservoir. Loosen the clamp and pull off the hydraulic fluid return line from the power steering unit. Discard drained fluid.

3. Detach the pressure line (arrowed). Seal off openings.

4. Unscrew left and right side nuts, and press off the tie rods where they connect to the spring struts. For most of these models, use a tool such as 32 0 070; however, for the M3, use 32 1 160 or equivalent.

5. Remove the bolts attaching the steering unit to the front axle carrier and remove it.

6. Install the steering unit to the front axle, keeping the following points in mind:

a. The steering unit bolts to the rear holes of the axle carrier. Use new self-locking nuts and torque them to 29-34 ft. lbs.

b. When reconnecting tie rods to the spring struts, make sure tie rod pins and strut bores are clean. Replace self-locking nuts, coat threads with Loctite® 270 or equivalent, and torque to 40-48 ft. lbs.

c. Replace the seals on the power steering pump connection, and torque the bolt to 29-32 ft. lbs.

d. Refill the fluid reservoir with specified fluid.

e. Idle the engine and turn the steering wheel back and forth until it has reached right and left lock 2 times each. Then, turn off the engine and refill the reservoir.

325iX (4 Wheel Drive)

NOTE: *To remove the steering gear on 4 wheel drive models, use a special tool to support the engine via the body. It is possible to use BMW Tool 00 0 200 or an equivalent device available in the aftermarket. It is also advisable to use a special tool to support the front axle carrier without damaging it. Another tool such as, BMW 00 0 200, would do this job. It is necessary to remove the entire front axle carrier to gain access to the mounting bolts for the steering gear on this model.*

1. Raise the car and support it securely off the ground via the body. Remove the splash guard. Remove the front wheels.

2. Remove the air cleaner. Use a clean syringe to remove the power steering fluid from the pump reservoir.

3. Attach the support tool and connect it to the engine hooks to be sure the engine is securely supported.

4. Remove the through bolts from the right and left engine mounts.

5. Disconnect both the hydraulic lines running from the power steering pump to the steering gear, and then plug the openings.

6. Loosen both the retaining bolts and then disconnect the steering column spindle off the steering gear.

7. Remove the retaining nuts on both sides and then use a tool such as 32 2 070 to press the tie rod ends off the steering knuckles. Be careful to keep grease out of the bores and off the tie rod ballstuds.

8. Remove the cotter pins, remove the retaining nuts on both sides and then use a tool such as 31 2 160 to press the control arm balljoint studs out of the steering knuckles. Be careful to keep grease out of the bores and off the control arm ballstuds.

9. Remove the 2 bolts on either side attaching the control arm brackets to the body.

10. Remove the 2 bolts and remove the stabilizer bar mounting brackets from the front axle carrier on both sides.

11. Support the front axle carrier with a floorjack, assisted by the special tool mentioned in the note above or by another safe means that will not put stress on the axle carrier. Then, remove the (2) mounting bolts on either side and remove the axle carrier. Remove the 3 mounting bolts and remove the steering gear from the axle carrier.

12. Install the steering gear to the axle carrier, noting these points:

  a. Clean the bores into which the axle carrier bolts are mounted. Use some sort of locking sealer and torque the bolts to 30 ft. lbs.

  b. Torque the mounting bolts holding the steering gear to front axle carrier to 30 ft. lbs.

  c. Install new cotter pins on the retaining nuts for the control arm ballstuds. Torque to 61.5 ft. lbs.

  d. Replace the self-locking nuts on the tie rod end ballstuds and connecting the steering column spindle to the steering box. Torque tie rod ballstud nuts to 24-29 ft. lbs.

  e. Replace the gaskets on power steering hydraulic lines. Refill the fluid reservoir with specified fluid. Idle the engine and turn the steering wheel back and forth until it has reached right and left lock 2 times each. Then, turn off the engine and refill the reservoir.

ADJUSTMENT

1. Remove the steering wheel center.

2. With the front wheels in the straight ahead position, remove the cotter pin and loosen the castle nut.

3. Press the center tie rod off the steering drop arm.

4. Turn the steering wheel to the left about one turn. Install a friction gauge and turn the wheel to the right, past the point of pressure and the gauge should read 8.5-10.5 in. lbs.

5. To adjust, turn the steering wheel about one turn to the left. Loosen the counter nut and turn the adjusting screw until the specified friction is reached when passing over the point of pressure.

Power Steering Pump
REMOVAL AND INSTALLATION
All Models Except 733i and 735i

NOTE: *On 5, 6 and 7 Series models built in 1986-88 and not equipped with anti-lock brakes, the power steering pump operates the power brakes. On these cars, depress the brake pedal repeatedly until all boost pressure has been discharged.*

1. Detach the steering pump hoses. Seal off all openings. Loosen the locknut and turn the adjusting bolt to release belt tension, and remove the belt.

2. On 1983-88 6 Series models, remove the splash guard. Remove bolts from the brackets holding the front and rear of the pump.

3. Install the pump in position and install the retaining bolts.

4. Torque pump mounting bolts to 16-17 ft. lbs. On 3 series cars with a toothed drive belt adjusting nut, torque the adjusting nut to 69-73 in. lbs. to get the correct belt tension.

NOTE: *Bleed the system and torque the hose connections to 35 ft. lbs. (29-32 ft. lbs. for the 318i and 325).*

733i and 735i

NOTE: *When the pump is damaged, the pressure control regulator must also be replaced.*

1. Discharge the hydraulic accumulator, by depressing the brake pedal with the force required for full stop breaking (about 20 times).

2. Use a syringe to draw the fluid out of the pump reservoir and discard it. Detach all hoses at the pump and plug the openings.

3. Loosen the 2 locknuts and turn the adjusting pinion nut to release the belt tension. Remove the drive belt.

4. Remove bolts from the brackets holding the pump in place at both top and bottom.

5. Install the pump and its mounting bolts. Reconnect the hoses to the pump in such a way that they will not rub against body parts. Note that on 1983-88 models, the belt tension is released or tightened by unscrewing the splash guard, loosening the locknut and bolts at top and bottom of the pump, and then turning the geared locking element.

6. In adjusting the belt, torque this locking element in the tightening direction to 69-73 in. lbs. and then tighten the locknut. Use new seals on the hydraulic lines.

NOTE: *Run the engine 10 minutes and turn the steering wheel several times from stop to stop. Operate the brake booster quickly, to obtain hard resistance, about 10 times to discard the oil leaving the return hose.*

7. Stop the engine, drain the oil from the tank and connect the booster return hose on the tank.

BELT ADJUSTMENT

Tighten the belt so that when pressure is applied to the belt, the distance between both belt pulleys is 5-10mm.

On 1983-88 733i and 735i models and the lat-

est 3 Series models, torque the geared locking element in the tightening direction to 69-73 in. lbs. and then tighten the locknut.

SYSTEM BLEEDING

1. Fill the reservoir to the edge with the proper fluid.

2. Start the engine and all oil until the oil level remains constant.

3. Turn the steering wheel from lock to lock quickly until air bubbles are no longer present in the reservoir.

4. On models incorporating a combination power steering and power brake system, operate the brake pedal to discharge the hydraulic accumulator until the oil level stops rising or noticeable resistance on the brake pedal is felt.

BRAKE SYSTEMS

Hydraulic System
BASIC OPERATING PRINCIPLES
Except Anti-Lock Braking System

Hydraulic systems are used to actuate the brakes of all modern automobiles. The system transports the power required to force the frictional surfaces of the braking system together from the pedal to the individual brake units at each wheel. A hydraulic system is used for two reasons. First, fluid under pressure can be carried to all parts of an automobile by small hoses-some of which are flexible-without taking up a significant amount of room or posing routing problems. Second, a great mechanical advantage can be given to the brake pedal end of the system, and the foot pressure required to actuate the brakes can be reduced by making the surface area of the master cylinder pistons smaller than that of any of the pistons in the wheel cylinders or calipers.

The master cylinder consists of a fluid reservoir and either a single or double cylinder and piston assembly. Double type master cylinders are designed to separate the front and rear braking systems hydraulically in case of a leak.

Steel lines carry the brake fluid to a point on the vehicle's frame near each of the vehicle's wheels. The fluid is then carried to the wheel cylinders by flexible tubes in order to allow for suspension and steering movements.

Each wheel cylinder contains two pistons, one at either end, which push outward in opposite directions. In disc brake systems, the cylinders are part of the calipers. One or four cylinders are used to force the brake pads against the disc, but all cylinders contain one piston only. All pistons employ some type of seal, usually made of rubber, to minimize fluid leakage.

A rubber dust boot seals the outer end of the cylinder against dust and dirt. The boot fits around the outer end of the piston on disc brake calipers, and around the brake actuating rod on wheel cylinders.

The hydraulic system operates as follows: When at rest, the entire system, from the piston(s) in the master cylinder to those in the wheel cylinders or calipers, is full of brake fluid. Upon application of the brake pedal, fluid trapped in front of the master cylinder piston(s) is forced through the lines to the wheel cylinders. Here, it forces the pistons outward, in the case of drum brakes, and inward toward the disc, in the case of disc brakes. The motion of the pistons is opposed by return springs mounted outside the cylinders in drum brakes, and by internal springs or spring seals, in disc brakes.

Upon release of the brake pedal, a spring located inside the master cylinder immediately returns the master cylinder pistons to the normal position. The pistons contain check valves and the master cylinder has compensating ports drilled in it. These are uncovered as the pistons reach their normal position. The piston check valves allow fluid to flow toward the wheel cylinders or calipers as the pistons withdraw. Then, as the return springs force the brake pads or shoes into the released position, the excess fluid reservoir through the compensating ports. It is during the time the pedal is in the released position that any fluid that has leaked out of the system will be replaced through the compensating ports.

Dual circuit master cylinders employ two pistons, located one behind the other, in the same cylinder. The primary piston is actuated directly by mechanical linkage from the brake pedal. The secondary piston is actuated by fluid trapped between the two pistons. If a leak develops in front of the secondary piston, it moves forward until it bottoms against the front of the master cylinder, and the fluid trapped between

Troubleshooting the Brake System

Problem	Cause	Solution
Low brake pedal (excessive pedal travel required for braking action.)	• Excessive clearance between rear linings and drums caused by inoperative automatic adjusters	• Make 10 to 15 alternate forward and reverse brake stops to adjust brakes. If brake pedal does not come up, repair or replace adjuster parts as necessary.
	• Worn rear brakelining	• Inspect and replace lining if worn beyond minimum thickness specification
	• Bent, distorted brakeshoes, front or rear	• Replace brakeshoes in axle sets
	• Air in hydraulic system	• Remove air from system. Refer to Brake Bleeding.
Low brake pedal (pedal may go to floor with steady pressure applied.)	• Fluid leak in hydraulic system	• Fill master cylinder to fill line; have helper apply brakes and check calipers, wheel cylinders, differential valve tubes, hoses and fittings for leaks. Repair or replace as necessary.
	• Air in hydraulic system	• Remove air from system. Refer to Brake Bleeding.
	• Incorrect or non-recommended brake fluid (fluid evaporates at below normal temp).	• Flush hydraulic system with clean brake fluid. Refill with correct-type fluid.
	• Master cylinder piston seals worn, or master cylinder bore is scored, worn or corroded	• Repair or replace master cylinder
Low brake pedal (pedal goes to floor on first application—o.k. on subsequent applications.)	• Disc brake pads sticking on abutment surfaces of anchor plate. Caused by a build-up of dirt, rust, or corrosion on abutment surfaces	• Clean abutment surfaces
Fading brake pedal (pedal height decreases with steady pressure applied.)	• Fluid leak in hydraulic system	• Fill master cylinder reservoirs to fill mark, have helper apply brakes, check calipers, wheel cylinders, differential valve, tubes, hoses, and fittings for fluid leaks. Repair or replace parts as necessary.
	• Master cylinder piston seals worn, or master cylinder bore is scored, worn or corroded	• Repair or replace master cylinder
Decreasing brake pedal travel (pedal travel required for braking action decreases and may be accompanied by a hard pedal.)	• Caliper or wheel cylinder pistons sticking or seized	• Repair or replace the calipers, or wheel cylinders
	• Master cylinder compensator ports blocked (preventing fluid return to reservoirs) or pistons sticking or seized in master cylinder bore	• Repair or replace the master cylinder
	• Power brake unit binding internally	• Test unit according to the following procedure: (a) Shift transmission into neutral and start engine (b) Increase engine speed to 1500 rpm, close throttle and fully depress brake pedal (c) Slow release brake pedal and stop engine (d) Have helper remove vacuum check valve and hose from power unit. Observe for backward movement of brake pedal. (e) If the pedal moves backward, the power unit has an internal bind—replace power unit

Troubleshooting the Brake System (cont.)

Problem	Cause	Solution
Spongy brake pedal (pedal has abnormally soft, springy, spongy feel when depressed.)	• Air in hydraulic system • Brakeshoes bent or distorted • Brakelining not yet seated with drums and rotors • Rear drum brakes not properly adjusted	• Remove air from system. Refer to Brake Bleeding. • Replace brakeshoes • Burnish brakes • Adjust brakes
Hard brake pedal (excessive pedal pressure required to stop vehicle. May be accompanied by brake fade.)	• Loose or leaking power brake unit vacuum hose • Incorrect or poor quality brakelining • Bent, broken, distorted brakeshoes • Calipers binding or dragging on mounting pins. Rear brakeshoes dragging on support plate.	• Tighten connections or replace leaking hose • Replace with lining in axle sets • Replace brakeshoes • Replace mounting pins and bushings. Clean rust or burrs from rear brake support plate ledges and lubricate ledges with molydisulfide grease. **NOTE:** If ledges are deeply grooved or scored, do not attempt to sand or grind them smooth—replace support plate.
	• Caliper, wheel cylinder, or master cylinder pistons sticking or seized • Power brake unit vacuum check valve malfunction	• Repair or replace parts as necessary • Test valve according to the following procedure: (a) Start engine, increase engine speed to 1500 rpm, close throttle and immediately stop engine (b) Wait at least 90 seconds then depress brake pedal (c) If brakes are not vacuum assisted for 2 or more applications, check valve is faulty
	• Power brake unit has internal bind	• Test unit according to the following procedure: (a) With engine stopped, apply brakes several times to exhaust all vacuum in system (b) Shift transmission into neutral, depress brake pedal and start engine (c) If pedal height decreases with foot pressure and less pressure is required to hold pedal in applied position, power unit vacuum system is operating normally. Test power unit. If power unit exhibits a bind condition, replace the power unit.
	• Master cylinder compensator ports (at bottom of reservoirs) blocked by dirt, scale, rust, or have small burrs (blocked ports prevent fluid return to reservoirs). • Brake hoses, tubes, fittings clogged or restricted • Brake fluid contaminated with improper fluids (motor oil, transmission fluid, causing rubber components to swell and stick in bores • Low engine vacuum	• Repair or replace master cylinder **CAUTION:** Do not attempt to clean blocked ports with wire, pencils, or similar implements. Use compressed air only. • Use compressed air to check or unclog parts. Replace any damaged parts. • Replace all rubber components, combination valve and hoses. Flush entire brake system with DOT 3 brake fluid or equivalent. • Adjust or repair engine

Troubleshooting the Brake System (cont.)

Problem	Cause	Solution
Grabbing brakes (severe reaction to brake pedal pressure.)	• Brakelining(s) contaminated by grease or brake fluid	• Determine and correct cause of contamination and replace brakeshoes in axle sets
	• Parking brake cables incorrectly adjusted or seized	• Adjust cables. Replace seized cables.
	• Incorrect brakelining or lining loose on brakeshoes	• Replace brakeshoes in axle sets
	• Caliper anchor plate bolts loose	• Tighten bolts
	• Rear brakeshoes binding on support plate ledges	• Clean and lubricate ledges. Replace support plate(s) if ledges are deeply grooved. Do not attempt to smooth ledges by grinding.
	• Incorrect or missing power brake reaction disc	• Install correct disc
	• Rear brake support plates loose	• Tighten mounting bolts
Dragging brakes (slow or incomplete release of brakes)	• Brake pedal binding at pivot	• Loosen and lubricate
	• Power brake unit has internal bind	• Inspect for internal bind. Replace unit if internal bind exists.
	• Parking brake cables incorrrectly adjusted or seized	• Adjust cables. Replace seized cables.
	• Rear brakeshoe return springs weak or broken	• Replace return springs. Replace brakeshoe if necessary in axle sets.
	• Automatic adjusters malfunctioning	• Repair or replace adjuster parts as required
	• Caliper, wheel cylinder or master cylinder pistons sticking or seized	• Repair or replace parts as necessary
	• Master cylinder compensating ports blocked (fluid does not return to reservoirs).	• Use compressed air to clear ports. Do not use wire, pencils, or similar objects to open blocked ports.
Vehicle moves to one side when brakes are applied	• Incorrect front tire pressure	• Inflate to recommended cold (reduced load) inflation pressure
	• Worn or damaged wheel bearings	• Replace worn or damaged bearings
	• Brakelining on one side contaminated	• Determine and correct cause of contamination and replace brakelining in axle sets
	• Brakeshoes on one side bent, distorted, or lining loose on shoe	• Replace brakeshoes in axle sets
	• Support plate bent or loose on one side	• Tighten or replace support plate
	• Brakelining not yet seated with drums or rotors	• Burnish brakelining
	• Caliper anchor plate loose on one side	• Tighten anchor plate bolts
	• Caliper piston sticking or seized	• Repair or replace caliper
	• Brakelinings water soaked	• Drive vehicle with brakes lightly applied to dry linings
	• Loose suspension component attaching or mounting bolts	• Tighten suspension bolts. Replace worn suspension components.
	• Brake combination valve failure	• Replace combination valve
Chatter or shudder when brakes are applied (pedal pulsation and roughness may also occur.)	• Brakeshoes distorted, bent, contaminated, or worn	• Replace brakeshoes in axle sets
	• Caliper anchor plate or support plate loose	• Tighten mounting bolts
	• Excessive thickness variation of rotor(s)	• Refinish or replace rotors in axle sets
Noisy brakes (squealing, clicking, scraping sound when brakes are applied.)	• Bent, broken, distorted brakeshoes	• Replace brakeshoes in axle sets
	• Excessive rust on outer edge of rotor braking surface	• Remove rust

Troubleshooting the Brake System (cont.)

Problem	Cause	Solution
Noisy brakes (squealing, clicking, scraping sound when brakes are applied.) (cont.)	• Brakelining worn out—shoes contacting drum of rotor • Broken or loose holddown or return springs • Rough or dry drum brake support plate ledges • Cracked, grooved, or scored rotor(s) or drum(s) • Incorrect brakelining and/or shoes (front or rear).	• Replace brakeshoes and lining in axle sets. Refinish or replace drums or rotors. • Replace parts as necessary • Lubricate support plate ledges • Replace rotor(s) or drum(s). Replace brakeshoes and lining in axle sets if necessary. • Install specified shoe and lining assemblies
Pulsating brake pedal	• Out of round drums or excessive lateral runout in disc brake rotor(s)	• Refinish or replace drums, re-index rotors or replace

Brake Specifications
All measurements in inches unless noted

Year	Model	Lug Nug Torque (ft. lbs.)	Master Cylinder Bore	Brake Disc Minimum Thickness	Maximum Runout	Standard Brake Drum Diameter	Minimum Lining Thickness Front	Rear
1970–71	1600	53–65	.810	.354	.008	7.87	.275	.079
1970–76	2000,2002	53–65	.810 ①	.354 ②	.008	9.06	.275	.079
	2500,2800 Bavaria,3.0 3000	60–66	.874	.827F/.709R	.008	9.84 ③	.275	.275 ④
1977–81	320i	59–65	.812	.827	.008	9.84 ⑤	.301	.118
1975–81	528i,530i	59–65	.937	.827F/.335R ⑦	.008	—	—	—
1977–81	630CSi,633	59–65	.937	.827F/.709R	.008	—	—	—
1978–81	733i	60–66	.937	.827F/.354R	.006	—	—	—
1982	320i	59–65	.812	.827	0.008	10.04	—	—
	633CSi	65–79	.936	.840F/.720R	0.008	—	—	—
	733i	65–79	.874	.840F/.360R	0.008	—	—	—
1983	320i	59–65	.812	.827	0.008	10.04	—	—
	533i	65–79	—	.787	0.008	—	0.079	0.079
	633CSi	65–79	—	.960F/.315R	0.008	—	0.079	0.079
	733i	65–79	—	.906F/.315R	0.008	—	0.079	0.079
1984	318i	65–79	—	.421	0.008	9.035	0.079	0.059
	533i	65–79	—	.787	0.008	—	0.079	0.079
	633CSi	65–79	—	.906F/.315R	0.008	—	0.079	0.079
	733i	65–79	—	.906F/.315R	0.008	—	0.079	0.079
1985	318i	65–79	—	.421	0.008	9.035	0.079	0.059
	325e	65–79	—	.421	0.008	—	0.079	0.079
	528e	65–79	—	.787F/.315R	0.008	—	0.079	0.079
	524td	65–79	—	.787F/.315R	0.008	—	0.079	0.079

Brake Specifications (cont.)

All measurements in inches unless noted

Year	Model	Lug Nug Torque (ft. lbs.)	Master Cylinder Bore	Brake Disc		Standard Brake Drum Diameter	Minimum Lining Thickness	
				Minimum Thickness	Maximum Runout		Front	Rear
1985	535i	65–79	—	.906F/.315R	0.008	—	0.079	0.079
	635CSi	65–79	—	.906F/.315R	0.008	—	0.079	0.079
	735i	65–79	—	.906F/.315R	0.008	—	0.079	0.079
1986	325e	65–79	—	.421	0.008	—	0.079	0.079
	528e	65–79	—	.787F/.315R	0.008	—	0.079	0.079
	524td	65–79	—	.787F/.315R	0.008	—	0.079	0.079
	535i	65–79	—	.906F/.315R	0.008	—	0.079	0.079
	635CSi	65–79	—	.906F/.315R	0.008	—	0.079	0.079
	735i	65–79	—	.906F/.315R	0.008	—	0.079	0.079
1987	325i	65–79	—	.421	0.008	—	0.079	0.079
	325iS	65–79	—	.421	0.008	—	0.079	0.079
	528e	65–79	—	.787F/.315R	0.008	—	0.079	0.079
	535i	65–79	—	.906F/.315R	0.008	—	0.079	0.079
	635CSi	65–79	—	.906F/.315R	0.008	—	0.079	0.079
	735i	65–79	—	.906F/.315R	0.008	—	0.079	0.079
	M5	65–79	—	1.102F/.315R	0.008	—	0.079	0.079
	M6	65–79	—	.906F/.315R	0.008	—	0.079	0.079
1988	325 (All)	65–79	—	.787F/.315R	0.008	—	0.079	0.079
	528e	65–79	—	.787F/.315R	0.008	—	0.079	0.079
	535i	65–79	—	.787F/.315R	0.008	—	0.079	0.079
	635CSi	65–79	—	.906F/.315R	0.008	—	0.079	0.079
	M3	65–79	—	.905F/.394R	0.008	—	0.079	0.079
	M5	65–79	—	1.102F/.315R	0.008	—	0.079	0.079
	M6	65–79	—	1.024F/.315R	0.008	—	0.079	0.079
	735i	65–79	—	.906F/.315R	0.008	—	0.079	0.079
	750iL	65–79	—	NAF/.709R	0.008	—	0.079	0.079

F Front
R Rear
① 2002ti and 2002tii: .9375
② 2002ti and 2002tii: .459
③ 2800CS only
④ 2800CS: .079
⑤ '80–'82: 10.00
⑥ '80–'82: 10.04
⑦ '75–'77 530i: .461F

the pistons will operate the rear brakes. If the rear brakes develop a leak, the primary piston will move forward until direct contact with the secondary piston takes place, and it will force the secondary piston to actuate the front brakes. In either case, the brake pedal moves farther when the brakes are applied, and less braking power is available.

All dual-circuit systems use a switch to warn the driver when only half of the brake system is operational. This switch is located in a valve body which is mounted on the firewall or the

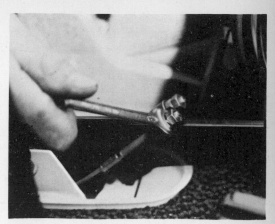

Location of brake adjusting bolt. A special tool is shown here, but a socket wrench with extension could also be used

Adjusting the handbrake at the adjusting nuts

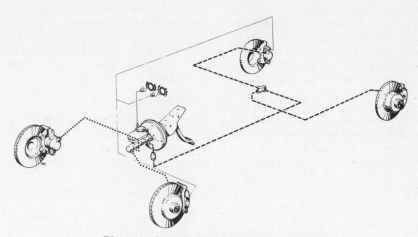

Diagram of standard brake system components

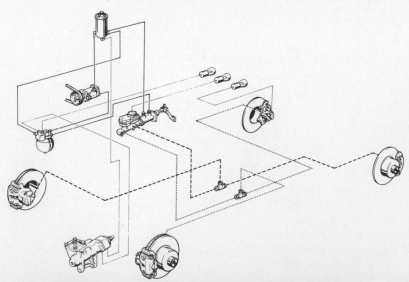

Diagram of hydraulically boosted-dual diagonal brake system

frame below the master cylinder. A hydraulic piston receives pressure from both circuits, each circuit's pressure being applied to one end of the piston. When the pressures are in balance, the piston remains stationary. When one circuit has a leak, however, the greater pressure in that circuit during application of the brakes will push the piston to one side, closing the switch and activating the brake warning light.

In disc brake systems, this valve body also contains a metering valve and, in some cases, a proportioning valve. The metering valve keeps pressure from traveling to the disc brakes on the front wheels until the brake shoes on the rear wheels have contacted the drums, ensuring that the front brakes will never be used alone. The proportioning valve controls the pressure to the rear brakes to avoid rear wheel lock-up during very hard braking.

Warning lights may be tested by depressing the brake pedal and holding it while opening one of the wheel cylinder bleeder screws. If this does not cause the light to go on, substitute a new lamp, make continuity checks, and, finally, replace the switch as necessary.

The hydraulic system may be checked for leaks by applying pressure to the pedal gradually and steadily. If the pedal sinks very slowly to the floor, the system has a leak. This is not to be confused with a springy or spongy feel due to the compression of air within the lines. If the system leaks, there will be a gradual change in the position of the pedal with a constant pressure.

Check for leaks along all lines and at wheel cylinders. If no external leaks are apparent, the problem is inside the master cylinder.

Anti-Lock Brake System

Certain BMW models are equipped with an anti-lock brake system. This system is designed to control the braking of the vehicle under all road conditions. In basic the system monitors the speed of each wheel as the vehicle is being braked. It does this with a sensor at each wheel reading the speed of that wheel. When the system determines that one or more wheels is losing traction under braking, it modulates the braking force to the wheel(s) which in turn prevents the wheel from locking up and the vehicle from going out of control.

The ABS system consists of a control unit, hydraulic unit, speed sensors and related wiring. The following is a description of each and its location:

Speed Sensors

Located behind each wheel on the vehicle, each sensor has gear wheel, which runs past the permanently magnetized edge of the sensor, and is installed in the wheel hub. The rotary

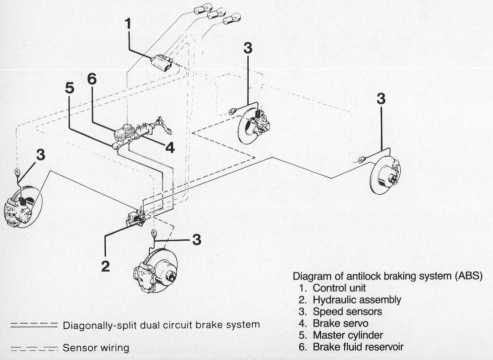

Diagram of antilock braking system (ABS)
1. Control unit
2. Hydraulic assembly
3. Speed sensors
4. Brake servo
5. Master cylinder
6. Brake fluid reservoir

===== Diagonally-split dual circuit brake system

—·—·— Sensor wiring

Diagram of anti-lock brake system

motion of the wheel is recorded and the electrical signal is sent to the control unit.

Electronic Control Unit

The control unit is located above the glove box. The control unit reads and interperts various wheel speed data from the speed sensors, it thens uses this data to determine wheel speed, loss of traction and excess grab. It takes all the data into account and adjusts the elctronically modulated valves accordingly. This enable the driver to maintain complete control of the vehicle under all operating conditions. All of the operation of the control unit takes place in milliseconds. ABS operation can be felt, as a brake pedal pulstaion by the driver, under extreme braking conditions, other wise its operation is not noticeable. There is also a warning light on the dash to indicate if the system is operating, if the light stays on, there is a problem with the system.

In the event of system failure normal braking will be maintained.

Hydraulic Unit

This is a hydraulic distributor and actuator that was added to the regular brake system. It is connected in series with the master cylinder and brake lines. It consists of electronically controlled valves that supply brake fluid to each of the wheels, as dictated by the ABS control unit. The hydraulic unit also has an eletronic return pump that that returns the brake fluid to the master cylinder while in operation. If the pump or the hydraulic unit fails, normal braking will be maintained. The hydraulic unit is located under the hood, in the area of the master cylinder.

SYSTEM SERVICE

The ABS should require no normal service and no out of the ordinary service when performing normal brake system repairs. The only exception is that the negative battery cable should be disconnected before brake system service, to protect the control unit.

If ABS system failure is suspected or the ABS warning indicator stays on, the vehicle should be taken to an authorized service station. ABS testing requires very expensive electronic testers and special troubleshooting procedures.

Disc Brakes

BASIC OPERATING PRINCIPLES

Instead of the traditional expanding brakes that press outward against a circular drum, disc brake systems utilize a disc (rotor) with brake pads positioned on either side of it. Braking effect is achieved in a manner similar to the way you would squeeze a spinning phonograph record between your fingers. The disc (rotor) is a casting with cooling fins between the two braking surfaces. This enables air to circulate between the braking surfaces making them less sensitive to heat buildup and more resistant to fade. Dirt and water do not affect braking action since contaminants are thrown off by the centrifugal action of the rotor or scraped off the by the pads. Also, the equal clamping action of the two brake pads tends to ensure uniform, straightline stops. Disc brakes are inherently self-adjusting.

There are three general types of disc brake:

1. A fixed caliper.
2. A floating caliper.
3. A sliding caliper.

The fixed caliper design uses two pistons mounted on either side of the rotor (in each side of the caliper). The caliper is mounted rigidly and does not move.

The sliding and floating designs are quite similar. In fact, these two types are often lumped together. In both designs, the pad on the inside of the rotor is moved into contact with the rotor by hydraulic force. The caliper, which is not held in a fixed position, moves slightly, bringing the outside pad into contact with the rotor. There are various methods of attaching floating calipers. Some pivot at the bottom or top, and some slide on mounting bolts. In any event, the end result is the same.

Drum Brakes

BASIC OPERATING PRINCIPLES

Drum brakes employ two brake shoes mounted on a stationary backing plate. These shoes are positioned inside a circular drum which rotates with the wheel assembly. The shoes are held in place by springs; this allows them to slide toward the drums (when they are applied) while keeping the linings and drums in alignment. The shoes are actuated by a wheel cylinder which is mounted at the top of the backing plate. When the brakes are applied, hydraulic pressure forces the wheel cylinder's actuating links outward. Since these links bear directly against the top of the brake shoes, the tops of the shoes are then forced against the inner side of the drum. This action forces the bottoms of the two shoes to contact the brake drum by rotating the entire assembly slightly (known as servo action). When pressure within the wheel cylinder is relaxed, return springs pull the shoes back away from the drum.

Most modern drum brakes are designed to self-adjust themselves during application when the vehicle is moving in reverse. This motion causes both shoes to rotate very slightly with

the drum, rocking an adjusting lever, thereby causing rotation of the adjusting screw.

Power Boosters

Power brakes operate just as standard brake systems except in the actuation of the master cylinder pistons. A vacuum diaphragm is located on the front of the master cylinder and assists the driver in applying the brakes, reducing both the effort and travel he must put into moving the brake pedal.

The vacuum diaphragm housing is connected to the intake manifold by a vacuum hose. A check valve is placed at the point where the hose enters the diaphragm housing, so that during periods of low manifold vacuum brake assist vacuum will not be lost.

Depressing the brake pedal closes off the vacuum source and allows atmospheric pressure to enter on one side of the diaphragm. This causes the master cylinder pistons to move and apply the brakes. When the brake pedal is released, vacuum is applied to both sides of the diaphragm, and return springs return the diaphragm and master cylinder pistons to the released position. If the vacuum fails, the brake pedal rod will butt against the end of the master cylinder actuating rod, and direct mechanical application will occur as the pedal is depressed.

The hydraulic and mechanical problems that apply to conventional brake systems also apply to power brakes, and should be checked for if the tests below do not reveal the problem.
Test for a system vacuum leak as described below:

1. Operate the engine at idle without touching the brake pedal for at least one minute.
2. Turn off the engine, and wait one minute.
3. Test for the presence of assist vacuum by depressing the brake pedal and releasing it several times. Light application will produce less and less pedal travel, if vacuum was present. If there is no vacuum, air is leaking into the system somewhere.
Test for system operation as follows:
1. Pump the brake pedal (with engine off) until the supply vacuum is entirely gone.
2. Put a light, steady pressure on the pedal.
3. Start the engine, and operate it at idle. If the system is operating, the brake pedal should fall toward the floor if constant pressure is maintained on the pedal.

Power brake systems may be tested for hydraulic leaks just as ordinary systems are tested.

CAUTION: *Brake linings contain asbestos. Asbestos is a known cancer-causing agent. When working on brakes, remember that the dust which accumulates on the brake parts and/or in the drum contains asbestos. Always wear a protective face covering, such as a painter's mask, when working on the brakes. NEVER blow the dust from the brakes or drum! There are solvents made for the purpose of cleaning brake parts. Use them!*

Adjustments
REAR DRUM BRAKE/HANDBRAKE
1600, 2000 2002 and 320i

Common adjustment of these two items is recommended at every major service (8,000 miles until 1974, 12,500 miles thereafter). In addition, if the handbrake can be pulled up more than four notches on 1970-74 cars, or five notches on later model years, adjustment should be performed.

1. Support the rear of the car securely on axle stands. Release the handbrake fully.
2. The brake adjusting bolt is located at the rear of the backing plate, right behind the drive axle. It is turned counterclockwise on the left side and clockwise on the right side to tighten. Spin the wheel and gradually tighten up on the adjustment until the wheel just stops and cannot be readily turned. Then, loosen exactly ⅛ turn; just to the point where there is no drag felt. Repeat on the other side.
3. Pull the handbrake lever up five notches (1975 and later vehicles) or four notches (earlier vehicles). Measure the distance between the middle of the handbrake lever and the driveshaft tunnel. It should be 109-119mm; otherwise, reset the handbrake into another notch until the dimension is correct.
4. Then, pull up the rubber boot, loosen the locknut on one side and tighten the adjusting nut until the wheel on that side is locked. Repeat for the other side. Tighten both locknuts.
5. Check to make sure the adjustment is correct by checking that the wheels are released completely when the brake is released and that both wheels are slowed at the same point as the lever is raised. Repeat the adjustments if necessary.

Brake Light Switch
REMOVAL AND INSTALLATION
All Models

1. Disconnect the negative battery cable. Disconnect the electrical connector to the switch.
2. Loosen the locknut and then turn the switch outward to remove it.
3. Screw the new switch in. Adjust the gap between the pedal and actuator on the switch to 5-6mm. Tighten the locknut.

Master Cylinder
REMOVAL AND INSTALLATION
1600, 2000, 2002, Bavaria, 3000, 3.0, 533i and 633i

1. Remove the air cleaner is necessary.
2. Drain and disconnect the brake fluid reservoir from the master cylinder. The brake fluid reservoir will be mounted in one of two ways: (1) assembled directly on top of the master cylinder; it is removed by tilting the reservoir to one side and lifting it off of the master cylinder, or (2) the reservoir is mounted in the engine compartment where it is attached to the inner fender sheet metal by means of attaching bolts; carefully disconnect the hoses leading to the master cylinder and allow the reservoir to drain.
CAUTION: *Exercise extreme care in handling brake fluid near the painted surface of vehicle as fluid will destroy the pain finish if allowed to come into contact with it.*
3. Disconnect all brake lines from the master cylinder.
4. Remove the master cylinder-to-power booster attaching nuts, and remove the master cylinder.
NOTE: *Observe the correct seating of the master cylinder-to-power booster seals (1).*
5. Bench bleed the master cylinder.
NOTE: *Check for proper seating of the master cylinder-to-power booster O-ring. Check the clearance between the master cylinder piston and push rod with a plastic gauge, and, if necessary, adjust to 0.05mm by placing shims behind the head of the push rod.*
6. Position the master cylinder onto the studs protruding from the power booster; install and tighten the attaching nuts.
7. Connect all brake lines.
8. Install the brake fluid reservoir and fill with brake fluid.
NOTE: *An alternate method to bench bleeding the master cylinder is to bleed the master cylinder in the vehicle by opening (only slightly) the brake line fitting at the master cylinder, and allowing the fluid to flow from the master cylinder into a container. However, this method should be considered as an ALTERNATE METHOD ONLY as it is more difficult to control the fluid leaving the master cylinder during bleeding, thereby increasing the chance of accidentally splashing brake fluid onto the painted surface of the vehicle.*
9. Bleed the brake system.

1. O-ring   2. Pushrod

Removing master cylinder from vacuum unit —2002

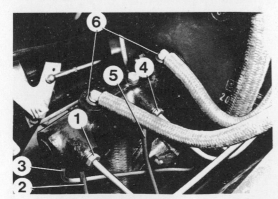

1. Right brake line—front
2. Left brake line—front
3. Brake line to rear wheel brakes
4. Right brake line—front (2nd circuit)
5. Left brake line—front (2nd circuit)

Removing the 600 series master cylinder

318i, 320i, 325, 325e, 325i and 325iS, 325iX, M3

1. Remove the fuel mixture control unit on the 320i. Disconnect the fluid level indicator plug.
2. Disconnect the clutch master cylinder hose at the fluid reservoir.
3. Drain and then disconnect the brake fluid reservoir from the master cylinder
4. Disconnect the brake lines from the master cylinder.
5. On the 320i, working from the underside of the left side inner fender panel (wheel opening area) remove the two master cylinder support bracket attaching nuts.
6. Remove the master cylinder-to-power booster attaching nuts, and remove the master cylinder. Inspect the rubber vacuum seal in the end of the unit and replace, if necessary.
7. Install the master cylinder to the power booster. Reconnect the brake lines and install the fluid reservoir. Connect the fluid level indicator.

NOTE: *Bench bleed the master cylinder prior to installation. Refer to the aforementioned note concerning an ALTERNATE bleeding procedure.*

8. Bleed the brake system.

524td, 528e, 535i, 635CSi, M5 and M6
WITH VACUUM POWER BRAKES

1. Using a syringe that is new or has been used only for brake fluids, draw off all brake fluid from the brake fluid reservoir. Disconnect the fluid line going to the clutch master cylinder and plug it.
2. Disconnect the two brake lines connected to the side of the master cylinder.
3. Remove the two mounting bolts and remove the master cylinder from the power booster.
4. Inspect the rubber O-ring located in the groove of the rear of the master cylinder. Replace it if it is damaged.
5. Install the master cylinder in position, on the booster. Reconnect the fluid lines. Bleed the system.

WITH HYDRAULIC POWER BRAKES

1. Operate the brake pedal with maximum force about 20 times to remove all residual hydraulic pressure. Using a syringe that is new or has been used only for brake fluids, draw off all brake fluid from the brake fluid reservoir.
2. Disconnect the hydraulic hoses and remove the fluid storage tank from the top of the master cylinder.
3. Remove the two bolts fastening the master cylinder to the booster and remove it.
4. Install the master cylinder on the booster and reconnect the brake lines. Fill the master cylinder and bleed the system.

733i and 735i

1. Drain and disconnect the fluid reservoir on 733i models built through 1982 and on 1986-88 models.
2. Disconnect the two brake lines from the outboard side of the master cylinder.

3. Remove the master cylinder-to-hydraulic booster attaching bolts, and remove the master cylinder.
4. Install the master cylinder on the booster and reconnect the brake lines. Install the fluid reservoir, if removed. Fill and bleed the brake system.

NOTE: *Bench bleed the master cylinder prior to installation. Refer to the aforementioned note concerning an ALTERNATE bleeding procedure.*

OVERHAUL
1600, 2000, and 2002

1. Remove the master cylinder as outlined under "Master Cylinder Removal and Installation."
2. Press in lightly on the piston (1) and remove the stop screw (2).
3. Remove the circlip (3) and withdraw the piston (1) from its bore. Then, pull off the stop washer (4), secondary sleeve (5), spacer ring (6), secondary sleeve (70, and stop washer (8).
4. Unscrew the retaining screw (9), and pull off the spring cap (10), spring (11), spring cap (12), pressure cup (13), and O-ring (14). Remove and discard the primary sleeve (8).

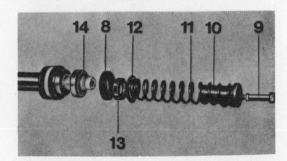

Disassembling master cylinder components: primary sleeve (8), retaining screw (9), spring cap (10), spring (11), spring cap (12), pressure cap (13), and O-ring (14)

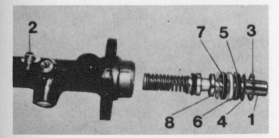

Removing master cylinder components—1600, 2002: piston (1), stop screw (2), circlip (3), stop washer (4), secondary sleeve (5), spacer ring (6), secondary sleeve (7), and stop washer (8)

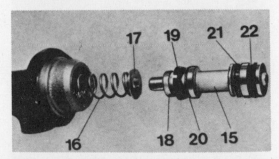

Removing master cylinder components: piston (15), spring (16), spring cap (17), pressure cap (18), primary sleeve (19), O-ring (20), secondary sleeve (21), primary sleeve (22)

Proper assembly sequence for sleeves 5 and 7

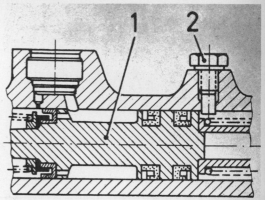

Note the positions of the piston (1) and the stop screw (2)—2800, 3.0

5. Using low pressure compressed air, push out the piston (15). Then, pull off the spring (16), spring cap (17), pressure cap (18), primary sleeve (19), and the O-ring (20). Lift out the secondary sleeve (21), and primary sleeve (22).

6. Clean all parts in methylated alcohol or clean brake fluid. Check the cylinder bore for surface defects. Replace any cylinder in questionable condition. Prior to assembly, thinly coat all parts with clean brake fluid.

7. Assemble the master cylinder by first clamping it vertically in a vise to prevent the pressure cap from slipping off during assembly. then assembling sleeves (5) and (7), make sure that they point in one direction. Coat the space between the secondary sleeve and spacer ring with silicone grease. Also, coat the piston shank with silicone grease. when installing the piston shanks in the bore, take care not to damage the rubber sleeves. Finally, push the piston assemblies into the bore, place a new copper washer under the stop screw, then screw in the stop screw, completing the assembly.

2500, 2800, Bavaria, 3000 and 3.0

1. Apply slight pressure to the piston. Remove the stop screw.

2. Remove the circlip, and then extract the piston.

3. Pull off the stop washer, secondary sleeve, intermediate ring, second secondary sleeve, and stop washer.

4. Remove the screw from the end of the spring cap, and then remove the spring cap, spring, spring cup, pressure plate, and spacer.

5. Build up air pressure carefully until the piston comes out of the bore.

6. Pull off the spring, spring cup, pressure plate, primary sleeve, and spacer.

7. Clean all parts in alcohol or clean brake fluid. Inspect the master cylinder bore for scratches or pits and replace is necessary.

8. Clamp the master cylinder vertically into a vise to prevent the pressure plate from slip-

The master cylinder

Disassembly of the master cylinder

ping during reassembly. Apply silicone grease to the new components, and to the piston rod.

9. Assemble the master cylinder, noting the following points:

a. A special tapered sleeve (such as BMW 6063) is available for installation of the piston back into the bore without damaging seals. Use some sort of sleeve or a least exercise extreme caution in reinstalling the piston so that seal lips do not fold back double.

b. Use a new copper gasket under the stop screw.

c. Note that the piston must be inserted

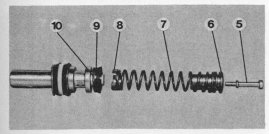

Further disassembly of the master cylinder

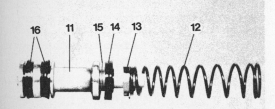

Disassembly of the master cylinder intermediate piston

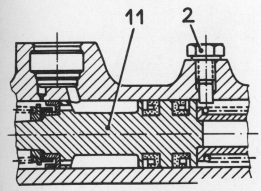

Cross section of the master cylinder showing the intermediate piston and stop screw

far enough into the bore to fully pass the stop screw before the screw is inserted.

All 3 Series

1. Push the piston (1) into the bore slightly and then remove the stop screw (2).

2. Remove the circlip (3) and pull out the piston.

3. Remove the bearing ring (1), secondary cups (2), intermediate ring (3) and the second bearing ring (4).

4. Loosen the connecting bolt (5), and pull off the spring retainer (6), spring (7), support ring (8), primary cup (9), and filler disc (10).

5. Then, remove the intermediate piston (11) by knocking the housing lightly against a block of wood. Pull off the spring (12), support ring (13), primary cup (14), the filler disc (15). Remove the separating cups (16).

6. Clean all parts in alcohol or clean brake fluid. Inspect the master cylinder bore and replace the unit if it is scored or pitted.

7. Reassemble the master cylinder, noting the following:

   a. Apply a very light coating of silicone lubricant or cylinder paste to new parts.

   b. The separating cups are marked with a ring of paint. Install them so their lips are opposite each other.

   c. Make sure both support rings (13) and (8) are positioned properly on the primary cups.

   d. When assembling parts to the primary piston (the piston with the rod which protrudes from the master cylinder after assembly), note the following sequence of installation: bearing ring (1); secondary cups (2) (both pointing in the same direction); intermediate ring (3); the bearing ring (4). Coat the space between the secondary cups and intermediate ring with silicone grease.

   e. When inserting pistons into the bore, use a tapered special tool such as BMW 343000, or be very careful to ensure that seal lips do not fold over.

   f. Coat the primary piston skirt with silicone grease. Put light pressure on the piston and then install the stop screw with a new copper seal. Make sure the intermediate piston (11) is beyond the stop screw (2).

5, 6 and 7 Series

1. Push the piston (1) inward using light pressure, and then remove the stop screw (7). Then remove the circlip (2) and pull out the piston. Remove the stop washer (3), secondary cup (5), intermediate ring (4) and bearing ring (6).

2. Loosen the connecting screw (9), and pull off the spring washer (10), spring (11), support (12), primary cup (8), and filler disc (13).

3. Remove the intermediate piston by knocking the housing against a wooden block lightly. then, remove the spring (15), support (16), pri-

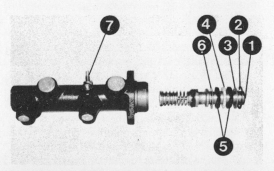

Disassembling the master cylinder—500, 600 and 700 series cars

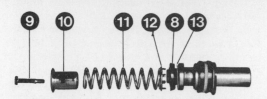

Further disassembly of 500, 600, and 700 series master cylinders

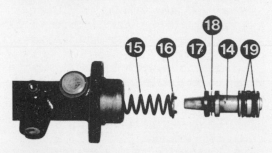

Disassembly of the intermediate piston and associated parts—500, 600, and 700 series master cylinders

mary cup (17), and filler disc (18) and separating cups (19).

4. Clean all parts in alcohol or clean brake fluid and inspect the bore of the master cylinder carefully for scoring or pitting. Replace if damaged.

5. To reassemble, first mount the cylinder in a vise with the bore facing downward at an angle, to prevent the support ring from slipping during assemble. If possible, use a tapered sleeve such as BMW part No. 34 3 000 to install the pistons. Otherwise, take care to ensure the seal lips do not double over during installation. Coat all parts with ATE Brake Cylinder paste or a similar silicone lubricant designed for this purpose. Also, keep the following points in mind:

  a. The separating cups are marked with a colored ring and must be installed with their lips opposite each other.

  b. Make sure both primary cup supports (12 and 16) are located in the primary cups correctly.

  c. Install both secondary cups in the same direction. Coat the space between the secondary cups and intermediate ring with silicone lubricant.

  d. When installing the piston, apply silicone lubricant to the piston rod and apply light pressure to the rod of the primary piston to push the intermediate piston past the location of the stop screw. Then, install the stop screw with a new copper washer.

Vacuum Operated Power Brake Booster

REMOVAL AND INSTALLATION

318i, 325, 325e, 325i and 325iS, 325iX, M3

1. Draw off brake fluid in the reservoir and discard.

2. Remove the reservoir and disconnect the clutch hydraulic hose.

3. Disconnect all brake lines from the master cylinder.

4. Remove the instrument panel trim from the bottom left inside the passenger compartment.

5. Remove the return spring from the brake pedal. Press off the clip and remove the pin which connects the booster rod to the brake pedal.

6. Remove the four nuts and pull the booster and master cylinder off in the engine compartment.

7. If the filter in the brake booster is clogged, it will have to be cleaned. To do this, remove the dust boot, retainer, damper, and filter, and clean the damper and filter. Make sure when reinstalling that the slots in the damper and filter are offset 180°.

8. Install the booster and master cylinder back into position. Connect the booster rod to the brake pedal. Complete the installation and adjust the stoplight switch for a clearance of 5-6mm.

9. Inspect the rubber seal between the master cylinder and booster and replace it if necessary.

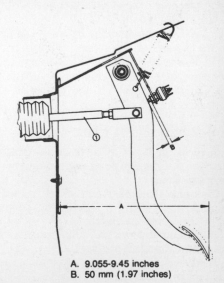

A. 9.055-9.45 inches
B. 50 mm (1.97 inches)

Brake Pedal Adjustment 528i, 528e, 630CSi, and 633CSi

320i

1. Remove the master cylinder.
2. Disconnect the vacuum line at the power booster.
3. Remove the brake pedal apply-rod to power booster push rod pin.
4. Remove the power booster attaching nuts, and remove the power booster.
5. Install the booster and connect the brake pedal rod. Install the master cylinder. Reconnect the vacuum line.

NOTE: *If the original power booster unit is to be reused, remove the dust boost and clean the silencer and filter. Position the slots in the silencer 180° away from the slots in the filter.*

6. Adjust the extended visible length of the brake light switch head to 5-6mm.

1983-85 528e, 533i and 633CSi

1. Remove the coolant reservoir.
2. Remove the master cylinder.
3. Disconnect the vacuum hose at the power booster.
4. Disconnect the power booster apply rod at the brake pedal.
5. Remove the power booster attaching bolts.
6. Remove the power booster.
7. Install the booster and connect the brake pedal rod. Install the master cylinder. Reconnect the vacuum line.

NOTE: *If the original power booster unit is to be reused, remove the dust boot and clean the silencer and filter. Position the slots in the silencer 180° away from the slots in the filter.*

8. Adjust the brake pedal distance to 230-240mm. Adjust the stop light switch distance as described below:

    a. Disconnect the electrical connector and loosen the locknut.

    b. Measure the distance between the button on the end of the switch and the brake pedal. It must be 5-6mm. If necessary, turn the stoplight switch to adjust the distance.

    c. Tighten the locknut and reconnect the electrical connector.

524td, 1986-89 528e, 535i, 635CSi, M5, M6

1. Remove all brake fluid from the master cylinder with a syringe or hose used only with clean brake fluid.
2. Disconnect the electrical plugs from the cap on the fluid reservoir. Disconnect the hose going to the hydraulic clutch.
3. Disconnect the two brake lines on the outboard side of the master cylinder.
4. Remove the instrument panel trim located in the bottom left area of the panel.
5. Disconnect and remove the pedal return spring. Then, remove the retaining clip and pull

out the clevis pin connecting the pedal linkage to the booster.

6. Remove the four nuts and washers from the firewall, under the brake pedal. Then, remove the booster and master cylinder from the engine compartment.
7. Remove the two mounting bolts and disconnect the master cylinder from the booster.

NOTE: *If the original power booster unit is to be reused, remove the dust boot and clean the silencer and filter. Position the slots in the silencer 180° away from the slots in the filter.*

8. Check the O-ring located in the end of the master cylinder and replace it if it is worn or cracked.
9. Install the booster and adjust the stoplight switch as described in the next step. Bleed the system.
10. To adjust the stoplight switch:

    a. Disconnect the electrical connector and loosen the locknut.

    b. Measure the distance between the button on the end of the switch and the brake pedal. It must be 5-6mm. If necessary, turn the stoplight switch to adjust the distance.

    c. Tighten the locknut and reconnect the electrical connector.

Hydraulically Operated Power Brake Booster

REMOVAL AND INSTALLATION

733i and 735i

1. Release the pressure in the hydraulic accumulator by operating the brake pedal (with the engine not running) 20 times with a force equivalent to that necessary to bring the vehicle to a complete stop. Use a syringe to draw off the brake fluid in the master cylinder reservoir.
2. Remove the lower left instrument panel trim.
3. Disconnect the power booster apply-rod at the brake pedal. This is done by pulling off the bayonet clip and then pulling the pin out of the piston rod.
4. Remove the master cylinder as describe above.
5. Disconnect the fluid lines at the brake booster.
6. Remove the four power booster to pedal base assembly attaching bolts, and remove the power booster.
7. Install the booster, then install the master cylinder. Reconnect the brake pedal apply rod. On 1983-88, the hydraulic return line connection must be tightened with 34 3 153 or equivalent and the pressure line with 34 3 152 or equivalent. The adjustments of Steps 8 and 9 are not required on those cars.

Remove the four arrowed bolts to remove the hydraulic brake booster (5-series cars)

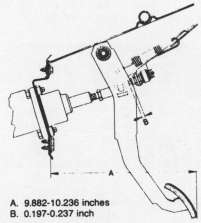

A. 9.882-10.236 inches
B. 0.197-0.237 inch

Brake pedal adjustment—733i

8. Adjust the distance between the brake pedal and the fire wall to 250-260mm.

9. Adjust the extended visible length of the brake light switch head (plunger) to 5-6mm.

Hydraulically Operated Power Brake Booster and Master Cylinder
REMOVAL AND INSTALLATION
524td, 528e, 535i, 635CSi, M5 and M6

NOTE: *Special wrenches must be used to tighten hydraulic lines for the hydraulic booster. Use BMW tools 34 3 153 and 34 3 152 or equivalent.*

1. With the engine off, discharge all pressure from the system by applying the brake pedal 20 times full force. Using a syringe or similar tool used only with brake fluids, draw excess brake fluid out of the reservoir.

2. Remove the lower left instrument panel trim. The, lift out the spring clip and remove the clevis pin fastening the piston rod to the brake pedal.

3. Disconnect the electrical connector and then pull of the reservoir.

4. Disconnect the brake hydraulic lines at the master cylinder. Disconnect the hydraulic hoses at the brake booster.

5. Remove the bolts from the driver's side of the pedal base assembly and remove the booster and master cylinder. To separate the master cylinder and booster to replace the booster, remove the two bolts.

6. Measure the distance from the end of the threads on the piston rod to the outer end of the forked fitting for the clevis pin. Then, transfer the fitting over to the new booster, screwing it on until the dimension is the same.

7. Install the booster in position, keeping the following points in mind:

a. When reattaching the hydraulic fittings to the booster, make sure everything is clean and use the special tools to tighten the fittings.

b. Check the rubber seals for the master cylinder reservoir and replace them is necessary.

c. Bleed the brakes. Test operation and boost of the system before driving the vehicle.

Proportioning Valve
REMOVAL AND INSTALLATION

2500, 2800, Bavaria, 3000 and 3.0

1. Siphon brake fluid out of the reservoir. If the fluid is to be reused, make sure the hose and container are clean and have not been used to contain other fluids.

2. Unscrew the left rear brake hose at the control arm and brake pressure regulator. Unscrew the brake lines at the pressure regulator limiter.

3. Remove the regulator mounting bolts at the underside of the body and remove the regulator.

4. Install the regulator and reconnect the lines. Bleed the system.

1. Front wheel brakes inlet
2. Front wheel brakes outlet
3. Rear wheel brakes inlet
4. Rear wheel brakes outlet

The 320i brake pressure regulator

318i, 325, 325e, 325i and 325iS, 325iX, M3

1. Draw off hydraulic fluid from the master cylinder with a syringe or hose used only with clean brake fluid.

2. Disconnect the brake lines at the top and bottom of the proportioning valve.

3. Remove the clamp from the valve and disconnect the pressure connection at the union.

4. Check day/year codes, reduction factor, and switch-over pressure to make sure the new valve is identical.

5. Install the valve and reconnect the brake lines. Bleed the system.

320i

1. Draw off brake fluid from the master cylinder with a syringe or hose used only with clean brake fluid.

2. Disconnect the four brake lines at the proportioning valve.

3. Unscrew the two mounting bolts from the inner front left wheel well. Replace this part with one bearing the code **25** and having a piston diameter of 18mm.

4. Install the valve and reconnect the brake lines. Bleed the system.

Bleeding The System

1600, 2000, and 2002

When a spongy brake pedal indicates that there is air in the system, or when any part of the hydraulic system has been removed for service, the system must be bled. In addition, if there are any fluid leaks, or if the level of fluid in the master cylinder reservoir is allowed to go below the minimum marks, air may enter the system, necessitating bleeding.

Be careful not to spill any brake fluid onto the disc, pads, drums or linings. If any brake fluid spills onto the paintwork, wipe it off immedi-

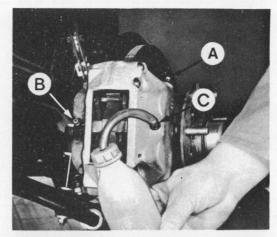

Bleeding sequence for the 500 and 600 series cars. Bleed A, then B. C is bleed port

Bleed the 733i brake calipers in the sequence shown (A, then B)

ately, as it will dissolve the finish. Always use brake fluid bearing the designation SAE 70R3 (SAE 1703), DOT 3 or DOT 4. Never reuse old brake fluid.

1. Fill the master cylinder reservoir to the maximum level with the proper brake fluid.

2. Remove all dirt and foreign material from around the 3 bleed screws on each front caliper and the one on each rear wheel cylinder. Remove the protective caps from the bleed screws.

3. The proper bleeding sequence always start with the brake unit farthest from the master cylinder and always ends with the brake unit closest to the master cylinder. Therefore, the sequence for you car will be; right rear, left rear, right front and then left front. Start out by inserting a tight fitting plastic tube over the bleed nipple for the right rear wheel (located on the backing plate), and inserting the other end of the tube in a transparent container partially filled with clean brake fluid.

4. Have a friend apply pressure to the brake pedal. Open the bleeder screw while observing

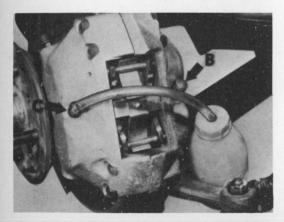

Bleeding sequence for front caliper—1600, 2002

the bottle of brake fluid. If bubbles appear in the container, there is air in the system. When your friend has pushed the pedal to the floor, have him hold it there, and immediately close the bleeder screw before he release the pedal. Otherwise, air or the brake fluid you just removed from the system, will be sucked back in. Repeat this procedure until no more bubbles appear in the jar. Periodically check the level of fluid in the reservoir to keep it at the maximum mark.

5. Repeat Step 4 for the left rear brake unit.

6. Jack up the front of the car and install jackstands beneath the reinforced boxmember area adjacent to the front jacking points. Remove the front wheel and tire assemblies. Each front caliper must be bled in a specified sequence. Starting with the right front caliper, attach the tube and bottle containing clean brake fluid to bleed the nippel **a** (see the illustration). Have a friend press down the pedal, and open the bleed screw. While the pedal hits the floor, close the bleed screw immediately. Once the brake fluid is free of bubbles, proceed to nipple **B**, and finally nipple **C**. It is imperative that this sequence (A, then B, then C) be used.

7. Recheck the level of fluid in the reservoir. Repeat Step 6 for the left front caliper.

8. Install the front wheels, remove the jackstands, and lower the car. The system should now be free of air bubbles. Road test the car and check brake operation.

3 Series

Follow the procedure for the 1600 and 2002 models described above. However, note that 3 series vehicles have only one bleed point on each wheel cylinder and one on each caliper. The calipers may be bled without removing the wheels.

All 6 Cylinder Models Except 528e and 733i

Follow the procedure for the 1600 and 2002 models described above. Note that these models have disc brakes at the rear. Bleed points for these calipers are at the top of the inside. when bleeding front calipers, follow the sequence (A, B, C) shown in the illustration.

528e

Follow the procedure for the 1600, 2000 and 2002 models described previously. However, note that the 528e has only one bleeder screw on each caliper, front and rear. The calipers may be bled without removing the wheel.

733i

Follow the procedure for the 1600 and 2002 models described above. Note that these models have disc brakes at the rear. Bleed points for

these calipers are located at the top of the inside. When bleeding front calipers, follow the sequence (A, B) shown in the illustration.

FRONT DISC BRAKES

CAUTION: *Brake shoes and pads contain asbestos, which has been determined to be a cancer causing agent. Never clean the brake surfaces with compressed air. Avoid inhaling any dust from any brake surface. When cleaning brake surfaces, use a commercially available brake cleaning fluid.*

Brake Pads
INSPECTION

Measure the thickness of the entire pad assembly or the lining itself as specified in the "Brake Specifications Chart" and replace a pad which is at or near the wear limit. In case local inspection law specifies more lining material as a minimum requirement, the local law should take precedence.

REMOVAL AND INSTALLATION
All Models Except 528e

1. Raise the front of the vehicle and support it with jackstands. Remove the wheel.

2. siphon a sufficient quantity of hydraulic fluid from the master cylinder reservoir to prevent the fluid from overflowing the master cylinder when removing the brake pads. This is necessary as the pistons must be forced back into the cylinder bore to provide sufficient clearance to remove the pads.

3. If so equipped, disconnect the electrical connector from the brake pad wear indicator and then pull the wires out of the clamp.

4. Remove the pad retaining pins and any retaining clips holding them.

5. Remove the anti-rattle and spreader

Driving the support pins out of the calipers

34 1 010

Removing the pads with BMW special tool

brakes into correct adjustment. Road test the vehicle.

NOTE: *If a firm pedal cannot be obtained, the system will require bleeding (see "Bleeding" in this section).*

528e

1. Raise and support the front of the vehicle on jackstands. Remove the wheel.

2. Siphon a sufficient quantity of hydraulic fluid from the master cylinder reservoir to prevent the fluid from overflowing the master cylinder while removing the pads. This is necessary as the pistons must be forced into the cylinder bore to provide sufficient clearance to remove the pads.

3. Grasp the caliper from behind and pull it toward you. This will push the piston back into the cylinder bore.

4. Disconnect the brake pad lining wear indicator.

5. Remove the plastic caps and then unscrew and remove the two socket head guide pins. Press out the pad clamp and then lift off the caliper and position it out of the way.

6. Remove the brake pads.

7. Check the brake disc (rotor) as detailed in the appropriate section.

8. Examine the dust boot for cracks or damage and push the piston back into the cylinder bore. If the piston if frozen of if the caliper is leaking hydraulic fluid, it will require overhaul or replacement.

9. Slip the new pads into the mounting bracket and then install the caliper in the reverse order of removal.

springs. note the correct positioning of the springs prior to removal. Replace if necessary.

6. Force the old pads away from the brake disc (rotor) for easy withdrawal and then lift the pads out of the caliper.

7. Check the brake disc (rotor) as detailed in the appropriate section.

8. Examine the dust boot for cracks or damage and push the pistons back into the cylinder bores. If the pistons are frozen or if the caliper is leaking hydraulic fluid, it will require overhaul or replacement.

9. Slip the new pads into the caliper and then install one pad retaining pin and clip. Position the anti-rattle springs and/or spreader springs and then install the other pad retaining pin and clip.

10. Refill the master cylinder with the correct brake fluid.

11. Replace the wheel and lower the vehicle. Pump the brake pedal several times to bring the

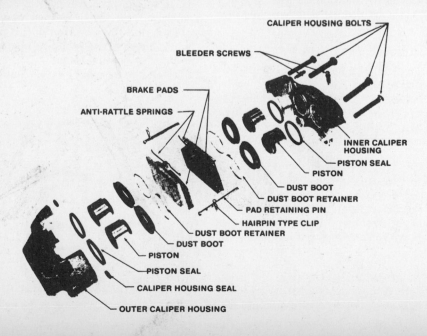

CALIPER HOUSING BOLTS

BLEEDER SCREWS

BRAKE PADS

ANTI-RATTLE SPRINGS

INNER CALIPER HOUSING

PISTON SEAL

PISTON

DUST BOOT

DUST BOOT RETAINER

PAD RETAINING PIN

HAIRPIN TYPE CLIP

DUST BOOT RETAINER

DUST BOOT

PISTON

PISTON SEAL

CALIPER HOUSING SEAL

OUTER CALIPER HOUSING

10. Refill the master cylinder with the proper brake fluid.

11. Replace the wheel and lower the vehicle. Pump the brake pedal several times to bring the brakes into correct adjustment. Road test the vehicle.

NOTE: *If a firm pedal cannot be obtained, the system will require bleeding (see "Bleeding" in this section).*

Front Brake Caliper
REMOVAL AND INSTALLATION
All Models Except 528e

1. Support the front of the vehicle in a raised position, and remove the front wheels.
2. Remove the brake pads.
3. Disconnect the brake lines at the caliper, and cap the lines to prevent brake fluid from escaping.

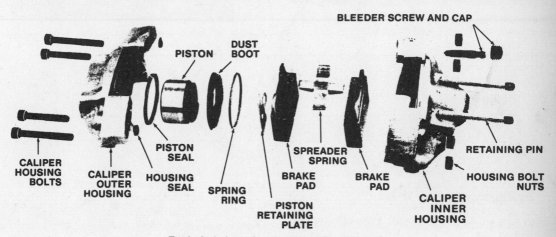

Exploded view of a two piston fixed caliper

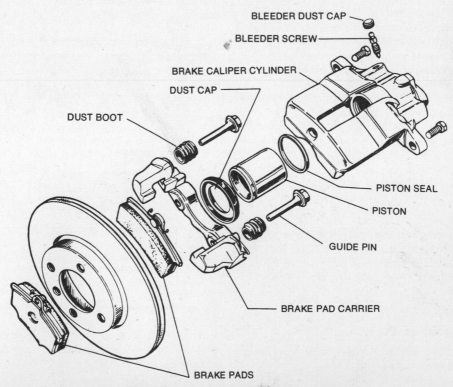

Exploded view of a floating caliper—528e

Remove the retaining pins (arrowed) and the cross spring (1)—600 and 700 series

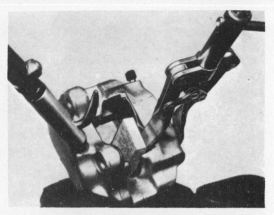

Removing pistons from their bores using compressed air and a wooden block

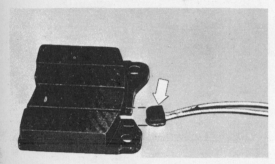

Installing a new pad wear indicator—600 and 700 series

Removing piston sealing rings

CAUTION: *If the fluid appears to be contaminated, discolored, or otherwise unusual in appearance, viscosity, or smell, then allow the fluid to drain from the uncapped brake lines, and flush the system.*

4. Remove the caliper-to-steering knuckle attaching bolts, and remove the caliper.

5. Install the caliper to the steering knuckle and install the attaching bolts.

6. Torque the Caliper-to-steering knuckle attaching bolts to 58-70 ft. lbs.

7. Reconnect the brake lines and install the brake pads.

8. Install the wheel and bleed the brake system.

528e

Caliper removal and installation procedures for the 528e are detailed in the "Pad Removal and Installation" section. Follow Steps 1-5 and then disconnect and plug the brake hydraulic line.

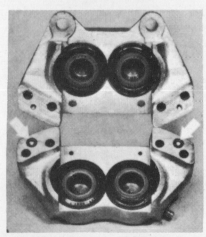

Separated caliper halves—typical. Arrows indicate fluid passages

OVERHAUL

All Models Except 320i, 528e, and 733i

1. Remove the protective dust boot snap ring, and remove the dust boot.

2. Using a BMW special tool 34-1-050 or an equivalent piston pressing device, press one piston into the caliper cylinder to the fully retracted position, and lock into place.

3. Insert a piece of hardwood, plastic, or any material of similar consistency, approximately 8mm thick, between the secured piston and the opposing piston.

4. Apply compressed air through the thread-

Piston dust boot (2) and snap ring (1) removed—733i

ed brake line port and into the circuit which controls the locked piston, thereby forcing the opposed piston out of the cylinder.

5. Remove the piston pressing tool, and plug the open cylinder bore with an Ate sealing plate and clamp or any similar sealing device.

6. Insert the protective block of wood between the remaining piston and the caliper housing, and, again, apply compressed air through the threaded brake line port and into the circuit which controls the remaining piston, thereby forcing the piston out of the cylinder.

CAUTION: *Apply compressed air through the circuit which corresponds with the piston to be removed. DO NOT apply compressed air to the other circuit unless the corresponding pistons are protected with the piece of wood previously mentioned.*

7. Repeat Steps 2 through 6 for the remaining pistons.

8. Carefully remove the piston O-ring.

9. Examine the pistons and cylinder bores for a scoring or binding condition. Replace if necessary.

NOTE: *The manufacturer specifically advises against machining either the piston or the cylinder bore. The recommended extend of overhaul should include only the examination of parts and/or the replacement of the dust boot and piston O-ring.*

The caliper halves should not be separated. An exception to this would be a problem involving a piston which is jammed in the cylinder bore. In this case it may be necessary to separate the cylinder halves in order to free the piston from the cylinder bore.

10. Lubricate the piston, cylinder wall, and piston O-ring with brake fluid prior to assembly.

11. Reassemble the caliper, and install it on the vehicle.

733i

The procedure for overhauling the four piston caliper on the 733i is the same in all respects as the procedure for overhauling the four piston caliper on the 2002, 2002tii, etc. with one major distinction. There is only one brake line to the caliper which attaches to a single line port as opposed to two brake lines with two brake line ports on the models. Because the dual circuit arrangement on the 2002 models it is possible to isolate two of the four pistons, thus facilitating piston removal. The circuits to the pistons on the 733i model can not be isolated, and it is for this reason that it is easier to remove two pistons at a time.

Instead of locking only one piston, two pistons (side by side) are locked into position in the cylinder bores, while the two opposed pistons are removed. A special sealing plate will be needed to seal the two open cylinder bores. Proceed as though overhauling a model 2002 four piston caliper.

320i

The caliper used on the 320i is similar in construction to the standard four piston caliper, however, it is comprised of only two pistons. Proceed as though overhauling a four piston caliper.

Brake Disc (Rotor)
REMOVAL, INSTALLATION AND INSPECTION

1600, 2000, 2002, 2500, 2800, Bavaria, 3000 and 3.0

1. Remove the hub cap and loosen the lug nuts a few turns. Jack up the front of the car and place jackstands beneath the reinforced boxmember area adjacent to the front jacking points.

2. Remove the wheel and tire assembly.

3. Remove the two bolts which retain the caliper to the spindle and slide it off the discs. Wire the caliper up out of the way so that the flexible brake hose is not strained.

4. Remove the grease cap from the hub. Remove the cotter pin, castellated nut, and washer retaining the disc and hub assembly to the spindle. Put off the wheel and hub assembly together with the wheel bearings and grease seal.

5. Remove the 4 or 5 allen head bolts which retain the disc to the hub and lift off the disc. If the disc is rested or otherwise fused to the hub, loosely bolt the wheel and tire back to the hub. then, (no grease fingers please) grasp the disc firmly and twist the disc back and forth briskly, while pulling up on the disc simultaneously. This should jerk the disc loose from the hub. A

Checking the disc runout with dial gauge

Measuring total variation in disc thickness with a micrometer

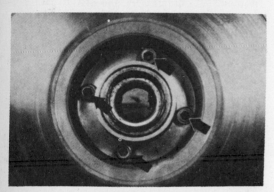

Removing allen bolts retaining disc to hub assembly

Note the balance weights (arrowed) and do not disturb their locations

little penetrating fluid on the lug nut studs will help also.

6. Check the disc for scoring or excessive corrosion. If the pads were ever allowed to run down to the bare metal, the disc will have to be refinished or replaced. Minimum disc thickness is 9mm on the 1600 and 2002, 11.5mm on the 500 series cars, 11.7mm on the 2800, and 21mm on the 3.0. If the refinishing operation cut the disc to less than the minimum thickness, the disc must be replaced. Also, the thick-

ness of the disc must not vary more than 0.2mm measured at 8 points on the contact surface with a micrometer. The contact surfaces of the disc should be absolutely clean of dirt, grease, or brake fluid.

7. At this time, it is good practice to remove, clean, repack and install the wheel bearings into the hub as outlined under "Wheel Bearings Removal and Installation".

8. Install the disc onto the hub. Tighten the allen bolts to 43 ft. lbs.

9. Install the disc and hub assembly onto the spindle. Adjust the wheel bearings as outlined under "Wheel Bearing Adjustment". Once the wheel bearings are properly adjusted, check disc run-out with a dual gauge. Maximum permissible run-out is 0.2mm.

10. Install the caliper, tightening the retaining bolts to 58 ft. lbs.

11. Install the wheel and tire assembly. Lower the car and perform a road test.

3, 5, 6 and 7 Series

1. Remove the lug bolts and remove the front wheel.

2. Detach the bracket and , on the 733i, the clamp, at the spring strut.

3. Remove the caliper mounting bolts, and tie the caliper up out of the way (brake line still connected).

4. With an allen wrench, remove the bolt retaining the disc to the hub. Then, remove the disc.

NOTE: *These discs are balanced. Be careful not to disturb the weights.*

5. To inspect the disc, reposition it on the hub, install the retaining bolt, and torque it to 36-42 in. lbs. (733i 23-24 ft. lbs.).

6. Adjust the wheel bearings as described below.

7. Use a dial indicator mounted at a point on the front suspension to measure the total run-out of the disc. Runout maximum is 0.2mm ex-

cept on the 733i; on that model, it is 0.15mm. Also, use a micrometer and measure the total variation in the thickness of the disc where the pads have worn it at 8 evenly spaced points around the disc. The allowance is 0.02mm on all models. If tolerances are greater than this, the disc must be machined.

8. Install the wheel.

Wheel Bearings

NOTE: *The wheel bearings for 318i and 325, 5 and 6 series for 1983-88, and 7 series for 1987-88 cannot be adjusted.*

ADJUSTMENT

1600, 2000, 2002, 320i, 630CSi, 633CSi, 733i and 735i

1. Raise the vehicle, support it an remove the front wheel.

2. Remove the end cap, and then straighten the cotter pin and remove it. Loosen the castellated nut.

3. While continuously spinning the brake disc, torque the castellated nut down to 22-24 ft. lbs. Keep turning the disc throughout this and make sure it turns at least two turns after the nut is torqued and held.

4. Loosen the nut until there is end play and the hub rotates with the nut.

5. Torque the nut to no more than 2 ft. lbs. Finally, loosen slowly just until castellations and the nearest cotter pin hole line up and insert a new cotter pin.

6 Make sure the slotted washer is free to turn without noticeable resistance; otherwise, there is no end play and the bearings will wear excessively.

2500, 2800, Bavaria, 3000, 3.0, 528i and 530i

1. Remove the wheel. Remove the locking cap from the hub by gripping it carefully on both sides with a pair of pliers.

Make sure the slotted washer can be turned freely, using a screwdriver, as shown

Assembly sequence for wheel bearing components

Force the outer bearing through the recesses (arrowed) in the wheel hub

2. Remove the cotter pin from the castellated nut, and loosen the nut.

3. Spin the disc constantly while torquing the nut to 7 ft. lbs. Continue spinning the disc a couple of turns after the nut is torqued and held.

4. Loosen the castellated nut ¼-⅓ turn; until the slotted washer can be turned readily.

5. Fasten a dial indicator to the front suspension and rest the pin against the wheel hub. Preload the meter about 1mm to remove any play.

6. Adjust the position of the castellated nut while reading the play on the indicator. Make the play as small as possible while backing off the castelled nut just until a new cotter pin can be inserted. The permissible range is 0.02-0.10mm.

7. Install the new cotter pin, locking cap, and the wheel.

528e

1. Raise the vehicle and support it safely. Remove the front wheels.

2. Remove the bearing cap and the self-locking nut.

3. Install a new nut and tighten it to specified torque.

4. Lock the nut by hitting it with a round punch several times on the outer lip.

5. Install the bearing cap and front wheels. Lower the vehicle.

REMOVAL AND INSTALLATION (PACKING)

Refer to Chapter 1 for all bearing removal and installation procedures.

REAR DRUM BRAKES

CAUTION: *Brake shoes and pads contain asbestos, which has been determined to be a cancer causing agent. Never clean the brake surfaces with compressed air. Avoid inhaling any dust from any brake surface. When cleaning brake surfaces, use a commercially available brake cleaning fluid.*

Brake Drums

REMOVAL, INSPECTION AND INSTALLATION

1. Support the rear of the car securely and remove the rear wheel. On the 320i, remove the allen bolt from the brake drum.

2. If the drum will not pull off, severe wear may have grooved it, causing the brake linings to prevent it from coming off. See the brake adjustment procedure at the front of this chapter, and loosen both the brake adjuster and the hand brake adjustment; then, pull the drum off the axle flange.

3. Check the contact surface of the drum for scoring and measure the inside diameter to check for ovality. Ovality must not exceed 0.5mm. The drum may be machined 0.5mm at a time to a maximum oversize of 1mm. Always cut the drums in pairs.

4. To check the drum for cracks, hang the drum by a piece of wood and tap with a small metal object. A cracked drum will sound flat.

5. Install the drum and adjust the brakes. Install the wheel.

Brake Shoes

REMOVAL AND INSTALLATION

1600, 2000, 2002 and 280CS

1. Remove the hub cap and loosen the lug nuts a few turns. Jack up the rear of the car and install jackstands beneath the reinforced boxmember area adjacent to the rear jacking points. Make sure that the parking brake is released.

2. Remove the wheel and tire assembly.

3. Pull off the brake drum.

4. Loosen the brake shoes by turning the brake adjustment screw at each backing plate clockwise (left hand side) or counterclockwise (right hand side).

5. Remove the cotter pin and castellated nut from the axle shaft. Using a hub puller, pull off the axle shaft drive flange.

Removing the axle shaft drive flange—1600, 2000, 2002 and 2800CS

Remove the allen bolt from the brake drum—320i

Disconnecting brake show spring

6. Disconnect the brake shoe spring at the bottom of the shoes. Lever the shoes together at the bottom end and remove the upper ends from the wheel cylinder.

7. Disconnect the thrust rod and parking brake cable. Lift off the brake shoes, noting their placement.

8. If the shoe linings are worn down to less than 3mm, the shoes must be replaced at the same time to provide even braking action. If the linings wore down to the point where the rivets made metal-to-metal contact with the brake drum, have the brake drum turned to remove the score marks. If the drums are cut, purchase new shoes to match the drum oversize. Also, at this time, check the wheel cylinder for leakage.

Inserting long end of spring between parking brake lever and brake shoe

Turn the retainers (arrowed) 90 degrees to release the retaining springs

Disconnecting the parking brake cable—320i

If any trace of brake fluid is found, remove and overhaul the brake cylinder as outlined under "Wheel Cylinder Overhaul."

9. Install the brake shoes, using the following installation notes:

　a. Take care not to contaminate the brake linings with dirt, grease, or brake fluid.

　b. When installation the shoes on the backing plate, insert the long end of the spring between the parking brake lever and the brake shoe (see the illustration).

　c. When installing the nut for the axle shaft drive flange, adjust the nut as outlined under step 8 and 9 of "Halfshaft Removal and Installation" in Chapter 7.

　d. Adjust the brakes as outlined under "Drum Brake Adjustment."

320i

1. Remove the brake drum as described above.

2. Turn the retainers 90° and remove the retaining springs at the center of both shoes.

3. Disconnect the return springs at the bottom with a return spring tool, noting their exact locations. Disconnect the bottoms of the shoes from the retainers.

4. Pull the tops of the shoes out of the brake cylinder piston rods, and pull slightly away from their mountings for clearance. Then, disconnect the parking brake cable from the actuating hook, and remove the shoes.

5. Measure the brake linings. Minimum thickness is 3mm. Also check the return spring for signs of heat damage and replace, if necessary.

6. Install in reverse order, making sure you connect the long end of the return spring between the parking brake lever and brake shoe.

Wheel Cylinders
REMOVAL AND INSTALLATION

1. Remove the brake drum as outlined under "Brake Drum Removal and Installation."

2. Loosen the brake shoes by rotating the adjustment screw at each backing plate. To loos-

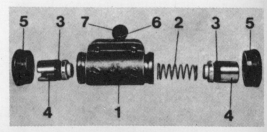

Wheel cylinder components—see text

en, turn the left hand screw clockwise and the right hand screw counterclockwise.

3. Disconnect and plug the brake line to the wheel cylinder. Remove the bleed screw and mounting screws for the wheel cylinder from behind the backing plate.

4. Push the wheel cylinder to the right and left out forward.

5. Reverse the above procedure to install, taking care to adjust the brakes as outlined under "Drum Brake Adjustment," and bleed the brakes as outlined under "Bleeding".

OVERHAUL

1. Remove the wheel cylinder as outlined under ''Wheel Cylinder Removal and Installation.''

2. Remove the protective rubber end caps (5) from the cylinder (1) and withdraw the piston (4), sleeves (3), and compression spring (2).

3. Clean all parts in clean brake fluid or methylated alcohol. Inspect the compression spring, pistons and cylinder bore. Replace the spring if it is distorted. Replace the pistons and cylinder if either is corroded or scored. Always use new rubber sleeves and protective end caps to assemble. Also, make sure that the grooves at the ends of the cylinder for the rubber caps are not damaged.

4. Dip the cylinder bore, pistons, and the new seals in clean brake fluid or Ate cylinder paste. Insert the piston and seal assemblies together with the compression spring into the bore. Install the new rubber end caps on the cylinder, making sure that the lips on the end caps seat fully in the cylinder grooves.

5. Install the wheel cylinder as outlined under "Wheel Cylinder Removal and Installation." Remember to adjust the brakes and bleed the hydraulic system.

REAR DISC BRAKES

CAUTION: *Brake shoes and pads contain asbestos, which has been determined to be a cancer causing agent. Never clean the brake surfaces with compressed air. Avoid inhaling any dust from any brake surface. When cleaning brake surfaces, use a commercially available brake cleaning fluid.*

Disc Brake Pads

INSPECTION

Measure the thickness of the entire pad assembly or the lining itself as specified in the "Brake Specifications Chart" at the beginning of this chapter, and replace a pad which is at or near the wear limit. In case local inspection law spec-

ifies more lining material as a minimum requirement, the local law should take precedence.

REMOVAL AND INSTALLATION

NOTE: *The position of the caliper piston must be checked with a special BMW gauge (or equivalent) 34 1 000 series (order by the model of your car) and, if necessary, aligned with a special tool such as 34 1 060 or equivalent. It would be best to price these tools and weigh their cost against the cost of having the repairs performed before proceeding. Do not attempt to perform the job without the special tools.*

All Equipped Models Except 528e, 6 and 7 Series

1. Support the rear of the vehicle in a raised position, and remove the rear wheels.

2. Drive out the retaining pins.

3. Remove the cross springs (anti-rattle clips).

4. Using a BMW special hook, tool 34-1-010 or an equivalent tool, pull the pads out and away from the caliper.

Checking the 20 degree position of the caliper piston—528i, 530i

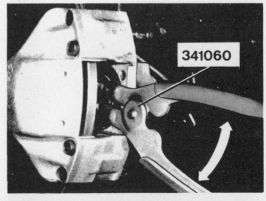

Correcting the angle of the caliper piston to 20 degrees with a special pair of pliers—528i, 530i

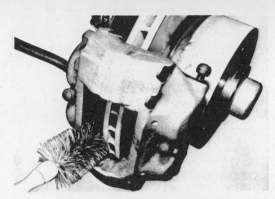

Use an alcohol soaked brush to clean the guide surface of the housing opening

5. Using a BMW special tool 34-10050, press the piston into the caliper to the fully retracted position. You may wish to drain fluid from the master cylinder first as doing this will displace fluid and raise the level there.

6. Check the 20° position of the caliper piston with a BMW special gauge 34-1-000 or an equivalent gauge. The 20° step must face the inlet or the brake disc.

7. Install the new brake pads, making sure to reinstall the anti-rattle clips. Install the rear wheel.

630CSi, 633CSi and 733i

NOTE: *The position of the caliper piston must be checked with a special BMW gauge (or equivalent) 34 1 000 series (order by the model of your car) and, if necessary, aligned with a special tool such as 34 1 060 or equivalent. It would be best to price these tools and weigh their cost against the cost of having the repairs performed before proceeding. do not attempt to perform the job without the special tools.*

1. Remove the rear wheel. Disconnect the right rear plug for the pad wear indicator. Take the wires out of the clamp.

2. Drive out the retaining pins and remove the cross spring.

3. Pull the pads straight out with a tool which will grab them via the backing plate holes. If the pads are to be reused, make sure not to mix them up-they must be reinstalled in the same place.

4. When ordering new pads, note both the color code and make. Replace all four pads on rear axle together if any pads are excessively worn.

5. Install a new wear sensor on the right side of the left brake pad (thicker side toward disc).

6. Use a brush and alcohol to clean the guide surface of the housing opening.

7. Force the pistons back into the caliper

with an appropriate special tool (for example BMW 34 1 050). Forcing the pistons back will displace the fluid in the caliper and raise the level in the master cylinder. Drain some fluid out of the master cylinder reservoir before proceeding.

8. The step on the piston must face the side of the caliper where the disc enters the caliper when the vehicle is moving forward. If necessary, correct the angle of the piston with a special tool such as BMW 34 1 060. Measure the angle with BMW gauge 34 1 100 or equivalent.

9. Reinstall pads in reverse order. Check the cross spring and retaining pins and replace if necessary. Pump the brake pedal until all motion has been taken out of the pads and they rest at the calipers. Keep the master cylinder fluid reservoir full while doing this.

528e

For rear pad removal and installation procedures, please follow those already detained under "Front Disc Brakes".

Disc Brake Calipers
REMOVAL AND INSTALLATION

All Models

For rear disc brake caliper removal and installation procedures, please follow those already detailed in the "Front Disc Brake" section. Caliper mounting bolt torque is 44-48 ft. lbs.

OVERHAUL
All Models Except 528e

1. Remove the caliper as described above. Remove the brake pads.

2. Remove the clamp and rubber piston seal on both sides.

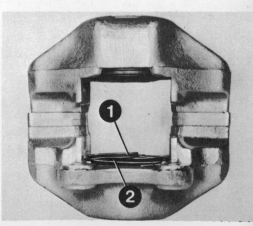

Remove the clamp (1) and rubber piston seal (2) on both sides

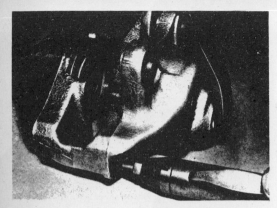

Plugging the brake line connecting hole in the caliper—2800, 3.0

Locations of the four ring seals

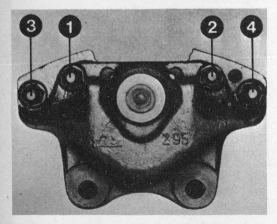

Tighten new stretch bolts in the numbered sequence

3. Place a felt pad or hardwood block in the caliper jaws and between the pistons.

4. On the 2800 and 3.0, plug the brake line connecting hole and retain the piston on the connecting hole side with brake pliers. On other models, hold the piston opposite the brake line

connecting hole with brake pliers and apply the compressed air to the connecting hole. Apply air pressure gradually to reduce the chance of personal injury, just until the first piston pops out.

5. Plug the open piston bore with some sort of sealing plate. On the 500, 600 and 700 series, also plug the connecting hole and switch the air pressure hose to the bleed hole. Then, force out the second piston in the same manner.

6. Lift out seals with a soft (plastic) probe.

7. Clean all parts in alcohol and dry with clean compressed air. Replace calipers with damaged bores and pistons with scored or pitted surfaces.

8. Reassemble in reverse order, using all new seals from an overhaul kit. Be careful not to cock pistons in the bores when reinstalling, and coat all parts with silicone lubricant.

9. Check the 20° position of the piston, install the calipers and pads, and bleed the system, as described above.

10. On the 2800, 3.0 and 528i and 530i, the calipers can be split for replacement of seals inside. Split the calipers and replace these four ring seals only if absolutely necessary. When reassembling, make sure to torque the bolts to 16-19 ft. lbs. only in the numbered order shown. Use new bolts only.

528e

For all caliper overhaul procedures, please refer to the "Front Disc Brake" section.

Brake Discs

REMOVAL AND INSTALLATION

All Models

1. Remove the rear wheel, and, if necessary, unclamp the brake line from the rear suspension. Remove the caliper as described above.

2. On the 2800, 3.0, 528i and 530i, simply pull the disc off the axle shaft. Note the position of the holes in the disc and axle shaft flange (on 500 series models, the large hole in the disc aligns with the large hole in the axle shaft flange.

3. On the 528e, the 600 and 700 series, remove the allen bolt and remove the disc.

4. Reverse the removal procedure to install. Torque allen bolts retaining the disc to 22-24 ft. lbs.

INSPECTION

1. Mount a dial indicator on the rear caliper with the pin against the disc. It may be convenient to pull the rear brake pads out and measure between the jaws of the caliper.

2. Measure the thickness of the disc at eight points around the diameter on the worn surfaces with a micrometer. Compare the thick-

CHILTON'S
AUTO BODY REPAIR TIPS

Tools and Materials • Step-by-Step Illustrated Procedures
How To Repair Dents, Scratches and Rust Holes
Spray Painting and Refinishing Tips

With a little practice, basic body repair procedures can be mastered by any do-it-yourself mechanic. The step-by-step repairs shown here can be applied to almost any type of auto body repair.

TOOLS & MATERIALS

You may already have basic tools, such as hammers and electric drills. Other tools unique to body repair — body hammers, grinding attachments, sanding blocks, dent puller, half-round plastic file and plastic spreaders — are relatively inexpensive and can be obtained wherever auto parts or auto body repair parts are sold. Portable air compressors and paint spray guns can be purchased or rented.

Auto Body Repair Kits

The best and most often used products are available to the do-it-yourselfer in kit form, from major manufacturers of auto body repair products. The same manufacturers also merchandise the individual products for use by pros.

Kits are available to make a wide variety of repairs, including holes, dents and scratches and fiberglass, and offer the advantage of buying the materials you'll need for the job. There is little waste or chance of materials going bad from not being used. Many kits may also contain basic body-working tools such as body files, sanding blocks and spreaders. Check the contents of the kit before buying your tools.

BODY REPAIR TIPS

Safety

Many of the products associated with auto body repair and refinishing contain toxic chemicals. Read all labels before opening containers and store them in a safe place and manner.
• Wear eye protection (safety goggles) when using power tools or when performing any operation that involves the removal of any type of material.
• Wear lung protection (disposable mask or respirator) when grinding, sanding or painting.

Sanding

1 Sand off paint before using a dent puller. When using a non-adhesive sanding disc, cover the back of the disc with an overlapping layer or two of masking tape and trim the edges. The disc will last considerably longer.

2 Use the circular motion of the sanding disc to grind *into* the edge of the repair. Grinding or sanding away from the jagged edge will only tear the sandpaper.

3 Use the palm of your hand flat on the panel to detect high and low spots. Do not use your fingertips. Slide your hand slowly back and forth.

WORKING WITH BODY FILLER

Mixing The Filler

Cleanliness and proper mixing and application are extremely important. Use a clean piece of plastic or glass or a disposable artist's palette to mix body filler.

1 Allow plenty of time and follow directions. No useful purpose will be served by adding more hardener to make it cure (set-up) faster. Less hardener means more curing time, but the mixture dries harder; more hardener means less curing time but a softer mixture.

2 Both the hardener and the filler should be thoroughly kneaded or stirred before mixing. Hardener should be a solid paste and dispense like thin toothpaste. Body filler should be smooth, and free of lumps or thick spots.

Getting the proper amount of hardener in the filler is the trickiest part of preparing the filler. Use the same amount of hardener in cold or warm weather. For contour filler (thick coats), a bead of hardener twice the diameter of the filler is about right. There's about a 15% margin on either side, but, if in doubt use less hardener.

3 Mix the body filler and hardener by wiping across the mixing surface, picking the mixture up and wiping it again. Colder weather requires longer mixing times. Do not mix in a circular motion; this will trap air bubbles which will become holes in the cured filler.

Applying The Filler

1 For best results, filler should not be applied over ¼" thick.

Apply the filler in several coats. Build it up to above the level of the repair surface so that it can be sanded or grated down.

The first coat of filler must be pressed on with a firm wiping motion.

Apply the filler in one direction only. Working the filler back and forth will either pull it off the metal or trap air bubbles.

REPAIRING DENTS

Before you start, take a few minutes to study the damaged area. Try to visualize the shape of the panel before it was damaged. If the damage is on the left fender, look at the right fender and use it as a guide. If there is access to the panel from behind, you can reshape it with a body hammer. If not, you'll have to use a dent puller. Go slowly and work

the metal a little at a time. Get the panel as straight as possible before applying filler.

1 This dent is typical of one that can be pulled out or hammered out from behind. Remove the headlight cover, headlight assembly and turn signal housing.

2 Drill a series of holes ½ the size of the end of the dent puller along the stress line. Make some trial pulls and assess the results. If necessary, drill more holes and try again. Do not hurry.

3 If possible, use a body hammer and block to shape the metal back to its original contours. Get the metal back as close to its original shape as possible. Don't depend on body filler to fill dents.

4 Using an 80-grit grinding disc on an electric drill, grind the paint from the surrounding area down to bare metal. Use a new grinding pad to prevent heat buildup that will warp metal.

5 The area should look like this when you're finished grinding. Knock the drill holes in and tape over small openings to keep plastic filler out.

6 Mix the body filler (see Body Repair Tips). Spread the body filler evenly over the entire area (see Body Repair Tips). Be sure to cover the area completely.

7 Let the body filler dry until the surface can just be scratched with your fingernail. Knock the high spots from the body filler with a body file ("Cheesegrater"). Check frequently with the palm of your hand for high and low spots.

8 Check to be sure that trim pieces that will be installed later will fit exactly. Sand the area with 40-grit paper.

9 If you wind up with low spots, you may have to apply another layer of filler.

10 Knock the high spots off with 40-grit paper. When you are satisfied with the contours of the repair, apply a thin coat of filler to cover pin holes and scratches.

11 Block sand the area with 40-grit paper to a smooth finish. Pay particular attention to body lines and ridges that must be well-defined.

12 Sand the area with 400 paper and then finish with a scuff pad. The finished repair is ready for priming and painting (see Painting Tips).

Materials and photos courtesy of Ritt Jones Auto Body, Prospect Park, PA.

REPAIRING RUST HOLES

There are many ways to repair rust holes. The fiberglass cloth kit shown here is one of the most cost efficient for the owner because it provides a strong repair that resists cracking and moisture and is relatively easy to use. It can be used on large and small holes (with or without backing) and can be applied over contoured areas. Remember, however, that short of replacing an entire panel, no repair is a guarantee that the rust will not return.

1 Remove any trim that will be in the way. Clean away all loose debris. Cut away all the rusted metal. But be sure to leave enough metal to retain the contour or body shape.

2 Grind away all traces of rust with a 24-grit grinding disc. Be sure to grind back 3-4 inches from the edge of the hole down to bare metal and be sure all traces of paint, primer and rust are removed.

3 Block sand the area with 80 or 100 grit sandpaper to get a clear, shiny surface and feathered paint edge. Tap the edges of the hole inward with a ball peen hammer.

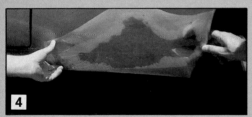

4 If you are going to use release film, cut a piece about 2-3" larger than the area you have sanded. Place the film over the repair and mark the sanded area on the film. Avoid any unnecessary wrinkling of the film.

5 Cut 2 pieces of fiberglass matte to match the shape of the repair. One piece should be about 1" smaller than the sanded area and the second piece should be 1" smaller than the first. Mix enough filler and hardener to saturate the fiberglass material (see Body Repair Tips).

6 Lay the release sheet on a flat surface and spread an even layer of filler, large enough to cover the repair. Lay the smaller piece of fiberglass cloth in the center of the sheet and spread another layer of filler over the fiberglass cloth. Repeat the operation for the larger piece of cloth.

7 Place the repair material over the repair area, with the release film facing outward. Use a spreader and work from the center outward to smooth the material, following the body contours. Be sure to remove all air bubbles.

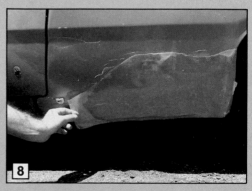

8 Wait until the repair has dried tack-free and peel off the release sheet. The ideal working temperature is 60°-90° F. Cooler or warmer temperatures or high humidity may require additional curing time. Wait longer, if in doubt.

9 Sand and feather-edge the entire area. The initial sanding can be done with a sanding disc on an electric drill if care is used. Finish the sanding with a block sander. Low spots can be filled with body filler; this may require several applications.

10 When the filler can just be scratched with a fingernail, knock the high spots down with a body file and smooth the entire area with 80-grit. Feather the filled areas into the surrounding areas.

11 When the area is sanded smooth, mix some topcoat and hardener and apply it directly with a spreader. This will give a smooth finish and prevent the glass matte from showing through the paint.

12 Block sand the topcoat smooth with finishing sandpaper (200 grit), and 400 grit. The repair is ready for masking, priming and painting (see Painting Tips).

Materials and photos courtesy Marson Corporation, Chelsea, Massachusetts

PAINTING TIPS

Preparation

1 SANDING — Use a 400 or 600 grit wet or dry sandpaper. Wet-sand the area with a 1/4 sheet of sandpaper soaked in clean water. Keep the paper wet while sanding. Sand the area until the repaired area tapers into the original finish.

2 CLEANING — Wash the area to be painted thoroughly with water and a clean rag. Rinse it thoroughly and wipe the surface dry until you're sure it's completely free of dirt, dust, fingerprints, wax, detergent or other foreign matter.

3 MASKING — Protect any areas you don't want to overspray by covering them with masking tape and newspaper. Be careful not get fingerprints on the area to be painted.

4 PRIMING — All exposed metal should be primed before painting. Primer protects the metal and provides an excellent surface for paint adhesion. When the primer is dry, wet-sand the area again with 600 grit wet-sandpaper. Clean the area again after sanding.

Painting Techniques

P aint applied from either a spray gun or a spray can (for small areas) will provide good results. Experiment on an

old piece of metal to get the right combination before you begin painting.

SPRAYING VISCOSITY (SPRAY GUN ONLY) — Paint should be thinned to spraying viscosity according to the directions on the can. Use only the recommended thinner or reducer and the same amount of reduction regardless of temperature.

AIR PRESSURE (SPRAY GUN ONLY) — This is extremely important. Be sure you are using the proper recommended pressure.

TEMPERATURE — The surface to be painted should be approximately the same temperature as the surrounding air. Applying warm paint to a cold surface, or vice versa, will completely upset the paint characteristics.

THICKNESS — Spray with smooth strokes. In general, the thicker the coat of paint, the longer the drying time. Apply several thin coats about 30 seconds apart. The paint should remain wet long enough to flow out and no longer; heavier coats will only produce sags or wrinkles. Spray a light (fog) coat, followed by heavier color coats.

DISTANCE — The ideal spraying distance is 8"-12" from the gun or can to the surface. Shorter distances will produce ripples, while greater distances will result in orange peel, dry film and poor color match and loss of material due to overspray.

OVERLAPPING — The gun or can should be kept at right angles to the surface at all times. Work to a wet edge at an even speed, using a 50% overlap and direct the center of the spray at the lower or nearest edge of the previous stroke.

RUBBING OUT (BLENDING) FRESH PAINT — Let the paint dry thoroughly. Runs or imperfections can be sanded out, primed and repainted.

Don't be in too big a hurry to remove the masking. This only produces paint ridges. When the finish has dried for at least a week, apply a small amount of fine grade rubbing compound with a clean, wet cloth. Use lots of water and blend the new paint with the surrounding area.

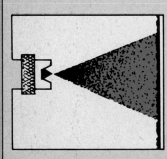

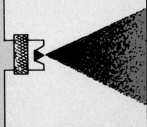

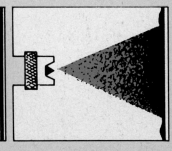

WRONG	CORRECT	WRONG

Thin coat. Stroke too fast, not enough overlap, gun too far away.

Medium coat. Proper distance, good stroke, proper overlap.

Heavy coat. Stroke too slow, too much overlap, gun too close.

ness readings and subtract the lowest from the highest. If this figure is greater than the maximum specification described in the specification chart at the beginning of this chapter, the disc must be machined. Note also the minimum thickness figures and the fact that, if the disc requires machining and cannot be cleaned up before the thickness drops below the minimum figure, it must be replaced.

3. Preload the dial indicator a small amount and measure the total runout of the disc as it rotates. Compare with specifications and if runout is excessive, have the disc machined (note that wheel bearing problems, if they exist, can show up as excessive runout).

PARKING BRAKE

Parking Brake Cable

ADJUSTMENT

Vehicles Equipped with Rear Drum Brakes

1. Support the rear of the vehicle in the raised position.
2. Fully release the handbrake.
3. On vehicles with adjustable brakes, while rotating the tire and wheel assembly, turn the left hand eccentric adjustment nut counterclockwise and the right hand eccentric adjustment nut clockwise until the brake shoes are tight against the drum and the wheel will no

longer rotate. On vehicles with self-adjusting brakes, simply operate the pedal hard several times to ensure automatic adjusters have taken up the slack.

4. Loosen the eccentric nuts by ⅛ of a turn,

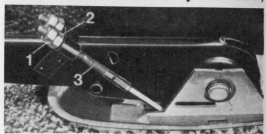

Parking brake lever components—1600, 2002

Gaining access to the rear brake shoe adjusting starwheel—733i

To disconnect the rear brake cable on the 735i, pull the spreader lock assembly (A) out of the housing and remove the pin at the lower end. Disconnect the cable at (B); pull the inner portion of the spreader lock (C) out of the housing.

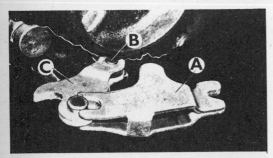

Removing the brake shoe expander—2800, 3.0

Loosening the footwell nozzle mounting screw (arrowed) on the 733i

so that the wheel is just able to turn, on vehicles with adjustable brakes.

5. Push up the rubber sleeve on the handbrake lever until the locknut is visible.

6. Loosen the locknut.

7. Pull up on the handbrake lever for a distance of five notches. Measure the distance between the middle of the handle and propeller shaft tunnel. This distance should be approximately 114mm ± 5mm.

8. Tighten the adjustment nut until the wheels are locked, and retighten the locknut. On the 318i, the wheels must be just beginning to drag, and resistance on both sides must be equal.

9. Release the handbrake. Make sure that the wheels turn freely when the handbrake is released.

Vehicles Equipped with Rear Disc Brakes Except 325, 325e, 325i, 325iS, 1983-84 733i and 735i

The procedure for adjusting the handbrake on vehicles equipped with rear disc brakes is similar to the procedure for adjusting the handbrake on vehicles equipped with rear drum brakes with one exception.

The mechanism for adjusting the brake shoes is a star wheel type adjuster. Insert a screwdriver through the 15mm hole, and turn the adjusting star wheel until the brake disc can no longer be moved. Proceed as though adjusting the handbrake on vehicles equipped with rear drum brakes.

325, 325e, 325i and 325iS, 325iX, M3

1. Remove one bolt on each rear wheel with the vehicle securely supported. Make sure the handbrake is off and cable properly adjusted.

2. Turn the wheels until the bolt hole is about 30° behind the 12 o'clock position. Then it is possible to reach the star wheel adjuster with a long screwdriver.

3. Turn the left side adjusting nut up, or the right side nut down, to tighten the adjustment until the shoes prevent the disc from being turned by hand. Now loosen the adjustment 3-4 threads. Make sure the disc turns easily.

733i (1983-84) and 735i

1. The parking brake should be adjusted when the lever can be pulled up more than 8 notches. First, remove the cover pate on the console (the handbrake lever protrudes through this plate). Then, loosen the locknuts and loosen the adjusting nuts (2) for the cables until they are nearly at the ends of the threads.

2. Support the car securely off the rear wheels. Remove one wheel bolt from each rear wheel. Then, rotate one wheel until the hole left by removing the bolt is about 45° counterclockwise from the 6 o'clock position. This will line the hole in the wheel with the star wheel which adjusts the rear brake shoes (used for parking only). If it is difficult to turn the star wheel it will help to remove the rear wheel and, if necessary, the brake disc.

3. Turn the adjusting star wheel with a screwdriver until the rear wheel or brake disc can no longer be turned. Then, back it off 4 to 6 threads.

4. In the passenger compartment, pull the handbrake up 4 notches. Then, turn the cable adjusting nuts in the tightening direction until the rear wheels can just barely be turned. Make sure the adjustment is uniform. Lock the adjusting nuts in position.

5. Release the handbrake and make sure the wheels can now be turned easily, repeating Step 4 to correct a failure to release if necessary.

REMOVAL AND INSTALLATION

318i and 320i

1. Remove the brake drum as described above. Pull off the rubber boot at the handbrake lever, loosen and remove the locknuts on the appropriate side, and disconnect the cable at the handbrake lever.

2. Remove the brake shoes as described in above.

3. Then, on 320i, pull the cable out of the holder toward the rear of the car. On 318i, disconnect the cable on the rear suspension arm,

compress the locking clamp, and disconnect the cable on the backing plate and pull it out.

4. Install in reverse order, making sure the cable holders are both located properly—one in the protective tube, and the other in the backing plate. On the 318i, make sure the clamp which locates the tube is properly connected. Adjust the brakes as described at the front of this chapter.

325, 325e, 325i and 325iS

1. Remove the rubber boot at the base of the handbrake by pulling up the clamp at the front and lifting it out at the rear.

2. Lift out the ashtray at the rear of the console. Remove the bolt located under the ashtray. Then, pull the console to the rear to disconnect it and remove it.

3. Unscrew and remove the parking brake cable nuts.

4. Remove the parking brake shoes. Locate the cable spread outboard of the brake disc. Pull the outer portion of the spreader to the rear and remove it. Then, press out the pin and pull the unit off.

5. Disconnect the brake cable at the trailing arm. Then, pull the cable out of the protective tube. Disconnect the cable support at the rear disc and then pull the assembly out.

6. Install in reverse order. The sliding surfaces of the cable spreader should be coated with Molykote® G paste or equivalent. Make sure the cable holder rests on the protective tube. To adjust the cable, pull the brake up just five notches, and then tighten the nuts until the right and left rear wheels just begin to drag uniformly. Release the brake and make sure the wheels turn freely.

1983-84 733i and 735i through 1986

1. Lift out the cover plate that surrounds the handbrake lever. Remove the locknuts and adjusting nuts from the front ends of the brake cables.

2. Remove the rear brake discs.

3. Disconnect the spreader locks from the backing plates: first, rock the lower end of the spreader lock outward, and then pull out the pin. Press the cable connection out of the spreader lock. Pull the spreader lock out of the housing. Pull the cable through the backing plate.

4. Detach the parking brake cable at the trailing arm and remove it.

5. To install, reverse the removal procedures, giving the sliding surfaces and pin of the spreader lock a light coating of an lubricant such as Molykote® G paste. Adjust the handbrake as described above.

1987-88 735i

1. Remove the rear brake discs.

2. Using brake spring pliers, disconnect the upper return spring for the parking brake shoes. Then, using a special tool 34 4 000 or the equivalent, turn the retaining springs for the parking brake shoes 90° to unlock them and then disconnect them.

CAUTION: *In performing the next step, watch the pin for the expander lock and keep it if it falls out.*

3. Separate the parking brake shoes at the top and then remove them from below.

4. Disconnect the spreader locks from the backing plates: first, rock the lower end of the spreader lock outward, and then pull out the pin. Press the cable connection out of the spreader lock. Pull the spreader lock out of the housing. Pull the cable through the backing plate.

5. Disconnect the parking brake cable at the trailing arm.

6. Working inside the car, remove the console cover as follows:

   a. Lift out the air grille and remove the two nuts underneath.

   b. Remove the cap and unscrew the mounting bolt that's located at the forward end of the console on the right side. Lift out the cover that the bolt retains.

   c. Remove the bolt on the left side of the forward end of the console. If the car has power windows, disconnect the plugs. Then, lift the console and remove air ducts.

   d. Turn the retainer 90° and peel the rubber cover downward. Now, unscrew the adjusting nuts on the parking brake cables and pull them out.

7. Install the cable and adjust the parking brake as described above.

All Others

1. Remove the parking brake shoes.

2. Disconnect the negative battery cable, loosen the mounting screw and pull off the footwell nozzle.

3. Unscrew mounting bolts, and pull the tray at the front of the footwell out far enough to disconnect the wires. Then, remove the tray.

4. Remove the rubber boot from the handbrake lever. Unscrew the locknuts and remove them and pull the cable out of the brake lever.

5. Working under the car, detach the brake cable at the suspension arm. Remove the two mounting nuts at the brake backing plate, and then pull the cable out of the protective tube.

6. Install the new cable in position and install the remaining components.

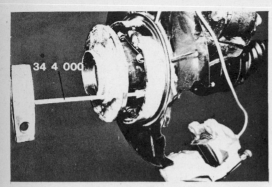

Turning the retaining springs with a special tool to remove rear parking brake shoes—typical

Parking Brake Shoes
Rear Disc Brakes

REPLACEMENT

Models Equipped

1. Remove the rear caliper.
2. Remove the rear brake disc.
3. Remove the bottom return spring.
4. Using a tool such as BMW special tool 34-4-000, turn the retaining springs 90°, and remove the springs.
5. Pull the brake shoes apart at the bottom, and left them out.
6. Install the new brake shoes and install the retaining springs. Install the rear brake disc and caliper.

EXTERIOR

Doors

There are 2 types of door mountings that can be on your vehicle, these are; exposed hinge mounting (generally found on the older model BMW's) and hidden hinge mounting (found on some older and all newer models).

Exposed hinge mounting is when the door hinges are mounted to the outside of the door body (not on the surface skin but on the inner, hanging surface). This type of door is easy to remove and adjust because of the ease of access to the mounting points.

Hidden hinge mounting is when the door half of the hinge is actually inside the door. This poses a problem for removal because the door trim and window components must now be removed before you can gain access to the mounting points.

Follow the below outlined procedure that fits the type of door mounting on your vehicle. Remember to very careful when working with the doors, so as not to damage painted surfaces or delicate trim pieces.

REMOVAL AND INSTALLATION

Models with Exposed Hinges

The door on these models can be removed without removing the window glass or trim panels, however if you are going to remove them anyway it is better to do it before removing the door.

1. Disconnect the negative battery cable.
2. Roll down the window, if not already removed.
3. Scribe the location of the hinges in relation to the door, this will make sure that the door is reasonably adjusted when it is installed.
4. If the door has a retainer strap to keep it from opening, remove the retainer strap. This may require drilling out the strap rivets. With a helper holding the door, to keep it from falling, remove the 3 upper and lower hinge-to-door retaining bolts.
5. Remove the door from the vehicle.
6. To install the door, again with a helper, place the door in position and loosely install the bolts.
7. Align the hinges with the scribe marks and tighten the bolts. Check the adjustment of the door and adjust if necessary.

Models with Hidden Hinges

The door on these models must first be stripped of all interior trim and the window and regulator or electric motor assemblies.

1. Remove the armrest and all door panel components, see the procedure later in this chapter.
2. Remove the plastic vapor shield from the door.
3. Remove the window glass and regulator.
4. Drill out the rivet on the door retainer strap anchor. Remove the retainer-to-door bolts and remove the retainer.
5. Disconnect any electrical leads going into the door.
6. Scribe the location of the hinge on the inside of the door. With the help of an assistant, remove the 3 upper and lower hinge bolts and remove the door.
7. Install the door in position and reinstall all removed components.
8. Check the adjustment of the door and correct as necessary.

ADJUSTMENT

Door adjustment is simple and can be done with relative ease. There are 2 basic door adjustments, the first is to adjust the door by loosening the hinges (which are usually slotted for adjustment) and moving the door appropriately to gain the correct adjustment.

The second adjustment is made by adjusting

Drill out the door retainer rivet (arrow)

Adjust the door striker by loosening the bolts (arrows) and moving it

Remove the retainer to door bolts and remove the retainer

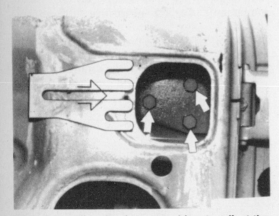

When reinstalling the door, use shims to adjust the door-to-body depth

the striker, which the door locks into, this adjustment is only to be made after the hinge adjustment since it can be affected by improper hinge adjustment.

To determine the correct door adjustment, use the body lines of the vehicle and adjust the door accordingly.

NOTE: *Improper adjustment of the striker*

plate can cause the door to latch improperly when closed, therefore always check the operation of the door after making any adjustments.

Hood

REMOVAL AND INSTALLATION

NOTE: *This procedure will require the aid of an assistant. Also, remember to use cardboard or a sheet to protect the hood when it is removed.*

1. Remove the front air intake hose and remove the windshield washer tank from the fender well.

2. Disconnect the plug for the engine compartment light, if equipped.

3. Scribe the location of the hinges on the inside of the hood, this will help during installation and making hood alignment easy.

4. Have your assistant support the hood and remove the bolt from the hood support arm mounts, note the location and position of any washers.

Hood hinge adjustment through the grille area with the grille removed

Adjust the hood lock plates for hood height

Use the rubber stops to pre-load the hood

Adjust the rear height of the hood by moving the catch assembly

5. Detach the left and right support arms from the torsion bars on the hood.

6. Loosen the hinge bolts and remove the hood.

7. Install the hood in position and install the hinge bolts loosely.

8. Reinstall the hood supports and check the hood for proper adjustment and alignment. Align or adjust as necessary.

ALIGNMENT

The hood must be aligned for correct height and centered in position, this can be done be a few simple adjustments.

The grille must removed to align the hood via the hinges, once the grille is removed, loosen the hinge bolts and adjust the front height of the hood and make sure it is centered evenly from side to side.

Next the lock stops on the side of the hood can be loosened and moved to adjust the height of the sides of the hood, so that it can be even with the top of the fenders.

To adjust the hood for correct operation the hood latch assembly can be moved be simply loosening the bolts and sliding it to the correct position, note that the latch can also be used to adjust the rear hood height on BMW vehicles.

The final adjustment is for preload, so that the hood will open when the release is pulled. This can be done by turning the 4 rubber stops at the corners of the hood. The hood should pop open but also close easily. It should also latch firmly.

NOTE: *Improper latch adjustment can cause the hood to latch too loosely and may cause it to open while in motion. Check that the hood is latched firmly after each adjustment.*

Trunk Lid

REMOVAL AND INSTALLATION

NOTE: *You will need an assistant for this procedure.*

1. Remove the inside liner from the hood. Disconnect the trunk light wire, if equipped.

2. Scribe the location of the trunk hinges on the trunk lid, this will make installation easy and adjustment much simpler.

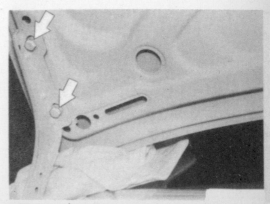

Adjust the trunk lid by loosening the bolts and moving the lid

3. Have an assistant hold the trunk lid while you remove the retaining bolts, remove the trunk lid.

4. Install the trunk lid in position and install the retaining bolts.

5. Check the alignment of the trunk lid and adjust as necessary.

Bumpers
REMOVAL AND INSTALLATION
Front

1. Disconnect fog light wires, if equipped.
2. Loosen both left and right bumper-to-body mounting bolts.
3. Remove the bumper bolts and remove the bumper by pulling it forward.
4. Install the bumper in reverse order, tighten the mounting bolts to 26 ft. lbs.

Rear

Remove the bolts that retain the bumper to the rear impact absorbers and remove the bumper. Install it in position and tighten the bolts to 22 ft. lbs.

Remove the center grille section by removing the 4 screws

Remove the side grille sections by removing the retaining screws (1 thru 4)

Grille
REMOVAL AND INSTALLATION

The grille is removed in 3 sections, one center and 2 side sections. The sections are held in place by screws. Remove the screws for the section you want to remove and remove that section. Note that on early 6 series vehicles the center section of the grille is spring loaded, so do not loose the springs when removing it.

Outside Mirrors
REMOVAL AND INSTALLATION

Remove the door mirrors by, first removing the triangular plastic cover from inside the door. Then unplug the mirror, on models with power mirrors. Remove the 3 retaining screws and remove the mirror.

On late model 5, 6 and 7 series with the radio speakers in this location, unplug the speaker and be careful not to puncture it when removing the trim from around it.

Antenna
REMOVAL AND INSTALLATION
Post Antenna

1. Disconnect negative battery cable.
2. Unplug the antenna from the radio, this may require radio removal on some models.
3. Pull the antenna wire through the firewall.
4. Using an adjustable wrench, remove the antenna base from the fender well and remove the antenna.
5. Install in reverse order, making sure to route the antenna wire carefully through the fire wall to prevent cutting the wire.

Disconnect the plug (1) and remove the mounting screws

Automatic Telescoping Antenna

1. Disconnect the negative battery cable.

2. Open the trunk and remove the side trim panel screws and remove the panel. Remove the spare tire and jack, on some models.

3. Unplug the antenna power lead and the antenna wire.

4. Carefully, using an adjustable wrench, remove the antenna mast mounting from the top of the rear fender.

5. Remove the antenna mounting bracket bolt inside the trunk and remove the antenna assembly by pulling it down and out.

6. Install the antenna in reverse order, check the operation of the antenna.

Typical door panel removal—unscrew the bottom then pull off

INTERIOR

Door Panels

REMOVAL AND INSTALLATION

1. Disconnect the negative battery cable.

2. Remove the power mirror switch, if equipped, py prying it carefully from the door panel. Disconnect the electrical lead from it.

3. If equipped with power windows, remove the window switch from the armrest. Disconnect the electrical wires from it.

4. If equipped with manual windows, remove the window crank.

5. Remove the screws retaining the armrest and remove the armrest from the door panel.

6. Remove the screw in the plate around the inside door handle. Remove the plate from around the door handle.

7. Remove the retaining screws at the bottom edge of the door panel and pull the panel off. Use care not to loose any of the retaining clips.

8. The top panel can now be removed by using the following procedures:

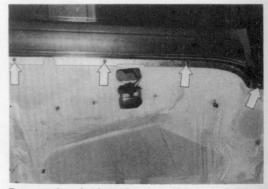

Remove the trim from the top trim panel and then pull it off

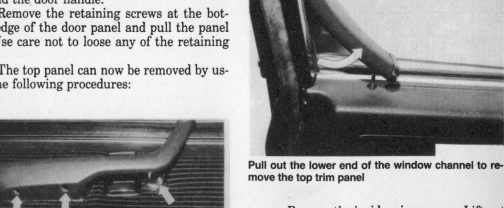

Pull out the lower end of the window channel to remove the top trim panel

a. Remove the inside mirror cover. Lift out the rear window channel slightly.

b. Remove the screws along the bottom edge of the top trim panel.

c. Remove the panel by lifting up on it and pulling out of the top of the door. Be careful not to loose any of the clips.

9. If work is going by done on the inside of the door, remove the plastic sheeting from the

Typical armrest removal

door. This panel must be reinstalled when finished, it serves as a water barrier for the door panel.

10. Install the top panel first, making sure the clips are fully seated.

11. Install the mirror cover and reinsert the window channel in position.

12. Install the door panel, top first, by pushing in the areas where there are clips then screw the bottom in place.

13. Complete the installation by installing the remaining components.

Door Locks

REMOVAL AND INSTALLATION

The procedure for door lock removal and installation is the same for both power and manual locks with the exception of the lock actuating switch and wiring on power lock systems.

1. Disconnect the negative battery cable.

2. Remove the front door panel.

3. Wind the window all the way up and pull the window guide out at the bottom. This can

Remove the lower window guide rail through the bottom opening (arrow)

Disconnecting the lock rods at the main lock assembly

Disconnect the lock assembly bracket (1) and remove the lock and bracket

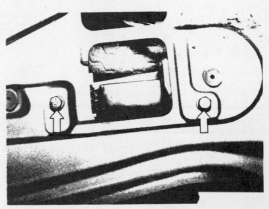

To remove the inside door handle remove the bolts and take the handle off, to the inside of the door

be reached through the bottom opening in the door panel.

4. Remove the bolt retaining the lower part of the window guide rail and take the guide rail out by pulling down, this will not cause the window to fall.

5. Locate the lock assembly bracket, on power lock equipped models this will also hold the lock actuator and wiring.

6. Loosen the retaining screw and remove the bracket, disconnect the actuator wire if equipped with power locks.

7. Disconnect the lock rod from the lock assembly, at the main door lock, the part of the lock that actually keeps the door closed.

8. Any of the other locking components can now be removed as necessary, these include the inside release handle, the locking mechanism linkages and the key lock assembly on front doors. The key lock is removed by twisting it 90 degrees and pulling it out to the inside of the door.

9. Reinstall any removed components then install the lock assembly bracket.

10. On models with power door locks, reconnect the wiring to the actuator.

11. Check all lock rods for binding or bent linkages. It is also a good idea to check the locking mechanism for proper operation before reinstalling the door panel.

12. After all components are in place and you are sure the locking system is working, reinstall the lower window rail and then install the door panel.

NOTE: *When installing the door panel the plastic sheeting MUST be reinstalled as this is a water barrier. If the sheeting is damaged, use a piece of heavy plastic to replace it.*

13. Reconnect the negative battery cable and recheck the operation of the door locks.

14. On models with power door locks, be sure the entire locking system is working.

Door Glass and Regulator
REMOVAL AND INSTALLATION

Models with Manual Window Controls

This procedure is good for both front and rear doors. Remember when removing window glass to use care when handling it. The glass should be placed out of the way to prevent the chance of damaging it.

1. Disconnect the negative battery cable.
2. Remove the door trim panel.
3. Locate the screws that hold the bottom lifting rail in place and remove them. Hold the window when doing this as it will become loose.
4. Tilt the window forward slightly and remove the lifting arm from the lifting rail.
5. Pull the window carefully out of the door.
6. The regulator can now be removed. This is done removing the bolts retaining it and pulling it out through the door.
7. Any of the window guide rails, molding or weatherstrip can now be removed.

Remove the bolts to remove the window glass from the lifting rail

Loosen the bolts and then turn the adjusting tool, 51 3 150, until the window slides are snug

The window travel should be limited by the stop (1)

8. Install any parts removed other than the window and regulator.
9. Install the window regulator and the lifting arm. Install the window by sliding it into the door.
10. Install the glass into the lifting arm and install the retaining screws.
11. Check the operation of the window and adjust it as necessary, using the following procedure:

    a. Put the window all the way up. Loosen the lifting rail bolts.

    b. Using special tool 51 3 150, turn the holder for the lifting rail so that both slides on the rail fit snugly. Tighten the rail bolts.

    c. Check the window travel, it should be limited by the stop on the regulator.

12. Install the door panel and check the operation of the window.

Door Glass and Electric Motor
REMOVAL AND INSTALLATION
Models with Electric Window Controls

This procedure is good for both front and rear doors. Remember when removing window glass to use care when handling it. The glass

should be placed out of the way to prevent the chance of damaging it.

1. Disconnect the negative battery cable.

2. Remove the door trim panel.

3. Locate the screws that hold the bottom lifting rail in place and remove them. Hold the window when doing this as it will become loose.

4. Tilt the window forward slightly and remove the lifting arm from the lifting rail.

5. Pull the window carefully out of the door.

6. The regulator and motor assembly can now be removed. This is done removing the bolts retaining it and pulling it out through the door.

7. The motor can be removed from the regulator assembly by pulling back the protective sleeve, turning the armature until the toothed gear is clear of the motor and removing the mounting screws. Pull the motor from the assembly.

8. Any of the window guide rails, molding or weatherstrip can now be removed. The motor control switch is also easy to remove now, disconnect the wires from it and pull it out of the door.

Removing the motor from the regulator assembly

The window travel should be limited by the stop (arrow)

9. Install any parts removed other than the window and motor, and regulator assembly.

10. Install the window regulator and motor assembly, and the lifting arm. Install the window by sliding it into the door.

11. Install the glass into the lifting arm and install the retaining screws.

12. Check the operation of the window and adjust it as necessary, using the following procedure:

   a. Put the window all the way up. Loosen the lifting rail bolts.

   b. Using special tool 51 3 150, turn the holder for the lifting rail so that both slides on the rail fit snugly. Tighten the rail bolts.

   c. Check the window travel, it should be limited by the stop on the motor.

12. Install the door panel and check the operation of the window.

Inside Rearview Mirror
REMOVAL AND INSTALLATION

To remove the inside mirror, remove the Allen head screw that keeps it attached to its base and slide the mirror off.

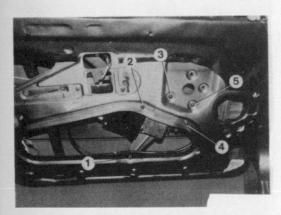

Remove the mounting bolts (1 thru 5) and remove the motor and regulator as an assembly

Remove the wires and remove the window control switch

How to Remove Stains from Fabric Interior

For rest results, spots and stains should be removed as soon as possible. Never use gasoline, lacquer thinner, acetone, nail polish remover or bleach. Use a 3' x 3" piece of cheesecloth. Squeeze most of the liquid from the fabric and wipe the stained fabric from the outside of the stain toward the center with a lifting motion. Turn the cheesecloth as soon as one side becomes soiled. When using water to remove a stain, be sure to wash the entire section after the spot has been removed to avoid water stains. Encrusted spots can be broken up with a dull knife and vacuumed before removing the stain.

Type of Stain	How to Remove It
Surface spots	Brush the spots out with a small hand brush or use a commercial preparation such as K2R to lift the stain.
Mildew	Clean around the mildew with warm suds. Rinse in cold water and soak the mildew area in a solution of 1 part table salt and 2 parts water. Wash with upholstery cleaner.
Water stains	Water stains in fabric materials can be removed with a solution made from 1 cup of table salt dissolved in 1 quart of water. Vigorously scrub the solution into the stain and rinse with clear water. Water stains in nylon or other synthetic fabrics should be removed with a commercial type spot remover.
Chewing gum, tar, crayons, shoe polish (greasy stains)	Do not use a cleaner that will soften gum or tar. Harden the deposit with an ice cube and scrape away as much as possible with a dull knife. Moisten the remainder with cleaning fluid and scrub clean.
Ice cream, candy	Most candy has a sugar base and can be removed with a cloth wrung out in warm water. Oily candy, after cleaning with warm water, should be cleaned with upholstery cleaner. Rinse with warm water and clean the remainder with cleaning fluid.
Wine, alcohol, egg, milk, soft drink (non-greasy stains)	Do not use soap. Scrub the stain with a cloth wrung out in warm water. Remove the remainder with cleaning fluid.
Grease, oil, lipstick, butter and related stains	Use a spot remover to avoid leaving a ring. Work from the outisde of the stain to the center and dry with a clean cloth when the spot is gone.
Headliners (cloth)	Mix a solution of warm water and foam upholstery cleaner to give thick suds. Use only foam—liquid may streak or spot. Clean the entire headliner in one operation using a circular motion with a natural sponge.
Headliner (vinyl)	Use a vinyl cleaner with a sponge and wipe clean with a dry cloth.
Seats and door panels	Mix 1 pint upholstery cleaner in 1 gallon of water. Do not soak the fabric around the buttons.
Leather or vinyl fabric	Use a multi-purpose cleaner full strength and a stiff brush. Let stand 2 minutes and scrub thoroughly. Wipe with a clean, soft rag.
Nylon or synthetic fabrics	For normal stains, use the same procedures you would for washing cloth upholstery. If the fabric is extremely dirty, use a multi-purpose cleaner full strength with a stiff scrub brush. Scrub thoroughly in all directions and wipe with a cotton towel or soft rag.

Remove the mounting bolts (arrows) to remove the seat from its base

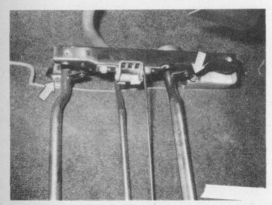

To remove the seat base, unbolt the 4 corners and remove it

On models with overhead consoles, remove the overhead console retaining screws and pull the console down. Disconnect the electrical lead and remove the console. Remove the Allen head screw and remove the mirror from its base.

Seats

REMOVAL AND INSTALLATION

Seat removal and installation is basically the same for both manual and power seat assemblies, with the exception of extra wiring for power seat equipped models. Also the driver and passenger seats are removed the same way.

Front

1. Disconnect the negative battery.
2. Slide the seat all the way back and locate the front 2 seat track-to-base mounting bolts.
3. Remove the front 2 mounting bolts.
4. Slide the seat all the way forward and locate the rear seat track-to-base mounting bolts.
5. Remove the bolts and tilt the seat backward.
6. Disconnect all of the electrical wiring and remove the seat from the vehicle.
7. The seat mounting base will still be in the vehicle, it can now be removed if desired. To do so, remove the 4 base mounting bolts and pull the assembly out of the vehicle.
8. Install the base, if it was removed. Install the seat back into the vehicle and reconnect the electrical leads.

Rear

To remove the rear seat, first Remove the base by pulling it up in the front and sliding it forward and out of the vehicle. Then remove the bolts at the bottom corners of the seat back and pull it up and out of the vehicle.

Power Seat Motor and Transmission

REMOVAL AND INSTALLATION

Power seat actually have more than one drive motor, most have 3. These motors are mounted on a separate base that is between the mounting base and the seat tracks, this is called the transmission. It is driven by cables from the motors. Therefore, the motors and transmission can be removed as an assembly.

Removal of the drive motor and transmission can be accomplished after removal of the seat (see above outlined procedure for seat removal). After the seat is removed, place it upside down on a clean work surface. Remove the transmission assembly by removing the 4 mounting bolts. After the transmission is removed the individual motors can be removed by unbolting them and disconnecting their drive cables. Install the transmission back onto the seat and reinstall the whole assembly into the vehicle.

Mechanic's Data

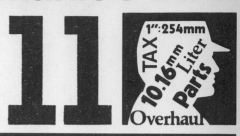

1":254mm
TAX
10.16mm
Liter
Parts
Overhaul

General Conversion Table

Multiply By	To Convert	To	
LENGTH			
2.54	Inches	Centimeters	.3937
25.4	Inches	Millimeters	.03937
30.48	Feet	Centimeters	.0328
.304	Feet	Meters	3.28
.914	Yards	Meters	1.094
1.609	Miles	Kilometers	.621
VOLUME			
.473	Pints	Liters	2.11
.946	Quarts	Liters	1.06
3.785	Gallons	Liters	.264
.016	Cubic inches	Liters	61.02
16.39	Cubic inches	Cubic cms.	.061
28.3	Cubic feet	Liters	.0353
MASS (Weight)			
28.35	Ounces	Grams	.035
.4536	Pounds	Kilograms	2.20
—	To obtain	From	Multiply by

Multiply By	To Convert	To	
AREA			
.645	Square inches	Square cms.	.155
.836	Square yds.	Square meters	1.196
FORCE			
4.448	Pounds	Newtons	.225
.138	Ft./lbs.	Kilogram/meters	7.23
1.36	Ft./lbs.	Newton-meters	.737
.112	In./lbs.	Newton-meters	8.844
PRESSURE			
.068	Psi	Atmospheres	14.7
6.89	Psi	Kilopascals	.145
OTHER			
1.104	Horsepower (DIN)	Horsepower (SAE)	.9861
.746	Horsepower (SAE)	Kilowatts (KW)	1.34
1.60	Mph	Km/h	.625
.425	Mpg	Km/1	2.35
—	To obtain	From	Multiply by

Tap Drill Sizes

National Coarse or U.S.S.

Screw & Tap Size	Threads Per Inch	Use Drill Number
No. 5	40	39
No. 6	32	36
No. 8	32	29
No. 10	24	25
No. 12	24	17
1/4	20	8
5/16	18	F
3/8	16	5/16
7/16	14	U
1/2	13	27/64
9/16	12	31/64
5/8	11	17/32
3/4	10	21/32
7/8	9	49/64

National Coarse or U.S.S.

Screw & Tap Size	Threads Per Inch	Use Drill Number
1	8	7/8
1 1/8	7	63/64
1 1/4	7	1 7/54
1 1/2	6	1 11/32

National Fine or S.A.E.

Screw & Tap Size	Threads Per Inch	Use Drill Number
No. 5	44	37
No. 6	40	33
No. 8	36	29
No. 10	32	21

National Fine or S.A.E.

Screw & Tap Size	Threads Per Inch	Use Drill Number
No. 12	28	15
1/4	28	3
6/16	24	1
3/8	24	Q
7/16	20	W
1/2	20	29/64
9/16	18	33/64
5/8	18	37/64
3/4	16	11/16
7/8	14	13/16
1 1/8	12	1 3/64
1 1/4	12	1 11/64
1 1/2	12	1 27/64

Drill Sizes In Decimal Equivalents

Inch	Decimal	Wire	mm
1/64	.0156		.39
	.0157		.4
	.0160	78	
	.0165		.42
	.0173		.44
	.0177		.45
	.0180	77	
	.0181		.46
	.0189		.48
	.0197		.5
	.0200	76	
	.0210	75	
	.0217		.55
	.0225	74	
	.0236		.6
	.0240	73	
	.0250	72	
	.0256		.65
	.0260	71	
	.0276		.7
	.0280	70	
	.0292	69	
	.0295		.75
	.0310	68	
1/32	.0312		.79
	.0315		.8
	.0320	67	
	.0330	66	
	.0335		.85
	.0350	65	
	.0354		.9
	.0360	64	
	.0370	63	
	.0374		.95
	.0380	62	
	.0390	61	
	.0394		1.0
	.0400	60	
	.0410	59	
	.0413		1.05
	.0420	58	
	.0430	57	
	.0433		1.1
	.0453		1.15
3/64	.0465	56	
	.0469		1.19
	.0472		1.2
	.0492		1.25
	.0512		1.3
	.0520	55	
	.0531		1.35
	.0550	54	
	.0551		1.4
	.0571		1.45
	.0591		1.5
	.0595	53	
	.0610		1.55
1/16	.0625		1.59
	.0630		1.6
	.0635	52	
	.0650		1.65
	.0669		1.7
	.0670	51	
	.0689		1.75
	.0700	50	
	.0709		1.8
	.0728		1.85

Inch	Decimal	Wire	mm
	.0730	49	
	.0748		1.9
	.0760	48	
	.0768		1.95
5/64	.0781		1.98
	.0785	47	
	.0787		2.0
	.0807		2.05
	.0810	46	
	.0820	45	
	.0827		2.1
	.0846		2.15
	.0860	44	
	.0866		2.2
	.0886		2.25
	.0890	43	
	.0906		2.3
	.0925		2.35
	.0935	42	
3/32	.0938		2.38
	.0945		2.4
	.0960	41	
	.0965		2.45
	.0980	40	
	.0981		2.5
	.0995	39	
	.1015	38	
	.1024		2.6
	.1040	37	
	.1063		2.7
	.1065	36	
	.1083		2.75
7/64	.1094		2.77
	.1100	35	
	.1102		2.8
	.1110	34	
	.1130	33	
	.1142		2.9
	.1160	32	
	.1181		3.0
	.1200	31	
	.1220		3.1
1/8	.1250		3.17
	.1260		3.2
	.1280		3.25
	.1285	30	
	.1299		3.3
	.1339		3.4
	.1360	29	
	.1378		3.5
	.1405	28	
9/64	.1406		3.57
	.1417		3.6
	.1440	27	
	.1457		3.7
	.1470	26	
	.1476		3.75
	.1495	25	
	.1496		3.8
	.1520	24	
	.1535		3.9
	.1540	23	
5/32	.1562		3.96
	.1570	22	
	.1575		4.0
	.1590	21	
	.1610	20	

Inch	Decimal	Wire & Letter	mm
	.1614		4.1
	.1654		4.2
	.1660	19	
	.1673		4.25
	.1693		4.3
	.1695	18	
11/64	.1719		4.36
	.1730	17	
	.1732		4.4
	.1770	16	
	.1772		4.5
	.1800	15	
	.1811		4.6
	.1820	14	
	.1850	13	
	.1850		4.7
	.1870		4.75
3/16	.1875		4.76
	.1890	12	
	.1890		4.8
	.1910	11	
	.1929		4.9
	.1935	10	
	.1960	9	
	.1969		5.0
	.1990	8	
	.2008		5.1
	.2010	7	
13/64	.2031		5.16
	.2040	6	
	.2047		5.2
	.2055	5	
	.2067		5.25
	.2087		5.3
	.2090	4	
	.2126		5.4
	.2130	3	
	.2165		5.5
7/32	.2188		5.55
	.2205		5.6
	.2210	2	
	.2244		5.7
	.2264		5.75
	.2280	1	
	.2283		5.8
	.2323		5.9
	.2340	A	
15/64	.2344		5.95
	.2362		6.0
	.2380	B	
	.2402		6.1
	.2420	C	
	.2441		6.2
	.2460	D	
	.2461		6.25
	.2480		6.3
1/4	.2500	E	6.35
	.2520		6.
	.2559		6.5
	.2570	F	
	.2598		6.6
	.2610	G	
	.2638		6.7
17/64	.2656		6.74
	.2657		6.75
	.2660	H	
	.2677		6.8

Inch	Decimal	Letter	mm
	.2717		6.9
	.2720	I	
	.2756		7.0
	.2770	J	
	.2795		7.1
	.2810	K	
9/32	.2812		7.14
	.2835		7.2
	.2854		7.25
	.2874		7.3
	.2900	L	
	.2913		7.4
	.2950	M	
	.2953		7.5
19/64	.2969		7.54
	.2992		7.6
	.3020	N	
	.3031		7.7
	.3051		7.75
	.3071		7.8
	.3110		7.9
5/16	.3125		7.93
	.3150		8.0
	.3160	O	
	.3189		8.1
	.3228		8.2
	.3230	P	
	.3248		8.25
	.3268		8.3
21/64	.3281		8.33
	.3307		8.4
	.3320	Q	
	.3346		8.5
	.3386		8.6
	.3390	R	
	.3425		8.7
11/32	.3438		8.73
	.3445		8.75
	.3465		8.8
	.3480	S	
	.3504		8.9
	.3543		9.0
	.3580	T	
	.3583		9.1
23/64	.3594		9.12
	.3622		9.2
	.3642		9.25
	.3661		9.3
	.3680	U	
	.3701		9.4
	.3740		9.5
3/8	.3750		9.52
	.3770	V	
	.3780		9.6
	.3819		9.7
	.3839		9.75
	.3858		9.8
	.3860	W	
	.3898		9.9
25/64	.3906		9.92
	.3937		10.0
	.3970	X	
	.4040	Y	
13/32	.4062		10.31
	.4130	Z	
	.4134		10.5
27/64	.4219		10.71

Inch	Decimal	mm
	.4331	11.0
7/16	.4375	11.11
	.4528	11.5
29/64	.4531	11.51
15/32	.4688	11.90
	.4724	12.0
31/64	.4844	12.30
	.4921	12.5
1/2	.5000	12.70
	.5118	13.0
33/64	.5156	13.09
17/32	.5312	13.49
	.5315	13.5
35/64	.5469	13.89
	.5512	14.0
9/16	.5625	14.28
	.5709	14.5
37/64	.5781	14.68
	.5906	15.0
19/32	.5938	15.08
39/64	.6094	15.47
	.6102	15.5
5/8	.6250	15.87
	.6299	16.0
41/64	.6406	16.27
	.6496	16.5
21/32	.6562	16.66
	.6693	17.0
43/64	.6719	17.06
11/16	.6875	17.46
	.6890	17.5
45/64	.7031	17.85
	.7087	18.0
23/32	.7188	18.25
	.7283	18.5
47/64	.7344	18.65
	.7480	19.0
3/4	.7500	19.05
49/64	.7656	19.44
	.7677	19.5
25/32	.7812	19.84
	.7874	20.0
51/64	.7969	20.24
	.8071	20.5
13/16	.8125	20.63
	.8268	21.0
53/64	.8281	21.03
27/32	.8438	21.43
	.8465	21.5
55/64	.8594	21.82
	.8661	22.0
7/8	.8750	22.22
	.8858	22.5
57/64	.8906	22.62
	.9055	23.0
29/32	.9062	23.01
59/64	.9219	23.41
	.9252	23.5
15/16	.9375	23.81
	.9449	24.0
61/64	.9531	24.2
	.9646	24.5
31/32	.9688	24.6
	.9843	25.0
63/64	.9844	25.0
1	1.0000	25.4

AIR/FUEL RATIO: The ratio of air to gasoline by weight in the fuel mixture drawn into the engine.

AIR INJECTION: One method of reducing harmful exhaust emissions by injecting air into each of the exhaust ports of an engine. The fresh air entering the hot exhaust manifold causes any remaining fuel to be burned before it can exit the tailpipe.

ALTERNATOR: A device used for converting mechanical energy into electrical energy.

AMMETER: An instrument, calibrated in amperes, used to measure the flow of an electrical current in a circuit. Ammeters are always connected in series with the circuit being tested.

AMPERE: The rate of flow of electrical current present when one volt of electrical pressure is applied against one ohm of electrical resistance.

ANALOG COMPUTER: Any microprocessor that uses similar (analogous) electrical signals to make its calculations.

ARMATURE: A laminated, soft iron core wrapped by a wire that converts electrical energy to mechanical energy as in a motor or relay. When rotated in a magnetic field, it changes mechanical energy into electrical energy as in a generator.

ATMOSPHERIC PRESSURE: The pressure on the Earth's surface caused by the weight of the air in the atmosphere. At sea level, this pressure is 14.7 psi at 32°F (101 kPa at 0°C).

ATOMIZATION: The breaking down of a liquid into a fine mist that can be suspended in air.

AXIAL PLAY: Movement parallel to a shaft or bearing bore.

BACKFIRE: The sudden combustion of gases in the intake or exhaust system that results in a loud explosion.

BACKLASH: The clearance or play between two parts, such as meshed gears.

BACKPRESSURE: Restrictions in the exhaust system that slow the exit of exhaust gases from the combustion chamber.

BAKELITE: A heat resistant, plastic insulator material commonly used in printed circuit boards and transistorized components.

BALL BEARING: A bearing made up of hardened inner and outer races between which hardened steel ball roll.

BALLAST RESISTOR: A resistor in the primary ignition circuit that lowers voltage after the engine is started to reduce wear on ignition components.

BEARING: A friction reducing, supportive device usually located between a stationary part and a moving part.

BIMETAL TEMPERATURE SENSOR: Any sensor or switch made of two dissimilar types of metal that bend when heated or cooled due to the different expansion rates of the alloys. These types of sensors usually function as an on/off switch.

BLOWBY: Combustion gases, composed of water vapor and unburned fuel, that leak past the piston rings into the crankcase during normal engine operation. These gases are removed by the PCV system to prevent the buildup of harmful acids in the crankcase.

BRAKE PAD: A brake shoe and lining assembly used with disc brakes.

BRAKE SHOE: The backing for the brake lining. The term is, however, usually applied to the assembly of the brake backing and lining.

BUSHING: A liner, usually removable, for a bearing; an anti-friction liner used in place of a bearing.

BYPASS: System used to bypass ballast resistor during engine cranking to increase voltage supplied to the coil.

CALIPER: A hydraulically activated device in a disc brake system, which is mounted straddling the brake rotor (disc). The caliper contains at least one piston and two brake pads. Hydraulic pressure on the piston(s) forces the pads against the rotor.

CAMSHAFT: A shaft in the engine on which are the lobes (cams) which operate the valves. The camshaft is driven by the crankshaft, via a

belt, chain or gears, at one half the crankshaft speed.

CAPACITOR: A device which stores an electrical charge.

CARBON MONOXIDE (CO): a colorless, odorless gas given off as a normal byproduct of combustion. It is poisonous and extremely dangerous in confined areas, building up slowly to toxic levels without warning if adequate ventilation is not available.

CARBURETOR: A device, usually mounted on the intake manifold of an engine, which mixes the air and fuel in the proper proportion to allow even combustion.

CATALYTIC CONVERTER: A device installed in the exhaust system, like a muffler, that converts harmful byproducts of combustion into carbon dioxide and water vapor by means of a heat-producing chemical reaction.

CENTRIFUGAL ADVANCE: A mechanical method of advancing the spark timing by using flyweights in the distributor that react to centrifugal force generated by the distributor shaft rotation.

CHECK VALVE: Any one-way valve installed to permit the flow of air, fuel or vacuum in one direction only.

CHOKE: A device, usually a moveable valve, placed in the intake path of a carburetor to restrict the flow of air.

CIRCUIT: Any unbroken path through which an electrical current can flow. Also used to describe fuel flow in some instances.

CIRCUIT BREAKER: A switch which protects an electrical circuit from overload by opening the circuit when the current flow exceeds a predetermined level. Some circuit breakers must be reset manually, while other reset automatically

COIL (IGNITION): A transformer in the ignition circuit which steps of the voltage provided to the spark plugs.

COMBINATION MANIFOLD: An assembly which includes both the intake and exhaust manifolds in one casting.

COMBINATION VALVE: A device used in some fuel systems that routes fuel vapors to a charcoal storage canister instead of venting them into the atmosphere. The valve relieves fuel tank pressure and allows fresh air into the tank as fuel level drops to prevent a vapor lock situation.

COMPRESSION RATIO: The comparison of the total volume of the cylinder and combustion chamber with the piston at BDC and the piston at TDC.

CONDENSER: 1. An electrical device which acts to store an electrical charge, preventing voltage surges.
2. A radiator-like device in the air conditioning system in which refrigerant gas condenses into a liquid, giving off heat.

CONDUCTOR: Any material through which an electrical current can be transmitted easily.

CONTINUITY: Continuous or complete circuit. Can be checked with an ohmmeter.

COUNTERSHAFT: An intermediate shaft which is rotated by a mainshaft and transmits, in turn, that rotation to a working part.

CRANKCASE: The lower part of an engine in which the crankshaft and related parts operate.

CRANKSHAFT: The main driving shaft of an engine which receives reciprocating motion from the pistons and converts it to rotary motion.

CYLINDER: In an engine, the round hole in the engine block in which the piston(s) ride.

CYLINDER BLOCK: The main structural member of an engine in which is found the cylinders, crankshaft and other principal parts.

CYLINDER HEAD: The detachable portion of the engine, fastened, usually, to the top of the cylinder block, containing all or most of the combustion chambers. On overhead valve engines, it contains the valves and their operating parts. On overhead cam engines, it contains the camshaft as well.

DEAD CENTER: The extreme top or bottom of the piston stroke.

DETONATION: An unwanted explosion of the air fuel mixture in the combustion chamber caused by excess heat and compression, advanced timing, or an overly lean mixture. Also referred to as "ping".

GENERATOR: A device which converts mechanical energy into electrical energy.

HEAT RANGE: The measure of a spark plug's ability to dissipate heat from its firing end. The higher the heat range, the hotter the plug fires.

HUB: The center part of a wheel or gear.

HYDROCARBON (HC): Any chemical compound made up of hydrogen and carbon. A major pollutant formed by the engine as a byproduct of combustion.

HYDROMETER: An instrument used to measure the specific gravity of a solution.

INCH POUND (in.lb. or sometimes, in. lbs.): One twelfth of a foot pound.

INDUCTION: A means of transferring electrical energy in the form of a magnetic field. Principle used in the ignition coil to increase voltage.

INJECTION PUMP: A device, usually mechanically operated, which meters and delivers fuel under pressure to the fuel injector.

INJECTOR: A device which receives metered fuel under relatively low pressure and is activated to inject the fuel into the engine under relatively high pressure at a predetermined time.

INPUT SHAFT: The shaft to which torque is applied, usually carrying the driving gear or gears.

INTAKE MANIFOLD: A casting of passages or pipes used to conduct air or a fuel/air mixture to the cylinders.

JOURNAL: The bearing surface within which a shaft operates.

KEY: A small block usually fitted in a notch between a shaft and a hub to prevent slippage of the two parts.

MANIFOLD: A casting of passages or set of pipes which connect the cylinders to an inlet or outlet source.

MANIFOLD VACUUM: Low pressure in an engine intake manifold formed just below the throttle plates. Manifold vacuum is highest at idle and drops under acceleration.

MASTER CYLINDER: The primary fluid pressurizing device in a hydraulic system. In automotive use, it is found in brake and hydraulic clutch systems and is pedal activated, either directly or, in a power brake system, through the power booster.

MODULE: Electronic control unit, amplifier or igniter of solid state or integrated design which controls the current flow in the ignition primary circuit based on input from the pickup coil. When the module opens the primary circuit, the high secondary voltage is induced in the coil.

NEEDLE BEARING: A bearing which consists of a number (usually a large number) of long, thin rollers.

OHM: (Ω) The unit used to measure the resistance of conductor to electrical flow. One ohm is the amount of resistance that limits current flow to one ampere in a circuit with one volt of pressure.

OHMMETER: An instrument used for measuring the resistance, in ohms, in an electrical circuit.

OUTPUT SHAFT: The shaft which transmits torque from a device, such as a transmission.

OVERDRIVE: A gear assembly which produces more shaft revolutions than that transmitted to it.

OVERHEAD CAMSHAFT (OHC): An engine configuration in which the camshaft is mounted on top of the cylinder head and operates the valve either directly or by means of rocker arms.

OVERHEAD VALVE (OHV): An engine configuration in which all of the valves are located in the cylinder head and the camshaft is located in the cylinder block. The camshaft operates the valves via lifters and pushrods.

OXIDES OF NITROGEN (NOx): Chemical compounds of nitrogen produced as a byproduct of combustion. They combine with hydrocarbons to produce smog.

OXYGEN SENSOR: Used with the feedback system to sense the presence of oxygen in the exhaust gas and signal the computer which can reference the voltage signal to an air/fuel ratio.

PINION: The smaller of two meshing gears.

DIAPHRAGM: A thin, flexible wall separating two cavities, such as in a vacuum advance unit.

DIESELING: A condition in which hot spots in the combustion chamber cause the engine to run on after the key is turned off.

DIFFERENTIAL: A geared assembly which allows the transmission of motion between drive axles, giving one axle the ability to turn faster than the other.

DIODE: An electrical device that will allow current to flow in one direction only.

DISC BRAKE: A hydraulic braking assembly consisting of a brake disc, or rotor, mounted on an axle, and a caliper assembly containing, usually two brake pads which are activated by hydraulic pressure. The pads are forced against the sides of the disc, creating friction which slows the vehicle.

DISTRIBUTOR: A mechanically driven device on an engine which is responsible for electrically firing the spark plug at a predetermined point of the piston stroke.

DOWEL PIN: A pin, inserted in mating holes in two different parts allowing those parts to maintain a fixed relationship.

DRUM BRAKE: A braking system which consists of two brake shoes and one or two wheel cylinders, mounted on a fixed backing plate, and a brake drum, mounted on an axle, which revolves around the assembly. Hydraulic action applied to the wheel cylinders forces the shoes outward against the drum, creating friction and slowing the vehicle.

DWELL: The rate, measured in degrees of shaft rotation, at which an electrical circuit cycles on and off.

ELECTRONIC CONTROL UNIT (ECU): Ignition module, module, amplifier or igniter. See Module for definition.

ELECTRONIC IGNITION: A system in which the timing and firing of the spark plugs is controlled by an electronic control unit, usually called a module. These systems have not points or condenser.

ENDPLAY: The measured amount of axial movement in a shaft.

ENGINE: A device that converts heat into mechanical energy.

EXHAUST MANIFOLD: A set of cast passages or pipes which conduct exhaust gases from the engine.

FEELER GAUGE: A blade, usually metal, of precisely predetermined thickness, used to measure the clearance between two parts. These blades usually are available in sets of assorted thicknesses.

F-Head: An engine configuration in which the intake valves are in the cylinder head, while the camshaft and exhaust valves are located in the cylinder block. The camshaft operates the intake valves via lifters and pushrods, while it operates the exhaust valves directly.

FIRING ORDER: The order in which combustion occurs in the cylinders of an engine. Also the order in which spark is distributed to the plugs by the distributor.

FLATHEAD: An engine configuration in which the camshaft and all the valves are located in the cylinder block.

FLOODING: The presence of too much fuel in the intake manifold and combustion chamber which prevents the air/fuel mixture from firing, thereby causing a no-start situation.

FLYWHEEL: A disc shaped part bolted to the rear end of the crankshaft. Around the outer perimeter is affixed the ring gear. The starter drive engages the ring gear, turning the flywheel, which rotates the crankshaft, imparting the initial starting motion to the engine.

FOOT POUND (ft.lb. or sometimes, ft. lbs.): The amount of energy or work needed to raise an item weighing one pound, a distance of one foot.

FUSE: A protective device in a circuit which prevents circuit overload by breaking the circuit when a specific amperage is present. The device is constructed around a strip or wire of a lower amperage rating than the circuit it is designed to protect. When an amperage higher than that stamped on the fuse is present in the circuit, the strip or wire melts, opening the circuit.

GEAR RATIO: The ratio between the number of teeth on meshing gears.

GENERATOR: A device which converts mechanical energy into electrical energy.

HEAT RANGE: The measure of a spark plug's ability to dissipate heat from its firing end. The higher the heat range, the hotter the plug fires.

HUB: The center part of a wheel or gear.

HYDROCARBON (HC): Any chemical compound made up of hydrogen and carbon. A major pollutant formed by the engine as a byproduct of combustion.

HYDROMETER: An instrument used to measure the specific gravity of a solution.

INCH POUND (in.lb. or sometimes, in. lbs.): One twelfth of a foot pound.

INDUCTION: A means of transferring electrical energy in the form of a magnetic field. Principle used in the ignition coil to increase voltage.

INJECTION PUMP: A device, usually mechanically operated, which meters and delivers fuel under pressure to the fuel injector.

INJECTOR: A device which receives metered fuel under relatively low pressure and is activated to inject the fuel into the engine under relatively high pressure at a predetermined time.

INPUT SHAFT: The shaft to which torque is applied, usually carrying the driving gear or gears.

INTAKE MANIFOLD: A casting of passages or pipes used to conduct air or a fuel/air mixture to the cylinders.

JOURNAL: The bearing surface within which a shaft operates.

KEY: A small block usually fitted in a notch between a shaft and a hub to prevent slippage of the two parts.

MANIFOLD: A casting of passages or set of pipes which connect the cylinders to an inlet or outlet source.

MANIFOLD VACUUM: Low pressure in an engine intake manifold formed just below the throttle plates. Manifold vacuum is highest at idle and drops under acceleration.

MASTER CYLINDER: The primary fluid pressurizing device in a hydraulic system. In automotive use, it is found in brake and hydraulic clutch systems and is pedal activated, either directly or, in a power brake system, through the power booster.

MODULE: Electronic control unit, amplifier or igniter of solid state or integrated design which controls the current flow in the ignition primary circuit based on input from the pickup coil. When the module opens the primary circuit, the high secondary voltage is induced in the coil.

NEEDLE BEARING: A bearing which consists of a number (usually a large number) of long, thin rollers.

OHM: (Ω) The unit used to measure the resistance of conductor to electrical flow. One ohm is the amount of resistance that limits current flow to one ampere in a circuit with one volt of pressure.

OHMMETER: An instrument used for measuring the resistance, in ohms, in an electrical circuit.

OUTPUT SHAFT: The shaft which transmits torque from a device, such as a transmission.

OVERDRIVE: A gear assembly which produces more shaft revolutions than that transmitted to it.

OVERHEAD CAMSHAFT (OHC): An engine configuration in which the camshaft is mounted on top of the cylinder head and operates the valve either directly or by means of rocker arms.

OVERHEAD VALVE (OHV): An engine configuration in which all of the valves are located in the cylinder head and the camshaft is located in the cylinder block. The camshaft operates the valves via lifters and pushrods.

OXIDES OF NITROGEN (NOx): Chemical compounds of nitrogen produced as a byproduct of combustion. They combine with hydrocarbons to produce smog.

OXYGEN SENSOR: Used with the feedback system to sense the presence of oxygen in the exhaust gas and signal the computer which can reference the voltage signal to an air/fuel ratio.

PINION: The smaller of two meshing gears.

PISTON RING: An open ended ring which fits into a groove on the outer diameter of the piston. Its chief function is to form a seal between the piston and cylinder wall. Most automotive pistons have three rings: two for compression sealing; one for oil sealing.

PRELOAD: A predetermined load placed on a bearing during assembly or by adjustment.

PRIMARY CIRCUIT: Is the low voltage side of the ignition system which consists of the ignition switch, ballast resistor or resistance wire, bypass, coil, electronic control unit and pick-up coil as well as the connecting wires and harnesses.

PRESS FIT: The mating of two parts under pressure, due to the inner diameter of one being smaller than the outer diameter of the other, or vice versa; an interference fit.

RACE: The surface on the inner or outer ring of a bearing on which the balls, needles or rollers move.

REGULATOR: A device which maintains the amperage and/or voltage levels of a circuit at predetermined values.

RELAY: A switch which automatically opens and/or closes a circuit.

RESISTANCE: The opposition to the flow of current through a circuit or electrical device, and is measured in ohms. Resistance is equal to the voltage divided by the amperage.

RESISTOR: A device, usually made of wire, which offers a preset amount of resistance in an electrical circuit.

RING GEAR: The name given to a ring-shaped gear attached to a differential case, or affixed to a flywheel or as part a planetary gear set.

ROLLER BEARING: A bearing made up of hardened inner and outer races between which hardened steel rollers move.

ROTOR: 1. The disc-shaped part of a disc brake assembly, upon which the brake pads bear; also called, brake disc.
2. The device mounted atop the distributor shaft, which passes current to the distributor cap tower contacts.

SECONDARY CIRCUIT: The high voltage side of the ignition system, usually above 20,000 volts. The secondary includes the ignition coil, coil wire, distributor cap and rotor, spark plug wires and spark plugs.

SENDING UNIT: A mechanical, electrical, hydraulic or electromagnetic device which transmits information to a gauge.

SENSOR: Any device designed to measure engine operating conditions or ambient pressures and temperatures. Usually electronic in nature and designed to send a voltage signal to an on-board computer, some sensors may operate as a simple on/off switch or they may provide a variable voltage signal (like a potentiometer) as conditions or measured parameters change.

SHIM: Spacers of precise, predetermined thickness used between parts to establish a proper working relationship.

SLAVE CYLINDER: In automotive use, a device in the hydraulic clutch system which is activated by hydraulic force, disengaging the clutch.

SOLENOID: A coil used to produce a magnetic field, the effect of which is produce work.

SPARK PLUG: A device screwed into the combustion chamber of a spark ignition engine. The basic construction is a conductive core inside of a ceramic insulator, mounted in an outer conductive base. An electrical charge from the spark plug wire travels along the conductive core and jumps a preset air gap to a grounding point or points at the end of the conductive base. The resultant spark ignites the fuel/air mixture in the combustion chamber.

SPLINES: Ridges machined or cast onto the outer diameter of a shaft or inner diameter of a bore to enable parts to mate without rotation.

TACHOMETER: A device used to measure the rotary speed of an engine, shaft, gear, etc., usually in rotations per minute.

THERMOSTAT: A valve, located in the cooling system of an engine, which is closed when cold and opens gradually in response to engine heating, controlling the temperature of the coolant and rate of coolant flow.

TOP DEAD CENTER (TDC): The point at which the piston reaches the top of its travel on the compression stroke.

TORQUE: The twisting force applied to an object.

TORQUE CONVERTER: A turbine used to transmit power from a driving member to a driven member via hydraulic action, providing changes in drive ratio and torque. In automotive use, it links the driveplate at the rear of the engine to the automatic transmission.

TRANSDUCER: A device used to change a force into an electrical signal.

TRANSISTOR: A semi-conductor component which can be actuated by a small voltage to perform an electrical switching function.

TUNE-UP: A regular maintenance function, usually associated with the replacement and adjustment of parts and components in the electrical and fuel systems of a vehicle for the purpose of attaining optimum performance.

TURBOCHARGER: An exhaust driven pump which compresses intake air and forces it into the combustion chambers at higher than atmospheric pressures. The increased air pressure allows more fuel to be burned and results in increased horsepower being produced.

VACUUM ADVANCE: A device which advances the ignition timing in response to increased engine vacuum.

VACUUM GAUGE: An instrument used to measure the presence of vacuum in a chamber.

VALVE: A device which control the pressure, direction of flow or rate of flow of a liquid or gas.

VALVE CLEARANCE: The measured gap between the end of the valve stem and the rocker arm, cam lobe or follower that activates the valve.

VISCOSITY: The rating of a liquid's internal resistance to flow.

VOLTMETER: An instrument used for measuring electrical force in units called volts. Voltmeters are always connected parallel with the circuit being tested.

WHEEL CYLINDER: Found in the automotive drum brake assembly, it is a device, actuated by hydraulic pressure, which, through internal pistons, pushes the brake shoes outward against the drums.

ABBREVIATIONS AND SYMBOLS

A: Ampere

AC: Alternating current

A/C: Air conditioning

A-h: Ampere hour

AT: Automatic transmission

ATDC: After top dead center

μA: Microampere

bbl: Barrel

BDC: Bottom dead center

bhp: Brake horsepower

BTDC: Before top dead center

BTU: British thermal unit

C: Celsius (Centigrade)

CCA: Cold cranking amps

cd: Candela

cm^2: Square centimeter

cm^3, cc: Cubic centimeter

CO: Carbon monoxide

CO_2: Carbon dioxide

cu.in., in^3: Cubic inch

CV: Constant velocity

Cyl.: Cylinder

DC: Direct current

ECM: Electronic control module

EFE: Early fuel evaporation

EFI: Electronic fuel injection

EGR: Exhaust gas recirculation

Exh.: Exhaust

F: Fahrenheit

F: Farad

pF: Picofarad

μF: Microfarad

FI: Fuel injection

ft.lb., ft. lb., ft. lbs.: foot pound(s)

gal: Gallon

g: Gram

HC: Hydrocarbon

HEI: High energy ignition

HO: High output

hp: Horsepower

Hyd.: Hydraulic

Hz: Hertz

ID: Inside diameter

in.lb.; in. lb.; in. lbs: inch pound(s)

Int.: Intake

K: Kelvin

kg: Kilogram

kHz: Kilohertz

km: Kilometer

km/h: Kilometers per hour

kΩ: Kilohm

kPa: Kilopascal

kV: Kilovolt

kW: Kilowatt

l: Liter

l/s: Liters per second

m: Meter

mA: Milliampere

mg: Milligram

mHz: Megahertz

mm: Millimeter

mm^2: Square millimeter

m^3: Cubic meter

MΩ: Megohm

m/s: Meters per second

MT: Manual transmission

mV: Millivolt

μm: Micrometer

N: Newton

N-m: Newton meter

NOx: Nitrous oxide

OD: Outside diameter

OHC: Over head camshaft

OHV: Over head valve

Ω: Ohm

PCV: Positive crankcase ventilation

psi: Pounds per square inch

pts: Pints

qts: Quarts

rpm: Rotations per minute

rps: Rotations per second

R-12: A refrigerant gas (Freon)

SAE: Society of Automotive Engineers

SO$_2$: Sulfur dioxide

T: Ton

t: Megagram

TBI: Throttle Body Injection

TPS: Throttle Position Sensor

V: 1. Volt; 2. Venturi

μV: Microvolt

W: Watt

∞: Infinity

<: Less than

>: Greater than

Index

F

G